Business Communication

Thomas L. Means

Contributing Author

Dianne S. Rankin

SOUTH-WESTERN
CENGAGE Learning·

Australia • Brazil • Japan • Korea • Mexico • Singapore • Spain • United Kingdom • United States

SOUTH-WESTERN
CENGAGE Learning™

Business Communications
Means

Vice President of Editorial, Business:
Jack W. Calhoun

Vice President/Editor-in-Chief:
Karen Schmohe

Acquisitions Editor: Jane Congdon

Senior Developmental Editor: Penny Shank

Consulting Editor: Dianne Rankin

Marketing Manager: Linda Kuper

Content Project Manager: Jared Sterzer

Senior Media Editor: Mike Jackson

Manufacturing Buyer: Kevin Kluck

Production Service: Pre-Press PMG

Copyeditor: Carol Ann Ellis

Compositor: Pre-Press PMG

Senior Art Director: Tippy McIntosh

Internal Designer: Ke Design, Mason, Ohio

Cover Designer: Ke Design, Mason, Ohio

Cover Image: © Getty Images/Vincent Hazat,
Photo Alto

Photography Manager: Darren Wright

Photo Permissions Acquisitions Manager:
Don Schlotman

Text Permissions Acquisitions Manager:
Tim Sisler

For product information and technology assistance, contact us at
Cengage Learning Customer & Sales Support, 1-800-354-9706

For permission to use material from this text or product,
submit all requests online at **www.cengage.com/permissions**
Further permissions questions can be emailed to
permissionrequest@cengage.com

States' Career Clusters Initiative, 2009, www.careerclusters.org

Access, Excel, Internet Explorer, Microsoft, Microsoft ActiveSync, Microsoft
Windows, MSN, Outlook, and PowerPoint are registered trademarks of
Microsoft Corporation.
Adobe, Fireworks, and Photoshop are registered trademarks of Adobe
Systems Incorporated.
CorelDRAW, Corel, and Quattro Pro are registered trademarks of Corel
Corporation.
dBASE is a trademark of dataBased Intelligence, Inc.
Eudora is a registered trademark of Qualcomm Incorporated.
Exam*View*® is a registered trademark of eInstruction Corp.
FileMaker is a registered trademark of FileMaker, Inc.
Google is a trademark of Google Inc.
Linux is a registered trademark of Linus Torvalds.
Lotus is a registered trademark of IBM.
Mac OS, Macintosh, and Power Mac are registered trademarks of Apple, Inc.
Netscape Navigator is a registered trademark of Netscape Communications
Corporation in the United States and other countries.
Norton 360 is a trademark of Symantec Corporation.
ResumeMaker is a trademark of Individual Software.
WinZip is a Registered Trademark of WinZip International LLC.

© 2010 Cengage Learning. All Rights Reserved.

ISBN-13: 978-0-538-44947-2

ISBN-10: 0-538-44947-0

South-Western Cengage Learning
5191 Natorp Boulevard
Mason, OH 45040
USA

Cengage Learning products are represented in Canada by
Nelson Education, Ltd.

For your course and learning solutions, visit **school.cengage.com**

Printed in Canada
1 2 3 4 5 6 7 13 12 11 10 09

Contents

Chapter 1   **Communicating in Your Life 2**

1.1   The Communication Process 4
The Communication Process 4,   Purposes of Communication 6,
Types of Business Communication 7

1.2   Overcoming Communication Barriers 11
Communication Barriers 11,   Overcoming Barriers 12

1.3   Reading in the Workplace 19
Importance of Reading 19,   Improving Reading Skills 23

Chapter 2   **Diversity and Ethics 32**

2.1   Diversity at Work 34
Overview of Diversity 34,   Diversity Trends 36,
The World as a Global Workplace 37

2.2   Differences 40
Cultural Differences 40,   Customs and Etiquette 43

2.3   Strategies for Effective Communication 45
Professional Attitude 45,   Cross-Cultural Communication 46,
Fairness and Sensitivity 49

2.4   Ethics in Business Communication 52
A Definition of Ethics 52,   Communicating in an Ethical Way 53

Chapter 3   **Nonverbal Communication and Teamwork 66**

3.1   Nonverbal Communication 68
The Roles of Nonverbal Communication 68,   Nonverbal
Symbols 70,   Nonverbal Symbols and Your Image 74,
Nonverbal Symbols in the Environment 77

3.2   Listening Skills 79
The Listening Process 79,   Types of Listening 80,
Barriers to Effective Listening 82,   Listening Effectively 84

3.3   Teamwork 89
Workplace Relationships 89,   Workplace Teams 91,
Working Effectively in Teams 93

Chapter 4   Basics of English Grammar 104

4.1   Parts of Speech and Sentences 106

Parts of Speech 106,   Sentence Parts 107,   Sentence Structure 111

4.2   Nouns, Pronouns, and Adjectives 114

Nouns 114,   Pronouns 115,   Adjectives 119

4.3   Verbs and Adverbs 123

Verbs 123,   Adverbs 128

4.4   Prepositions, Conjunctions, and Interjections 131

Prepositions 131,   Conjunctions 132,   Interjections 133

Chapter 5   Mechanics of Writing 140

5.1   External Marks and the Comma 142

Punctuation 142,   The Period 142,   The Question Mark 143,
The Exclamation Point 144,   The Comma 145

5.2   Other Internal Marks 150

The Semicolon 150,   The Colon 151,   The Dash 153,
The Hyphen 154,   Quotation Marks 155,   Parentheses 157,
The Apostrophe 158

5.3   Abbreviations, Capitalization, and Number Expression 161

Abbreviations 161,   Capitalization 164,   Number Expression 165

Chapter 6   The Writing Process 174

6.1   Planning and Organizing Messages 176

Planning Messages 176,   Organizing Messages 179

6.2   Composing Messages 182

Effective Messages 182,   Courteous Messages 182,
Correct Messages 186,   Concise Messages 187,
Clear Messages 188,   Complete Messages 189

6.3   Editing and Publishing Messages 192

Stages in the Writing Process 192,   Editing Messages 192,
Proofreading Messages 194,   Publishing Messages 198

Chapter 7   Writing Memos, E-mail, and Letters 208

7.1   Business Correspondence 210

Types of Business Correspondence 210,   Purposes for
Correspondence 214,   Planning and Organizing Messages 216

7.2   Memos 219

Writing Memos 219,   Editing and Publishing Memos 226

7.3   E-mail and Instant Messaging 228

       E-mail 228,   Instant Messaging 235

7.4   Letters 239

       Writing Letters 239,   Editing and Publishing Letters 245

Chapter 8   Writing to Clients and Customers 256

8.1   Neutral or Positive Messages 258

       Planning Neutral or Positive Messages 258,   Organizing Neutral or Positive Messages 259,   Writing Neutral Messages 260,   Writing Positive Messages 264

8.2   Negative Messages 274

       Planning Negative Messages 274,   Organizing Negative Messages 275,   Writing Negative Messages 280,   Writing Messages with Both Positive and Negative News 283

8.3   Persuasive Messages 286

       Planning Persuasive Messages 286,   Organizing Persuasive Messages 287,   Writing Persuasive Messages 292,   Planning Proposals 296,   Organizing and Writing Proposals 297

Chapter 9   Writing Reports 310

9.1   Planning Reports 312

       Types of Reports 312,   Defining the Report 313,   Collecting the Data 315,   Processing the Data 321

9.2   Writing Informal Reports 327

       Organizing Informal Reports 327,   Outlining and Writing Informal Reports 328,   Formatting Informal Reports 331

9. 3   Writing Formal Reports 338

       Organizing and Writing Formal Reports 338,   Parts of a Formal Report 339

Chapter 10   Graphics and Visual Aids 362

10.1   Using Graphics and Visual Aids 364

       The Importance of Graphics and Visual Aids 364,   Use of Visual Aids in Documents 365,   Choosing the Correct Visual Aid 369

10. 2   Developing Graphics 372

       Creating Graphics Electronically 372,   Tables 373,   Charts 374,   Other Visual Aids 381

Chapter 11   Technical Communication 392

11.1   Writing to Instruct 394

The Purpose of Instructions and Manuals 394,   Parts of Effective
Instructions 394,   Writing and Editing Guidelines 398,   Parts of
Effective Manuals 401

11.2   Writing to Describe 407

Types of Description Writing 407,   Object Descriptions 408,
Process Descriptions 412

Chapter 12   Technology in the Workplace 424

12.1   Computer Hardware and Software 426

Technology at Work 426,   Computer Software 430,   File Storage and
Management 433,   Peripherals 437

12.2   Other Technologies 443

The Connected World 443,   The Internet 444,   Security 445,
Document Transmittal 448,   Pagers 449,   Voice Mail 450,   Cell
Phones 450,   VoIP 455,   Digital Cameras 456,   Global Positioning
Systems 456,   Conference Technologies 458,   Training Technologies 458

12.3   Workplace Safety and Ergonomics 462

Workplace safety 462,   Computer Use and Ergonomics 464,
Ergonomics and the Computer Workstation 465

Chapter 13   Presentations and Meetings 478

13.1   Oral Presentations 480

Short Oral Presentations 480,   Formal Oral Presentations 481,
Delivery of Oral Presentations 488

13.2   Visual Aids in Presentations 494

Types of Visual Aids 494,   Choosing Appropriate Visual Aids 497,
Preparing Visual Aids 498,   Presenting Your Visual Aids 500

13.3   Effective Meetings 504

Types of Meetings 504,   Meeting Documents 505,   Participation in
Meetings 508,   Organize Productive Meetings 513,   Lead Meetings
Effectively 518

Chapter 14   Communicating with Customers 528

14.1   Customer Service 530

Importance of Customer Service 530,   Customer Service
Culture 531,   Customer Interaction 534,   Managing Challenging
Situations 539

14.2   Face-to-Face Communication 544

Communication and Your Voice 544,   Parts of a Conversation 546,
Guidelines for Success 548

14.3   Telephone Communication 551
Effective Telephone Communication 551,   Outgoing Calls 553,
Incoming Calls 556

Chapter 15   Getting a Job 566

15.1   Job Search 568
Your Goals 568,   Job Qualifications 570,   Job Opportunities 572

15.2   Resume 578
Preparing a Resume 578,   Alternative Resumes 586

15.3   Application Letter and Form 592
Application Letter 592,   Application Forms 597

15.4   Interview and Follow-Up Messages 600
The Job Interview 600,   Follow-Up Messages 606

Appendix A   Glossary 618

Appendix B   Proofreaders' Marks and Document Styles 625

Appendix C   Checkpoint Answers 630

Index 647

Business Communication, 2e

More Focused. More Readable. More Concise.

Employers regularly list communication as one of the most important skills they look for in job applicants. *Business Communication, 2e* equips students with the communication tools they need for success in the workplace!

Every chapter has been reviewed, and here's what reviewers are saying...

"This textbook is a fantastic introduction to business communication. Thank goodness someone's finally addressing issues such as cell phone etiquette. It's also great to see an easy-to-understand example of verbal and nonverbal communication. Students need to know how to respond professionally."

Regarding Chapter 1, Communicating in Your Life:

"It couldn't be better. As an instructor, I appreciate the flow in which the chapter is designed and how easy it is to prepare lessons that accommodate the information."

Regarding Chapter 2, Diversity and Ethics:

"Good job dealing with real-world issues which need to be discussed on a regular basis. The part on plagiarism is a MUST READ for students today. The language and culture section is also essential in the global marketplace we now live in. "

Regarding Chapter 3, Nonverbal Communication and Teamwork:

"Analyzing speaking behavior was the strength of this chapter, in my opinion. This shows students how important what they say is." *(Azzie Olds, Business Department Chairperson, North Caddo Magnet High School)*

Regarding Chapter 3, Nonverbal Communication and Teamwork:

"The successful teamwork section is FANTASTIC! In the collaborative culture we live in, students desperately need this information." *(Mary Beth Lee, Rider High School)*

Organized for Success…

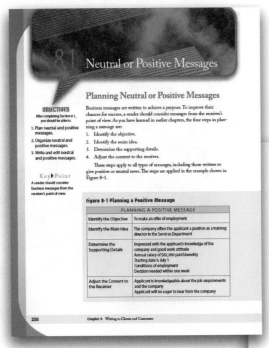

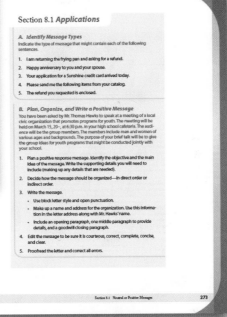

15 Chapters…

For readability and ease of teaching, each chapter is organized into sections. Sections begin with a set of objectives and conclude with applications for assessment of student learning.

A **Chapter Summary**, vocabulary terms exercise, Critical Thinking Questions, applications, Editing Activities, and case studies are provided at the end of each chapter to reinforce the material presented.

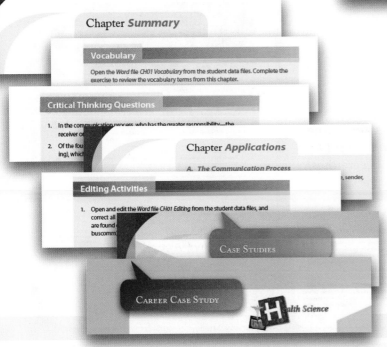

3 Appendices…

Appendix A: Glossary lists and defines key terms introduced in the chapters.

Appendix B: Proofreaders' Marks and Documentation Styles provides a list of commonly used proofreaders' marks and documentation examples for APA, MLA, and Chicago Manual of Style formats.

Appendix C: Checkpoint Answers provides answers to the checkpoints that appear in the chapters so students can verify their answers.

What's New...

Business Communication, 2e **introduces new chapters and topics; revised, expanded, and updated chapters; engaging features; and an attractive new layout while retaining its foundation of strong and user-friendly content.**

A revised **Chapter 2 deals with diversity issues** students are likely to encounter at work, such as understanding, communicating, and working with clients and colleagues from other cultures.

An **expanded discussion of ethics** explores contemporary issues in confidentiality, privacy, electronic rights, security of information, honesty, and plagiarism.

Reading skills are emphasized in a new section in Chapter 1 and *Reading Skills* exercises in other chapters.

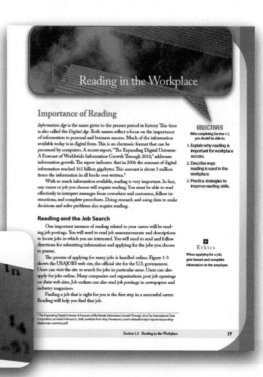

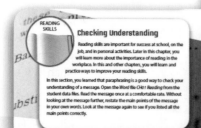

Two new chapters increase the emphasis on **English grammar and writing mechanics.** Editing activities are provided in every chapter to reinforce these skills.

CHAPTER 4

Basics of English Grammar

4.1 Parts of Speech and Sentences

4.2 Nouns, Pronouns, and Adjectives

4.3 Verbs and Adverbs

4.4 Prepositions, Conjunctions, and Interjections

CHAPTER 5

Mechanics of Writing

5.1 External Marks and the Comma

5.2 Other Internal Marks

5.3 Abbreviations, Capitalization, and Number Expression

CHAPTER 12

Technology in the Workplace

12.1 Computer Hardware and Software

12.2 Other Technologies

12.3 Workplace Safety and Ergonomics

Technology in the Workplace is a new chapter that focuses on technologies students are likely to encounter at work, such as e-mail, cell phones, message systems, networks, laptops, tablets, and training materials.

Powerful Tools for Teaching Business Communication...

Easy-to-read style.
The text is written in everyday language. Bulleted and enumerated lists highlight important concepts.

Engaging and useful illustrations.
Color photos and figures provide visual reinforcement and act as a starting point for class discussion.

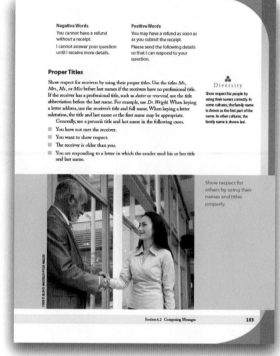

Document formats.
Numerous model documents in **Office 2007** formats show students how to format letters, memos, reports, resumes, and other documents.

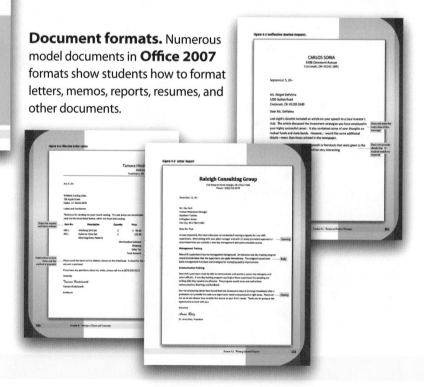

Integration of technology.
Chapter 12 is a new chapter devoted to workplace technologies. In addition, technology concepts and exercises requiring the use of technology are integrated throughout the text.

The 16 Career Clusters.

The *Career Case Studies* at the end of every chapter represent the 16 Career Clusters, allowing students to learn about the role of communication in a wide range of careers.

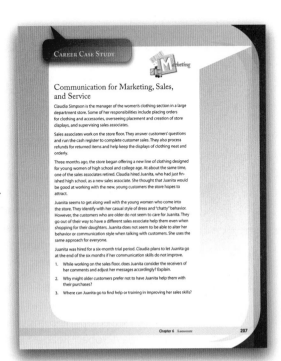

Communication for Marketing, Sales, and Service

Claudia Simpson is the manager of the women's clothing section in a large department store. Some of her responsibilities include placing orders for clothing and accessories, overseeing placement and creation of store displays, and supervising sales associates.

Sales associates work on the store floor. They answer customers' questions and run the cash register to complete customer sales. They also process refunds for returned items and help keep the displays of clothing neat and orderly.

Three months ago, the store began offering a new line of clothing designed for young women of high school and college age. At about the same time, one of the sales associates retired. Claudia hired Juanita, who had just finished high school, as a new sales associate. She thought that Juanita would be good at working with the new, young customers the store hopes to attract.

Juanita seems to get along well with the young women who come into the store. They identify with her casual style of dress and "chatty" behavior. However, the customers who are older do not seem to care for Juanita. They go out of their way to have a different sales associate help them even when shopping for their daughters. Juanita does not seem to be able to alter her behavior or communication style when talking with customers. She uses the same approach for everyone.

Juanita was hired for a six-month trial period. Claudia plans to let Juanita go at the end of the six months if her communication skills do not improve.

1. While working on the sales floor, does Juanita consider the receivers of her comments and adjust her messages accordingly? Explain.

2. Why might older customers prefer not to have Juanita help them with their purchases?

3. Where can Juanita go to find help or training in improving her sales skills?

Chapter 6 Assessment   207

NET Bookmark

Purdue University provides an Online Writing Lab called OWL. A link to OWL is given on the Web site for this book that is shown below. Use the link to go to the OWL site. Select the link for **Professional, Technical, and Job Search Writing.** Then select **Business Letters, Accentuating the Positives.** Review the information on this page.

1. Why does this resource suggest that you use positive wording in business letters?

2. What steps are suggested for softening the effects of negative news?

www.cengage.com/school/bcomm/buscomm

Internet research. A new *Net Bookmark* feature provides chapter-related activities for students to complete using information found on the Internet.

check point 3

1. What two things can you do to make a good first impression on customers?

2. List five things you can do to provide quality customer service.

Check your answers in Appendix C.

Feedback. *Checkpoints* in chapters provide immediate feedback, thereby enhancing learning.

Editing Activity

Open and edit the *Word* file *CH06 Editing* from the student data files. Correct all spelling, punctuation, and grammar errors.

Opportunities to write and revise.

Many opportunities to write, edit, revise, and proofread are provided throughout the text.

B. Write a Persuasive E-mail

1. Assume that you work for a large shoe manufacturer. Write an e-mail to your coworkers, persuading them to join a new sports team or club that is being organized. (You choose the sport or club.)

2. Use an e-mail address provided by your instructor (or save the message as a draft and do not send it.)

3. Make sure you mention benefits that will appeal to the wide range of people who work at your company.

4. Tell the readers what you want them to do. Request that they send you a reply within five days stating whether or not they want to play on the sports team or join the club.

5. Edit the message to be sure it is courteous, correct, complete, concise, and clear.

6. Proofread the message and correct all errors.

B. Bias-Free Messages

Rewrite each sentence, using positive, bias-free words.

1. Alberto is afflicted with smallpox.

2. The Asian-American teacher was recognized for excellence in teaching.

3. The old lady purchased a bag of oranges.

4. The policeman studied the site of the robbery.

5. The male nurse cared for the infant.

B. Plan, Organize, and Write a Positive Message

You have been asked by Mr. Thomas Hawks to speak at a meeting of a local civic organization that promotes programs for youth. The meeting will be held on March 15, 20--, at 6:30 p.m. in your high school cafeteria. The audience will be the group members. The members include men and women of various ages and backgrounds. The purpose of your brief talk will be to give the group ideas for youth programs that might be conducted jointly with your school.

Comprehensive student and instructor resources complete the package.

For the Student...

Study Guide – serves as a tool for review and a resource for additional enrichment activities. This workbook includes matching, multiple-choice, short-answer, and true/false questions in addition to writing exercises.

Text/eBook Bundle – Adobe® eBook provides the same content as the printed text. It can be viewed on the computer or handheld with the free Acrobat® Reader® and looks exactly like the printed version, including content, photos, graphics, and rich fonts.

Web Site – The companion Web site www.cengage.com/school/bcomm/buscomm contains:
- Data files for use in completing applications
- Web links for chapter applications that require Internet use
- Vocabulary flash cards
- Additional grammar, punctuation, number usage, and spelling exercises for extra review
- Files for a continuing case
- Document formats

For the Instructor...

Instructor's Manual – includes an overview of the instructional package, including:
- General teaching suggestions
- Guidelines for assessment
- Objectives for each chapter
- Chapter outlines
- Answers and solutions to chapter questions and applications

ExamView® – test bank provides an objective 40-question test bank for every chapter. Instructors can add, delete, or change questions.

Instructor's Resource CD – offers the following:
- PDF file of the Instructor's Manual
- Data files in Word 2003 format for use with editing exercises and applications
- Solution files for selected applications
- Lesson plans in Word files

- Transparency masters with document formats for traditional and Word 2007
- Study Guide Answers and sample solutions in PDF
- One test per chapter provided in PDF
- One PowerPoint slide show per chapter to introduce or review the chapter
- Supplemental grammar, punctuation, number usage, and spelling exercises
- A continuing case as supplemental material

Web Site – The companion Web site www.cengage.com/school/bcomm/buscomm. Everything on the IRCD will be included on the instructor password-protected portion of the Web site.

Reviewers

Susan Butts
Effective Communications Instructor
Greenville High School
Greenville, Ohio

Tammi Campbell
Business Education Teacher
Newberry County Career Center
Newberry, South Carolina

Scott Christy
Business Education Instructor
Green Bay Public Schools
Green Bay, Wisconsin

Karen Conrad
Business Education Instructor
North Star High School
Boswell, Pennsylvania

Michael Crawford
Marketing, Advertising &
  Entrepreneur Instructor
GASC Technology Center
Flint, Michigan

Kay Lynn Holmes
Business Education Teacher
Uintah High School
Vernal, Utah

Mirriam Larson
Educator, Business,
Comp. Tech. Department
  Southwest Education Academy
Cedar City, Utah

Mary Beth Lee
Publications Adviser, Teacher
Rider High School
Wichita Falls, Texas

Jallane Link
Business Office Technology
  Instructor
Canadian Valley Technology Center
Chickasha, Oklahoma

William McAndrews
Business Department
PROGRESS High School
  for Professional Careers
Brooklyn, New York

Sarah Meece
Business Teacher / CTE Coordinator
Larry A. Ryle High School
Union, Kentucky

Azzie L. Olds
Business Department Head
North Caddo Magnet High School
Vivian, Louisiana

Marti Shirley
Business/Computer/Math Instructor
Lake Park High School
Roselle, Illinois

Nancy Stewart
Instructor, English IV
  Communication for Life
Riverdale High School
Murfreesboro, Tennessee

Shani Watkins
Coordinator, BAS-ITAM program,
Lecturer
Central Washington University /
  Tacoma Public Schools
Lynnwood, Washington /
  Tacoma, Washington

Mary Williamson
Business Teacher / Adjunct Professor
Peabody Magnet High School /
  Northwestern State University
Alexandria, Louisiana

CHAPTER 1

Communicating in Your Life

1.1 *The Communication Process*

1.2 *Overcoming Communication Barriers*

1.3 *Reading in the Workplace*

Antonio's Mistake

Antonio Perez, a recent high school graduate, has been working at the law firm of Washington and Kim for almost two months. He loves his job and tries to do his best. Last week, Mr. Kim told Antonio that he is quite happy with Antonio's performance.

Cecile Garcia also works at the law firm of Washington and Kim. Cecile has worked at the firm for almost a year and has the same responsibilities as Antonio. When Antonio has a question about how to do something, he asks Cecile for help. Antonio and Cecile have become friends. They have gone to lunch together several times. Recently, they started seeing each other for dates after work.

Today Antonio is very busy. He is writing a report for Mr. Kim who needs the report by 2:00 p.m. today. Antonio really wants to talk with Cecile, but he knows he should stay focused on his work. The time is already 1:30 p.m., and the report is not finished. However, Antonio cannot resist stopping to talk with Cecile for just a few minutes. While Antonio is in Cecile's cubicle, Mr. Kim walks in to talk with Cecile. Antonio is embarrassed. He excuses himself quickly and returns to his desk to work on the report.

A few minutes later, Mr. Kim arrives at Antonio's desk and asks Antonio whether the report is finished. When Antonio explains that the report is not complete, Mr. Kim is very upset. Mr. Kim says, "Antonio, I am disappointed that you took time to socialize with Cecile when you have not finished the report." Then Mr. Kim turns and walks away.

Questions

1. What was Antonio's first mistake?

2. Should Antonio go and apologize to Mr. Kim? If so, what should he say?

3. Should he go to Mr. Kim and tell him that he was visiting Cecile to ask about a work-related issue even though he was not?

The Communication Process

The Communication Process

Communication is the process used to send and interpret messages so they are understood. Talking with teachers and fellow students is a form of communication. Sending an e-mail message, writing a report, and listening to a song are also forms of communication. Communication is important because it allows people to share ideas, ask questions, and enjoy artistic works, such as a poem or movie. Communication allows people to fill social needs—to have contact with others. Without communication, people would not be able to share information and work together to perform daily activities. The elements of the process are defined in Figure 1-1.

Message

A **message** is an idea expressed by a set of symbols. **Verbal symbols** are words used in a spoken or written message. A message sent without words is a nonverbal communication. **Nonverbal symbols** are actions or conditions that express a meaning. Gestures, posture, facial expressions, color, and lighting are examples of nonverbal symbols. Nonverbal symbols add meaning to a message. The tone of voice used by a speaker tells the listener the mood or

Key▶Point

Most messages contain both verbal and nonverbal symbols.

Figure 1-1 Each element in the communication process is important.

ELEMENTS OF THE COMMUNICATION PROCESS	
Message	An idea composed of a set of symbols, such as words or gestures
Sender	A person who creates and shares a message
Receiver	A person who hears or reads and interprets a message
Channel	The mode used to send a message, such as a letter or speaking to someone
Feedback	The response of a receiver to a message, such as a comment or a nod of the head

attitude of the speaker. The appearance of a letter that has smudges or misspelled words tells the reader that the writer is not careful with written messages.

Sender and Receiver

A **sender** is a person who creates and shares a message. When you write and send an e-mail message, you are the sender. When you ask a friend a question, you are the sender in the communication process.

A person who hears, sees, or reads symbols and interprets a message is the **receiver**. A receiver must interpret the meaning of the verbal and nonverbal symbols used by the sender. The meaning receivers give to messages depends on their backgrounds. Factors such as education, opinions, and emotional states affect how a receiver interprets a message.

Channel

The mode or form used to send a message is called the **channel**. To send messages, people speak and write. To receive messages, people listen and read. Letters and reports are common channels for written messages. Face-to-face conversations and telephone calls are common channels for spoken messages. E-mail and voice mail are common channels for written and spoken electronic messages. All forms of communication are important. However, many people spend more time listening to spoken messages than using any other communication channel.

Key▶Point

A sender may use more than one channel for a message. For example, a telephone call may be followed by a letter to provide more details.

Feedback

Feedback is the response of a receiver to a message. Feedback can be nonverbal (a smile or a nod of the head) or it can be verbal (a comment related to the message). Any response—even no response—is feedback.

Feedback is important because it helps the sender determine whether the receiver has understood the message. If the receiver looks confused (nonverbal feedback), the sender may need to clarify the message by providing more information.

check point 1

1. What are the five elements of the communication process?

2. What must a receiver do for communication to occur?

Check your answers in Appendix C.

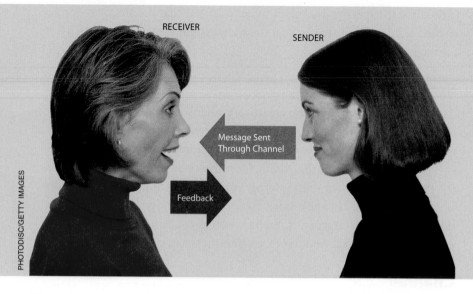

The main components of communication are sender, message, channel, receiver, and feedback.

RECEIVER

SENDER

Message Sent Through Channel

Feedback

Purposes of Communication

People communicate for many different purposes. The focus of your learning in this course will be on business communication. **Business communication** is sending and interpreting messages related to products, services, or activities of a company or an organization. Effective communication is important for business success.

Obtain or Share Information

Information is one of the most valuable resources people and companies have. Communication is used to obtain and share information. One of the main goals of most businesses is to make a profit—to earn more money than is spent operating the business. If a company does not make a profit, it may soon go out of business. To make a profit, a business must understand what its customers want. The employees of a business learn what customers want by communicating. They ask questions and listen to feedback from customers. Employees must also share information to plan and carry out the activities of the business.

Build Goodwill and Image

Goodwill is a positive feeling or attitude toward others. In the business world, goodwill refers to the good reputation or positive image of a company. When employees communicate in a positive and effective way with others, they are building goodwill for the company. When others feel goodwill toward you or a company, they are more likely to share information, grant requests you make, or offer support in other ways. When a company has a positive image, the public is more likely to buy products or services from the company.

Diversity

A sender should consider the receiver's background and experiences when trying to build goodwill.

Persuade

To persuade means to convince others to adopt an opinion or take a certain action. The sender must often convince others of the benefits of taking the action. For example, a company may try to persuade a customer that a particular product is better than other similar products. Advertising often focuses on benefits to the customer of owning the product.

Build Relationships and Self-Esteem

People have various types of relationships with others. Personal relationships include those with family and friends. Work relationships include those with coworkers, clients, and the public. Communicating effectively helps build positive relationships. For example, providing correct and timely information to a client gives the impression that you are competent in your job. This impression strengthens your relationship with the client.

Positive comments or reactions from others increase your self-esteem. Such positive reinforcement causes you to feel good about yourself. That confidence has a positive impact on how you interact with others.

> **check point 2**
>
> 1. List four purposes for business communication.
>
> 2. Why are goodwill and a positive image important for business success?
>
> Check your answers in Appendix C.

Types of Business Communication

Business employees communicate with people inside the company. They also send messages to customers and others outside the company. Messages sent to people within the company are called internal communication. Messages created within the company and sent to people outside the company are called external communication.

Formal and Informal Communication

Communication within a company can be formal or informal. An e-mail sent by a supervisor to those whom she leads is a formal communication. Informal communication does not follow lines of authority in a company. It can be written or spoken. Talking with fellow employees during lunch is an example of informal communication. Informal communication is usually fast. However, it is not always accurate. Informal communication is sometimes called the **grapevine.**

Ethics

Repeating rumors about coworkers or business affairs may be unethical.

PHOTODISC/GETTY IMAGES

Communication Direction

Communication travels down, across, or up lines of authority. Communication that travels from managers to employees is called downward communication. For example, a policy prepared by company officers and sent to employees is a downward communication.

Communication among peers—people of the same status—is called lateral communication or horizontal communication. A memo from one team member to another is an example of lateral communication. This type of communication usually results in cooperation within a company.

Upward communication refers to messages from workers to managers of the company. When employees convey their ideas to their supervisors, they are communicating upward.

Written and Oral Communication

Written messages can be internal or external. Letters, memos, and reports are common forms of written business communication. Written messages can be composed, edited, and transmitted on computers, for example by e-mail. They can be printed and sent by U.S. mail or interoffice mail.

Written communication is often the best channel for a message for these reasons:

- Written messages provide a record of information exchanged. For example, a price quoted in a written bid cannot be disputed.

- The message can be revised until it is logical and clear. Revision is especially important when complex data must be explained.

- A written message allows the receiver to read the message and refer to it as many times as necessary.

Of all types of communication, oral communication is the fastest. It provides immediate feedback to the sender. Oral communication is used in face-to-face and telephone conversations. Oral messages can be sent by telephone and stored electronically for playback later on a voice mail system.

Key ▶ Point
Oral communication is fast and allows the receiver to give immediate feedback to the sender.

check point 3

1. Is a letter from the company president to employees an example of an informal communication or a formal communication?

2. Give two reasons why using written communication may be appropriate.

Check your answers in Appendix C.

ETHICS

Protecting Confidential Information

Confidential information is data that should be kept private or secret. Patient health records, employee salaries, and plans for a new product are examples of confidential business information. Employees often read or hear private information in the course of their work. They have a duty to refrain from sharing this information with people who are not authorized to have it. Consider the following situation.

Mary Ann works in the Human Resources Department of a small company. Her friend, Jacob, works in the Marketing Department. As Mary Ann and Jacob are having lunch, Jacob confides that he is very anxious to learn whether he will be promoted to the position of marketing manager. Mary Ann reviewed a list of job promotions this morning. She knows that Jacob's name is on the promotions list. "I wouldn't be too anxious if I were you," Mary Ann says to Jacob. "I think everything is going your way this week."

Has Mary Ann acted in an unethical way? Why or why not? How will Mary Ann feel if the list of employees selected for promotions changes and Jacob is not promoted? How will Jacob feel toward Mary Ann?

Section 1.1 *Applications*

A. *The Communication Process*

Read the paragraphs below. Identify the sender, receiver, message, channel, and feedback in the situation described.

> Tom Wilson spoke to his coworker, Alice Wong, by telephone this morning.
>
> Tom: "Good morning, Alice. I am calling to let you know that the meeting scheduled for 9 a.m. today has been rescheduled. It will be held at 2 p.m. tomorrow at the same location."
>
> Alice: "Thanks, Tom. I will make a note of the time change."

B. *Access the Web Site for This Textbook*

INTERNET

A companion web site with information related to the textbook is available. The web site contains data files, vocabulary flashcards, links, and other information that you will use as you complete the activities in this textbook. You will need to visit this site often.

1. Access the Internet. Start your web browser such as *Internet Explorer*®. Access the web site at **www.cengage.com/school/bcomm/buscomm**.

2. When the site appears, click a hyperlink, such as **Student Resources**. Quickly scan the new page to see the information that is provided. Click the **Back** button to return to the welcome page.

3. Locate and access the **Links** information on the site. These links to other sites can be used as you complete activities. Whenever a web site is mentioned in an activity in the textbook, look for the link to that site on this page.

4. Return to the welcome page for the site. Locate and access the student data files on the site. You will download and use these files to complete activities.

5. Return to the welcome page for the site. Add this site to your Favorites or Bookmarks list. Use this Favorites or Bookmarks link whenever you need to access this site for later activities.

1.2 Overcoming Communication Barriers

Communication Barriers

The primary goal of communication is for the receiver to interpret the message as the sender intended. Often that goal is not achieved. **Communication barriers** are things or conditions that interfere with communication. Learning to recognize communication barriers will help you overcome them.

External Barriers

Conditions outside the receiver and the sender that hinder communication are called **external communication barriers**. Poor lighting, heat or cold, humidity, uncomfortable seating, and noise are examples of these barriers.

The appearance of a document can be a barrier to communication. For example, a document can have smudges or contain many spelling errors. You may become so distracted with the appearance of the document that you fail to comprehend its contents.

A "closed" climate within a company can be a barrier to communication. In such a climate, decisions are often made without input from employees. Workers may stop offering suggestions because they believe that making them is useless. In an "open" climate, ideas and information are welcomed, and communication flows easily. Workers believe that managers want to hear their ideas. This climate makes communication easier.

Internal Barriers

Conditions within a receiver or sender that hinder communication are called **internal communication barriers**. People have different educational backgrounds, experiences, and biases that affect how they send and receive messages. For example, a person who knows many technical terms may use the terms in a message. If the receiver does not know the terms, the message may not be interpreted correctly.

Lack of motivation or interest on the part of the receiver can hinder communication. A receiver who is interested in the topic will listen and take part in the discussion. A receiver who is not interested may not contribute or listen.

OBJECTIVES

After completing Section 1.2, you should be able to:

1. List the two types of barriers to communication and identify examples of each.

2. Describe how senders and receivers can overcome communication barriers.

Key▶Point

Communication barriers interfere with successful communication.

check point 4

1. What is an external communication barrier? Give examples.

2. What is an internal communication barrier? Give examples.

Check your answers in Appendix C.

Overcoming Barriers

Communication is a two-party process between senders and receivers. Both senders and receivers can take steps to help overcome communication barriers. Each party has important duties in the communication process.

The Sender's Duties

Because the sender begins the communication process, he or she selects the channel for the message. The sender also selects the verbal and nonverbal symbols that make up the message. Therefore, the sender has these duties:

1. Analyze and understand the receiver, using a process called audience analysis

2. Analyze and understand the message environment

3. Select symbols that the receiver will understand and select a channel

4. Encourage and interpret feedback

Audience Analysis

Audience analysis is the process used to create a profile of the intended receivers of a message. All receivers are different, unique individuals. However, receivers can share common traits or experiences. Knowing factors about the receiver helps the sender create a message the receiver will understand. For example, suppose the receivers for a message are all medical doctors. Knowing this fact allows the sender to use medical terms that would not be appropriate for a message sent to a general audience.

When preparing an audience analysis, consider the factors listed below.

- Age and gender
- Background, education, and experience
- Interests and concerns
- Attitudes
- Emotional state

Figure 1-2 shows questions you can answer to create an audience profile.

Key ▶ Point

Knowing factors about the receiver can help the sender create a clear message.

Figure 1-2 Audience Profile

AUDIENCE PROFILE QUESTIONS	
Age and Gender	• What is the age of the receiver? • What is the gender of the receiver?
Background, Education, and Experience	• Have I interacted with this receiver before? If so, what is our relationship? • Does the receiver have experience or education that relates to the topic of the message? If so, how much? • How much education does the receiver have?
Interests and Concerns	• What are the concerns and needs of the receiver? • Does the receiver have a particular motive in this situation? • Does the receiver have a certain outcome in mind?
Attitudes	• What are the beliefs, biases, values, and viewpoints of the receiver? • What will make a positive impression? a negative impression? • What ideas, if any, can be used to communicate effectively with the receiver?
Emotional State	• Will the message make the receiver happy? sad? pleased? upset? • Will the message affect the receiver at all? • Will the receiver's mood enhance his or her willingness to receive the message? • If not, do I have time to delay sending the message?

Key▶Point

A receiver's emotional state can affect how a message is interpreted.

After answering the questions about your receiver, you are ready to adjust your message based on the audience profile. Though you may not realize it, you probably have used audience analysis in the past. For example, have you ever postponed giving someone a message because that person was in a bad mood? If so, you used audience analysis to make your decision. You considered the receiver's emotional state when deciding to delay the message.

Message Environment

Another factor a sender should consider is the message environment. **Message environment** refers to the physical and social setting in which a message is sent or received. Being aware of the environment can help you overcome barriers.

Key ▶ Point

When in a meeting or other group setting, turn off your cell phone or set it to alert you silently to calls so as not to be a distraction to others.

Diversity

Appropriate times and places for discussing business vary by culture. Do research to ensure that you will behave appropriately when meeting with people from other cultures.

When selecting a physical location where you will speak to listeners, consider questions such as:

- Is the location quiet and free of distracting noise?
- Is the location comfortable with appropriate temperature, light, and seating?
- Is the location one in which interruptions are unlikely?

When considering the physical environment, the sender must ask this question: Is the environment such that the message will be understood and will receive the desired reaction? If the answer is yes, the message should be sent. If the answer is no, the message should be delayed, if possible, until a more favorable time. For example, when your supervisor is in a bad mood, this might not be a good time to make suggestions on how to improve procedures.

Another factor of message environment is the social setting. For example, an office party is not typically a good place to discuss serious business matters. However, a business lunch is a good time to offer new ideas. When an important project is behind schedule, your manager may be worried about whether the team will complete it on time. This may not a good time to ask your manager about planning a company picnic. The sender should analyze the message environment and then react accordingly.

Symbol and Channel Selection

After considering the audience and the message environment, the sender is ready to select the words and nonverbal symbols for the message. Each verbal and nonverbal symbol has a meaning to the receiver. If any of

The message environment affects how listeners receive a message.

DIGITAL VISION/GETTY IMAGES

these meanings differ from those of the sender, this can be a barrier to communication. Therefore, the sender should select words and other symbols carefully.

The sender must select a channel for the message. The channel used should be one that has the best chance for successful communication. For example, suppose the receiver reads the sender's language well but speaks it poorly. In this case, a written message would be the best channel.

Seeking Feedback

Interpreting feedback can help senders overcome barriers. For example, feedback can show that a listener does not understand the message. The sender can take steps to improve communication. The sender could do one of the following:

- Use different words or symbols to make the message clear.
- Use a different example that relates to the listener's experiences.
- Eliminate noise or other distractions.
- Correct problems with temperature or lighting that make it hard for the listener to focus on the message.

Senders should let receivers know that they are sincerely interested in the receiver's needs and concerns. This increases the sender's chances of getting honest feedback.

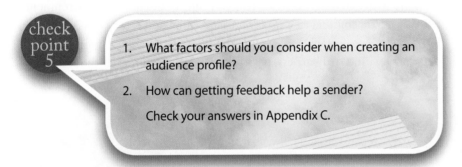
The Receiver's Duties

The receiver has a duty to aid the communication process by trying to overcome barriers. The receiver often has more control over her or his part of the process than does the sender. Basically, the receiver's duties are to read and to listen effectively.

Reading

Reading is the process of seeing and interpreting written words and other symbols. Focusing and ensuring understanding are the keys to effective reading. Receivers should try to overcome external and internal barriers that can interfere when reading.

Key ▶ Point

When preparing to read, select a location that is quiet and free of outside distractions.

To overcome external barriers when reading:

■ Select a location that is quiet and free of outside distractions.

■ Make sure the lighting is appropriate for reading.

■ Select comfortable seating.

■ Set the heat or air conditioning to a comfortable temperature, if possible.

A reader's mental state or physical well-being can affect the ability to focus on a message. To overcome internal barriers when reading:

■ Clear your mind of distracting thoughts.

■ Attempt to ignore tiredness, minor aches, or physical discomforts.

■ Be open to new ideas.

■ Avoid letting biases or previous experience prevent you from considering other viewpoints.

Diversity

Employers may need to provide assistance for workers who are hearing impaired. Interpreters and special telephone equipment can assist hearing-impaired employees.

Listening

Listening is the process of hearing and focusing attention to understand an oral message. Gaining information from listening can be more challenging than from reading. You can read a passage again if you become distracted and do not focus on the message. When listening, you may have only one opportunity to hear the message.

Receivers should try to overcome external and internal barriers that can interfere with listening. As when reading, control the physical environment as best you are able. Select a location that is quiet and free of outside distractions. Select comfortable seating. Set the temperature at a comfortable level. To overcome internal barriers, try to clear your mind of other thoughts and

Readers should select a quiet location that is free from distractions.

BLEND IMAGES/GETTY IMAGES

focus on the message. Avoid letting biases or previous experience prevent you from considering other views or new ideas.

If possible, give feedback to the sender when you do not understand a message. Ask questions that will help clarify your understanding. Be sure to ask questions at an appropriate time. In a group setting, wait until the speaker offers to answer questions or asks for feedback. In a one-to-one conversation, wait until the speaker pauses to comment or ask a question.

To check your understanding of a message, restate the main points of the message in your own words. This is called paraphrasing. When in a group setting, paraphrase silently when there is a pause in the message. In a one-to-one conversation, you could paraphrase when the speaker asks if the message is clear. If a message is not understood, paraphrasing will bring this to light. The speaker can then try to clarify the message.

Key▶Point

At an appropriate time, ask questions that will help clarify your understanding of the message.

check point 6

1. What are a receiver's duties in the communication process?

2. Why may understanding a spoken message be more challenging than understanding a written message?

    Check your answers in Appendix C.

READING SKILLS

Checking Understanding

Reading skills are important for success at school, on the job, and in personal activities. Later in this chapter, you will learn more about the importance of reading in the workplace. In this and other chapters, you will learn and practice ways to improve your reading skills.

In this section, you learned that paraphrasing is a good way to check your understanding of a message. Open the *Word* file *CH01 Reading* from the student data files. Read the message once at a comfortable rate. Without looking at the message further, restate the main points of the message in your own words. Look at the message again to see if you listed all the main points correctly.

Section 1.2 *Applications*

CRITICAL
THINKING

A. *Overcoming Communication Barriers*

For each situation described below, indicate whether the barrier to communication is internal or external. Tell how the sender or receiver might overcome the barrier in each situation.

1. The receiver is feeling slightly ill.

2. The receiver is peering out a window that overlooks a beautiful lake and snowy mountains.

3. The air conditioning is broken, and the room is extremely hot.

4. The computer system is down, and no e-mail messages can be sent.

5. The sender of a message is distracted with worry about her sick child.

B. *Audience Analysis*

Assume that you are planning to deliver a message to the members of your class. The purpose of the message is to persuade the listeners to try your favorite hobby or sport. Create an audience profile of the class. Include information from the following categories in the profile of class members.

• Age and gender

• Background, education, and experience

• Interests and concerns related to the topic

• Attitudes related to the topic

• Emotional state

If you do not know some of your classmates very well, you may not be able to cite information for all the categories. This is often the case when a sender creates an audience profile. Include information you know or can conclude from observing classmates. For example, you can often tell whether a person is happy, sad, frustrated, or mad from observation.

C. *External Communication Barriers*

TEAMWORK

Work with a classmate to complete this activity. Consider your current setting, whether in the classroom or another location. Make a list of the external communication barriers present in this setting. For each barrier, note whether a person in this setting is able to control or eliminate the barrier.

Reading in the Workplace

Importance of Reading

Information Age is the name given to the present period in history. This time is also called the *Digital Age*. Both names reflect a focus on the importance of information to personal and business success. Much of the information available today is in digital form. This is an electronic format that can be processed by computers. A recent report, "The Expanding Digital Universe: A Forecast of Worldwide Information Growth Through 2010," addresses information growth. The report indicates that in 2006 the amount of digital information reached 161 billion gigabytes. This amount is about 3 million times the information in all books ever written.[1]

With so much information available, reading is very important. In fact, any career or job you choose will require reading. You must be able to read effectively to interpret messages from coworkers and customers, follow instructions, and complete procedures. Doing research and using data to make decisions and solve problems also require reading.

Reading and the Job Search

One important instance of reading related to your career will be reading job postings. You will need to read job announcements and descriptions to locate jobs in which you are interested. You will need to read and follow directions for submitting information and applying for the jobs you choose to pursue.

The process of applying for many jobs is handled online. Figure 1-3 shows the USAJOBS web site, the official site for the U.S. government. Users can visit the site to search for jobs in particular areas. Users can also apply for jobs online. Many companies and organizations post job openings on their web sites. Job seekers can also read job postings in newspapers and industry magazines.

Finding a job that is right for you is the first step in a successful career. Reading will help you find that job.

OBJECTIVES

After completing Section 1.3, you should be able to:

1. Explain why reading is important for workplace success.

2. Describe ways reading is used in the workplace.

3. Practice strategies to improve reading skills.

Ethics

When applying for a job, give honest and complete information to the employer.

Figure 1-3 USAJOBS is the official job site of the U.S. government.

Source: USAJOBS, United States Office of Personnel Management, accessed February 6, 2008, available from http://jobsearch.usajobs.gov/jobsearch.asp.

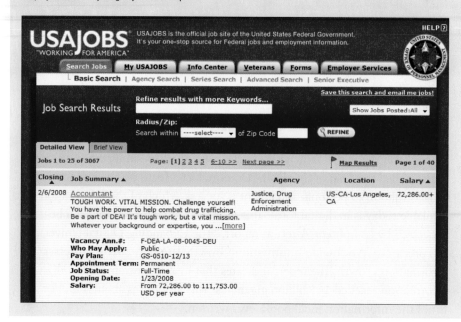

Reading on the Job

Once you find a job, you will need to read for many reasons. You will read for background information, to locate specific data, and to learn new procedures. You will also read to gather data for use in making decisions or solving problems. In some cases, you will need to share the information you read with coworkers or clients. The paragraphs that follow describe a few situations in which reading on the job is important.

Staying Informed

Although every job requires reading, some jobs involve more reading and paperwork than others. In any job, however, you will want to read about your company. Newsletters, magazines articles, the company web site, and other sources will help you learn about the company. Being informed about the company and its activities will make you a better employee.

Technology and methods of doing things in business and other fields change on an ongoing basis. You may need to read journals, newsletters, or articles to keep current in your field. You may also need to take seminars or continuing education courses that will involve reading. Staying aware of current methods will help you in your present job and may prepare you for a higher-level position or a job in a related field.

Ethics

Ethical employees focus on work activities while at work. They do not read personal e-mails and other material.

Following Procedures

Many jobs require workers to perform various procedures. You will need to read instructions or procedures manuals to learn or review the steps to follow. For example, an office worker may be assigned to oversee the use and upkeep of an office copier. The worker will need to read the copier manual to learn how to perform tasks, such as changing the toner or ink and clearing paper jams. An engineer may use computer software to design buildings. When a new version of the software is released, the engineer will need to read the software manual or help files to learn procedures for using the software. In both examples, reading helps the worker complete tasks and be a more effective employee.

In some jobs, an employee's safety may depend on reading and following procedures correctly. For example, employees must read material safety data sheets when working with or near dangerous chemicals to avoid injury.

K e y ▶ P o i n t

Employees must read and follow procedures carefully to avoid injury when working with hazardous materials.

Handling Transactions

Exchanging goods or services for payments is the basis of most business affairs. Workers must read to verify that transactions are completed as planned. For example, Angela Jones works in the Warehouse Department of a small company. She reads packing slips that come with shipments of goods or products. Then Angela compares the packing slip with the goods actually received. Next she reads the order for the goods and compares it to the packing slip. If all three agree, the order has been filled correctly. If not, Angela must take steps to correct the problem.

DIGITAL VISION/GETTY IMAGES

Workers in the Warehouse Department must read orders and packing slips.

Connie Chang works in the Accounting Department for the same small company. Part of her job is to read invoices (bills) for items the company has bought. She must read the goods received list and compare it with the invoice to be sure the company is being charged correctly.

Providing Customer Service

Ramon Garcia works in the Shipping Department of his company. Ramon must read the orders received from customers and pack the goods for shipment. Filling orders correctly is very important for keeping customers satisfied and ensuring future orders. Ramon must also read the procedures provided on when to use various shipping services to fill orders.

Reading also plays a role in keeping customers happy after the sale. Customer service associates must read e-mails and letters from customers to answer questions and provide other support.

Diversity

Companies operate in a global marketplace with customers from around the world. Employees must communicate effectively to serve customers from diverse backgrounds and cultures.

Making Decisions and Solving Problems

One of the most important purposes of reading in the workplace is to gain information for making decisions or solving problems. Figure 1-4 gives a few example situations.

Figure 1-4 Information gained by reading is critical for making decisions.

READING TO MAKE DECISIONS AND SOLVE PROBLEMS
• Read to understand material from several sources on a certain topic. Make a recommendation as requested by your manager.
• Read several accounts of how a product failed to perform properly to find the underlying cause of the problem.
• Read research reports and market forecasts to help decide whether to produce a new product.
• Read employee evaluations and manager comments to select a person for promotion to a higher-level job.
• Read information on employee benefits, such as health care plans, to help you choose appropriate options.

check point 7

1. Explain how reading is important for workplace success.

2. Describe four ways reading is used in the workplace.

Check your answers in Appendix C.

Improving Reading Skills

To be an effective reader, you must read at an appropriate rate, understand what you read, and remember what you read. Reading speed can be improved with practice. Expanding your vocabulary can help you improve your reading comprehension (understanding of what you read).

Types of Reading

Basically, there are three types of reading: skimming, scanning, and careful reading. Different reading speeds are appropriate for each type of reading.

Skimming is looking over material quickly to locate specific data. For example, you may skim a ten-page report to find one paragraph about improving customer service. When the data is located, read the material carefully at a comfortable rate.

Scanning is an attempt to get a basic understanding of the objectives and the important points of the material you are going to read. To scan, read main headings, subheadings, and the first sentence of each paragraph. Look at figures and read their captions. Scan lists and numbered items since they often add depth to content. When you scan, read very quickly. You will read more slowly when carefully reading the material.

Careful reading is used when trying to understand and remember the material that is read. In the workplace, you need to exercise careful reading much of the time.

Key ▶ Point

Different reading speeds are appropriate for scanning and for careful reading.

NETBookmark

Several web sites provide free reading tests online. Go to a search engine such as Google™. A link to Google is provided on the web site for this book that is shown below. Search for *speed reading test*. Go to one of the sites in the search results and take a free test to find your reading speed.

1. What is your reading speed as shown by the free online test?

2. How does your score compare with the speeds discussed in the text on page 24?

www.cengage.com/school/bcomm/buscomm

Improving Speed and Comprehension

Many people read at an average speed of from 200 to 350 words per minute. With practice and improved vocabulary, readers can improve to 350 to 800 words per minute. Exceptional readers may read at 1,000 words per minute or more. Reading speed must be balanced with comprehension. Reading quickly but not understanding or remembering what you have read is fruitless. Seminars, books, and computer software designed to improve reading speed and comprehension are available. However, with dedicated effort, you can do much on your own to improve your skills. To improve the speed and comprehension of careful reading, follow these tips:

Key ▶ Point

Both reading speed and comprehension are important for effective reading.

- Select a location that is conducive to reading. If a room is not comfortable or has distractions, you cannot focus on what you are reading.

- Scan the item you are to read. Getting an overview of the information will help improve your understanding of the material.

- Use a dictionary to look up words you do not know. Building your vocabulary will help improve your reading speed and comprehension.

Diversity

When reading messages from people for whom English is a second language, assume that the formal, dictionary definitions of words apply.

- If you are a word-for-word reader, try to learn to read in groups of words. Silently pronouncing each word slows reading speed. Try to grasp the meaning of phrases and clauses without focusing on individual words.

- Find the main idea in every paragraph. The rest of the sentences in a paragraph usually provide additional details about the main idea.

- Recognize the order of events in a situation. This understanding will allow you to reconstruct the entire situation.

- Take notes or highlight information while reading. Study your notes to help you recall what you read.

- To check your understanding and create a frame of reference, compare the information you read to what you already know.

Reading Skills exercises, such as the one on page 17, are found throughout this textbook. Completing these exercises will help you improve your careful reading skills.

check point 8

1. What is scanning when reading? How does scanning help improve reading comprehension?

2. Describe three things you can do to help improve your careful reading skills.

Check your answers in Appendix C.

Section 1.3 *Applications*

A. *Purposes for Reading on the Job*

For each situation described below, indicate the primary purpose for reading.

1. A new employee wants to learn general information about the company

2. A salesperson needs to know answers to a customer's questions

3. A worker needs to know how to operate a new piece of machinery

4. Company managers must review sales figures to see whether a product rebate is resulting in increased sales and decide whether to continue the program

5. An accounts payable associate needs to know whether the correct payment discount has been taken when paying a bill

B. *Practicing Reading Skills*

When you begin a new job, you will need to complete forms related to payroll and taxes. One of these is Form W-4, which lists tax exemptions.

1. Open and print the *Word* file *CH01 Form W-4* found in the student data files. This file contains Form W-4 for 2008. (The student data files are found on the companion web site or may be provided by your instructor.)

2. Scan the information on page 1 of the form. What three types of information are provided on page 1? Scan page 2. What two worksheets are shown on page 2?

3. Skim the information at the top of page 1 to find the section that describes a head of household. Read that section carefully. Write a summary of who may be a head of household in your own words.

4. Skim the information at the top of page 1 to find the section that discusses nonwage income. What are the two examples of nonwage income given in this section?

5. Skim page 2. Who should use the Two-Earner/Multiple Jobs Worksheet?

6. Read carefully the directions in the Personal Allowances Worksheet section. Complete the Employee's Withholding Allowance Certificate using your personal information and following the directions you have read.

Chapter *Summary*

1.1 The Communication Process

- The elements of the communication process are the message, the sender, the receiver, the channel, and feedback.

- The purposes of business communication are to obtain or share information, build goodwill and image, persuade, and build relationships and self-esteem.

- Business communication can be formal or informal and written or oral.

- Business messages can be used for upward, downward, or lateral communication.

1.2 Overcoming Communication Barriers

- Communication barriers are things or conditions that interfere with communication. Communication barriers can be internal or external.

- To help overcome barriers, the sender can analyze and understand the receiver and the message environment.

- The sender should select an appropriate channel and symbols that the receiver will understand.

- Encouraging and interpreting feedback are important duties of the sender.

- To help overcome barriers, the receiver can read and listen effectively.

1.3 Reading in the Workplace

- Reading is important for career success. Any career or job you choose will require reading.

- Reading is used for many purposes in the workplace, such as to locate specific data, learn new procedures, and gather data for use in making decisions or solving problems.

- To be an effective reader, you must read at an appropriate rate, understand what you read, and remember what you read.

- Reading speed and comprehension can be improved with practice.

Vocabulary

Open the *Word* file *CH01 Vocabulary* from the student data files. Complete the exercise to review the vocabulary terms from this chapter.

audience analysis

business communication

channel

communication

communication barriers

confidential information

external communication barriers

feedback

goodwill

grapevine

internal communication barriers

listening

message

message environment

nonverbal symbols

reading

receiver

scanning

sender

verbal symbols

Critical Thinking Questions

1. In the communication process, who has the greater responsibility—the receiver or the sender? Justify your answer.

2. Of the four forms of communication (speaking, writing, listening, and reading), which form is the most important to you? Explain why.

3. When you send a message and receive no feedback, how do you interpret this response?

4. Do internal or external barriers affect your communication skills the most? Explain your answer.

5. Describe a situation in which you used reading to learn a new process or procedure. Would improved reading skills have made the learning easier?

6. Identify a job that you may like to have in the future. Describe how reading skills could help you be successful in that job.

CRITICAL THINKING

Chapter *Applications*

A. *The Communication Process*

Identify the element of the communication process (message, sender, receiver, channel, or feedback) described in each situation.

1. A person who is reading an e-mail
2. The content of a letter
3. The use of a memo to send a message to a coworker
4. A person who uses a computer to relay a message over a network
5. The smile of someone listening to a speaker

B. *The Purposes of Communication*

Indicate the purpose of each business communication described below.

1. A customer newsletter article describing improved customer service
2. A memo to a coworker describing the parts needed for a new product
3. A letter to a client urging the client to buy a product
4. An e-mail to a coworker thanking him for helping you with a project

C. *Communication Direction*

Indicate whether each message described below is upward, lateral, or downward communication.

1. A memo to a coworker with the same job as yours
2. A report from a department supervisor to a vice president
3. An e-mail from a supervisor to all department employees
4. A telephone call from a manager to an administrative assistant

D. *Verbal and Nonverbal Messages*

Indicate whether each message contains verbal or nonverbal symbols or both.

1. A telephone call to a supplier
2. No verbal response to a spoken message
3. An e-mail
4. A written report sent to a company president

E. Internal Barriers

1. Analyze yourself as a communicator. Identify internal barriers that are a challenge for you as you speak, write, listen, or read.

2. Write a paragraph explaining why you find these barriers challenging. Describe steps you can take to help overcome these barriers.

CRITICAL THINKING

F. Reading for Safety

Reading and understanding safety procedures is very important. You probably have a school handbook or notices posted in your school that contain valuable information for how to proceed in an emergency.

1. Skim your school handbook (or posted notices) to find the section that deals with a fire emergency. Read this section carefully.

2. In your own words, explain the steps you should take in a fire emergency.

REAL WORLD

G. Reading about Communication Barriers

Communication barriers are things or conditions that hinder communication. Practice your reading skills while learning more about communication barriers.

1. Open an Internet search engine. Search for articles using the keywords *communication barriers*.

2. Open and scan several articles shown in the search results list. Select one article to read carefully.

3. Read the article carefully and answer the following questions.

INTERNET

- What is the title of the article or web page?

- What is the web page address where the article can be found?

- Who is the author of the article (if an author is given)?

- Does the article discuss internal communications barriers, external communication barriers, or both types of barriers?

- What are the main points of the article?

Editing Activities

1. Open and edit the *Word* file *CH01 Editing* from the student data files, and correct all spelling, punctuation, and grammar errors. (The student data files are found on the companion web site (www.cengage.com/school/bcomm/buscomm) or may be provided by your instructor.

A. Contacting a Customer

As a sales representative with your company, you want to send a message to an important customer, Mr. Park. He is a good friend of the company's president and regularly orders supplies from your company. In your opinion, the two of you have a very good relationship. However, the last time you visited him, he seemed impatient with you. You got the feeling that he was anxious to get back to his work. Now, two days after your visit, your company launches a sales campaign. Many of the products that Mr. Park purchases from you are on sale. The prices are good, but the sale will last only two weeks.

1.   Should you contact this customer?

2.   If yes, will you contact him by letter? by e-mail? with a personal visit? with a telephone call? Justify your answer.

B. Handling Sensitive Information

Maria works for a large, local company. She is an administrative assistant to the director of the Human Resources Department, the person who hires new employees. Many people come into her office every week. She loves her work and really admires the director. Recently, several men and women have come into the office and interviewed for an area sales manager position. One of the men who interviewed for the position was a person whom she knew when she worked for another company. Unfortunately, she knows that this man was fired because he provided false information to make himself and others within his district look good.

1.   If you were in Maria's position, what would you do? Would you tell the director or would you not get involved?

2.   If you choose to tell the director, should you share this sensitive information in an e-mail? a memo? a face-to-face conversation? Why would you use the channel you chose?

ealth Science

Communication for Health Science Careers

Since her childhood, Julia Rodman has wanted to be a nurse. Four years ago, after a lot of schooling and work, her dream came true. She graduated from Stone Creek College with a degree in nursing. After a short time, Julia realized that her job would be more secure if she were a registered nurse (RN). Julia went back to school. Two years ago, she completed her RN training.

Last week, a member of the hospital's administration called Julia into her office to discuss a new job opportunity—head nurse for the second floor. As Julia thinks about the job opportunity, she wonders if she has the skills necessary for the new position. She enjoys talking and working with patients and is a successful RN—partly because of her interpersonal skills. Julia wants a second opinion. She has come to you and asked, "What do you think I should do?"

1. In Julia's present job, how are communication skills important?

2. In the new position offered to her, are communication skills important? Justify your answer.

3. How do the communication skills required for the two positions differ?

4. Should this difference be an important consideration in Julia's decision? If so, why?

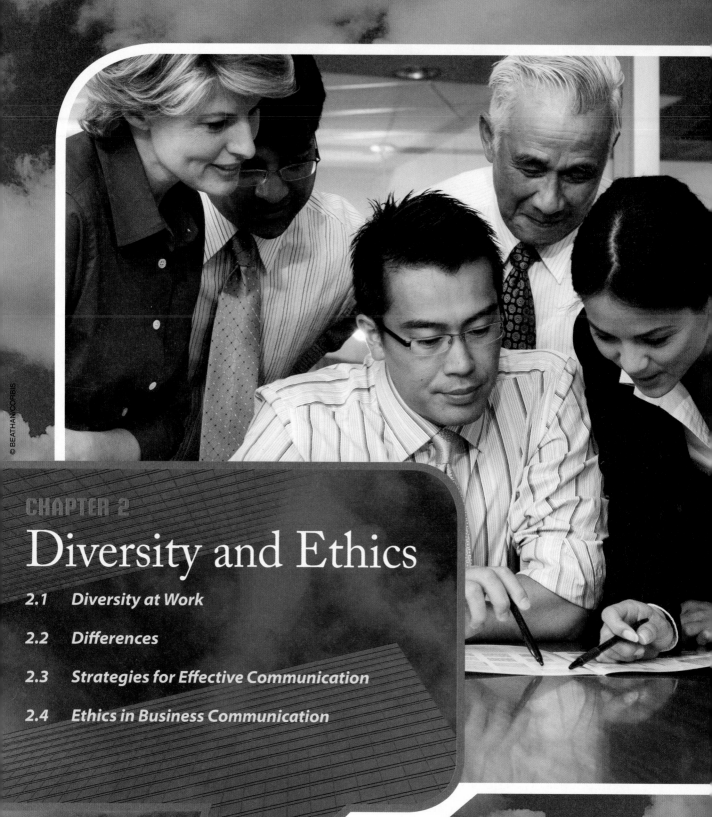

CHAPTER 2
Diversity and Ethics

2.1   Diversity at Work

2.2   Differences

2.3   Strategies for Effective Communication

2.4   Ethics in Business Communication

Succeeding in a Global Business

The company where Anita Boaz works has recently been acquired by a German company. Anita has a new supervisor, Hans Dortmann, who moved to the area from Germany.

Anita's first meeting with Mr. Dortmann was set for Friday, which is casual dress day at the office. Anita chose some nice slacks to wear instead of jeans. Traffic was unusually heavy, and Anita was a few minutes late for the meeting. The door to the meeting room was closed when Anita arrived. She knocked once and went in. Mr. Dortmann and the other executives, who were all dressed in business suits, were sitting at the conference table. Anita reached out her hand to Mr. Dortmann and said with a smile, "Good Morning, Hans. I'm Anita Boaz. It's good to meet you."

Mr. Dortmann rose hesitantly, then responded with a brief greeting and sat down. Anita was baffled by his chilly reaction. Then she decided that maybe he was not used to working with women at the management level. She came away thinking Mr. Dortmann and the other executives were very cool and unfriendly.

Anita decided to do some research about business customs in Germany. From her research, she learned that business executives in Germany tend to have a high regard for authority and structure. They typically greet each other formally. They tend to separate business and leisure activities. With her new understanding of German business customs, Anita was better able to understand Mr. Dortmann's behavior. She began to interact with Mr. Dortmann in a more formal manner. Over time, she and Mr. Dortmann developed a cooperative and respectful working relationship.

Questions

1. What communication barriers existed between Anita and Mr. Dortmann? Did Anita do the right thing to overcome those barriers? Explain.

2. How might Anita and her new supervisor benefit from their differences? What must they do to recognize and learn from each other's strengths?

2.1

Diversity at Work

Overview of Diversity

OBJECTIVES

After completing Section 2.1,
you should be able to:

1. Define *diversity* and
   identify its benefits
   and challenges in the
   workplace.

2. Discuss the diversity of
   the U.S. population and
   workforce.

3. Discuss how globalization
   affects the workforce.

Diversity refers to the presence of a wide range of variation in qualities or attributes of people or things. People in the United States live and work in a diverse society. Coworkers, customers, and business associates come from different backgrounds. They may have different customs, values, manners, beliefs, and languages. A company in the United States may be owned by a company based in Europe or Asia. Some fellow employees may have been transferred from company headquarters in London or Taipei. Coworkers or customers may have immigrated to the United States in recent decades.

Wherever people are from, they have unique backgrounds and personalities. They have their own ideas about how things should be done. Accommodating and benefiting from the diversity of employees and customers is one of the greatest challenges in the workplace today.

Diversity Benefits

Key ▶ Point

A diverse workforce makes companies better able to meet the needs of customers.

A diverse workforce makes employers better able to meet the needs of growing global markets and an increasingly diverse U.S. population. Having a diverse workforce enhances the reputation of a company. It also helps the company attract talented employees and keep customers. Diverse work groups may be more creative and innovative than groups that are not diverse.

A diverse workforce can help a company understand its customers' needs.

DIGITAL VISION/GETTY IMAGES

Figure 2-1 Diversity refers to qualities or attributes of people.

TERMS RELATED TO DIVERSITY	
Race	The division of people into groups based on physical characteristics, such as skin or hair color
Ethnicity	The division of people into groups that share a common ancestry, history, or culture
Culture	A set of beliefs, attitudes, practices, and social customs that distinguishes a group of people
Inclusion	Seeing and valuing the contributions of everyone in a workplace and treating everyone fairly

Traditional definitions of diversity have centered on race, gender, age, and disability. Today diversity has a broader definition—one that includes differences in ethnicity, culture, background, and personality. Figure 2-1 defines several terms related to diversity.

Diversity Challenges

Companies have found that lack of attention to diversity issues can be costly. Employees who believe that their employer is indifferent or is hostile to workers "like them" may seek jobs elsewhere. Companies that do not have a diverse workforce may not understand what a diverse group of customers wants or needs. This lack can result in missed opportunities for new markets and loss of customers. Failing to recognize workers' differences and needs can result in lower productivity and low morale. Claims of discrimination may be made by workers who think they are receiving unfair treatment.

Ethics

Discriminating against workers because of their gender, age, or ethnicity is unethical.

Diversity

To succeed at work you need to be able to get along with many different kinds of people. The inability to work with others is a common reason employees are fired.

check point 1

1. What is the definition of *diversity*?

2. What are some benefits of having a diverse workforce?

3. What are some challenges related to diversity in the workplace?

Check your answers in Appendix C.

Diversity Trends

The United States is more culturally diverse than ever before, partly because of a rise in immigration. According to the Center for Immigration Studies, the 1990s saw more immigration than any other period in American history.[1] States such as Florida, Texas, and California have traditionally had large immigrant populations. Today, immigrants settle in many states. Many cities now have a large number of immigrant residents.[2]

Population Predictions

The U.S. Census Bureau makes several predictions for the future of a diverse U.S. population. According to these population projections, the following trends will occur:

- The country's population will continue to grow, increasing to 419.9 million in 2050.

- The nation's Hispanic and Asian populations will triple over the next half century.

- Non-Hispanic whites will represent about one-half of the total population by 2050.

- The black population will rise to 61.4 million in 2050, an increase of about 26 million.

- The country's population will become older. By 2030, about one in five people will be 65 or older.

- The female population will continue to outnumber the male population, having 213.4 million females and 206.5 million males by mid-century.[3]

The Diverse Workforce

Today's workforce reflects the recent changes in the nation's population. The civilian labor force is already more diverse than it was when your parents took their first jobs. The following projections from the *Monthly Labor Review* show that the U.S. workforce will become even more diverse.

- By 2012, the number of persons working or looking for work is expected to reach 162.3 million.

- Women will make up close to half the labor force.

Key▶Point

The Hispanic and Asian populations in the United States are predicted to triple over the next half century.

Key▶Point

By 2012, women will make up close to half the labor force.

---

[1]"Where Immigrants Live," Center for Immigration Studies, accessed February 26, 2008, available from http://www.cis.org/articles/2003/back1203.html.

[2]Audrey Singer, "The Rise of New Immigrant Gateways," Center on Urban and Metropolitan Policy, The Brookings Institution, accessed February 28, 2008, available from www.brookings.edu/urban/pubs/20040301_gateways.pdf.

[3]"More Diversity, Slower Growth," U.S. Census Bureau News, accessed February 26, 2008, available from http://www.census.gov/Press-Release/www/releases/archives/ population/001720.html.

- White non-Hispanics will continue to make up about 66 percent of the labor force.

- More than 30 percent of the workforce will consist of African-American, Latino, and Asian-American people. By 2012, nearly one in three workers will belong to one of those groups.

- Older workers make up a large part of the labor force. Workers 55 and older will compose 19.1 percent of the labor force in 2012, up from 14.3 percent in 2002. [4]

check point 2

1. Is the U.S. population becoming more or less diverse?

2. Does the United States have more male or female citizens?

3. By 2012, African-American, Latino, and Asian-American people will make up about what percentage of the U.S. workforce?

4. Is the U.S. workforce as a whole getting younger or older?

Check your answers in Appendix C.

The World as a Global Workplace

Globalization is the integration of activities among nations in areas such as commerce and culture. Improved communication technologies make doing business globally easier and cheaper than ever before. Favorable trade agreements, such as the North American Free Trade Agreement (NAFTA), also improve trade among countries.

Globalization affects the workforce in many ways. When applying for a job, individuals may have to compete with job candidates from around the world. This can be an advantage to companies, as it may give them a larger group of qualified candidates. However, it may make getting a job harder for some people. Once on the job, there is a good chance employees will interact

Diversity

Globalization makes understanding other cultures important for business success.

---

[4]Mitra Toossi, "Labor Force Projections to 2012: The Graying of the U.S. Workforce," *Monthly Labor Review* (February 2004), accessed February 28, 2008, available from http://www.bls.gov/opub/mlr/2004/02/art3full.pdf.

OCCUPATIONAL SUCCESS

Work/Life Balance

The U.S. workforce has become very diverse. Women make up about half of the workforce. There are more families with two working parents than in the past. Single-parent families are also on the rise. Many of the activities once handled by a nonworking parent must now be handled by a working parent.

The term *work/life balance* describes the need workers have to balance work with other aspects of life. Different careers make different demands on workers and their families. Some jobs may require much travel, overtime, or a long commute. These conditions reduce time available to spend with family or for taking part in other activities. In many jobs, taking time off to care for a sick child or for other personal needs is not an option.

When employees do not have enough time to take care of their personal matters, they bring stress to the workplace and may be less productive. Many companies address this problem by creating a workplace that is supportive of workers' needs. For example, some companies have childcare facilities on-site. Other companies create positions with flexible work hours. More companies are also providing benefits for part-time workers.

When choosing a career, consider how your choice will affect all aspects of your life. When choosing an employer, consider whether the company fits your needs as well as whether you fit the needs of the company.

Diversity

Millions of U.S. employees work for foreign multinational companies doing business in the United States.

with coworkers and customers from other countries. This situation may require that employees be trained in dealing with people from other cultures. It may also require companies to have employees who speak several languages.

Some employees work for a **multinational company**—a company that conducts business in at least two nations. PepsiCo, for example, is headquartered in Purchase, New York. PepsiCo brands are available in nearly 200 countries. Other successful multinational companies include Disney, Microsoft, and Sony. Employees of multinational companies may be asked to move to a different country to continue working for the company.

Some companies move all or part of their operations to foreign countries to take advantage of favorable conditions, such as lower labor costs or better-trained workers. This often means that workers in the home country lose their jobs. However, new job opportunities may be created as companies from foreign countries move all or part of their operations to the workers' home country.

Section 2.1 *Applications*

A. *Globalization*

Write a paragraph that discusses how globalization affects U.S. workers. Address these questions:

- How might globalization affect people who are looking for jobs?
- How might globalization affect workers on the job?
- How might globalization affect employees of multinational companies?

B. *Diversity in Your State*

The U.S. Census Bureau provides information on population diversity. Learn about the diverse population of the country and your state.

1. Access the Internet and the Web site for this textbook. On the Links list, select the link for USA QuickFacts.

2. Select the name of your state from the drop-down list or click your state on the map. The table that appears shows data for your state and the entire country.

3. Answer the following questions about the population. (If you do not have access to the Internet, open the *Word* file *CH02 USA QuickFacts* from the student data files. Answer the questions using data for the entire country.)

   - For what year or years are the census data shown?
   - What is the population estimate for your state? for the country?
   - What percentage of the population of your state is female? How does this number compare to the percentage for the entire country?
   - Black persons make up what percentage of the population of your state? of the country?
   - Persons of Hispanic origin make up what percentage of the population of your state? of the country?
   - Persons of Asian origin make up what percentage of the population of your state? of the country?
   - Persons of your race and/or ethnicity make up what percentage of the population of your state? of the country?

INTERNET

REAL WORLD

2.2 Differences

Cultural Differences

OBJECTIVES

After completing Section 2.2, you should be able to:

1. Describe examples of differences among cultures.

2. Explain the importance of respecting customs and practicing etiquette.

Key▶Point

Cultural differences can be communication barriers.

People from cultures different from your own are likely to have different values. They are likely to make different assumptions than you do. For example, a medical assistant explaining a procedure to a patient may assume that when the patient nods and smiles, the patient understands. In some cultures, however, nodding and smiling is a way of showing respect. It does not indicate understanding. Consider another example: A person who recently emigrated from a country where police are brutal and corrupt is likely to react with suspicion and fear to police officers in the United States.

To communicate effectively, you must recognize barriers to communication. Cultural differences can be communication barriers. They can prevent or hinder an effective exchange of ideas or information. All people want to feel they are valued, respected, and understood. The challenge is knowing what words or actions will be seen as respectful and helpful.

Language

Language is a common communication barrier. Though English is widely spoken across the globe, it is the native language of only a handful of countries. In the 2000 U.S. census, after English and Spanish, Chinese was the language most commonly spoken at home followed by French and German. Nearly 11 million people indicated that they did not speak English well or did not speak English at all.[5]

Although English is studied widely outside the United States, many people do not speak the language well or at all. Some of the most widely spoken languages in the world include Mandarin Chinese, Spanish, English, Arabic, Hindi, Portuguese, Bengali, Russian, Japanese, and German.[6]

Some of your fellow employees, clients, and business associates may not speak English or may not speak it well. Even within the same language, accents and the use of different words for the same ideas can make speech difficult to understand, especially when the speaker is talking rapidly.

---

[5]Hyon B. Shin and Rosalind Bruno, "Language Use and English-Speaking Ability: 2000," Census 2000 Brief, accessed February 28, 2008, available from http://www.census.gov/prod/2003pubs/c2kbr-29.pdf.

[6]Matt Rosenberg, "Most Popular Languages," About.com: Geography, accessed February 28, 2008, available from http://geography.about.com/od/culturalgeography/a/10languages.htm.

Body Language

Body language can be a barrier to communication. The facial expressions, gestures, or postures that accompany a person's words often have greater meaning than the words themselves. In addition, the less people understand English, the more they rely on body language.

Do not assume that people from different cultures know and use the same nonverbal symbols that you do. The *OK* gesture used in the United States would likely be perceived as poor manners by someone from France, where it signifies *worthless* or *zero*. In other countries, the OK sign represents an obscene comment. Here are several more examples:

■ In many countries and religions, people consider the feet unclean. If you touch someone with your foot, apologize. Do not cross your feet at the ankles. Doing so displays the soles of your feet, which is considered rude.

■ The way people indicate yes and no differs significantly in various cultures. To say yes, a Greek may tilt his or her head to either side. To say no, the person may nod upward slightly or just lift his or her eyebrows.

■ You may think that greeting people would be a simple procedure. How hard can it be to smile, look pleasant, and shake hands? In fact, people from various cultures have their own ideas about the proper way to greet others. A smile can show displeasure, embarrassment, or other feelings depending on the place and situation.

■ Americans tend to maintain steady eye contact while talking. In many other cultures, less eye contact is considered more respectful.

Diversity

Nonverbal symbols can mean different things in different cultures.

STOCKBYTE/GETTY IMAGES

Greeting colleagues appropriately is important.

Building Vocabulary

Your vocabulary is the words and terms you recognize and understand. When you are reading, look up words that you do not understand. Building your vocabulary will help improve your reading speed and comprehension.

In this chapter, you are learning about the importance of diversity in the workplace. Some companies are so committed to having a diverse workforce that they have a diversity director. This position may also be called *EEO (Equal Employment Opportunity) officer* or *affirmative action coordinator*.

Open the *Word* file *CH02 Reading* from the student data files. This file contains material from the *Occupational Outlook Handbook*. Read the job description, which includes EEO officer. Several words and terms in the job description are underlined. Using a dictionary, the Internet, or the information in the document, write definitions for each of the ten words or terms.

Personal Space

Personal space is the area near a person within which other people should not intrude. The amount of personal space with which people are comfortable varies depending on individual preference and cultural background. Most Americans appreciate personal space of 18 inches to 4 feet.

Moving into someone's personal space may make that person uncomfortable. In some cultures, though, people are at ease with less personal space. They may be insulted if an American steps back to create more space.

check point 3

1. What are three differences in culture that may be barriers to communication?

2. Give two examples of body language that may have different meanings in different cultures.

Check your answers in Appendix C.

Customs and Etiquette

Etiquette is a set of rules of behavior for a particular place or situation. Customs (beliefs, traditions, and practices of a group of people) and etiquette vary from country to country and culture to culture. The following examples highlight some differences.

- Americans are accustomed to business meetings starting on time. In some countries, punctuality is less important. When invited to meetings in these countries, Americans should arrive on time and be prepared to wait graciously.

- Americans are casual with business cards. In other countries, such as China and Japan, business cards are taken very seriously. They are presented with care, read carefully, and not immediately put away.

- Proper attire matters. In Saudi Arabia, for example, American women can show their respect for local customs by dressing conservatively, with high necklines, long sleeves, and skirts well below the knee.

Your job may involve working with someone from another country or culture. When this is the case, do research to learn the appropriate etiquette to follow. Show respect for other people and their cultures. Remember, however, that things you read about a group of people may not apply to every person in that group. Pay attention to individuals and listen to what they say. Observe what they do, and ask questions when you do not understand comments or actions.

In some cases, discomfort in dealing with others arises from a stereotype. A **stereotype** is an oversimplified belief about a group of people. For example, thinking of older people as unable to adapt to change is a stereotype. Stereotypes lead to judging people as members of a group rather than as individuals.

A related problem is prejudice. **Prejudice** is a bias that prevents objective thought about a person or thing. Prejudice can hinder communication. Remember that although people within a group may share some characteristics, each person is unique in personality, experience, ability, and life situation.

Key ▶ Point

Stereotypes lead to judging people as members of a group rather than as individuals.

check point 4

1. What is *etiquette*? Why is following proper etiquette important?

2. What is a stereotype? What is prejudice? How can both hinder communication?

Check your answers in Appendix C.

Section 2.2 *Applications*

A. Stereotypes

"All teenagers are trouble-makers!" "What do kids know?" These two state-ments reflect stereotypes related to a person's age.

1. Describe a situation in which a person allowed a stereotype related to age to affect something that was said or done. The situation can be a real one you have witnessed or one you have read about or seen on TV.

2. Explain how the stereotype hindered the communication process.

3. Explain how the communication could have been handled differently to avoid using stereotypes.

B. World Languages

English is studied widely outside the United States; however, many people do not speak English well or at all. Some of the most widely spoken languages in the world are listed in the table below. These are approximate numbers for first-language speakers for that language.

LANGUAGE	SPEAKERS (In Millions)
Mandarin Chinese	882
Spanish	325
English	312 to 380
Arabic	206 to 422
Hindi	181
Portuguese	178
Bengali	173
Russian	146
Japanese	128
German	96

Source: Matt Rosenberg, "Most Popular Languages," About.com: Geography, accessed February 28, 2008, available from http://geography.about.com/od/culturalgeography/a/10languages.htm.

1. Use spreadsheet or presentation software to create a column chart that compares the number of people (from the table above) who speak each language.

2. Use **COMPARISON OF POPULAR LANGUAGES** as the chart title. Use **Speakers in Millions** as the chart subtitle.

3. For languages that have a range for the number, use the lowest number. Add data labels to show the value for each column.

2.3 Strategies for Effective Communication

Professional Attitude

In a diverse world, effective communication at work begins with having a professional attitude. Having a professional attitude reduces barriers to communicating with others. Figure 2-2 lists traits of a person who has a professional attitude.

Consider this example: Louise is a bookkeeper in a social service agency. She is 71 years old. All the other employees are less than 30 years old. Many of their attitudes about work, beliefs, and ideas are different from Louise's. When Louise was hired, most of the employees had not worked with an older person before. "At first," Louise says, "they didn't know what to expect. Then they got to know me." Louise has never had problems working with the younger employees. "They respect me, talk to me, and ask questions. They like that an older person respects their points of view. They like to be treated as equals. I have to understand their points of view even though I might not think they are valid. I listen to them and try to understand the way they think and feel."

Not being offended easily is one of the most important aspects of having a professional attitude. If a coworker says something that sounds offensive, stop and think. Was the offense intentional? Did you understand the remark correctly? How often has someone interpreted something you said differently than you intended? Is it possible that could be the case here, too?

Figure 2-2 Professional attitude helps avoid communication barriers.

INDICATORS OF A PROFESSIONAL ATTITUDE
A person who has a professional attitude:
• Refrains from making judgments about others
• Keeps an open mind
• Does not make assumptions or jump to conclusions
• Keeps emotions in check
• Is slow to take offense
• Gives others the benefit of the doubt

check point 5

1. What traits and actions indicate that a person has a professional attitude?

2. How can having a professional attitude help you communicate successfully?

Check your answers in Appendix C.

Cross-Cultural Communication

Cross-cultural communication occurs when people from different cultures share messages verbally, nonverbally, or in writing. Because the individuals do not belong to the same culture, they often do not share the same language. Their values, beliefs, customs, or assumptions about what is and is not proper may also differ. Those differences add challenges to the process of communicating.

Learning

If you work with people from other cultures, spend time learning about those cultures. Use Internet sources, read books and magazines, and see foreign movies. Visit ethnic neighborhoods. Enroll in diversity training or other diversity-related programs offered by your employer. Take every opportunity to talk to people from those cultures. Often, you will find that they appreciate your interest and will be glad to tell you about themselves and their backgrounds.

Be aware of a culture's forms of nonverbal communication. Recognize that even seemingly harmless gestures such as a smile or a nod may send a message other than what you intend.

Language

Because most Americans do not speak a language other than English, the first barrier to cross-cultural communication is often language. Some companies offer foreign-language courses for their employees. Language classes are also available at colleges. Merely learning how to greet someone and to say good-bye, along with a few polite expressions, such as *please* and *thank you*, can open the door to good relations with people from other cultures.

When sharing messages with people from other cultures, keep your language simple and to the point. Use simple vocabulary (*help* instead of *facilitate*, for example). Slow down a little if you normally speak quickly. Speak clearly and pronounce words carefully. Keep sentences short.

Key ▶ Point

The Internet, books, and magazines are good sources of information about people of other cultures.

Avoid acronyms and other abbreviations, as well as idioms, slang, and jargon. Acronyms are shortened forms of words or expressions typically formed from the first letter of each word. For example, the medical acronym *APGAR* stands for *activity, pulse, grimace, appearance,* and *respiratory effort*. This is a test used to assess a newborn infant's health.

Idioms are expressions that cannot be understood from simply reading the words that make them up. The expression *get your feet wet* is an example. It does not mean literally to get wet feet, but rather to gain a little experience at something. Slang is a word or expression that is not considered standard language. Slang words and terms are often understood only by people in a particular group or geographic region. Idioms and slang can be very confusing to people from other cultures.

Jargon is technical language used in a particular kind of work. *Acute myocardial infarction* (heart attack) and *toxic tort* (an injury resulting from exposure to a toxic substance) are examples of jargon. If you must use jargon, make sure the person with whom you are communicating understands it.

Guidelines for Cross-Cultural Communication

The following guidelines will help you be successful when speaking and corresponding with people from other cultures.

■ Remember not to make assumptions. Statements you have read about a culture may not be true of the particular person with whom

Diversity

Acronyms, idioms, slang, and jargon may be difficult for people of other cultures to understand.

Key▶Point

Statements you have read about a culture may not be true of the particular person with whom you are dealing.

When talking with people from other cultures, keep your language simple and to the point.

PHOTODISC/GETTY IMAGES

you are dealing. For example, do not assume that a person from Puerto Rico shares the same cultural background as a person from Mexico just because both are Latino. Use your knowledge of culture as a general guide and deal with individuals.

Key ▶ Point

With people whose cultures are more formal than yours, adapt your style to theirs.

- Be adaptable. American communication tends to be informal and direct. With people whose cultures are more formal, adapt your style to theirs.

- Avoid politics, religion, and other potentially sensitive topics. Remember that not everyone celebrates U.S. holidays, such as Thanksgiving and Independence Day. Similarly, Christmas and Easter are Christian holidays that not everyone observes.

- Be careful about using humor. A joke may seem funny to you, but it may seem senseless or, worse, offensive to your readers or listeners.

- Maintain personal contact. In some cultures, people tend to prefer face-to-face communication. When possible, meet in person. If distance is a barrier, talk by phone and arrange an occasional videoconference.

- Listen actively. Focus on what the speaker is saying. Carefully observe his or her body language for additional cues.

- Use visual aids. When language is a barrier, a sketch or drawing can be helpful. Sometimes it helps to write down a difficult word. The person's understanding of written English may be greater than his or her understanding of spoken English.

Use patience, sensitivity, understanding, and tolerance when communicating with people from other cultures. Do not correct people's English unless they have asked you to do so. Though your intentions are good, correcting someone's speech can be viewed as snobbish. Remember not to talk down to people who do not speak your language fluently. Instead, think of new ways to communicate that help you and your listener understand and become comfortable with each other.

CRITICAL
THINKING

check point 6

1. What methods can you use to learn about other cultures?

2. Why should you avoid acronyms, idioms, slang, and jargon in cross-cultural messages?

3. Which of the guidelines given for cross-cultural communication do you think is the most important? Why?

Check your answers in Appendix C.

DIGITAL VISION/GETTY IMAGES

When language is a barrier, use visual aids that are easily understood.

Fairness and Sensitivity

The two most important things you can do to show fairness and sensitivity toward others at work are to have a professional attitude and treat everyone with respect. Several of the guidelines for communicating with people from other cultures presented earlier apply to interactions with any client, coworker, or business associate.

- Do not make assumptions.
- Be adaptable.
- Avoid politics, religion, and other sensitive topics.
- Be careful about using humor.
- Listen actively.

Be sure to understand and follow your company's guidelines for dealing with clients and coworkers. In some companies, interactions are more formal than in others. For example, employees may address one another by first names or more formally by titles and last names. Clients or customers may also be addressed by first or last names, depending on the business or situation. Even in informal situations, using terms of endearment is not appropriate. Words such as *honey*, *dear*, and *sweetheart* are not appropriate when addressing a coworker or client.

Sometimes people are treated differently from what they expect or think is appropriate. Bad feelings and even charges of discrimination can result. **Discrimination** is unfair treatment of a person or group on the basis of prejudice. Title VII of the Civil Rights Act of 1964 makes it illegal to discriminate in employment on the basis of race, color, religion, sex, or national origin. Other laws forbid discrimination on the basis of age, medical conditions, or disabilities.

Ethics

Treating others unfairly because of their sex, age, or race is unethical.

A recent story in the news concerned an African-American woman who was wrongly accused of using fake checks in a store. She had recently moved to the area. She used a preprinted starter check to pay for her purchases. Her check was approved by the automatic verification service at the register. However, the cashier called over an assistant manager. The manager told the woman they could not accept the check and took it to an office. After 30 minutes, the assistant manager returned and said that he would accept the check.

When the customer left the store, police officers who had been called by store employees were waiting to arrest her. Finally, the customer was let go. She filed complaints with the state Department of Human Rights. The store admitted that it was in error and that its employees did not follow the company's policy.

When speaking or writing, treat your customers and business associates as individuals. Do not refer to race, ethnicity, gender, age, disability, or religion unless it is relevant to your topic. When you do refer to those subjects, do so with sensitivity and respect. The following examples show how to use tact in communications.

Do Not Say	the Vietnamese patient in Room 122
Say	the patient in Room 122
Do Not Say	the boys in the Sales Department
Say	the employees in the Sales Department
Do Not Say	Steve is a male nurse.
Say	Steve is a nurse.
Do Not Say	the bagger with Down's syndrome
Say	the bagger at Register 4

Key▶Point

In business communications, do not refer to race, ethnicity, gender, age, disability, or religion unless it is relevant to your topic.

Section 2.3 *Applications*

A. *Sexual Harassment*

Sexual harassment is a form of sex discrimination that violates Title VII of the Civil Rights Act of 1964. Open the *Word* file *CH02 Harassment* from the student data files. This file contains information about sexual harassment from the U.S. Equal Employment Opportunity Commission. After reading the information, answer the questions below.

1. What conditions or actions constitute sexual harassment?

2. Does the victim have to be of the opposite sex from the harasser?

3. What types of people may be the harasser?

4. Should the victim ignore the harasser's comments or actions? Explain.

5. What can employers do to prevent sexual harassment in the workplace?

REAL WORLD

B. *Tactful Communications*

In business communications, do not refer to race, ethnicity, gender, age, disability, or religion unless it is relevant to your topic. The statements below are not tactful or respectful of others. Rewrite the statements to show sensitivity and respect.

1. The crippled worker was unable to walk without crutches.

2. The firemen saved three people from a burning building.

3. Joan, dear, would you call my attorney for me.

4. The Jewish store owner handled the sale quickly.

5. The old woman paid her bills promptly.

C. *Discrimination Policies*

Many companies and organizations post their policies regarding discrimination on their Web sites.

1. Search the Internet using the term *discrimination policy*. Find and read the policy for two companies or organizations.

2. What do the two policies have in common? How are the two policies different? Be prepared to share your findings with the class.

REAL WORLD

INTERNET

2.4 Ethics in Business Communication

A Definition of Ethics

Key ▶ Point

A code of ethics states how an organization or group should treat clients, employees, or members.

Ethics are principles of right and wrong. Everyone has his or her own set of personal ethics. Personal ethics are influenced by your experiences and the culture and society in which you learn and grow.

Many ethical principles are widely shared. For example, many people believe that stealing is wrong. When many people in a community, state, or nation agree on an ethical principle, it is often made a law. Although an action may not violate a law, it may be unethical. Persuading a home buyer to take a loan he or she cannot afford is unethical but may not be illegal.

Businesses and professions have their own sets of ethical guidelines. They may be published in the form of a code of ethics. This code states how the group should treat clients, employees, or members. A growing number of organizations distribute annual reports that describe their ethical policies and corporate conduct. Employees are expected to respect their company's code of ethics while doing business for the company.

While some groups have written ethical guidelines, every organization and profession has its own unwritten code of conduct. For example, employees may be expected to refrain from reading others' e-mail. It is important to be aware of the written and the unwritten ethical guidelines of your employer.

Stories about business scandals frequently appear in newspapers. However, the majority of business dealings are done in an ethical manner. Companies know that dealing fairly with others promotes goodwill. Most people want to treat customers, coworkers, and employers in an ethical manner.

check point 7

1. What is the definition of *ethics*?

2. What factors influence personal ethics?

3. Why should employees be aware of the code of ethics of their employers?

Check your answers in Appendix C.

Communicating in an Ethical Way

A company's ethics affects how it deals with employees, customers, and the public. These ethics are also reflected in the company's communications. Companies and their employees have an obligation to tell the truth. Lying and withholding facts is always unethical. It is also often illegal.

Honesty

Honesty is an ethical issue that influences business communication. When dealing with clients, be honest about the products or services you or your company offers. Do not overstate or promise more than you can deliver. Follow these guidelines to help ensure that your statements to customers are truthful ones.

Ethics

When dealing with clients, be honest about the products or services you offer.

■ Learn about the products or services your company offers.

■ Inform yourself about company policies and procedures. Know the rules of your organization. Learn exactly what you can and cannot do for clients.

■ Offer facts, not opinions. Remember that facts can be proven with evidence to be true.

Instead of	This is the best treatment plan for you.
Say	This treatment plan has been successful for 87 percent of our patients.
Instead of	This product is better than any other on the market.
Say	This product received top ratings from consumer testing groups.

PHOTODISC/GETTY IMAGES

Be truthful when communicating with customers.

Just as employees should be honest with clients, employees have an obligation to be honest with their employers. Examples of unethical employee behavior include:

- Lying about the need for sick days
- Arriving to work late or leaving early
- Using work time for personal activities
- Using company resources for personal use
- Doing less than one's best work
- Taking credit for the work of others
- Giving false information about projects, products, or work conditions

Consider the following example. Tom Lee is a social worker. His duties include making bimonthly visits to all his clients. Once or twice a week he leaves the office, telling his employer that he will be seeing clients. Instead, he spends his time running personal errands. Tom tells himself that he does enough for his clients already and that many of them do not need to be seen as often as twice a month. Tom's behavior is clearly unethical. He is not being honest with his employer. He is also not giving clients the attention they are scheduled to receive.

Confidential Information

Confidential information is private, secret information that is not to be shared with anyone except those authorized to know it. The confidentiality of medical records and other types of information is an important ethical issue in the workplace today.

Medical Information

The content of medical records is protected by law for two reasons. First, medical data is very private. Knowing that their medical data will not be shared with others helps people speak honestly with healthcare providers. Second, people can use medical information to discriminate against others in violation of the law.

A federal law related to health care data is the Health Insurance Portability and Accountability Act of 1996 (HIPAA). It prohibits sharing a patient's medical and billing information without the patient's written consent. Exceptions include sharing data with others providing health care to the patient. Data can also be shared with insurance companies in some instances.

Other Types of Information

Information a person shares with his or her attorney is confidential. It may not be disclosed by that attorney or his staff except under special circumstances. This attorney-client privilege allows clients to speak more freely with attorneys.

Financial companies, such as banks, handle private data from clients. These companies must not share certain client data without the client's consent. They must also protect client data from illegal use. For example, private data, such as Social Security numbers and credit card numbers, can be stolen and used illegally. This is called **identity theft** and is a growing crime.

Some court records are open and can be viewed by the public. Other court records are confidential. These records may relate to juveniles or be sealed by a judge for some reason. The federal government and some states also safeguard educational records, including transcripts, financial statements, and recommendations.

Trade secrets are information that gives a business a competitive advantage and that it makes reasonable efforts to keep secret. Employees who work with trade secrets may be asked to sign a nondisclosure agreement. In this agreement, they promise not to share trade secrets with others for a certain period of time. You can learn more about trade secrets online. Figure 2-3 shows information about trade secrets provided by Business.Gov.

Key▶Point
Identity theft is a criminal offense. It occurs when a person uses another's private data for illegal acts.

Figure 2-3 Theft of trade secrets is a crime.

Source: Patents, Trademarks, and Copyright, Business.Gov, accessed February 26, 2008, available from http://www.business.gov/guides/business_law/intellectual_property.html.

Trade Secrets

A trade secret is information that has value because it is not generally known and is the subject of efforts to keep it secret. State law protects against disgruntled ex-employees, sabotage by current employees, or simple carelessness about the risk and possible protections of your trade secrets. Protection for trade secrets does not expire, as it does for copyright. As long as the owner makes reasonable efforts to keep the information secret, the information is protected.

- The model Uniform Trade Secrets Act has been passed in whole or in part by 45 states. You should consult a local attorney for the specific provisions that apply to your business.
- The Economic Espionage Act of 1996 makes the theft or misappropriation of a trade secret a federal crime.

You can protect your trade secrets by requiring employees and others with whom you share the information to sign a nondisclosure agreement (NDA). SCORE provides the following resources on how to protect your trade secrets using a nondisclosure agreement:

- Protect Your Trade Secrets with a Nondisclosure Agreement
  Information on how to protect your business' trade secrets using an NDA.
- Sample Non-Disclosure Agreement
  Basic nondisclosure agreement you can use in your business.

Protecting Confidential Data

Employees should use discretion in handling confidential and sensitive information. Make sure you understand your organization's policies and the law. The consequences of sharing confidential data may be loss of trust or respect from clients, coworkers, or supervisors; loss of business; loss of a license; loss of a job; or legal prosecution.

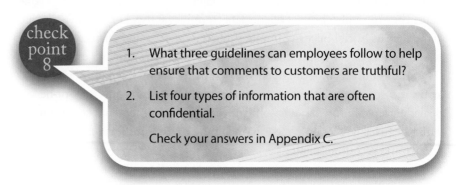

check point 8

1. What three guidelines can employees follow to help ensure that comments to customers are truthful?

2. List four types of information that are often confidential.

Check your answers in Appendix C.

Privacy and Electronic Rights

Employees should be protective of data stored on computers and networks. When you leave your desk, close files that contain confidential information. If you have been working on a network, log off. Keep passwords secure. Do not share them or leave written copies where others can find them. Change passwords often, and use passwords that will be hard for people to guess.

E-mail and instant messaging (IM) are popular means of sending messages. Both e-mail and instant messages are quick and informal. Some people mistakenly believe that these messages are private and that once an e-mail is deleted or an instant message is sent, it disappears forever. As a result, comments and data that people would never include in a business letter or memo sometimes appear in e-mail or instant messages.

Many employers monitor e-mail their employees send and receive. Monitoring helps ensure that employees are not spending too much work time on personal messages. It also helps ensure that confidential information is not being sent outside the company. Some employers have fired employees for e-mail misuse.

Ethics

Offensive materials, jokes, and gossip should not be sent in an e-mail or instant message.

Be aware of purposes for which e-mail and IM should not be used. Do not send confidential information or offensive material, such as jokes or gossip. Do not send anything by e-mail or IM that you would not want to see with your name on a company bulletin board.

Treat senders and recipients of e-mail ethically. Respect their privacy and the confidentiality of any information you receive. Do not forward an e-mail without the sender's permission.

check point 9

1. Why is it important to keep computer passwords secret?

2. Should you make a comment in an e-mail or instant message that you would not put in a printed letter? Why or why not?

Check your answers in Appendix C.

Plagiarism

Plagiarism is the act of claiming someone else's words or ideas as your own. The following situations are examples of plagiarism because no credit is given to the source of the information.

- Avery copies three sentences from an online encyclopedia and pastes them into his report.

- Keiko uses an economist's description of capitalism in an essay. She rewrites the description in her own words.

- Gloria takes some graphics from the Internet to illustrate her story.

- Dean is writing a history paper. He has read his source material several times. As a result, some of the author's wording has stuck in his mind. Without realizing it, he uses the wording in his paper.

Plagiarism is unethical and illegal; it can have serious consequences: Journalists have had their careers ruined because of plagiarism. Distinguished scientists and historians have lost the respect of their colleagues and have had all of their work called into question. Employees have resigned or have been dismissed. Students have been failed or expelled. Graduates have had their degrees revoked.

Avoiding Plagiarism

Avoiding plagiarism is easy. While doing research, note the source of any information that you think you might use. Put quotation marks around text you have written down word for word or copied from the Internet. Check your final draft against your sources to be sure you have not used another writer's words or ideas without giving credit to the source.

Figure 2-4 lists types of sources for which credit should be given. Note that for paraphrasing, it does not matter how many words you change. If the material represents someone else's words or ideas, you need to acknowledge the source.

Ethics

The ease with which material can be copied and pasted from the Internet contributes to plagiarism.

Figure 2-4 Always give credit for information that is not your original work.

SOURCE MATERIALS
• Direct quotations, no matter how brief
• Material that is paraphrased or restated in your own words
• Factual information that is not widely available or generally known
• Summaries

Copyright and Fair Use

In most of the world, books, articles, stories, photographs, music, and other works are protected by copyright laws. **Copyright** is the legal right of someone, usually the author or artist, to use or reproduce a work. Copyright protection lasts many years. During that time, anyone wanting to use the work—for instance, to quote at length from a book or to excerpt a chapter—must obtain the author's written permission.

An exception to that rule is fair use. The fair use doctrine allows limited use of copyrighted material without the author's permission. Fair use may apply, for example, if you want to use material in the course of teaching, researching, or news reporting.

The rules for what constitutes fair use are vague. Generally, the use should be not for profit, and the material used should be a small portion of the work. Quotes used in papers written for school generally fall under the fair use doctrine. After a certain number of years, the copyright to a work may expire. The work is then said to be in the public domain. Even when you have written permission from the author or when a work is out of copyright and in the public domain, you still need to credit the source.

check point 10

1. How can writers avoid plagiarism?

2. What is copyright protection? Are copyrighted works protected forever?

Check your answers in Appendix C.

Section 2.4 *Applications*

A. Ethical Communications

For each situation, tell why the communication or behavior is unethical.

1. A nurse is discussing a patient's medical care on a cell phone.

2. A worker submits as his own a report written by another person.

3. A secretary leaves a client's file displayed on a computer screen.

4. A product brochure makes untrue claims for a product.

5. A bank employee faxes private client data to the wrong number.

6. An employee uses an office phone list to solicit customers for a personal business.

B. Identify Ethical Issues

Sanjay is proud of his personal Web site. It includes cartoons and articles he found on the Web. Some funny jokes, some of his favorite music, and humorous descriptions of his supervisor and a few coworkers are also included. Sanjay sometimes works on his Web site in his spare time at work.

1. Is Sanjay behaving ethically?

2. Write a description of the ethical issues related to Sanjay's actions.

C. Discuss Ethical Situations

1. Search the Internet, magazines, or newspapers to find an article related to business or government actions that may be unethical.

2. Record the title and source of the article. Write a summary of the main points of the article.

3. Discuss the article with a group of your classmates. State whether you think the actions were ethical or not and explain your position.

REAL WORLD

TEAMWORK

Chapter *Summary*

2.1 Diversity at Work

- Diversity refers to the presence of a wide range of variation in qualities or attributes of people or things.

- Accommodating and benefiting from the diversity of employees and customers is one of the greatest challenges in the workplace today.

- The United States is more culturally diverse than ever before.

- Globalization affects the workforce in many ways.

2.2 Differences

- People from cultures different from your own are likely to have different values and assumptions than you do.

- Cultural differences, such as those in language, body language, and required personal space, can be communication barriers.

- Customs and etiquette vary from country to country and culture to culture.

- Learning about other cultures and following proper etiquette are important for successful communication.

2.3 Strategies for Effective Communication

- In a diverse world, effective communication at work begins with having a professional attitude.

- Differences in culture and languages add challenges to the process of cross-cultural communication.

- Individuals should show fairness and sensitivity toward others at work by having a professional attitude and treating everyone with respect.

2.4 Ethics in Business Communication

- Businesses and professions have ethical guidelines. Employees are expected to respect their company's code of ethics while doing business for the company.

- A company's ethics are reflected in the company's communications.

- Companies and employees should be honest and make efforts to keep confidential information secure.

- Plagiarism is the act of claiming someone else's words or ideas as your own. Plagiarism is unethical and may be illegal.

Vocabulary

Open the *Word* file *CH02 Vocabulary* from the student data files. Complete the exercise to review the vocabulary terms from this chapter.

copyright

cross-cultural communication

culture

discrimination

diversity

ethics

ethnicity

etiquette

globalization

identity theft

inclusion

multinational company

plagiarism

prejudice

race

stereotype

trade secret

Critical Thinking Questions

1. People from different cultures celebrate different religious and secular holidays. How can a company create a holiday schedule (for paid days off) that will accommodate workers from many different cultures?

2. When a person from another country takes a job in the United States, should that person be expected to learn English and the customs of the local area? Why or why not?

3. Does globalization benefit or hurt U.S. workers? Explain your reasoning.

4. How can you tell that you are invading someone's personal space? What clues might the person give you?

5. "That's not me; that's my job." Some people draw a line between the ethical standards that govern their personal lives and those that govern their work lives. Is it possible or right to have one set of ethical values for home and another for work? Explain your answer.

CRITICAL THINKING

Chapter *Applications*

REAL WORLD

TEAMWORK

A. *Multinational Company*

1. Work with a classmate to complete this activity. Search the Internet, magazines, or newspapers to find information or an article about a multinational company.

2. Record key information about the company, such as its name, home office location, countries or number of countries in which it does business, and primary products or services it offers.

3. Be prepared to share this information with the class.

B. *Cross-Cultural Communication*

Edit the following sentences so they are bias-free or would be easily understood by someone whose first language is not English. Invent details as needed.

1. Please send me the results of your study ASAP.

2. We want to hit the ground running on this project.

3. Ralph Colter, a deaf student at Grand Vista College, won the prize.

4. Filling out this form will enable us to expedite your services.

5. Jean is one of our best female lab technicians.

6. Which advertising campaign will give us the most bang for the buck?

7. Your son will need a tonsillectomy.

8. We plan to hire two Latino policemen.

9. Mariana, you have the floor.

10. I will give you an answer after I crunch the numbers.

INTERNET

REAL WORLD

C. *Business Etiquette*

1. Suppose you will be traveling to a foreign country on business. Choose a country and research it on the Internet. Keying the name of the country and the words *business etiquette* into a search engine will yield good results.

2. Develop a one-page checklist of helpful information for your stay. Include information on topics such as:

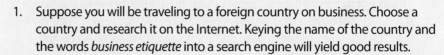

- Currency
- Time differences
- Customs for greeting and saying good-bye to people

- Cues about body language
- Meeting and dining protocol
- Business dress

D. Languages

Many Americans do not speak a language other than English. This can be a barrier to cross-cultural communication.

1. What languages other than English are spoken by you and your class-mates? by their family members? Survey the class and record your findings.

2. What language courses are available in your school or community? Make a list of the languages taught.

3. Some colleges and other postsecondary schools require that students complete language courses before enrolling. Select a college or other postsecondary school that you might want to attend. Do research to find what language courses must be completed by students before enrolling.

4. Identify a career that you might want to pursue after finishing your education. Would being able to speak languages other than English be helpful to you in this career? Which languages would be helpful?

E. Copyright and Fair Use

An important aspect of copyright rules is the fair use doctrine. The doctrine has developed through a number of court decisions over the years. Open the *Word* file *CH02 Fair Use* from the student data files. Read the document. For each situation described below, indicate whether you think the use would be acceptable under the fair use doctrine.

1. A student included a paragraph from a copyrighted article in a report and did not give credit to the source.

2. A teacher copied one page from a copyrighted book to use in a class lesson and gave credit to the source.

3. A school club is selling copies of a copyrighted song to raise money for a school project. Permission was not received from the copyright holder.

4. A student quoted two lines from a copyrighted book in a school report and gave credit to the source.

5. A student bought a research report from a Web site and submitted it to his teacher as his own work.

Editing Activity

Open and edit the *Word* file *CH02 Editing* from the student data files, and correct all spelling, punctuation, and grammar errors.

CASE STUDIES

A. Confidential Information

Shariq Malouf is close to being hired for a job he really wants. The position is project manager in the IT Department of a large corporation. He is on his third interview with Alicia Rhodes, who would be his supervisor. Ms. Rhodes asks for a detailed account of Shariq's most recent projects. Shariq signed a nondisclosure agreement with his current employer, who happens to be one of the corporation's competitors. He explains this fact to Ms. Rhodes. She says, "I need to know that you are capable of handling this job. Anything you say won't leave this room, I assure you."

1. Should Shariq give information about his recent work? Why or why not?

2. Would your answer would change if:

   - Shariq knew and trusted Alicia Rhodes

   - Shariq had been dismissed unfairly from his last job

   - The two companies were not competitors

   - The nondisclosure agreement were about to expire

B. Body Language

Elaine was visiting Mexico on business. During a crowded cocktail party, she noticed her business client waving to her from across the room. Talking with someone else, she saw the wave and thought, "How friendly!" She waved back. A little while later he waved again—more urgently and vigorously. Again, she waved back more enthusiastically. In the days that followed, her client would not return phone calls and canceled appointments with her.

1. Why do you think the client became cool to her?

2. What could Elaine have done to prevent this misunderstanding?

Agriculture, Food & Natural Resources

Communication for Agriculture, Food, and Natural Resources

Mary Blake started a landscaping business in Atlanta about ten years ago. Her company has grown, and it now has eight full-time employees. The company has another dozen seasonal employees. When she hires seasonal help, Mary is careful to choose people who are willing to work hard and who have some interest in landscaping and in working with their hands.

For the past several seasons, most of the company's seasonal employees have been Hispanic. Mary has been pleased with their work. The workers follow directions well, learn new skills willingly, and work hard. The problem, though, is getting the seasonal workers to work well with the full-time employees.

Most of the full-time employees are landscape designers. They often go to job sites to supervise the work crews. Though it seems to Mary that the seasonal workers are respectful, the designers have complained that the workers are disrespectful. Mary guesses that the designers simply feel left out. When the workers talk among themselves, they speak in Spanish. They bring their own lunches and keep to themselves during breaks and lunchtime. In addition, the company office manager seems to have difficulty communicating with the seasonal workers about withholding taxes and other payroll issues.

The business has been growing and Mary would like to expand her full-time staff. A couple of her seasonal workers are her first choices for those positions. However, Mary is worried about whether the Hispanic workers will feel part of the company team.

1. What can Mary do to help the current full-time staff feel more comfortable with the seasonal workers?

2. If Mary hires some of the seasonal workers as full-time staff, what further steps can she take to ensure that all her employees work well together?

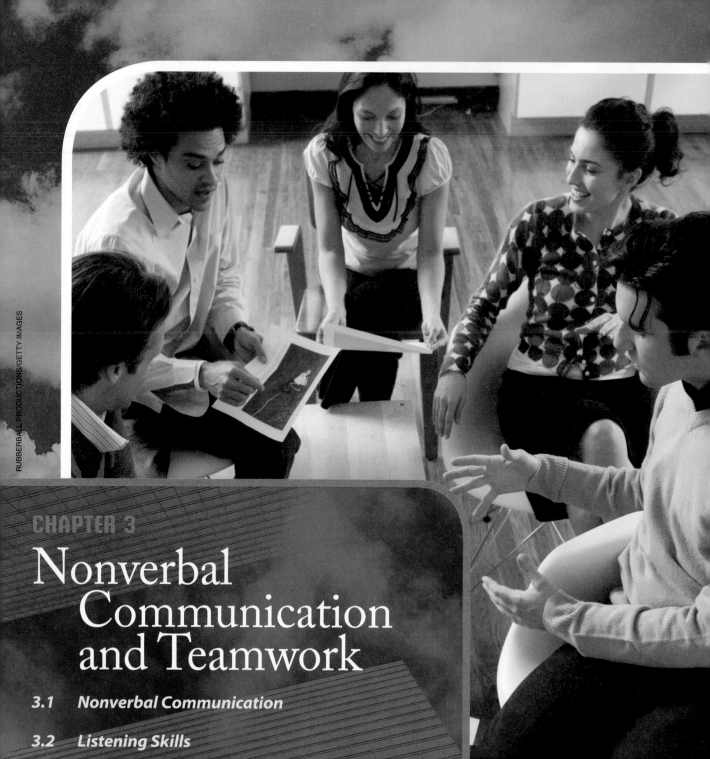

CHAPTER 3
Nonverbal Communication and Teamwork

3.1   *Nonverbal Communication*

3.2   *Listening Skills*

3.3   *Teamwork*

Nonverbal Communication on the Job

Miguel works as a supervisor at a hair salon, Maria's Boutique. He plans to evaluate two relatively new employees tomorrow.

The first employee, Carrie, is from the United States. English is her first language, and she understands it well. Sometimes Carrie does not get to work on time. However, the only time she misses work is when she is sick. Her uniforms are usually a little wrinkled, her shoes are unpolished, and she likes to wear long earrings that jingle. She is quiet and does not talk much with the customers while she works. The quality of most of her work is acceptable. However, sometimes she is a bit careless when using hair dyes because she has not listened or did not understand instructions. She is not very friendly with her coworkers and does not socialize much. She does not seem to care very much about her job.

The other employee, Chi, is from Myanmar. Chi has been in this country for about one year. She speaks English but not well. When she is given instructions on the usage of hair dyes and supplies, she listens intently, smiles, and nods her head "yes." However, many times she does not understand. As a result, she often needs help in learning how to use the chemicals and supplies correctly. Otherwise, Chi's work is very good. Her uniforms are somewhat worn but always clean and tidy. Unlike Carrie, Chi is very friendly. However, she is limited in her ability to socialize and develop friendships with coworkers because of her English skills. Coworkers seem to like her and enjoy her enthusiasm for life in the United States.

Questions

1. How important are listening skills to helping Carrie and Chi complete work successfully?

2. How important is nonverbal language to helping Carrie and Chi communicate?

3. Which employee seems to be a better teammate, Carrie or Chi? Why?

Nonverbal Communication

The Roles of Nonverbal Communication

Nonverbal communication is composed of the messages sent without or in addition to words. These messages have a strong impact on receivers. Often, actions speak so loudly that they drown out spoken words. This action happens because people use nonverbal symbols as a means to determine what the sender really thinks or feels. Nonverbal symbols can also indicate the degree of importance the sender attaches to a message.

Spoken or written symbols make up the verbal part of a message and are accompanied by nonverbal symbols. However, a nonverbal message may not have a verbal counterpart. Nonverbal symbols—body language, appearance, touch, space, time, voice—exist in written and oral communication and in the environment.

Receivers interpret nonverbal symbols by using their senses: sight, hearing, touch, taste, and smell. If you hear a person say, "Great!" and see the person smile while looking at a letter, you will conclude that the letter contains good news. If you hear a frowning person say, "Great!" in a disgusted tone when looking at a letter, you will probably conclude that the letter contains disappointing news. The receiver interprets the message based on sight (seeing the smile or frown) and hearing (the tone of voice).

People's opinions are often based on the nonverbal symbols they see and how they interpret them. Verbal and nonverbal symbols should be interpreted in relation to each other. Nonverbal symbols may reinforce, contradict, or substitute for verbal symbols. They may also regulate the verbal part of a message.

Key▶Point

Nonverbal symbols may reinforce, contradict, regulate, or substitute for verbal symbols.

Reinforcing a Verbal Message

Nonverbal symbols usually reinforce the verbal message. Pointing to a door as you state, "The office is the second door on the left" reinforces the verbal message. Pounding the table while making a statement also reinforces a verbal message.

Nonverbal symbols, such as a smile, can reinforce verbal symbols.

DIGITAL VISION/GETTY IMAGES

Contradicting a Verbal Message

Sometimes verbal and nonverbal symbols do not agree. You may say, "That's fine," but if your voice is strained and you look away from the receiver, which symbol will the receiver believe—the verbal or the nonverbal? When verbal and nonverbal symbols conflict, the receiver usually believes the nonverbal message.

Substituting for a Verbal Message

Nonverbal symbols sometimes act as substitutes for verbal messages. Gritting your teeth or throwing your hands in the air indicates frustration. Clenching your fists indicates anger. Tapping your foot or a pencil indicates impatience. Nodding or smiling indicates agreement.

Regulating a Verbal Message

Nonverbal symbols may be used to regulate or control oral communication between the sender and receiver. These regulators may signal when you want to speak, when you want others to continue speaking, or when you want to withdraw from a conversation. For example, nodding in agreement encourages another person to continue. However, checking your watch or closing a portfolio means you are through listening.

Ethics

Is it ethical to agree with someone in words when you really do not agree? How may the nonverbal symbols you send show that you do not agree?

check point 1

1. How are nonverbal symbols used in relation to verbal symbols?

2. Give an example of how a nonverbal symbol may contradict verbal symbols.

Check your answers in Appendix C.

Nonverbal Symbols

Though used the same way in most cultures, nonverbal symbols differ among cultures. In some cultures, for example, arriving late for a social or business engagement is polite; in others, it is considered rude.

Another common difference involves personal space. **Personal space** is the nearby area around a person or the area the person considers his or her territory. The personal space North Americans prefer is larger than the personal space people from other cultures generally prefer.

Diversity

The meanings of body language and other nonverbal symbols vary among cultures.

Nonverbal Symbols in Written Messages

The appearance and correctness of a written document send critical nonverbal messages and deserve careful attention. Letterhead sheets, plain sheets, and envelopes should be made of quality bond paper and be of the same color. The design of the letterhead and company logo should convey a professional image. Drawings, pictures, charts, and graphs should be appropriate to the content. The print should be crisp and easy to read.

Documents should not have errors and should be in an appropriate format. Check capitalization, grammar, and spelling carefully. Make sure all facts, such as dates and amounts, are correct. Error-free documents send a positive message that the sender is reliable and considers quality important.

Nonverbal Symbols in Spoken Messages

Several nonverbal symbols have an impact on spoken messages. These symbols are described in Figure 3-1 and in the following paragraphs.

Body Language

Body language includes facial expressions and gestures. Interpreting body language is complex. A single motion can have many different meanings.

People can reveal their feelings through various facial expressions. A frown usually indicates negative feelings; a smile, happy feelings. Nervous smiles convey weakness or insecurity.

Figure 3-1 Nonverbal symbols affect spoken messages.

NONVERBAL SYMBOLS	
Body language	Facial expressions, gestures, and posture
Touching	Shaking hands, back slapping, placing a hand on someone's shoulder, and hugging
Space	The physical distance between individuals
Time	Being punctual for appointments or completing tasks by the date requested
Paralanguage	Qualities of voice (such as pitch and volume), rate of speech, and actions (such as laughing or sighing)

Eyes provide revealing facial expressions and often are called "the windows of the soul." Eyes reveal feelings, such as excitement, boredom, and concentration. Eyebrows also send various messages. Raised eyebrows may mean nervousness, surprise, or questioning. Pinched together they may imply confusion or indecision.

Direct eye contact conveys interest, friendship, or confidence. A lack of eye contact may mean disinterest or boredom. In business, the amount of eye contact varies depending on a person's status. Because subordinates want to tell their supervisors that they like them, they generally make more eye contact.

A **gesture** is the use of your arms and hands to express an idea or feeling. Crossed arms may indicate concentration or withdrawal. A hand placed against the side of the head can imply forgetfulness. Trembling or fidgeting hands sometimes indicate nervousness.

Leaning toward a person who is speaking conveys an open attitude. Nodding confirms listening and sometimes agreement. However, folding your arms or shaking your head from side to side indicates a closed attitude or disagreement.

People use gestures to determine the real meaning in a message. No matter what words you may use, your eyes and your face reveal what your true feelings are. When people attempt to use gestures to deceive or hide the truth, they will undermine the message.

Touching

A handshake is the most acceptable form of touching for both men and women in the American business environment. It is a gesture used to greet someone and to close a discussion. A person who gives a firm handshake and makes eye contact projects a cordial, confident image. However, a weak, soft

Diversity

Facial expressions and gestures are very culturally oriented. For example, an Asian generally greets one with a bow of the head; the American offers to shake your hand.

Ethics

Sexual harassment is an ethical issue because it infringes on personal freedom and can have a demeaning or demoralizing effect on the victim.

handshake suggests listlessness or mental dullness. A cold, wet handshake may indicate nervousness and possibly a feeling of inferiority.

Other forms of touching, such as hugging or backslapping, are generally not acceptable in business. A person of higher rank, however, may put his or her hand on a subordinate's shoulder as a sign of encouragement or support. A coworker could do the same thing with another coworker. A coworker should not put his or her hand on the shoulder of the supervisor. Such action could be considered too familiar. Everyone should avoid touching that could be interpreted as condescending or as sexual harassment.

Personal Space

One aspect of personal space is the physical distance between individuals. In general, people stand relatively close to people they like. People tend to leave more space between themselves and people they fear or do not like. When unable to arrange space comfortably, as in a crowded elevator, people adjust by using other nonverbal symbols, such as avoiding eye contact. They may stare at the passing floor numbers or remain silent. People avoid speaking or making eye contact in these situations because their territory, or their own space zone, is being violated. The size of this space depends on the activity and the relationships with the other persons involved. Typical space zones for North Americans are shown in Figure 3-2.

The social zone is common for most business meetings or social gatherings. When people converse in their social zone, they have some reason for speaking. If a stranger enters a social zone, people usually break eye contact or turn away. For example, if you notice a stranger as you walk on the sidewalk, you watch the stranger from a distance of about 20 feet. As the stranger approaches, however, you break eye contact. If you speak to a stranger who is within your social zone, you use a formal, businesslike voice.

Key ▶ Point

A comfortable personal space zone for talking with colleagues is 18 inches to 4 feet.

Figure 3-2 Use of personal space sends a nonverbal message.

NONVERBAL SYMBOLS	
Intimate Zone 0 to 18 inches	Comfort zone for talking with close friends or relatives
Personal Zone 18 inches to 4 feet	Comfort zone for talking privately with colleagues and acquaintances
Social Zone 4 to 12 feet	Comfort zone for talking with others at most business meetings or social gatherings
Public Zone 12 feet or more	Comfort zone between a speaker and an audience at a meeting or presentation

Communication between a speaker and an audience is within the public zone. From a distance of more than 12 feet, people may look at each other, but they do not maintain eye contact. Interaction is avoided.

When a coworker stands too close or too far from you, he or she probably thinks your relationship is on a different level than you do. You may think the relationship is on a personal level, but he or she thinks it is on a social level. Consistently standing too close to a coworker could be interpreted as sexual harassment.

In an office setting, the size, location (corner office, distance from the top manager's office, and so forth), and use of space may be a sign of a person's status. Generally, the more spacious a person's office is, the higher the person's status is.

Time

The use of time is another aspect of nonverbal communication. Suppose someone asks you to do a task as soon as possible. If you complete the action right away, you send a positive message to the other person. Ignoring an urgent request can send a negative message.

In American culture, promptness is considered important. Being on time for a meeting shows your respect for others. In some other cultures, arriving several minutes after a stated time may be considered appropriate.

Paralanguage

Maybe you have heard the saying, "It's not what you say, but how you say it that counts." **Paralanguage** is the nonverbal symbols that accompany a verbal message and reveal the difference between what is said and how it is said. Paralanguage includes pitch, stress, rate, volume, inflection, rhythm, and pronunciation. It also includes laughing, crying, sighing, grunting, yawning, and coughing. Even silence, pauses, and hesitations are part of paralanguage. Paralanguage is critical to the correct interpretation of a message.

Key▶Point

Paralanguage involves how a message is said rather than the words spoken.

check point 2

1. What are some examples of nonverbal symbols sent in written messages?

2. What are some nonverbal symbols sent in spoken messages?

3. When judging attitudes, do people give more importance to how words are spoken or to the words themselves?

Check your answers in Appendix C.

Nonverbal Symbols and Your Image

Your nonverbal communications are extremely important. Whether you realize it or not, you use them to establish your image. If you ask yourself, "What kind of worker do others think I am?" you are examining your image. Important aspects of your image are based on level of confidence, friendliness, enthusiasm, sincerity, appearance, eye contact, and posture.

Level of Confidence

Confidence means trust or freedom from doubt. **Self-confidence** means belief in yourself and your abilities. "No one knows you as well as you do." Because this statement is true, others use your self-confidence level as a basis for determining your competence and abilities. If others think that you have confidence in yourself, they will believe that you are competent unless you prove otherwise.

Too Much Self-Confidence

Being too self-confident can hinder your communications and hurt your image. Others may see you as arrogant, inflexible, or a "know it all." They may think you are unrealistic about your own abilities. They may have serious questions about your ability to work with others or complete tasks. They may wonder whether you have a personality that allows you to learn and grow.

Displaying self-confidence can help you communicate successfully.

STOCKBYTE/GETTY IMAGES

Too Little Self-Confidence

Having too little self-confidence can also hinder communication and hurt your image. If people think you do not believe in yourself, they will question why they should believe in you. Being too nervous in a normal situation shows low self-confidence. This nervousness is reflected by a quivering voice, shaking hands, perspiration, or the inability to think or respond clearly. When people think you are not confident about your message, they will be less likely to believe you.

Negative thinking and unrealistic expectations are two causes of a lack of confidence. Remember that everyone makes mistakes—forgetting details, overlooking things, and so forth. However, people need to feel positive about themselves. No matter who you are, you can make a contribution. Identify your strengths and build on them. Identify your weaknesses and make a plan to improve on them.

Friendliness

Friendliness is an important aspect of an effective image. **Friendliness** is defined as being supportive, helpful, or kind. When you are cordial, pleasant, or kind to others, they are more likely to respond to you in a positive way. This positive response may make communication easier.

To be perceived as friendly often means that you must focus on the needs of others rather than on your own needs. You send nonverbal messages that say "friend" when you smile, when you have a relaxed approach, and when you desire honest, open feedback.

Enthusiasm

Enthusiasm is an aspect of image that can set you apart from others. **Enthusiasm** means showing excitement or a lively interest. Real enthusiasm is contagious. When you enthusiastically present your ideas, receivers will sense your enthusiasm and feel positive about those ideas and you. When you are truly excited about an idea and eagerly present it, your feelings spread quickly to others. Smiles, raised eyebrows, and eyes that are wide open and sparkle are nonverbal symbols that show enthusiasm.

Sincerity

Sincerity means being open and genuine or earnest. Being seen as sincere helps you build a positive image. For you to be credible, you must be perceived as sincere—which may take time. Open, honest communication sends a nonverbal message that you are sincere. In order to think that you are sincere, receivers need time to observe you. If your actions and words contrast with one another, you will be viewed as insincere. If they match, you will be considered credible and sincere.

Ethics

Do you know someone who is phony or insincere? How do you feel about that person? Many unethical people are judged so because they are seen as phony or insincere.

Appearance

Key ▶ Point

Your appearance is critical to your image. This does not mean that you should always dress in a formal fashion. Dress appropriately for the particular work or social situation.

Your appearance is critical to your image. It helps to create the first impression others have of you. Proper diet, rest, and exercise can help you maintain a healthy body and present a confident image. Being clean and neatly dressed and wearing clothing and accessories that are tasteful generally create a favorable impression. In addition, your clothing should be appropriate for your work and for your organization. In many businesses, appropriate clothes are conservative in fabric, color, and style. Being poorly groomed or dressed in a way that is not appropriate can create a negative image.

Eye Contact

Eye contact is one of the most important nonverbal symbols. As already mentioned, eye contact can send a message of confidence, interest, honesty, or sincerity. It can also send a message of the lack of confidence, weakness, boredom, fear, insincerity, or dishonesty.

In one-to-one situations, effective eye contact builds interpersonal trust and confidence in each other. In small-group situations, look each person in the eye, keeping eye contact long enough to give that person a feeling that you are talking with him or her personally. In large-group settings, make sure that you look at individuals in all parts of the room. This action makes members of the group feel that they are being included and not ignored.

Posture

Posture is the way you stand or sit. It can convey your confidence level or your interest in a situation or topic. Poor posture may be a sign of timidity, laziness, or lack of interest. To project a positive self-image, sit and stand naturally but straight and tall. Sitting or standing erect and leaning in can signal that you are interested in the topic being discussed.

check point 3

1. What are some nonverbal symbols that affect a person's image?

2. Why is having the right amount of self-confidence important?

3. Why is it important to dress appropriately for your work setting?

Check your answers in Appendix C.

Reading for Comprehension

Reading comprehension means understanding what you have read. A reader's mental state or physical well-being can affect the ability to focus and to understand a message. To overcome internal barriers when reading:

- Clear your mind of distracting thoughts.

- Attempt to ignore tiredness, minor aches, or physical discomforts.

- Be open to new ideas.

- Avoid letting biases or previous experience prevent you from considering other viewpoints.

Open the *Word* file *CH03 Reading* from the student data files. Read the message once at a comfortable rate. Without looking at the message, answer the questions about the message. Look at the message again to see if you answered the questions correctly.

Nonverbal Symbols in the Environment

Characteristics of a physical setting can send nonverbal messages. Furnishings and decor; the arrangement of tables and chairs; the level of lighting, temperature, and sound; and the use of color contribute to the way people feel in a setting.

Furnishings and decor often are a part of a business strategy. For example, in a typical fast-food restaurant, the tables are close together, the lighting is bright, and the seats are molded plastic. The environment is carefully planned to encourage fast turnover of customers. In contrast, a fine restaurant may have a more spacious setting, dim lighting, padded armchairs, fine china, tablecloths, and fresh flowers. This setting encourages diners to linger.

Color establishes a mood within an environment. Soothing colors, such as beige, off-white, or light yellow, are especially suitable where people perform stressful or tedious work. Excessive use of light blue can have a dulling effect, tending to make workers feel sluggish. Red and orange are stimulating colors, appropriate for areas where people spend a short amount of time (a cafeteria, for example) or perform creative work.

Ethics

Do you think it is ethical for businesses to use color, lighting, and music to influence the behavior of customers? Why or why not?

Section 3.1 *Applications*

A. *Analyze Speaking Behavior*

Robert spoke to his coworker, Sherry, this morning. "Good morning, Sherry," Robert said in a quiet voice as he slouched by Sherry's desk. "I think I can complete the reports you requested by Thursday," he added as he looked down at her with a frowning face. "I will appreciate it if you can get the data to me by this afternoon," Robert said with a sigh as he walked away.

1. What nonverbal symbols were part of Robert's communication with Sherry?

2. Do Robert's nonverbal symbols indicate that he is pleased to prepare the reports Sherry requested? Explain your answer.

3. Rewrite the conversation. Change the nonverbal symbols to alter the meaning of Robert's message to show that he is pleased to help with the reports.

CRITICAL THINKING

B. *Identify Nonverbal Symbols in Written Messages*

The appearance and correctness of a written document send nonverbal messages to the reader. Writers should consider the appearance of documents as well as the content before sending them to others.

1. Open and print the *Word* file *CH03 Letter* from the student data files.

2. Do you think this document will make a favorable impression on readers? Why or why not?

3. What nonverbal symbols does this document contain?

REAL WORLD

C. *Identify Nonverbal Symbols in the Environment*

Aspects of a physical setting can send nonverbal messages. Furniture, the level of lighting, temperature, sound, and the use of color can affect people in the setting.

1. Identify a public setting that you will use for this activity, such as your school cafeteria or a fast-food restaurant.

2. List all the nonverbal symbols you can identify in the setting. Consider furniture, lighting, temperature, sound (music or noise), and colors. Tell how you think each symbol affects people in this setting.

Listening Skills

The Listening Process

What is the most frequent form of communication—reading, writing, speaking, or listening? If you said listening, you are correct. Research indicates that many people spend more than half of their waking time communicating. Much of this time is spent listening. Managers often spend much of their workday listening. Generally, the higher your position in a company, the more time you may spend listening to others.

The listening process involves hearing, focusing attention, understanding, and remembering. These steps are described in Figure 3-3. Listening also requires noticing nonverbal cues. The speaker's tone of voice, gestures, facial expressions, and posture can add meaning to a message. The following situation provides an example of the steps used in listening.

1. Jose sends a message by speaking to Betty.

2. Betty listens to Jose's words and to the way he uses them. She also watches the nonverbal cues sent by Jose's face, hands, and so forth.

3. Betty analyzes the verbal and nonverbal messages and decides what she thinks Jose is saying.

4. Betty summarizes to Jose what she thinks was his intended message.

OBJECTIVES

After completing Section 3.2, you should be able to:

1. Explain the listening process.

2. Identify types of listening and describe the reasons for which they are used.

3. List barriers to effective listening.

4. Describe effective listening techniques.

figure 3-3 Listening involves hearing and understanding a message.

THE LISTENING PROCESS	
Hearing	Detecting sounds. In an office, you may hear people talking, telephones ringing, a door closing, or other sounds.
Focusing Attention	Concentrating on the speaker and what he or she says. You must ignore unrelated sounds, background noise, and other distractions.
Understanding	Attaching meaning to the speaker's message.
Remembering	Recalling a message you have seen or heard.

5. Jose decides whether Betty's summary is correct. If Betty is correct, Jose signals that it was correct. If Betty's summary is incorrect, Jose restates the message. At this point, Betty repeats steps 2 through 5. This process is repeated until Jose agrees with Betty's summary.

check point 4

1. What activities are involved in the listening process?

2. What is the difference between hearing and listening?

Check your answers in Appendix C.

Types of Listening

People listen for many reasons—to relax, obtain information, express interest, and discover attitudes. When you listen to music, usually you are listening to relax. Listening to directions for a task, taking part in an interview, and getting feedback from a customer are examples of listening to obtain information. You listen to let people know that you are interested in what they have to say and that they are important. Listening and responding to friends during lunch sends the message that their thoughts and feelings are important to you. Attitudes often are expressed in the nonverbal cues of a message. Alert listeners observe these cues and try to identify the speaker's real feelings.

People use different types of listening when listening for different purposes. The listening may be casual or active.

Casual Listening

Casual listening is hearing and understanding a message but not trying to remember the message in the long term. Casual listening is sometimes called passive listening. Listening while watching a movie or making small talk at lunch are examples of casual listening. The casual listener expends little energy or effort. Although the listener may understand the message, remembering it for a long time is not important. Casual listening is relaxed. When you are talking with others, however, you must be careful not to listen so casually that others think you are not paying attention.

Active Listening

Active listening is hearing and trying to understand and remember a message. It has purpose. Active listening may be informative, evaluative, emphatic, or reflective.

Casual listening is relaxed and involves little energy or effort.

Informative Listening

Informative listening is used to obtain specific information or understand a message. Doctors use informative listening when talking with their patients. Interviewers actively listen to what an applicant says. These are examples of informative listening. Recall a time when you listened very intently because you had something to gain from what was said. You listened actively because you were motivated by your interests.

Evaluative Listening

Evaluative listening involves judging the importance or accuracy of what a speaker is saying. Suppose you listen to a presidential candidate's speech. As you listen, you judge the sincerity and truthfulness of the message. You are using evaluative listening. This type of listening is also called critical listening.

Key ▶ Point

Critical listening involves judging the importance or accuracy of what a speaker says.

Emphatic Listening

Emphatic listening involves trying to understand the speaker's point of view, attitudes, and emotions. The listener is trying to understand something about the person as well as the spoken message. This type of listening can be important in resolving conflicts or disputes. Suppose a customer calls a help support line to complain about a printer that does not work properly. The support person might say, "I understand how disappointing it can be when a new product does not work properly. Let me ask some questions to learn what the problem might be." The support person is showing understanding of the customer's frustrations with the new printer. This understanding makes resolving the problem easier.

Diversity

Cultural differences make effective listening—understanding and recalling a message—more challenging.

Reflective Listening

Reflective listening involves understanding and restating the speaker's message. A reflective listener responds to the speaker with genuine concern. However, the listener does not try to give a different point of view or judge the speaker or the message. The listener simply lets the speaker know that the message has been understood. The listener may repeat or paraphrase what was said or make statements that reflect the speaker's feelings. This type of exchange is also known as parallel talk. Parallel talk can help the listener understand the speaker and help the speaker clarify thoughts or feelings. A guidance counselor may use reflective listening when talking with a student about career goals. This approach may help the student clarify his or her thoughts about this topic.

check point 5

1. How is casual listening different from active listening?

2. Describe four types of active listening and give an example of when each type may be used.

Check your answers in Appendix C.

Barriers to Effective Listening

Missing an important appointment, overlooking the feelings behind the words, and interpreting a situation incorrectly are just a few examples of problems that occur because of poor listening. Deafness or a partial hearing loss is a physical barrier to listening. Various other conditions and actions create barriers to good listening. As you read about these barriers, evaluate yourself as a listener.

- **Attitudes About the Speaker.** Attitudes about the speaker can be a barrier to listening. A speaker's appearance, mannerisms, tone of voice, and body language can distract the listener. Poor grammar or inappropriate word choice also can cause individuals to stop listening and mentally criticize the speaker. When listeners let their attitudes be a distraction, they miss what the speaker is saying.

- **Attitudes About the Topic.** "I can't program using C11; programming is too complex." "Oh, insurance! Don't talk to me about that dull subject." Messages that sound technical often intimidate listeners. Uninteresting or boring messages cause people to tune out the speaker. In a similar manner, listeners often lose patience with messages that are too detailed or too long.

- **Prejudices or Differing Opinions.** Most people have preconceived ideas about certain topics. If a speaker challenges a strongly held belief, the listener may simply tune out the speaker. Often the listener begins preparing a response even before the speaker has finished.

- **Assumptions.** Assumptions made in advance can account for a decline in listening. People often disregard messages when they think they already know the information.

- **Environmental Distractions.** Have you ever attended a luncheon at which the speaker began a presentation while the desserts or beverages were being served? Have you ever tried to finish a conversation with the telephone ringing in the background? If so, you know that unrelated activities and noise can interfere with your ability to listen.

- **Physical Discomfort.** A headache or another temporary physical discomfort can inhibit listening. Room temperature that is too warm or cool can also be distracting.

- **Divided Focus.** Failing to focus on the message hinders effective listening. Worrying about a personal problem or daydreaming about more interesting ideas can cause your mind to wander. Note-taking techniques can create a divided focus. The listener is dividing his or her focus between listening and recording information. While writing notes about one point, the listener may miss the speaker's next point.

Ethics

Some people allow prejudices to color their remarks about a person or group. Making unfavorable and untrue remarks about a person or group is unethical.

DIGITAL VISION/GETTY IMAGES

Worrying about a personal problem can keep you from listening effectively.

check
point
6

1. List eight barriers to effective listening.

2. How can note-taking become a barrier to listening?

Check your answers in Appendix C.

Listening Effectively

Listening affects the quality of your relationships with others. Through listening, you can better understand your own feelings and beliefs, as well as those of others. Friendships thrive when people take the time to understand each other. Likewise, effective listening helps businesses develop an important resource—their employees.

Employees who believe their opinions count develop greater self-esteem. They want to contribute to the organization. Customers who think a company understands and meets their needs will return for future business dealings. Customers who feel ignored will not return.

To be productive, people need to become effective listeners. Understanding the listening process and knowing the barriers to effective listening are not enough. To become a good listener, you must practice good listening habits. Suggestions for improving your listening skills are discussed in the following paragraphs.

Key▶Point

Listening to customers is important. Customers who feel ignored or misunderstood may take their business to another company.

Share the Responsibility

The speaker has most of the responsibility for conveying meaning during the communication process. Listeners have the vital role of attaching meaning to what has been said. People typically talk at a rate of about 100 to 150 words a minute. People can process information mentally at a rate of about 300 to 500 words a minute. Thus, the listener has spare time available. Rather than letting their minds wander, effective listeners use this spare time in ways that increase understanding.

Focus on the Main Idea

Some speakers develop their points in a disorganized manner, mixing the unimportant with the important. Therefore, to be a good listener, you must be willing to wait for the main idea and not be distracted by unimportant details. Separate fact from opinion. When taking notes, record the main ideas and enough supporting information to make the main ideas meaningful. Concentrate on the message, not on the speaker's delivery or appearance.

Evaluate the Message

Compare the speaker's message with the information you already know or believe about the topic. When you have some knowledge of the topic, do not ignore the speaker by assuming you already know what he or she will say. Instead, relate what you already know to what the speaker is saying. Do not judge a speaker until he or she is finished.

The International Listening Association (ILA) is a professional organization. Its members seek to learn about the impact that listening has on human activity. A link to the Web site for the ILA is provided on the Web site for this book that is shown below. Use that link to go to the ILA site and explore the site.

1. When was ILA formed?

2. In what areas do the members of ILA work?

3. What are some activities of the ILA?

www.cengage.com/school/bcomm/buscomm

Observe the speaker's nonverbal symbols. A natural, relaxed style and good eye contact show that the speaker feels confident about the message. On the other hand, nervous mannerisms may cause you to question the validity of the message.

Provide Feedback

When you understand the message, smile or nod your head to give the speaker feedback. Feedback tells the speaker that you are listening and that you understand the message. To assure understanding, ask questions, summarize main ideas, paraphrase the message, or restate the message as you understand it. Statements such as, "If I understand you correctly, you mean that . . ." can provide valuable feedback and aid understanding.

Take Notes

Effective notes can be an important aid to remembering messages. Notes are especially important when you need to remember specifics of a message. For example, you may need to follow spoken instructions for completing a task.

When you take notes, write the main points of the message. Then write supporting details as time allows. Do not become so focused on taking notes that you miss something the speaker is saying. When listening to instructions, ask questions at the appropriate time to be sure you have understood the instructions.

Key▶Point

Do not become so focused on taking notes that you miss something the speaker is saying.

When taking notes, you may be writing quickly, and your notes may be somewhat disorganized. Later when time allows, you may want to organize the notes in outline form with details listed under main points. Use phrases, abbreviations, and subject titles rather than complete sentences to save time when taking notes. Later, spell out any abbreviations and add details you think you may have trouble remembering.

Another note-taking technique uses two columns for notes. Main points are written in the left column. Supporting details or questions are written in the right column. Again, save time by using phrases to express your ideas rather than complete sentences.

Overcome Poor Listening Habits

Listening is a skill that requires practice. Becoming an effective listener requires changing attitudes toward speakers, attitudes toward topics, and personal habits that result in poor listening. Some strategies for becoming a better listener are shown in Figure 3-4.

Listening in Specific Situations

In the business world, you will find two common listening situations— listening in a small group and listening in a conference setting.

Figure 3-4 Practice listening skills to become a better listener.

LISTENING STRATEGIES
• Find common interests with the speaker or topic.
• Judge the content—not the delivery—of the message.
• Delay judgment until the speaker is finished.
• Listen for the main ideas of the message.
• Take notes on the important points.
• Concentrate on listening; stay alert.
• Avoid or ignore physical and environmental distractions.
• Listen with an open mind. Do not let prejudices or assumptions cause you to miss the message.
• Ask questions or give feedback, if appropriate.
• Review and evaluate or analyze the message after the speaker is finished.

Listening in a Small Group

When in a small group, all of your communication skills, including your listening skills, are important. Practice active listening. Listen for both ideas and feelings. Use effective eye contact and body language that indicate to others that you are listening. Check your understanding by asking questions or restating ideas as appropriate.

Listening in a Conference Setting

As an employee, you will continue to learn new skills and information related to your job. You may attend meetings, seminars, or conferences designed to improve your skills and knowledge. In such a setting, you will need to listen effectively in order to learn. Follow these guidelines for taking part in a seminar or conference.

- Clearly understand your reasons for being at the conference. What do you need to learn or accomplish at the conference?
- Choose comfortable seating.
- Choose seating where you can see the speaker and any visual aid that may be used.
- Avoid judging the speaker's subject, ability to present, and appearance before hearing the message.
- Take notes effectively.
- Ask questions when permitted.
- Review the content of your notes and add more details after the session.

Diversity

Be aware of cultural differences when communicating in a small group. Appropriate eye contact and desired personal space may vary by culture.

check
point
7

1. List four techniques for improving listening skills.

2. Describe two ways to organize notes taken during listening.

3. What steps can you take to practice active listening when in a small group?

Check your answers in Appendix C.

Section 3.2 *Applications*

A. *Follow Spoken Instructions*

In the workplace, spoken instructions are often given for a task or procedure. In this application, you will practice listening to and following spoken instructions.

1. Listen to instructions for a task read by your instructor. (Instructions are provided in the *Instructor's Manual.*)

2. When listening to the instructions, note the task or procedure to which they apply. Record the main points as they are given.

3. After you have finished listening, add details to your notes. Organize the notes so they will be easy to follow.

4. Ask questions of your instructor to clarify any point you did not understand.

5. Complete the task following the spoken directions and using your notes.

B. *Analyze Listening Behavior*

CRITICAL
THINKING

Joyce is a customer service associate for a retail company. She is attending a seminar to learn how to use a new software program for her job. The software will allow her to access information to answer customers' questions and to record details of the calls. Joyce has already seen a demo of the software and thinks she probably will not learn anything new. She wishes she did not have to waste her time at the seminar.

As the seminar begins, Joyce notices that the presenter seems nervous. She wonders whether the speaker has much experience with the software. As the seminar continues, Joyce takes notes, trying to record almost everything the speaker says. When the speaker asks whether there are questions, Joyce has several because she missed some points while she focused on taking notes. Because Joyce has so many notes and they are somewhat hard to read, she never puts them into an organized form. When she refers to them later, she has to scan several sections to find the information she needs.

1. What behavior contributed to listening effectively?

2. What behaviors were barriers to effective listening?

Teamwork

Workplace Relationships

In the workplace, individuals may have relationships with managers, co-workers, and customers. Knowing your role in each type of relationship is important.

Employee and Manager Relationships

Most employees, even those who are managers themselves, report to a manager or supervisor. What is your role in your relationship with your manager? What should your manager expect of you? Your manager is in a position of authority. You should respect this authority by being an honest and loyal employee. Your manager should expect that you will do your work to the best of your ability, keep confidential information secure, and support the efforts of your company and workgroup.

Part of keeping a good relationship with your manager is respecting lines of authority in communicating with other employees. For example, suppose you learn about a problem that will affect several people in the company. You may think the problem is too far-reaching for your manager to handle. However, your manager is the person to whom you should give information about the problem. Your manager will, in turn, let her or his manager know about the situation. Thus, the information travels up through the company along lines of authority until it reaches the person who can handle the problem. Suppose a problem or issue affects only a few coworkers or people who report to you. Handling the issue and letting your manager know the action that has been taken would be appropriate.

What can you, an employee, expect of your manager? Your manager should provide you with the appropriate direction and support to do your job well. What this direction consists of will vary from job to job. In some jobs, an employee may receive very detailed instructions for completing tasks. In other jobs, only general instructions may be given with the employee being expected to decide the best way to handle the tasks or projects. Your manager should treat you with respect and give you regular feedback about your work and how well you have completed your duties. If you do not receive feedback about your work, tactfully ask your manager how you are doing. Having good feedback may allow you to avoid repeating mistakes and to improve your work in the future. Open and honest communication is essential for good employee and manager relationships.

Coworker Relationships

A coworker may be considered anyone who works for the same company as you do. You may work closely and regularly with some coworkers. Other coworkers may work with you only occasionally. Follow these guidelines for dealing with coworkers.

- Be fair and honest in your dealings with coworkers. However, remember to keep confidential information secure, even from coworkers.
- Be helpful. If a coworker requests your help with a rush project, give your help if you can do so without creating problems for other projects that have a higher priority.
- Be tactful when communicating with coworkers. If work has errors or must be redone, state this information in a positive and constructive way.
- Acknowledge your mistakes. Do not attempt to hide your mistakes or blame others for your errors.
- Show appreciation and acknowledge good work done by others.
- Try to resolve conflicts with coworkers before the problem becomes serious. A **conflict** is a disagreement or quarrel. Figure 3-5 lists strategies that can help resolve conflicts.

Figure 3-5 Being able to resolve conflicts is important for coworker relationships.

STRATEGIES FOR RESOLVING CONFLICTS

- Listen and talk with coworkers to be sure you all have the same information about the situation.
- Identify the real reason or the underlying cause of the conflict.
- Center your discussions on the issues or behaviors involved, not on the people involved. Be tactful.
- Think objectively about your role in the situation. Be willing to admit your mistakes and apologize when you hurt someone's feelings.
- Focus on resolving the problem, not on assigning blame. Discuss possible solutions with coworkers or managers.
- Be willing to do your part to make the proposed solution work.

Diversity

Be aware of cultural differences when dealing with coworkers. Get to know each person as an individual—not just as part of a group.

Customer Relationships

In some jobs, employees deal with customers or others outside the organization. For example, a teacher may talk regularly with parents of students and develop relationships with them. Communicating effectively is important for developing these relationships. Be honest and respectful in dealing with others. Know your employer's policies and what you are (and are not) allowed to do for customers or other people. The guidelines given earlier for dealing with coworkers also apply to your relationships with customers and others. More about dealing with customers is presented in Chapter 14.

check point 8

1. List three types of workplace relationships.

2. Describe what a manager should expect of an employee and what an employee should expect of a manager.

3. List five guidelines for dealing with coworkers.

Check your answers in Appendix C.

Workplace Teams

Teamwork is two or more people acting together to achieve a goal. Various types of teams are common in the workplace. An employee and a manager may be considered a team. They work together to complete tasks and projects as discussed earlier. The employees in a department of a company, such as the Marketing Department or the Accounting Department, may be considered a team. Their combined efforts accomplish the goals of the department.

Workgroup teams are a trend in American companies. These teams may have members from one or several departments of the company. The goals of the team are related to accomplishing the work of the business. For example, a publishing company may form a team to handle the writing, production, and marketing of a book about how to use a software program. The team may include technical writers, desktop publishers, manufacturing associates, and marketing managers. Each person is part of a different department and reports to a different manager. However, they work together as a team to complete the tasks needed to produce and market the book.

> **Key▶Point**
> Workgroup teams are a trend in American companies. The goals of the team are related to accomplishing the work of the business.

Special Teams

Other workplace teams may be organized to accomplish more specific or specialized goals. A team that is set up to work on an ongoing basis is often called a committee. A committee may handle various projects or tasks

Workplace teams are a trend in American companies.

related to its primary goal. For example, a committee may be formed to deal with employee benefits, such as vacation time and health care insurance. The team members may be from several departments of the company. The goals of the committee may be to identify benefits that the company might offer and to discover which benefits employees need or want. Because the benefits available will change and the employee needs may change, the work of the committee needs to be ongoing.

A project team is formed to handle a specific task or assignment. This type of team typically operates for a set period until its goals are achieved. For example, a project team might be formed to design procedures and training for using a new telephone system the company has installed. Once the procedures are written and the training is complete, the team is no longer needed.

Advantages and Disadvantages of Teams

Using teams to achieve goals can have several advantages. Members of a team bring different skills and knowledge to the group. Team members who work well together often create synergy. This **synergy** allows the team to be more creative and productive than the individuals would be working separately. Team members may be able to help one another if a part of the project is behind schedule or not working as planned. A team with culturally diverse members may be better able to understand the needs of culturally diverse customers.

Using teams to achieve goals can also have disadvantages. If the team is disorganized or the members do not understand their goals or tasks, the team may accomplish little. Poor communication among team members can also be a problem that limits the team's accomplishments. This situation is especially true for a virtual team. A **virtual team** is one with members who do not share a physical workspace. The members work together using communications technology, such as telephone and e-mail.

check point 9

1. List three types of workplace teams.

2. Describe advantages and disadvantages of using workplace teams.

Check your answers in Appendix C.

Working Effectively in Teams

Effective workplace teams do not just happen. Team members must be selected who have the skills and knowledge needed to accomplish the goals of the team. Once the team is formed, the team members may need to learn about each other. The team needs to know the skills and experiences of each member. Some teams may be formed of employees who have worked together in the past. These team members have the advantage of knowing each other from the beginning. Workgroup teams whose members are of about the same rank in the company are known as peer group teams. Other teams may include people of different ranks. One person is typically identified as the team leader. This person may or may not be the one of the highest rank.

Team Roles

To be successful, a team has several roles that must be filled. Teams are made up of individuals who have different skills and backgrounds. Each person who is part of a team fulfills some sort of role on that team. Figure 3-6 describes those roles and how each one contributes to the team. Aside from the leader and the recorder, these roles are usually not assigned. However, most groups include people who naturally assume these positions. Some people may fill more than one role or may fill different roles at different times.

Learning to Work Together

Learning how to work together is the most challenging part of team development. It begins with establishing ground rules and procedures. For example, the team may decide to hold meetings on a regular schedule and to call additional meetings to discuss critical issues. Members may determine that only one person can talk at a time, with no side discussions, and that

Key ▶ Point

Members of a virtual team work in different locations and communicate by telephone, e-mail, or other means.

Diversity

Teams are made up of individuals who have different skills and backgrounds. This can make the team more creative and productive.

Figure 3-6 Team members assume different roles to ensure team success.

TEAM ROLES	
Leader	This person makes sure all members understand the goals of the team and their tasks and duties.
Challenger	This person tries to improve the team's methods or plans by asking questions and offering new ideas.
Doer	This person keeps the team focused on its goals and tasks.
Thinker	This person carefully considers other members' ideas and makes tactful suggestions.
Supporter	This person eases tensions and helps members have a good working relationship.
Recorder	This person keeps a written record of the team's meetings and plans.

the content of meetings is confidential. The team leader should encourage all team members to take part in discussions.

The team members need to understand how decisions will be made. On some teams, such as peer group teams, the members may discuss options and reach a consensus or agreement. On other teams, members work together and make suggestions regarding decisions. However, the leader may be a person of higher rank. The leader may make final decisions after considering comments from the team members. Once decisions are made in whatever manner, all team members should support the decisions.

Guidelines for Team Success

Workplace teams are formed for many reasons and have many different goals. Communicating openly and tactfully is one of the most important guidelines for the success of any team. Other guidelines that can help team members work together effectively are stated in the following list.

- Identify the goals of the team. State clearly what the team plans to accomplish. State how the team will know when the goals are achieved.
- Determine tasks or steps needed to accomplish the goals. The team may need to break large tasks into small parts.
- Identify resources needed to complete the tasks. Get any approvals that are needed before proceeding.
- Assign duties and tasks to team members. Set times for when each task should be accomplished.
- Communicate regularly with team members about the progress of tasks.

Key▶Point

In some teams, decisions are reached by consensus. In other teams, the leader makes decisions with input from team members.

Key▶Point

Team members should identify resources needed and get any needed approvals before committing to tasks.

- Resolve conflicts that arise. (See Figure 3-5 on page 90.) Do not let prejudice and assumptions that may be incorrect hinder communication.

- Brainstorm ideas for solving problems that arise. Figure 3-7 gives basic steps for solving a problem.

- Evaluate procedures. Periodically, look at how the work has progressed. Individual team members should reflect on the procedures used and ways to improve them. The team should consider how well the members work together and how procedures and relationships can be improved.

- Celebrate success. When significant parts of the project or an entire project is completed, recognize efforts of group members.

OCCUPATIONAL SUCCESS

Leadership

Leadership is providing guidance and inducing others to act. It is a vital skill that companies seek in employees. Leadership is important for managers and for employees in many non-management positions. Some people are more naturally prone to be leaders than others. However, leadership skills can be developed. Good leaders have these qualities:

- Leaders are committed to their work. They show discipline and initiative.

- Leaders have integrity. They are honest and live by high ethical standards.

- Leaders are enthusiastic. They take on assignments and tackle problems eagerly.

- Leaders have self-confidence and inspire others to trust them.

- Leaders care about others. They have good communication and teamwork skills.

A good way to begin building your leadership skills is by joining career-related student organizations. One organization for high school students is FBLA (Future Business Leaders of America). By taking part in organizations like FBLA, you learn to work with others, set goals, improve communication skills, and build self-confidence. Many student organizations provide information about their goals on a Web site. Search the Internet using the term *student organization* and a career area (such as *nursing*) to find groups that interest you.

Figure 3-7 Following logical steps can help teams solve problems.

PROBLEM-SOLVING STEPS
1. Identify the problem. Write a statement that clearly describes the problem.
2. Describe effects of the problem. What situations or behaviors are occurring because of the problem?
3. Brainstorm ideas for how to solve the problem. At this stage, record all ideas without spending time evaluating them.
4. Evaluate the possible solutions. Identify the one that seems most practical and most likely to solve the problem.
5. Test the solution. Apply the proposed solution for the problem.
6. Evaluate the results. Is the problem solved satisfactorily? If not, evaluate and test other possible solutions.

Standout Team Members

Key▶Point

Each team member should do his or her best to make the team successful.

Some teams you belong to will be effective and some will not. Many facets of a team are outside your control, but your own attitudes and actions are within your control. Strive to be a good team member and have a professional attitude. Your positive example is likely to help the team improve. Follow these guidelines for being a good team member.

- Set aside personal goals and focus on the team's goals.
- Do your work as well as you can. Be reliable and responsible.
- Contribute your ideas and opinions to team discussions.
- Find roles that you can fill and be ready to step into other roles, including leadership roles, when you are needed.
- Be supportive of your team members. Keep the team's affairs confidential.
- Do not take it personally when others disagree with you or criticize your ideas.

check point 10

1. List guidelines teams can follow to help them be successful.

2. List things you can do as a team member to contribute to team success.

Check your answers in Appendix C.

Section 3.3 *Applications*

A. *Participate in a Group Discussion*

1. Work in a team with three or four other students to complete this activity.

2. As a team, select a current business topic and ask your instructor to approve your choice. Identify one or two questions related to the topic that the team will consider. Examples of topics and questions are listed below.

   - What *green* (or *greening*) practices are being used by businesses? Are they really beneficial to the environment? to the business?

   - Is the U.S. economy currently growing stronger or weaker? What indicators support your position?

   - Is the use of telecommuting for employees increasing or decreasing? What are the advantages of telecommuting to a company? to the employee?

3. Use the Internet or other resources to do research on the selected topic. Read articles from magazines, newspapers, or the Internet. Each team member should do research independently.

4. Discuss the selected topic with team members. Share the information you have found with the group. Give your position on the topic, making your points tactfully.

5. Reach a consensus on the answers to the questions posed about the topic. Key the questions and answers your team has discussed.

TEAMWORK

INTERNET

REAL WORLD

B. *Evaluate Workgroup Procedures*

Jason Roberts has been part of a workgroup team for four months. The team's primary goal is to develop a marketing plan for a new product. Tami Wong, a marketing manager, typically assumes the leadership role in the team. However, the team has not formally identified a leader. The team members meet twice a month. They discuss ideas for how to sell and advertise the product. Team members have volunteered to do research or other tasks. Jason and two other team members have reported on their progress. Others have said they have not yet had time to do their part of the project. The deadline for completing the marketing plan is only two months away, and much work remains to be done. Clearly, the team needs to evaluate its methods.

1. What questions should Jason consider as part of a self-evaluation of his work with the team?

2. What suggestions could Jason make to the team members for improving the way the team functions?

Chapter *Summary*

3.1 Nonverbal Communication

- Nonverbal communication is composed of the messages sent without or in addition to words. Nonverbal symbols may reinforce, contradict, regulate, or substitute for verbal symbols.

- Nonverbal symbols, such as body language and use of personal space, and their meanings differ among cultures.

- The appearance and correctness of a written document can send critical nonverbal messages.

- Important aspects of your image are conveyed by nonverbal symbols.

- Characteristics of a physical setting, such as furnishings and color, can send nonverbal messages.

3.2 Listening Skills

- The listening process involves hearing, focusing attention, understanding, and remembering.

- People use different types of listening when listening for different purposes. The listening may be casual or active.

- Active listening may be informative, evaluative, emphatic, or reflective.

- Deafness or a partial hearing loss is a physical barrier to listening. Various other conditions and actions create barriers to good listening.

- To become a good listener, you must practice good listening habits.

3.3 Teamwork

- In the workplace, individuals may have relationships with managers, coworkers, and customers.

- Teamwork is two or more people acting together to achieve a goal. Various types of teams are common in the workplace.

- Team members should be selected who have the skills and knowledge needed to accomplish the goals of the team.

- Communicating openly and tactfully is one of the most important guidelines for team success.

- Individuals should strive to be good team members and have a professional attitude.

Open the *Word* file *CH03 Vocabulary* from the student data files. Complete the exercise to review the vocabulary terms from this chapter.

active listening	nonverbal communication
casual listening	paralanguage
conflict	personal space
emphatic listening	posture
enthusiasm	reflective listening
evaluative listening	self-confidence
friendliness	sincerity
gesture	synergy
informative listening	teamwork
leadership	virtual team

Critical Thinking Questions

1. What nonverbal symbols can you use to help create a positive professional image?

2. When listening to a speaker, what may be the result of taking too few notes? of taking too many notes?

3. Of the four parts of listening—hearing, focusing, understanding, and remembering—which is most important? Why?

4. Why is self-reflection by each team member about his or her performance important for team success? Why is peer evaluation of the performance of team members important for team success?

5. How important is following the guidelines for effective teamwork to completing group projects? to making group decisions? Why? What may happen if one or more of the guidelines is not followed? Give examples.

CRITICAL THINKING

Chapter *Applications*

A. *Casual and Active Listening*

Identify the type of listening demonstrated in each situation.

1. A career counselor is listening to a student discuss career goals. The counselor uses parallel talk to help the student clarify goals.

2. Several people are watching and listening to a movie.

3. An employee is listening to a manager give instructions for a task.

4. Jury members are listening to a witness testify about actions of an alleged robber.

5. Adam and Elena are discussing a problem related to work. Adam is listening and trying to understand Elena's point of view.

B. *Conflict Resolution*

Betty and Joe work in the same office. Betty, Joe, and several other employees share a network printer. Betty is working on a report that her manager needs by noon. She finishes keying the report at 11:15 a.m. and sends it to the printer. She thinks she will have plenty of time to proofread the report, make corrections, and print a final copy by 11:45 a.m.

Betty goes to the printer to get the report. "Oh, no!" she exclaims. "The printer is out of paper again. I just filled it an hour ago." Betty refills the paper tray, and printing resumes. However, it is not her report that is printing but a technical manual that contains 250 pages. Betty looks at the printer cue and sees that Joe is the person who sent this document to the printer. Storming over to Joe's desk, Betty angrily says, "Joe, how do you expect anyone else to get any work done when you keep hogging the printer and never refill the paper tray?" Joe calmly says, "Betty, I don't know what you are talking about, but I don't like your tone. Perhaps we should discuss this matter after you calm down."

1. Do Joe and Betty have the same information or understanding of the situation? Why or why not?

2. What is the underlying cause of the conflict?

3. How could Betty have tactfully brought the problem to Joe's attention?

4. Is Betty objectively considering her role in the situation? Explain your answer.

5. Should Betty apologize to Joe for her angry comments?

6. What are some possible solutions you could suggest for resolving this conflict?

C. Team Behavior

Every team is different, depending on the personalities and styles of its individual members. What is it that makes one team productive and another not productive? Read the following profiles of two teams. Look for similarities and differences between the two teams.

TEAM 1

The members of Team 1 hum along in their daily tasks without much fanfare. They pass work back and forth to each other, verify information by telephone, or work in pairs on specific projects—all with little wasted effort.

Team 1 members know what they do well and what other members do well. When they meet, they are relaxed. They accomplish work easily and laugh a lot. The team's results have had a visible impact on company performance. In a crisis, Team 1 rallies to do what it takes to accomplish the immediate goal, but its everyday functioning is not in "crisis mode." People find being on this team satisfying. Other employees wish they could be part of Team 1.

TEAM 2

Team 2 members work hard. They seem to be in meetings every day. They have motivating team slogans on the wall. However, they often leave meetings angry, frustrated, or disgusted. When team members get together in pairs, they spend time blaming others for the team's failures and do not get much accomplished. Several members have approached their supervisor about having one of the team members removed.

1. What are the similarities between Team 1 and Team 2?

2. What are the differences between Team 1 and Team 2?

3. What can Team 2 do to become more productive?

Editing Activity

Open and edit the *Word* file *CH03 Editing* from the student data files. Correct all spelling, punctuation, and grammar errors.

Listening Behavior

You have an acquaintance named Wilson. You have known him for more than ten years. He feels very close to you and considers you a good friend. However, you do not feel the same way about him. One of the reasons that you do not feel close to him is that he is always talking and never listens to you. Even when he does let you talk, his mind seems to wander. He seems to be thinking about what he will say next. At times, he seems to think he knows what you are going to say and does not want to hear your comments.

Wilson has commented that he cannot listen to people who are dressed strangely or have annoying habits. You wonder what he says about you when talking with others. Probably his most irritating trait is his inability to agree. If you say "yes," he says "no;" if you say "no," he says "yes."

Wilson has just been fired from his second job in three months. The same reason was given each time: "You do not listen." In a moment of humility, he approaches you as his friend and asks, "Am I really a bad listener? If I am, how can I learn to listen better?" He sincerely wants you to be honest with him.

1. What would you tell Wilson about his listening behavior?

2. What specific suggestions would you give Wilson to help him improve his listening skills?

Communication in Law, Public Safety, Corrections, and Security

Shane Correa is especially excited to go to work today. Shane is a new police detective, and he solved his first crime yesterday. He and his partner, Lee Park, solved a bank robbery case.

A local bank was robbed two days ago. Mid-afternoon is the time when tellers usually have the most money in their cash drawers. The robbery occurred at 2:15 p.m. The robber got away with $48,556 in cash.

Shane suspected that the robbery was an "inside job" because of the timing of the robbery. Sheila, one of the bank tellers, seemed very nervous when she was questioned about the robbery. She sat tensely in the chair, tapped her pencil, and perspired heavily. She also seemed hesitant when answering questions and would not make eye contact. Shane's partner, Lee had noticed the same things. He commented to Shane that Sheila seemed unusually nervous when she was being questioned.

Because of their suspicions, Shane and Lee examined Sheila's background. They quickly discovered that Sheila's boyfriend had a criminal record and had spent some time in prison for robbery. When looking at the bank's tapes of the robbery, they recognized the robber as Sheila's boyfriend. Sheila and her boyfriend had planned the robbery together. Today, Shane will fill out the paperwork on the case so that charges can be filed against the couple.

1. What role did nonverbal communication play in solving the case?

2. What role did teamwork play in solving the case?

3. Do you think listening and observing nonverbal cues are important in law enforcement? Why or why not?

CHAPTER 4

Basics of English Grammar

4.1   Parts of Speech and Sentences

4.2   Nouns, Pronouns, and Adjectives

4.3   Verbs and Adverbs

4.4   Prepositions, Conjunctions, and Interjections

To Hire or Not to Hire?

Chara has been in the United States for two years, and she loves living here. Since being a young girl in Africa, she has wanted to be an assistant to a lawyer. Chara graduated from high school in her native country. She entered a business school as soon as she arrived in the United States. Chara graduated from Coastal Banks Business College with a 3.5 grade point average. Her grades in English were very good. Now she is applying for her dream job—an assistant to a lawyer.

Chara is going to her first interview. When Chara enters the law office, she is a little nervous. During the interview, Chara makes the following statement, "When I lived in Africa, I taked English in high school and received straight A's. While in business school, I took courses that prepared me to be a lawyer's assistant. Thus, I feel that I speak English good and that my thorough understanding of the law would enable me to function good in a law office." She also indicates that her African heritage would be beneficial to the firm because many people in the surrounding neighborhoods are from her native land.

Because the position will require a lot of writing, the law firm looked at Chara's application form very carefully. When filling out the form, Chara quoted a friend. She wrote, "A friend indicated that my English is real solid, and she do not think that I would have trouble being an excellent assistant to a lawyer."

Questions

1. For this job, is speaking and writing English correctly important? Why or why not?

2. What other characteristics about Chara (which are not given in the case) would affect your decision about whether to hire her?

3. If you were the lawyer in this case, would you hire Chara? Why or Why not?

4.1 Parts of Speech and Sentences

OBJECTIVES

After completing Section 4.1, you should be able to:

1. Identify the eight major parts of speech.
2. Identify subjects and predicates in sentences.
3. Identify clauses and phrases in sentences.

Key ▶ Point

Understanding the parts of speech will help you communicate more effectively.

Parts of Speech

Every word in a message has a use. Familiarity with the parts of speech will help you choose appropriate words. The eight parts of speech are listed below. You will study each one in more detail later in this chapter.

- ■ A noun names a person, place, or thing. *Car, girl,* and *clock* are examples of nouns.

- ■ A pronoun takes the place of a noun. *She, he,* and *they* are examples of pronouns.

- ■ An adjective describes a noun or pronoun. *Big, red,* and *cool* are examples of adjectives.

- ■ A verb is a word or phrase that describes the action, state of being, or condition of a person, place, or thing. *Run, is,* and *talk* are examples of verbs.

- ■ An adverb describes a verb, an adjective, or another adverb. *Quickly, late,* and *now* are examples of adverbs.

- ■ A preposition connects a noun or pronoun to other words to form a phrase. *To, from,* and *for* are examples of prepositions.

- ■ A conjunction joins words, phrases, or clauses. *And, but,* and *so* are examples of conjunctions.

- ■ An interjection expresses surprise or strong feeling. *Oh!* and *Help!* are examples of interjections.

check point 1

1. Which of the eight parts of speech modifies an adjective?

2. Which of the eight parts of speech joins words, phrases, or clauses?

3. Explain the difference between a noun and a pronoun.

Check your answers in Appendix C.

Sentence Parts

A **sentence** is a group of related words that contains a subject and a predicate and expresses a complete thought. The sentence is the core of all communication. When forming sentences, the parts of speech are arranged into subjects and predicates.

Sentence Subjects

A **subject** of a sentence is the person who is speaking, the person who is spoken to, or the person, place, or thing spoken about. A simple subject is the main word in the *complete subject* that specifically names what the sentence is about. The simple subject of a sentence is never in a prepositional phrase. The simple subject is in italics in the following examples.

Key ▶ Point
A simple subject specifically names what the sentence is about.

> *John*, the young journalist, writes articles.
>
> The *chair* behind the girl is vacant.

A complete subject includes the simple subject plus all the sentence that is not part of the *complete predicate*. The complete subjects are in italics in the following sentences.

> *John* writes articles.
>
> *John, the young journalist,* has written articles.

A compound subject is two or more simple subjects joined by conjunctions, such as *and, or, nor, not only/but also,* and *both/and.*

> *John* and *Halle* work for our company.
>
> His *brother* or my *sister* will accompany us.

When two nouns in a subject refer to one person, the article *the* (or *a*) is omitted before the second noun.

> The *teacher* and *counselor* is my friend.

When two nouns in a subject refer to two people, the article *the* (or *a*) is placed before both nouns.

> The *teacher* and the *counselor* are my friends.

Sentence Predicates

The complete **predicate** is everything in the sentence said by, to, or about the subject. It always includes the main verb of the sentence. Whatever is not included in the *complete subject* of a sentence belongs in the *complete predicate.*

Key ▶ Point
The complete predicate always includes the main verb of a sentence.

John *writes articles.*

John, the young journalist, *has written articles.*

The simple predicate is the verb in the *complete predicate.*

John *writes* articles.

John, the young journalist, *has written* articles.

A compound predicate consists of two or more verbs with the same subject. The verbs are connected by conjunctions, such as *and, or, nor, not only/but also,* and *both/and.*

John and Halle *discussed* the matter and *concluded* that we are handling this situation incorrectly.

The engineer not only *complained* but also *refused* to finish the project.

Sara agreed to *mow* the lawn and *trim* the shrubs for Jack.

Objects and Subject Complements

Objects and subject complements help to complete the thought expressed by a subject and simple predicate.

Objects

An object is a noun, pronoun, clause, or phrase that functions as a noun. It may be direct or indirect. A **direct object** helps complete the meaning of a sentence by receiving the action of the verb. In fact, only action verbs can take direct objects. Direct objects answer the questions *what?* or *whom?* raised by the subject and its predicate.

Louis closed the *door.* (Louis closed *what?*)

The boy lost his *mother.* (The boy lost *whom?*)

K e y ▶ P o i n t
A sentence cannot have an indirect object without a direct object.

An **indirect object** receives the action that the verb makes on the direct object. A sentence cannot have an indirect object without a direct object. Neither the direct object nor the indirect object can be part of a prepositional phrase. The indirect object usually answers the question *to whom is this action being directed?* You can locate the indirect object by inverting the sentence and adding *to.* In the following sentences, the direct object is in *italics* and the indirect object is in **bold**.

Rafael gave **Thomas** the *candy bar.* (The candy bar was given by Rafael to Thomas.)

Nancy brought the **twins** their *broccoli.* (The broccoli was brought *to* the twins by Nancy.)

Lacy sold **Andrew** her *car.* (The car was sold to Andrew by Lacy.)

Subject Complements

A subject complement is either a noun or pronoun that renames the subject or an adjective that describes the subject. In either case, it always follows a state-of-being or linking verb (such as *am, is, are, was, were, has been, seems, appears, feels, smells, sounds, looks,* and *tastes*). In the following examples, the subject and subject complement are in *italics* and the linking verb is in **bold**.

> *Peter* **is** an honest *banker.* (The noun *banker* renames *Peter.*)
>
> *We* **have been** *sleepy* before. (The adjective *sleepy* describes *we.*)
>
> *Her writing* **appears** *magical.* (The adjective *magical* describes *writing.*)

check point 2

Identify the simple subject and the simple predicate in each sentence.

1. Brandon ran three marathons this year.
2. Lucille is a trained nurse.
3. Ramon and Maria work at this company.
4. We have been to every store in the mall.
5. Elena will finish her report on time.

Check your answers in Appendix C.

Clauses, Phrases, and Fragments

A **clause** is a group of words with a subject and a predicate; a **phrase** is a group of related words with no subject or predicate.

Clauses

An independent clause can stand alone as a complete sentence. A dependent clause must be attached to an independent clause to make sense.

Independent Clause	One of our sales managers has developed an excellent training manual
Dependent Clause	Which we plan to use in future training sessions
Complete Sentence	One of our sales managers has developed an excellent training manual, which we plan to use in future training sessions.

Key▶Point

A dependent clause does not express a complete thought.

Phrases

A phrase is a group of related words that does not contain both a subject and a predicate. A prepositional phrase is a group of words that begins with a preposition and ends with a noun or a noun substitute.

Place both cartons *on the desk.*

The boxes *in the office* belong *to him.*

Key ▶ Point

A verb phrase consists of a main verb and one or more helping verbs.

Frequently, sentences have a main verb and helping verbs. The combination of a main verb, either action or linking, preceded by a helping verb or verbs forms a verb phrase. The most common helping verbs are forms of the verb *to be* and forms of the verb *to have.* Examples are *is, are, was, were, has, have,* and *had.*

Julita *spoke* to her peers. (The verb is *spoke.*)

Julita *has spoken* to her peers. (The main verb is *spoken;* the helping verb is *has;* thus the verb phrase is *has spoken.*)

Additional helping verbs include *can, could, may, might, must, ought, should, will,* and *would.*

Julita *could have spoken* to her peers. (The main verb is *spoken;* the helping verbs are *could have;* the verb phrase is *could have spoken.*)

For a verb to be classified as a helping verb, it must have a main verb to help. Compare the following sentences.

Jim *has assisted* Ms. Wang. (The helping verb *has* precedes the main verb *assisted.*)

Jim *has* a new computer. (The verb is *has.*)

Ms. Madena *will be looking* for it. (The helping verb *will be* precedes the main verb *looking.*)

Ms. Madena *will be* here. (The linking verb is *will be.*)

Fragments

Key ▶ Point

A fragment is an incomplete sentence.

A **fragment** is an incomplete sentence that may or may not have meaning. Fragments that have meaning in context (*Good luck on your trip!*) can be used in business messages. However, do not use fragments that have no meaning.

Fragment	Sam, the vice president's brother.
Sentence	Sam, the vice president's brother, got a hefty raise.
Fragment	Because the beds were uncomfortable.
Sentence	Because the beds were uncomfortable, she slept on the floor.

check point 3

Identify the independent clause and the dependent clause in each sentence.

1. She took many pictures on her trip, which lasted a month.

2. The report that you wrote contains valuable information.

3. I will go if I am invited.

4. Since John will be out of town, he will not attend the meeting.

5. The work will be completed as soon as time allows.

Check your answers in Appendix C.

Sentence Structure

Your messages will be more interesting if you vary the types of sentences you write. Sentence structures are classified on the basis of the number and type of clauses they have.

Recall that the two types of clauses are independent (main) and dependent (subordinate). As an effective writer, you can put emphasis on an idea by placing it in an independent clause. You can de-emphasize an idea by placing it in a dependent clause.

Simple Sentences

A simple sentence contains one independent clause and no dependent clauses. There may be any number of phrases in a simple sentence. A simple sentence can be a clear, direct way to present an idea because there are no distracting dependent clauses. However, if overused, too many simple sentences in one paragraph can sound monotone or abrupt. The following examples are simple sentences.

Key ▶ Point

A simple sentence may contain a number of phrases but only one clause.

Theodore sings. (simple sentence)

Theodore and Jason sing. (simple sentence with compound subject)

Theodore sings and acts. (simple sentence with compound predicate)

Theodore Carson, a famous tenor, sings like an angel. (simple sentence with various phrases)

Compound Sentences

A compound sentence contains two or more independent clauses and no dependent clauses. In other words, two main ideas share equal importance. Note in the following examples that the two independent clauses are joined by a coordinating conjunction, a conjunctive adverb, or a semicolon.

> Mr. Feinstein is the founder, and he was the first president of FSI.
>
> It's getting late; however, I am glad to stay here and finish this project.
>
> Erin loves to ride horses; Manuel loves to draw horses.

Complex Sentences

A complex sentence contains one independent clause and one or more dependent clauses. The less important or negative ideas can be de-emphasized by using a complex sentence structure. In the following examples, the dependent clauses are in *italics*.

> *Although it is important to proofread a written message,* many people feel they do not have the time.
>
> Renaldo, *who cannot swim,* hates wading in Lake Waldo *because he thinks it is polluted.*

A compound-complex sentence contains two or more independent clauses and one or more dependent clauses. In the following examples, the independent clauses are in **bold** and the dependent clauses are in *italics*.

> *Since Noni left the folders on the desk,* **her assistant decided to finish up,** and **he did a good job**, *even though he was very tired.*
>
> **Sierra and Casey**, *who are cousins,* **play together often**; however, **their fathers**, *who are brothers,* **don't see enough of each other**.

check point 4

Indicate whether each sentence has simple, complex, or compound structure.

1. The beautiful butterfly landed on a flower.

2. The string beans, which were planted early, yielded a good harvest.

3. The meeting lasted two hours, and I was late for my next appointment.

4. Because he was hungry, he ordered a large meal.

5. You should review the report before the meeting.

Check your answers in Appendix C.

Section 4.1 *Applications*

A. *Parts of Speech*

Identify the nouns, pronouns, and verbs in the sentences.

1. You did an excellent job, Catherine.
2. Sign the voucher and attach it to your order.
3. All coaches will follow her instructions.
4. Dr. DeMarco spoke to us.
5. Shawn and I were delayed in London.

B. *Subjects and Predicates*

Identify the complete subject and the complete predicate in each sentence.

1. The leadership committee will meet soon.
2. The park was named last summer.
3. You will receive a copy of the report.
4. That company makes small engine parts.
5. I doubt that the proposal will be approved.

C. *Clauses and Phrases*

Identify the dependent clause in each sentence.

1. After I bake the cookies, we will go to the party.
2. The bicycle was left behind because it had a flat tire.
3. You will receive a copy of the report, which was prepared yesterday.
4. Later in the day, the game will resume.

Identify the verb phrase (main and helping verbs) in each sentence.

5. With practice, you can improve your reading skills.
6. The club members could have voted to take the trip.
7. The winner will be named next month.
8. You have cleaned your room well.

4.2

Nouns, Pronouns, and Adjectives

Nouns

OBJECTIVES

After completing Section 4.2, you should be able to:

1. Identify nouns, pronouns, and adjectives.

2. Create the plural form of nouns.

3. Use nouns, pronouns, and adjectives correctly in sentences.

A **noun** is a word used to name people, places, or things. A proper noun names a specific person, place, or thing. Proper nouns are always distinguished by capital letters. Examples of proper nouns are *Mary Ann*, *Seattle*, and *Pepsi*.

A common noun is a word that identifies a person, place, or thing in a general way. *Girl*, *team*, *rock*, and *car* are examples of common nouns.

Common nouns can be made up of more than one word. These nouns are called compound nouns. *Editor in chief*, *pocketbook*, *son-in-la*w, and *board of directors* are examples of compound nouns. Note that some compound nouns are hyphenated and others are not.

Singular and Plural Nouns

A singular noun is one that refers to one person, place, or thing. A plural noun is one that refers to more than one person, place, or thing. Plural nouns are formed in various ways. Refer to a dictionary when you are unsure of the correct plural form of a word.

Diversity

English does not have masculine and feminine forms of nouns, but many other languages, such as French and Spanish, do.

- Many plural nouns may be formed by adding *s* to the end of the singular form. Examples of these nouns are *books* and *guys*.

- Some plural nouns are formed by adding *es* to a singular noun that ends in *s*, *x*, *z*, *sh*, *ch*, or *o*. Examples of these nouns are *lenses*, *bushes*, *taxes*, and *potatoes*.

Key▶Point

A plural noun refers to more than one person, place, or thing.

- Some plural nouns are formed by changing a *y* at the end of the word to *i* and then adding *es*. Examples of these nouns are *cities* and *territories*.

- Some nouns have irregular plural forms. These nouns are formed by changing letters in the word. Examples of these nouns are *man* and *men*, *child* and *children*, *foot* and *feet*.

- Some nouns are always singular. Examples of these nouns are *advice* and *information*.

- Some nouns are always plural. Examples of these nouns are *pants* and *goods*.

■ A **collective noun,** such as *tribe* or *jury,* represents a group that usually acts as a single unit. These words are treated as singular nouns. *The jury eats in the cafeteria at noon.*

Possessive Nouns

Possessive nouns are ones that show ownership. To form a possessive noun, add an apostrophe plus *s* (*'s*) to a singular noun. Examples of possessive nouns are shown below.

man	+ 's	=	man's opinion
Ms. Lopez	+ 's	=	Ms. Lopez's car
district attorney	+ 's	=	the district attorney's actions

Add only an apostrophe (') to a plural noun if it ends in *s.*

executives	+ '	=	three executives' goals
district attorneys	+ '	=	the district attorneys' ideas

Irregular plural nouns and some compound plural nouns do not end in s. Add an apostrophe plus *s* (*'s*) to form the possessive of these nouns.

men	+ 's	=	the men's coats
brothers-in-law	+ 's	=	my two brothers-in-law's cars

Key ▶ Point

Possessive nouns show ownership.

check point 5

1. What is a noun?

2. Explain the difference between a proper noun and a common noun. Give examples of each one.

3. What is the plural form of each of these nouns?

   woman, cat, brush, facility, sister-in-law, district attorney

4. What is a collective noun? Give an example of a collective noun.

5. What is the possessive form of each of these nouns?

   men, dog, tables, sister-in-law, district attorney

   Check your answers in Appendix C.

Pronouns

Pronouns are words used in the place of nouns. A personal pronoun is a substitute for a noun that refers to a specific person or thing. Personal pronouns may be in the nominative case, objective case, or possessive case.

Key ▶ Point

A personal pronoun is a substitute for a noun that refers to a specific person or thing.

Key ▶ Point

An objective case pronoun may be used as a direct or indirect object of a verb or as the object of a preposition.

- A nominative case pronoun (*I, we, you, he, she, it, who, whoever*) may be used as a subject or a predicate nominative in a sentence. A predicate nominative is a noun or pronoun that refers to the subject and follows a form of the verb *to be* (*am, is, are*).

- An objective case pronoun (*me, us, you, him, her, it, them, whom, whomever*) may be used as a direct or indirect object of a verb or as the object of a preposition.

- A pronoun that indicates ownership is a possessive case pronoun (*my, mine, our, ours, your, yours, his, her, hers, its, their, theirs, whose*). Unlike nouns, pronouns do not need an apostrophe to signal possession.

Note these examples:

Nominative Case	Anita and *I* voted for him.
	It is *she* who received all the attention.
Objective Case	Please send *them* by express mail.
	Lamar brought *her* a burrito.
Possessive Case	These are *our* folders.
	The fancy clothes are *hers*.

Intensive and Reflexive Pronouns

Key ▶ Point

Intensive pronouns are used to provide emphasis in a sentence.

An intensive pronoun (*myself, yourself, herself, himself, itself, ourselves, yourselves, themselves*) is a compound pronoun created by joining a pronoun with *self* or *selves*, such as *myself* and *yourselves*. Use intensive pronouns to provide emphasis in a sentence.

I *myself* completed the project in two days.

Only you *yourselves* are responsible for this budget.

A reflexive pronoun is also a compound pronoun that ends in *self* or *selves*. However, a reflexive pronoun refers to a noun or pronoun that appears earlier in a sentence.

We found *ourselves* reminiscing at the reunion. (The reflexive pronoun *ourselves* refers to *we*.)

Interrogative and Demonstrative Pronouns

An interrogative pronoun begins a question that leads to a noun or pronoun response. Interrogative pronouns are *who, whose, whom, which,* and *what*.

Who is in your office?

Whose books are these?

What are your plans?

Whom do you want to call you?

Which of those are important?

A demonstrative pronoun is used to point to a specific person, place, or thing. The four demonstrative pronouns are *this*, *that*, *these*, and *those*.

Do you prefer *this* monitor or *that* one?

These books should be moved next to *those* shelves.

check point 6

Edit the sentences for correct use of nominative, objective, and possessive case pronouns. Write *correct* if a sentence has no errors.

1. These are they books.

2. Buy extra pencils for Jane and I.

3. Give the report to whoever you find at home.

4. My horse won the race.

5. Mark and I left work on time.

6. Gloria and me went to the movies.

Check your answers in Appendix C.

Pronoun-Antecedent Agreement

The noun or noun phrase that is replaced or referred to by the pronoun is called the **pronoun antecedent**. The pronoun must agree with its antecedent in person, number, and gender.

▦ Use a first-person pronoun to represent the persons speaking (*I*, *we*). Use a second-person pronoun to represent the persons spoken to (*you*). Use a third-person pronoun to represent the persons spoken about (*he*, *she*, *it*, *they*).

▦ Use a singular pronoun (*he*, *she*) to refer to an antecedent that is a singular noun. Use a plural pronoun (*they*) to refer to an antecedent that is a plural noun.

▦ Use a masculine pronoun (*he*, *his*) to refer to an antecedent that is a masculine noun. Use a feminine pronoun (*she*, *her*) to refer to an antecedent that is a feminine noun.

▦ Use a gender-neutral pronoun (such as *it*) to refer to an antecedent that is a gender-neutral noun (such as *table*).

▦ When the gender of the antecedent in a sentence is not obvious, writers can use both masculine and feminine pronouns (*he* or *she*). Another option is to change the antecedent to a plural form and use the gender-neutral plural pronoun (*they*, *their*).

Key ▶ Point

A pronoun must agree with its antecedent in person, number, and gender.

Diversity

Use gender-neutral nouns and pronouns when the gender is not known. For example, use *police officer* instead of *policeman*.

In the following examples, the antecedents are in *italics* and the pronouns are in **bold**.

> *Kim* encouraged **his** staff.
>
> *Anyone* can state **his** or **her** opinion on the matter.
>
> The British *man* **who** completed the two projects received a promotion.
>
> A good *manager* consults with **his** or **her** staff.
>
> A *doctor* tends to **his** or **her** patients without favoritism.
>
> The *students* completed **their** software installation on time.
>
> The *astronauts* cooperate 100 percent with **their** peers at NASA.
>
> The *panel* submitted **its** report.

Compound Antecedents

A compound antecedent is one that consists of two or more elements. Determining agreement in number may present a problem when an antecedent is compound. To eliminate errors when this occurs, follow these guidelines.

- When two or more elements are connected by *and*, use a plural pronoun to refer to the antecedent.

  > After *Shawn and I* drafted the proposal, **we** sent it to Ms. Jones.
  >
  > The *manager and the word processor* planned **their** itinerary.
  >
  > After *Joe and Robert* played ball, **they** went home.
  >
  > The *teacher and the coach* discussed **their** assignments.
  >
  > *Maria and Yuki* practiced **their** songs for the play.

- Two or more elements of a compound antecedent may be joined by *or/nor*, *either/or*, and *neither/nor*. Use a singular pronoun if all elements are singular. Use a plural pronoun if all elements are plural.

  > *Faye or Tom* can work on **her or his** papers now.
  >
  > *Neither Mateo nor Hal* has completed **his** book report.
  >
  > *The trainees or their supervisors* will finish **their** statistical computations.
  >
  > *Neither the men nor the women* plan to share **their** profits on the sale.

- When one part of the antecedent is singular and the other is plural, the pronoun must agree with the part that is closest to the verb.

  > *Neither the women nor the man* expressed **his** opinion.
  >
  > *Either the engineers or Ms. Mendoza* will give **her** suggestions for renovation.
  >
  > *Neither the manager nor the boxers* expressed **their** opinions.
  >
  > *Either the architect or the engineers* will give **their** suggestions for renovation.

Indefinite Pronoun Agreement

An indefinite pronoun refers in general terms to people, places, and things. Some pronouns in this category are always singular, such as *one*, *each*, *every*, *anybody*, and *anything*. They require a singular pronoun. Other indefinite pronouns are always plural, such as *many*, *few*, *both*, and *several*. They require a plural pronoun. Some pronouns (*all*, *some*, *more*) can be singular or plural.

Key▶Point
Some indefinite pronouns are always singular and some are always plural.

Every person had an opportunity to ask **his** or **her** questions.

Many will hand in **their** questionnaires.

Some will return **their** books on time.

> **check point 7**
>
> Edit the sentences for correct pronoun and antecedent agreement. Write *correct* if a sentence has no errors.
>
> 1. Alice Wong delivered his speech well.
> 2. The manager and employees read his bulletins.
> 3. Each of the boys ate their lunch.
> 4. Bill or Ray can complete their assignment.
> 5. Mr. Lau and I took my seats on the airplane.
>
> Check your answers in Appendix C.

Adjectives

An **adjective** is a word that describes or limits nouns, pronouns, and phrases that act as nouns. Adjectives answer questions about nouns, such as the following.

- Which one? *this* proposal, *those* appointments
- How many? *six* calls, *few* tourists
- What kind? *ambitious* student, *creative* teacher

Articles

Key▶Point
The adjectives *the*, *a*, and *an* are also called articles.

Although classified as adjectives, the words *the*, *a*, and *an* are also called articles. *The* denotes a specific noun or pronoun. *A* and *an* denote a nonspecific noun or pronoun.

- Place the article *the* before a noun to designate that the noun is specific, not general.

The man (a specific man)

The toy (a specific toy)

- Place the article *a* before a noun that begins with a consonant sound to designate that the noun is general, not specific.

  A man (a nonspecific man)

  A toy (a nonspecific toy)

- Place the article *an* before a noun that begins with the sound of a vowel.

  an honorable leader

  an attractive child

Nouns and Pronouns Used as Adjectives

Key▶Point

Nouns and pronouns can be used as adjectives.

Nouns or pronouns that precede and modify other nouns and answer questions, such as *which one* or *what kind* are used as adjectives.

Luis had four *theater* tickets. (*Theater* serves as an adjective describing the kind of tickets.)

Our family thoroughly enjoys *Thanksgiving* dinner. (*Thanksgiving* is used as an adjective to identify which dinner.)

Compound Adjectives

A compound adjective is two or more hyphenated words that precede and modify nouns.

The *well-known* mystery writer is signing copies of his book.

Vivian is selling *long-term* service plans.

Ms. Woo will attend a *high-level* meeting.

Comparison of Adjectives

✚

Ethics

Companies often use the superlative degree (*excellent, best*) for adjectives that describe their products when the positive (*good*) or comparative (*better*) degree would be more accurate. Is this practice unethical?

Regular adjectives have three degrees of comparison: the *positive* degree, the *comparative* degree, and the *superlative* degree. The positive degree describes one item. The comparative degree describes two items. The superlative degree describes three or more items.

To create the comparative degree of regular adjectives, add *er, more,* or *less* to the positive degree form. To create the superlative degree of regular adjectives, add *est, most,* or *least* to the positive degree form.

Positive Degree   The box is a *big* carton.

Montel is an *efficient* worker.

He is as *big* as you.

Comparative Degree	The box is a *bigger* carton than the first one.
	Montel is *less efficient* than Charles.
	He is bigger than you.
Superlative Degree	The box is the *biggest* carton of the three.
	Montel is the *least efficient* of the new employees.
	He is the *biggest* boy in his class.

A few frequently used adjectives do not form their comparisons in the usual manner (adding *er, more, est,* or *most*). Examples are *good, bad, little, many,* and *much*.

Positive	Comparative	Superlative
good book	*better* book	*best* book
many reports	*more* reports	*most* reports
little amount	*less* amount	*least* amount

Absolute Adjectives

Some adjectives cannot be compared because they do not have degrees; they are already at their highest level. These adjectives are referred to as absolute adjectives. Some examples of absolute adjectives are *immaculate*, *perfect*, *square*, *round*, *complete*, *excellent*, and *unique*. When you use these words in your sentences, use them alone or precede them with the terms *more nearly* or *most nearly*.

The food at Benito's restaurant is *excellent*.

Your yard is *more nearly square* than your neighbor's yard.

Key▶Point

Absolute adjectives do not have degrees. They are already at the highest level.

check point 8

Edit the sentences for correct use of adjectives. Write *correct* if a sentence has no errors.

1. Kim is efficienter than Robert.

2. Of the three books, the first one is the better one.

3. Your performance was more excellent than mine.

4. Her daughter is an pretty child.

5. His speed was the fastest of all the runners.

Check your answers in Appendix C.

Section 4.2 *Applications*

A. *Proper, Common, and Possessive Nouns*

Write ten sentences using each of the following proper, common, and possessive nouns.

1. bank
2. First National Bank
3. college
4. Union College
5. children
6. Mr. Smith
7. Mr. Smith's
8. memo's
9. telephones'
10. editor in chief's

B. *Pronoun Case*

Edit the sentences to correct errors in nominative, objective, and possessive case pronouns.

1. Gloria's outdated typewriter was her to keep.
2. Did Bettina ask for the operator whom assisted her?
3. We voted for they for treasurer and parliamentarian.
4. It's Appendix F is incomplete.
5. Him working on the budget keeps him busy.

C. *Adjectives*

Identify the adjectives in each sentence.

1. The brick house is obviously the largest and most beautiful on the block.
2. We invited Jeremy, a friend, to join us at the cottage.
3. The antiques dealer appraised the teak chest at $6,000.
4. Liberty Place is the taller of the two new buildings downtown.
5. A quick-witted applicant is needed for this job.
6. Patricia has a bigger payment than her brother.

4.3 Verbs and Adverbs

Verbs

The most important part of speech in a sentence is probably the verb. A **verb** expresses action, a state of being, or a condition of the subject of the sentence. No sentence is complete without a verb, and some sentences have more than one verb.

Types of Verbs

Every sentence must have a verb in order to be complete. Verbs are either action or linking verbs. Linking verbs include state-of-being verbs and condition verbs.

Action verbs help to create strong, effective sentences. Action verbs may take objects and indirect objects.

> Mr. Gomez *teaches* me Finance 102.
>
> Juanita *purchased* a stock certificate.
>
> Alana *wrote* legibly.

State-of-being linking verbs, sometimes called *to be* verbs, do not have objects or indirect objects. Instead, these verbs have *predicate nominatives* and *predicate adjectives*. The verb *to be* has many different forms to denote the present, past, or future state of being.

> The new president *is* Mr. Chow. (The predicate nominative, *Mr. Chow*, is linked to the subject by the verb *is*.)
>
> The old software programs *were* expensive. (The predicate adjective is *expensive*.)

A condition linking verb does not have an object or an indirect object. Instead, it connects an adjective to the subject. Condition linking verbs either refer to a condition or appeal to the senses. Examples are *taste*, *smell*, *seem*, *appear*, and *become*.

> The assistant *appears* cooperative.
>
> The health food *tastes* delicious.

OBJECTIVES

After completing Section 4.3, you should be able to:

1. Identify types of verbs.
2. Identify adverbs and words they modify.
3. Use verbs and adverbs correctly in sentences.

Key ▶ Point

Every sentence must have a verb to be complete.

Verb Tenses

There are six verb tenses in English. The **verb tense** indicates the time an action takes place. These six tenses are categorized into two groups, simple and perfect.

Simple Tenses

The simple tenses are called *present*, *past*, and *future*. A present tense verb expresses present occurrences (what is happening now).

> Computer services *sell* information.
>
> Georgia *is teaching* a course in merchandising.
>
> Rachel *sings* in the shower.

A past tense verb expresses action recently completed.

> Restless, the commander *walked* all night.
>
> Tammy *was visiting* her bedridden father.
>
> Joe *ate* lunch before noon.

A future tense verb expresses action or condition yet to come. Future tense is formed by placing the helping verb *will* before the main verb.

> I *will* vote on election day.
>
> The accountants *will be consulting* with their clients.
>
> The president *will take* office on January 20.

Perfect Tenses

A perfect tense verb describes the action of the main verb in relation to a specific time period that is in the past, from the past to the present, or in the future. The three perfect tenses are *present perfect*, *past perfect*, and *future perfect*. Form the perfect tense by preceding the past participle form of the main verb with either *have*, *has*, or *had*.

A present perfect tense verb indicates continuous action from the past to the present. *Has* or *have* precedes the past participle form of the main verb.

> George *has voted* in every election since 1986.
>
> They *have been jogging* every day since the beginning of the month.

A past perfect tense verb indicates action that began in the past and continued to the more recent past when it was completed. *Had* precedes the past participle form of the main verb.

> George *had voted* in every election until last week.
>
> They *had been jogging* every day until this past Monday.

A future perfect tense verb indicates action that will be completed at a specific point in the future. *Will have* precedes the past participle form of the main verb.

Including next year, George *will have voted* in every election since 1986.

By next Tuesday, they *will have been jogging* for a month.

By the end of the day, the train *will have reached* Phoenix.

Transitive and Intransitive Verbs

A transitive verb is a verb that must have an object to complete the meaning of a sentence.

Corrina *suggested* (Suggested what? Not complete)

Corrina *suggested* a profitable method. (Complete)

William *has rejected* (Rejected what? Not complete)

William *has rejected* our help. (Complete)

Jason *promised* (Promised what? Not complete)

Jason *promised* to return by Tuesday. (Complete)

An intransitive verb is a verb that does not need an object to complete the meaning of a sentence.

The recruits *laughed*.

The merchandise *is* here.

He *will be* treasurer. (*Treasurer* is a predicate nominative.)

> Key ▶ Point
>
> A transitive verb needs an object to complete the meaning of the sentence.

Active and Passive Voice

Voice indicates whether the subject is doing the action or receiving the action of a verb. **Active voice** means that the subject of a sentence is doing the action.

Mr. Park *completed* his report using his computer.

The young sprinter *won* the race.

Gloria *presented* the sales figures.

Passive voice means that the subject of a sentence is receiving the action. Passive voice is more indirect than active voice.

The ball *will be caught* by Yoko.

The report *was completed* by Mr. Park.

The poem *is recited* by the young actor.

> Key ▶ Point
>
> Active voice means that the subject of a sentence is doing the action.

Identify the verbs in the sentences. Tell the tense of each verb.

1. Since joining the restaurant, he has worked as a chef.

2. Our local high school will play in the basketball tournament.

3. I am happy about the change.

4. My team won the race.

5. She is our new teacher.

Check your answers in Appendix C.

Subject-Verb Agreement

Good communicators make sure that their subjects and verbs always agree (*he walks*, *they walk*). Grammatical errors in subject-verb agreement label the person who erred as a careless writer or speaker.

Agreement in Number

Key ▶ Point

Subjects and verbs should agree in number.

Third-person singular pronouns and singular nouns require a singular verb that ends in *s* when the present tense is used.

> Lora *telephones* her parents daily.

> Geraldo *drives* to his client's warehouse every Monday.

Third-person plural pronouns and plural nouns require a plural verb that does not end in *s* when the present tense is used.

> Joy's parents *telephone* her daily.

> The musicians *record* their music when they have a chance.

If a sentence is inverted (the predicate precedes the subject), putting the sentence in normal order will help you check subject-verb agreement:

Inverted Order   In the box *are* two *bags* of apples.

Normal Order   Two *bags* of apples *are* in the box.

Intervening Phrases

Intervening words do not affect subject-verb agreement and should be ignored. In the following examples, the intervening words are in **bold** and the subjects and verbs are in *italics*.

> The *manager* **of the sports teams** *is traveling* to New Orleans.

> The *members* **of the audience** *have* different reactions.

A Number, The Number

When used as a subject, the expression *a number* is considered plural and needs a plural verb. When used as a subject, the expression *the number* is considered singular and needs a singular verb.

A number of inquiries **come** to our office each day.

There **are** *a number* of tourists at our concert.

The number of inquiries **has decreased** since last month.

The number of attorneys in Philadelphia **is** on the rise.

Names of Companies

Names of companies are usually considered singular. Although a firm's name may end in *s* or include more than one individual's name, it is still one business and should have a singular verb.

Gordon, Rodriguez, and Ramirez **is representing** the plaintiff.

Silkowski and Daughters **manufactures** computer chips.

Park and Sons **sells** hardware and supplies.

Amounts

An amount that is plural in form takes a singular verb if the amount is considered one item. An amount that is plural in form takes a plural verb if the amount is considered to be more than one item.

One hundred dollars **is** a generous wedding gift.

Fifty-one books **are** on my shelf.

Twelve students do not have their work completed.

Compound Subjects

Errors in subject-verb agreement commonly occur with compound subjects. Usually a compound subject joined by *and* is plural and requires a plural verb. Sometimes, however, compound subjects are treated as one item and require a singular verb.

Francesca and Lorenzo **are visiting** their parents in Wuxi.

Peanut butter and jelly **is** popular in the middle school.

If *each*, *every*, *many a*, or *many an* precedes a compound noun, always use a singular verb. When a compound subject is joined by *or*, *nor*, *either/or*, or *neither/nor*, the verb agrees with the subject that is closest to the verb.

Many an investor and homeowner **has supported** this tax increase.

Tracey or *Hal* **seems** to be well qualified for the position.

Either George or *his sisters* **are** catering the buffet.

Neither the supervisors nor *the security guard* **has seen** the criminal.

Key ▶ Point

Compound subjects may require a plural or a singular verb depending on the use intended.

check point 10

Correct errors in subject and verb agreement in the sentences.

1. Ben or Jan need to finish the report.

2. Fifty dollars are the amount we paid.

3. The team members races to the finish.

4. Malloy and Moss manufacture toys.

5. A number of bills is past due.

Check your answers in Appendix C.

Adverbs

An **adverb** is a word that modifies an action verb, an adjective, or another adverb. Most adverbs end in *ly*. An adverb answers the questions *how, when, where, how often*, or *to what extent*.

> He wrote the report *correctly*. (How?)
>
> He wrote the report *yesterday*. (When?)
>
> He wrote the report *here*. (Where?)
>
> He wrote the report *twice*. (How often?)
>
> He wrote the report *very quickly*. (To what extent? How?)

K e y ▶ P o i n t

Adverbs modify action verbs, but they do not modify linking verbs.

Modifying Verbs, Adjectives, and Other Adverbs

Adverbs modify action verbs (but not linking verbs). Because adverbs modify action verbs and verb phrases that include action verbs, adverbs such as *never* or *always* frequently appear in the middle of verb phrases.

> She gave it to me *gladly*.
>
> The dog sat up and begged *just once*.
>
> Ned is *always* writing e-mail messages.
>
> That has *already* been ordered.

An adverb can modify an adjective. An adverb usually answers the question *to what extent* about an adjective that it modifies.

> The cookies Granny bakes are *very* good.
>
> That new project is *tremendously* complex.

An adverb can modify another adverb. An adverb often answers the question *to what extent* about another adverb in a sentence.

The middle school pupil did her work *too quickly*.

We purchased the new printer *very recently*.

Conjunctive Adverbs

A conjunctive adverb is a transitional word that joins two independent but related sentences. Examples of conjunctive adverbs are *therefore, moreover, however, nevertheless,* and *furthermore*.

They remained at work late; *therefore,* they were able to complete the project.

The student works after school as a messenger; *moreover,* she waits on tables in the evening.

Key▶Point

A conjunctive adverb joins two independent but related sentences.

Comparison of Adverbs

Like adjectives, adverbs have three degrees of comparison: positive, comparative, and superlative. To create the comparative form of an adverb, add *er, more,* or *less* to the simple form (positive degree). To create the superlative form of an adverb, add *est, most,* or *least* to the simple form.

Positive	Comparative	Superlative
arrived *late*	arrived *later* than she	arrived *latest* of all
clearly written	*more clearly* written	*most clearly* written
keyed *fast*	keyed *faster* than he	keyed *fastest* of all

check point 11

Identify the adverbs in each sentence. Indicate the word the adverb modifies.

1. The children read quietly.

2. The car was traveling very fast.

3. The really big dog chased the cat.

4. He watched the movie today.

5. The work has already been completed.

Check your answers in Appendix C.

Section 4.3 *Applications*

A. *Types of Verbs*

Identify the verbs in each sentence. Indicate whether each verb shows action or a state of being.

1. The man is tired.
2. The cows are grazing in the field.
3. Ten robins flew into the yard.
4. I am ready to begin.
5. The lamp shines brightly in the night.

B. *Verb Tenses*

Indicate the tense of the verbs in each sentence.

1. The water is boiling.
2. Madison baked cookies yesterday.
3. Ashley will travel to Madrid.
4. Alice Wong has walked to school every day this week.
5. By Saturday afternoon, I will have completed the quilt.

C. *Adverbs*

Write a sentence that correctly uses each adverb.

1. here
2. now
3. highly
4. too
5. therefore

4.4 Prepositions, Conjunctions, and Interjections

Prepositions

A **preposition** connects a noun or pronoun to other words to form a phrase. *About, after, at, before, below, between, from, for, into, on, under,* and *up* are examples of prepositions. A preposition usually indicates direction, position, or time.

Direction	She walked *into* the classroom.
Position	She stood *behind* the open gate.
Time	She left work *before* lunch.

A prepositional phrase begins with a preposition and ends with a noun or noun substitute that functions as the object of the preposition. One or more adjectives that modify the object may appear in a prepositional phrase. The prepositional phrases in the following sentences are in italics.

Place the carton *behind the tall cabinet.*

Mr. Fong believes that learning a spreadsheet program is *beyond him.*

Prepositional phrases may modify nouns (acting as adjectives) or action verbs, adjectives, or adverbs (acting as adverbs).

Roberto is *among those here. After lunch,* Jalicia filed the papers.

Ms. Torres is very knowledgeable *about the subject.*

OBJECTIVES

After completing Section 4.4, you should be able to:

1. Identify prepositions, conjunctions, and interjections.

2. Use prepositions, conjunctions, and interjections correctly in sentences.

Key ▶ Point

A prepositional phrase may act as an adjective or an adverb.

check point 12

Identify the prepositional phrases in each sentence.

1. Effective reading is important for workplace success.

2. The item was found under the desk.

3. Please finish this work for me.

4. Before eating, always wash your hands.

5. Come into the garden and through the back gate.

Check your answers in Appendix C.

Conjunctions

A **conjunction** is a word or phrase that joins two or more words, phrases, or clauses. Examples of conjunctions are *and, but, either/or,* and *when.* Different types of conjunctions are used to join words, phrases, and clauses.

Coordinate Conjunctions

A coordinate conjunction joins words, phrases, and clauses that are the same part of speech. These words, phrases, or clauses are considered to be equal in rank. The coordinate conjunctions are *for, and, nor, but, so, or,* and *yet.*

The teacher *and* the principal spoke outside the room.

Rafael did not agree with Craig, *nor* did he agree to take part in the arrangements.

Leo is studying computer science, *for* he plans to be a systems analyst.

Rosario wanted to attend the workshop, *but* she couldn't spare the time.

Janice loves him, *so* she said she would marry him.

They will swim *or* hike this weekend.

Helida says she loves to travel, *yet* she has never been on an airplane.

Correlative Conjunctions

A correlative conjunction also connects words, phrases, and clauses of equal rank. However, they are always used in pairs for emphasis. Examples of these conjunctions are *both/and, neither/nor, either/or,* and *not only/but also.*

Both Clinton *and* Barbara applied for the teaching position.

Either Clinton *or* Barbara applied for the teaching position.

Neither Clinton *nor* Barbara applied for the teaching position.

Not only Clinton *but also* Barbara applied for the teaching position.

Subordinate Conjunctions

A subordinate conjunction joins elements of unequal rank. These conjunctions are used primarily to connect dependent clauses with independent clauses. Examples of subordinate conjunctions are *after, as though, provided, though, whenever, although, because, since, unless, where, as, before, so that, until, while, as if, if, that,* and *when.*

Although we couldn't attend, we sent a donation.

They saw her *as* they were leaving the factory.

As if we could solve the problems, the men asked us for help.

Jules and Jalicia will visit *provided* they are allowed.

Parallel Construction

For messages to be clear, sentences should use parallel construction. A construction that is not parallel will have a conjunction that joins unmatched elements. Note the correct and incorrect uses of parallel construction in the following examples.

Incorrect	The exercise program was *rigorous* and *a challenge*.
Correct	The exercise program was *rigorous* and *challenging*.
Incorrect	The expert works *cleverly* and *with speed*.
Correct	The expert works *cleverly* and *speedily*.
Incorrect	Jack must *wash*, *iron*, and *to fold* the clothes.
Correct	Jack must *wash*, *iron*, and *fold* the clothes.
Incorrect	The apple was *juicer* and *more sweet* than the pear.
Correct	The apple was *juicer* and *sweeter* than the pear.
Incorrect	*Keying, writing,* and *addition* are skills needed for the job.
Correct	*Keying, writing,* and *adding* are skills required for the job.

Key ▶ Point

Sentences that use parallel construction are easier to understand than those that do not.

Interjections

An **interjection** is a word or expression that has no grammatical relationship with other words in a sentence. An interjection is used primarily to express strong emotion. Therefore, it is often followed by an exclamation point.

Hey, get your coffee cup off my monitor!

Help! Do you hear that comment daily from your customers?

Your idea is sure to work. *Super*!

In specific situations, such as sales promotions, interjections add color and vitality. However, interjections should not be used routinely in business writing.

Key ▶ Point

Interjections should not be used routinely in business writing.

check point 13

Identify the conjunctions and interjections in each sentence.

1. Oh! This present is lovely.

2. Mario and Jill attended the basketball game.

3. Help! The house is on fire.

4. Although I would like to go, I must stay here.

5. Both Raji and Kapoor ran for office.

   Check your answers in Appendix C.

Section 4.4 *Applications*

A. *Prepositions*

Write a sentence that correctly uses each preposition.

1. about
2. before
3. after
4. below
5. between
6. from
7. for
8. into
9. on
10. under

B. *Conjunctions*

Write a sentence that correctly uses each conjunction.

1. and
2. but
3. or
4. yet
5. so
6. either/or
7. unless
8. although
9. before
10. until

Chapter *Summary*

4.1 Parts of Speech and Sentences

- The eight parts of speech are nouns, pronouns, adjectives, verbs, adverbs, prepositions, conjunctions, and interjections.

- A sentence is a group of related words that contains a subject and a predicate and expresses a complete thought.

- An object is a noun, pronoun, clause, or phrase that functions as a noun. It may be direct or indirect.

- A clause is a group of words with a subject and a predicate; a phrase is a group of related words with no subject or predicate.

- Sentences may be simple, compound, or complex in structure.

4.2 Nouns, Pronouns, and Adjectives

- A noun is a word used to name people, places, or things. A proper noun names a specific person, place, or thing. A common noun identifies a person, place, or thing in a general way.

- Pronouns are words used in the place of nouns. A personal pronoun is a substitute for a noun that refers to a specific person or thing.

- An adjective is a word that describes or limits nouns, pronouns, and phrases that act as nouns.

4.3 Verbs and Adverbs

- A verb expresses action, a state of being, or a condition of the subject of the sentence. The subject and verbs in a sentence should agree in number.

- An adverb is a word that modifies an action verb, an adjective, or another adverb.

4.4 Prepositions, Conjunctions, and Interjections

- A preposition connects a noun or pronoun to other words in the sentence to form a phrase.

- A conjunction is a word or phrase that joins two or more words, phrases, or clauses.

- For messages to be clear, sentences should use parallel construction.

- An interjection is a word or expression that shows strong emotion.

Open the *Word* file *CH04 Vocabulary* from the student data files. Complete the exercise to review the vocabulary terms from this chapter.

active voice	passive voice
adjective	phrase
adverb	possessive noun
clause	predicate
collective noun	preposition
conjunction	pronoun
direct object	pronoun antecedent
fragment	sentence
indirect object	subject
interjection	verb
noun	verb tense

Critical Thinking Questions

CRITICAL
THINKING

1. Grammar checkers in word processing programs can identify possible mistakes. Do you need to proofread for errors if you use a grammar checker? Why or why not?

2. What would language be without adjectives? Would you be able to express your thoughts well without them? Explain.

3. How are adjectives and adverbs similar? How are they different?

4. Why would a writer want to avoid using interjections in most business writing?

Chapter *Applications*

A. *Parts of Speech*

Identify the correct part of speech for each italicized word in the paragraph.

Ms. Callens *is* very efficient and knows a *great* deal about the *situation*. However, *a* discussion with her *should focus* on the principles. *Totally* omit any miscellaneous details, except *for* the grievance. The case *is scheduled* for court on February 22.

B. *Plural and Possessive Nouns*

Indicate the word that correctly completes each sentence.

1. Only three of the (prototypes, prototype's) are available.

2. This brochure explains all the (HMOs, HMO's) policies.

3. They plan to review all the (expenses, expenses').

4. We will replace the (headsets, headset's) next year.

5. The (booth's, booths') prime location ensured heavy customer traffic during exhibit hours.

C. *Verb Use*

Write each sentence. Correct any errors in verb use. Write *correct* if the sentence is correct.

1. The nurse gone out of his way to care for the sick child.

2. After you get the mail, lie it on the kitchen counter.

3. Some residents of the town has traced their ancestry.

4. Frieda learned the business and begins looking for customers.

5. The officers am budgeting an extra $5,000 for taxes next year.

6. I choose the materials last week.

7. The delegates should rise from their seats when Mr. Li arrives.

Editing Activities

Open and edit the *Word* file *CH04 Editing* from the student data files. Correct all spelling, punctuation, and grammar errors in the two activities.

Writing Skills

Since his graduation from Glenview Coast Community College, Diego Flores has been looking for a job in which he can use his writing skills. He currently works in the produce section at a local market. That part-time employment provides just enough income to provide for his basic needs.

A friend mentions to Diego that her aunt, Akina Hamacho, manages the Publications Department at Expert Services Group, a large computer consulting firm. She tells Diego that Ms. Hamacho is looking for someone to help with editing and writing tasks.

Diego applies for the job. He polishes his resume, checking it several times for grammar, formatting, and spelling errors. He is very happy when he gets a call from Expert Services Group to schedule an interview with Ms. Hamacho. After the interview, Diego senses that it went well. He takes an editing and proofreading test. At Ms. Hamacho's request, he submits some writing samples.

Several weeks pass before Diego receives a routine form letter from the company. The position he wanted so badly has been given to another applicant.

After pleading with his friend to ask her aunt whether he might speak with her, Diego is able to talk with Ms. Hamacho. She tells Diego that there were only a few errors in Diego's editing and proofreading test. However, the three writing samples Diego submitted contained numerous grammar and spelling errors.

1. What message did the grammar and spelling errors send to Diego's potential employer?

2. Why did Ms. Hamacho put so much emphasis on the mistakes Diego made in the writing samples?

Communication for Hospitality and Tourism

Peter Chapman has been employed in the hospitality and tourism industry for nine years. He recently took a job in the Marketing Department at a new resort. The resort, which is in Branson, Missouri, is building phase three of its apartment units. The resort is also doubling the size of its health club. Peter has been hired to lead the marketing effort that will advertise these changes. The resort has a beautiful lake that is perfect for swimming, boating, and fishing. Other on-site amenities at the resort include:

- An indoor pool
- Racquetball and tennis courts
- An 18-hole golf course
- A restaurant

Peter's main task is to design advertising materials that will attract guests to the resort. The ads should also encourage people to buy timeshare condominium units. When buying a timeshare, a person pays a one-time purchase price. A typical price is $12,000 to $20,000. The buyer may also have to pay low yearly upkeep fees. This purchase gives the buyer certain rights, typically for occupying the unit one or two weeks per year. The unit can be sold to another person or willed to a relative.

1. How can Peter promote the resort amenities to potential buyers?
2. How can Peter show the benefits of timeshare ownership over other vacation formats, such as staying in hotels or camping?
3. What would be the effect of having grammatical errors in the advertising materials that Peter and his staff will develop?

+ Ethics

Some companies that sell condos use high-pressure sales techniques. They offer buyers lower prices if they will make a purchase on the same day they tour the resort. This gives buyers little time to read or evaluate the fine print in the contract. Is this practice ethical?

Hospitality & Tourism

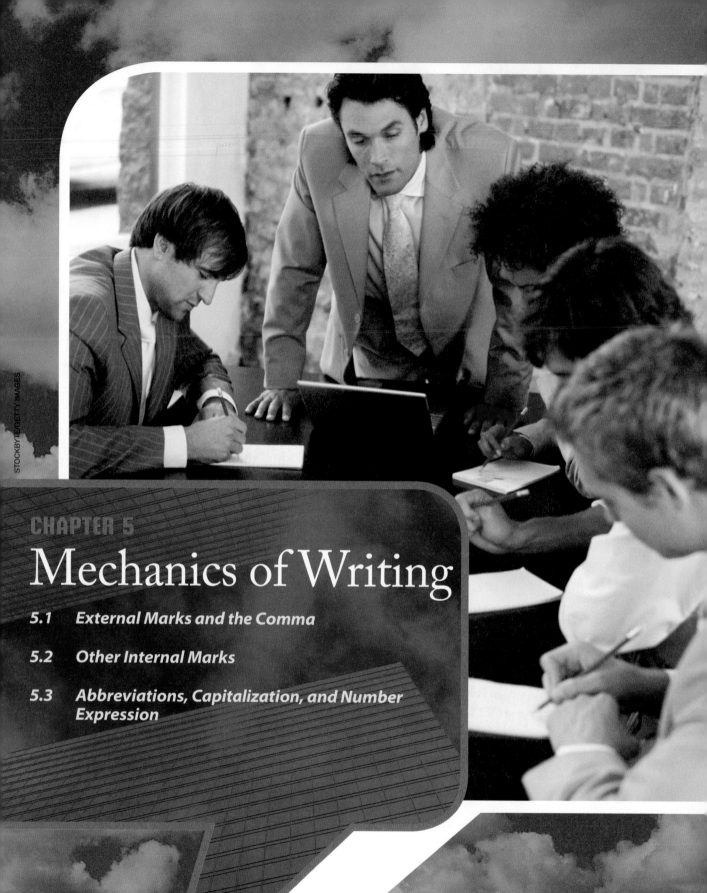

CHAPTER 5
Mechanics of Writing

5.1 *External Marks and the Comma*

5.2 *Other Internal Marks*

5.3 *Abbreviations, Capitalization, and Number Expression*

Comma Use or Comma Misuse

Chantelle and her family had a great vacation this past summer. They camped in both Yellowstone National Park and Glacier National Park. They saw buffaloes, elk, deer, grizzly bears, black bears, moose, swans, ducks, geese, and other animals. They viewed beautiful mountains and lakes. They also saw geysers and bubbling mud pots. The vacation was fun and interesting.

Today, the summer ends and school begins. Chantelle's little brother, Brandon, is in the second grade. As usual, he has to write a paragraph telling what he did during the summer. He has written his report and asked Chantelle to proofread it for him. Here is his paragraph:

> "This summer my family and I went to some national parks. One was in Wyoming the other was in Montana. They were really neat parks we saw elk deer moose and buffaloes. Because she loves to run Chantelle my oldest sister would get up every morning and go for a two mile run. One morning she saw a grizzly bear some wolves and a moose. So that morning she got scared and cut her run short. One morning I had pancakes bacon strawberries and whipped cream for breakfast."

Questions

1. Does Brandon know how to use punctuation yet?

2. Does accurate punctuation help the reader understand what the writer intends?

3. How is the reader's understanding of the message affected when the writer does not use punctuation properly?

External Marks and the Comma

Punctuation

For readers to interpret your ideas and questions as you intend, you need to use correct punctuation in every message you write. Punctuation tells your readers where one thought ends and the next begins. It clarifies and adds emphasis.

Punctuation includes external marks, such as periods, question marks, and exclamation points. Punctuation also includes internal marks, such as commas, semicolons, colons, quotation marks, parentheses, dashes, apostrophes, and hyphens.

The Period

A **period** is a punctuation mark used to signal the end of a sentence or an abbreviation. It is also used after numbers or letters in a list.

At the End of Sentences

A period is used at the end of a sentence. Types of sentences and examples are shown in the following list.

- A **declarative sentence** makes a statement.

  Gloria and Jamal are upgrading their software programs.

  The choir members will sing in Italy during the holiday season.

- A **mild command** is a stern request from the writer to the reader.

  You should watch your step or you will fall.

  Return the defective hard disk to the plant today.

- An **indirect question** is a statement that contains a reference to a question.

  They inquired how your parents are feeling since their accident.

  The judge asked whether the prosecutor had questions for the witness.

Key ▶ Point

A courteous request should end with a period rather than a question mark.

- A **courteous request** is a polite way to ask for action on the part of the reader; it does not ask for a *yes* or *no* answer. Whether to use a period or a question mark in such a sentence will depend on the intent of the writer.

  Would you be kind enough to revise the proposal and return the corrected copy to me as soon as possible.

With Abbreviations

Periods are placed after many commonly used abbreviations to indicate that the words are shortened forms of longer words.

Mr. (Mister)	Jr. (Junior)	Dr. (Doctor)
Ltd. (Limited)	Inc. (Incorporated)	Sr. (Senior)

Diversity

The abbreviation *Ltd.* (Limited) is England's equivalent to America's *Inc.* (Incorporated).

In Lists

When numbers or letters are used in a vertical list, periods are placed after each number or letter.

Your child will need the following items for the outing:

1. One change of clothing
2. Bathing suit, swim cap, sandals, towel, and sunscreen lotion
3. Money to buy snacks

Key ▶ Point

Periods are used after numbers or letters in vertical lists. If the items in the list are complete sentences, use periods at the end of the items.

check point 1

Write each sentence, using periods correctly.

1. The team won the game by a narrow margin
2. Return all borrowed equipment to the proper location
3. Will you please close the door on your way out
4. Mr and Mrs Levi arrived on time
5. Dr Patel is on vacation

Check your answers in Appendix C.

The Question Mark

A **question mark** is a punctuation mark used after a direct question and after each part in a series of questions. The response may be a single word, or it may be one or more sentences.

After Direct Questions

Use a question mark after a complete or incomplete sentence that asks a direct question.

Do you agree that summer seems to pass more quickly than winter?

Have you considered relocating to find suitable employment?

Why not?

Key ▶ Point

By ending each part in a series of questions with a question mark, the writer emphasizes each part of the question.

In a Series

Occasionally a series of questions may be useful in your writing. For emphasis, follow each segment in the series with a question mark.

> Were all the votes counted? all the winners notified? all the losers contacted?

> Did she apply to Temple University? to Boston College? to Florida International University?

check point 2

Write each sentence, using question marks correctly.

1. When will the project be completed
2. Have you already eaten lunch
3. Have you keyed the report the letter the flyer
4. Will you return before noon
5. Can she lift the box

Check your answers in Appendix C.

The Exclamation Point

Key ▶ Point

Use exclamations sparingly in business documents.

An **exclamation point** is a punctuation mark that shows strong emotion. It may follow a word, a group of words, or a sentence. When an expression shows excitement, urgency, or anger, use an exclamation point. Use exclamations sparingly in all writing, but especially in business documents.

> Quick! Here's an opportunity to make money!

> I'll never do that again!

check point 3

Write each sentence, using exclamation points correctly.

1. Oh no I forgot my keys
2. Help The store is being robbed
3. Surprise Happy birthday
4. Great I knew you could do it
5. Hold on We're falling

Check your answers in Appendix C.

The Comma

External punctuation marks tell the reader whether a sentence is a statement, a question, or an exclamation. Internal punctuation marks clarify the message intended by the writer.

The **comma** is an internal punctuation mark used to separate items in a sentence. Commas also are used to indicate the omission of words and to promote clarity in sentences. Notice how the comma in the second example below makes the sentence clear.

| Not Clear | Shortly after the teacher left the classroom. |
| Clear | Shortly after, the teacher left the classroom. |

With Introductory Elements

Introductory elements add meaning to a sentence. They come before the main clause of the sentence. Insert a comma after an introductory word, phrase, or clause.

Meanwhile, I will begin the next phase of the project.

Before running, the teenager warms up her leg muscles.

Because we have no record of the sale, we cannot help you.

K e y ▶ P o i n t

An introductory element comes before the main clause in a sentence and should be followed by a comma.

In Compound Sentences

Independent clauses in a compound sentence may be joined by a coordinate conjunction. Examples of coordinate conjunctions are *for*, *and*, *nor*, *but*, *or*, and *yet*. Precede a coordinate conjunction in a compound sentence with a comma. When each independent clause in a compound sentence has fewer than four words, however, no comma is needed.

I will go to the hockey game on Friday, or I will babysit for my niece.

The new order forms are on legal-size paper, and the quantity we bought should last for three months.

We thought he was guilty at first, but now we have changed our minds.

Megan spoke and they responded.

I rode but he walked.

With Interrupting Elements

Interrupting elements are phrases or clauses that break the flow of a sentence. In some cases, the element is essential to the meaning of the sentence. In other cases, it is not. Nonessential elements are set off from the rest of a sentence with commas.

To determine whether the information is essential, temporarily omit it. If the meaning of the sentence stays the same, set off the nonessential word, phrase, or clause with commas. If the meaning of the sentence is not clear when the information is omitted, do not set off the information with commas.

Nonrestrictive and Restrictive Elements

A **nonrestrictive element** is a phrase or clause that gives information that is not essential to the meaning of the sentence. These words are set off from the rest of the sentence with commas. In the following examples, nonessential elements are shown in *italics*.

The most interesting part of the movie, *I believe,* is the chase scene.

He should, *on the other hand,* separate the items in the box.

Jeff Chang, *who graduated from Loyola,* is my neighbor.

We plan to order Part 643, *which Marcos recommended.*

A **restrictive element** is a phrase or clause that gives information that is essential to the meaning of a sentence. An essential phrase or clause is not set off with commas. In the following examples, the essential phrases are shown in *italics*. These words are needed to make the meaning of the sentence clear.

Ask the nurse *who was on duty that night.*

The man *who was just hired* is part of my team.

Appositives

An **appositive** is a noun or phrase that renames and refers to a preceding noun. As with other interrupting elements, appositives may provide essential or nonessential information. When an appositive provides nonessential information, set it off from the rest of the sentence with commas. In the following examples, the appositives are shown in *italics*.

The paper contained the forecasts for the next quarter, *July through September.*

Ruby Munoz, *the council member,* will attend the meeting.

Mr. Rodriguez, *the famous baseball player,* signed autographs.

Takashi, *a certified mechanic,* installed a new alternator in the car.

When an appositive provides essential information, do not set it off from the rest of the sentence with commas. In the following examples, the appositives are shown in *italics*.

My brother *Mario* is touring the factory.

The singer *Alice Johns* will be performing at the concert.

The substitute teacher *Ms. Johnson* will teach the class today.

check point 4

Write each sentence, using commas correctly.

1. After lunch we will continue our meeting.

2. The item in the package was broken and I refused delivery.

3. Please remember I need the data this afternoon.

4. He played and I sang.

5. The reports all of which were late supported his plan.

Check your answers in Appendix C.

With Direct Address

To personalize a message, a writer may use direct address. **Direct address** means speaking directly to someone, usually calling the person by name. The name can appear in the beginning, middle, or end of the sentence. Because the name is not needed to convey the meaning of the sentence, it is set off with commas.

> *Dr. Oakes*, you have been exceedingly helpful to my family.
>
> Have I told you, *Gwen*, that we appreciate your purchase?
>
> *Mr. James,* please meet Mrs. Park.
>
> Where will you go, *Maria?*

Key ▶ Point

Because a noun of direct address is not needed to convey the meaning of the sentence, it is set off with commas.

In a Series

Use a comma to separate three or more items in a series of words, phrases, or clauses. Although some experts omit the comma before a conjunction in a series, including the comma avoids confusion.

> Evan's college essay was thoughtful, humorous, and brief.
>
> I will go to the movies, to the mall, or to my grandparents' home.
>
> Wake up early, prepare and serve breakfast, and go to work.

Between Adjectives

Use a comma between two adjectives that modify the same noun when the coordinate conjunction *and* is omitted. If the word *and* would not make sense between the adjectives, do not insert a comma.

> The short, thin teenager envied the tall, husky football players.
>
> Reggie's royal blue suit is inappropriate attire for a job interview.

With Omission of Words

Occasionally, a writer may omit words that are understood by the reader. Inserting a comma at the point of omission provides clarity. In the example below, the word *is* is omitted twice in the sentence. Commas are inserted at the points of omission. Semicolons are used to separate the items in the series because the items have commas within them.

> The treasurer is Yoshi; the secretary, Elena; and the president, Warren.

In Numbers and Dates

Key▶Point

Do not use commas in the decimal part of a number.

Use commas to indicate a whole number in units of three. Do not use commas in the decimal part of a number.

> $2,468   34,235 hot dogs   526,230 pins   278,249   0.567258

Commas are used with a complete date that appears in a sentence.

> On May 3, 2010, the day was overcast and chilly.

With Abbreviations

Diversity

Some people who have *Jr.* in their names may omit the comma before *Jr.* Some companies that have *Inc.* in their names omit the comma before *Inc.* Follow the wishes of the people or companies in those cases.

In a series, insert a comma before *etc.* when it appears at the end of a sentence. Use commas before and after *etc.* when it appears within a sentence.

> We will be taking camping clothes: shorts, boots, swimwear, etc.
>
> Maps, tools, supplies, etc., will be needed.

Generally, place a comma before *Jr.*, *Sr.*, and *Inc.* in a name. Also insert commas after the abbreviations in the middle of a sentence.

> Harry Larkin, Jr., was elected to the presidency.
>
> Able, Inc., is owned by a conglomerate in New York.

check point 5

Write each sentence, using commas correctly.

1. I see Maria that you have completed the report the letter and the memo.

2. The fast quiet printer was a welcome addition to the office.

3. Tom Wilson Sr. talked with Ms. Mendez from Boston Cards Inc.

4. Grammar punctuation spelling etc. will be counted on the test.

Check your answers in Appendix C.

Section 5.1 *Applications*

A. External Punctuation

Write each sentence, using correct punctuation.

1. Mae Wong left the office to attend a dinner meeting

2. Will you please call me when you are ready to discuss this issue

3. Wow This cake is great

4. How many people do you expect to attend the seminar

5. Dr. Chu and Mrs. Tong are working together on this project

6. Complete the steps in this order:

   a   Select a time for the meeting

   b   Reserve a conference room

   c   Notify the team members about the arrangements

B. Commas

Write each sentence, using correct punctuation.

1. Jose implied Miguel is not trustworthy.

2. After all you have accomplished more than anyone I know.

3. The menu includes chicken rice salad and cake.

4. Personally I think the color is beautiful.

5. To Jill Robert seemed upset.

6. Give me the report and I will deliver it to the main office.

7. After we left work we went directly to the restaurant.

8. Do you want eggs or cereal or pancakes for breakfast?

9. Bennington Inc. makes toys and children's clothing.

10. The order totaled $23456.75.

5.2 Other Internal Marks

The Semicolon

OBJECTIVES

After completing Section 5.2, you should be able to:

1. Use internal punctuation marks correctly in sentences.

2. Use internal punctuation marks correctly in letters, dates, numbers, and time.

A **semicolon** is a punctuation mark used to denote a pause. Semicolons are stronger than commas but weaker than periods.

Between Clauses

A semicolon can be used between two related independent clauses instead of using a comma and a coordinate conjunction.

> George is studying economics; his brother Javier is majoring in accounting.

> Elaine will attend the July convention; she then will vacation in London.

Use a semicolon before a coordinate conjunction in a compound sentence when one or both of the clauses have commas. The sentence might be misread if a comma is inserted before the conjunction.

> I requested a return call, information about a particular check, and the teller's extension number; instead, I received a past-due notice, a reference to the wrong check, and an incorrect telephone number.

> On Wednesday, March 12, 2004, the group will meet; but Florio will not officiate.

Use a semicolon before a conjunctive adverb (*moreover*, *nevertheless*, *however*, *consequently*) that joins two independent clauses. Conjunctive adverbs, which act as transitional expressions, introduce the second clause.

> His report is too long; therefore, he cannot submit it until he revises it.

> Getting information from Amtrak can be easy; however, the voice-mail system tends to confuse some callers.

In a Series or List

Use semicolons to separate items within a series when any of the items already contain commas.

> Those in attendance were Jesus Canseco, President; Larry Tripp, Vice President; Rob Healy, Secretary; and Juanita Hall, Treasurer.

Key ▶ Point

Use a semicolon before a conjunctive adverb that joins two independent clauses.

The mortgage company has branches in Newport, Rhode Island; Atlanta, Georgia; and Chicago, Illinois.

Use a semicolon before expressions, such as *for example*, *that is*, and *for instance*, when they introduce a list of examples.

You can attend some interesting functions; for example, an art show, a dance performance, or a special film screening.

They must follow smart money management principles; that is, save part of their income, make purchases they can afford, and avoid buying inferior goods.

check point 6

Write each sentence, using correct punctuation.

1. The meeting will end at noon lunch will be served after the meeting

2. She planned to leave work early however her boss asked her to work late

3. The seminars will be held in Lexington Kentucky Cincinnati Ohio and Knoxville Tennessee

4. I ordered a printer a fax machine and three ink cartridges but I received only a printer

5. The quilters chose a variety of block patterns for example lone star, log cabin, flying geese, and birds in the air.

Check your answers in Appendix C.

The Colon

A **colon** is a punctuation mark that directs the reader's attention to the material that follows it. The material that follows the colon completes or explains the information that comes before the colon.

Key▶Point

A colon directs the reader's attention to the material that follows it.

Before a Series or List

Use a colon when the words *the following*, *as follows*, and *are these* are near the end or at the end of a sentence that introduces a series of items.

Each person will need the following: a computer, a printer, a set of instructions, and a writing tablet.

The new automobile's special features are as follows: antilock brakes, a built-in CD player, and leather upholstery.

Use a colon before a vertical, itemized list. As with a series, the words *the following*, *as follows*, or *are these* may precede the colon.

> Your instructions for Monday are these:
>
> 1. Open the office at 9 a.m.
> 2. Check Saturday's mail, and call me if Irene's check arrives.
> 3. Answer the telephone until noon.

Ethics

Always give credit to the source of quotes or paraphrased material used in documents or presentations.

Before a Long Quotation

Use a colon to introduce a long quotation of more than two lines.

> Chien remarked: "When I think of my home in Beijing, I can just picture the hundreds of people riding their bicycles to work in the early morning light."

Between Independent Clauses

Use a colon to separate two independent clauses when the second clause explains the first. In the following situations, a colon replaces a semicolon.

> Lucia is a skilled artist: She won an award for sketching animals.

After a Salutation

When using mixed punctuation in a letter, use a colon after a salutation.

> Dear Sir: Dear Dr. Santiago: Dear Ms. Linden:

In Times

Use a colon between the hour and the minutes when expressing time.

> Let's meet at 11:30 a.m. in the lobby of the office building.

check point 7

Write each sentence, using colons correctly.

1. Each camper will need the following items a sleeping bag, a pillow, a backpack, and a rain tarp.
2. The game will begin at 130 p.m.
3. The copier's special features are these fast printing speed, reduction mode, and duplexing.
4. The group is well-traveled they toured Europe last year.
5. This horse is fast he set a track record.

   Check your answers in Appendix C.

The Dash

A **dash** is a punctuation mark used to show a sudden change of thought. Formed by keying two hyphens, a dash is an informal punctuation mark. A dash can also be used for emphasis rather than a comma or colon in some situations.

Key ▶ Point

A dash is an informal punctuation mark. It can be used for emphasis rather than a comma or colon in some situations.

With a Sudden Change of Thought

Use a dash to indicate a sudden change of thought or a sudden break in a sentence.

> Here is the perfect suit for work—and it's on sale, too!
>
> "Then we both agree that—oh no, now what's wrong?" asked Amy.

For Emphasis

A dash can be used for emphasis instead of a comma or a colon in some situations. Examples are discussed in the following list.

■ For emphasis, a dash can be used to set off appositives and other nonessential elements from the rest of the sentence. Some of the nonessential elements may have internal commas.

> The stockbroker's office—newly equipped, nicely decorated, and spacious—is perfect for the hospitality reception.
>
> There is a special ingredient in my recipe—sage.

■ A dash can be used after a listing at the beginning of a sentence that is followed by a summarizing statement. The dash provides strong emphasis. Summarizing statements usually begin with the words *all* or *these*.

> A nurturing manner, a love of people, and an unselfish attitude—these are three traits school counselors need.
>
> Precision in mechanics, vocabulary, and facts—all are necessary for effective communications.

■ A dash can be used to set off a listing or an explanation that provides details or examples.

> The restaurant features exotic desserts—Polynesian pudding, Hawaiian coconut sherbet, and Samoan almond supreme cake.

■ A dash can be used to give strong emphasis to a related clause.

> The referee's call was unfair—and you know it!
>
> I do the work—she gets the pay.

check point 8

Write each sentence, using dashes correctly.

1. Do you believe that yes, I guess you do.

2. Bobby Chin he's the one in the red shirt is our best player.

3. The park's attractions are these swimming pools, tennis courts, picnic tables, and hiking trails.

4. One key element is missing money.

5. Dallas, Houston, and San Antonio all are important markets for us.

Check your answers in Appendix C.

The Hyphen

A **hyphen** is a punctuation mark used after some prefixes and in forming some compound words. A hyphen is also used to divide words between syllables at the end of a line in letters, reports, and other documents.

After Prefixes

Use a hyphen after prefixes in some words. If you are unsure whether a word needs a hyphen, consult a dictionary.

ex-president	pro-American	semi-invalid
de-emphasize	co-coordinator	

In Compound Words

Key ▶ Point

Some compound words are hyphenated; others are not. Check a dictionary when in doubt about whether to use a hyphen.

Use a hyphen in some compound words. In the English language, some compound words are written as one word, others are written as two words, and others are hyphenated. Some examples of hyphenated compound words are shown here.

up-to-date reports	self-confident speaker
well-informed reporter	two-year-old child

Some compound adjectives, such as *up to date*, *well informed*, and *two year old*, are hyphenated when they come before the noun they modify. They are not hyphenated when they follow the noun.

The report is up to date.

Our up-to-date equipment improves productivity.

check point 9

Write each sentence, using hyphens correctly.

1. Watch this station for up to the minute reports.

2. My father in law is retired.

3. Margie is the cocoordinator for the project.

4. One fourth of the building has been painted.

5. Please keep the team up to date on your progress.

Check your answers in Appendix C.

Quotation Marks

Quotation marks indicate a direct quotation, a definition, nonstandard English, or a title. They may also be used to indicate a word or phrase used in an unusual way.

With Quotations

When stating someone's exact words, enclose the words within opening and closing quotation marks.

> Betty exclaimed, "It's getting late; let's go!"
>
> "We'll leave now," answered Jeff. "We don't want to miss the train."
>
> "You may watch television after you finish your homework," Mother said.

Use single quotation marks to enclose a quotation within a quotation.

> Amanda stated, "They listened carefully to the president when he said, 'Our competition is getting ahead of us.' "

With Definitions and Nonstandard English

Use quotation marks to designate a term that is defined in the same sentence in which the term appears. Use quotation marks to enclose slang words or expressions.

> A "couch potato" is someone who watches television all day and all evening.
>
> He referred to his car as "old red."
>
> A "blog" is a word derived from *web* and *log*.

Diversity

Avoid using slang words or colloquialisms in business documents, especially when writing to a diverse audience or to those whose first language is not English.

With Titles

Use quotation marks to enclose the titles of parts of whole works, such as magazine articles and chapters in books. Quotation marks also are used to enclose titles of lectures, songs, sermons, and short poems.

> I read the article "The New Subcompact Cars" in *Consumer's Digest*.
>
> Gregory's lecture "E-Mail Versus Voice Mail" created a stir in the crowd.

With Other Punctuation Marks

When placing ending quotation marks, follow these guidelines.

- Place periods and commas within ending quotation marks.

   > "I concur," said the investor, "with your suggestion."

- Place semicolons and colons outside ending quotation marks.

   > His best lecture is called "Psychoanalysis in the 1990s"; have you had an opportunity to hear it?
   >
   > Enjoy the "beauty of San Diego": ideal temperatures and clear skies.

- Place question marks and exclamation points inside the ending quotation marks when the quoted material is a question or an exclamation.

   > She shouted, "Watch out!"
   >
   > He replied, "What's happening?"

- Place question marks and exclamation points outside the ending quotation marks when the sentence, but not the quoted material, is a question or an exclamation.

   > Did Angelique actually say, "I will attend the seminar"?
   >
   > What a deplorable situation; he's just "goofing off"!

Key ▶ Point

Periods and commas always go inside ending quotation marks. Semicolons and colons always go outside ending quotation marks.

check point 10

Write each sentence, using quotation marks correctly.

1. She asked, Will you be home early?

2. Did he say, I was home alone?

3. I agree, said the teacher, that your work has improved.

4. She wrote the article The New Math for the school newspaper.

5. A hacker is someone who accesses a computer network without authorization.

Check your answers in Appendix C.

Parentheses

A parenthesis is a punctuation mark used in pairs to set off nonessential words, phrases, or clauses. The pair is called **parentheses**. Parentheses also are used with abbreviations, references and directions, and numerals and letters in lists.

With Nonessential Elements

Nonessential elements in a sentence may be placed in parentheses. Words in parentheses have less emphasis than words separated by commas or dashes. When the items in parentheses appear at the end of a sentence, place the external mark after the ending parenthesis.

> A high percentage of the alumni (73 percent of those surveyed) opposed changing the name of the college.

> We received a visit from our ex-president (1997–1998).

When a complete sentence is placed in parentheses, capitalize the first word and end the sentence with an external punctuation mark. Place the external punctuation mark inside the closing parenthesis.

> Luis and Ramona relocated to Brooklyn. (Didn't you meet them in San Juan?)

When a dependent clause is followed by words within parentheses, place the comma after the ending parenthesis. Place the external punctuation mark inside the closing parenthesis.

> When they arrive at the airport (around 6 p.m.), Tak will meet them.

> When buying an item online (using a credit card), be sure the site is secure.

With Numbers and Abbreviations

Primarily in legal documents, parentheses are used to enclose numerals following numbers written in words. The number is repeated for clarity.

> Mr. Perez will deposit the sum of five hundred dollars ($500) in the escrow account.

> I leave to my nephew, Steven Rogers, the sum of ten thousand dollars ($10,000).

Parentheses are used to enclose abbreviations that follow names. They are also used to enclose names that follow abbreviations.

> The Association for Business Communication (ABC) had selected Sandra Chung as its director.

> FBLA (Future Business Leaders of America) is a popular student organization.

> The American Institute of Certified Public Accountants (AICPA) has thousands of members.

Key ▶ Point

Words in parentheses have less emphasis than words separated by commas or dashes.

With References and Directions

Use parentheses to set off references and directions to minimize their importance in a sentence.

> You may consult the appendix (page 345) for the correct format.
>
> This trip (see the enclosed brochure) is a once-in-a-lifetime opportunity.

With a List

Key ▶ Point

Parentheses may be used to enclose the numerals or letters in a horizontal list.

When numerals or letters are used to list items in a sentence, parentheses may be used to enclose the numerals or letters.

> Please include (a) your date of birth, (b) your Social Security number, and (c) your mother's maiden name.

check point 11

Write each sentence, using parentheses correctly.

1. The vast majority 95 percent of the members voted to accept the contract.

2. Homonyms are words that sound alike but have different meanings. See a dictionary for word definitions.

3. The American Marketing Association AMA has thousands of members.

4. On the report title page, include a your name, b your class, and c the date.

5. Refer to Chapter 4 page 56 to review this information.

Check your answers in Appendix C.

The Apostrophe

Key ▶ Point

Apostrophes are used in contractions to indicate the omission of letters.

The **apostrophe** is a punctuation mark used to indicate the omission of characters or possession. An apostrophe is also used with some lowercase letters and abbreviations to form the plural.

In Contractions

Because contractions are considered informal, use contractions sparingly in business documents. To indicate a contraction, insert an apostrophe in the space where the missing letter or letters belong.

> don't (do not)   didn't (did not)   we'll (we will)

To indicate an omission in a number, insert an apostrophe in the space where the missing number or numbers belong.

> Martin graduated in '99. (1999)
>
> The reunion was planned for this year but rescheduled for '09. (2009)

In Possession

Apostrophes are used in nouns to indicate possession. In general, if a noun ends in *s*, add an apostrophe to show possession. If a noun does not end in *s*, add an *'s* to show possession.

> The boys' suits need pressing. (plural possessive)
>
> The boy's suit needs pressing. (singular possessive)

Add an *'s* to an indefinite pronoun, such as *someone* or *everyone,* to show possession. In compound words, add the apostrophe to the last word to indicate possession.

> Someone's monitor has been left on.
>
> My brother-in-law's education prepared him for his career.

Add an *'* or *'s* to *dollar*, *day*, *week*, *month*, and *year* to indicate each word's relationship with the noun that follows it.

> A week's salary is needed to pay the rent.
>
> Buy ten dollars' worth of produce at the farmer's market.

Key ▶ Point

In compound words, add the apostrophe to the last word to indicate possession.

In Plurals

Add an *'s* to lowercase letters and to some abbreviations to form the plural.

> We sometimes find it difficult to distinguish her *a's* from her *o's*.
>
> Do not include so many *etc.'s* in your listings.

check point 12

Write each sentence, using apostrophes correctly.

1. Last years rainfall exceeded this years rainfall.

2. Jamals plan has the best chance of success.

3. My mother was born in 55.

4. I dont think the children are in school today.

5. The jurys verdict was delivered earlier today.

Check your answers in Appendix C.

Section 5.2 *Applications*

A. *Internal Punctuation*

For each number, write a sentence that correctly uses the punctuation mark(s) given. A sentence may include other marks in addition to the one listed. For each sentence, tell why this use is a correct application of the mark.

1. comma
2. semicolon
3. colon
4. dash
5. hyphen
6. quotation marks
7. parentheses
8. apostrophe

B. *Numbers and Punctuation*

Write the sentences using correct punctuation related to numbers.

1. The children should be in bed by 930 pm.
2. One half of the votes have been counted.
3. The sum of four hundred dollars $400 is due at closing.
4. You may consult the glossary page 35 to find the meaning of these terms.
5. The stadium was built in 06.

C. *Quotation Marks and Other Punctuation*

Write the sentences, using quotation marks correctly with other punctuation marks.

1. Before you go, said the client, give me your telephone number.
2. He asked calmly, Have you finished painting my car?
3. Stop! he shouted. That chemical is dangerous.
4. The teacher said, Read the text about atoms (page 42).
5. This morning you said, I will send the document right away; it has not arrived yet.

Abbreviations, Capitalization, and Number Expression

Abbreviations

An **abbreviation** is a shortened form of a word or a group of words. Shortened forms should be used sparingly in business letters. They sometimes obscure the writer's meaning. They also present an informality that may offend the reader. Although many abbreviations are followed by periods, some abbreviations are not.

Titles and Degrees

Abbreviate a personal title that precedes a person's name. The title *Messrs.* is the plural of the title *Mr. Ms.* is a title for a woman that omits reference to marital status; it does not have a full-length form. *Ms.* is not an abbreviation for *Miss* or *Mrs.*

> Messrs. White and Rome represent our firm at the negotiations.
>
> We will interview Ms. Violeta Ruiz.

Abbreviate family designations, such as *junior* and *senior,* that appear after a person's name. Commas usually set off the family designations.

> Carl Brockman, Jr., is the first speaker on the program.

Sometimes people use an initial to indicate the first letter of their first name or middle name.

> I. H. Roth uses his first and middle initials, not his first name.
>
> Gladys S. Blackwood insists that her middle initial appear on all correspondence.

Some professional titles are abbreviated in business writing. Academic and professional degrees that follow a person's name may also be abbreviated.

> Dr. Anna Silva is an internist in private practice.
>
> The company lawyer, Diego Ramos, Esq., has an office here.
>
> Luisa Barnes, Ed.D.   Letitia Anderson, M.D.
>
> Steven Park, Ph.D.   Edwina Jeffreys, D.D.S.

OBJECTIVES

After completing Section 5.3, you should be able to:

1. Use abbreviations correctly in documents.

2. Use correct capitalization in documents.

3. Express numbers correctly in sentences and other formats.

Key▶Point

Academic and professional degrees that follow a person's name may be abbreviated.

Addresses

In business correspondence, do not abbreviate the words *street*, *avenue*, *boulevard*, *road*, *lane*, *north*, *south*, *east*, and *west*. However, do abbreviate compass designations after street names.

> Our new address is 123 South Main Street.
>
> The meeting will take place at 4 Spring Boulevard.
>
> Our president lives at 1605 Bird Lane NW.

Key ▶ Point

Two-letter postal abbreviations are used for state names in full addresses within the text of a letter. However, they are not used when a state name appears in a sentence by itself.

Two-letter postal abbreviations for states appear in all capital letters without punctuation. Use these abbreviations with the appropriate nine-digit ZIP Codes in your correspondence. Two-letter postal abbreviations are used in full addresses within the text of a letter. However, they are not used when a state name appears in a sentence by itself.

> Please send the letter to Ms. Lucy Sands, 1004 Clemens Avenue, Roslyn, PA 19001-4356.
>
> The cellular phone must be shipped directly to Pennsylvania.

Companies, Organizations, and Departments

You may abbreviate the names of companies and organizations if the institutions themselves use the abbreviations. This policy also applies to U.S. government departments.

ABC	American Broadcasting Company
AMA	American Management Association
FBI	Federal Bureau of Investigation
IBM	International Business Machines
IRS	Internal Revenue Service
YWCA	Young Women's Christian Association
Black, Inc.	Black, Incorporated

Expressions of Time

The abbreviations *a.m.* and *p.m.* may be used to designate time when they accompany numerals. The abbreviation a.m. stands for the Latin term *anno meridian*. It is used to indicate times of the day before noon. The abbreviation p.m. stands for the Latin term *post meridian*. It is used to indicate times of the day after noon.

> The next meeting is called for 8 a.m. on Tuesday.
>
> The concerts will be held at 9:00 a.m. and 2:30 p.m.
>
> The class begins at 11:20 a.m. and ends at 1:20 p.m.

Miscellaneous Abbreviations

The abbreviations *No.* (Number) and *Acct.* (Account) may be used in technical documents and also in business correspondence when they are followed by numerals.

> Please refer to our check No. 654.
>
> This information pertains to Acct. 6J843.

Some abbreviations that are acceptable in statistical documents, lists, or business forms should not be used in business letters. Names of days and months fall into this category. Other examples are listed below.

Key ▶ Point

Abbreviations such as *reg., pd.,* and *bal.* should not be used in business letters.

mfg.	manufacturing	reg.	registered
bal.	balance	mdse.	merchandise
pd.	paid	whlse.	wholesale
mph	miles per hour	in.	inches
oz.	ounce	ft.	feet
lb.	pound	kg.	kilogram
cm.	centimeter	yd.	yard

check point 13

Write each sentence, making correct use of abbreviations.

1. Mister Brown will meet with Miss Vega.

2. Albert P. Jones, Junior, is the first member to volunteer.

3. Doctor Anna Sanchez is in charge of this case.

4. The patient lives at 6 Elm Ave.

5. Come to the family reunion, which will be held in TX.

6. The Federal Bureau of Investigation will review the case.

7. The bal. to which I referred earlier in this letter has been pd.

8. Retrieve invoice number 398, and check the payment date.

9. The mdse. was purchased whlse.

10. Thank you for agreeing to speak to our group on Mon., Dec. 7.

Check your answers in Appendix C.

Capitalization

Diversity

Conventions for the capitalization of words vary among languages and cultures.

Capitalization is using uppercase letters in writing. Using correct capitalization in letters, reports, and other documents is important. Capital letters signal the reader that a new sentence or quote is beginning. They also signal proper names, titles, and headings. The following list gives rules and examples for capitalization.

▥ Capitalize the first letter of the first word of a sentence.

The tax collector is at the door.

When did this problem begin?

▥ Capitalize the first word of a direct quotation.

He said, "Let me help you perform the end-of-month audit."

"We should congratulate Toni," James stated, "on her recent promotion."

▥ Capitalize the names of specific people, places, and things.

Bill and I are always together.

Have you crossed the Atlantic Ocean?

She is a veteran of World War II.

Have you studied the Constitution of the United States?

On Monday, we are having a Fourth of July picnic.

Key ▶ Point

Capitalize all titles of family members, such as *Mother* and *Dad*, when they are used as proper nouns.

▥ Capitalize all titles of family members when they are used as proper nouns.

Let's visit Grandmother this morning.

▥ Capitalize professional titles that precede proper names.

Dr. Theresa Torres and Governor Lou Chin will speak.

▥ Capitalize compass points (*north*, *south*, *east*, and *west*) only when they refer to a geographical area or a definite region.

The corporate office is in the South.

Travel east to the river and then drive south to the farm.

▥ Capitalize most nouns that precede numbers or letters. Exceptions to this guideline include *line*, *paragraph*, *verse*, *size*, *page*, and *note*.

Does Flight 643 seat 150 passengers?

A word is missing in paragraph 2 on page 24.

▥ In a letter salutation, capitalize the first letter of the first word, the person's title, and the proper name. Capitalize the first word in a complimentary close for a letter.

| Dear Sir | Ladies and Gentlemen | Dear Ms. Morales |
| Yours truly | Cordially | Sincerely |

■ Capitalize the names of nationalities (American), races (Caucasian), religions (Catholicism), and languages (Latin).

Many Mexican tourists visit San Diego.

Students learned about Judaism, Christianity, and Buddhism in Comparative Religion 101.

Her job at the World Bank requires her to learn both French and Russian.

check point 14

Write each sentence using correct capitalization.

1. joe and i left work early.

2. "we hope you will visit us soon," will said, "after you recover from your illness."

3. on monday, alicia will leave for a cruise on the pacific ocean.

4. is mom home yet?

5. dr. roberts and ms. thomson are in room 3.

6. the south is having a severe drought.

7. please turn to page 34 and read about french cuisine.

Check your answers in Appendix C.

Diversity

Be sensitive to names used to describe cultural or ethnic groups. Strive to use names the persons in the groups will consider positive or neutral.

Number Expression

Number expression is the way numbers are written—as words or numerals. Numbers generally are written as words in very formal documents (wedding invitations) and in some literary works. Numbers are shown as words or numerals in business and personal writing, depending upon the number and its use.

The following list gives rules and examples for number usage.

■ Write numbers ten and lower in words. Write numbers eleven and higher in numerals.

Mail three copies of the proposal to us.

Charles received 16 inquiries the first day of the session.

■ Use words to express indefinite or approximate numbers.

Several thousand people attended the concert.

Approximately thirty-five students complained to the department head.

Key ▶ Point

In business writing, numbers are shown as words or numerals, depending upon the number and its use.

When a sentence has some numbers that are ten and lower and some that are eleven and higher, use numerals for all the numbers.

Our inventory list of paint shows 18 cans of white, 24 cans of eggshell, and 9 cans of light blue.

When two related numbers appear next to each other in a sentence, write the shorter number in words and the other in numerals. If two unrelated numbers appear next to each other in a sentence, separate them with a comma to avoid confusion.

Ms. Chan received 160 two-inch samples.

Oscar brought twelve 36-inch pieces to the classroom.

In 2000, 18 girls made the All-State Team.

Key ▶ Point

Use words to express a number that begins a sentence. If the words will be very long, reword the sentence to move the number within the sentence.

Use words to express a number at the beginning of a sentence.

Eighty-one questionnaires were returned.

Twenty employees applied for the new health-care benefit.

When a day follows a month, express the day in numerals. Use ordinals (such as *d* or *th*) with the day when the day precedes the month and when the month and the year are omitted.

Kim's presentation will be on March 26.

The 26th of March is her graduation date.

In ordinary text, use numerals to express house and building numbers except for the number *one*. Use words for streets numbered first through tenth and numerals with ordinals for streets numbered 11th and higher.

I live at One East Grayson Place.

The package was delivered to 634 South 21st Street.

Write sums of $1 or more in numerals preceded by a dollar sign ($). For sums less than one dollar, use numerals followed by the word *cents*. In a series of amounts in the same sentence, use a consistent format.

The baseball game program costs $5.

Our total expenses are $5.00 for the program and $3.50 for snacks.

The small tablet costs 75 cents.

Be sure to budget $57.00 for the textbook, $3.50 for the pens and markers, and $0.99 for the paper clips.

Key ▶ Point

Repeat words such as *million* after each amount. *The project will cost either $3 million or $4 million.*

Use a combination of words and numerals to express very large amounts of money.

They won a $20 million prize last Tuesday.

- Use numerals followed by the word *percent* (not %) to express percentages in sentences. The percent sign may be used with numbers in tables.

  The department store is offering a 40 percent discount.

- Express decimals in numerals. Express simple fractions in words.

  The strip measures 0.457 inches.

  Move the marker one-half inch to the right.

- Use figures to express a mixed number (a whole number and a fraction) unless it appears at the beginning of a sentence.

  Completing the job will take 2 ½ hours.

  Two and one-half pounds of coffee are enough for the group.

- When expressing time, use words before *o'clock*. Use numerals before *a.m.* and *p.m.* To express the time on the hour, omit the colon and two zeros before *a.m.* or *p.m.* if all times in the sentence are on the hour.

  A meeting that begins at ten o'clock could extend past noon.

  One session begins at 9 a.m.; the other begins at 1 p.m.

  One session begins at 9:00 a.m.; the other begins at 1:30 p.m.

Key ▶ Point

When expressing time, use words before *o'clock*. Use numerals before *a.m.* and *p.m.*

check point 15

Write each sentence, using correct number expression.

1. I ordered fifteen cartons of paper.

2. The 4 new employees were assigned network passwords.

3. The box held four rulers, 11 notebooks, and twenty rolls of tape.

4. Nan's birthday is April 15th.

5. I sent the order to 1 Maple Street.

6. Lemonade costs $0.50 per cup.

7. The meeting begins at ten a.m. and will last two and a half hours.

8. She will get 50% of the $3,000,000 prize.

Check your answers in Appendix C.

Section 5.3 *Applications*

A. *Abbreviations*

For each number, write a sentence that correctly uses abbreviations.

1. Mister Lee, Doctor Paul
2. Lena Bridge, Medical Doctor
3. 45 Main Street Northwest
4. Monticello, KY 42633
5. check number 245

B. *Capitalization*

For each sentence, write *Yes* if the capitalization is correct or *No* if it is not.

1. the room contains 24 desks.
2. He said, "Let me help you with that box."
3. Ashley will cruise on the pacific ocean.
4. Turn to page 48, and read about the French revolution.
5. The frozen North is no place for a southern girl.

C. *Number Usage*

For each number, write a sentence that correctly uses each number or series.

1. 4, 9, 25
2. 25%
3. $5,000,000
4. April 12
5. 1 North Peyton Place

Chapter *Summary*

5.1 External Marks and the Comma

- External punctuation marks include the period, the question mark, and the exclamation point.

- External punctuation marks signal the end of a sentence, indicate a question, or show strong emotion.

- The comma is an internal punctuation mark used to separate items in a sentence and to promote clarity in sentences.

5.2 Other Internal Marks

- A semicolon is used to denote a pause. Semicolons are stronger than commas but weaker than periods.

- A colon directs the reader's attention to the material that follows it.

- A dash shows a sudden change of thought. A dash can also be used for emphasis rather than a comma or colon in some situations.

- A hyphen is used after some prefixes, in forming some compound words, and in dividing words at the end of a line.

- Quotation marks indicate a direct quotation, a definition, nonstandard English, or a title.

- A parenthesis is a punctuation mark used in pairs (parentheses) to set off nonessential words, phrases, or clauses.

- An apostrophe is used to indicate the omission of characters or possession.

5.3 Abbreviations, Capitalization, and Number Expression

- An abbreviation is a shortened form of a word or a group of words. Shortened forms should be used sparingly in business letters.

- Capitalization is using uppercase letters in writing. Using correct capitalization in letters, reports, and other documents is important.

- Number expression is the way numbers are written—as words or numerals. Numbers are shown as words or numerals in business and personal writing, depending upon the number and its use.

Vocabulary

Open the *Word* file *CH05 Vocabulary* from the student data files. Complete the exercise to review the vocabulary terms from this chapter.

abbreviation	hyphen
apostrophe	nonrestrictive element
appositive	number expression
capitalization	parentheses
colon	period
comma	question mark
dash	quotation marks
declarative sentence	restrictive element
direct address	semicolon
exclamation point	

Critical Thinking Questions

CRITICAL
THINKING

1. What impression may a writer who does not follow standard rules for number usage give the reader?

2. Would messages be harder to read without external punctuation marks? Why or why not?

3. In some situations, a writer might choose a comma, a dash, or parentheses to set off nonessential elements, depending on the emphasis or meaning intended. Give an example of this type of sentence, showing it punctuated the three different ways.

4. Why would a writer want to avoid using many abbreviations in business letters?

Chapter *Applications*

A. *Appositives*

Write each sentence, setting off the nonessential elements with proper punctuation.

1. Mrs. Roberts my friend and I will discuss the plans.

2. The author Elias Grey will sign his books in the store lobby.

3. The corrections shown in red were made by the editor; the ones in blue were made by the author.

4. The luncheon which was served on the patio was informal.

5. The company president Mrs. Lui discussed benefits with the employees.

B. *Business Documents*

Identify whether the statement is true or false.

1. In a business letter with mixed punctuation, a colon follows the salutation.

2. The proper way to key the date on a letter is: 12/10/09.

3. Using the abbreviation *Acct.* 124 (for *account*) is acceptable in a business letter.

4. In a business letter with mixed punctuation, a comma follows the complimentary close.

5. This example shows the proper way to use capitalization in a letter salutation: dear mrs Park.

C. *Word Division Rules*

1. Work with a classmate to complete this project.

2. Search the Internet or other sources to find guidelines for word division in business documents. Key a list of at least seven guidelines.

3. Share the guidelines you found with the class. With your instructor's guidance, prepare one list of guidelines to follow when creating documents for this class.

TEAMWORK

IINTERNET

Editing Activity

Open and edit the *Word* file *CH05 Editing* from the student data files. Correct all spelling, punctuation, and grammar errors.

Good Presentations or Flawed Documents?

Bob Lin and Celia Juarez own World of Copiers. Their company sells photocopy materials to small businesses. To increase sales, Bob and Celia are attending a seminar sponsored by Sales Trainers. This company teaches salespeople to be more effective. If Bob and Celia are impressed with the seminar, they will book seminars for their sales staff.

The seminar begins well. Several company associates give excellent presentations. During a break, Celia and Bob begin reading the handouts about Sales Trainers. The high-quality paper, ink, and graphics are impressive. When browsing through the written materials, however, Celia and Bob begin to exchange glances. The introductory letter has a paragraph that reads:

> Sales Trainers believes that sucessful business relationships begin with a commitment to quality, and customer service. For example, Dr. Hannah Lotte, Ph,.D. Vice President of Customer Services, personnally reviews the status of each customer on a regular basis.

When Bob and Celia review the materials, they see the following table.

SALES TRAINERS MAKE A DIFFERNECE

Customer	Sales Before	Sales After	Closing Data
Copy Universe, Inc.	$214,000	$288,00	June 5, 20--
Luxury cars, inc,	987,000	1,428,000	June 12, 20--
schott's Hardware	197,950	256,250	June 25 20--

1. Do you think Bob and Celia are more likely to remember the flawed paragraph and table or the excellent presentations? Why?

2. How might Celia and Bob tactfully communicate their thoughts about Sales Trainers' written materials?

3. What steps might employees of Sales Trainers take to ensure that company materials are error-free?

Business Management & Administration

Communication for Business Management and Administration

Sue Sadinski is the director of the Human Resources Department for a company that makes athletic shoes. Sue supervises employees that have a wide range of duties. The department seeks to achieve these goals:

- Hire and retain skilled workers

- Provide training and development opportunities for employees

- Manage pay and benefit issues

- Handle labor relations issues

- Enhance morale and productivity

- Limit job turnover

- Increase employees' satisfaction with their jobs and working conditions

In the past three years, the company has had a 20 percent turnover rate for its manufacturing employees. This high turnover rate means that the company is sometimes short of trained employees. To meet production contracts, workers are often asked to work overtime, which is costly for the company. Advertising to find new workers and training new workers is also costly.

An associate from the Human Resources Department conducts exit interviews with each employee who leaves the company. However, Sue thinks that many of these employees have not provided complete information about their reasons for leaving. She has decided to address the problem by sending each person that leaves the company a memo with an attached survey. In the memo, Sue stresses that the answers to the questions on the survey will be kept confidential. She hopes this action will give her insights to the reasons for the high turnover rate.

1. Is a memo with an attached questionnaire a good way to gather the information Sue needs? Why or why not?

2. Why might people leaving the company be reluctant to discuss their real reasons for leaving the company?

CHAPTER 6

The Writing Process

6.1   Planning and Organizing Messages

6.2   Composing Messages

6.3   Editing and Publishing Messages

What Did He Say?

This is tax season, the busiest time of the year at Green's Accounting Service. Several changes were made in the tax laws for the previous year. Making sure these changes are taken into account requires extra time in preparing clients' tax returns. The Tax Department is behind schedule on its work during the most critical time of the year for the company.

On Tuesday morning, Collin, the supervisor of the Tax Department, is feeling very stressed. He has been called into his manager's office. Yesterday, he wrote and sent a memo to the employees in the Tax Department. In the memo, Collin made the following statements: "You are behind schedule and must catch up by April 15. If this means that you must work overtime, I expect you to do so. However, do not expect overtime pay. There is no money remaining in the department's budget for overtime."

After the memo was sent, it took about five minutes for upset workers to talk with Collin's manager. They felt Collin blamed them for being behind schedule. Also, they pointed out that a company cannot expect workers on an hourly wage to work overtime without overtime pay. To have these employees work overtime and not pay them for it is illegal.

Questions

1. Is Collin being fair in blaming the employees for the work being behind schedule? Explain.

2. Is the content regarding overtime pay in Collin's message correct? Explain.

3. Does Collin's memo show empathy for the receivers of the message? Justify your answer.

6.1 Planning and Organizing Messages

Planning Messages

OBJECTIVES

After completing Section 6.1, you should be able to:

1. Plan messages by identifying the objective, main idea, and supporting details.

2. Adjust messages for the planned audience.

3. Organize messages in direct, indirect, or direct-indirect order.

K e y ▶ P o i n t

Every business message should promote goodwill for the company.

Have you ever sent a message that you wished you had not sent? Maybe you wished you had stated your ideas differently. Do you feel uneasy about your written communications? If so, the problem may be that you do not take time to plan before you begin to compose. Planning a message involves these four steps: identify the objective, determine the main idea, select supporting details, and adjust the message for the receiver.

Identify the Objective

An **objective** is a goal or an outcome you want to achieve. The objective of a message may be to promote goodwill, inform, request, record, or persuade.

Every business message should promote goodwill. Goodwill is a positive feeling or attitude toward others or the positive reputation or image of a company. It contributes to the success of the company and to the stability of your job because it strengthens business relationships. Goodwill helps attract and keep customers and encourages good working relationships.

You can determine the other objective(s) of a message by asking yourself what you hope to accomplish with the message. Figure 6-1 shows objectives and examples of business messages.

Figure 6-1 Every business document should achieve an objective.

OBJECTIVES OF BUSINESS MESSAGES	
Objectives	**Examples**
Inform	A message tells a customer when a package will be delivered.
Request	A letter asks for the price of a road bike.
Record	A memo confirms the time and place of a meeting that was discussed earlier.
Persuade	A brochure describes the features and quality of a product.

Determine the Main Idea

After determining the objective(s) of a message, the next step is to identify its main idea. The main idea is the central theme or most important thought. For example, in a message informing a customer about the delivery of pet supplies, the main idea is the time the delivery will arrive. In a request for furniture prices, the main idea is the price of the furniture. The main idea of a record of a telephone conversation is the topic discussed. In a message to persuade readers to buy an appliance, the main idea is that readers should buy the appliance from this particular merchant.

Choose Supporting Details

Supporting details include essential facts that explain, reinforce, or justify the main idea. Details should be stated in terms receivers can understand and from which they can benefit. Make sure receivers have all of the information they need to respond to your message. To select supporting details, answer these questions:

- What does the receiver need to know about the main idea to respond completely to my message?
- How will the message benefit the receiver?

Adjust the Message for the Receiver

Consider the audience for the message and adjust the content of the message to meet the needs or gain the interest of the receivers. Practice **empathy**—put yourself in the place of the receiver. Through empathy, you can see a situation from the receiver's point of view and compose a message accordingly. When you adjust the content of your messages, you will write considerate, receiver-oriented messages. Writing in this style is called the *you approach*.

Answer the following questions to help you adjust a message for your receiver.

- What is the age and gender of the receiver?
- How much knowledge, experience, and education does the receiver have about the subject of the message?
- What does the receiver need to know about the subject?
- What opinions or attitudes might the receiver have about the subject?
- How does the receiver feel about me or my department, company, or product?
- How can my message benefit the receiver?

Diversity

When writing to a diverse audience, consider what the receivers may have in common that will help them relate to your message.

STOCKBYTE/GETTY IMAGES

Consider the receivers and adjust the message accordingly.

The following message is written in two ways to reach two different receivers. Message A is written to a small business owner who is not familiar with the subject of the message. Message B is written to an advertising executive who knows a great deal about the subject. The objective of both messages is to persuade. The main idea is to promote television advertising as the most effective and economical way to increase business.

Message A	Television advertising can increase your business substantially. It will allow you to reach more buyers more times and for fewer dollars than any other advertising medium.
Message B	As you know, the cost of television advertising is justified on the basis of reach, frequency, and cost.

Another way to orient messages to your receivers is to address them directly. Use their names and second-person pronouns (you and your) instead of first-person pronouns (I and we). Review Chapter 1 for examples of how to create receiver-oriented messages that display the *you* approach.

check point 1

1. List the four steps in planning a message.

2. What is involved in adjusting a message for the receiver?

Check your answers in Appendix C.

Providing Complete Information

Businesses that sell products and services often describe them in advertisements and on Internet sites. The information provided is not always accurate or complete. This situation may be because of an honest mistake or because the company intentionally leaves out details about the item. The company's return policy for products may also be vague or intentionally unclear. Consider the following situation.

Lois Ann ordered a sewing machine from a company online. The machine was described as having a hard case. Lois Ann thought the case would be good for carrying the machine to sewing classes. When the machine arrived, the item described as a case did not completely enclose the machine. It only loosely covered the machine and had no bottom.

Lois Ann was not pleased. She contacted the company and asked to be allowed to return the item for a full refund because the item was not, in her opinion, as advertised. The company refused to give a full refund. They agreed to give Lois Ann a store credit for the purchase prices less a 25 percent restocking fee. "But your return policy states that a store credit or refund will be given," Lois Ann said to the customer service associate. "Yes, but the choice of which one to give is up to us," replied the associate.

Has the company acted in an unethical way? Why or why not? Do you think the company is intentionally giving vague or unclear information? Do you think Lois Ann will buy from this company in the future? Why or why not?

Organizing Messages

After identifying the content of the message, your next step is to determine the order in which to present the information. The order depends on how you expect the receiver to react (favorably or unfavorably) to the message. Business messages are organized using direct, indirect, or direct-indirect order.

Direct Order

To organize a message using direct order, present the main idea first and follow it with supporting details. Favorable, positive, and neutral messages should be organized in direct order. By beginning with a positive statement, the sender establishes a positive tone for the message. Routine messages are

Key ▶ Point

The way you expect the receiver to react to the message should help determine which writing order you use.

often neutral and also should be organized in direct order. It is assumed that the receiver will respond in a positive or neutral manner. The first paragraph of a positive message presented in direct order is shown in the following example. Supporting details would follow in the second paragraph.

> Thank you, Ms. Perez, for agreeing to speak to our class about career goals. Your insights will be valuable to us as we explore various careers.

Indirect Order

A message organized in indirect order presents the supporting details before the main idea. Unfavorable, negative, and persuasive messages should be written using the indirect order. Stating supporting information before presenting the bad news helps prepare the receiver for the negative message. This preparation helps the receiver accept the negative message. The negative message in the following example uses an indirect approach.

> Thank you, Mr. Wong, for applying for a loan with our bank. Your business is important to us.
>
> In reviewing your records, we find that your reported sources of income do not support our granting you another loan at this time. When you have repaid your existing loans, you may qualify for the loan you seek. Please contact us again at that time.

Direct-Indirect Order

Use direct-indirect order when you have both good news and bad news for the receiver. In those situations, present the good news first, using direct order. Then present the bad news using indirect order. Give the reasons for the bad news; then state the bad news itself. Use of the direct-indirect approach increases the chance that the receiver will understand the message and accept its outcome.

Ethics

Do not make promises or statements that may be incorrect or overly optimistic in an effort to soften the impact of bad news.

Key▶Point

If the negative news in a letter is about a very serious or significant matter, limit the message to this one topic.

check point 2

1. When a message has only good news, which order should be used for the message?

2. When a message has both good news and bad news, which order should be used for the message?

3. When a message has only bad news, which order should be used for the message?

   Check your answers in Appendix C.

Section 6.1 *Applications*

A. *Analyze an Effective Message*

1. Read the paragraphs below, which are in the body of a letter sent to a potential customer. What is the objective of the message?

2. What order is used for the message?

3. What is the main idea of the message? What are the supporting details?

4. Is the message you-oriented? Explain your answer.

   Thank you for ordering a Good Sound telephone. It is a favorite with customers because it is so easy to use.

   Because of high demand, our supply of the Good Sound telephone is depleted. However, a new shipment will arrive on Thursday, May 20, 20--. Your phone will be shipped to you that day by overnight express.

   When you receive your Good Sound telephone on Friday, you can begin to enjoy its clear, static-free sound. Please let me know if you have any questions about the phone after you receive it.

B. *Review a Business Message*

1. Describe one business message you or a family member has received. (Select a message that is not confidential.)

2. What is the objective of the message?

3. What is the main idea of the message?

4. How is the message organized—direct, indirect, or direct-indirect order?

5. Is the message *you* oriented? Justify your answer.

REAL WORLD

C. *Select a Message Order*

You have been asked to write a message to students who applied for a scholarship to summer camp. Three students will receive a scholarship, and six students will not. You must deliver the news to each student.

1. What order should you use for messages to the students who will receive the scholarships?

2. What order should you use for messages to the students who will not receive the scholarships?

Composing Messages

Effective Messages

Effective business messages are those that build goodwill and achieve their objectives. Effective business messages have several traits in common. They are courteous, correct, concise, clear, and complete. Courteous messages help build goodwill—a goal of all business messages. Concise messages show respect for the reader's time. They do not include unrelated details that waste the reader's time and distract from the real message. Being correct, clear, and complete improves the chances that the message will be understood as the sender intends. Composing messages with these traits is discussed in the following pages.

Courteous Messages

Courteous messages are positive, considerate, and bias-free. They use the receivers' proper titles. They capture the receivers' attention and encourage a positive response. Remember, an important step in showing courtesy is saying *please* and *thank you*.

Courteous words show receivers that you appreciate them. This message is important whether the receiver is a customer, a coworker, or some other person. The sentences in the second column are examples of the polite way to express information.

Less than Courteous	Courteous
You inquired about . . .	Thank you for inquiring about . . .
Send me . . .	Please send me . . .
I know you are willing to . . .	Your willingness to . . . is appreciated.

Positive Words

Key ▶ Point

Courteous messages help build goodwill.

As you have already learned, one purpose of every business message is to promote goodwill. Use a courteous and positive tone even when your message contains negative news. State what can be done rather than what cannot be done. Discuss what something is rather than what it is not. The receiver will have a positive response (or at least a less negative one) when the tone of the message is positive. Consider the following examples.

Negative Words	**Positive Words**
You cannot have a refund without a receipt.	You may have a refund as soon as as you submit the receipt.
I cannot answer your question until I receive more details.	Please send the following details so that I can respond to your question.

Proper Titles

Show respect for receivers by using their proper titles. Use the titles *Mr.*, *Mrs.*, *Ms.*, or *Miss* before last names if the receivers have no professional title. If the receiver has a professional title, such as *doctor* or *reverend*, use the title abbreviation before the last name. For example, use *Dr. Wright*. When keying a letter address, use the receiver's title and full name. When keying a letter salutation, the title and last name or the first name may be appropriate.

Generally, use a person's title and last name in the following cases.

- You have not met the receiver.
- You want to show respect.
- The receiver is older than you.
- You are responding to a letter in which the sender used his or her title and last name.

Diversity

Show respect for people by using their names correctly. In some cultures, the family name is shown as the first part of the name. In other cultures, the family name is shown last.

BLEND IMAGES/JUPITER IMAGES

Show respect for others by using their names and titles properly.

Use a person's first name in the following situations.

- You have met the receiver more than once and believe he or she would not be offended by your using the first name.
- The receiver is about the same age as or younger than you.
- The receiver has previously identified himself or herself to you by first name.

Bias-Free Words

Courteous business messages do not offend the receiver by showing biases. A **bias** is a belief or opinion that hinders fair and impartial actions or judgments. Courteous messages do not make the receiver feel singled out in a negative way. Biases to beware of include those related to gender, race, age, and disability.

Gender Bias

Diversity

Women make up almost half of the U.S. labor force and work in many different jobs.

Men and women can be hired for any jobs for which they are qualified. Women are pilots, police officers, engineers, doctors, and lawyers. Men are nurses, secretaries, elementary school teachers, and the principal caretakers of young children. The words used for workers should be free of gender bias to reflect the reality of the workforce. Use neutral words to identify workers as shown in Figure 6-2.

Figure 6-2 Use gender-neutral words in business messages.

GENDER-NEUTRAL WORDS	
Gender-Biased Words	**Neutral Words**
actress, female vocalist	actor, vocalist
foreman	supervisor
office girls, businessman	office workers, businessperson
waiter/waitress, stewardess	server, flight attendant
salesman, policeman	salesperson, police officer
mankind	people
manmade	manufactured, synthetic
executives and their wives	executives and their spouses

Neutral pronouns should be used to refer to neutral nouns. If you use a singular neutral noun, the pronoun will need to include both masculine and feminine forms to be neutral, as in the phrase *his* or *her*. You can avoid using two pronouns by using a plural noun. Plural pronouns, such as *them* or *theirs*, are neutral. These sentences eliminate double pronouns by using neutral nouns.

Singular Noun	**Plural Noun (neutral)**
Each student sat in his or her chair.	The students sat in their chairs.
A doctor uses her or his expertise with every patient.	Doctors use their expertise with every patient.

Race and Age Bias

A simple way to avoid biases of race and age is to avoid mentioning race or age unless it is essential to the message. The following sentences show how to avoid race and age biases.

Biased Words	**Unbiased Words**
We hired an Asian-American baker.	We hired an experienced baker.
Have you met the little old man?	Have you met the man?

Disability Bias

Avoid disability bias by avoiding reference to a disabling condition. If you must mention the condition, use unbiased words as shown in the following examples.

Biased Words	**Unbiased Words**
afflicted with, suffering from	has
crippling defect, disease	condition

Ethics

Discrimination in the workplace on the basis of gender, race, age, or disability is unethical. Federal and state laws prohibit such practices.

check point 3

1. What characteristics make a message courteous?

2. Name four types of biases that writers should avoid.

   Check your answers in Appendix C.

Correct Messages

Correct messages are those that do not contain errors or omit needed information. Correct messages create a positive impression of the writer. Messages that contain errors create a negative impression of the writer. When creating messages, make sure the main idea and the supporting details are correct.

The Main Idea

Key ▶ Point

Be sure you understand and convey the main idea in a business message correctly.

When identifying the main idea of a message, be sure you understand the facts correctly. For example, when you say in a letter that your company will bid on a work project, this is a commitment on the part of your company. If you have misunderstood and the company managers do not want to pursue this job, you may lose goodwill for your company later when you do not submit a bid. Getting the main idea of a message wrong can result in lost goodwill, lost business, or lost money for the company.

Supporting Details

Check all the supporting details included in a business message. Pay special attention to dates and numbers. If you ask Mr. White, a potential business partner, to come to a meeting on March 12 and the meeting is really scheduled for March 21, you will create a problem situation. When Mr. White arrives on March 12, the person he needs to meet with, Ms. Alvarez, might be out of town. If Ms. Alvarez is in the office, she likely will not be prepared for the meeting. Both situations will create confusion and loss of goodwill for your company. If the meeting cannot take place, your company managers may think the least they can do is pay Mr. White's travel expenses. This cost may be small, however, compared to the lost opportunity of working with Mr. White.

Key ▶ Point

Correctness is important in routine messages to coworkers just as it is in messages to clients and others outside the company.

Dates and money amounts are particularly important in contracts and project bids. A **project bid** is a document that describes work to be done, completion times, charges, and related details. If you make an error in a date on a project bid, your company's employees may have to work overtime to complete the project on time. If you make an error in a contract related to an amount to be paid or received, your company could lose a substantial amount of money.

Correctness is also important in routine messages to coworkers. Suppose you tell a coworker that you will finish a project by a certain date. Your coworker may plan other work around receiving the project on time from you. If you do not deliver the work as indicated, you may create a problem for other workers and lose their goodwill.

TETRA IMAGES/GETTY IMAGES

Effective messages are easy to understand; they do not confuse the reader.

check point 4

1. What characteristics make a message correct?

2. Give an example of how an incorrect date or amount in a message could create a problem for the writer or reader.

Check your answers in Appendix C.

Concise Messages

Good business messages are concise. **Concise messages** are brief and to the point. They do not contain unrelated material that can distract the reader from the important points of the message. *Brief* is a term that means short; however, concise messages are not so short that they omit important details or seem rude.

Unnecessary Elements

Business messages should use concise sentences. When you write, express one clear thought in each sentence. Unnecessary sentence elements, such as redundancies, empty phrases, and unneeded words, weaken business messages. As you adjust your message to be concise, keep in mind the information the receiver already knows and the information she or he needs to know.

Key▶Point
Redundancies and empty phrases are not found in concise messages.

Redundancies

Redundancy is needless repetition. Sometimes writers use two or three words whose meanings overlap when one word is all that is needed. For example, say *gift* instead of *free gift*. Say *to* instead of *for the purpose of*.

Empty Phrases

Empty phrases clutter sentences without adding meaning. *I believe, in my opinion,* and *for the purpose of* are examples of empty phrases. The meaning behind those phrases is usually implied, so you do not need to use them when you write. Cut down on sentence clutter by using a word or short phrase rather than a longer clause. The following sentences show how to avoid empty phrases and wordiness.

Empty Phrase	I believe the best plan is to establish guidelines for situations such as this.
Better	We should establish guidelines for such situations.

Active Voice

To cut down on wordiness, use active voice rather than passive voice in your messages. When you write in the active voice, the subject of the sentence performs the action of the verb. In passive voice, the subject receives the action. Using active voice creates a direct message and keeps sentences from being too wordy.

Passive	The best idea was submitted by Vernon.
Active	Vernon submitted the best idea.

check point 5

1. What characteristics make a message concise?

2. What is a redundant expression? Give an example.

Check your answers in Appendix C.

Clear Messages

Clear messages are specific, precise, and complete. They use concrete words and terms rather than vague words and terms. They provide all the information needed for receivers to understand the message. They do not contain contradictory information.

Clear Words and Sentences

Vague words, such as *many, better, bigger, fast, later,* and *soon,* provide some information. However, they are not specific or precise. Rather than saying that something is better, tell what makes it better. Instead of saying a project will be finished soon, give a completion date.

Clear messages state information in a way that will not be easily misunderstood. For example, suppose you get a message on Thursday afternoon that asks you to come to a meeting next Friday. You may wonder whether the sender wants you to attend a meeting tomorrow or a week from now. Instead, the sender should say, "… attend a meeting on Friday, April 12."

Contradictory Information

Clear messages do not contain contradictory information that will be confusing to readers. **Contradictory** means inconsistent or opposing. Suppose the first paragraph of a letter you receive says, "Thank you for agreeing to speak to our group on December 10." Other details about the meeting are given. In the last paragraph, the letter says, "Please let me know if you need directions to our location. We look forward to seeing you on December 8." The dates are inconsistent, and you would likely be confused about when the meeting will take place.

Key ▶ Point

Contradictions in times, dates, amounts, or other details make a message unclear.

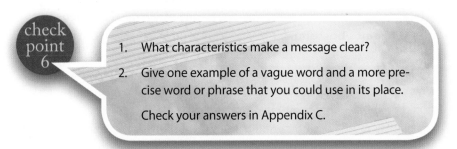

check point 6

1. What characteristics make a message clear?

2. Give one example of a vague word and a more precise word or phrase that you could use in its place.

Check your answers in Appendix C.

Complete Messages

Complete messages contain all the information needed to achieve the objectives of the sender. To compose complete messages, consider what your readers need to know. Dates, times, locations, addresses, quantities, amounts, and other details may be needed. Leaving out even one detail from a letter or memo can make it useless to the recipients.

The Five Ws

Complete business messages often include the five Ws: who, what, where, when, and why. A message that contains the five Ws can be as concise as the following sentence.

> Marsha, please attend a meeting in Room 421 at 3 p.m. on Tuesday, August 28, to discuss sales goals.

Many business messages require several paragraphs to cover the five Ws. Adjust the message for your receiver. In some cases, the receiver may not need all five pieces of information because some details are already known.

Complete Paragraphs

In business writing, the beginning sentence of a paragraph is usually a topic sentence. It gets right to the point by stating the paragraph's main idea. Middle sentences develop the topic sentence or main idea of the paragraph. These sentences give the receiver a description, an example, or other information to support the main idea. The ending sentence brings the paragraph to a close. It may be a short summary of the other sentences or restate the beginning sentence in a different way.

Message Structure

A message can consist of only one paragraph. However, most complete business messages have opening, developmental, and closing paragraphs. The opening paragraph identifies the subject of the letter or memo. An opening paragraph should be short—only two to five keyed lines.

One or more developmental paragraphs follow the opening paragraph. A developmental paragraph contains important information or details about the main idea of the message. These paragraphs are usually longer than the opening paragraph.

The closing paragraph ends a message. It may summarize the message or refer to the main idea stated in the opening paragraph. The writer may thank the reader or ask the reader to take some action in this paragraph. The closing paragraph also can build goodwill.

NET Bookmark

Purdue University provides an Online Writing Lab called OWL. A link to OWL is given on the Web site for this book that is shown below. Use the link to go to the OWL site. Select the link for **Professional, Technical, and Job Search Writing**. Then select **Business Letters, Accentuating the Positives**. Review the information on this page.

1. Why does this resource suggest that you use positive wording in business letters?

2. What steps are suggested for softening the effects of negative news?

www.cengage.com/school/bcomm/buscomm

check point 7

1. What characteristics make a message complete?

2. What are the five Ws a message should contain to be complete?

Check your answers in Appendix C.

Section 6.2 *Applications*

A. *Courteous Messages*

The paragraphs below are not written in a courteous tone. Rewrite the paragraphs using a courteous tone and the *you* approach.

> I did not receive all the information related to the item you want to return. I cannot authorize a return without the product number and the exact reason for the return. These facts are clearly stated in our return policy. Didn't you read the return policy?
>
> I will wait to hear from you regarding the missing information. If you will be more careful about providing complete information in the future, your returns can be processed more quickly.

B. *Bias-Free Messages*

Rewrite each sentence, using positive, bias-free words.

1. Alberto is afflicted with smallpox.
2. The Asian-American teacher was recognized for excellence in teaching.
3. The old lady purchased a bag of oranges.
4. The policeman studied the site of the robbery.
5. The male nurse cared for the infant.

C. *Concise and Clear Messages*

Rewrite each sentence, making the information concise and clear. Use a positive tone. Add any necessary details.

1. It is my belief that most homes in this area cost about $250,000.
2. Chenda is tired because she is very weary.
3. Ms. Curie suggested several alternatives that could be applied.
4. Past history teaches us that the people of certain societies are generally and usually trustworthy.
5. Tony interrogated Suzanne by asking how long it would take her to complete the electrical work.
6. A pound of chocolates costs a lot of money.
7. Stock in that company is very expensive.
8. We regret to inform you that we won't be able to complete your cabinets until next month.

6.3 Editing and Publishing Messages

OBJECTIVES

After completing Section 6.3, you should be able to:

1. Describe the stages of the writing process.

2. Edit and revise business messages.

3. Use effective proofreading methods and proofreaders' marks.

4. Select appropriate ways to publish business messages.

Key▶Point

Each stage in the writing process is important for creating effective business messages.

Stages in the Writing Process

Writing is a process that involves planning, composing, editing, proofreading, and publishing messages. Each stage of the process is important for creating effective business messages. Earlier in this chapter, you learned how to plan messages and select an appropriate order for presenting information. You also learned how to compose messages that are courteous, correct, concise, clear, and complete. In this section, you will learn how to edit and proofread messages. You will also learn about publishing messages.

Editing Messages

Editing is reviewing and revising (changing) a message to improve it. Editing is so important that you should plan to spend as much time editing as you do composing. When you edit, focus on the main ideas and the content of your message. Consider the following questions as you edit a message.

■ Have you considered the reader? Have you included what the reader needs or wants to know?

■ Is the message courteous? Are the words and tone of the message positive and bias-free?

■ Is the message correct and complete? Have you checked all the facts included in the message? Have you included all the needed information?

■ Is the message concise and clear?

■ Is the message written in an interesting style? You will hold your readers' attention if you use variety in the length and structure of sentences and paragraphs.

■ Have you used appropriate transitions? A **transition** is a word or phrase that connects sentences in paragraphs and, in turn, connects paragraphs in a message. Transitions help the reader move easily from one thought to the next. Figure 6-3 contains a list of common transition words and phrases.

Figure 6-3 Transition words and phrases increase the clarity of a message.

TRANSITION WORDS AND PHRASES		
Relationship	**Words and Phrases**	
Contrast	but however in spite of	on the contrary on the other hand nevertheless
Cause and Result	because of consequently for this reason	hence therefore thus
Explanation	also for example for instance	to illustrate too
Listing	besides first, second, etc.	in addition moreover
Time	since finally	first, second, …, last
Similarity	likewise	similarly

When editing you can key changes directly in the word processing file. This option is fine when you are working alone and other people do not need to see the changes that are made. When others need to see the edits or you want to have a record of the edits, you can mark changes in the electronic file. For example, *Word's* Track Changes feature allows users to indicate words to be deleted or inserted in the file. The insertions and deletions appear in a different font color to make them easy to follow. You or another user can look at each suggested change and accept or reject the change. Figure 6-4 on page 194 show edits marked using *Word's* Track Changes feature. Insertions are shown in red, and deletions are shown in blue.

Key▶Point

Some word processing programs allow users to track changes made to a file.

check point 8

1. What are the five stages in the writing process?

2. What is the purpose of editing a message?

Check your answers in Appendix C.

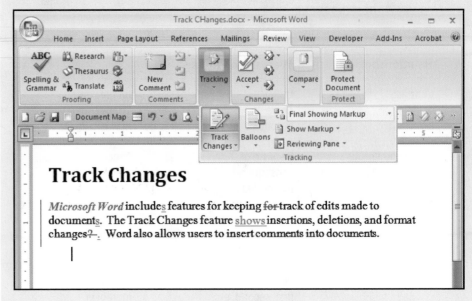

figure 6-4 Tracking changes is easy in Word.

Proofreading Messages

Proofreading is reviewing and correcting the final draft of a message. Proofreading differs from editing in that it mainly involves looking for errors or omissions rather than improving writing style or tone. Proofreading is usually the last step in preparing a message. Allow time for proofreading so you can produce error-free messages. Errors reflect badly on you and may cause confusion for your receivers.

A message may contain many kinds of errors. When you proofread, look for one kind of error at a time. You may want to begin by looking for general content errors. Content errors include missing, repeated, or substituted words; transposed words; incorrect proper names; incorrect numbers; and incorrect use of words.

Next, look for mechanical errors. Common mechanical errors are incorrect spacing, missing parts of a business letter, misspelled words, incorrect or missing punctuation, and incorrect capitalization. Mechanical errors may be difficult to catch. It takes a careful proofreader to find all errors in a message.

Proofreading Methods

The following list describes effective proofreading methods.

- Scroll the screen. Move the cursor down the screen of your computer monitor as you proofread each line. Moving the cursor down one line

Key ▶ Point

Allowing time for proofreading and correcting errors in messages is important.

at a time helps you slow down and focus on each line without getting distracted by other things on the page.

- Read aloud. Reading aloud forces you to slow down and examine words more carefully. Hearing the words can help you catch awkward sentences as well as omitted or repeated words.

- Compare drafts. Check the current draft against the previously edited copy. This method also helps ensure that you made all edits when you revised.

- Proofread the hard copy. It is a good idea to proofread the printed document, even if you have proofread on the screen. In particular, you may detect format errors that were not apparent on the screen.

- Read from right to left. Proofread each line from right to left. Instead of seeing the words that you remember writing, you will see each word separately. This method is effective when you are checking for spelling and keying errors.

- Use two proofreaders. One proofreader reads aloud from the previously edited copy while the other checks the final copy. The reader indicates punctuation, format changes, and special type treatment (such as bold or italics). The reader also spells out proper names and unfamiliar words.

Ethics

Be careful to protect confidential information. Make sure that a person you ask to help you proofread is authorized to know the information in the document.

READING SKILLS

Reading Goals

Before you read a message, ask yourself, "What is my goal? Why am I reading this material?" Effective reading can be done at different speeds and with different methods depending upon the goal you are trying to achieve. When your goal is to read for understanding of new material, viewing words in groups is more effective than looking at each word individually. Avoiding subvocalization (saying each word silently) also speeds reading. When your goal is to proofread a final draft of a message, looking at each word individually is an effective reading method. Reading aloud or saying each word silently also helps you identify errors.

Open the *Word* file *CH06 Reading* from the student data files. Follow the directions given in the file to practice effective proofreading.

Spelling and Grammar Checkers

Almost all word processing programs include a spelling checker, and many include a grammar checker as well. These programs or functions are useful; therefore, you should make a habit of using them. Do not assume, however, that they can replace your own editing or proofreading. Spelling checkers catch obvious spelling or keying errors. They do not find errors for most proper nouns, nor do they help with word substitutions. For example, you might key *estate* instead of *state* or *stripes* instead of *striped*. As shown in Figure 6-5, these errors are not found by the *Microsoft Word's* spelling checker. Only the writer can detect such errors by proofreading carefully.

The same is true of grammar checkers. Most of these programs detect repeated words, and they may point out an especially long sentence. Some programs point out the use of passive voice and offer an alternative in active voice. You must decide whether to revise sentences as suggested. Grammar checkers cannot evaluate your choice of words or the logic of your sentences. A writer must edit and proofread carefully to make sure that a message is error-free.

Diversity

You may use certain foreign words or names regularly in business messages. In some programs, you can add these words to a custom dictionary that is used for checking the spelling in a document.

Figure 6-5 A spelling checker may not find substituted words.

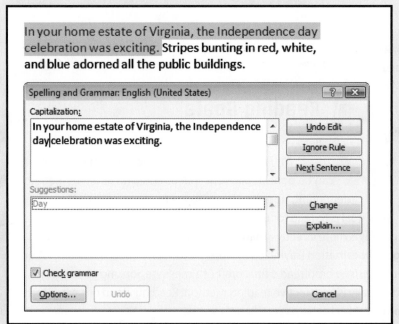

Proofreaders' Marks

Proofreaders' marks are words and symbols used to mark edits on hard copy documents. Common proofreaders' marks are shown in Figure 6-6.

figure 6-6 Proofreaders' marks are used to edit printed documents.

PROOFREADERS' MARKS

SYMBOL		MARKED COPY	CORRECTED COPY
‖	Align	$298,000 $117,000	$298,000 $117,000
∼∼	Bold	The meaning is important.	The **meaning** is important.
≡	Capitalize	bobbie caine	Bobbie Caine
◡	Close up space	Use con cise words.	Use concise words.
✗	Delete	They are happpy.	They are happy.
∧	Insert	Please make copy.	Please make a copy.
#	Space	Show alot of examples.	Show a lot of examples.
___	Italicize	The Sacramento Bee	The *Sacramento Bee*
stet	Ignore correction	He is an effective writer.	He is an effective writer.
/	Lowercase	Sincerely Yours	Sincerely yours
↺	Move as shown	I am only going tomorrow.	I am going only tomorrow.
⊏ ⊐ ⊓ ⊔	Move left, right, up, or down	Mr. Herschel King 742 Wabash Avenue Skokie, IL 60077	Mr. Herschel King 742 Wabash Avenue Skokie, IL 60077
⌗	Paragraph	The file is attached.	The file is attached.
⬭ sp	Spell out	7209 E. Darrow Avenue	7209 East Darrow Avenue
∽	Transpose	The down up and motion	The down and up motion
⌐	Use initial cap only	FORMATTING A MEMO	Formatting a Memo

check point 9

1. How does proofreading differ from editing?

2. What is the purpose of proofreaders' marks?

Check your answers in Appendix C.

Publishing Messages

Up until now, you have been paying attention to composing your message and making sure it is logical and mechanically correct. Now you are ready to publish your work. To **publish** a message is to send it to the receiver or make the message available to the receiver. Sending an e-mail message, mailing a letter, and posting a page on a Web site are examples of ways to publish a message.

Appropriate Methods

Key▶Point

Selecting an appropriate method for publishing a message is important.

Selecting an appropriate method for publishing a message is important. For example, a message to a coworker that contains sensitive or confidential data should not be sent in an e-mail message. A printed memo should be used instead. Letters are considered to be more formal than e-mail messages or memos. Letters are typically used to send messages to people outside the organization. Web sites are used by many companies to provide information about products or services to customers.

Many companies publish messages for employees on an intranet. An **intranet** is a communications network within an organization. It is

Sending a letter is a typical way to publish a formal business message.

© ORANGE LINE MEDIA/SHUTTERSTOCK

meant for the use of its employees or members. For example, a manual that describes company policies may be posted on the company intranet. The pages of the intranet may look like pages on a typical Web site. However, they are available only to company employees. Team members may be able to post messages for coworkers on the intranet. Progress reports, product updates, and new procedures are examples of these messages. An example of an intranet page is shown in Figure 6-7.

Appearance Counts

To make sure you are ready to publish, you must evaluate your message from a physical or visual viewpoint. Your finished product should not only sound good; it should also look good.

Paper

For printed documents, the paper should not be thin, nor should it be wrinkled or stained. The ink on the paper, whether from a pen or a printer, should be dark, not faded. There should be no stray ink marks or smudges on the page.

    The quality of paper you use varies with the type of business message you are sending. Resumes and formal business letters should be printed on the highest quality paper. The company you work for will likely have letterhead on high-quality paper that is preprinted with the company's logo, name, address, and so on. Internal memos and routine reports are usually printed on a lower quality paper. Nonetheless, they must be neat and attractive.

Key▶Point

Select paper of an appropriate quality for printed business messages. Use inexpensive paper for routing memos to coworkers. Use quality letterhead for messages to clients.

figure 6-7 Business messages may be published on a company intranet.

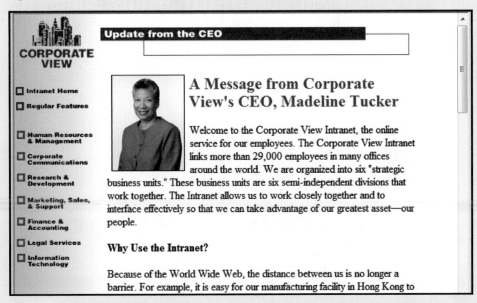

Virgin or recycled paper that is high in cotton content is suitable for formal business letters and for letterhead. The speckled or marbled varieties can be attractive, but they may detract from your message.

Format

Take a look at any book or magazine around you. Notice that each page contains a certain amount of white space. A reader's eye needs this white space to help focus on the printed words. Notice, too, that the printed lines of text are not usually more than about 4.5 inches wide—and they are often much shorter. You need to set up your business documents with these same ideas in mind. You want your document to be easy for the receiver to read. In addition, you want it to be attractive.

Having some white space in a document makes it more attractive than if the page is crowded with text and figures. Most of the white space will be in the top, bottom, and side margins of the pages. Software programs usually have default margins. Common defaults are one inch on all four sides of the page. These margins are appropriate for most business correspondence. Using default margins and other settings saves time in formatting a document.

You will learn specific formatting guidelines for memos, letters, reports, and other documents in later chapters. Check to make sure the document follows the formatting guidelines. Editing, proofreading, and checking the format may seem like a lot of trouble for a simple memo. However, appearance and correctness is just as important for that document as it is for an annual report or a job application letter.

Many companies request that job applicants submit applications and resumes in electronic format. For these documents, ease of scanning information is more important than an attractive printed format. You may need to use a simple design and save the resume in a plain text format. If you plan to submit a resume in electronic format, follow any guidelines given on the site. You may also want to read articles available online that provide tips for electronic resumes. More information about resumes is presented in Chapter 15.

Key ▶ Point

Default margins for word processing programs are appropriate for most business messages. Using default settings saves time in formatting a document.

check point 10

1. Give two examples of ways to publish a business message.

2. Should paper of the same quality be used for all printed business messages? Why or why not?

Check your answers in Appendix C.

Section 6.3 *Applications*

A. *Editing a Message*

1. Key the paragraphs below or open the *Word* file *CH06 Camp* from the data files.

2. Edit the paragraphs to make them correct, clear, and concise. Add any needed details. Use proofreaders' marks on a printed copy of the text, or use *Word's* Track Changes feature to indicate changes to be made.

3. Make the edits (if using a printed copy and proofreaders' marks) or accept the changes if using Track Changes, and save the file using a new name. Submit both the edits and the final copy to your instructor.

CRITICAL
THINKING

Thank you for submitting a request for an application to attend our summer camp for students'. The deadline for the application is next week, so you have written just in time.

The summer camp will be conducted for two weeks in mid-May. Students should plan to arrive on a sunday and leave two weeks later. Most, but not all, camping gear will be provided. Some items should be brought to the camp by the students. The charge for the camp is $10 per day for a total of $150.

Please let me know if you have any questions about the enclo-seed application. I can be reached at 606-555-0124 during regular business hours.

B. *Publishing Messages*

What is an appropriate way to publish each message? List more than one method when appropriate.

1. A message about routine work to your supervisor

2. An answer to a request from an important client

3. An announcement about a change in vacation days from the company managers to all employees

4. A message to a coworker that contains confidential information

5. A reply to a question about a product that you received from a customer by e-mail

Chapter *Summary*

6.1 *Planning and Organizing Messages*

- To plan a message, identify the objective, determine the main idea, select supporting details, and adjust the message for the receiver.

- The objective of a message may be to promote goodwill, inform, request, record, or persuade.

- Writers should consider the audience for the message and adjust the content of the message to meet the needs or gain the interest of the receivers.

- Business messages are organized using direct, indirect, or direct-indirect order.

6.2 *Composing Messages*

- Effective business messages are those that build goodwill and achieve their objectives.

- Effective business messages are courteous, correct, concise, clear, and complete.

- Business messages should use a courteous and positive tone even when they contain negative news.

- Courteous business messages do not offend the receiver by showing biases.

6.3 *Editing and Publishing Messages*

- Writing is a process that involves planning, composing, editing, proof-reading, and publishing messages.

- Editing is reviewing and revising a message to improve it.

- Transition words and phrases help the reader move easily from one thought in a message to the next thought.

- Proofreading is reviewing and correcting the final draft of a message.

- Publishing a message is sending it to the receiver or making the message available to the receiver.

Vocabulary

Open the *Word* file *CH06 Vocabulary* from the student data files. Complete the exercise to review the vocabulary terms from this chapter.

bias

clear message

complete message

concise message

contradictory

correct message

courteous message

editing

empathy

intranet

objective

project bid

proofreaders' marks

proofreading

publish

redundancy

transition

Critical Thinking Questions

1. How might the receiver react to a good-news message in which you used the indirect order? How might he or she react to a bad-news message in which you used the direct order?

2. Why should every business message promote goodwill?

3. What may result when a message is not properly planned or organized?

4. Do you think that incomplete messages can be expensive? Explain your answer.

5. Explain the importance of each step in the writing process—planning, composing, editing, proofreading, and publishing.

CRITICAL
THINKING

Chapter *Applications*

A. Revise and Publish a Message

For years, Evan has dabbled in carpentry—just simple projects. He has found the activity relaxing and rewarding. Recently, he agreed to build a playhouse for his neighbor's children. He enjoyed the work so much that he spent more time than he had intended and added special details. The children were delighted. In fact, everyone in the neighborhood thought the playhouse was wonderful. Several people have encouraged Evan to market his design or offer his services to others. He dismissed the idea at first. However, he kept thinking about it and imagining how great it would be to get paid for designing playhouses.

Evan conducted a search for playhouse designs on the Web. Several companies offer playhouses in different designs, but no one seems to offer custom-designed playhouses. Evan decided to post his own site on the Internet to market his services as a playhouse designer.

Because Evan's playhouse design service seems to be a new concept, he was not sure what information to include on his site. He decided to keep the information simple as shown below.

> Playhouses by Evan
>
> I can design any playhouse you want. I have done carpentry as a hobby for years. Recently, I built a playhouse for a neighbor. Everyone in the neighborhood said it was great. Send an e-mail if you want me to design a playhouse for you.

1. Has Evan left anything out of the message?

2. Describe the audience you think Evan is trying to reach with his message.

3. What is the objective of Evan's message? What is the main idea?

CRITICAL THINKING

4. Edit and correct Evan's message to improve it. The finished message should be courteous, correct, concise, clear, and complete. Add any missing details.

5. Save the message as a single file Web page that could be published on the Internet. Preview the message in a Web browser to see how it will look when viewed on the Internet. Make changes to the fonts, colors, or other design elements to create an attractive and interesting Web page. For example, you could add a photo or clip art of a playhouse.

B. Use Proofreaders' Marks

TEAMWORK

1. Work with a classmate to complete this project. Open and print the *Word* file *CH06 Mortgage* from the data files.

2. Working together, proofread the message to correct errors and make the message concise, courteous, and complete. Use proofreaders' marks (on each person's copy) to indicate changes.

3. Using the marked copy, make the changes indicated and print the corrected message.

4. Exchange corrected messages with your teammate. Proofread the final copy and mark other changes, if necessary. Teammates should exchange messages and revise until they agree that both copies are correct.

REAL WORLD

C. *Research Data for a Complete Message*

1. Read the e-mail to Anna Sanchez shown below.

2. Do research on the Internet to find the information Anna needs to reply to the message. Use search terms such as *letterhead paper* and *business stationery* to find appropriate sites.

3. Using the data from your research, compose an answer to the message as if you were Anna.

INTERNET

From:	Jim Hari
Date:	May 5, 20--
To:	Anna Sanchez
Subject:	Letterhead Supplies

Thank you for your suggestions regarding ways to save money on office supplies. Your suggestions were discussed at our team meeting, along with those from other employees.

Printing our own letterhead stationery instead of buying it preprinted sounds like a promising idea. Our star logo and company name and address can easily be inserted into document files. We may also be able to save money by buying inexpensive paper to use for drafts of documents and memos that go to people within the company.

Please search the Web and find prices for quality paper appropriate for letterheads and second sheets. The paper should be at least 24 lb. weight. Also, look for prices for marbled or other "designer" paper that would be appropriate for letterheads. Matching envelopes will also be needed. Select three different papers that you recommend. Give the name, a description, and the price per ream (500 sheets) for each. Include prices for matching envelopes. Also, indicate the source from which the paper can be ordered.

Editing Activity

Open and edit the *Word* file *CH06 Editing* from the student data files. Correct all spelling, punctuation, and grammar errors.

Letter to Temporary Employees

Dresden Press is a company that offers desktop publishing services to clients. The staff produces items such as newsletters, brochures, programs, and catalogs. A staff of ten full-time employees stays busy planning projects with customers. They oversee projects and supervise the desktop publishers who use computers to create the documents. Cher Markham, the president, hires desktop publishers on a temporary basis. These employees have special skills and are paid well. Cher finds it is too expensive to keep them on staff as regular employees.

Each employee signs a contract stating that she or he will be paid a certain rate for working on a specific project for a certain length of time. The contract also states that the employee will be given notice two weeks prior to his or her job termination. As project end dates approach, the desktop publishers begin to worry and become anxious. They wonder whether the project they are working on will be completed on schedule. They also hope the company will have another project they can work on. Finally, when Cher decides it is time, a letter is sent to the desktop publishers whose projects are ending and whose services will no longer be needed. She knows she is likely to need these people again, but right now, she does not have any big projects they can work on.

1. What order should Cher use for the letter to the desktop publishers? Is the letter a good news or bad news message?

2. How can Cher promote goodwill and keep the person interested in working for her company in the future?

Communication for Marketing, Sales, and Service

Claudia Simpson is the manager of the women's clothing section in a large department store. Some of her responsibilities include placing orders for clothing and accessories, overseeing placement and creation of store displays, and supervising sales associates.

Sales associates work on the store floor. They answer customers' questions and run the cash register to complete customer sales. They also process refunds for returned items and help keep the displays of clothing neat and orderly.

Three months ago, the store began offering a new line of clothing designed for young women of high school and college age. At about the same time, one of the sales associates retired. Claudia hired Juanita, who had just finished high school, as a new sales associate. She thought that Juanita would be good at working with the new, young customers the store hopes to attract.

Juanita seems to get along well with the young women who come into the store. They identify with her casual style of dress and "chatty" behavior. However, the customers who are older do not seem to care for Juanita. They go out of their way to have a different sales associate help them even when shopping for their daughters. Juanita does not seem to be able to alter her behavior or communication style when talking with customers. She uses the same approach for everyone.

Juanita was hired for a six-month trial period. Claudia plans to let Juanita go at the end of the six months if her communication skills do not improve.

1. While working on the sales floor, does Juanita consider the receivers of her comments and adjust her messages accordingly? Explain.

2. Why might older customers prefer not to have Juanita help them with their purchases?

3. Where can Juanita go to find help or training in improving her sales skills?

CHAPTER 7
Writing Memos, E-mail, and Letters

7.1   Business Correspondence

7.2   Memos

7.3   E-mail and Instant Messaging

7.4   Letters

The Wrong Recipients

Alex Green heads the Technology Development Department at his company. The employees in this department use advanced computer design programs along with the latest, powerful computers.

Last week Alex was notified that Jennifer Tinsley, one of his most creative and productive employees, has an infectious disease and cannot work for a month. Jennifer is working on the design for a new program that is to be presented to an important client in one month. With Jennifer out of the office for four weeks, having the design ready on time is a problem. Alex is very upset as he discusses the situation with his supervisor, Ms. Aragon. She suggests that other employees in the department complete Jennifer's work.

After thinking about this suggestion and while he is still upset, Alex sends an e-mail to Ms. Aragon. He states that the other employees are "not as creative as Jennifer and might botch up her work." To provide a record, Alex decides to send a copy of the message to the company's president. However, Alex accidentally selects the team's group e-mail address instead of the president's address. He sends the e-mail not only to Ms. Aragon but also to members of his department. When department members see the e-mail, they are very upset.

Questions

1. Is e-mail the best channel to be used for all in-house messages? Why or why not?

2. What other method could Alex have used to communicate this message to Ms. Aragon?

3. What can Alex do to prevent such a situation from happening again?

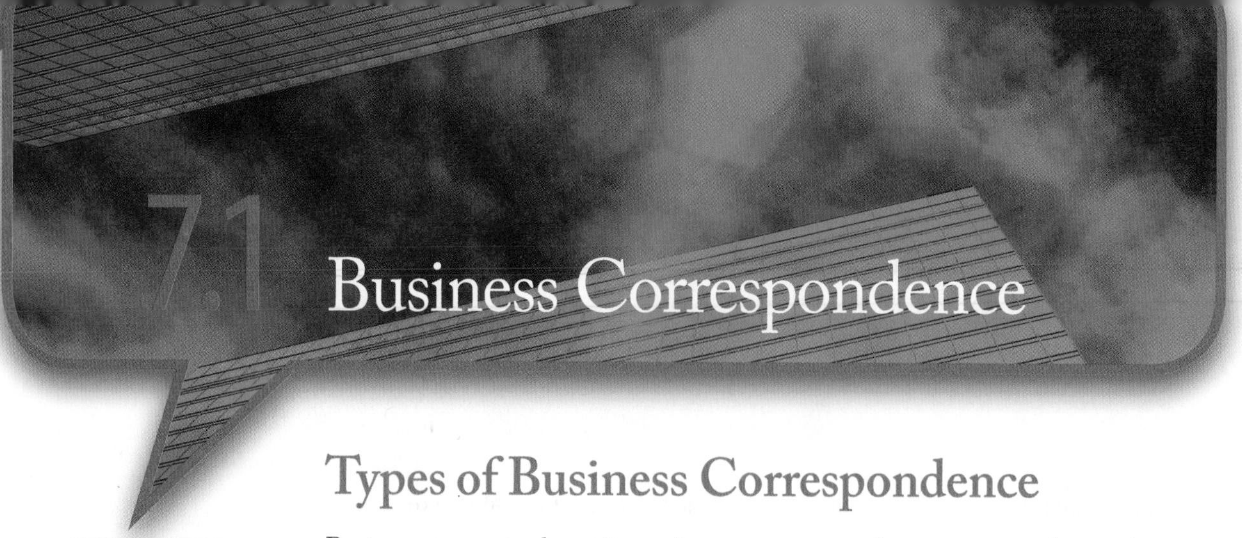

7.1 Business Correspondence

OBJECTIVES

After completing Section 7.1, you should be able to:

1. Describe types of business correspondence.
2. Name purposes for business correspondence.
3. Plan and organize effective business correspondence.

Key ▶ Point

A memo may be sent by interoffice mail or by U.S. Mail.

Types of Business Correspondence

Business correspondence is a written message, such as a memo or letter, that deals with business matters. These documents are written to share or request information. The audience for the message or request may be persons within or outside the company or organization.

Memos and E-mails

Memos and e-mail messages are the documents most commonly written for use within an organization. A **memo**, more formally called a memorandum, is an informal document that is sent to someone within your company or group. Memos usually are keyed in word processing software, printed, and sent to the

Figure 7-1 Memos are used to communicate within an organization.

Star Industries

TO: Linda Cheng

FROM: Ray Posner

DATE: June 3, 20--

SUBJECT: Charitable Giving

Thank you for your proposal that we provide laptop computers to the Farraday Women's Shelter. Our company is strongly committed to supporting the community through charitable giving. Your proposal fits well with our corporate mission.

For tax purposes, all allocations for direct grants must be made by April 15. Since our funds for this year already have been allocated to other projects, we are not able to approve your proposal at this time. We strongly encourage you to resubmit it next January. A submission form is enclosed.

eb

Enclosure

receiver. Memos are often sent by interoffice mail. However, they may also be sent by U.S. Mail. Figure 7-1 shows a memo that delivers a negative message. Memo parts and formatting for memos are discussed in Section 7.2.

An **e-mail** (electronic mail) is an informal message written, sent, and received on a computer. Some cell phones and handheld computers also allow users access to e-mail. Memos were once the most common type of internal document used in companies. Today e-mail messages are used more often than memos are. Figure 7-2 shows an e-mail sent to a coworker. The message contains an attachment, and a copy is sent to another person. E-mail parts and writing e-mails are discussed in Section 7.3.

Increasingly, e-mail is being used instead of letters to send certain types of routine positive or neutral messages to people outside the organization. Examples of these messages include acknowledgments and order confirmations.

Letters

A business **letter** is a document used to send a written message to someone outside an organization. Letters also are used to send formal written messages to employees or members within an organization. Business letters are considered more formal than memos or e-mail messages.

Key▶Point

E-mail is used more often than memos to send business messages.

Key▶Point

A business letter is a more formal document than a memo or e-mail.

Figure 7-2 E-mail is used to send messages within an organization.

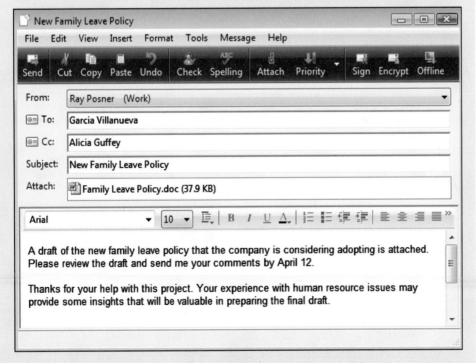

Business letters are typically printed on high-quality stationery and include a letterhead. The letterhead may be preprinted or printed as part of the document file. The letterhead contains the company name, address, and telephone number. The letterhead may include other information, such as the company's logo, fax number, Web site address, and e-mail address. Appearance is important because a receiver starts to form an opinion of the sender and the company from looking at the letter. A business letter is shown in Figure 7-3. Writing letters and formatting are discussed in Section 7.4.

Personal business letters are written by individuals (rather than companies) to deal with business matters. A letter of application for a job and a request for replacement of a faulty CD player are examples of personal business letters.

Key ▶ Point

A personal business letter is written by an individual rather than a company employee.

figure 7-3 A letter is a formal document sent to persons inside or outside the organization.

OVERSEAS, INC.

16 Glover Street, Lexington, KY 40509-0016
Phone: (859) 555-0142

January 17, 20--

Ms. Cindy Dau
142 Front Street
Lexington, KY 40502-0142

Dear Ms. Dau

Thank you for inquiring about internships at our company. Our internship program has been in operation since 1998. Over the years, our interns have described their time here as a valuable learning experience.

A brochure that describes the internship program in detail is enclosed. Please complete the enclosed application and send it to me along with your resume. This material should be mailed in time to arrive no later than February 1, 20--.

The professional experience you gain as an intern will help you prepare for a successful career. Please consider applying to join our program.

Sincerely

Joseph Wilson
Internship Coordinator

Enclosures

Other Documents

Other business documents are also sent to share information with employees and customers. For example, an agenda is sent to let people know the topics that will be discussed at a meeting. Minutes of a meeting are sent after a meeting to summarize meeting discussions. You will learn to prepare an agenda and minutes in Chapter 13.

Several business documents are related to processing orders and payments. For example, an **invoice** is a bill for items or services purchased from a company. A sample invoice is shown in Figure 7-4. The items or services, charges, and related information are shown on the invoice. These documents are typically prepared using a standard form. Creating the document with correct and complete information is very important. Any directions included with the form should be clear and concise. Little composition is involved with this type of document. However, the sender may have an opportunity to be courteous by using statements such as, "Your business is important to us. Please let us know if you have any questions about this invoice."

Key ▶ Point

Routine business documents, such as invoices, are often prepared using a standard form.

Figure 7-4 An invoice is a bill for items or services purchased.

INVOICE

JOHNSON OFFICE SUPPLY
2200 New Bedford Road
Delray Beach, FL 33445-2200
(561) 555-0145

Date: July 17, 20--
Invoice No.: JOS 107726
Customer No.: 5690-1278
Ship Via: UPS Ground
Terms: 2/10, net 30

Sold to:

Jackson and Jackson, Inc.
1068 Wabashaw Court
Ferguson, KY 42502-4664

Ship to:

Same

Item No.	Quantity	Description	Unit Price	Total
SR100	10	Personal shredder with waste bin	$ 89.00	$ 890.00
SR 203	10	Console shredder	399.00	3,990.00

Subtotal	$4,880.00
Shipping	130.00
Taxes	244.00
Total	$5,254.00

Your business is important to us. Please let us know if you have any questions about this invoice.

check point 1

1. How are memos and e-mail messages alike? How are they different?

2. What is the most commonly used business document for internal messages?

3. Which document is more formal—a letter or a memo?

Check your answers in Appendix C.

Purposes for Correspondence

Business documents are written to achieve a purpose or an objective. As you learned in Chapter 6, all business messages should promote goodwill. Other purposes for business messages may be to:

- Provide a record
- Advise, direct, or state a policy
- Inform
- Request information or reply to requests
- Persuade

Provide a Record

Key ▶ Point

Memos and e-mail are often used to provide a record of plans or discussions.

Business documents are used to record events that have occurred or things people have said. For example, suppose your supervisor asks you to make major changes to a project you are working on. You explain that making these changes will mean that the project is completed two weeks later than originally planned. Your supervisor says that this delay is acceptable. After the discussion, you might send an e-mail to your supervisor summarizing the changes discussed. This e-mail provides a record of the conversation. It documents what you have been asked to do and the new completion date.

Advise, Direct, or State a Policy

Business documents also are used to advise or direct employees. For example, your team leader might send you an e-mail advising you about how to solve a problem with your work. A memo from your supervisor might direct you to make travel arrangements for his or her upcoming trip.

Business documents also are used to state policy and explain procedures. For example, a manager might send a letter to employees explaining changes in the company policy regarding gifts from vendors.

Keep the purpose of the message in mind when creating business documents.

Inform

Business documents frequently are used to inform. For example, suppose that Nita, one of the workers in your department, will be on medical leave for two months. Her supervisor might write a memo informing department members of the leave and naming the person who will perform Nita's duties during her leave.

Request

Employees frequently need to request information. They also need to reply to requests made by coworkers, supervisors, or customers. Memos, e-mails, and letters can be used for this purpose. For example, you might send an e-mail to a coworker asking when a certain report is needed. Your coworker may reply, giving you the date.

Persuade

Business messages sometimes are sent to persuade others of your point of view. For example, you might send a memo to your supervisor to persuade him or her to consider allowing department employees to have flexible working hours. You might send a letter to a customer urging him or her to place an order while sale prices are in effect.

Ethics

Memos or letters should be used to share confidential information rather than e-mails. The reason for Nita's leave should be shared only if Nita has approved release of this information to coworkers.

Key ▶ Point

Goodwill messages are sent to congratulate, welcome, apologize, express thanks, and extend invitations.

Promote Goodwill

Although all business messages should promote goodwill, some messages are written primarily for that purpose. For example, a team leader might write a memo to thank all the team members who worked on a recently completed project. Goodwill messages also are sent to congratulate, welcome, apologize, and extend invitations.

> **check point 2**
>
> 1. What are six purposes or objectives for which business messages are used?
>
> 2. Give an example of a situation in which a message might be sent to inform a coworker or customer.
>
> Check your answers in Appendix C.

Planning and Organizing Messages

Some messages require less planning than others. For example, a memo inviting a coworker to a retirement lunch for your supervisor needs little planning. For anything other than simple messages, however, adequate planning is essential. Remember to include the five Ws (who, what, where, when, and why) when planning messages. Using the correct order to present the information is also important.

Planning Messages

In Chapter 6, you learned a four-step process for planning messages. Use this process to plan your memos, e-mail messages, and letters.

1. Identify the objective. What do you hope to accomplish by sending the message?

2. Determine the main idea. What is the central theme or most important thought?

3. Choose supporting details. What does the receiver need to know about the main idea?

4. Adjust the message for the receiver. How can you present the message to address the receiver's point of view?

Diversity

Consider the age, gender, and culture of the recipient when planning a message.

Organizing Messages

In Chapter 6, you learned about the direct and indirect order for organizing messages. Use the guidelines you learned earlier for selecting the proper order for memos, e-mails, and letters.

Confused and Misused Words

Readers can become confused when writers use words incorrectly. Readers can also misunderstand a message when they do not know the correct meaning of a word. Being aware of words and terms that are often confused or misused can help readers understand messages correctly and recognize when words may not be used properly.

Building your vocabulary can help improve both your reading speed and comprehension. In this exercise, you will learn or review several words and terms that are often confused or misused. Open the *Word* file *CH07 Reading* from the student data files. Follow the directions given in the file to complete the exercise.

Use direct order in a message that contains good or neutral news or a routine request or answer. Remember that in direct order, the main idea is presented first, followed by supporting details and a goodwill closing.

Use indirect order for messages that contain bad news or that try to persuade the receiver. As you have learned, indirect order means that the supporting information appears before the main idea. For negative messages, putting the supporting details first helps prepare the reader for the bad news (the main idea). In persuasive situations, receivers are more likely to do as you ask when they know the reasons before the request is made.

A message that is organized indirectly has a neutral opening. The opening is followed by the supporting information, the main idea, and a goodwill closing. The neutral opening should not state or imply the main idea. Instead, it should introduce the topic of the message. The memo shown in Figure 7-1 on page 210 uses an indirect approach.

Key▶Point

Correspondence that contains routine or neutral messages should use direct order.

check point 3

1. What are the five Ws that you should consider when planning the details for a message?

2. When the supporting information appears before the main idea in a message, which order is being used?

Check your answers in Appendix C.

Section 7.1 *Applications*

A. *Purposes for Business Correspondence*

Business messages are used to provide a record, advise or direct, state a policy, inform, request information or reply to requests, persuade, and promote goodwill. Indicate which of these purposes is the primary one intended for each message described below.

1. A memo reminding employees of the rules regarding use of company cars

2. An e-mail thanking a coworker for her support on a project

3. A memo to an administrative committee that recommends the purchase of new equipment

4. A letter giving a client the date, time, and place for a meeting

5. An e-mail answering a coworker's questions about credit terms

6. A memo detailing plans discussed at a meeting

7. A letter to a client congratulating the client on an award he has won

8. An e-mail to an administrative assistant telling her to arrange a meeting between her manager and a client

B. *Planning and Organizing a Message*

You are the head of a committee formed to consider ways your company can use green practices. Green practices are those that are friendly to the environment or that save resources. Company managers have selected six employees to serve on this committee with you. These employees do not yet know about the committee or its purpose.

1. Plan a message to be sent as an e-mail to these employees. What is the primary objective of the message? What is the main idea?

2. Should you use a direct or indirect approach for the message?

3. What are the supporting details? Assume the committee will meet soon for the first time. Give a date, time, and place for the first committee meeting. (Make up these details.)

4. Compose the paragraphs of the message you have planned and organized.

7.2 Memos

Writing Memos

After you have planned and organized your message, you are ready to write. A memo consists of heading lines and a body and may contain one or more notations. Each part of a memo serves an important purpose. The parts of a memo and guidelines that will help you compose effective memos are discussed in the following paragraphs.

Heading Lines

The heading consists of the To, From, Date, and Subject lines. Begin the heading lines at about 2 inches from the top of the page. If the paper has a preprinted company name or a name in the header, begin at least ½ inch below the name. Use default side margins. Key the heading words (TO, FROM, DATE, and SUBJECT) in bold and all caps at the left margin. Follow each heading word with a colon. Align the data that follows the heading words at the first tab after *SUBJECT*. If your software does not leave blank space after each paragraph, tap ENTER to leave one blank line between heading lines. The heading lines are indicated in Figure 7-5 on page 220.

To Line

The To line contains the name(s) of the person(s) to whom the memo is written. Often, just the first and last names are included without titles.

TO: Preston Wheat

In some organizations, names in the To line include job titles, department names, or degrees and courtesy titles, such as *Ms.* Follow the preference of your organization.

Memos can be addressed to everyone who holds a particular job or everyone in a particular department.

TO: Service Managers

TO: All Customer Service Personnel

OBJECTIVES

After completing Section 7.2, you should be able to:

1. Compose effective memos.

2. Format, edit, and publish memos.

Key ▶ Point

Use default side margins and line spacing when creating memos. Begin the To line about 2 inches from the top of the page.

Diversity

If you work for an international company, using titles may be considered important, even in a memo.

Figure 7-5 Interoffice Memo.

TO: Linda Cheng

FROM: Ray Posner

Heading lines ········ **DATE:**   November 3, 20--

SUBJECT: Charitable Giving

Thank you for your proposal that we provide laptop computers to the Farraday Women's Shelter.

Body ········ Our company is strongly committed to supporting the community through charitable giving. Your proposal fits well with our corporate mission.

For tax purposes, all allocations for direct grants must be made by April 15. Since our funds for this year already have been allocated to other projects, we are not able to approve your proposal at this time.

Linda, we encourage you to resubmit your proposal next January. A blank submission form is enclosed. Please include these items for our consideration:

Bulleted List ········
- A completed submission form
- A general description of the Farraday Women's Shelter and its mission
- A summary of how the computers would be used at the shelter

Reference Initials ········ eb

Enclosure Notation ········ Enclosure

When sending a memo to more than one person, either separate the names by commas or set them in a list. Alphabetize the names unless your organization prefers that persons be listed by rank.

TO: Dino Arellano, Arlene Little, Preston Wheat

TO: Dino Arellano
                Arlene Little
                Preston Wheat

For a long list of recipients, use a distribution list. Key the words *Distribution List* in the To line. List the recipients alphabetically by last name at the end of the memo below any notations. If your software automatically adds space after a paragraph, remove the space after paragraphs in the list of names.

TO: Distribution List

FROM: Robert James

DATE: June 10, 20--

SUBJECT: Planning Meeting

[body of memo]

Distribution List

    Dino Arellano
    Kathy D'Alfonso
    Alberto Diaz
    Arlene Little
    Ray Wong

> **Key ▶ Point**
> Use a distribution list when a memo is sent to several people.

From Line

The sender's name appears in the From line. As in the To line, usually just the first and last name are included.

FROM: Lisa Sage

Do not use a courtesy title with your own name unless that is your company's policy. However, you may need to include one or more pieces of information (for example, a job title, department, location, or telephone extension) to help the reader understand the source of the message or for the reader's convenience.

FROM: Lisa Sage, Security Manager

FROM: Lisa Sage, Ext. 988

> **Key ▶ Point**
> Helpful information, such as a department name or telephone number, may be added after your name on the From line.

Date Line

Key or insert the current date on the Date line. Spell out the month, use a numeral for the day, and follow with the year.

DATE: March 6, 20--

You may want to create a memo template to use when you write memos. With *Microsoft Word* and some other programs, you can insert a date code. You can set the date code to insert the current date automatically when you open the file. Figure 7-6 on page 222 shows the date options for *Word*.

Subject Line

Restrict a memo to one idea or topic. Supervisors and coworkers are busy people. Including more than one topic in a memo poses the risk that one of the topics will be ignored or forgotten. When you need to discuss another

Figure 7-6 The date in a memo can be formatted to update automatically.

Date and Time

Available formats:

4/12/2008
Saturday, April 12, 2008
April 12, 2008
4/12/08
2008-04-12
12-Apr-08
4.12.2008
Apr. 12, 08
12 April 2008
April 08
Apr-08
4/12/2008 8:48 PM
4/12/2008 8:48:18 PM
8:48 PM
8:48:18 PM
20:48
20:48:18

Language:

English (United States)

☑ Update automatically

Default...   OK   Cancel

idea, write another message. The exception to this guideline is a memo report, which may be several pages long. Reports formatted as memos are discussed in Chapter 9.

Compose a short, clear, specific subject line. The **subject line** of a memo states the main idea or topic of the message. The sentence that contains the main idea and the subject line should be similar, and they should use the same keywords. Note that the subject line is not a complete sentence. Make the subject brief and to the point so your receiver can quickly identify the purpose of the memo.

Subject Line	Planning Committee Meeting
Sentence	The next Planning Committee meeting will be held on Friday, November 10, at 2 p.m. in Room 312.

Body

The **body** of a memo contains the paragraphs. A memo should be written clearly enough for the receiver to understand it even if he or she does not read the subject line. The body should be courteous, correct, concise, clear, and complete.

Key▶Point

The subject line of a memo should be short, clear, and specific to the message.

Begin each line of the body at the left margin. Do not indent paragraphs. Leave a blank line between paragraphs if your software does not automatically leave extra space after a paragraph. The memo in Figure 7-5 on page 220 uses the *Microsoft Word* default setting of 10 point spacing after each paragraph.

Use bulleted or numbered lists to present details clearly. Use bullets when the order of the items does not matter—in a list of needed supplies, for example. Use numbers when the order of the items does matter. For instance, use numbers for directions that must be completed in a certain order or for items listed by priority. Do not leave extra space between listed items if they are short. If they are long, leave (or add) extra space between listed items.

Key ▶ Point
Do not indent the paragraphs of a memo. Begin each paragraph at the left margin.

Key ▶ Point
Use numbers rather than bullets for a list when the items should be presented or done in a specific order.

Some background on the options will help the committee to conduct its review. Please research the following benefits:

● Flextime

● Leave sharing

● Matching 401(k) plans

● On-site flu vaccinations

● Stock options

Use tables, graphs, and charts when you need to share statistical information or other numerical data. If the table or chart is large, it can be included as an attachment rather than in the body of the memo. You will learn more about graphics and visual aids in Chapter 10.

Sales in all regions have increased over the past five years. The pie chart below shows the percentage of sales for each region for the past year.

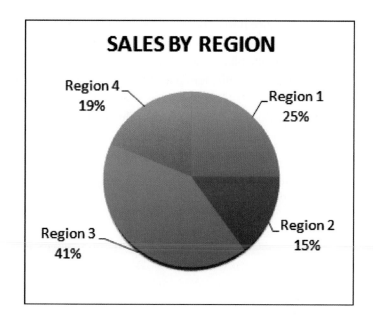

SALES BY REGION

Region 4 — 19%
Region 1 — 25%
Region 2 — 15%
Region 3 — 41%

Notations

The body of a memo may be followed by one or more notations. These notations appear at the left margin below the body of the memo. Leave one blank line between notations if your software does not automatically leave blank space after a paragraph.

Reference Initials

Key ▶ Point

Do not include reference initials for a memo you composed and keyed.

Reference initials are the initials of the person who keyed the memo. You should include reference initials only on memos you key for someone else. Memos that are from you and that you key yourself should not contain reference initials. Reference initials are lowercase (*xx*) and appear below the last paragraph of the memo body. Leave one blank line before the reference initials if your software does not automatically leave space after each paragraph.

Some organizations prefer to have the writer's initials included. The writer's initials are keyed in capital letters, followed by a colon and the initials of the person who keyed the memo (*JB:xx*).

Attachment or Enclosure Notations

An **attachment notation** tells the recipient that another separate document is attached to the memo. The document may be attached to the memo with a staple or paper clip. Key the word *Attachment* at the left margin below the reference initials or below the last paragraph if there are no reference initials.

Key ▶ Point

Details about the attachment or enclosure, such as the number of pages, may be included in the notation.

An **enclosure notation** tells the recipient that a document is included with the memo but not attached to it. Key the word *Enclosure* at the left margin below the reference initials or below the last paragraph if there are no reference initials. An enclosure notation is shown in the memo in Figure 7-5 on page 220. Leave one blank line before an attachment or enclosure notation if your software does not automatically leave space after each paragraph.

Attachments or enclosures may be listed, or the total number of enclosures may be given. Key the word (for example, *Enclosures*), tap TAB, and key the text that follows.

Enclosures: Check #245
               Order form

Attachment: Application form

Enclosures: 3

Attachment: Contract

Copy or Blind Copy Notations

A **copy notation** indicates that a copy of the memo is being sent to the person(s) named. A copy notation consists of the letter *c* followed by the name(s) of the person(s) receiving a copy. Key the notation below an attachment or enclosure notation. If there are no other notations, key the copy notation below the reference initials. If there are no reference initials, key the copy notation below the last paragraph in the body. Leave one blank line before a copy notation if your software does not automatically leave space after each paragraph.

> The research phase of this project must be completed before we can move forward. Please have your report to me by April 12.
>
> Enclosure
>
> c   Dora Marcos
>   Janet Woo

A **blind copy notation** indicates that a copy of the memo is being sent to the person(s) named without the recipient's knowledge. A blind copy notation consists of the letters *bc* followed by the name(s) of the person(s) receiving a copy. Key the notation as the last item on the memo following the same style as a copy notation. Be sure the notation appears only on your file copy and the copy sent to the person named in the bc notation—not on the copy sent to the recipient named in the To line.

Second Page Headings

Try to limit a memo to one page. When a memo requires more than one page, use a heading as shown in Figure 7-7 for all pages after the first page. In the

Figure 7-7 Use a heading on all pages after the first page of a memo.

> Mr. Alberto Diaz
> Page 2
> February 12, 20--
>
> The research phase of this project must be completed before we can move forward. Please have your report to me by April 12. Once we have all the necessary information, the construction phase of the project will begin. We plan to have construction finished by November 30, 20--.

Ethics

Some people question whether it is ethical to send a copy of correspondence to another person without letting the recipient know about the copy. When might sending a blind copy be ethical? When might it be unethical?

document header, key the recipient's name, insert the page number, and key the date. Leave a blank line after the date and before the body. Suppress the header on the first page of the document.

Memo Templates

Many organizations have a template or standard format for memos that they require employees to use. Memos may be prepared on plain paper or on company memo letterhead. Letterhead content varies. As an example, it might include the company name as shown in Figure 7-1 on page 210 or the words *Interoffice Memo*.

If your company does not have a standard memo format, use the format shown in Figure 7-5 on page 220. You also may want to review the templates provided with your word processing software and adapt one for your use.

check point 4

1. What is a distribution list? When should a distribution list be used?

2. What important step must be completed so that the heading for a two-page memo appears only on page 2?

Check your answers in Appendix C.

Editing and Publishing Memos

Key▶Point

Use the procedures you learned in Chapter 6 to edit and proofread a memo before mailing it.

Follow the procedures you learned in Chapter 6 to edit the memo. Be sure the memo is courteous and includes complete and correct information. Make the memo concise, but not so short as to seem abrupt or discourteous. Proofread the final draft carefully and correct all errors. Print a copy to keep for your files and one for each recipient.

Publishing a memo is typically accomplished by placing it in an envelope and sending it by interoffice mail. If you are working away from the company offices, you may need to send the memo by U.S. Mail. Instructions for preparing envelopes to be sent by U.S. Mail are given later in this chapter.

Section 7.2 *Applications*

A. *Format a Memo*

1. Review the instructions for margins and formatting for a memo given in this section and the memo example on page 220.

2. Key the information given below in correct memo format. Proofread the memo and correct all errors. Print the memo.

    Date: Current date

    Subject: Sales Projections

    From: Joann Tipton

    To: Alice Yung

    The sales projections you requested are shown on the attached page. These figures include actual sales numbers for the first three quarters of this year and estimates for the fourth quarter of this year.

    Please let me know if you need additional information.

B. *Compose a Memo*

1. You need to respond to a memo from an employee who requests information about the company's family medical leave policy. Open the *Word* file *CH07 Wilson Memo* from the data files. Print and read the memo.

2. Open and print the *Word* file *CH07 FML Policy* from the data files. This document contains the information you will need about the company's family medical leave policy.

3. Plan your reply message (writing as if you were Roger). Identify the main objective of the message and the order (direct or indirect) that will be appropriate for this message.

4. Identify the main point and an appropriate subject line for the memo. Identify supporting details for the message. Read the FML Policy to find the information you need to respond to the questions.

5. Compose and key the message. Refer to Figure 7-5 on page 220 and the instructions in this section for formatting guidelines. Indicate that a copy of the family medical leave policy is enclosed with the memo.

6. Edit the message to be sure it is courteous, correct, concise, clear, and complete.

7. Proofread the message carefully and correct all errors. Print the memo.

CRITICAL THINKING

7.3 E-mail and Instant Messaging

E-mail

OBJECTIVES

After completing Section 7.3, you should be able to:

1. Compose effective e-mail messages.

2. Describe business uses for instant messages.

E-mail messages are written, sent, and received on a computer. The sender keys the message in e-mail software. With the click of a button, the message is sent almost instantly to the receiver's electronic mailbox, where he or she can read it and respond, also using e-mail.

E-mail has several advantages compared to other types of written messages.

■ Because e-mail is an informal means of communicating and requires little formatting, it can be composed quickly.

■ E-mail messages usually require little transmission time. A message can be sent, replied to, and acted on in minutes—more quickly than a memo sent through interoffice mail.

■ E-mail is inexpensive. It requires no use of paper or ink to create and no postage to send.

Many organizations use software such as *Microsoft Outlook*® or *Eudora*® to create and send e-mail messages. Some firms have their own privately-owned e-mail systems. A company may have an internal network on which e-mail messages are transmitted or messages may be sent over the Internet.

Most e-mail programs are compatible with other e-mail programs. A message written in *Microsoft Outlook*, for example, can be received and read in *Netscape Navigator*®.

Parts of an E-mail Message

An e-mail message consists of two parts: the header and the body. The header identifies the subject of the message and tells to whom, from whom, and when the message was sent. An e-mail message is shown in Figure 7-8 on page 229.

To Line

Key▶Point

The text in an e-mail address may be case sensitive. Key addresses exactly as given to you including capital and lowercase letters.

The recipient's e-mail address is entered on the To line. To avoid having messages go to the wrong address, you should enter the address exactly as written.

If the address is	mriviera@pandora.net
Do not key	MRiviera@Pandora.net
Or	MRIVIERA@PANDORA.NET

Figure 7-8 E-mail Message.

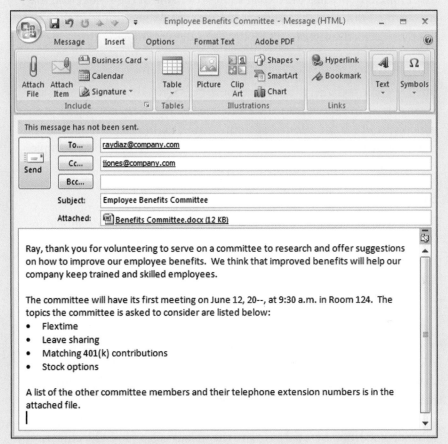

Many e-mail programs have an address book feature. Names and e-mail addresses of people to whom you write are stored in the address book. You can select a name from the address book for the To line. Selecting names from an address book can reduce errors. The name has to be keyed and checked carefully only once—when it is entered into the address book. When a recipient is selected from an address book, the person's name, rather than the person's e-mail address, may appear on the To line as shown in Figure 7-2 on page 211.

Figure 7-2 on page 211.

Cc and Bcc Lines

The Cc line is used to enter the e-mail address of someone to whom you want to send a copy of the message. *Cc* stands for *carbon copy*, from the days when people used carbon paper to make copies of letters as they keyed them on a typewriter. The Bcc (blind carbon copy) line is used when you do not want the individual to whom the e-mail message is addressed to know that a copy has been sent to someone else.

Blind carbon copy should be used carefully. A typical business use is to protect the privacy of a group of customers by hiding their e-mail addresses from each other and from spammers.

> **Key▶Point**
>
> E-mail addresses may be selected from an address book rather than keyed on the To line. Using the address book saves time and reduces the chances of keying errors.

Diversity

Some people have two or more e-mail accounts that are used for different purposes. For example, one account may be used to receive feedback from Spanish-speaking customers. Another account may be used to send messages to investors in Japan.

If you have more than one e-mail account, you may need to select an account name to appear in the From line.

Ethics

Do not create, send, or forward spam messages. To do so is considered unethical.

From Line

The From line contains the e-mail address or name of the sender. You may not see the From line as you compose a message. When you send the message, your e-mail software will insert your address automatically.

Date Line

The Date line contains the date the message is sent. The time the message is sent may also appear. Like the From line, the date does not appear in the window in which you compose your message. It is inserted automatically by the software when the message is sent as shown in the following example:

> Thursday, October 16, 2008 4:47 PM

Subject Line

Text for the Subject line is entered by the sender. A subject line should indicate the topic or main idea of the message. Remember that subject lines should be short, specific, and clear. The following examples are appropriate subject lines.

> Wilson Project Bid
> Budget Meeting Rescheduled
> Invoice 23975 Attached

All messages received by e-mail software are placed in the recipient's inbox, where they are listed by subject line, sender, and date. Many people receive many e-mail messages each day, including unsolicited junk messages called **spam**. A vague subject line may cause a message to be ignored or deleted or its importance to be misunderstood. Some e-mail programs cut off long subject lines. Identify the effective and ineffective subject lines in the inbox shown in Figure 7-9.

Body

Keying a message in e-mail software is very much like keying in a word processor. Key the message body in blocked, single-spaced paragraphs.

Figure 7-9 E-mail Inbox

Subject	Sender	Date	Priority
Horizons Committee Meeting	Jack Delgado	4/8/20-- 9:02 AM	Normal
Contact	Sunita Narayan	4/8/ 20-- 9:45 AM	Normal
You Won't Believe This!	Caleb Schira	4/8/ 20-- 1:30 PM	Normal
FW: Last Week to Sign Up for	Lynette Johns	4/8/ 20-- 2:37 PM	Normal
Annual Report Draft Attached	Nicolett Hafner	4/8/ 20-- 3:09 PM	High
Spring Sale	Crosby Gardens	4/9/ 20-- 4:05 AM	Normal
Weekly Status Report	Patrick Wilson	4/9/ 20-- 9:35 AM	Normal
Need Your Response	Hui Ying Zhao	4/9/ 20-- 1:15 PM	High

Double-space between paragraphs to set them apart. Many features, such as bold and italic, work just as they do in word processing software. Some programs have features for bullets and numbering. Other formatting, such as various fonts, may be available. However, they may not be compatible with your recipient's software.

Work-Friendly Features

Some features of e-mail software are especially useful at work. They include the address book, signature file, spelling checker, attachment, draft, reply, forward, priority, and return receipt features.

Address Book

As discussed earlier, e-mail addresses can be entered into an electronic address book. When you compose an e-mail message, you can choose an address from the address book instead of keying the address. An address book is also a convenient place to store regular mailing addresses, phone numbers, and other information about your correspondents.

With some programs, you can use an address book to create customized e-mail lists. You might create lists for groups of people, such as teams, committees, or work groups. When you write to a group, the software automatically enters the e-mail addresses of all members. Using the group address saves you time and reduces the chance that you will mistakenly omit a member or send the message to someone not in the group. Examples of group e-mail addresses are shown below.

Accounting Department
Benefits Committee
Product Research Team A

With some programs, placing an address in your address book will prevent a message from that address from being treated as spam or junk mail. For example, you may want to receive e-mail messages about sales and new products from a particular company. Your e-mail software or Internet provider may suspect that these messages are spam and delete them or place them in a spam folder. Placing the address of the company in your address book tells the program that this address is one from which you want to receive mail.

Signature File

Some e-mail programs allow you to create a signature file. A signature file is a short block of text placed at the end of an e-mail message. Signature files usually contain useful contact information, such as your full name, title, company name, address, and phone number. You can create different signature blocks to use for messages to different groups of people. When you have more than one signature block, you must select the signature block to use for each message. A signature block is shown in Figure 7-10 on page 232.

Diversity

As when writing any business message, consider the age, gender, culture, and customs of the recipients to create a courteous message.

Key ▶ Point

Placing an address in your address book may prevent a message from that address from being treated as spam or junk mail.

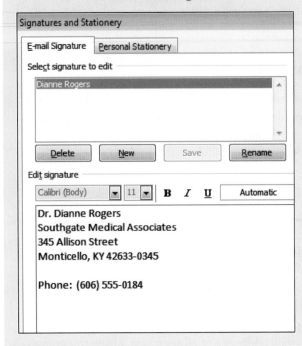

Figure 7-10 Users can create a signature block to insert in e-mail messages.

Spelling Checker

Like the feature in word processing software, the spelling checker in e-mail software checks the text of an e-mail message for spelling errors. Always run the spelling checker for an e-mail message. Also, proofread the message and correct all errors before sending it.

Attachment

The Attachment feature lets you send files created in other programs with an e-mail message. Many types of files, such as word processing, spreadsheet, database, and graphics files, can be sent as attachments. Always check the size of a file you want to send as an e-mail attachment. Some e-mail systems will not accept large files as attachments. Figure 7-8 on page 229 shows a file attachment.

Draft

The Draft option lets you save an e-mail message. The message is not sent to the recipient. It is stored on your computer or network. You can open the message later, finish it, and send it. This feature is useful when you are interrupted while writing a message or find that you need to check facts or get more information to finish a message.

Key▶Point

Do not send large files as e-mail attachments unless you know the receiving system can handle the large files. Large file attachments can stall some e-mail programs, preventing access to e-mail for hours.

Reply and Reply All

The Reply feature is used when you want to answer an e-mail message you have received. The e-mail address will appear automatically in the To line. Depending on the settings in your software, the text of the message you received may appear in the response below your reply message. For example, suppose you have received an e-mail containing driving directions, and you have some questions about them. Including the original driving directions along with your questions is a courtesy to the person to whom you are writing. The reader can refer to the directions when answering your questions.

Reply All is the same as Reply, except that it sends your response to the person who wrote to you and to anyone listed in the Cc or Bcc lines of the e-mail. For both Reply and Reply All, the e-mail addresses of recipients are entered automatically. Use Reply All only when the persons who received copies of the message need to see your answer.

Forward

The Forward feature allows you to send a message you have received to a recipient you specify. You might use this feature when someone else needs to have the information in the e-mail and/or to respond to it.

Priority

You can assign a priority to an e-mail you compose. The default setting, which is used for nearly all messages, is normal or routine priority. In Figure 7-9 on page 230, most of the messages are rated as normal priority. Two messages are rated as high priority. Typically, a normal or routine priority is automatically assigned to messages. You change the priority to let a recipient know when a message is urgent. Assign a high priority to a message only when necessary.

Return Receipt

The return receipt feature is useful when you want to make sure the recipient has opened your e-mail message. When you request a return receipt, a message will appear when the recipient opens the message. A *Windows Mail* message is shown in Figure 7-11 on page 234. When the receiver clicks *Yes*, a message is sent to the original sender indicating that the e-mail has been opened.

E-mail Netiquette

Netiquette is a set of informal guidelines for behaving courteously online. Using netiquette when you are composing and sending e-mail messages shows consideration for the receiver. For example, quoting only enough of an original message in your reply so that the receiver will understand shows that you recognize the importance of his or her time.

Key▶Point
Do not routinely use Reply All when answering messages. Many times, only the person who sent the message needs your reply.

Key▶Point
Request a return receipt for important messages when you want to be sure they are read.

Figure 7-11 Users can request a return receipt for an e-mail message.

Key▶Point

Using proper netiquette is very important. If you do not use proper netiquette, the receiver may think that you are rude or do not know how to communicate courteously online.

Follow these netiquette guidelines to communicate courteously:

▪ Assign a high priority to a message only when it is truly urgent.

▪ Ask for approval from the recipient before sending a message with large attachments or several attachments.

▪ Before forwarding a message, get the writer's consent.

▪ Use the Bcc feature cautiously.

▪ Do not use e-mail to send confidential or sensitive information or to communicate personal criticism.

▪ Do not use all capital letters when keying an e-mail message. Using all capitals is considered shouting.

▪ Do not send **flames**, which are angry or insulting messages.

▪ Do not send or forward spam.

▪ Do not use emoticons in business e-mails. An **emoticon** is a combination of keyboard characters or icons used in messages to indicate emotion. For example, a smiley face icon ☺ indicates that a comment is made in jest.

▪ Use correct grammar, spelling, and punctuation. Do not use informal abbreviations, such as *TTYL* for *talk to you later*.

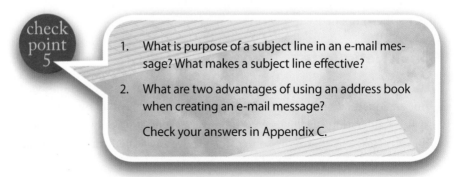

check point 5

1. What is purpose of a subject line in an e-mail message? What makes a subject line effective?

2. What are two advantages of using an address book when creating an e-mail message?

Check your answers in Appendix C.

Instant Messaging

Instant messaging (IM) is a means of communicating electronically via text messages with one or more people in real time. The exchange is immediate, like a telephone conversation, when both or all parties are online. Comments are keyed rather than spoken. Some companies use IM to communicate with clients, customers, and suppliers. At an online clothing retailer, for example, a customer who is not sure what size shirt to order can "talk" with a customer service representative, using a chat feature. The customer can get an answer that otherwise would involve a telephone call or several exchanges of e-mail messages.

Most often, IM is used at work to communicate with coworkers. It is especially popular with young adults who have used the technology at home and school for years. IM can save communication time and improve teamwork.

Instant messages are sent over the Internet or via private company networks. Some IM programs are not compatible with other IM programs. A person using *MSN® Messenger*, for example, may not be able to chat with someone using a different program.

IM conversations are very informal. They are truly conversations—not documents like letters or memos. Instant messages may use jargon, abbreviations, elliptical sentences such as *A bit small,* and emoticons.

Key▶Point

Some companies use IM to communicate with clients, customers, and suppliers. Most often, IM is used at work to communicate with coworkers.

IM Basics

Like an e-mail composition window, the window for composing an instant message generally includes a To line and a text area where the message is keyed. You can key the recipient's name or select the name on a contacts list. Once you send your message and the other person responds, the conversation begins. Several people can take part in a single conversation using a chat feature. At work, however, only two people typically take part in the conversation.

Key▶Point

Several people can take part in a single conversation using an IM chat feature.

Buddy, Contacts, or Friends List

A **contacts list** is a list of people with whom you communicate. For example, you might create a contacts list for coworkers with whom you communicate frequently, another for members of a committee on which you are serving, and another for people on your production team. In some programs, the contacts list is called a *buddy list* or *friends list.* When you connect to your messaging server and choose a contacts list, you can see at a glance which people on that list are online and available to talk with you. Those people can see that you, too, are available to talk.

Chat Window

Key▶Point

Using informal abbreviations and incomplete sentences is considered appropriate in IM.

The chat or conversation window displays everything keyed in the current chat session. Comments are listed in the order made, and the person who made each comment is identified. The window also includes a space in which you enter the comments you would like to add to the discussion. Notice that abbreviations for *thanks* (*thx*) and *talk to you later* (*TTYL*) are used in the message shown in Figure 7-12.

Figure 7-12 Instant Messaging Chat Window

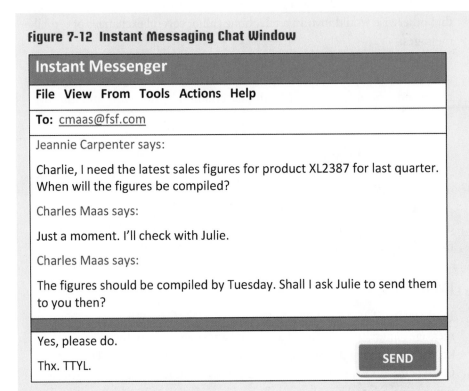

> **Instant Messenger**
>
> File View From Tools Actions Help
>
> **To:** cmaas@fsf.com
>
> Jeannie Carpenter says:
>
> Charlie, I need the latest sales figures for product XL2387 for last quarter. When will the figures be compiled?
>
> Charles Maas says:
>
> Just a moment. I'll check with Julie.
>
> Charles Maas says:
>
> The figures should be compiled by Tuesday. Shall I ask Julie to send them to you then?
>
> Yes, please do.
>
> Thx. TTYL.
>
> SEND

Work-Friendly IM Features

Like e-mail, IM has several features that are especially useful at work. Status options show whether a person is available to talk. Options vary with the software. Examples are Available, Away, Busy, Be Right Back, Out to Lunch, and On the Phone. Some software allows you to create personalized status messages. Other features, such as the ability to save messages, spelling checker, attachment, forward, and return receipt, are similar to those found in e-mail programs.

IM Netiquette

Many of the rules of netiquette for e-mail also apply to IM. The primary rule is to be considerate of others. Additional rules of IM netiquette are listed below.

Key ▶ Point

IM transmissions may not be secure or private. Do not communicate confidential, sensitive, or personally critical information by IM.

- Do not use all capital letters.

- Be sensitive to the possibility that other users may have slower systems.

- Do not communicate confidential, sensitive, or personally critical information by IM.

- Be brief. IM is best for short messages. Use other methods for long messages.

- Use status options to let people know about your availability and respect the status option listings of others.

- Even when someone's status is Available, it is polite to begin a conversation by asking whether now is a good time to talk.

- Consider your receiver in the level of formality of your comments, as well as in your use of abbreviations and emoticons.

- Do not leave other people waiting for your response. When you start a chat, be prepared to carry it through with little or no interruption.

- Protect your privacy and the privacy of others by learning about and using the security features of your system.

check point 6

1. Describe business uses for instant messages.

2. What is the primary IM netiquette rule?

Check your answers in Appendix C.

Section 7.3 *Applications*

CRITICAL THINKING

A. *Compose an E-mail*

Each December, the members of your department attend a holiday luncheon. You have been asked to make the luncheon plans and share them with your coworkers.

1. Create an e-mail message that will be sent to all the employees in your department. (If you do not have e-mail software, key the message as a memo.) Use an address provided by your instructor in the To line.

2. The message will be from you on the current date. Key an appropriate subject line.

3. Organize the information you will need to tell your coworkers. Select a date and time for the luncheon. Select a local restaurant where the luncheon can take place. Do research to find the address and phone number.

4. Key the body of the e-mail. Remember to make the message courteous and to include the five Ws—who, what, where, when, and why.

B. *Review E-mail Netiquette*

Review the e-mail netiquette guidelines given in this chapter. Then, read the e-mail message shown below. Does this message follow netiquette guidelines? What problems with the message can you identify?

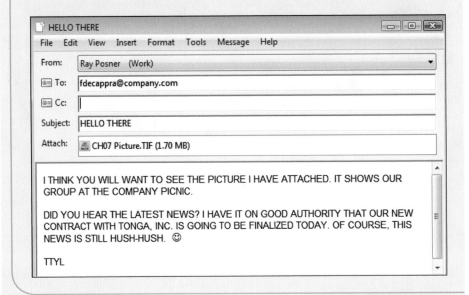

Letters

Writing Letters

After you have planned and organized your message, you are ready to write. Every letter should contain certain standard parts. Several optional letter parts may be used when needed. Each part of a letter serves an important purpose. The parts of a letter and formatting guidelines for letters are discussed in the following paragraphs.

Standard Letter Parts

The standard parts of a letter are the date, letter address, salutation, body, complimentary close, writer's name and title, and reference initials. Figure 7-13 on page 240 illustrates these standard letter parts.

Date

The date indicates when the letter was composed. Begin the date at about 2 inches from the top of the page or center the page vertically. If the paper has a preprinted company letterhead or a letterhead in the header, begin at least ½ inch below the letterhead. Use default side margins.

Use the same format for the date as you do in memos. Spell out the month, use a numeral for the day, and follow with the year. Key the date or use a feature such as *Word's* Date and Time to insert the date.

If your software leaves 10 points of blank space after each paragraph, tap ENTER twice. If the software does not add space after a paragraph, tap ENTER three times to leave blank lines after the date.

Letter Address

The letter address contains the name and address of the receiver. For a business letter, it generally consists of the receiver's name and job title, followed by the company, street address, city, state, and ZIP Code. Key one space between the two-letter state abbreviation and the ZIP Code. Use the ZIP+4 Code if you know the last four digits. If you do not know the ZIP Code for an address, you can find it by looking on the U.S. Postal Service Web site. Enter the search term *ZIP Code lookup* in an Internet search engine to quickly find the site.

OBJECTIVES

After completing Section 7.4, you should be able to:

1. Format, edit, and publish letters.
2. Prepare envelopes for business letters.

Key ▶ Point

These standard parts should be included in every letter:

- Date
- Letter address
- Salutation
- Body
- Complimentary close
- Writer's name and title

Figure 7-13 This block letter has open punctuation.

Letterhead ········ **Park Systems**

303 Park Avenue
New York, NY 10033-1784
Phone: (800) 555-0150

Date ········ January 8, 20--

Letter Address ········ Mr. William Delaney
Delaney Financial Services
105 High Street
Columbus, OH 43230-9017

Salutation ········ Dear Mr. Delaney

Body ········ Thank you for giving us the opportunity to prepare a cost analysis and bid for your new office
system. You should receive our bid by special courier within the next ten days.

Brochures describing our Model 4000 office system that you requested are enclosed. Please call
me at (800) 555-0150 if you have any questions about the system.

Complimentary Close ········ Sincerely

Martina Garcia

Writer's Name and Title ········ Martina Garcia
Sales Manager

Reference Initials ········ jk

Enclosure Notation ········ Enclosure

If your software leaves 10 points of blank space after each paragraph, tap ENTER once after the last line of the address. Remove the blank space after the other lines in the address. See Figure 7-13 for an example address format. If the software does not add space after a paragraph, tap ENTER two times to leave a blank line after the address.

Include the receiver's personal or professional title (*Mr., Ms., Dr.*) in the letter address. If you are writing to a woman and do not know which personal title she prefers, use *Ms.* A job title can appear on the same line with the name or on the line below, whichever makes the letter address block look more balanced.

Ms. Maeve Saunders, Treasurer
Central Tennessee Bank
396 West Street
Franklin, TN 37064-7109

Salutation

The salutation serves as a greeting to the receiver. It usually consists of *Dear* and the receiver's personal or professional title and last name (*Dear Dr. Sanjabi*). If you and the person you are writing to are on a first-name basis, use the first name instead. Use the name you would use if you were addressing the person face-to-face.

If you are writing to a company and do not know the name of the appropriate person to receive the letter, use the salutation *Ladies and Gentlemen.* If the letter is addressed to a job title, use the title in the salutation.

| Dear Mrs. Nunez | Ladies and Gentlemen |
| Dear Frederick | Dear Service Manager |

You may use one of two punctuation styles for the salutation and complimentary close. **Open punctuation** means that no punctuation follows the salutation or complimentary close. Open punctuation is often used with block letter style; however, it is also appropriate for modified block letter style. **Mixed punctuation** means that a colon follows the salutation and a comma follows the complimentary close. Mixed punctuation is appropriate for both block and modified block letter styles.

Open Punctuation	Mixed Punctuation
Dear Dr. Lombardi	Dear Mr. Van Nuys:
Sincerely	Sincerely,

If your software leaves 10 points of blank space after each paragraph, tap ENTER once after the salutation. If the software does not add space after a paragraph, tap ENTER two times to leave a blank line after the salutation.

K e y ▶ P o i n t

If your software leaves 10 points of blank space after each paragraph, remove the blank space after the lines within the address. (Do not remove space after the last line.)

K e y ▶ P o i n t

The salutation should be appropriate for the letter address. When writing to a company, use the salutation *Ladies and Gentlemen.*

Body

The body contains the paragraphs of the letter. The body should be courteous, correct, concise, clear, and complete. Begin each line of the body at the left margin. Leave a blank line between paragraphs if your software does not automatically leave extra space after a paragraph. The letter in Figure 7-13 on page 240 uses the *Microsoft Word* default setting of 10 point spacing after each paragraph.

As in memos, use bulleted or numbered lists to present details clearly. Use bullets when the order of the items does not matter—in a list of needed supplies, for example. Use numbers when the order of the items does matter.

Complimentary Close

The complimentary close is the formal closing. Only the first letter of the first word is capitalized. Key a comma after the complimentary close when using mixed punctuation. Do not insert any punctuation when using open punctuation. Frequently used complimentary closes include the following:

Sincerely   Sincerely yours   Cordially

If your software leaves 10 points of blank space after each paragraph, tap ENTER twice. If the software does not add space after a paragraph, tap ENTER three times to leave blank lines after the close.

Writer's Name and Title

Key the writer's name below the complimentary close. Remove space after the paragraph if your software automatically adds space after a paragraph. Key the title on the next line. Personal or professional titles usually are not included unless the writer wants to indicate his or her gender and the first name does not do so (for example, *Ms. Dale Normington*). However, a degree or another professional designation after a name is acceptable. A personal business letter does not include a job title.

Place the writer's job title next to the keyed name or on the line below it, whichever looks more balanced. If a department or another division is included, arrange it for balance as well.

Jenny Kaplan, Ph.D.   Leng Xiong, Director
Program Coordinator   City Youth Program

Reference Initials

Reference initials indicate who keyed a letter. They appear two lines below the writer's title (or the printed writer's name if no title is used). As in memos, reference initials in letters are lowercase. Include them only when you key a letter for somebody else.

Key ▶ Point

Key a comma after the complimentary close when using mixed punctuation. Do not insert any punctuation when using open punctuation.

Diversity

In some languages, a person's family appears first in the name. If you are unsure about a name, do research to learn about the person and his or her name before replying to a letter.

check point 7

1. What are the standard parts of a business letter?

2. What top and side margins should be used for a business letter?

Check your answers in Appendix C.

Optional Letter Parts

A business letter may include one or more of these optional parts: attention line, reference or subject line, enclosure or attachment notation, copy or blind copy notation, and postscript. Personal business letters may have these same optional letter parts.

Notations, such as enclosure, attachment, copy, and blind copy, follow the same rules as those for memos and appear in the same location. Other optional letter parts are discussed in the following paragraphs.

Attention Line

An attention line is used when a letter is not addressed personally to an individual, but rather to an organization. The attention line directs the letter to a position or department within the organization. A letter from a radio station offering special prices on ads to a public relations agency might use an attention line in one of the ways shown here.

Attention Media Buyer   Attention Marketing Department
Pinciaro Consulting   Pinciaro Consulting
62 Broughton Street   62 Broughton Street
Hartford, CT 06109-3405   Hartford, CT 06109-3405

Note that when an attention line is used, it is the first line of the letter address. The proper salutation is *Ladies and Gentlemen*. An attention line is shown in Figure 7-14 on page 244.

Reference Line

A reference line directs the reader to a source document, such as an invoice, that is included with the letter. The reference line appears below the letter address, before the salutation.

Ms. Myra Quigley
Quigley Dry Cleaners
570 Orion Road
Northbrook, IL 60062-4110

Re: Invoice 84295

Dear Ms. Quigley

Key▶Point

An attention line is used when a letter is not addressed personally to an individual, but rather to an organization.

Figure 7-14 This modified block letter has mixed punctuation.

Park Systems

303 Park Avenue
New York, NY 10033-1784
Phone: (800) 555-0150

January 8, 20--

Attention Line .... Attention Office Manager
Delaney Financial Services
105 High Street
Columbus, OH 43230-9017

Ladies and Gentlemen:

Subject Line .... BID FOR OFFICE SYSTEM

Thank you for giving us the opportunity to prepare a cost analysis and bid for your new office system. You should receive our bid by special courier within the next ten days.

Brochures describing our Model 4000 office system that you requested are enclosed. Please call me at (800) 555-0150 if you have any questions about the system.

Sincerely,

Martina Garcia

Martina Garcia
Sales Manager

jk

Enclosure Notation .... Enclosure

Copy Notation c   Joshua Cohen

Postscript .... If you would like our regional salesperson to visit your office and talk with your staff, contact Mr. Cohen at (614) 555-0134.

Subject Line

As in a memo, the subject line of a letter provides the letter's topic. The subject line appears between the salutation and the body. It may be keyed in all capital letters or using initial capitals. The word *Subject* is optional.

> Dear Mr. Petrocelli
>
> TOULOUSE-LAUTREC EXHIBIT
>
> There has never been a better time to renew your Briarley Museum membership. This fall, the museum will host an exhibition of more than 200 works by Henri de Toulouse-Lautrec. This exhibit . . .

Postscript

For emphasis, you may add a postscript. A **postscript** is a sentence or paragraph at the end of the letter that reinforces the message or provides additional information. Postscripts rarely are used in routine business letters, but they often are used in sales letters. Position the postscript below the last notation.

> Enclosure
>
> Remember that if you order by November 1, you will receive a 15 percent discount and free shipping.

check point 8

1. What are the optional parts that may be included in a business letter?

2. What is the purpose of a postscript, and where is it placed in a business letter?

Check your answers in Appendix C.

Editing and Publishing Letters

Follow the procedures you learned in Chapter 6 to edit letters. Be sure the letter is courteous and includes complete and correct information. Proofread the final draft carefully and correct all errors. Print a copy to keep for your files and one for each recipient.

Publishing a letter is typically accomplished by placing it in an envelope and sending it by interoffice mail, U.S. Mail, or a private mail carrier.

Key ▶ Point

Use reference and subject lines correctly. A reference line directs the reader to a source document, such as an invoice. A subject line indicates a letter's topic.

Key ▶ Point

Postscripts rarely are used in routine business letters, but they often are used in sales letters.

Key ▶ Point

Use the procedures you learned in Chapter 6 to edit and proofread a letter before mailing it.

Business Letter Formats

Business letters may be prepared in block or modified block format. In block format, all lines begin at the left margin. A block letter is shown in Figure 7-13 on page 240. In modified block format, all lines begin at the left margin except for the date, complimentary close, and writer's name and title. These items begin at the horizontal center of the page. Figure 7-14 on page 244 shows a modified block letter.

Like business letters, personal business letters may be written in block or modified block format. They may be keyed on plain paper or personal letterhead.

Some business or personal business letters exceed one page. For these letters, use a heading on the second page. The heading is the same as for the second page of a memo. See Figure 7-7 on page 225. Use plain paper of the same quality as the letterhead for the second page.

Business Envelopes

When preparing a business envelope, use the same address that appears in the letter. If the letter address contains an attention line, key that information as the first line of the address on the envelope.

Address Format

Using U.S. Postal Service format—keying the address in all capital letters with no punctuation—can result in more efficient processing of your letter. This format is shown in Figure 7-15 on page 247. However, using the traditional uppercase and lowercase letters and punctuation for the address is also acceptable.

With a standard size 10 business envelope (4 ⅛" x 9½"), the receiver's name and address should begin about 2 ½ inches from the top. Key the information single-spaced in block style. Begin the letter address about ½ inch left of the center, as shown in Figure 7-15.

Businesses often use envelopes with a preprinted return address. If your company does not, key the return address in the envelope's upper left corner.

Self-adhesive labels often are used when letters are mailed to many recipients. For example, labels may be used for a mailing to customers, telling them of an upcoming sale. These labels should be placed approximately in the same spot on the envelope as the recipient's address would be keyed.

Mail may be sent by private mail carriers, such as FEDEX or UPS. When sending mail by a private carrier, complete the form provided by the carrier. Forms vary, but they typically include the name, address, and telephone number for both the sender and the receiver. The class of service, such as Overnight Mail, is also shown on the form.

Envelope Feature

Most word processing software has an Envelope feature. This feature copies the letter address from a letter you have keyed. The address is

Key▶Point

Using block letter format saves time because no tab settings are required. All lines begin at the left margin.

Key▶Point

Some companies direct employees to use the format recommended by the U.S. Postal Service for envelope addresses. Other companies prefer the traditional format that uses punctuation and capital and lowercase letters.

Key▶Point

Key the return address in the envelope's upper left corner if it is not printed on the envelope.

OCCUPATIONAL SUCCESS

Using Mail Merge

Successful workers use efficient methods for completing work tasks. Using the mail merge feature of your word processing software allows you to create mailings efficiently.

Suppose you need to send letters to 120 people. Each letter will tell the recipient a date when membership in your organization expires. You could key 120 different letters or manually edit the first letter for each additional recipient. Using mail merge would be a more efficient way that would require much less time.

Mail merge allows you to create personalized letters for recipients. The parts of the letter that are the same for each recipient are keyed in one file. The names, addresses, membership expiration dates, and any other data that are different for each recipient are keyed in a different file. Field codes for the variable data are also keyed in the letter file. The mail merge process integrates the variable information into the letter file to create personalized letters. Read the Help information that is available in your word processing software to learn more about using mail merge.

automatically inserted on an envelope page or printed. The envelope feature also can insert a return address and accommodate single envelopes, mass mailings, and address labels. Some software can add a postal barcode that speeds mail handling.

Key ▶ Point

Using the Envelope feature of word processing software to create envelopes saves times and reduces the chance of keying errors in the address.

Figure 7-15 Size 10 Envelope

Grant Memorial Hospital
10245 Central Boulevard
Bisbee, AZ 85603-2176

MR JIAN WANG
49 RED CANYON ROAD
BISBEE AZ 85603-1890

| Envelopes and Labels | ? ✕ |

Envelopes   Labels

Delivery address: 📖 ▼

Mr. Thomas Delaney
Delaney Financial Services
105 High Street
Columbus, OH 43230-9017

☐ Add electronic postage

Return address: 📖 ▼ ☐ Omit

Rosa Diaz
32 State Street
Monticello, KY 42633

Preview

Feed

Before printing, insert envelopes into the following printer tray: Auto Select.

[Print] [Add to Document] [Options...] [E-postage Properties...]

[Cancel]

Folding Letters

Business letters should be folded neatly before being inserted into envelopes. Follow these steps to fold and insert a letter.

1. With the letter face up, fold slightly less than one-third of the letter up toward the top.

2. Fold down the top of the letter to within ½ inch of the bottom fold.

3. Insert the letter into the envelope with the last crease toward the bottom of the envelope.

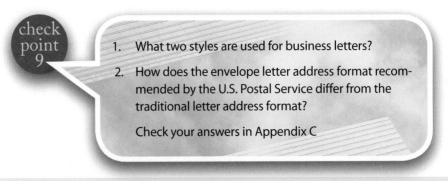

check point 9

1. What two styles are used for business letters?

2. How does the envelope letter address format recommended by the U.S. Postal Service differ from the traditional letter address format?

Check your answers in Appendix C

Section 7.4 *Applications*

A. Letter Parts and Format

REAL WORLD

1. Bring to class a business letter that you or someone in your family has received. (Select a letter that does not contain confidential information.)

2. Which letter format, block or modified block, does the letter use? If the format does not conform to either style shown in this textbook, describe how it is different.

3. What letter parts are included in the letter?

4. What punctuation style is used in the letter?

5. If the letter has a letterhead, what information is included in the letterhead?

B. Block Letter

1. Key the information shown below as a block letter with open punctuation. Assume the letter will be printed on letterhead paper. Refer to Figure 7-13 on page 240 for an example block letter.

2. Proofread the letter carefully and correct all errors.

    June 15, 20--

    Mr. Rob DeSousa | 89 Gateway Street | Seattle, WA 98104-3428

    Dear Mr. DeSousa

    Your new Main Street Clothing credit card and credit agreement are enclosed. You may use this card in both our Seattle and our Tacoma stores. Because of your good credit record, you will be able to charge as much as $5,000 at a time on your card.

    Plan to take advantage of our annual summer clearance sale that begins on July 1. Many items will be 25 percent off the regular price. You can use the enclosed coupon to purchase one item at 50 percent off the regular price.

    Thank you for becoming a Main Street Clothing credit customer. Please let me know if you have any questions about your new account.

    Sincerely

    Mary Ann Loudon
    Credit Manager

    xx
    Enclosures

Chapter *Summary*

7.1 Business Correspondence

- Business correspondence is a written message, such as a memo or letter, that deals with business matters.

- Purposes for business messages may be to provide a record, advise, direct, state a policy, inform, request information, reply to requests, persuade, or promote goodwill.

- To plan a business message, identify the objective, determine the main idea, choose supporting details, and adjust the message for the receiver.

- Use direct order in a message that contains good or neutral news. Use indirect order in a message that contains bad news or that tries to persuade the receiver.

7.2 Memos

- A memo is an informal document that is sent to someone within your company or group.

- A memo contains heading lines and a body. It may also contain one or more notations.

- The subject line of a memo states the main idea or topic of the message. It should be short, clear, and specific.

7.3 E-mail and Instant Messaging

- An e-mail (electronic mail) is an informal message written, sent, and received on a computer. E-mail is a fast and inexpensive way to send business messages.

- Using netiquette when you are composing and sending e-mail messages shows consideration for the receiver.

- Instant messaging (IM) is a means of communicating electronically via text messages with one or more people in real time.

7.4 Letters

- A business letter is a document used to send a formal written message to someone inside or outside the organization.

- The standard parts of a letter are the date, letter address, salutation, body, complimentary close, writer's name and title, and reference initials.

- Business letters may be formatted in block or modified block style.

Open the *Word* file *CH07 Vocabulary* from the student data files. Complete the exercise to review the vocabulary terms from this chapter.

attachment notation	invoice
blind copy notation	letter
body	memo
contacts list	mixed punctuation
copy notation	netiquette
e-mail	open punctuation
emoticon	postscript
enclosure notation	reference initials
flame	spam
instant messaging (IM)	subject line

Critical Thinking Questions

1. Should your company e-mail account be used to send personal messages? Why or why not?

2. Confidential information should not be sent in an e-mail message. Why is this so?

3. You need to let your supervisor know that a client has decided to place a large order with a competitor rather than with your company. What type of written message should you use?

4. Identify a job that you may like to have in the future. What types of letters or memos do you think a person in this job might need to write?

CRITICAL
THINKING

Chapter *Applications*

A. *Modified Block Letter*

1. Refer to Figure 7-14 on page 244 to review modified block letter style.

2. Open the *Word* file *CH07 Carson Letter* from the data files. Format the text in the file as a modified block letter with mixed punctuation.

3. Read the edits and accept or reject the changes so the letter uses correct grammar, spelling, and punctuation. Proofread and correct all errors. Print the letter.

B. *Phishing Alert Memo*

1. Open and print the *Word* file *CH07 Phishing Memo* from the student data files. Key the information in correct memo format.

2. Proofread the memo and correct all errors. Print the memo.

C. *E-mail Safety*

INTERNET

TEAMWORK

1. Work with a classmate to complete this activity. Search the Internet for articles about using e-mail safely. The article might be about phishing, spam, identity theft, passwords, computer viruses, or other matters involving e-mail.

2. Key a summary of the main points of the article. Give complete source information (author, article name, Web site name, Web site address, and date accessed). Be prepared to share what you have learned with the class.

D. *E-mail to Contact Group*

TEAMWORK

1. Format the following message as an e-mail.

2. Work with another student and send your e-mails to each other. Use the Reply feature to reply to your partner's e-mail and suggest any corrections.

3. Create a contacts group or mailing list to include six students in your class. Send the final, corrected e-mail to the group or mailing list with a copy to your instructor.

   Fire lanes are an important part of our school's emergency plan. They are designed to allow fire engines and other emergency equipment easy access to the buildings and grounds.

   Recently, an increasing number of cars have been parked in fire lanes and left unattended. Parking in fire lanes, even for a short time, is prohibited by law. It endangers our students, staff, and visitors. Effective next Monday, [insert next Monday's date], any car parked in a fire lane, no matter how briefly, will be ticketed by metro police and towed at the owner's expense.

Our three parking lots provide ample space for student and staff parking, as well as parking for visitors. In addition, short-term parking is available in designated spaces in front of the main building. Please join us in our effort to keep the school safe and to set a good example for other drivers.

E. Envelopes for Business Letters

1. Open the letter you created in Application B on page 252.

2. Use your software's envelope or mailings feature to create an envelope for the letter. Use the all capitals, no punctuation style recommend by the U.S. Postal Service for the letter address. Key your address as the return address.

3. Add the envelope to the letter file if you have that option. Print the envelope. (Use paper cut to 4 ⅛" x 9 ½" to simulate a standard size 10 business envelope if envelopes are not available.)

4. Open the letter you created in Application A on page 251.

5. Use your software's envelope or mailings feature to create an envelope for the letter. Use the traditional style (initial caps and punctuation) for the letter address. Key the name and address shown in the letterhead in the return address.

6. Add the envelope to the letter file if you have that option. Print the envelope. (Again, use paper cut to size if envelopes are not available.)

F. Personal Business Letter

REAL WORLD

1. Select a product or service you have used that you like very much or that you do not like. Do research to find the seller of the product or service and an address where you can write to the company. Some products have a company address on the label. For other products or services, you may need to do research on the Internet.

2. Write a personal business letter to the company, thanking them for making such a good product or telling them why you do not like the product. Give details about why you like or do not like the product and suggestions for changes.

3. Create a letterhead with your name and address in the document header.

4. Edit the letter to be sure it is courteous, correct, concise, clear, and complete. Proofread and correct all errors. Create an envelope for the letter.

Editing Activity

Open and edit the *Word* file *CH07 Editing* from the student data files. Correct all spelling, punctuation, and grammar errors.

Planning Messages

Alicia Perez is the public relations director of a regional theater. She would like to start a tradition of offering twice-yearly matinees of selected shows for students. After a performance, the actors would answer questions and hand out box lunches. Offering the matinees might seem like a simple matter, but it will require a good deal of planning. Alicia already has the approval of the artistic director and business manager. She needs to complete several tasks to accomplish her goal:

- Find corporate sponsors to pay for tickets and to donate box lunches.

- Secure the cooperation of the shows' stage managers and casts.

- Inform the house manager to ensure that the theater remains open and staffed for the extra time after performances.

- Invite schools to participate.

- Make the box office aware of the special ticketing arrangements.

1. What type of message (letter, memo, or e-mail) would Alicia need to write to accomplish each task?

2. What order (direct or indirect) would be appropriate for each message?

Communication for Architecture and Construction

James graduated from high school a year ago and began looking for a job in construction. Initially, finding a job was somewhat difficult. To improve his chances for finding a job in construction, James took several construction-related courses at a local technical college. One of the courses was Safety in Construction.

James is now working at Patterson Construction Company as part of a framing crew. His job is to help construct the frame of new buildings. His crew is currently working on a new apartment complex. As he is working on the project, James notices several violations of safety codes that he learned about in his safety course. For example, many workers do not wear safety glasses when cutting wood for the frames. Also, items that could cause a worker to fall are sometimes left on temporary stairs between floors within the complex.

1. What should James do? Should he report the violations to his supervisor?

2. What might happen if James reports the violations to his supervisor?

3. If James reports the violations to his supervisor, what method of communication should he use? Why?

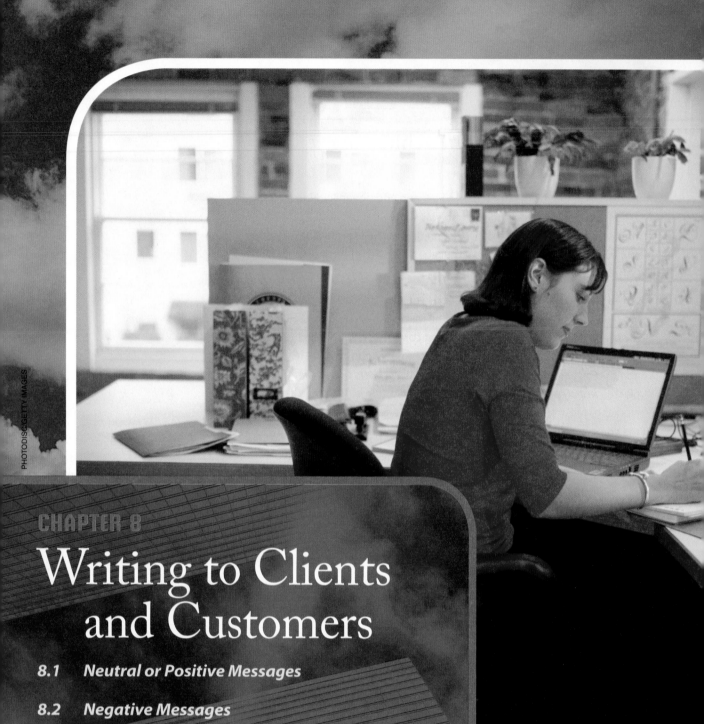

CHAPTER 8

Writing to Clients and Customers

8.1   *Neutral or Positive Messages*

8.2   *Negative Messages*

8.3   *Persuasive Messages*

Rosita's Reactions to Letters

Recently, Rosita Hernandez changed jobs. After completing her business technology degree, she left her position as a clerk at a local supermarket. Now she works as an administrative assistant at a financial services office in San Diego, California.

In her new job, Rosita keys letters for the members of her work team. The letters often contain specific formatting instructions, which vary from letter to letter. Some of the letters look quite different from the letter formats Rosita learned to use in her college classes. She has suggested to the team members that using only one or two letter formats would give the company's letters a consistent look. This approach would also speed processing of the letters. However, the team members do not seem interested in changing letter styles.

Rosita keys letters written in English only. Most of the recipients of these letters are in the United States. However, some recipients live in Mexico. Some of the letters are very short, and they seem a little blunt and tactless to Rosita. Some letters are long and wordy, sometimes running to two and three pages. Rosita wonders whether the people writing the letters consider the receiver's culture and try to adjust the message to fit the receiver.

Questions

1. Are Rosita's concerns about the varying formats justified? Is there one correct format?

2. If there is more than one correct letter format, how do you determine which one to use?

3. Should a writer consider the reader's culture or nationality when writing his or her letters? Why or why not?

8.1 Neutral or Positive Messages

Planning Neutral or Positive Messages

Key ▶ Point

A sender should consider business messages from the receiver's point of view.

Business messages are written to achieve a purpose. To improve their chances for success, a sender should consider messages from the receiver's point of view. As you have learned in earlier chapters, the four steps in planning a message are:

1. Identify the objective.

2. Identify the main idea.

3. Determine the supporting details.

4. Adjust the content to the receiver.

These steps apply to all types of messages, including those written to give positive or neutral news. The steps are applied in the example shown in Figure 8-1.

Figure 8-1 Planning a Positive Message

PLANNING A POSITIVE MESSAGE	
Identify the Objective	To make an offer of employment
Identify the Main Idea	The company offers the applicant a position as a training director in the Services Department
Determine the Supporting Details	Impressed with the applicant's knowledge of the company and good work attitude Annual salary of $62,000 paid biweekly Starting date is July 1 Conditions of employment Decision needed within one week
Adjust the Content to the Receiver	Applicant is knowledgeable about the job requirements and the company Applicant will be eager to hear from the company

Organizing Neutral or Positive Messages

After identifying the content for a message, the writer should select the correct order for the information. Messages with positive or neutral news should be organized in direct order. In direct order, the main idea is presented first, followed by the supporting details and the closing.

Main Idea

In effective messages with positive, neutral, or routine news, the main idea should appear in the first or second sentence. The main idea should be stated clearly and concisely. Emphasize the main idea by keeping the introductory paragraph short—one or two sentences (usually no longer than four lines).

Supporting Details

After giving the main idea in the first paragraph, the writer should provide details that can clarify the main idea and help the receiver. Supporting details should furnish necessary explanations, state conditions of the main idea, or answer the receiver's questions.

This section may have one or more paragraphs. For clarity, make sure each paragraph has a central idea, repeats key words, and lists important points. To make your messages appealing, keep these middle paragraphs short—about eight lines or less for each one.

Goodwill Closing

The closing of a message provides an opportunity to build goodwill. The closing should be friendly and courteous. It should leave a favorable impression with the receiver. In addition, it should identify any action required. Remember, using the receiver's name adds a personal touch. The following closing paragraph uses this technique.

> Elizabeth, we eagerly await your reply and hope that you will accept our offer. If you have any questions, call me at 864-555-0185.

Closings in messages from a company that sells products or services may include a soft sell. A **soft sell** is an attempt to sell a product or service, but it is not strong or pushy. Instead, a subtle or low-pressure appeal is used. The following goodwill closing contains a soft sell message.

> Thank you, Mr. Ming, for your order. You may want to visit our store during our Anniversary Sale during May 15 to 29. All personal computers will be reduced 25 percent.

check point 1

1. What are the steps in planning a message?

2. For a positive or neutral message, what order should be used to present the information?

    Check your answers in Appendix C.

Writing Neutral Messages

Some documents, such as routine requests or claims, contain neutral messages. In a message with neutral news, the main idea is neither positive nor negative. The senders of these neutral messages think the receivers will respond as requested. The receivers are not being persuaded to do something.

Routine Requests

Key ▶ Point

The message containing a routine request should be presented in direct order.

In a **routine request**, the sender asks for an action that will be done willingly. This type of request is presented in a direct order. "Will you . . ." is the main idea of a routine request. To aid the receiver in the response, the writer must provide enough details for the receiver to understand the request and respond easily. Providing details means anticipating the receiver's questions and responding to them. For example, if you ask someone to speak at an event, you need to provide the receiver with the following details:

▨ The topic

▨ The background, knowledge, and expected size of the audience

▨ The date, time, and location of the presentation

▨ The amount the speaker will be paid, if appropriate

▨ Details about travel arrangements

In a routine request, reveal the main idea early in the message. Provide the necessary supporting details concisely. Close in a polite, helpful manner. The following plan is used for routine requests.

Main Idea	State the request politely and directly and provide the reason for the request if appropriate.
Details	Provide the information required to obtain a complete response, such as times, dates, benefits to the receiver, and terms of payment.
Closing	End pleasantly and indicate the action the receiver should take.

Figure 8-2 on page 261 contains an example of an ineffectively written routine request. Figure 8-3 on page 262 contains a well-written routine request.

Figure 8-2 Ineffective Routine Request.

CARLOS SORIA
6308 Claremont Avenue
Cincinnati, OH 45242-1841

September 5, 20--

Ms. Abigail DePalma
1002 Sutton Road
Cincinnati, OH 45230-2640

Dear Ms. DePalma

Last night's *Gazette* included an article on your speech to a local investor's club. The article discussed the investment strategies you have employed in your highly successful career. It also contained some of your thoughts on mutual funds and state bonds. However, I would like some additional details—more than those printed in the newspaper.

Does not state the main idea of the message

Do you have any copies of your speech or handouts that were given to the club? I'm sure the information will be very interesting.

Does not provide details the receiver needs to respond

Sincerely

Carlos Soria

Carlos Soria

Figure 8-3 Effective Routine Request.

CARLOS SORIA
6308 Claremont Avenue
Cincinnati, OH 45242-1841

September 5, 20--

Ms. Abigail DePalma
1002 Sutton Road
Cincinnati, OH 45230-2640

Dear Ms. DePalma

Please send me a copy of the handouts you provided at your recent presentation to the Queen City Investment Club. If you have handouts on your investment strategies and your insights on mutual funds, please send those also.

Unfortunately, I had to miss the meeting and your presentation. I read the article in last night's *Gazette*. Although the article was very complimentary, it did not contain many details. Because several members have told me that I missed some very valuable information, I am making this request.

A self-addressed, stamped envelope is enclosed for your convenience in sending the materials to me. Thank you for being willing to share your expertise with others.

Sincerely

Carlos Soria

Carlos Soria

Enclosure

States the request clearly

Explains why the request is made

Makes it easy for the receiver to respond

Claims

A **claim** is a message that requests a refund, an exchange, or a discount on merchandise or services. Customers and clients use a direct order in claims to communicate to the receiver that they expect an adjustment—a positive settlement to a claim.

Main Idea	Ask for an adjustment
Details	Explain the problem or the reason for the request and identify the damage (if damage occurred)
Closing	End with a positive statement and indicate how to correct the situation

A claim message should have a positive but firm tone. Claims may be submitted using e-mail or an online form as well as by letter. Figure 8-4 shows a well-written claim message sent by e-mail.

Ethics

Be fair and honest in dealing with claims. Request an adjustment only when the seller is at fault. For example, saying that you did not receive part of an order when you did receive all the items would be unethical.

check point 2

1. What are two types of letters that contain neutral messages?

2. What is a claim?

Check your answers in Appendix C.

Figure 8-4 Claim Message

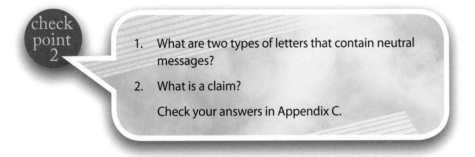

To:	Claims@OfficeSupplies.net
Cc:	
Subject:	Claim for Order No. 26834

Thank you for sending my recent order No. 26834 so promptly. There is a problem with the order that requires an adjustment.

The order was for 15 printer cartridges and several other items. All the items that arrived for the order were correct except the printer cartridges (item MBT 23976). The box contains only 12 cartridges—not the 15 cartridges as ordered.

Please send me the three missing printer cartridges (item MBT 23976). If the cartridges are not available, please credit my account for the cost of the three missing cartridges. If you have any questions about this claim, please call me at (513) 555-0129.

Mr. Ray Posner
Posner Associates
734 Elmore Street
Cincinnati, OH 45202

Writing Positive Messages

Key ▶ Point

A positive message is one that the receiver will be glad to read. Use direct order for positive messages.

A receiver will react favorably to a message that contains positive news. Examples of documents that contain positive messages are orders, positive responses to requests, friendship messages, and acknowledgments. For those messages, use direct order.

Main Idea	Say yes to the receiver
Details	Provide information the receiver needs to carry out specific instructions
Closing	End with a helpful, positive closing; if the sender sells goods or services, the closing may contain a soft sell

Orders

Key ▶ Point

An order is a message that requests the receiver to sell goods or services to the sender.

Companies usually place an order by using a form called a *purchase order*. Occasionally, a small company or an individual will use a letter or e-mail to place an order. "Please send me . . ." is the main idea of an **order**.

Provide complete supporting details to ensure that an order will be filled correctly and to avoid wasting time and money. For each item ordered, indicate:

▪ The stock number or catalog number

▪ A description (including the size and color if applicable)

▪ Quantity ordered, unit cost, and total cost

▪ Method of shipment

▪ Buyer's name and shipping address

▪ Method of payment

In an order, formatting the middle paragraph as a table can be helpful. Use direct order in this type of message.

Main Idea	Ask the receiver to fill the order
Details	Supply specific information needed by the receiver
Closing	End with a statement indicating the action the receiver should take

The letter shown in Figure 8-5 on page 265 is an ineffectively written order. The first paragraph does not state plainly that this is an order. The second paragraph does not state clearly what is being ordered and where the items should be sent. Figure 8-6 on page 266 illustrates a well-written order.

The first paragraph makes clear that the letter is an order. The items ordered are presented in a table. The sender provides complete details needed for shipping the items.

Figure 8-5 Ineffective Order Letter

Tamara Hindelworth
4509 Keynote Drive
Texarkana, AR 71854-9051

July 9, 20--

Whitlock Catalog Sales
708 Apple Street
Ogden, UT 84244-0076

Ladies and Gentlemen

I was looking at your recent sales catalog and became very excited when I saw that you had Winthrop drill sets for $99. I could use three sets of these drills as gifts for my sons.

> Does not state clearly that this is an order

Also, I saw that you carry Osborne dishes. I love the Morning Glory pattern. I want two sets of eight place settings each for $125 each. These dishes will be used as gifts for my daughters.

> Does not state clearly the items being ordered or where to send the items

I have enclosed a check for the total amount, which includes the $25 shipping fee. Thank you.

Sincerely

Tamara Hindelworth

Tamara Hindelworth

Enclosure

Figure 8-6 Effective Order Letter

Tamara Hindelworth
4509 Keynote Drive
Texarkana, AR 71854-9051

July 9, 20--

Whitlock Catalog Sales
708 Apple Street
Ogden, UT 84244-0076

Ladies and Gentlemen

Thank you for sending me your recent catalog. The sale prices are remarkable. Please send me the items listed below, which are from that catalog.

States the request and items ordered

Item No.	Description	Quantity	Price	Total
456-1	Winthrop Drill Set	3	$ 99.00	$ 297.00
9071	Osborne China Set (Morning Glory Pattern)	2	125.00	250.00
			Merchandise Subtotal	547.00
			Shipping	25.00
			Sales Tax	36.10
			Total Amount	$ 608.10

States where to send items and the method of payment

Please send the items to the address shown on the letterhead. A check for the total amount is enclosed.

If you have any questions about my order, please call me at (870) 555-0122.

Sincerely

Tamara Hindelworth

Tamara Hindelworth

Enclosure

Positive Responses to a Request

A positive response tells the receiver the sender is saying yes to a request. Direct order is used for positive responses. If the sender is a business, the closing may include a soft sell.

Main Idea	Give a positive response to the request.
Details	Provide necessary information so the receiver knows what the sender is offering and expects; also make necessary requests
Closing	End with a courteous, positive statement and possibly a reminder of any action the sender wants the receiver to take

Figure 8-7 on page 268 contains an example of an ineffectively written positive response. The letter does not use direct order and takes too long to give the positive response. Figure 8-8 on page 269 contains an example of a well-written positive response. Note that the supporting information confirms details, such as the date, time, and place, and makes a request of the receiver.

The following example contains a positive response to a credit request. However, it is ineffectively written because it uses indirect order—the main idea follows the supporting information.

> Thank you for your application for a charge account at Top-Notch Building Supplies. When we receive such applications, we always examine them very carefully.
>
> All our accounts have credit terms of 2/10, net/30. After examining your credit background, we find that you have an excellent credit history. As a result, we are giving you a $15,000 limit on your account.
>
> We hope to see you soon.

The following example is a well-written positive response to a credit request. The supporting information, which follows the main idea, includes a description of restrictions on the account and the payment terms. The closing includes an effectively written soft sell.

> Your Top-Notch Building Supplies charge account has been activated and is ready for your use. Thank you for your interest in our products.
>
> For new accounts, the terms are 2/10, net/30. Because your credit rating and references are excellent, the limit for your account is $15,000.
>
> Our most recent catalog is enclosed. If you have questions about our products, call 1-800-555-0199. Our trained salespeople will be happy to help you.

Key ▶ Point

Use direct order when writing a positive response to a request.

Ethics

Do not send a positive response to a request unless you are reasonably sure you can do what the response indicates. Failing to keep appointments or commitments without good cause is considered unethical.

Figure 8-7 Ineffective Positive Response

Computer Services

13450 Hillcrest Boulevard
Greenville, SC 29615-1345
864.555.0185   Fax 864.555.0186

October 18, 20--

Ms. Elizabeth Somers
4103 Walker Avenue
Greenville, SC 29605-4303

Dear Elizabeth:

We appreciate your coming to interview for the position of training director in the Office Services Department. There were many well-qualified individuals who applied for the position.

During your visit, we were impressed with your knowledge of the company and of the management techniques we use. Your positive attitude is very apparent. Thus, we would like to offer the position to you. Your starting date will be December 12 if you accept the offer. Your annual salary will be $48,600, and you will be paid biweekly.

Please let us know your decision in writing by November 15, 20--. If you have any questions, call me at 864.555.0185.

Sincerely,

Ray Park

Ray Park

rk

Does not use direct order

Takes too long to give the positive response

Figure 8-8 Effective Positive Response

Computer Services
13450 Hillcrest Boulevard
Greenville, SC 29615-1345
864.555.0185   Fax 864.555.0186

October 18, 20--

Ms. Elizabeth Somers
4103 Walker Avenue
Greenville, SC 29605-4303

Dear Elizabeth:

Congratulations! You have been selected for the position of training director in the Office Services Department.

Gives the positive response immediately

During your visit, we were impressed with your knowledge of the company and of the management techniques we use. If you accept our offer, your starting date will be December 12. Your annual salary will be $48,600, and you will be paid biweekly.

Provides supporting details

Please let us know your decision in writing by November 15, 20--. If you have any questions, call me at 864.555.0185.

States action to be taken

Sincerely,

Ray Park

Ray Park

rk

Goodwill Messages

A **goodwill message** can be an acknowledgment or a friendly message designed to build relationships. Effective goodwill messages help increase the receiver's positive feelings toward the sender. Goodwill messages may express congratulations, sympathy, welcome, or appreciation. They may also extend invitations or acknowledge an order or receipt of something. The expression of goodwill is the main idea of this type of message.

Friendship Messages

A friendship message says nonverbally to your receiver, "I want a positive relationship with you." This type of message may or may not need supporting details. For example, when expressing sympathy, details are not appropriate. Yet details in an invitation are important. The receiver needs to know who is invited, when and where the occasion will be held, and how to dress.

The following congratulatory message needs no supporting details.

Main Idea	Congratulations on your recent promotion to supervisor of Office Services.
Closing	You have served the company well in your previous jobs. I am confident you will be successful in your new position.

The following invitation includes the necessary supporting details.

Main Idea	You are invited to a small surprise party celebrating Arianne Hanson's promotion.
Details	The party will be held in the cafeteria at 4:30 p.m. on Tuesday, March 24.
Closing	Come and help us congratulate Arianne. RSVP by Friday, March 20, ext. 4456.

Diversity

Consider the culture and customs of the receiver when deciding how formal or informal a friendship message should be.

STOCKBYTE/GETTY IMAGES

Friendship messages, such as birthday cards, are sent to build goodwill.

Acknowledgments

An **acknowledgment** is a message that tells a sender that a message or item has been received. The objective of an acknowledgment is to maintain or build goodwill. An acknowledgment also may be used to inform the receiver that a request cannot be filled right away. These messages often are used to acknowledge orders and credit applications. The supporting information usually reveals the reasons for the delayed response. The goodwill closing may contain a soft sell, as shown below.

Key▶Point

An acknowledgment lets the sender know that a message or an item has been received.

Main Idea	Thank you for your order. We are pleased to have you as one of our customers.
Details	The demand for the earthenware plant holders has far exceeded our supply. Your order will be sent on May 15, the day we expect our shipment.
Closing	In the meantime, look over the enclosed flyer announcing our Spring Fling Sale. Place your order now to enjoy 50 percent savings on several popular items.

The checklist shown on the following page will help you compose effective neutral or positive messages.

check point 3

1. What are four types of letters that contain positive messages?

2. What is an acknowledgment?

Check your answers in Appendix C.

CHECKLIST FOR POSITIVE OR NEUTRAL MESSAGES

PLAN

❏ Have I identified the objective of the message?

❏ Have I determined the main idea?

❏ Have I selected supporting details?

❏ Have I adjusted the message for the reader?

WRITE

❏ Is the main idea presented in the first paragraph?

❏ Are the supporting details presented after the main idea?

❏ Is the closing courteous?

❏ Is a soft sell message in the closing appropriate?

EDIT AND PROOFREAD

❏ Is the language clear and concise?

❏ Are the details correct?

❏ Are the format, grammar, punctuation, and spelling correct?

❏ Is each paragraph an appropriate length?

❏ Does the message use the you approach?

❏ Have I proofread the document and corrected all errors?

Section 8.1 *Applications*

A. *Identify Message Types*

Indicate the type of message that might contain each of the following sentences.

1. I am returning the frying pan and asking for a refund.

2. Happy anniversary to you and your spouse.

3. Your application for a Sunshine credit card arrived today.

4. Please send me the following items from your catalog.

5. The refund you requested is enclosed.

B. *Plan, Organize, and Write a Positive Message*

You have been asked by Mr. Thomas Hawks to speak at a meeting of a local civic organization that promotes programs for youth. The meeting will be held on March 15, 20--, at 6:30 p.m. in your high school cafeteria. The audience will be the group members. The members include men and women of various ages and backgrounds. The purpose of your brief talk will be to give the group ideas for youth programs that might be conducted jointly with your school.

1. Plan a positive response message. Identify the objective and the main idea of the message. Write the supporting details you will need to include (making up any details that are needed).

2. Decide how the message should be organized—in direct order or indirect order.

3. Write the message.

   - Use block letter style and open punctuation.

   - Make up a name and address for the organization. Use this information in the letter address along with Mr. Hawks' name.

   - Include an opening paragraph, one middle paragraph to provide details, and a goodwill closing paragraph.

4. Edit the message to be sure it is courteous, correct, complete, concise, and clear.

5. Proofread the letter and correct all errors.

Negative Messages

Planning Negative Messages

After completing Section 8.2, you should be able to:

1. Plan negative messages.
2. Organize negative messages.
3. Write and edit negative messages.

Key▶Point

A negative message should be written in a positive tone that considers the receiver's point of view.

A negative message conveys news that will disappoint the receiver. Messages that deny requests, decline to supply information, refuse credit, or reject a proposal are examples of this type of message. Careful planning and organizing are required to give the bad news and yet maintain goodwill. Achieving this goal is challenging, especially when the receiver of the message has a different culture or customs than those of the writer. For example, people from some cultures may view a writer's use of concise writing as somewhat short and abrupt.

The tone of a negative message should reflect a sincere concern for the receiver's interests. The objective is to present the unfavorable news in a positive light; in a manner the receiver will view as fair; and, if possible, in the receiver's best interests. The writer should give reasons for the negative news before stating the negative news. This strategy helps prepare the reader to accept the negative news. Details supporting the negative news also help the reader to see the negative decision as a fair one. The steps for planning a negative message are shown in Figure 8-9.

Figure 8-9 Planning a Negative Message

PLANNING A NEGATIVE MESSAGE	
Identify the Objective	Give the negative news
Identify the Main Idea	State the negative news in a positive tone that reflects an interest in the reader
Determine the Supporting Details	Give logical reasons for the bad news Identify benefits to the reader, if possible Identify other details that may be helpful to the reader
Adjust the Content to the Receiver	Consider the reader's concerns and probable reaction to the bad news

Organizing Negative Messages

After identifying the content for a message, the writer should select the correct order for the information. Messages with negative news should be organized in the indirect order. Indirect order presents the reasons or details that explain the negative news before stating the news. The reasons are presented first to prepare the receiver for the bad news.

Key ▶ Point
Messages with negative news should be organized in the indirect order.

When using indirect order for a message that gives unfavorable news, follow these steps:

1. Begin with a neutral opening.
2. Explain the reasons for the negative news.
3. State or imply the negative news.
4. Close on a positive note; if possible, offer an alternative.

Neutral Opening

The objectives of the opening are to establish trust and to focus the receiver's attention on the topic of the message. To establish trust, begin with a **neutral opening**. Do not imply a positive or a negative response to the receiver. A neutral opening does not mislead the receiver into thinking the response is positive, nor does it discourage the receiver by revealing the negative news.

Key ▶ Point
The neutral opening in a message with negative news should not imply a positive or a negative response to the receiver.

In the opening, maintain a positive tone by avoiding the use of negative words or phrases, such as *unable, regret to tell you, a problem exists,* or *unfortunately*. Instead, use positive, neutral words and phrases, such as *appreciate, agree with you,* and *thank you*.

Avoid opening a message containing negative news by referring to the date of the receiver's previous message. The examples shown below on the left are not effective openings. They do not introduce the topic of the message. The examples on the right introduce the topic.

Ineffective Opening	**Effective Opening**
Thank you for your letter of August 10.	Your application for a charge account received our immediate attention.
We received your request dated May 5.	Your request for a refund has been reviewed by our Customer Service Department.
Your letter of June 12 has been received.	Your application for a loan has received our careful consideration.

A neutral opening in a letter builds trust and does not give bad news.

BLEND IMAGES/GETTY IMAGES

Assume that the sender is writing to refuse a request to serve on a committee. Ineffective and effective neutral openings for that situation follow.

Ineffective Openings	**Effective Openings**
Serving on such an important committee would be a real pleasure.	Thank you for asking me to serve on the Improvements Committee.
The Improvements Committee is an important committee on which to serve.	As you pointed out, the Improvements Committee is very important.
I wish I could serve on the Improvements Committee.	Thank you for the opportunity to serve on the Improvements Committee.

Reasons for the Negative News

The supporting details in a negative-news message provide the reasons for the negative news. This section may have one or two paragraphs, depending on the complexity of the message. Present the receiver with a logical explanation of the reasons for the negative news. Keep the message unified by focusing on one or two main reasons.

If possible, tell how the reasons will benefit the receiver. Do not state company policy as the reason for denying a request. Although citing company policy may be appropriate in some cases, always explain the reasons for

Ethics

Be tactful and honest in your response to a request. Making up reasons why you cannot grant a request is unethical.

the policy. If the message does not explain reasons for the company policy, the goodwill between a company and its customers may be damaged.

In the following examples, the reasons on the left are company-oriented rather than receiver-oriented. The reasons on the right are you-oriented.

Ineffectively Written Reasons	**Well-Written Reasons**
We would like to repair your cell phone, but company policy forbids it.	Providing free repair of cell phones out of warranty would add greatly to the retail prices of our phones. For example . . .
If we replaced your sprinkler or refunded your money, we would be doing the work of the shipping company. Write to the shipping company for a refund of your money. It has insurance to cover its costs.	We choose the company that ships our merchandise carefully. This shipper guarantees its service, yet keeps costs low. Because the product was damaged during shipping, you will need to contact the shipping company to request a replacement or refund.

The Negative News Itself

After learning the reasons for the negative news, the receiver should be mentally prepared to receive the actual refusal or other bad news. If the reasons are logical, the reader will expect the negative news. In some cases, it may be appropriate to soften the negative message by implying the negative news

Diversity

Use care when writing to a receiver whose first language is not English. The reader may not understand negative news that is only implied and not stated directly.

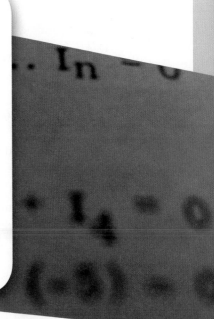

READING SKILLS

Facts or Opinions

People often read to gain information to help them solve problems or make decisions. In such cases, being able to tell facts from opinions in the material you read is very important. **Facts** are statements that can be proved to be true or correct. **Opinions** are views or conclusions reached by someone. Generally, facts are more valuable for solving problems or making decisions. However, opinions can be helpful when they come from a person who is trained or has experience on the subject.

When you read, be aware that the material may contain both facts and opinions. Consider the source of the information to help you judge its value. Open the *Word* file *CH08 Reading* from the student data files. Follow the directions given in the file to complete the exercise about facts and opinions.

rather than stating it directly. Convey the message quickly, using positive language if possible.

To imply the bad news and to avoid using words with a negative tone, use an *if* clause as shown in the example below. Use the passive voice or focus on "what you can do" rather than "what you cannot do."

If you must use negative language, avoid using personal pronouns—*I, me, my, mine, we, our, ours, us, you, your,* and *yours.* Those personal pronouns combined with negative language can offend the receiver.

In the following examples, the responses on the left are ineffectively written. The responses on the right are well written.

Ineffectively Written "No's"	Well-Written "No's"
I cannot send your order today.	If I could, I would send your order today. Your order will be sent as soon as we receive the shipment from our supplier.
Because your camera is no longer under warranty, I cannot grant your request for a replacement.	If your camera were still under warranty, it would be replaced. Only cameras under warranty are replaced free of charge.

The Closing

The closing of a message containing negative news should be courteous and helpful. The purpose of the closing is to maintain or rebuild goodwill. After presenting or implying the negative news, change the emphasis and close on a positive note.

To maintain a positive tone, do not mention or remind the receiver of the negative news again. Do not apologize because you cannot accommodate the receiver. If a mistake has not been made, an apology is inappropriate. If you did make a mistake, you owe the receiver an apology. However, place the apology in the middle paragraphs—not in the closing.

The closing should have a sincere tone. Avoid overused closings such as *If you have any questions, please don't hesitate to call.* Use a similar statement but with a positive tone: *If you have any questions, please call.* Avoid using conditional words such as *hope, think,* and *maybe.*

Offer the receiver another option. Most problem situations have more than one solution. Presenting another option shifts the emphasis from the negative news to a positive solution. If another option is not available at the present, mention an option that may be available in the future. The following example provides such as option.

You may apply for the loan again at a later date when you have improved your credit score.

The following examples illustrate both ineffectively written and well-written closings.

Ineffectively Written Closings

Even though we cannot fill your order, I have enclosed our newest catalog.

I am sorry that I cannot fill your order, but I have enclosed our newest catalog.

Even though I cannot fill your order, if there is anything else I can do, please let me know.

Well-Written Closing

Because Part No. 1403 is no longer being manufactured, part No.1402 is being used as a substitute. The substitute part is only $15 and works just as well as Part No. 1403. If you would like to order Part No. 1402, call me at 1-800-555-0155.

Your order will be shipped the day you place your order.

If the receiver is a customer, you may close the message with a soft sell by mentioning a related product, a discount, or some other relevant item that would interest the receiver. In this situation, your job is to get the customer to come into the store or to use your services again.

Key ▶ Point

An effective letter can deliver bad news and include a closing designed to get the customer to come into the store or to use your services again.

Ineffectively Written Closings

Some of our materials are being offered at greatly reduced prices. Come in and see them soon.

We appreciate your business. Come in and see us soon.

Our lowest sale prices of the year will be in effect all next week.

Well-Written Closing

Our latest sales brochure is enclosed. Note that some of our materials are reduced by as much as 50 percent. Come in and see them soon.

Join us on November 12 when three local authors will be signing their new books. All books by these authors will be reduced 25 percent.

Our Fall Fix It Sale will be from October 31 through November 6. All merchandise for home repair will be reduced 25 percent. All items for the lawn and garden will be reduced 20 percent. Customers will receive a free package of tulip bulbs for fall planting with a purchase of $20 or more.

check point 4

1. Give three examples of negative messages.

2. What steps should you follow when using indirect order for a negative message?

Check your answers in Appendix C.

Writing Negative Messages

Many situations call for messages that contain negative news. Some messages containing negative news need special attention. They are messages that deny a request and messages that refuse credit.

Denying a Request

In a **request denial**, you are saying *no* to another person's request. The reasons for declining a request are an important aspect of this type of message. The success of the message depends on whether the receiver judges the reasons to be valid. Figure 8-10 on page 281 illustrates an ineffectively written message that declines a request. Figure 8-11 on page 282 illustrates a well-written message that declines a request.

Refusing Credit

A **credit refusal** is a message that denies credit to an applicant. Credit may be refused for several reasons. The credit application may contain incomplete details or lack credit references. The applicant's employment record may show a frequent change of jobs. The applicant may already be in debt, be behind on payments, or have insufficient income to warrant a loan.

If credit must be refused, the receiver has a right to know why. The sender should explain the reasons tactfully. The goal is to refuse credit but maintain the person as a customer. An example of the body of a well-written message that denies credit is shown below.

> Thank you for your order for Stonecut Flooring. You have selected a quality product that is extremely durable.
>
> Your credit application has been reviewed. Based on your income and existing debts, you do not qualify for a credit purchase with our company at this time. Please let us know if you would like to place a cash order instead.
>
> In addition to flooring, we have many other quality products for your home at low discounted prices. As a cash customer, you will receive quality merchandise, courtesy, and low prices.

Notice that the message above has a neutral opening and uses positive language. It is written in indirect order, giving the reason for the negative news before the negative news is stated. The customer is offered an alternative—placing a cash order. The checklist on page 284 will help you compose effective messages that contain negative news.

Figure 8-10 Ineffective Negative Message

Lemmon's Electronics
906 Comet Street
Billings, MT 59105-0906
406-555-0185   Fax 406-555-0186

April 26, 20--

Mr. Eugene Anderson
3692 Stoner Point
Billings, MT 59105-3692

Dear Mr. Anderson

I received your request for a refund of $59.58 for a DVD player you bought at our recent clearance sale. I am sorry, but your request cannot be granted.

> Opening should not include a negative response

When we hold a clearance sale, signs are posted all over the store that clearly state that all sales are final. If the DVD does not function properly, please bring it to the store for a replacement.

Mr. Anderson, I am sorry for the misunderstanding. Please come in and see us again. We are having a big sale next week.

> Closing should not include an apology

Sincerely yours

Clayton Lemmon

Clayton Lemmon
Manager

Figure 8-11 Effective Negative Message

Lemmon's Electronics

906 Comet Street
Billings, MT 59105-0906
406-555-0185   Fax 406-555-0186

April 26, 20--

Mr. Eugene Anderson
3692 Stoner Point
Billings, MT 59105-3692

Dear Mr. Anderson

Opening is neutral

Your request for a refund of $59.58 for a DVD player was brought to my attention. You bought an excellent product when you purchased the M-100.

Provides reasons for the negative news and an alternate solution

When items are sold at clearance prices, they may be returned only if they are defective. This allows us to offer products to our customers at greatly reduced prices. During clearance sales, signs are posted many places in the store, stating that all sales are final. However, if the DVD does not function properly, please bring it to the store for a replacement.

Closing includes a soft sell and an incentive for the customer to return

Mr. Anderson, a certificate for 25 percent off your next purchase at Lemmon's is enclosed. Presently, we are having a sale on computers. Please come in and use your certificate to take advantage of great savings.

Sincerely yours

Clayton Lemmon

Clayton Lemmon
Manager

Writing Messages with Both Positive and Negative News

Once in a while, you may have to write a message that contains both positive and negative news. The steps for planning that type of message are the same as for other messages. However, in these situations, you will have two main ideas instead of just one—the positive news is the first idea, and the negative news is the second. When organizing these messages, use indirect order with the good news as the opening. In the following example, the positive news is used as the opening of a bad-news message. The positive news is followed by the reasons for the bad news and the bad news itself.

Key ▶ Point

In a letter that has both positive and negative news, present the positive news first.

Good-News or Neutral Beginning	Thank you for your order of four Kiley Fisher CDs and three Viewmaster CDs. The four Kiley Fisher CDs are being shipped to you today.
Reasons for the Bad News	The demand for the Viewmaster CDs has far exceeded our expectations. As a result, these CDs are presently out of stock.
The Bad News	However, a new shipment will arrive on Thursday of this week. Your Viewmaster CDs will be mailed to you the day they arrive.
Soft Sell	A catalog of our new arrivals is enclosed. Some CDs are as much as 50 percent below retail prices. Find those you would like and send us your order soon.

check point 5

1. What are two types of letters that contain negative news?

2. How should a message that contains both positive and negative news be organized?

Check your answers in Appendix C.

CHECKLIST FOR NEGATIVE MESSAGES

PLAN

❑ Have I identified the objective of the message?

❑ Have I determined the main idea?

❑ Have I selected supporting details?

❑ Have I adjusted the message for the reader?

WRITE

❑ Is the opening neutral? Does it introduce the topic of the message?

❑ Does the supporting information focus on one or two receiver-oriented reasons for the negative message?

❑ Have I used positive language? Is the closing courteous?

❑ Have I used an if clause or passive voice if possible?

❑ Have I told the receiver what could be done rather than what could not be done?

❑ Have I avoided using personal pronouns and negative words?

❑ Is the closing helpful and courteous?

❑ Does the closing offer an alternative, contain no apology, and avoid reminders of the negative message?

EDIT AND PROOFREAD

❑ Is the language clear and concise?

❑ Are the details correct?

❑ Are the format, grammar, punctuation, and spelling correct?

❑ Is each paragraph an appropriate length?

❑ Have I proofread the document and corrected all errors?

Section 8.2 *Applications*

A. *Identify Message Types*

Indicate the type of message that might contain each of the following sentences.

1. My schedule does not allow me to accept any speaking engagements for the next three months.

2. Our research shows that you have two outstanding loans, and payments on both loans are past due.

3. All our grant money for the current year has been designated for other projects.

4. Since you purchased the item more than 30 days ago, the time for requesting a refund has passed.

B. *Plan, Organize, and Write a Negative Message*

Mayfield Printing Service prepared and printed a resume for Mr. Luther Donaldson. The resume was printed exactly as Mr. Donaldson specified. He proofread the resume. However, he overlooked a mistake in the spelling of a previous employer's name. The resume was printed with the mistake. After receiving the resumes, Mr. Donaldson has asked for a refund. As manager of Mayfield Printing Service, write a message to Mr. Donaldson denying his request.

1. Plan a negative response message. Identify the objective and the main idea of the message. Write the supporting details you will need to include (making up any details that are needed).

2. Decide how the message should be organized—in direct order or indirect order.

3. Write the message.

   - Create a letterhead for the company, making up an address and phone number.

   - Create a letterhead using your name and address in the document header.

   - Use block letter style and open punctuation.

   - Mr. Donaldson's address is 1607 North Bernard Avenue, Bartlesville, OK 74006-0551.

4. Edit the message to be sure it is courteous, correct, complete, concise, and clear.

5. Proofread the letter and correct all errors.

Persuasive Messages

Planning Persuasive Messages

A **persuasive message** tries to convince the reader to take an action. In a work setting, people often try to persuade other people to do things. A team leader tries to persuade his or her team members to work overtime on a special project. One employee tries to persuade other employees to use a new form. A salesperson tries to persuade customers to place orders. The Collections Department tries to persuade customers to pay their bills. Much of this persuasion occurs in letters, memos, messages, and proposals.

To persuade people to do something, you must be able to identify a reason for them to do it. People will act to meet their own needs, so you must show your readers they have a need to do what you want them to do. That need must be theirs, not yours. For example, if you ask other employees to fill out a new form because it will make your job easier, they are unlikely to be persuaded. However, if you show them how using the form will make their jobs easier, they will be more willing to do as you ask. Needs vary among people; but those needs are often linked to achievement, recognition, comfort, convenience, physical well-being, or money. When planning a persuasive message, analyze the audience to determine their needs. Relate the action you want readers to take (or not take) to those needs.

Key ▶ Point

An effective persuasive message addresses needs of the reader.

The steps for planning a persuasive message are applied in the example shown in Figure 8-12.

Figure 8-12 Planning a Persuasive Message

PLANNING A PERSUASIVE MESSAGE	
Identify the Objective	Get the receiver to take an action or refrain from taking an action
Identify the Main Idea	Show that the requested action will benefit the receiver
Determine the Supporting Details	Give information that will convince the receiver to do as you request
Adjust the Content to the Receiver	Consider the reader's concerns, needs, and probable reaction to the request

check point 6

1. Give an example of a persuasive message.

2. What is the purpose of the supporting details in a persuasive message?

Check your answers in Appendix C.

Organizing Persuasive Messages

Like negative messages, most persuasive messages are organized in an indirect order. That means that you must describe the need convincingly before making your request. In that way, you prepare the reader for the main message before presenting it. After readers understand the need, they are more likely to agree to the solution—acting as you request. Some messages, such as urgent collection messages, are written in direct order.

To organize a persuasive message in indirect order, follow these steps:

1. Gain the reader's attention.

2. Show the reader that he or she has a need or will benefit from fulfilling the request.

3. Explain your solution to that need—in other words, your request.

4. Present the supporting information.

5. Ask for a specific action.

Figure 8-13 on page 288 shows what can happen if these steps are ignored. Figure 8-14 on page 289 shows how much more persuasive a message can be when the writer follows the steps.

Gain the Reader's Attention

Introduce the topic of your message in an interesting and relevant way. Remember that the goal is to capture your reader's interest, not to make the request. Here are some possible approaches:

- Describe a problem related to your request that the reader has experienced or mentioned recently. For example, perhaps your supervisor has noted that your department is behind in processing orders.

- Remind the reader of a goal related to your request. For example, your department has set a goal of calling 80 potential customers a day.

- Present a "what if" situation related to your request. For example: What if there was a no-cost way to cut the number of customer complaints in half?

- Tell your coworkers that you know of an opportunity they will not want to miss.

Key ▶ Point

Most persuasive messages should be organized in indirect order.

Key ▶ Point

The first paragraph of a persuasive message should introduce the topic. It should not make a request.

Figure 8-13 Ineffective Persuasive Memo

TO: Belinda Lopez, Human Resources Director

FROM: Rita James, Customer Service Supervisor

DATE: November 13, 20--

SUBJECT: Additional Staff

Does not use indirect order ·····

Does not present supporting details ·····

In spite of the company's hiring freeze, my department needs additional staff immediately. We are ten days behind with our correspondence, and we are getting further behind every day. Although I have tried everything I know to alleviate the situation, I am convinced there is no hope of solving this problem with our present staff. In view of these circumstances, please consider hiring more staff for this department.

Figure 8-14 Effective Persuasive Memo

TO: Belinda Lopez, Human Resources Director

FROM: Rita James, Customer Service Supervisor

DATE: November 13, 20--

SUBJECT: Additional Staff

At our last staff meeting, you mentioned that the Customer Service Department is getting behind in answering inquires and complaints. I share your concern because we are now ten days behind. Our goal is to answer customer messages within four days; we are not meeting that goal.

Opening paragraph gains the reader's attention

During the past three months, customer messages have increased 115 percent. In large part, this increase is due to questions about our latest software release. In the same period, a worker from our department left the company. We have only five full-time employees in the department. Although all of us have been working overtime, we are getting further behind.

Explains the need from the reader's point of view

If we hired another full-time staff member, I estimate that we would be only six days behind by the end of the first month. By the end of the second month, we would be meeting our goal and no longer be behind on answering messages. If we also hired a temporary worker for at least one month, we could get back on schedule even sooner.

Explains the solution

I realize that the company has a freeze on hiring. However, I think we could hire both a full-time worker and a temporary worker for the same salary that was being paid to our former staff member. The money spent would be well worth the goodwill we would create by answering customer messages promptly. A prompt response to inquiries encourages customers to order from us again.

Provides supporting details

Will you meet with me on November 18 to discuss my request? The sooner we hire additional staff, the sooner we can deliver the prompt service our customers expect.

Asks for specific action

Diversity

Understanding the culture and customs of the reader is important when trying to establish a need.

Ethics

Be honest and give complete information when describing the solution you can provide.

Key▶Point

Obstacles typically involve time, money, or the reader's resistance to change.

Show a Need

Explain the need from the reader's point of view. For example, if you are writing a memo to your supervisor, you might point out an increase in customer complaints, a backlog in the Service Department, the errors that result from the current method of entering orders, or the high cost of repairing the copier during the past three months. Because the supervisor is responsible for the efficient operation of your department, he or she has an interest in solving those problems.

Explain Your Solution

Now that your reader understands the need, explain how he or she can meet that need—by doing as you request. For example, you might suggest a small product change to reduce customer complaints. Perhaps you could recommend a simpler procedure to allow staff to catch up with a backlog.

Do your homework before writing this part of your persuasive message. The more details you include, the easier it is for readers to visualize your solution and the more likely they are to agree to it. For example, you would describe the product change in as much detail as your readers need. You would outline the new procedure step-by-step.

If you are requesting a purchase, such as a new copier, suggest specific models and provide approximate rental or purchase costs. You might even attach brochures for the two copier models that best meet your department's needs. Make it easy for the reader to grant your request.

Present Supporting Details

To encourage readers to agree to your request, you must do two things: address any obvious obstacles and emphasize your primary appeal—the benefit that will appeal most to the reader.

Address Obstacles

An **obstacle** is something that hinders or prevents progress or achieving a goal. The most common obstacles or objections involve a resistance to change and a lack of time, energy, and/or money. Assume that you are asking other staff members to fill out new forms. You must overcome their resistance to change and their concern about the time required to complete the forms. You might point out that the new forms will greatly reduce the current errors that consume so much of the employees' time. If you are suggesting that your department needs a new copier, point out how the purchase will eliminate the high repair costs for the old copier. If you are suggesting a new procedure, explain how the procedure will save time or money or decrease costs.

In a persuasive message, the writer must overcome resistance to change.

Emphasize the Primary Appeal

You must identify the benefits that match the values and concerns of your readers. Think of benefits to the readers personally, not just to the company. Suppose your request is to make a small product change. The benefits might include increased sales and fewer customer complaints. What if you are asking for a new copier? The benefits, in addition to saving money on repairs, might include having reliable equipment and improving staff morale.

From all of the possible benefits, determine the primary appeal. The **primary appeal** is the most convincing point in a persuasive message. That is the appeal that is most likely to attract readers' attention and motivate them to act. Perhaps you are trying to convince a coworker to serve on a committee. The primary appeal for one person might be the opportunity to influence office policies in general. The primary appeal for another coworker might be the opportunity to work toward a certain goal, such as having flexible working hours.

Do not assume that readers will automatically recognize the benefits of doing as you request. Point out the benefits and help your readers visualize them in their own lives. Depending on the values and needs of your readers, you might provide research findings that support your request. You might also mention other departments or other companies that have made the same change and benefited from it. Try to anticipate any objections the readers will have. Point out benefits that will counter the objections. Understanding benefits will make readers more likely to grant your request.

Key▶Point

The primary appeal is the one that is most likely to attract readers' attention and motivate them to act.

Ask for a Specific Action

Writers sometimes end their persuasive messages and memos with vaguely hopeful sentences such as these:

> I hope you will give my request serious consideration.
>
> Please let me know if you have any questions about my request.

Key▶Point

The closing of a persuasive message should clearly indicate the action the reader must take to approve or grant the request.

Those writers are not asking for a specific response. They are likely to get no response at all. The closing of a persuasive message should clearly indicate the action the reader must take to approve or grant the request. The action suggested should be easy to do, such as initialing the memo and returning it to you.

If your request is major or expensive, you might end by asking for an appointment to talk about it. You might ask for your request to be discussed at the department's weekly meeting. You could also tell the reader that you will call in two days to discuss your request.

If possible, encourage the reader to act promptly by including a deadline of some kind. Explain how quickly approving your request will save time and/or money. For example, you might mention that the copier you recommend is on sale. Purchasing it by the end of the month will reduce the cost by 10 percent. You could also point out that as soon as the new forms are created and distributed, the number of errors will begin to drop.

check point 7

1. In what order are most persuasive messages organized?

2. What steps should you take to organize a persuasive message?

Check your answers in Appendix C.

Writing Persuasive Messages

Persuasive requests are common in the business environment. They might be sent from one employee to another or from an employee to a customer or supplier. Sales messages and collection messages are two special kinds of persuasive messages.

Sales Messages

Key▶Point

A sales message should establish a need and show how a product or service can meet that need.

A **sales message** tries to persuade a potential customer to purchase a product or service. Like other persuasive messages, it involves gaining the reader's attention. The message should establish a need and show how a product or service will meet that need. Supporting details and an easy way for the reader to respond should also be included. A sales message might appeal to readers' senses by describing how something looks, sounds, feels, smells, or tastes. This appeal can range from the warm, cinnamon smell of apple pie to the silky feel of a new blouse. Figure 8-15 on page 294 shows an effective sales message.

Collection Messages

The purpose of a **collection message** is to persuade a customer to pay a past-due bill. Collection messages have four stages as listed below.

1. The reminder stage
2. The strong reminder stage
3. The discussion stage
4. The urgency stage

The reminder message assumes that the customer has simply forgotten to make a payment. It is written in indirect order, as shown in the following message.

Key ▶ Point

Collection messages proceed through four stages from a routine reminder to a strong demand for payment.

> Dear Customer
>
> Thank you for your prompt payments during all of 2006. A copy of your January 2007 statement is enclosed.
>
> Did you overlook this payment, which was due February 10? An addressed, postage-paid envelope is enclosed for your convenience in sending this payment.
>
> Thank you for your attention to this matter.

A strong reminder is sent when the customer has not responded to the first reminder. This collection message is serious and firm, as shown in the following example.

> Dear Customer
>
> Thank you for your prompt payments during all of 2006. A copy of your January 2007 statement is enclosed.
>
> As you can see, your February 10 payment is overdue. By sending a check for $700, you will bring your account up to date and preserve your credit rating. A postage-paid return envelope is enclosed.
>
> Please send your payment today to clear your account.

Figure 8-15 Effective Sales Message

Comfy Feet Inc.
798 Newell Street
Salt Lake City, UT 84119-2450
801-555-0126   Fax 801-555-0127

May 3, 20--

Ms. Lu Wang
12 Merryweather Lane
Eureka, KS 67045-7112

Dear Ms. Wang

Gains attention and establishes a need ...... On your feet for eight hours or more a day, but not foot-weary? Is that how you would like to feel at the end of your workday?

Explains the solution ...... Through extensive research and testing, a new kind of shoe has been developed with you in mind. These comfortable, attractive shoes have shock-absorbing features that cushion and protect your feet all day. More than 80 percent of doctors and nurses who tried our shoes wanted to keep them! Many people wanted to order a pair for a friend or relative.

Provides supporting details ...... As an introductory offer, these quality leather shoes are available for only $79.95 a pair. As you can see from the enclosed brochure, they come in styles and colors to please everyone.

Asks for specific action ...... To place your order, call 1-800-555-0100 or return the enclosed, postage-paid order form by mail. You will be slipping into your new shoes within a week and enjoying new freedom from tired feet!

Sincerely

Todd Roseman

Todd Roseman, Vice President

ch

Enclosures

The purpose of the discussion-stage collection message is to obtain full payment or partial payment as a temporary measure. An explanation of why the customer has not made the appropriate payment is also sought. This message is organized in an indirect way as a last attempt to persuade the customer to discuss the problem.

Key ▶ Point

The discussion-stage collection message is a last attempt to persuade the customer to discuss the problem.

Dear Customer

Your home loan with First Western Bank has been beneficial to both of us. In the past, your payments have been prompt and consistent. In fact, you have been one of our best customers.

Two months have passed, however, since your last payment. Although we have sent you two reminders, we have not received a reply. Is there some reason why you cannot make a payment?

You can preserve your credit rating in one of these ways:

- Make your past-due payments totaling $1,400 within ten days.

- Send one payment of $700 immediately and send the other payment by March 30.

- Call within one week to let us know why you have missed your last two payments and to explain your plans for correcting the situation.

Please respond so that this matter can be resolved.

The purpose of the urgency-stage collection message is to obtain payment. The message also tells the customer what will happen if payment is not made immediately. In this message, use direct order and a firm tone. Earlier reminder messages may have been signed by someone in the Accounting Department. The urgency-stage collection letter may be signed by a manager or owner of a business to stress the importance of the letter.

Key ▶ Point

The urgency-stage message tells the customer what will happen if payment is not made.

Dear Customer

Although we have sent you three reminders, your account with us is still past due. You have not communicated with us to tell us why you are unable to make the payments.

The enclosed statement shows the amount now due, $2,100. Unless we receive full payment by April 30, your account will be turned over to the Emerson Credit Agency, a collection company.

To prevent this negative situation, send us your full payment immediately.

Chain Letters

One type of persuasive message is the chain letter. Like other persuasive messages, a chain letter tries to convince the receiver to take some action. The request typically involves sending the letter or e-mail message to several other people. It may also ask the receiver to send the writer money. The idea is that other people (to whom the receiver writes) will send money and pass the letter on to others. The money the sender hopes to receive is the incentive for giving money to the original writer and forwarding the letter to others.

Chain letters that are sent by U.S. Mail are illegal if they request money or other items of value.[1] Chain letters that are sent over the Internet may also be illegal if they require that money be sent by U.S. Mail. Do not create, send, or forward chain letters that request money or items of value. To do so is unethical and, depending on the circumstances, is likely to be illegal. If you receive a chain letter that asks for money or items of value, give the letter to your local postmaster. To learn more about chain letters, visit the U.S. Postal Inspection Service Web site.

check point 8

1. What is the purpose of a sales message?

2. What is the purpose of a collection message?

3. What are the four stages of collection messages?

Check your answers in Appendix C.

Planning Proposals

Key▶Point

A proposal may be written to address needs within a company or to address needs of clients.

Proposals are another type of persuasive writing. A **proposal** is a formal document that describes a problem or need and recommends a solution. The writer establishes a need and tries to convince the reader to meet that

---

[1] "Chain Letters," U.S. Postal Inspection Service, accessed May 8, 2008, available from http://www.usps.com/postalinspectors/fraud/chainlet.htm.

need by taking a specific action. Proposals may be internal, such as from an employee to a supervisor. Proposals may also be external, such as from a consulting firm to a company.

Sometimes a company asks for proposals to meet a need. Those proposals are solicited. The company sends out a **request for proposal (RFP)** that outlines what it needs. For example, a company might ask suppliers to provide proposals giving the price, delivery time, quality, and other details for goods or services. The company then uses the proposals to select a company from which to buy the goods or services.

Other proposals are unsolicited. The receiver has not requested the proposal. The writer of an unsolicited proposal must work hard to establish a need for the proposed action. For example, a researcher might write a proposal to request money from a company. The money will be used to investigate a specific problem related to the company's products.

Key ▶ Point

An unsolicited proposal must clearly establish a need for the proposed action.

An effective proposal clearly states the benefits for the receiver. If the proposal is solicited, the receiver already sees the need. However, you must present your solution to that need. For example, you may be able to provide lower costs or higher quality than another company can provide.

Organizing and Writing Proposals

The organization and content of a proposal will vary depending on what you are proposing. Most, but not all, proposals contain the following elements.

1. **Introduction.** Briefly summarize what you are proposing, what your proposal will accomplish, and what types of information are included in your proposal. Immediately begin to stress the benefits to the receiver.

Key ▶ Point

The introduction of a proposal should briefly describe the need or problem and summarize the proposed solution.

2. **Background.** In this optional section, you might describe the events that led to the current situation, such as changes in the company structure or in a product line.

3. **Need.** From the receiver's point of view, describe the problem that your proposal will solve or the need it will meet.

4. **Scope of project.** Outline your plan or solution to meet the need.

5. **Action plan.** List the steps that must be taken to carry out your proposal.

6. **Schedule.** Discuss the amount of time needed to complete the project and the deadline for each step in the action plan.

7. **Cost.** Explain the proposal's total cost and link the cost to the benefits the reader will receive.

8. **Qualifications.** Describe your own qualifications (if you will carry out the proposal personally) or those of your company.

9. **Call for action.** Just as in a persuasive message, end with a specific request for the receiver to do something, such as scheduling a meeting to discuss your proposal.

10. **Supporting information.** Include any necessary supporting information, such as the names of references, in an appendix.

An RFP usually lists the information that must be included in a solicited proposal. Follow the RFP closely. If you do not, the proposal may be eliminated because of the way you presented the information. If your proposal is unsolicited, use subheadings to make the document inviting to read and easy to skim, as shown in Figure 8-16 on pages 299 and 300.

Use the checklist shown on page 301 to help you write convincing persuasive letters, memos, reports, e-mails, and proposals.

Key▶Point

A solicited proposal should provide all the information requested in the RFP.

check point 9

1. What is a proposal?

2. What elements are included in most proposals?

Check your answers in Appendix C.

An effective proposal clearly states the benefits for the receiver.

DIGITAL VISION/GETTY IMAGES

Figure 8-16 Solicited Proposal in Letter Form

INFO FIND

100 Broadmoore Way
Omaha, NE 68112-1844
402-555-0150   Fax 402-555-0157

July 12, 20--

Ms. Leslie Carroll
Director of Consumer Affairs
The Foodworks Market
600 Dunstable Highway
Omaha, NE 68111-6409

Dear Ms. Carroll

As you requested, here is our proposal for conducting an Internet survey. The survey is to determine consumer interest in the posting of nutritional information in your store's produce area. The objective of the project is to provide the research you need to decide whether to post this information. This proposal describes the need for and the scope of the project. It also outlines the action plan we would carry out to obtain the customer feedback that will help you make your decision.

Background
Consumers are concerned about their health. Many people want to use more fresh fruits and vegetables in the meals they prepare at home. However, because produce is not packaged in containers, consumers cannot check the labels for nutritional value. Thus, they have no source of nutritional information at the point of sale.

Need
Your store has positioned itself as the market leader in customer service. To maintain that position, you want to investigate whether posting detailed nutritional information in the produce area would be of value to customers.

Scope of Project
To learn what adult consumers think about the posting of nutritional information, we propose to plan and conduct a comprehensive survey. It would include the following:

- Identifying people to interview
- Preparing a form for an Internet survey
- Processing completed surveys and preparing a final report for Foodworks' management

To get a balanced sampling, we recommend surveying at least 300 adults. We will need the names and addresses of 900 adults so we can be assured of 300 responses.

Figure 8-16 Solicited Proposal Continued

Ms. Leslie Carroll
July 12, 20--
Page 2

Action Plan
After you approve the project, Info Find will require about three working days to prepare, test, and revise the form for the survey. After testing the survey on 25 contacts and making any necessary changes, we will obtain 300 or more completed surveys. One week after obtaining the completed surveys, we will provide an analysis of the results and a written summary of our findings and recommendations.

Schedule
We can begin this project within a week of receiving your approval. You will receive our analysis and summary about three weeks after we begin.

Cost
Our price for planning, completing, and analyzing the survey is $10,000.

Info Find has been privileged to conduct more than a dozen surveys for Foodworks during the past three years. As always, we welcome the opportunity to help you identify and meet the needs of your customers. Thank you for asking us to submit this bid.

Will you meet with us sometime during the next two weeks to discuss any questions you may have? Please call Beth at 402-555-0150 to set up a time that is convenient for you.

Sincerely

Lawrence Sweeney

Lawrence Sweeney
Vice President of Research

dm

CHECKLIST FOR PERSUASIVE MESSAGES

PLAN

❏ Have I identified the objective of the message?

❏ Have I determined the main idea?

❏ Have I selected supporting details?

❏ Have I considered my receiver's needs and determined the primary appeal of the message?

WRITE

❏ Does the opening gain the receiver's attention and introduce the topic?

❏ Is my solution to the need clear, logical, and practical?

❏ Did I focus on the identified primary appeal?

❏ For a proposal, have I included all of the appropriate components?

EDIT AND PROOFREAD

❏ Is the language clear and concise?

❏ Are the details correct?

❏ Are the format, grammar, punctuation, and spelling correct?

❏ Have I proofread the document and corrected all errors?

Section 8.3 *Applications*

A. *Identify Message Order*

Indicate whether these sentences from persuasive messages should be in an opening paragraph, a middle paragraph (supporting information), or a closing paragraph.

1. At the last manager's meeting, you mentioned that your department was overstaffed.

2. Visit our Web site at www.smithcoshoes.com and order your comfortable air-float work shoes today.

3. Your account is overdue in the amount of $2,359.86.

4. This manufacturing process will allow you to make the product in half the time and at a reasonable cost.

5. Use the enclosed coupon to save 25 percent on your next purchase.

B. *Write a Persuasive E-mail*

1. Assume that you work for a large shoe manufacturer. Write an e-mail to your coworkers, persuading them to join a new sports team or club that is being organized. (You choose the sport or club.)

2. Use an e-mail address provided by your instructor (or save the message as a draft and do not send it.)

3. Make sure you mention benefits that will appeal to the wide range of people who work at your company.

4. Tell the readers what you want them to do. Request that they send you a reply within five days stating whether or not they want to play on the sports team or join the club.

5. Edit the message to be sure it is courteous, correct, complete, concise, and clear.

6. Proofread the message and correct all errors.

Chapter *Summary*

8.1 Neutral or Positive Messages

- To plan a neutral or positive message, identify the objective, identify the main idea, determine the supporting details, and adjust the content to the receiver.

- Messages with positive or neutral news should be organized in direct order. The main idea is presented first, followed by the supporting details and the closing.

- Examples of documents that contain positive messages are orders, positive responses to requests, friendship messages, and acknowledgments.

8.2 Negative Messages

- A negative message conveys news that will disappoint the receiver.

- Messages with negative news should be organized in an indirect order. Indirect order presents the reasons or details that explain the negative news before stating the news.

- Messages that deny requests, decline to supply information, refuse credit, or reject a proposal are examples of a negative message.

- In a letter that has both positive and negative news, the positive news should be presented first.

8.3 Persuasive Messages

- A persuasive message tries to convince the reader to take an action.

- Most persuasive messages should be organized in an indirect order.

- Sales letters and collection letters are examples of persuasive messages.

- A proposal is a formal document that describes a problem or need and recommends a solution.

Open the *Word* file *CH08 Vocabulary* from the student data files. Complete the exercise to review the vocabulary terms from this chapter.

acknowledgment	order
claim	persuasive message
collection message	primary appeal
credit refusal	proposal
fact	request denial
goodwill message	request for proposal (RFP)
neutral opening	routine request
obstacle	sales message
opinion	soft sell

Critical Thinking Questions

CRITICAL
THINKING

1. Why should positive or neutral messages be organized in direct order?

2. Why is a goodwill closing important for all types of messages?

3. Why is it important to present negative news using positive language?

4. Should a persuasive message be more receiver-oriented than a negative message? Explain.

5. Why are most persuasive messages organized in an indirect order?

Chapter *Applications*

A. *Routine Request*

You are visiting your cousin in another city during summer vacation. You planned to stay with your cousin for ten days. You brought three good books along to read during your stay. The books were checked out at your local public library. Now your plans have changed. You have decided to stay with your cousin for another ten days.

1. Write an e-mail to your local public library. (Save the message as a draft. Do not actually send it.)

2. Provide information about yourself, such as your name and library account number, and the books you have checked out. (You select books for the message.)

3. Explain that you would like the librarian to extend the due date of the books to a certain date (two weeks beyond the original due date).

4. You expect the librarian to grant this request willingly, so use direct order for the message. Remember to include a goodwill closing.

B. *Credit Refusal Letter*

Assume that you are a loan officer for Lumberton First National Bank. You have received a request for a $50,000 home improvement loan from Mr. and Mrs. Thomas Banuelos. After reviewing their application, their income, and their credit score, the bank has determined that they do not qualify for a $50,000 loan. The bank is willing to loan them $20,000.

1. Write a letter to Mr. and Mrs. Banuelos. Thank them for being long-time customers of the bank. Let them know the bank's decision regarding the loan.

2. Use the appropriate order for the letter.

3. Use block letter style and open punctuation.

4. Make up an address for the bank and create a letterhead in the document header.

5. The letter address is:

   Mr. and Mrs. Thomas Banuelos
   973 East Ashbrooke Drive
   Lumberton, MS 39455-3735

6. Edit the message to be sure it is courteous, correct, complete, concise, and clear.

7. Proofread the letter and correct all errors.

C. Customer Response Letter

1. The message shown below was written to a customer who has requested the replacement of two sets of sheets.

2. Write a list that describes the problems with the letter.

3. Edit and revise the message so it is well written. Use modified block format with mixed punctuation. Proofread the letter and correct all errors.

January 12, 20--

Mrs. J. T. Tokuda
444 North Summit Street
Bowling Green, OH 43402-0601

Dear Mrs. Tokuda,

We received the two sets of midnight blue no-wrinkle sheets that you returned to us. You requested that we exchange them for new ones.

We can imagine how disappointed you must have been, but we can explain the difficulty. You have been sending the sheets to a laundry that evidently washes them using a standard wash cycle.

The washing instructions, clearly visible on the label, say "WASH IN GENTLE CYCLES ONLY." Some laundries use gentle cycles only when specifically asked to do so. Using a standard cycle keeps other cotton fabrics clean; but on these sheets, the standard cycle causes wrinkling.

In view of your past record with us, however, we are sending you two new sets of midnight blue no-wrinkle sheets free of charge. If you follow the instructions on the label, the sheets will last a long time.

Cordially

Paco Carrasquillo
Complaint Department Manager

D. Goodwill Message

1. Compose an e-mail congratulating a friend on a recent promotion, an anniversary, a birthday, or another event. Supply all necessary information.

2. Edit the message to be sure it is courteous, correct, complete, concise, and clear. Proofread the message and correct all errors.

E. Good News Message

1. Write a letter to Ms. Reanna Coyle, telling her that her credit application with Katina's Fashions has been approved. Her account will have a $1,500 limit. The interest on the unpaid balance at the end of each 30-day billing period is 18 percent a year. More details are provided on the enclosed credit agreement.

2. Select an appropriate order for the message.

3. Select a letter style and punctuation style to use for the letter.

4. Create a letterhead in the document header for the company:

   Katina's Fashions
   391 East Kamala Lane
   Los Gatos, CA 95030-7432

5. Ms. Reanna Coyle's address is:
   4391 North Plum Tree Avenue
   Hollister, CA 95024-0413

6. Edit the message to be sure it is courteous, correct, complete, concise, and clear. Proofread the message and correct all errors.

F. Persuasive Message

1. Work with a classmate to complete this activity.

2. Search the Internet to find the Web site of a travel agency or a car dealership. Study the information provided for one or more tours or cars.

3. Write a one-page sales letter to potential customers, urging them to take a certain tour (trip, cruise, or vacation package) or to buy a certain car. Remember to establish a need and then describe how the product can fill that need.

4. Use indirect order for this persuasive message.

5. Select a letter format and punctuation style.

6. Make up a company name and address for the letterhead. Use your name and address as the letter address.

7. Edit the message to be sure it is courteous, correct, complete, concise, and clear. Proofread the message and correct all errors.

INTERNET

TEAMWORK

REAL WORLD

Editing Activities

Open and edit the *Word* file *CH08 Editing* from the student data files. Correct all spelling, punctuation, number expression, and grammar errors.

CASE STUDY

Up Close and Personal

Erika Tasmajian recently took over management of her grandfather's produce business, Fresh Everyday. Erika was eager to apply what she had learned in her college marketing classes.

Fresh Everyday had a number of long-time customers. However, it had been slowly losing business to national chains. Erika's strategies were designed to expand the Fresh Everyday client list. She created a Web page listing specials and bulk prices for restaurants. She automated the telephone system to answer calls more quickly. She also added a fax machine and equipment for video conferencing. Fresh Everyday did attract new customers, but Erika noticed fewer orders from long-time customers.

Over dinner, Erika discussed the problem with her grandfather. She learned that he had always kept in touch with his customers through letters. Courtesy letters accompanied each invoice. Informational letters advised customers of special sales. Thank-you letters sent after major holidays thanked customers for their business.

1. Do you think there is a connection between fewer orders from long-term customers and fewer letters being sent to customers? Why or why not?

2. Fresh Everyday has embraced several new technologies to further its business. Do you think these technologies can take the place of sending letters to communicate with its customers? Why or why not?

Communication for Finance

Joan has worked at Logan Savings and Loan for three years. A week ago, she was promoted to the position of loan officer. When someone comes into the office and wants a loan, she has the customer fill out the proper papers. She verifies the information given by the applicant and enters data into a computer that will analyze the customer's financial situation. Using this information, Joan makes a recommendation about whether to make or reject the loan. When the loan is approved or rejected, Joan writes a letter to the customer informing her or him of the decision. Because Joan is very busy, her letters are usually short.

Last week, Mr. Park, one of the company's customers, came in and filled out an application for a loan. Today, Joan must write to tell him that the company cannot loan him the money he requested. The body of the letter she wrote is shown below.

Dear Mr. Park

Thank you for using Logan Savings and Loan when applying for your loan. I wish we could grant you your loan, but we cannot. When your credit score improves, please contact us again.

1. What kind of letter has Joan written? Positive news? Neutral news? Negative news?

2. Is the letter written in the correct order?

3. How do you think Mr. Parker feels about Joan? About Logan Savings and Loan?

4. Why does he feel that way?

CHAPTER 9

Writing Reports

9.1   *Planning Reports*

9.2   *Writing Informal Reports*

9.3   *Writing Formal Reports*

Writing Reports—
A Major Expense

Luigi Rossi owns a profitable business—Rossi's Property Management. Business is strong, but it requires Luigi and his staff to work long, hard hours. The work is mentally stressful. The company manages the construction of building projects. It also manages the day-to-day operations of large and small apartment complexes.

Many of Luigi's clients are retired businesspeople who have large investments in their rental properties. The clients usually are very concerned about the properties and how they are being managed. To provide clients with feedback, Luigi and his staff write reports. Writing these reports takes a lot of time.

This past week, Luigi and his staff put in more than twenty hours writing a formal report to a client who is building a large apartment complex. Luigi is managing the project. The report includes information on the status of the project, costs, completion date, and other details.

The previous week was the first week of the month. During this week, reports on the previous month's activities are sent to owners. Thus, the staff worked overtime about fifteen hours.

At last, the weekend is here, but Luigi finds himself at the office on Saturday. He is completing a special report for a client who is considering selling her property. She wants Luigi to provide information on the profit of the property for the last five years.

While Luigi is taking a short break to relax, he starts thinking about his business and how the time spent preparing reports is growing. He wonders if there is anything he can do. He decides he will ask his staff members if they have any ideas on Monday.

Questions

1. How important do you think effective reports are to the success of Luigi's business?

2. If you were a staff member, what suggestions would you give Luigi?

9.1 Planning Reports

Types of Reports

OBJECTIVES

After completing Section 9.1, you should be able to:

1. Classify reports according to their style, purpose, and format.

2. Identify the steps in planning a report.

A **report** is a document that provides facts, opinions, or ideas about a specific topic or problem. Reports are business tools that help managers make decisions and solve problems. Reports can be classified according to their style, purpose, and format.

Style

The two styles of reports are formal and informal. Formal reports generally are long and contain preliminary parts. A title page, a summary, and a table of contents may appear in a formal report. A bibliography and an appendix may also be included.

An example of a formal report is a company's annual report to stockholders. A report to a government agency may be a formal report. Another example is an external proposal. This type of report analyzes a problem and recommends a solution.

Informal reports are typically shorter than formal reports. They are written in a less formal style. Typically, they have no preliminary pages except a title page. The everyday matters they discuss often require little background information.

A sales report is an example of an informal report. In a sales report, the writer summarizes sales for a specific period. An internal proposal is another type of informal report. Also known as a justification report, it is used to analyze an internal problem and recommend a solution.

Key ▶ Point

Informational reports are used to present facts. Analytical reports are used to analyze a problem and present recommendations.

Purpose

Reports can be designed to give information or an analysis of a problem. **Informational reports** present facts. They include very little analysis. For example, a bank manager may ask the head cashier to prepare an informational report about the average number and value of money orders sold each day. The parts of an informational report are the topics (subjects) or the areas investigated.

Analytical reports analyze a problem and present facts. They also draw conclusions and make recommendations. An analytical report suggests ways to solve the problem. The parts of the report are the problem's probable causes and solutions.

Format

Informal reports can be written in several different formats. Memo, letter, and manuscript formats are all used. Formal reports are longer and more complex than informal reports. They are written in manuscript format. Section 9.2 provides more information about formatting reports.

check point 1

1. What type of report presents facts but includes very little analysis?

2. What type of report analyzes a problem, presents facts and conclusions, and makes recommendations?

Check your answers in Appendix C.

Defining the Report

Before writing a report, you must do some planning and research. Even if you are simply reporting facts, you must gather those facts. You must arrange the facts in an easy-to-follow, logical sequence. The steps for planning a report are shown in Figure 9-1.

Key▶Point

For both informational and analytical reports, planning is an important first step.

Identify the Problem or Topic

The first step is to identify the problem or topic to be studied and the objective of the report. As in planning letters and memos, determine why you are writing

Figure 9-1 Planning a Report

PLANNING A REPORT
1. Identify the objective, problem, or topic.
2. Determine the scope of the report.
3. Develop a timeline.
4. Collect the data.
5. Develop a preliminary outline.
6. Analyze the data.
7. Draw conclusions and make recommendations.

the report and what you hope to accomplish. Write a question or statement that clearly expresses the problem or topic.

Question	Should the company buy new computers for the Accounting Department?
Statement	This report will examine whether the company should buy new computers for the Accounting Department.

Identify the areas or aspects of the problem or topic that you will investigate. Develop a list of questions you need to answer to achieve the objective of the report.

Determine the Scope

The next step is to decide exactly what to investigate or discuss. **Scope** refers to the boundaries of the report—what will be included and what will not. A problem or topic may be very broad or have many aspects. For example, a report about the use of computers in all company departments will require more research and have a wider scope than a report that examines computer use in just two departments.

Develop a Timeline

Develop a schedule for collecting the data, analyzing the results, and writing the report. Identify the date when the report must be completed. Then develop a timeline to help you complete the research and report on time. A **timeline** is a schedule that lists the dates by which each task and phase of a project must be completed. An example timeline is shown in Figure 9-2. To set up a timeline, it is easiest to begin at the completion date and work backward.

Figure 9-2 Report Timeline

Tasks	Completion Dates
Identify the problem or topic and areas to investigate.	April 21
Determine the scope of the report.	April 21
Develop a timeline.	April 22
Collect the data.	April 30
Develop a preliminary outline.	May 2
Analyze the data.	May 9
Draw conclusions and make recommendations.	May 9
Write the first draft of the report.	May 13
Make revisions and create the final draft report.	May 15

check point 2

1. List seven planning steps for creating a report.

2. What is the scope of a report?

Check your answers in Appendix C.

Collecting the Data

The next step in creating a report is to do research by collecting appropriate data. Two sources of data are available—primary sources and secondary sources. **Primary research** involves gathering new data. **Secondary research** involves locating data that already have been gathered and reported.

Primary Research

If the facts you need are not available in books, magazines, Internet pages, or other sources, you may need to conduct primary research. To conduct this type of research, you might use interviews, surveys, or observations.

An **interview** is a conversation between two or more people. Questions are asked by an interviewer to gain facts, ideas, or opinions from the people who are being questioned. You might interview experts in the field, employees of a business, or customers. From these people, you may gain valuable data that may not be available from other sources. Many companies regularly seek their customers' opinions on their products, prices, and services to help them better serve their markets.

A **survey** is a set of questions or statements used to learn facts or opinions. Surveys can be given in person, in writing, or by telephone. Surveys should use a carefully worded questionnaire. Designing and distributing the questionnaire can be expensive. Compiling the completed questionnaires also takes time and money. Therefore, before selecting this method of research, it is important to know that you have enough time and money to complete the project.

Observation means watching or monitoring people or things in an effort to learn something. For example, by observing people on the job, you may discover facts related to the workflow or operating procedures. You may be able to use these facts to draw conclusions about how to improve procedures. By observing customers using a product, you may learn which product features they like or dislike. This information can be used to improve future versions of the product. Like surveys, observations also take time and money. If more than one person will make the observations, standards or training may be needed to ensure that all observers report the same information in the same way.

Key ▶ Point

Primary research can be conducted using interviews, surveys, or observation.

Diversity

Survey questions must be carefully worded to avoid bias relating to gender, age, race, or national origin.

Secondary Research

Research completed by others can be useful in creating reports. Data from research is available in print and online. Consult printed books, encyclopedias, periodicals, and other reports to gather information. Many libraries have database services. These databases offer a thorough listing of resources. Three databases that give information on business topics are listed below. Use these databases to help you find printed materials.

- *Business Periodicals Index*
- *Reader's Guide to Periodical Literature*
- *The Wall Street Journal Index*

When conducting online research, using a search engine is a good way to find information on your research topic. A screen from Google, a popular search engine, is shown in Figure 9-3. Use the following steps to find information using a search engine. You can use a similar process to find information on Web sites for companies or organizations.

1. Access the search engine in your browser software.

2. Identify keywords or phrases that relate to the topic. For example, use the keyword *telecommuting* for articles about this topic.

3. Enter the keywords into the search box. Start the search.

Key ▶ Point

Secondary research involves locating data that already have been gathered and reported.

Figure 9-3 Google is a popular Internet search engine.

Source: Google, accessed May 22, 2008, available from http://www.google.com.

4. Review the list of search results, called the hit list. Some search engines display the number of hits. Notice in Figure 9-3 that results 11–20 of 3,850,000 are displayed.

5. Click a link in the hit list that seems to provide the information you want. Sponsored links may appear at the top or side of the list. A company or organization has paid to have these links appear with the keywords you entered. They may or may not contain useful information.

6. Review the material from this source.

7. Go back to the hit list. Review other sources.

8. Try other keywords if the hit list does not contain the information you seek. To narrow the results, you may need to use the advanced search features of the program. See the Occupational Success article in this chapter for information on advanced search techniques.

Key▶Point

When conducting online research, try other keywords if the hit list does not contain the information you seek.

Some of the most useful sources of information are found inside a company. Internal reports, memos, and reports to stockholders can provide valuable data. Many companies post their annual reports on their Web sites. Annual reports contain information about a company, such as directors and officers, financial highlights, new initiatives, and future plans.

The U.S. government is another good source of information. It publishes reports on a variety of subjects. For example, the U.S. Census Bureau provides data about the people and the economy of the United States. Figure 9-4 shows a screen from the U.S. Census Bureau Web site.

figure 9-4 The U.S. Census Bureau provides data on the U.S. population.

Source: U.S. Census Bureau, accessed May 16, 2008, available from http://www.census.gov/.

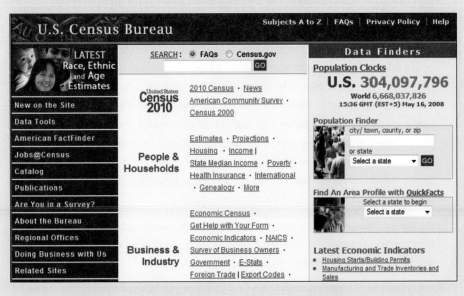

Searching for Data Online

Being able to find relevant data online quickly will help you prepare reports efficiently. When searching for data online, clearly focus your search to locate the information that will be most useful to you. Using advanced search techniques will allow you to enter more than one keyword or phrase. Boolean operators may be used to connect two or more keywords or phrases. The most common Boolean operators are *OR*, *AND*, and *NOT* (or *AND NOT*).

Using the term *OR* broadens your search. A larger list of sources (hit list) will result because only one of the search terms you enter needs to be present. For example, suppose you enter the terms *chocolate OR candy*. The software will return a list of sites containing either the word *chocolate* or the word *candy*. However, both words may not be within the same result.

The Boolean operator *AND* is used to narrow a search. When *AND* is used, all search terms must be present in each source on the hit list. For example, if you entered *branch AND tree*, the list would include only hits containing both the word *branch* and the word *tree*. Hits containing only one of the terms would not be listed. This strategy produces a shorter hit list with articles that may be more on target. Be careful, however, not to eliminate some useful sources that may not include both terms in the text.

When you want to eliminate a specific term from the hit list, it may be appropriate to use the Boolean operator *NOT* or *AND NOT*. For instance, suppose you enter the search terms *tree AND NOT bonsai*. The resulting hit list would include all sources containing the word *tree* but not those referring to bonsai trees.

Truncation is a method of broadening a search. A base or root word is followed by a wildcard that allows the software to search for several similar keywords that begin with the same root. A **wildcard** is a symbol, such as an asterisk (*) or a question mark, used in conducting searches. A wildcard tells the software to return a list of sources containing all words that begin with that root or base word. For example, entering the search term *pollut** would result in a hit list containing all the terms beginning with the base word *pollut*, including *pollutant*, *pollute*, *polluter*, and *pollution*. This is a handy tool to use when there are a number of similar words that may be relevant to your search.

Because some search engines or subject indexes handle advanced searches differently, you should review instructions at each search engine or subject index site before proceeding with an advanced search.

Evaluating Data Sources

When using data from secondary sources, you should evaluate the information you find. Ask yourself these questions:

- Is the information relevant to the topic or problem?
- Is the information true and accurate?
- Is the information reliable? Is it provided by a reputable source?
- Is the information current or useful?
- Is the information biased?

To be useful, the information must be relevant to the topic or problem you are researching. Although the data might be interesting, it cannot help you if it is not related to the topic or problem.

Always check the validity and reliability of your sources. Validity means that the data presented give accurate facts. Reliability indicates that the information is free of errors. If several sources you find offer the same or similar information, that is a good indication that it is reliable. If there is one source that offers dramatically different data, you should question its reliability.

Check to see if the information is provided by a reputable source. Is the research data provided by a university or a government agency? Can you tell who publishes the Web site? Are the name, title, affiliation, and contact information clearly listed? If the information you have found is outdated, it may be of little use to your research project. Pay attention to dates of publication as well as the dates on which the information was placed on a Web site.

Finally, ask yourself if the information from the article, book, or Web page is well balanced and lacks bias. You may discover bias relating to age, gender, race, or national origin. You also may notice bias simply in the way information is slanted in the presentation. Anyone can publish information giving his or her own viewpoint. Avoid using information that presents an obvious bias.

Bibliography Notes

As you conduct your research, you should use a method of identifying your sources. This method is called **documentation**. A **bibliography** is a list of sources used in preparing the report. You can document sources by preparing a note, as shown in Figure 9-5 on page 320, for every source. These notes provide the details for the bibliography that the formal report will include. The notes in Figure 9-5 have been keyed in a word processing program. If you have access to a computer, you may be able to key or handwrite notes for printed sources as you do your research. If not, you may need to handwrite the notes on paper.

Key ▶ Point

When using data from secondary research, make sure the data are current and come from a reliable source.

Key ▶ Point

When doing research for a report, prepare a bibliography note for each source you use.

Figure 9-5 Bibliography Notes

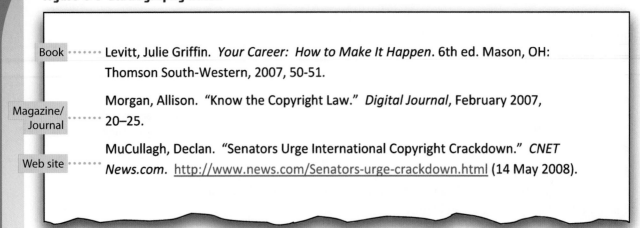

Book .... Levitt, Julie Griffin. *Your Career: How to Make It Happen.* 6th ed. Mason, OH: Thomson South-Western, 2007, 50-51.

Magazine/ Journal .... Morgan, Allison. "Know the Copyright Law." *Digital Journal*, February 2007, 20–25.

Web site .... MuCullagh, Declan. "Senators Urge International Copyright Crackdown." *CNET News.com.* http://www.news.com/Senators-urge-crackdown.html (14 May 2008).

For each source that you use, prepare a note similar to the one shown in Figure 9-5. For books, list the author's full name (last name first), the book title (in italics), the publisher's location and name, the publication date and the page numbers.

When you use information from a magazine article, list the author's full name (last name first), the article title (in quotation marks), the magazine title (in italics), the publication date, and the page numbers. An example is shown in Figure 9-5.

When you use an electronic source, list the author's name (if given) and the title of the article or Web page. List the name of the Web site. List the Web site address (URL) and the date you access the site. Indicate that the source is a CD-ROM instead of the URL if that is the case. All this information may not be available. List as much of the information as you can. An example is shown in Figure 9-5.

Ethics

Always give credit to the source of information you use in reports. Refer to Chapter 2 for more information on copyrights and plagiarism.

Research Notes

Prepare a separate note for each point you plan to mention in your report. In many cases, you will summarize the information you locate in a secondary source, as illustrated in Figure 9-6 on page 321. When you want to use a direct quote, copy the text exactly as shown in the source.

Avoid plagiarism (using another's work as your own) by clearly identifying your sources. Copyright laws protect the interests of the person who created the work. Even if the information does not fall under copyright protection, ethical behavior requires you to give credit to the source. You may want to briefly summarize the main points of all articles you read, even if you do not think you will use the material in your report. You can review these notes along with the others when you write the report to make sure you are not including material without crediting the source.

Figure 9-6 Research Note

Levitt, Julie Griffin

Your Career: How to Make It Happen

The Impact of Globalization

Globalization will impact your career development. During the beginning of the 21st century, experts expect global trade among nations to increase three or four times faster than individual national economies. p. 50.

check point 3

1. How does primary research differ from secondary research?

2. What three methods can be used to do primary research?

3. When using data from secondary sources, what questions can you ask to help evaluate the information you find?

Check your answers in Appendix C.

Processing the Data

Once the data has been collected, organize the data in a meaningful way. Analyze the data and use your findings to draw conclusions. Make recommendations based on your findings and conclusions.

Create a Report Outline

An **outline** is a listing of topics in a logical order. Prepare a preliminary outline to organize the facts you found in your research. This outline is not the final outline used to write your report. It is simply a way of organizing the information you gathered. The outline for an informational report can be arranged in several ways.

■ **Chronological Order.** Organize the facts in relation to time; that is, what happened first, next, and so forth.

Key▶Point

Use an outline to organize data for an informational report in some logical order.

- **Order of Importance.** Arrange the facts in order of importance, from the most to the least important or vice versa.
- **Logical Sequence.** Group the facts according to a logical order of steps—first, second, third, and so forth.
- **Category.** Separate the facts into categories; for example, stocks, bonds, and certificates of deposit.
- **Geographical Order.** Organize the facts by location.

When outlining analytical reports, you can organize the facts in one of two ways. One method is to use a hypothesis. A **hypothesis** is a possible solution for a problem or situation that can be tested. The second method is to use alternatives. An **alternative** is a possible solution or course of action that may be selected from those available.

Key▶Point

An outline based on a hypothesis should include questions to be answered to prove or disprove the hypothesis.

When working from a hypothesis, include each possible explanation in your outline. The following outline shows two hypotheses (the plural of *hypothesis*) for a drop in auto sales. Under each hypothesis are the questions that must be answered to prove or disprove the hypothesis.

I. Our prices are too high. (Hypothesis)
- A. What are our prices?
- B. What are our competitors' prices?
- C. How important is price to our customers?

II. The quality of our product is low. (Hypothesis)
- A. What is our repair record?
- B. How does our repair record compare with that of competitors?
- C. What are the results of product evaluations?

Key▶Point

An outline based on alternatives should include questions related to each alternative.

To examine alternatives to a problem, list them in your preliminary outline. For example, suppose you want to determine where to install new computers in your school building. One alternative is to research the number of courses in each subject that uses computers.

Another alternative is to research the number of students enrolled in each course that uses computers.

I. Number of classes taught using computers (Alternative)
- A. Paralegal courses
- B. Business courses
- C. Health technology courses

II. Number of students enrolled (Alternative)
- A. Paralegal courses
- B. Business courses
- C. Health technology courses

Research can involve direct observation, such as counting the number of rooms that have computers.

The preliminary outline follows either a topical format or a discussion format. In a topical outline, headings—the words that start each section—describe in a few words the topics you have investigated. A discussion outline provides more information about the topics and the subtopics—the topics that are included under each heading. A discussion outline takes longer to write, but it is often more helpful when writing the report.

Key▶Point

A topical outline or a discussion outline can be used in planning a report.

Topical Outline

I.   Characteristics of IM

   A.   Speed

   B.   Cost

   C.   Equipment

Discussion Outline

I.   IM offers the latest technology for sending messages.

   A.   It offers speed.

   B.   It is often free via the Internet.

   C.   All that is needed is a computer.

Analyze the Data

Analyze means to examine, study closely, or evaluate in order to understand something better than before. Take an initial look at the data. Are any of the findings surprising or unusual? Can you answer any of the questions you listed with the data in this form?

To analyze the data, look for logical links between facts and figures. If you are working with numbers, compare and contrast figures. When you look at answers from interviews or surveys, you can ask questions such as the following:

- How many times was this answer given?
- What percentage of the people responding gave this answer?
- What is the average rating this answer received?
- What response to this question occurs most often?
- What response to this question occurs least often?

READING SKILLS

Reading for Research

Reading is an important skill that you will use when looking for secondary research materials. You may have to review many articles and Web pages to find the data you need. Before reading an entire article or page carefully, scan the material to see if it is relevant to your research.

Many people read only the headline and first paragraph of news articles. For this reason, magazine and newspaper articles (found in print or online) are typically written in direct order. The main ideas are presented early in the article. Supporting details follow in later paragraphs. Articles that present opinion or ideas, rather than news reports, may use an indirect approach. You may need to scan to the end of the article to find the main ideas.

The information that is presented in an article may not be complete. The writer may focus on points the reader will find interesting or "newsworthy." As you scan an article, look for keywords or phrases you can use to search for related information. Use the questions presented in this chapter to evaluate the information you find for relevance, accuracy, reliability, bias, and timeliness.

Open the *Word* file *CH09 Reading* from the student data files. Follow the directions in the exercise to scan a news article, find the main idea, and identify keywords for further research.

Organize the data in a logical way. For example, you could arrange sales figures by region from lowest to highest. You could arrange the responses to a survey question by most favorable to least favorable answers. Suppose you researched the high turnover rate of production supervisors in your company. You might put the data into three categories as shown below.

■ Salaries of different supervisory jobs in the company

■ Salaries offered by competing manufacturers

■ The number and kinds of promotions supervisors have received at each job level

Key ▶ Point

Organize the data in a logical way that will help you draw conclusions.

Draw Conclusions and Make Recommendations

Use the data you have analyzed to try to answer your list of questions developed earlier. Do the results make sense? Are there any standards to which they can be compared? Do they seem logical based on what you know about the problem or topic? If not, more research or analysis may be needed.

If the results seem to be reasonable, try to reach some conclusions. A **conclusion** is an opinion you form that is based on studying the data. A possible conclusion for the study about production supervisors is shown in the following example.

Key ▶ Point

Recommendations in a report should be related to conclusions that are based on the research findings.

> Production supervisors in our company have limited advancement opportunities.

Include recommendations in a report if you have been asked to do so. A **recommendation** offers a suggestion of what should be done. Recommendations should be related to conclusions, as in the following example.

> I recommend that supervisory positions within our company be reorganized to provide opportunities for career advancement.

check point 4

1. List five ways the outline for an informational report can be arranged.

2. List two ways the outline for an analytical report can be arranged.

3. How does a discussion outline differ from a topical outline?

Check your answers in Appendix C.

Section 9.1 *Applications*

A. *Types of Report*

Indicate whether you would use an informational or an analytical report in response to each request.

1. Send me a memo report on our sales for the past six months. I want the data organized by region.

2. I need a report on possible solutions for the problems our department is having with the reporting system.

3. Prepare a report that examines the alternatives available for providing life insurance coverage for employees.

4. Create a report that summarizes the progress we have made on converting to the new accounting software.

5. Do some research and send me a report with your recommendation for how to solve the customer support problems we are having.

B. *Report Style and Format*

Indicate the style (formal or informal) and format (letter, memo, or manuscript) for each report.

1. Send me a memo with details on our returned goods for the past three months.

2. Prepare a report that examines the alternatives available for buying versus renting office copy machines.

3. Send a letter to the director of the Human Resources Department that reports on training programs completed by employees in our department.

C. *Report Research*

You have been asked to do research for a report on ways your company can improve customer service.

INTERNET

1. Search the Internet or other sources to find an article on customer service.

2. Prepare a topic outline of the article.

3. Place a bibliography note below the outline.

4. Prepare a research note that gives a short, direct quote from the article.

Writing Informal Reports

Organizing Informal Reports

Most business reports are informal reports that have one of two purposes. They present information that has been requested, or they analyze a problem and report the findings. The organization and the format of these reports vary depending on the nature of the message and the recipients.

Like business letters and memos, informal reports are organized around a main idea. Supporting information is included about the main idea. If the report is an informational report, the main idea is that you are providing data that has been requested. If the report is analytical, the main idea is its recommendation.

Informal reports may be organized in direct order or indirect order. The order you choose depends on how you expect your reader to receive the message. Sometimes you cannot know which order to use until you have completed the planning process described in Section 9.1.

OBJECTIVES

After completing Section 9.2, you should be able to:

1. Explain when to use direct or indirect order for reports.

2. Create a report outline.

3. Name the parts of an informal report.

4. Write an informal report.

DEX IMAGE/GETTY IMAGES

Reports written in direct order give the main idea early in the report.

Direct Order

K e y ▶ P o i n t

Use direct order when the report is routine or when you expect the reader to respond favorably.

If the report is routine (a weekly sales report, for example) or if you expect the reader to respond favorably, use direct order. Present the main idea first. Follow with supporting details. Busy managers prefer reading this type of report since the main idea appears at the beginning.

Informational reports, such as progress reports, commonly use direct order. In those reports, the results (or main ideas) appear at the beginning. Analytical reports that are likely to have a favorable response also are organized in direct order. The main ideas appear first, followed by the supporting information.

Indirect Order

K e y ▶ P o i n t

Use indirect order for a report when you expect an unfavorable response.

Use indirect order when you expect an unfavorable response. When the receiver may need persuasion to accept the main idea, use indirect order. You can buffer the main idea by presenting the data and the reasons first. For example, use indirect order in an internal proposal when managers are likely to be hesitant about approving the project or the budget. You might also use indirect order for a troubleshooting report. This is a type of analytical report in which you investigate a problem and propose a solution.

check point 5

1. When should direct order be used for a report?

2. When should indirect order be used for a report?

Check your answers in Appendix C.

Outlining and Writing Informal Reports

Once you decide how to organize your report, you are ready to write an outline. Outlining helps you identify and position the topics and subtopics you will include. After placing the main idea and the supporting information in a logical sequence, you can begin writing the report.

K e y ▶ P o i n t

Outlining helps you identify and position the topics and subtopics you will include in a report.

Report Outlines

As you start to outline an informal report, use the preliminary outline you developed to guide your research. The outline will need some revision because of what you learned from collecting and analyzing the data. Once you have revised the outline, use it as a guide for writing the final report.

Outlines for informal reports organized in direct or indirect order are shown in Figures 9-7 and 9-8.

Figure 9-7 is an outline for an informational report organized in direct order. Notice that the main idea comes first, followed by the findings.

Figure 9-7 Informational Report Outline in Direct Order

I. Introduction

II. Main idea: Clay State Bank, preferred bank for our firm

III. Areas investigated

IV. Findings: banking needs at our firm

    A. Low-cost check writing

    B. Online account availability

    C. Online loan payment system

    D. Courteous, friendly service

V. Findings: comparison to other local banks

    A. Second County Bank

    B. Monroe and Hayes National Bank

    C. Citywide Bank

    D. Tondo Savings and Loan

VI. Closing

Figure 9-8 on page 330 is an outline for an analytical report. The report is organized in indirect order. The findings and supporting details are presented first. The conclusion and recommendation follow the details.

Writing Style

Informal reports usually are written in a relatively personal style. Personal pronouns and contractions are often used in this style. If your report is about a serious problem or if it is going to a senior manager, you may want it to be more formal. In that case, you would write your report in an impersonal style, without using first- or second-person pronouns and contractions.

The impersonal style keeps a report from sounding like one person's opinion. It does not refer to *I, me,* or *you.* A report written in an impersonal style emphasizes the facts rather than the writer. The report sounds more objective than a report written in a personal style.

Diversity

Using a personal style may not be appropriate when the report is written for readers from other cultures.

Figure 9-8 Analytical Report Outline in Indirect Order

I. Introduction

    A. Report objective

    B. Area investigated

II. Findings and supporting details

    A. Production supervisors' salaries compare favorably with those of competing organizations.

    B. Fringe benefits are satisfactory.

    C. Opportunities for advancement are limited.

III. Conclusion: Production supervisors in our company have have limited advancement opportunities.

IV. Recommendation: Supervisory positions should be changed to provide opportunities for career advancement.

V. Closing

When writing about the data you have collected, use the present tense or the past tense. Use the past tense when writing about events in the past and the present tense when writing about events that are still occurring. Avoid switching back and forth between tenses when presenting the data. Switching can confuse your readers, who may have difficulty following the timing or sequence of events.

check point 6

1. What writing style is typically used for informal reports?

2. When should an impersonal writing style be used for a report?

3. Does a personal or an impersonal writing style make a report seem more objective?

Check your answers in Appendix C.

Formatting Informal Reports

Informal reports have three basic formats. They may be formatted like letters, memos, or manuscripts. The format depends on the receiver and the length of the report.

Parts of an Informal Report

Regardless of the format used, informal reports have three main parts: the opening, the body, and the closing.

The length of the opening will vary according to the purpose of the report. For a brief memo report, the opening might be only a subject line. For other informal short reports written in direct order, the opening may include the following information:

- The subject and purpose of the report (the reason the report is important)
- Recommendations
- A preview of the sections of the report
- The summary of findings or the conclusions

The body of a report includes the findings and supporting details that resulted from the research. Your revised outline will provide the organizational plan for this section. This section is usually the longest and must be well organized so the report is easy to understand.

The closing of a report is important because it is the final opportunity to impress the reader. If you are writing a report in direct order, you should reemphasize the main idea in this last section.

When using indirect order, present the objective of the report and the area investigated. Then give a summary of findings. Finally, give the conclusions and recommendations (analytical reports). Make sure that the conclusions are supported by the data. If the report includes several conclusions or recommendations, use a list format for simplicity.

Letter Reports

External reports, those written for people outside the organization, often are written in letter format. (See Chapter 7 for details on formatting letters.) These reports are called letter reports. In general, an informal report written in letter format should be five pages or less. Remember to include a heading on each page of the letter after the first page. The heading should contain the recipient's name, the page number, and the date. If you need more than five pages, use the manuscript format. Manuscript format allows you to separate the various parts of the report so readers can follow the organization of the material.

✛ Ethics

Confidential data may be used in some reports. Be careful to share the report only with people who are authorized to see the data.

Key ▶ Point

Letter reports are typically written for people outside the organization.

The opening may mention who asked for the report and the date the report was assigned. The report body includes findings and supporting details. It may include an analysis of the situation being studied and recommendations to resolve problems. The ending is similar to the closing in a letter. If possible, the ending should mention some expected action on the part of the reader or writer. See Figure 9-9 on page 333 for an example of a letter report.

Memo Reports

Key ▶ Point

Memo reports are typically written for people inside the organization.

A memo report is a short internal report written in memo format. It is sent to others within the organization. These reports are informal primarily because of their format, not necessarily because of their content. If a memo report is longer than one page, use a heading on all pages after the first page. The page headings should contain the recipient's name, the page number, and the date. Side headings may be used within the body of the report to facilitate locating information.

Use the memo format for routine internal reports that are five pages or less. (See Chapter 7 for detailed information on formatting memos.) If the report needs to be longer, use the manuscript format. An example of a memo report is shown in Figure 9-10 on page 334.

Manuscript Reports

Key ▶ Point

Manuscript reports may be written for people inside or outside the organization.

Informal manuscript reports are short reports written in manuscript format. They are usually longer than memo or letter reports but not as long as formal reports. They can be used either internally (a proposal to a supervisor) or externally (a report to a client).

The opening may include the following information:

- The subject of the report
- The purpose of the report (the reason the subject is important)
- A preview of the sections of the report

If you are writing in direct order, include the summary of findings (informational report) or the recommendations (analytical report) in the opening. See Figure 9-11 on pages 335 and 336 for an example of a manuscript report.

check point 7

1. What parts are included in an informal report?

2. What information is typically included in the opening for an informal short report written in direct order?

Check your answers in Appendix C.

Figure 9-9 Letter Report

Raleigh Consulting Group

216 Marginal Road, Raleigh, NC 27612-7643
Phone: (919) 555-0170

December 11, 20--

Mr. Ray Park
Human Resources Manager
Southern Textiles
6 Kingston Street
Elm City, NC 27822-1463

Dear Mr. Park

As you requested, this report discusses recommended training programs for new shift supervisors. After talking with your plant manager and with 12 newly promoted supervisors, I recommend that you consider a two-day management and communication course. ···· Opening

Management Training

New shift supervisors have no management background. An intensive one-day training program would provide ideas that the supervisors can apply immediately. The program would cover basic management functions and strategies for managing quality improvement. ······ Body

Communication Training

New shift supervisors must be able to communicate with workers, peers, top managers, and union officials. A one-day training program would give these supervisors the speaking and writing skills they need to be effective. This program would cover oral and written communication, listening, and feedback.

Our manufacturing clients have found that two consecutive days of training immediately after a promotion can provide the tools new supervisors need to be productive right away. Please call ···· Closing me so we can discuss how to tailor this course to your firm's needs. Thank you for giving us the opportunity to work with you.

Sincerely

Anna Ruiz

Dr. Anna Ruiz, President

Figure 9-10 Memo Report

TO: All Dieticians

FROM: Isadora Villegas, Chief Dietician

DATE: August 29, 20--

SUBJECT: High School Visits

Every high school in School District 3 has signed up for our free annual menu consultation. With the information we provide about menu items, serving size, and ingredients, the schools are better able to plan their monthly food purchases. In turn, we learn more about the students' and teachers' special dietary needs.

Because of the need to complete these visits before school begins, I have arranged the following schedule for high school visits.

Dietician	Schools	Dates
Allman, Thelma	Central High School	August 19
	Auburn Regional High School	August 20
Moroni, Lonzo	Campbell High School	August 19
	Morrow High School	August 20
Sogo, Kamal	Avondale High School	August 19
	MLK High School	August 20
Lanese, Kent	Forest Park High School	August 19
	Riverdale High School	August 20

Figure 9-11 Manuscript Report

Credit Records Storage Facility

The Credit Department proposes that a new credit records storage facility be created in the regional office. This facility will handle seasonal variations in credit volume. It will also allow for future growth in credit sales. The facility would store credit and collection records for up to 1,000 regional customers. This recommendation is made after the analysis of physical specifications, environmental factors, a construction schedule, and a file transfer schedule. `··· Opening`

Physical Specifications

The proposed storage facility should meet the specifications described in the following sections. `········ Body`

Space
An area of 7,000 to 9,000 square feet is needed for the storage facility.

Furniture and Equipment
Two rectangular workstations with seating for two at each station are needed. Each workstation should be equipped with two desktop computers, two scanners, and one printer. The computers should be linked with the central credit processing system. Each workstation requires two chairs. In addition, one 3' x 6' table for file preparation is required.

Credit applications must be retained for two years. To hold these records, provide 10 linear feet of reinforced steel shelving. The shelving should be 8' high with 16" between shelves. The lowest shelf must be positioned at least 3' above floor level.

Customer correspondence about credit disputes or collections must be stored. Provide six four-drawer letter-size file cabinets for these records. To hold returned mail from credit and collection accounts, provide two rolling storage bins.

One multiline telephone should be installed at each workstation. These telephones should be linked with the regional office's voice mail system.

Provide one fax machine for sending credit documents. The fax must be equipped with a 30-page document feeder and a letter-size tray to hold incoming faxes.

Security
The file storage facility must be secure both day and night. Provide one card-activated locking system with a manual override in case of power failure.

Figure 9-11 Continued

2

Wiring

Appropriate writing should be provided for the following equipment:

- Desktop computers and printers
- Scanners
- Fax equipment

Environment Factors

The file storage area should meet the certain standards. The heating, ventilation, and air conditioning system must allow a temperature range between 68 and 78 degrees Fahrenheit. A humidity level of 40-60 percent is required. Indirect lighting and task lighting is needed at the workstations. For all other areas in this facility, provide standard ceiling lighting.

Construction Schedule

Every year the Credit Department has heavier demand for records storage. This demand is because of increased credit and collection activity during the fall and winter months. To handle this seasonal demand, the facility should be ready by September 15.

File Transfer Schedule

The Credit Department will require two business days to transfer the current customer records from the downtown office to the new storage facility in the regional office. Customer correspondence records and files will be moved on the first day. Customer applications will be moved on the second day.

Summary

A storage facility constructed as described in this report would allow the Credit Department to handle records for all our customers. With the use of this storage facility, both seasonal storage demands and expected growth in records for future credit sales can be handled effectively.

Closing ······

Section 9.2 *Applications*

A. Analyze Data for a Report

You work at Kids First, a center that provides day care for children who are ages three to six years old. The center is small but successful. There is a waiting list of parents who want to place their children in the center. The owner, Louise Park, is considering increasing the number of children the center cares for each day. You have been asked to analyze the related information and prepare a report.

1. Analyze the following information to determine how much the center will gain or lose each month by caring for two additional children.

    *   The center charges $125 per week to care for each child.

    *   The center can care for two additional children per week with no increase in the number staff members.

    *   The center will need to purchase additional nap mats and blankets if additional children are accepted. The one-time cost will be about $200.

    *   A staff member meets with a parent of each child once a week for about 15 minutes to discuss the child's care. The staff member is paid for this meeting at the rate of $12 per hour.

    *   Fixed costs, such as rent, will not be increased by caring for two additional children. Increases in variable costs, such as water and electricity, are estimated at $10 per child per month.

    *   Food for each child is estimated at $100 per month.

2. What other factors should be considered? For example, staff members will have an increased workload if the center cares for two additional children.

B. Create an Outline and a Report

1. Write an outline for a memo report. The objective of the report is to present the information you analyzed about the Kids First center and your recommendation. Organize the information in direct order.

2. Write a memo report using the outline you created. Give your conclusions about the data in the opening paragraph. Also, give your recommendation about whether the center should care for two additional children in the opening paragraph. Give an explanation of your analysis in the following paragraphs.

9.3 Writing Formal Reports

Organizing and Writing Formal Reports

OBJECTIVES

After completing Section 9.3, you should be able to:

1. Decide when to use a formal report.
2. Identify parts of a formal report.
3. Plan and prepare a formal report.

Formal reports are more complex than informal reports. They are used when the report will be long or the research involved is extensive. Formal reports are used to report to top managers or to persons outside the company. They have preliminary and supplementary parts not found in informal reports. Because of the amount of time required to write formal reports, they are used only when absolutely necessary.

As with an informal report, the organization and writing style you choose for a formal report can vary. They depend on the nature of the message and the people who will receive it. Since formal reports are longer and more complex than informal reports, formal reports are formatted differently. Special manuals have been written for the formatting of formal reports. Some of them are the *Publication Manual of the American Psychological Association* (APA), the *MLA Handbook for Writers of Research Papers* (MLA), and *The Chicago Manual of Style*. The formal report shown in this text uses a traditional business format. The MLA guidelines are used for documentation.

Direct and Indirect Order

Key▶Point

Formal informational reports are usually organized in direct order.

When organizing a formal report, you can use either direct or indirect order. Formal informational reports usually follow direct order. They contain information that readers expect. Readers, therefore, should react favorably. Formal analytical reports that will likely receive a favorable response also are organized in direct order. On the other hand, indirect order is used in a formal report when you expect an unfavorable response. Indirect order is also used when you may need to persuade the reader to accept the main idea.

Writing Style

Key▶Point

Formal reports usually are written in an impersonal style, which makes the report sound objective.

Many important business decisions are made on the basis of the information presented in formal reports. With so much at stake, these reports need to sound impartial and professional. Thus, formal reports usually are written in an impersonal style. They do not use personal pronouns such as *you* and *I*. An impersonal writing style focuses attention on the facts rather than on the writer. It also makes the report sound objective.

Objective reports help managers make business decisions.

check point 8

1. Why are formal reports, rather than informal reports, used only when absolutely necessary?

2. Why are formal reports usually written in impersonal style?

Check your answers in Appendix C.

Parts of a Formal Report

A formal report has three major parts: preliminary parts, body or text, and supplementary parts. These parts are described in the following sections.

Preliminary Parts

The preliminary parts are the parts of a formal report that appear first, providing the reader with information about the report body. Preliminary parts include a letter or memo of transmittal, a title page, a table of contents, and an executive summary.

A letter of transmittal or a memo of transmittal introduces a formal report to the reader. This document conveys what you would say if you were handing the report directly to the reader. Therefore, it is usually less formal than the report itself. A letter of transmittal may accompany a report to readers inside or outside the organization. A memo of transmittal would accompany a report for internal use. Use direct order for the letter or memo of transmittal. Begin

Key▶Point

Preliminary parts are the parts of a formal report that appear first, providing the reader with information about the report body.

Diversity

Consider the readers' positions in the company and their cultures and customs when deciding how formal or informal a transmittal letter should be.

Ethics

If others helped you, give credit to the people who help you write a report. Presenting the report as if it is all your work is unethical.

with a statement such as *Here is the report you asked me to prepare about . . . .* Include a brief restatement of the report's objective, followed by a short summary of the report. End by thanking the person who requested the report and offering assistance if needed. Figure 9-13 on page 342 shows a sample letter of transmittal.

A title page shows the report title; the name, title, and organization of the person for whom the report was written; the writer's name, title, and organization; and the date the report is submitted. Figure 9-14 on page 343 shows a sample title page. You may use the title page as the report cover when the report is short or when the report is for internal use. Otherwise, use a cover made of heavy paper or plastic. Label the cover with the report title and, if desired, with the writer's name and the date.

A **table of contents** is a list of what the report includes. Prepare the table of contents after the report is written by listing the main headings shown in the report and the page number where each heading occurs. Figure 9-15 on page 344 provides an example of a table of contents.

If you use *Word's* styles to create the headings in the report, you can generate a table of contents automatically. Figure 9-12 shows options for a table of contents.

Figure 9-12 Microsoft Word Table of Contents Options

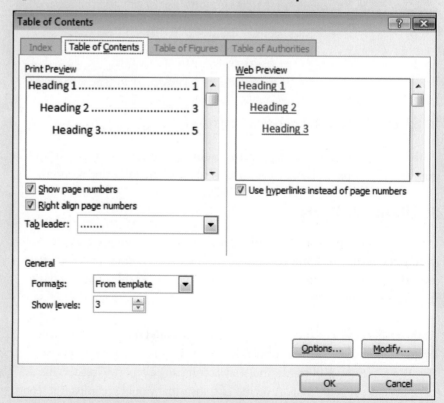

An **executive summary**, sometimes called a *synopsis* or an *abstract*, is a brief overview of the report. The purpose of an executive summary is to give the key points of the report to the reader. An executive summary is especially important when a report is long and technical. It allows busy readers to grasp the main points quickly without reading the entire report. An executive summary should use an indirect approach for reports written in indirect order. It should use a direct approach for reports written in direct order. Figure 9-16 on page 345 is an example of an executive summary.

Key ▶ Point

In reports written for school or for scholarly journals, the executive summary is often called a synopsis or an abstract.

The Report Body

The report body, which contains the text of the report, consists of three parts: the introduction; the findings and analysis; and the summary, conclusions, and recommendations.

The introduction states the purpose of the report. Figure 9-17 on page 346 shows an introduction to the body of the report. The introduction discusses several topics, including any or all of the following:

Authorization	Statement of who authorized the report and the time and manner of authorization
Statement of the Problem	Reasons for writing the report and the goals to be accomplished
Scope	Information the report does and does not cover
Limitations	Factors affecting the scope of the report, such as a limited amount of time or a limited budget
Definitions	List of unfamiliar terms and their definitions

The findings and analysis section of the report body comes next. It presents the findings and the supporting details and examines those results. See Figure 9-18 on pages 347–349 for an example. The summary, conclusions, and recommendations section comes last. It gives the report objectives, summarizes the findings, draws conclusions, and makes recommendations. Figure 9-19 on page 350 provides an example of this section.

Ethics

Be honest in your evaluation and reporting of research findings. Do not leave out data that fails to support your position.

Supplementary Parts

A formal report may also contain supplementary parts that follow the report body, such as a bibliography or an appendix. The bibliography is a list of sources used in preparing the report. The sources are shown in alphabetic order by authors' names. This page is called "Works Cited" when using MLA report format. Figure 9-20 on page 351 provides a sample Works Cited page.

Figure 9-13 Letter of Transmittal

Lamps, Inc.

7892 Gessner Drive
Austin, TX 78753
512-555-0125

May 5, 20--

Mr. Greg C. Gibson, Director
Human Resources Department
Lamps, Inc.
7892 Gessner Drive
Austin, TX 78753

Dear Mr. Gibson

On April 15, 20--, you asked me to research telecommuting programs. You also asked me to recommend whether to begin a telecommuting program at our Austin location. After completing my research, I recommend that the company begin a telecommuting program. The initial program should be only for employees in the Customer Service Call Center. The company may consider expanding the program later if it goes well with this department.

Several books and articles give information on the advantages and disadvantages of telecommuting. A summary of this information is included in the report. I also analyzed the monetary costs and benefits to the company to reach this recommendation.

If you have any questions about the report or telecommuting, please call me at extension 2891. I think employees in the Customer Service Call Center will be excited about a telecommuting program.

Sincerely

Katelyn Parker

Katelyn Parker
Human Resources Associate

Figure 9-14 Title Page

Telecommuting Program for Lamps, Inc.

Prepared for
Mr. Greg C. Gibson
Director of Human Resources
Austin Operations Center
Lamps, Inc.

Prepared by
Katelyn Parker
Human Resources Associate
Austin Operations Center
Lamps, Inc.

May 5, 20--

Figure 9-15 Table of Contents

Table of Contents

Executive Summary... iii

    Methodology iii

    Summary and Conclusions iii

    Recommendations.. iii

Introduction 1

    Statement of the Problem.. 1

    Scope 1

    Limitations 1

    Definitions 1

Findings and Analysis 2

    Advantages of Telecommuting.. 2

    Disadvantages of Telecommuting 2

    Employee Interest 3

    Costs and Benefits 3

Summary, Conclusions, and Recommendations.. 5

Works Cited... 6

Appendix 7

ii

Figure 9-16 Executive Summary

Executive Summary

The Austin Operations Center of Lamps, Inc., is considering implementing a telecommuting program for some employees. The purpose of this study was to determine whether or not telecommuting is feasible for some workers in the Customer Service Call Center.

Methodology

The possible advantages and disadvantages of telecommuting were identified from secondary research. A review of the company's current records provided costs for rent, taxes, and utilities for office space. Research was done to find approximate costs for a training program for employees and for new equipment and services that employees will need.

Summary and Conclusions

A telecommuting program for ten employees from the Customer Service Call Center at the Austin Operations Center will save the company about $41,980 in the first year of operation. In addition to the cost savings for the company, employees who take part in the program will have lower travel costs. They may also be more productive and satisfied with their jobs. These conditions may result in benefits to the company of more productive workers and less employee turnover. The teleworkers may use fewer sick days than they would if they were working at the company offices, which could save the company money.

Recommendations

The following recommendations are made based on the conclusions of this study:

- The company should implement a telecommuting program for ten employees from the Customer Service Call Center at the Austin Operations Center.

- The company should provide training for the employees who will telecommute and their supervisors. The training should detail what the company expects of teleworkers. It should also detail what teleworkers can expect from the company.

- The company should provide the equipment, telephone service, and Internet access needed by the employees who telecommute.

iii

Figure 9-17 Report Introduction

Introduction

Lamps, Inc. has successfully run an operations center in Austin, Texas, for the past 30 years. This manu-facturing, sales, and operations center has over 250 employees. Employees average five years or longer with the company.

Recently, the company has become interested in ways to save money and implement green practices. Green practices are those that are friendly to the environment. Telecommuting, which lowers harmful pollutants released by cars, is one such practice. Employees are interested in the benefits they can gain from telecommuting, such as lower travel costs.

Statement of the Problem

The objective of this report is to determine whether or not telecommuting is feasible for this branch of Lamp, Inc. To achieve this objective, the advantages and disadvantages of a telecommuting program will be identified. Costs and savings will be analyzed. Based on the analysis, conclusions will be drawn. Then a recommendation will be made.

Scope

This report discusses the possibility of using telecommuting at the Austin Operations Center. Employees that take part in the program would be from the Customer Service Call Center.

Limitations

This report is limited to the Austin Operations Center. Other branches of Lamps, Inc., were not part of this study.

Definitions

These definitions are listed to assist the reader.

- Telework is defined as "a variety of business situations where individuals use technology to work from somewhere other than a traditional workplace."

- Telecommuting is defined as "performing work at a place other than a traditional workplace in accordance with the terms of an employee and employer agreement" (Fulton-Calkins, 58-59).

Figure 9-18 Findings and Analysis

Findings and Analysis

A review of secondary research provided a list of possible advantages and disadvantages of telecommuting programs. A review of the company's current records provided costs for rent, taxes, and utilities for office space. Research was done to determine costs for a training program for employees and for new equipment and services that employees will need. A survey was used to determine employee interest in telecommuting.

Advantages of Telecommuting

There can be several advantages to telecommuting for both the company and the employees. Some advantages for employees and employers are listed below.

- No commuting time is required. Employees have more time to work or do other activities. Employees save money on fuel and upkeep for cars.

- Employees may experience lower stress levels. The home or other off-site setting may be more relaxing for workers than an office setting. There is no stress from driving or heavy traffic.

- Fewer interruptions may mean more productive work time for employees. Scheduling may be flexible, depending on the job.

- Companies may have lower costs for office space, furnishings, and other overhead items.

- Employees may find a telecommuting program attractive. Companies may be able to keep employees longer and have less turnover. This means lower hiring and training costs.

- Employees may take fewer sick days for minor illnesses or injuries. Bad weather will not prevent employees from working when they cannot travel to the company location ("Telecommuting Advantages").

Telecommuting programs can also provide advantages for the community. According to Tom Harnish, who studies the effects of telework, "Telecommuting offers the community less highway congestion, lower greenhouse gas pollution, and less dependence on foreign oil" ("New Study").

Disadvantages of Telecommuting

Although there are advantages of telecommuting, there can also be disadvantages. Some of the disadvantages are shown in the following list.

Figure 9-18 Findings and Analysis Continued

3

- Telecommuting works for some jobs but not for others (Weisman, 16). For example, when machinery is required for production of a product, workers must go to the machinery to do their work. Those workers cannot telecommute.

- Managers and employees must adjust to a lack of direct supervision of workers. Job performance must be measured by whether work is completed correctly and in a timely manner (Weisman, 16).

- Telecommuting involves security risks. Teleworkers often connect to a company network using a computer at home. The home computer may be at higher risk for viruses, Trojan horses, spyware, and other destructive programs. (Pelgrin)

- Some teleworkers may feel isolated. Some people enjoy the social aspects of the workplace and miss interacting with other employees in person.

- A separate telephone line is needed at the worker's home to handle business calls. Family members and others in the home must understand that this line is only for the teleworker's use (Fawkner). Other equipment, such as a printer or fax machine, and Internet access may also be needed.

Employee Interest

A questionnaire was given to employees in the Customer Service Call Center to determine their interest in a telecommuting program. The questionnaire is provided in the Appendix. Of the 30 employees, 15 employees indicated that they would like to take part in a telecommuting program. However, a certain number of employees are needed in the office to deal with situations that teleworkers may not be able to handle. Some employees may not have the discipline or organization skills that are needed for successful teleworkers. Therefore, the company must decide the number of employees to be part of the initial program.

Costs and Benefits

The following data relate to savings and costs for implementing a telecommuting program.

- The company pays $27 per square foot per year for office space at the Austin Center. The company pays about $15.90 per square foot of office space per year for related utilities and taxes.

- The company will no longer need to rent 1,200 square feet of office space if ten employees from the Customer Service Call Center telecommute.

- Teleworkers will need a separate telephone line and Internet access at their homes. This service will cost approximately $50 per month per worker.

- Teleworkers will use the computers that they now use at work, so no additional cost will be incurred for computers.

Figure 9-18 Findings and Analysis Concluded

- The company's telephone system can be set up to forward customer service calls to the teleworkers' home telephone at no additional cost.

- Teleworkers share a printer at the office. Teleworkers will need printers at home. A printer/fax machine will cost about $150 per worker. This will be part of the startup costs for the program.

- Employees who will telecommute will take a two-day training course related to telework and what the company expects of them. This course will cost the company $2,000 for ten teleworkers and three supervisors.

Table 1 shows the analysis of the cost data. Note that a net savings of $41,980 will result the first year. Changes in rental, utility, and tax rates and the need to replace equipment (computers or printers) may result in different figures for later years. If other employees take part in the program in future years, the training program may be needed again.

TABLE 1
SAVING AND COSTS OF IMPLEMENTING A TELECOMMUTING PROGRAM

Savings		Costs	
$ 27.00	Office Rent	$ 50.00	Telephone and Internet
15.90	Utilities and Taxes	12	Months per Year
$ 42.90	Total	$ 600.00	Total
		10	Number Required
1,200	Sq. Ft. Office Space No Longer Required	$6,000.00	Total
		$ 150.00	Printer/Fax Cost
		10	Printers Required
		$1,500.00	Total
		$2,000.00	Training Program Cost
$51,480.00	Total Saving First Year	$9,500.00	Total Costs First Year

Figure 9-19 Summary, Recommendations, and Conclusions

5

Summary, Conclusions, and Recommendations

The Austin Operations Center of Lamps, Inc., is considering implementing a telecommuting program for some employees. The purpose of this study was to determine whether or not telecommuting is feasible for some workers in the Customer Service Call Center. The possible advantages and disadvantages of telecommuting were identified from secondary research. A review of the company's current records provided costs for rent, taxes, and utilities for office space. Research was done to find approximate costs for a training program for employees and for new equipment and services that employees will need. A survey was used to determine employee interest in telecommuting.

The report findings support several conclusions. A telecommuting program for ten employees from the Customer Service Call Center at the Austin Operations Center will save the company about $41,980 in the first year of operation. In addition to the cost savings for the company, employees who take part in the program will have lower travel costs. They may also be more productive and satisfied with their jobs. These conditions may result in benefits to the company of more productive workers and less employee turnover. The teleworkers may use fewer sick days than they would if they were working at the company offices, which could save the company money.

The following recommendations are based on these conclusions:

- The company should implement a telecommuting program for ten employees from the Customer Service Call Center at the Austin Operations Center.

- The company should provide training for the employees who will telecommute and their supervisors. The training should detail what the company expects of teleworkers. It should also detail what teleworkers can expect from the company.

- The company should provide the equipment, telephone service, and Internet access needed by the employees who telecommute.

- The company's Information Technology Department should work with the teleworkers to be sure their home computers and/or networks have the proper security measures in place.

Figure 9-20 Works Cited

6

Works Cited

Fawkner, Elena. "The Telecommuting Alternative." *A Home-Based Business Online.* 29 May 2008
   <http://www.ahbbo.com/telecomalternative.html>.

Fulton-Calkins, Patsy and Karin Stulz. *Procedures and Theory for Administrative Professionals.* Ohio:
   Cengage, South-Western, 2009.

"New Study Quantifies Pollution Reduced by Telecommuters." *Business Wire* 17 April, 2008. 29 May
   2008 <http://findarticles.com/p/articles/mi_m0EIN/is_2008_April_17/ai_n25335034>.

Pelgrin, William F. "Telecommuting Security Risks." *Cyber Security Tips Newsletter* July 2007. 29 May
   2008 <http://www.msisac.org/awareness/news/2007-07.cfm>.

"Telecommuting Advantages—For You and Your Company." *MsMoney.com.* 26 May 2008
   <http://www.msmoney.com/mm/career/finding_balance/telecommute_adv.htm>.

Weisman, Robyn. "Trends in Telecommuting." *Processor* 15 December 2006.

Figure 9-21 Appendix

7

Appendix

Employee Questionnaire on Telecommuting

Respond to each question by checking the appropriate column.

	Agree	Disagree	No Opinion
1. I believe that telecommuting would lower my travel costs.	____	____	____
2. I believe that telecommuting helps the environment.	____	____	____
3. I believe that telecommuting will allow me to be more productive.	____	____	____
4. I believe that telecommuting will allow me to experience less job-related stress.	____	____	____
5. I believe that my job can be performed effectively from my home office.	____	____	____
6. I believe that I have the discipline and organization needed to be a successful teleworker.	____	____	____
7. I believe that telecommuting will make me feel isolated from my coworkers and have a negative impact on my work.	____	____	____
8. I believe that I will be happier with my job situation if I am given the opportunity to telecommute.	____	____	____
9. I believe that not all job situations lend themselves to telecommuting.	____	____	____
10. I am interested in taking part in a telecommuting program.	____	____	____

An **appendix** contains supplementary materials that are placed at the end of a document or book. These related materials are too long to be included in the body. Examples of appendix items include questionnaires and a glossary of terms. Figure 9-21 on page 352 shows a sample appendix.

Formatting Formal Reports

Formal reports generally follow specific formatting guidelines. A company may develop its own style manual. A style manual is a set of guidelines for formatting documents. This manual helps report writers plan the appropriate margins, spacing, headings, and other details.

Margins and Spacing

For an unbound report, use a top margin of 2 inches on the first page and on the first page of new sections, such as a Works Cited page. On the other pages, use a top margin of 1 inch. Use 1 inch for side and bottom margins for all pages. If the report will be bound, increase the left margin on all pages to 1.5 inches.

Follow the spacing guidelines given for the particular format being used. For example, MLA style requires double spacing for paragraphs. The example report in this section uses the *Word 2007* default spacing of 1.15 lines with 10 points of space after a paragraph.

Headings

Use headings to help organize and present data. Headings help the reader follow the line of thought as they move from point to point in the report. A first-level heading is a heading that opens a major section. For example, a first-level heading is a heading identified with a Roman numeral in the report outline. A second-level heading is a heading that introduces a subtopic below a first-level heading.

The headings of the same level within a section, such as second-level headings in an outline, should be parallel in form. Parallel headings show readers that the ideas are grouped for a reason. If one heading begins with a noun,

NETBookmark

Reports for school are often prepared in MLA (Modern Language Association) style. The *MLA Handbook* shows details of using this report style. The MLA provides a Web site with many types of information. A link to the MLA site is provided on the Web site for this book that is shown below. Go to the MLA site.

1. When was MLA founded? (See the About MLA page.)

2. About how many people are members of MLA?

3. Locate the frequently asked questions about the *MLA Handbook*. (Use the search box.) Read the list of questions. Select one of the questions and give a brief summary of the answer.

www.cengage.com/school/bcomm/buscomm

Key▶Point

Follow the guidelines for the report style you are instructed to use. The report shown in this section uses an appropriate format for a business report.

Key ▶ Point

The headings of the same level within a report should be parallel in form.

all headings at that level should begin with a noun. If one heading begins with a verb, all other headings should begin with a verb. This usage makes the headings parallel. In addition, each level should have a minimum of two headings. Examples of parallel headings and headings that are not parallel are shown below.

Headings Are Parallel

I. Steps in planning

    A. Defining the objective

    B. Determining the project leader

        1. Vendor

        2. Outside consultant

II. Feasibility study

Headings Are Not Parallel

I. Plan the study

    A. Defining the objective

    B. Determine project leader

        1. Vendor

        2. Hiring an outside consultant

II. Feasibility study

Visual Aids

Key ▶ Point

Visual aids (graphs, tables, and pictures) help the reader understand and interpret written data.

Most formal reports (and many informal reports) include visual aids and graphics. Charts, graphs, tables, pictures, and photos help the reader understand and interpret written information. With computers, producing graphics is easy and inexpensive. Visual aids and their use in reports are described in Chapter 10.

check point 9

1. What are the preliminary parts of a formal report? Are these parts placed before or after the report body?

2. What are two supplementary report parts that follow the report body?

Check your answers in Appendix C.

Section 9.3 *Applications*

A. *Formal or Informal Report*

Indicate whether you would use a formal or an informal report in response to each request.

1. Send me a report on our returned goods for the past six months. I want the data organized by region.

2. We are considering a telecommuting program for our customer service associates. Do an extensive study of costs and benefits to present to senior managers.

3. Prepare a report that examines the alternatives available for training on the new telephone system we have installed.

4. Create a report that summarizes the progress we have made on transferring files to the new storage location.

5. Create a report with your recommendation for how to change our running shoes to increase sales. You will need to do both primary and secondary research. The report will be evaluated by company senior managers.

B. *Parts of a Formal Report*

Indicate the part of a formal report that is described.

1. A part that tells the conclusions reached

2. A part that introduces the report to the reader

3. A part that lists the sections included in the report

4. A part of the body that states the purpose of the report

5. A part of the body that gives the limitations of the report

6. A part of the body that describes the data and how it was handled

7. A part of the body that advises the reader how to proceed

8. A part of the report that contains a list of source materials used in the report

9. A part of the report that contains supplementary material related to the report

10. A part of the report that tells what is and is not covered in the report

Chapter *Summary*

9.1 *Planning Reports*

- A report is a document that provides facts, opinions, or ideas about a specific topic or problem.

- Before writing a report, the writer must do planning and research.

- Primary research involves gathering new data. Secondary research involves locating data that already has been gathered and reported.

- Once the data for a report has been collected, it should be organized in a meaningful way.

- Data are analyzed and the findings are used to draw conclusions. Recommendations are made based on the conclusions.

9.2 *Writing Informal Reports*

- Most business reports are informal reports. They present information that has been requested, or they analyze a problem and report the findings.

- Informal reports may be organized in direct order or indirect order.

- An outline is used to identify and position the topics and subtopics in a report.

- Informal reports usually are written in a relatively personal style. If a report is about a serious problem or if it is going to a senior manager, it should be written in an impersonal style.

- Informal reports have three main parts: the opening, the body, and the closing. They may be formatted like letters, memos, or manuscripts.

9.3 *Writing Formal Reports*

- Formal reports are more complex and longer than informal reports.

- Formal reports may be organized in direct or indirect order.

- Formal reports usually are written in an impersonal style.

- A formal report has three major parts: preliminary parts, body or text, and supplementary parts.

- The report format should follow the guidelines of the report style the writer has been instructed to use.

Vocabulary

Open the *Word* file *CH09 Vocabulary* from the student data files. Complete the exercise to review the vocabulary terms from this chapter.

alternative	observation
analytical report	outline
analyze	primary research
appendix	recommendation
bibliography	report
conclusion	scope
documentation	secondary research
executive summary	survey
hypothesis	table of contents
informational report	timeline
interview	wildcard

Critical Thinking Questions

1. The longer and more complex the report, the more important outlining is. Do you agree with that statement? Why or why not?

2. Why is it important to express the objective or topic of a report in a single statement?

3. Which is more difficult to do, primary research or secondary research? Why?

4. Why is evaluating the data you find an important part of the research phase of preparing a report?

5. *Paraphrasing, plagiarism,* and *documentation* are terms associated with reports. Discuss how these terms relate to one another.

CRITICAL THINKING

Chapter *Applications*

A. *Plan a Formal Report*

1. Identify a topic or problem to be researched and studied for a formal report. The report can be an informational report or an analytical report. Ask your teacher to approve the topic.

2. Write a statement or question that identifies the objective of the report.

3. Determine the scope of the report. Decide what related areas will and will not be included in the report. You may need to modify the scope after you begin doing research.

4. Develop a timeline for completing the report. Start with the date your teacher gives you for completing the report. Work backward from that date to create a timeline.

INTERNET

B. *Conduct Research for a Report*

1. Decide whether primary research, such as collecting data from a survey, or secondary research is appropriate for the report. You might want to do both types of research.

2. Gather the data. Evaluate each source of data that you use to determine whether it is relevant, accurate, current, reliable, and unbiased.

3. Create a bibliography note and one or more research notes for each secondary data source you use.

REAL WORLD

C. *Analyze Data for a Report*

1. Prepare a preliminary outline to organize the data you found in your research.

2. Decide whether to use hypotheses or alternatives in the outline if you are doing an analytical report. Develop a list of questions you want to answer using the data.

3. Compile, compute, compare, contrast, or evaluate the data as appropriate for your project.

D. *Draw Conclusions and Make Recommendations*

CRITICAL THINKING

1. Use the data you have analyzed to try to answer your list of questions developed earlier.

2. Using the data analysis, reach one or more conclusions about the topic or problem.

3. Prepare recommendations based on the conclusions if that is appropriate for your report.

E. *Write a Formal Report*

1. Create an outline for the report you have planned and researched. The outline may be a topic outline or a discussion outline.

2. Write the report using the outline you prepared earlier.

    - Create a letter or memo of transmittal for the report. Address the letter or memo to your teacher.

    - Prepare a title page and a table of contents. You will need to update the table of contents with the page numbers after you complete the report body.

    - Create an executive summary for the report.

    - Create the report body to include an introduction section; a findings and analysis section; and a summary and conclusions section. Also, include recommendations if that is appropriate for your report.

    - Prepare a Works Cited or Bibliography page.

    - Format the report like the one shown in the figures in Section 9.3 of this chapter unless your teacher requests that you use another format. Use the MLA style for citations in the text unless your teacher requests that you use another format.

    - Include an appendix at the end of the report if needed.

    - Work with a classmate to edit and proofread the report to be sure it is courteous, correct, concise, clear, and complete.

TEAMWORK

Editing Activity

Open and edit the *Word* file *CH09 Editing* from the student data files. Correct all spelling, punctuation, and grammar errors.

CASE STUDY

Repair Shop Report

As manager of the automotive repair shop for a local car dealer, you have a thriving business. Yesterday the owner of the dealership, Mr. Alvarez, asked you to prepare a report summarizing the past year's activities in the shop. You saw some successes this past year, but you also had some problems.

The positives for the year were as follows:

- The 12 shop employees completed at least two training courses, preparing them to work on the new models coming out in the fall.

- On a questionnaire given to all customers, the average rating of the services rendered by workers in the shop was 5.5, with 7.0 being the highest score possible. That rating fell in the "very good" range.

- Just over 95 percent of the repairs to vehicles were completed within the time frame stated to customers.

- Income from the automotive repair shop increased 25 percent.

The negatives for the year were these:

- The customers' overall rating of the mechanical aspects of cars sold by the dealership fell 25 percent—from 5.0 to 3.75, with 7.0 being the highest score possible.

- The average rating by customers for parts was only 3.4, with 7.0 being the highest score possible. This rating fell in the "poor" range.

- While income for the automotive repair shop increased, profit from the shop fell 20 percent. (Costs increased 40 percent.)

- Labor turnover within the shop continues to be a problem. This year the turnover rate was 60 percent. The average number of years a worker has been employed in this shop is 1.4 years. When workers were asked about their reasons for leaving, most gave "wages" as the main reason. Some indicated that they could make as much as $3 an hour more in other shops. Also, some (40 percent) indicated that the "working atmosphere" of other shops was much better.

1. If you were writing the report, what order (direct or indirect) would you use? Why?

2. Should the report be an informational or analytical report? Why?

3. Should the report be formal or informal? Should it be written in memo, letter, or manuscript style? Why?

4. Should the report be prepared in personal or impersonal writing style? Why?

Transportation, Distribution & Logistics

Communication for Transportation, Distribution, and Logistics

Alice Cleveland is an experienced flight attendant at an international airline. Three months ago, she was asked to head a company-wide committee related to passenger safety. She was very pleased to be asked to head the committee.

The company's leaders are very much aware that when flight attendants give their government-required presentations, passengers are not paying attention. These talks explain the use of seat belts and oxygen masks and positions of exits of the airplanes. As a result, if an emergency were to arise, many passengers would not know what to do. Alice's committee is to investigate the problem and make recommendations on how to get passengers to listen.

The committee's research has been completed. Now Alice must report the committee's findings to her supervisors—both orally and in a written report. She is nervous, but she knows her supervisors well and thinks that they will be supportive.

1. What type of report should Alice write to her supervisors? Should it be formal or informal? Should it be in memo, letter, or manuscript format?

2. If the report was directed to the company's top management, would the type of Alice's report change? If so, how?

3. Is the objective assigned to the committee easy to accomplish? Why or why not?

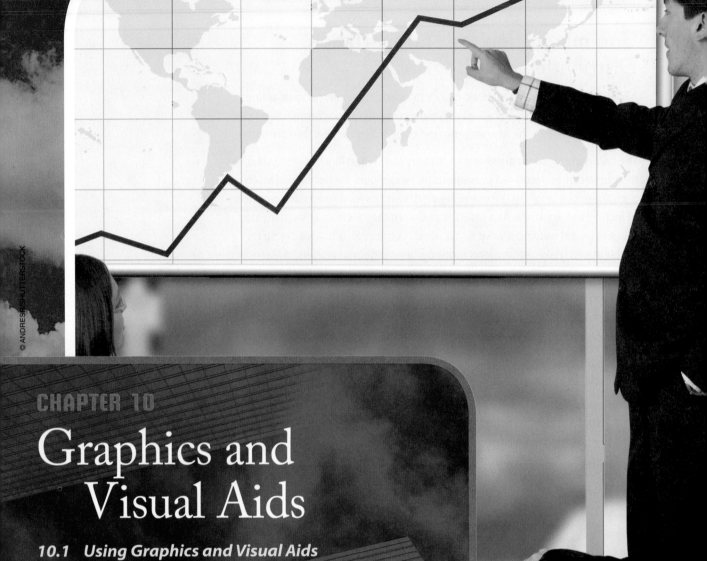

CHAPTER 10

Graphics and Visual Aids

10.1 Using Graphics and Visual Aids

10.2 Developing Graphics

Presenting a Progress Report

Lucia Lu has acted as her team's spokesperson for the past six months. Each month she gives her team's progress report on a major computer project to the company's top management. Today, as she leaves the meeting, she remembers the day she first volunteered to give the report for the team. She did not intend to become the team's spokesperson. Lucia intended to take her turn and then let others take their turns.

Now Lucia finds herself with an unwritten job responsibility—official team spokesperson. In fact, after her first presentation, no one ever raised a question about who would give the monthly presentation—it would be Lucia. Whenever the team raises a question about the content of the monthly progress report, they always look to Lucia for the answer.

Lucia thinks she is doing a good job when giving the information on the project. However, she is not quite sure that she is doing as well as she would like. The handout she prepares for her presentation each month is full of important numbers and statistics. When giving the oral presentation, she follows the handout.

Because she has worked with the numbers during the month, Lucia is very familiar with them by the time she presents them in the meeting. She is concerned, though, by the vacant look she has observed in many audience members during the part of her report in which she gives the numbers and statistics.

Lucia decides that between now and next month's meeting, she will try to find a better way to present the numbers and statistics of the progress report.

Questions

1. Why do audience members often lose interest when a great deal of numbers and statistical data are included in a report?

2. What would you recommend to Lucia to improve the way she presents numbers and statistics?

3. How might Lucia apply the Chinese proverb, "One showing is worth a hundred sayings"?

Using Graphics and Visual Aids

Key ▶ Point

Using graphics and other visual aids can help improve your communications.

The Importance of Graphics and Visual Aids

Many people remember information they see much longer and better than information they hear. For this reason, using graphics and other visual aids can help you improve your communications. These aids provide a visual image related to the words in a message.

The meaning of the terms **graphic** and **visual aid** overlap in general usage. A visual aid is any object, picture, drawing, map, poster, chart, or other image that helps the audience or reader understand data or concepts. A visual aid should provide an image that stimulates thought and interest. The term *graphic* is more narrow in scope. In this chapter, graphic will be used to mean a table or a chart. A graphic can be an efficient means of presenting large amounts of data. Communicators are using more visual aids than in the past for these reasons:

◼ Audiences expect messages to be delivered in clear, easy-to-understand, and visually stimulating ways. For example, few people return to an Internet site that contains only text. Magazines that have no photographs are not very popular.

◼ Creating and using visual aids is easier than ever before. Several software programs include features that allow you to create colorful, easy-to-understand graphics. These programs also allow you to insert visual aids into reports and letters or to use them in electronic slides.

◼ Communicators improve their chances of keeping the audience's attention when they use graphics and other visual aids. Important points can be made with visual aids.

check point 1

1. Why is it important to use graphics and other visual aids in the communication process?

2. Give five examples of visual aids.

Check your answers in Appendix C.

Visual aids can help readers and listeners understand a message.

Use of Visual Aids in Documents

When you use visual aids in documents, you should identify them and place them in an appropriate location. Doing so will ensure that the reader gains as much benefit from them as possible.

Placing Visual Aids

A visual aid, such as a chart or photo, can be placed in the body of a document. Graphics, such as tables or charts, are sometimes placed in an appendix. However, if the graphic is not important enough to be placed in the body of a document, it may not be important enough to be included at all. Place a visual aid in a document where the reader would prefer and most benefit from its placement. When a visual aid relates to a major point being presented, place it in the body of the document. If the purpose of a table or chart is to provide details that only some readers would need, place it in an appendix.

When you place a graphic within a document, include a reference to the graphic before the graphic appears. Make the reference to the graphic flow smoothly into your discussion, as illustrated in the following examples.

> As Figure 4 illustrates, the demand for plumbers has increased 7 percent in each of the past two years.

> Whenever the data you use in a graphic comes from another source, include a source line with the graphic as shown in Figure 10.

Diversity

Visual aids can be particularly helpful for readers for whom English is a second language.

When a graphic is placed in an appendix, mention the graphic in an appropriate place in the body of a document. The following example introduces a graphic in an appendix.

> The demand for plumbers over the past two years has increased an average of 7 percent. (See Figure 4 in the Appendix for a comparison by region.)

When placing a graphic in the body of a document, place the graphic on the same page as its reference, if possible. When that placement is not possible, place the graphic on the next page following its first reference. Avoid dividing a graphic between pages. Leave about one blank line (10 or 12 pts.) of space before and after a graphic in a document, such as a letter, memo, or report. Figure 10-1 shows a table in a report.

Photographs and clip art can be placed in documents to add interest or help illustrate a point. **Clip art** is a drawing or image that has been saved as an electronic file. For example, a flyer that announces a company picnic might contain clip art of a park, food, or a picnic basket. Clip art is available with word processing programs, in collections, and on the Internet. Some clip art is free and can be used in personal or business documents. Other clip art may be used for a fee. Be sure to check the use restrictions for clip art you find on the Internet that is listed as free. Free use may be limited to personal documents.

Ethics

Follow all copyright restrictions when using clip art. Using clip art without proper permission is unethical.

Figure 10-1 A table can be used to summarize data in a document.

2

Dirt Bike Sales

Sales of our most popular dirt bike, Model XX45, have increased by 10 percent over last quarter. The largest number of units was sold in the South region. Sales units by region are shown in Table 1.

Table 1

DIRT BIKE, MODEL XX45

Region	Sales in Units
Northwest	1,596
Northeast	2,200
Central	2,584
West	3,215
South	3,506
Total Sales	13,101

A reference statement often is not needed for photos or clip art. However, the image should be placed near the related text. A reference to the image can be made in the text if including the statement helps make a point.

Identifying Visual Aids

When several graphics or other visual aids are placed in a document, a numbering system is needed to identify each one. Giving each graphic a title helps readers understand the images. When the image or data used to create an image comes from another source, a source line is used. The source line tells where the data came from and gives credit to the creator or owner of the data.

Numbering System

When a document has only one graphic, no numbering system is needed. When a document has more than one graphic, a numbering system is necessary. Choose a numbering system and be consistent with the format throughout the document. For example, you may choose to identify all graphics as *Figures* and number them throughout. Another option is to use two designations. You might use the term *Table* for graphics that are in table format and the term *Figure* for graphics that are charts.

When a document contains only one section or chapter, number the figures consecutively (Figure 1, Figure 2, Table 1, Table 2, etc.). When there is more than one section or chapter, use a system such as *Figure 1.1, Figure 1.2* for the first section; *Figure 2.1, Figure 2.2* for the second section; etc. The number is usually placed along with a title above or below the graphic.

Titles for Visual Aids

A title should briefly describe a graphic. The title should contain enough information for the reader to understand the graphic aid without having to read an explanation in the text. However, the title should not be too long. The title may be shown in all uppercase letters or in uppercase and lowercase

Key▶Point

Use a numbering system and titles to identify graphics when more than one appears in a document.

letters. The title may also be in bold letters as shown below. Be consistent throughout the document in whatever format you choose for titles.

Figure 11-1 Growing Demand for Plumbers

Figure 9.2 Jobs for Plumbers

Key ▶ Point

When using data or graphics from secondary research, be sure you have permission to use the data or graphic.

Source Lines

When you have created the data and graphic (you are the original source), you do not need to include a **source line**. Whenever you obtain material from another source, you must include a source line. The line includes the word *source* followed by a colon and the source of the data or graphic. A figure and source line are shown in Figure 10-2. If the information is copyrighted, be sure you have permission to use the data or graphic.

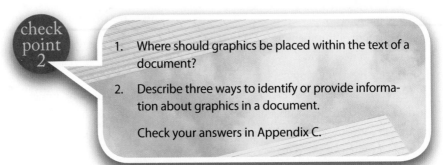

check point 2

1. Where should graphics be placed within the text of a document?

2. Describe three ways to identify or provide information about graphics in a document.

Check your answers in Appendix C.

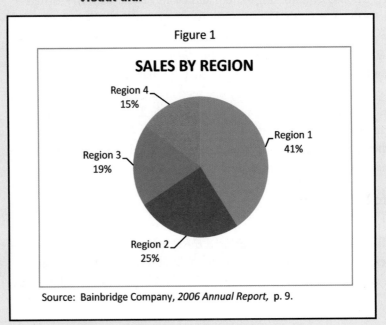

Figure 10-2 A source line identifies the creator of data or a visual aid.

Figure 1

SALES BY REGION

Region 4
15%

Region 1
41%

Region 3
19%

Region 2
25%

Source: Bainbridge Company, *2006 Annual Report,* p. 9.

Reading Charts

Employees often need to read charts found in reports or other documents. Understanding the parts of a chart can help you interpret the chart correctly.

A pie chart is used to show the relationship of a part to a whole. For example, a pie chart could be used to show the sales in each region as part of the total sales. The pieces in a pie chart are often shown as percentages. It is important to remember that the values for the pieces should add up to 100 percent or a total number that is given.

Column, bar, and line charts (also called graphs) are used to show a comparison of different items or of the same item over time. These charts have a value axis and a category axis. The value axis shows a number scale. The category axis shows the items being compared. It is important to read the scale as well as look at the columns, bars, or lines to understand a chart. The chart may have a legend. A chart **legend** identifies the items the columns, bars, or lines represent.

Open the *Word* file *CH10 Reading* from the student data files. Follow the directions provided to read charts and answer questions about them.

Choosing the Correct Visual Aid

To choose the most appropriate graphic or visual aid, you must identify what you want your receiver to understand. You must identify an objective and choose a graphic or other visual aid that is best suited for that purpose. The types of graphics and other visual aids covered in this chapter and the strength of each are presented briefly in the following list. You will learn about creating some of these visual aids in the next section.

Key▶Point

To choose the most appropriate graphic or visual aid, identify an objective you want to achieve with the visual aid.

- **Tables.** Tables show exact figures or present detailed information in an organized, easy-to-follow format.
- **Organization charts.** Organization charts show lines of authority and relationships among employees or job positions.
- **Flowcharts.** Flowcharts illustrate the steps in a procedure or process. Different shapes are used in indicate types of activities in some charts.

- **Pie charts.** Pie charts show how the parts of a whole are distributed.

- **Line charts.** Line charts show changes in amounts over time.

- **Bar charts.** Bar charts show a comparison of amounts. Bars extend from left to right in a bar chart. Items or categories being compared are placed on the vertical axis. Values are placed on the horizontal axis.

- **Column charts.** Column charts show a comparison of amounts. Columns extend vertically from bottom to top in a column chart. Items or categories being compared are placed on the horizontal axis. Values are placed on the vertical axis. Some programs and documents call both bar and column charts *bar charts*.

- **Maps.** Maps show geographic regions such as cities, states, or countries.

- **Photographs.** Photographs, also called pictures, show a realistic view of an item, person, or place. Using a digital camera provides photographs in electronic format than can easily be placed in documents.

- **Drawings.** Drawings are clip art or line art images that add interest or show specific details of an object.

check point 3

1. What type of graphic shows lines of authority and relationships among employees in a company?

2. What type of graphic shows geographic regions such as cities, states, or countries?

3. What type of graphic shows the steps in a procedure or process?

Check your answers in Appendix C.

Section 10.1 *Applications*

A. *Choose Visual Aids*

Identify the type of visual aid that would be appropriate for each situation described.

1. A chart to compare yearly sales in Texas for the past four years

2. An image to place on an invitation to a holiday luncheon

3. A chart to illustrate the steps in processing an order

4. A chart to show changes in amounts of overtime worked over the past six months for three departments

5. An image that shows the geographic region where the company has offices

6. An image that shows the lines of authority and relationships among employees in the Manufacturing Department

7. A realistic view of our new office building

8. A chart that shows the percentage of returned goods for each department

9. A graphic that shows prices for items in the new product line in an organized, easy-to-follow format

B. *Research Visual Aids*

1. Work with a classmate to complete this application.

2. Access the Internet. Use a search engine to find an article or report that uses charts, tables, maps, or other visual aids (other than photos). For example, you might search using the keywords *population growth chart* or *baseball stats*.

3. Record the name of the Web site and the article or page name.

4. Describe the visual aids that are used.

5. Are the visual aids used effectively? Why or why not?

INTERNET

TEAMWORK

REAL WORLD

Developing Graphics

Creating Graphics Electronically

Key ▶ Point

Word processing, spreadsheet, and graphics programs can be used to create visual aids.

Computer programs allow users to create and edit professional-looking graphics. The programs are easy to use and can be learned quickly. Word processing programs, such as *Microsoft Word*, come with clip art that can be used in documents. *Word* also provides a gallery of Table Styles that aids users in creating attractive tables. Figure 10-3 shows the Table Styles and a formatted table.

Spreadsheet programs, such as *Microsoft Excel*®, provide an easy way to create various kinds of charts. Charts created in one program can often be placed into documents created in other programs. For example, a chart created in *Excel* can be pasted into a *Word* document.

Some computer programs are designed specifically for creating and editing photos and graphics. *CorelDRAW*® *Graphics Suite*, *Adobe*® *Photoshop*®, and *Fireworks*® are examples of these programs. More time is required to learn how to use these programs than to learn the graphics features of word processing or spreadsheet programs. However, these programs have advanced

Figure 10-3 Table Styles in Microsoft Word

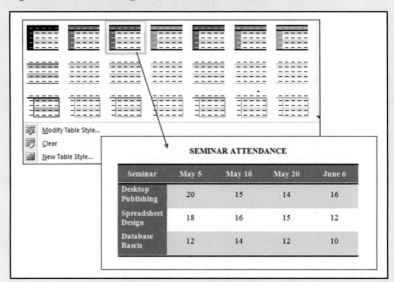

SEMINAR ATTENDANCE

Seminar	May 5	May 10	May 20	June 6
Desktop Publishing	20	15	14	16
Spreadsheet Design	18	16	15	12
Database Bascis	12	14	12	10

Modify Table Style...
Clear
New Table Style...

features that allow users to be very creative. Presentation software, such as *Microsoft PowerPoint®*, allows users to create charts, insert clip art and photos, and select various designs for electronic slides. You will learn more about using visual aids on electronic slides in Chapter 13.

Tables

A **table** is an arrangement of data organized in rows and columns. Rows extend horizontally across the table. Columns extend vertically. Tables are a valuable visual aid in reports and other documents because they show data in a way that is easy to understand. Tables can be created in word processing or spreadsheet programs.

Formats for tables vary. Use a format that makes the data easy to read and understand. Some general guidelines for creating an effective table are listed below. Refer to Figure 10-4 for a table illustration.

- Number tables if more than one table appears in a report. For example, key *Table 1* above the table title.

- Use a title for the table that is clear and concise. Key the title in bold, all capital letters and center it over the table.

- Use column headings to label the columns. Center the headings over the columns or match the alignment of the text or numbers in the columns.

Figure 10-4 Table

Table 1

NEW YORK YANKEES TEAM RESULTS
2000-2007

Year	Wins	Losses	Attendance
2007	94	68	4,271,083
2006	97	65	4,243,780
2005	95	67	4,090,440
2004	101	61	3,775,294
2003	101	61	3,465,600
2002	103	58	3,465,807
2001	95	65	3,264,847
2000	87	74	3,227,657
	773	519	29,804,508

Source: The Official Site of the New York Yankees, accessed June 5, 2008, available from http://newyork.yankees.mlb.com/nyy/history/year_by_year_results.jsp.

■ Align columns of text at the left. Align columns of numbers at the right or at the decimal point if the numbers have decimals.

■ Place a single line, also called a rule, under the last number when two or more numbers are calculated. Place a double rule under numbers that are totals or final amounts.

■ Include a source note for tables to show the source of the data. If the data are your original numbers, a source note is not needed.

Ethics

Using data without giving credit to the source is unethical. Include a source note to show where data in a table comes from when the data is not original.

check point 4

1. Why are tables a valuable visual aid for reports and other documents?

2. Name two types of programs that can be used to create tables.

3. What goal should be kept in mind when selecting a format for a table?

Check your answers in Appendix C.

Charts

In business documents, several types of charts are commonly used. Organization charts and flowcharts are often included in company manuals. Pie charts, line charts, and bar charts are used in reports, memos, and oral presentations.

Organization Charts

Key ▶ Point

An organization chart shows the lines of authority and communication in a company.

An **organization chart** shows the relationships of employees, positions, and departments. It shows lines of authority and communication in a company. The chart can show the entire company or only one section or department. Figure 10-5 on page 375 illustrates an organization chart. The boxes in the chart may list position titles or employee names and position titles. In general, the higher the level of the box in the chart, the higher the level of authority that position has within the organization.

The solid lines between boxes show lines of authority and formal communication. Dotted lines can be used to show positions that are not part of a line of authority. For example, a president of a company may have an assistant and a secretary. In the chart, those two positions are placed below the level of president and above the level of vice presidents. However, those two positions are not above the vice presidents in authority.

Figure 10-5 Organization Chart

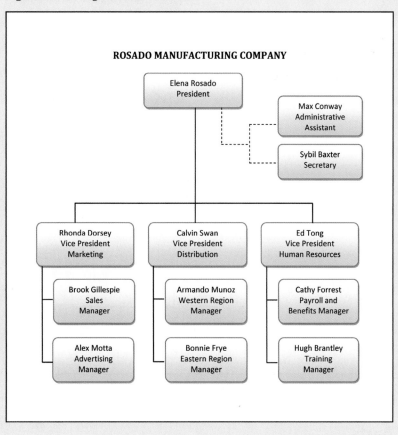

Flowcharts

A **flowchart** is a step-by-step diagram of a procedure or process. The flowchart allows the user to see the order in which the steps must be completed. For example, suppose a new procedure is described in eight paragraphs of text. Reading a flowchart that shows each step of the procedure would help employees follow the steps. Figure 10-6 on page 376 is a flowchart that shows the procedure for processing an order.

Tables and charts can be presented in either portrait or landscape orientation. In **portrait orientation**, the short edge of the image is at the top. Letters and memos are created using portrait orientation. The chart in Figure 10-5 uses portrait orientation. In **landscape orientation**, the long edge of the image is at the top. Wide tables and advertising flyers are often created using landscape orientation. The chart in Figure 10-6 uses landscape orientation. You should choose the orientation that works best to display the table or chart.

Key▶Point

A flowchart is used to show the steps in a procedure or process.

Figure 10-6 Flowchart for an Order Process

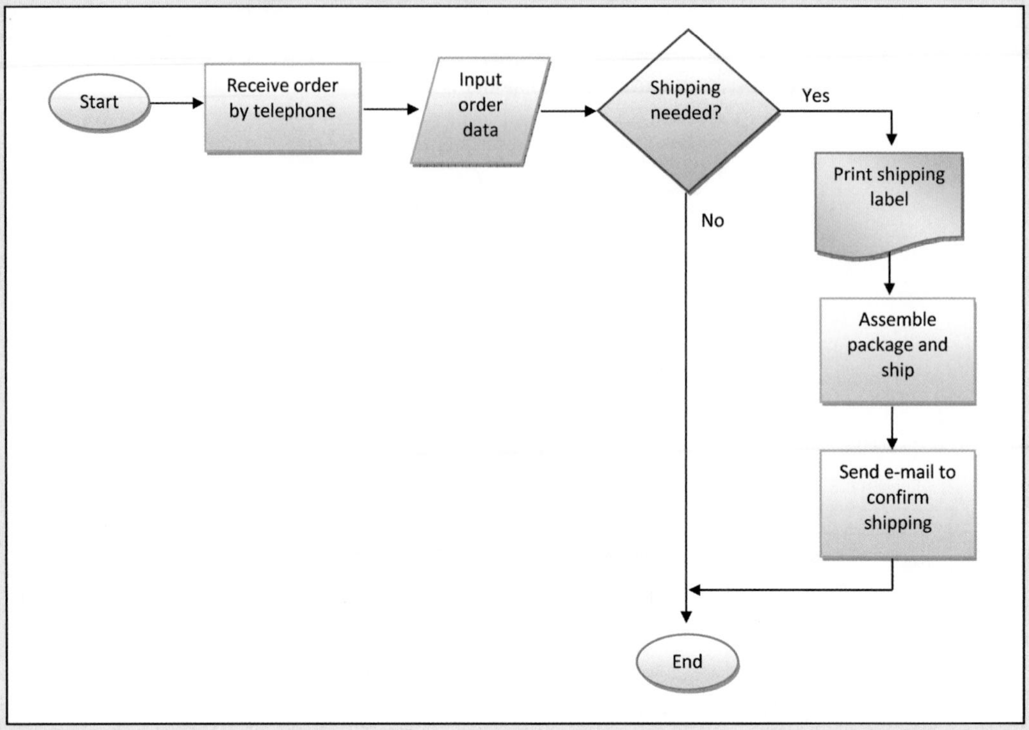

Pie Charts

A **pie chart** shows how the parts of a whole are distributed and how the parts relate to one another. Figure 10-7 on page 377 shows two pie charts. Often, the parts are shown as percentages. A pie chart can clearly present data, such as sales or earnings by company regions or departments.

A pie chart is suitable for displaying data when there are a small number of parts. When you make a pie chart, arrange the data in some logical order. You could arrange sales percentages by region numbers as shown in Figure 10-7. This method would be a good way to show data if you also have a pie chart that shows earnings by region. This arrangement would make it easy to compare data from the two charts. You might place the data (and pie sections) in order from largest to smallest. This order would be good for looking at attendance records for seminars given during one year.

Include a specific, clear title when creating a pie chart. The title should contain enough information for the reader to understand the pie chart without having to read an explanation in the text. Use a chart legend to show the name of each piece or label the pieces. You can also label the pieces to show values.

Key▶Point

When creating a pie chart, use a chart legend to show the name of each chart piece or label the pieces.

Figure 10-7 Pie Charts

Figure 1

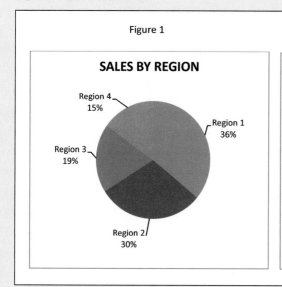

SALES BY REGION

Region 4
15%

Region 1
36%

Region 3
19%

Region 2
30%

Figure 2

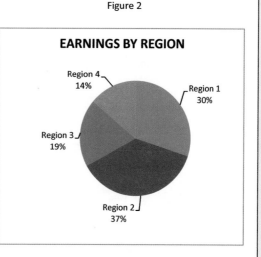

EARNINGS BY REGION

Region 4
14%

Region 1
30%

Region 3
19%

Region 2
37%

Line Charts

A **line chart** shows changes in quantity or value over time. This type of chart is often used to show ups and downs or trends over a period of time. In charts that show trends, the category (horizontal) axis is used to show the time or quantity measured. The value (vertical) axis is used to show amounts.

A single-line chart shows the movement of only one quantity or value over time. Shading or coloring may be used to add emphasis to the single-line chart. This type of chart is also called an *area chart*.

A multiple-line chart shows the movement of two or more quantities or values over time. In this type of chart, you can choose a different line style or color for each category. Use a legend to identify what each line represents, as shown in Figure 10-8 on page 378. You can also label points on the lines to show values.

as shown in Figure 10-8 on page 378.

K e y ▶ P o i n t

A line chart may show values for only one set of data or for two or more sets of data.

check point 5

1. What type of data is shown in an organization chart?

2. What is the purpose of a flowchart?

3. In what order should data be arranged in a pie chart?

Check your answers in Appendix C.

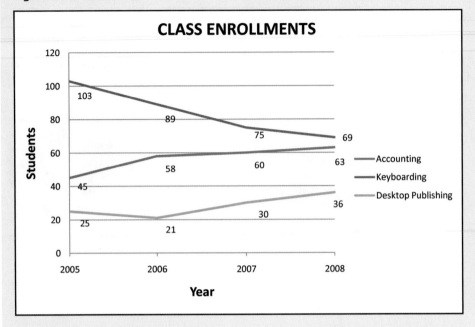

Figure 10-8 Line Chart

CLASS ENROLLMENTS

(Chart showing Students vs. Year)

- Accounting
- Keyboarding
- Desktop Publishing

Accounting: 103 (2005), 89 (2006), 75 (2007), 69 (2008)
Keyboarding: 45 (2005), 58 (2006), 60 (2007), 63 (2008)
Desktop Publishing: 25 (2005), 21 (2006), 30 (2007), 36 (2008)

Bar and Column Charts

Key ▶ Point

Both bar charts and column charts are used to compare data for different items or categories.

Bar charts and column charts are used to compare different groups of data to each other through the use of bars or columns that represent each group. The length of the bars or columns relate directly to their value. In a **bar chart**, bars extend from left to right. Items or categories being compared are placed on the vertical axis. Values are placed on the horizontal axis as shown in Figure 10-9 on page 379.

In a **column chart**, columns extend vertically from the bottom to the top of the chart. Items or categories being compared are placed on the horizontal axis. Values are placed on the vertical axis as shown in Figure 10-9. Some programs and documents call both bar and column charts *bar charts* or *bar graphs*.

A simple bar or column chart compares only one set of data. The width or height of the bar or column indicates quantity. Bar and column charts can also compare two or more sets of data. Different colors can be used for the different sets of data to make reading the chart easy. A legend identifies what each color represents. Limit the number of data sets used in one chart. Comparing more than four sets of data in one chart makes the chart too cluttered and difficult to read. If the chart will be placed on an electronic slide, use colors for the bars or columns that contrast well with each other and the chart background color. You may need to adjust the font size for titles or captions in the chart to make them easy to read.

Figure 10-9 Bar Chart and Column Chart

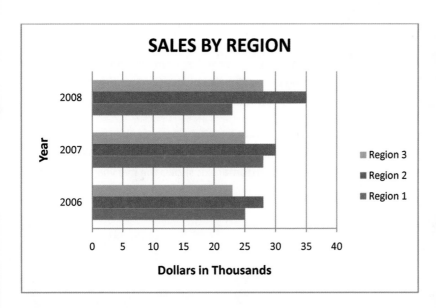

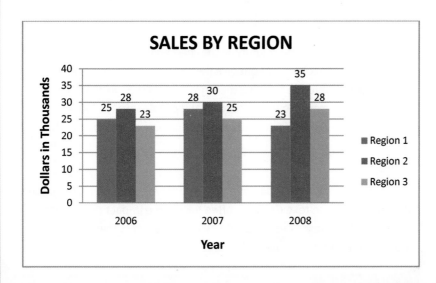

Charts That Mislead

Generally, writers use charts that represent data clearly. However, readers who do not look at charts carefully can be misled. Misleading charts may result when the writer is careless or not skilled in creating charts. Misleading charts can also be used on purpose to influence readers. This practice is unethical.

Compare the two charts show below. They illustrate the same data. In these two charts, the vertical axis shows the number of people who attended a conference. The horizontal axis shows the five years for which attendance figures were provided.

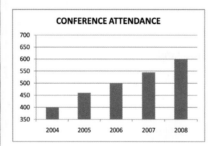
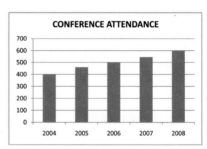

Look at the heights of the columns in the chart on the left. The difference in the heights of the columns might give the impression that nearly four times as many people attended in 2008 than in 2004. This change would be an increase of 400 percent. However, notice that the scale starts at 350. The chart on the right provides a clearer picture of the increase in attendance. The scale begins at 0 rather than 350. The actual increase is 50 percent over the five-year period, not 400 percent.

Some readers only skim a document, giving more attention to the graphics than to the written text. Graphics often have more impact on the reader than the related text does. Be careful to create graphics that give readers a clear and accurate picture of the data.

check point 6

1. What type of chart is used to show ups and downs or trends over a period of time?

2. How is a column chart different from a bar chart?

Check your answers in Appendix C.

Other Visual Aids

In addition to tables and charts, other types of visual aids can enhance documents. The visual aids discussed here are maps, photographs, and drawings.

Maps

A map shows geographic relationships. A map is especially useful when your audience may not be familiar with the geographic areas being discussed. A map, as shown in Figure 10-10, communicates information in an easy-to-grasp, interesting format. This map is from the National Atlas Web site, which provides several types of maps. The maps can be used for personal, school, and business documents.

Diversity

Maps can be helpful visual aids when sharing information with people from other regions or countries.

Figure 10-10 Map of Kentucky Congressional Districts

Source: National Atlas of the United States, accessed June 5, 2008, available from http://nationalatlas.gov/printable/images/pdf/congdist/KY05_110.pdf.

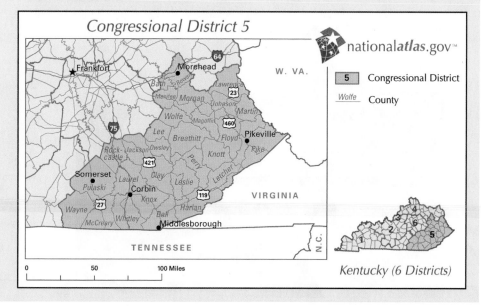

Photographs

A photograph is used to provide a realistic view of a specific item or place. Photographs can make a document more appealing to read. Four sources of easy access to photographs are a digital camera, professional photograph collections available on CD-ROM, a scanner, and the World Wide Web.

- A digital camera stores images digitally (in a format a computer can use) rather than recording them on film. Once you take a picture, you can download the photograph to your computer or printer. You can edit the photograph and insert it into a document. You can print the document or print just the photograph.

- CD-ROM collections, such as *ClipArt&More 3.5Million*, provide quality photographs. Some collections also include clip art, fonts, sound clips, and animations. Depending on the source of the photographs and how you are using them, you may have to pay a fee for their use.

- A scanner captures images from printed documents or objects. Photographs, posters, and magazine pages can be scanned. Some scanners come with software that lets you resize or modify a captured image. The image can be printed or inserted into a document.

- The World Wide Web is another excellent source of photographs. Many Web sites provide photographs that you may download for free. Other sites charge a fee for the photographs you use.

See Figure 10-11 for a photograph used to give a realistic view of people in a meeting.

⊞

Ethics

You may have to pay a fee to use photographs from CD-ROM collections or from the Internet. Read and follow the usage rules carefully when buying or downloading photographs.

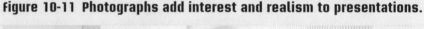

figure 10-11 Photographs add interest and realism to presentations.

IMAGE SOURCE BLACK/JUPITER IMAGES

Drawings

A drawing is useful for showing details or a procedure. Makers of bicycles, for example, provide consumers with detailed drawings. These drawings assist consumers in putting the bicycles together. A photograph of the assembled bicycle would not provide enough detail. Consumers would not be able to tell how to put the bicycle together properly.

The drawing in Figure 10-12 shows how to tie an underwriter's knot. This type of knot is used in wiring a lamp. The drawing provides more detail about the procedure than a photograph showing the finished knot could provide. A specific, detailed drawing, such as the one shown in Figure 10-12, may need to be created especially for particular use.

Clip art files contain drawings that can be used in documents and on electronic slides. Many different images are available. Writers can often find an image that is appropriate for the document or slide and do not need to create new art.

Ethics

Read and follow the usage rules carefully when buying or downloading clip art.

Figure 10-12 A drawing can show details or steps in a process.

Tying an Underwriter's Knot

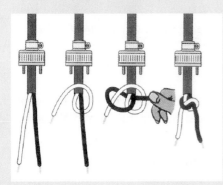

check point 7

1. What type of visual aid shows geographic relationships?

2. What type of visual aid is used to provide a realistic view of a specific item or place?

3. Why is a drawing sometimes a more effective visual aid than a photograph?

Check your answers in Appendix C.

Section 10.2 *Applications*

CRITICAL THINKING

TEAMWORK

A. Use Photographs or Clip Art

You have been asked to design a flyer that announces the annual company picnic.

1. Select a date for the picnic and a location. The location could be a city park, a water park, an amusement park, or other site in your area.

2. Create an attractive, full-page flyer that tells employees everything they need to know about the picnic. (Make up the details. Ask the five Ws to be sure all details are included.)

3. Include an appropriate photograph or clip art on the flyer.

4. Use landscape orientation for the flyer. Print the flyer on colored paper, if available.

5. Ask a classmate to review your flyer and offer suggestions for improvement. Make edits, proofread carefully, and correct all errors. Print a final copy of the flyer.

B. Create an Organization Chart

Create an organization chart for Jamison Company, using the details given below.

• The company president is Arthur Jamison.

• Three executives report directly to Mr. Jamison: Bill Wong, Vice President of Finance; Amy Wallace, Vice President of Manufacturing; and Alicia Diaz, Director of Human Resources.

• Bill Wray, Director of Accounting, and Tammy Chang, Budget Analyst, report to Bill Wong.

• Jack Greene, Plant Manager, and Wilson Jones, Maintenance Manager, report to Amy Wallace.

• Iris Diego, Training Specialist, and Anna Anderson, Benefits Manager, report to the Alicia Diaz.

• Georgia Rivers, Administrative Assistant, and Tom Brown, Secretary, report to Mr. Jamison.

Chapter *Summary*

10.1 Using Graphics and Visual Aids

- Using graphics and other visual aids can help improve communications.

- A visual aid is any object, picture, drawing, map, poster, chart, or other image that helps the audience or reader understand data or concepts.

- A visual aid, such as a chart or drawing, can be placed in the body of a document or in an appendix.

- When placing a graphic in the body of a document, include a reference to the graphic. Place the graphic on the same page as its reference, if possible.

- Use a numbering system and titles to identify graphics when more than one appears in a document. Whenever you obtain material for a graphic from another source, include a source line.

- To choose the most appropriate graphic or visual aid, consider what you want the receiver to understand.

10.2 Developing Graphics

- Computer programs allow users to create and edit professional-looking graphics.

- Tables are a valuable visual aid in reports and other documents because they show data in a way that is easy to understand.

- An organization chart shows the relationships of employees, positions, and departments.

- A flowchart is a step-by-step diagram of a procedure or process.

- A pie chart shows how the parts of a whole are distributed and how the parts relate to one another.

- A line chart shows changes in quantity or value over time.

- Bar charts and column charts are used to compare different groups of data to each other through the use of bars or columns that represent each group. The length of the bars or columns relate directly to their value.

- Maps, photographs, and drawings are visual aids that can enhance documents.

Vocabulary

Open the *Word* file *CH10 Vocabulary* from the student data files. Complete the exercise to review the vocabulary terms from this chapter.

bar chart	line chart
clip art	organization chart
column chart	pie chart
flowchart	portrait orientation
graphic	source line
landscape orientation	table
legend	visual aid

Critical Thinking Questions

CRITICAL THINKING

1. Why is the placement of a graphic important? What happens if a writer places a graphic in a report before he or she makes a reference to it?

2. Why do graphics often have more impact on their receivers than the related text?

3. Why is it important to follow the use restrictions for clip art, photographs, and other visual aids that you buy or download?

4. What can you do to make your graphics easy to understand?

Chapter *Applications*

A. *Report with Map*

You have been asked to prepare a report that gives information about your congressional district. You will find and download a map to use in this report.

INTERNET

REAL WORLD

1. Access the Internet and go the National Atlas Web site. A link to this site is provided on the Web site for this book. You can also search for *National Atlas*.

2. Go the page that has printable maps. Select the link for congressional districts.

3. Select the link that allows you to view and print maps.

4. Select your state from the list, and then select your congressional district. Choose to preview the map to make sure you have selected the correct one.

5. With the preview map on the screen, right-click on the preview map and select **Save Picture As**.

6. Enter a filename. Enter a location where the image will be saved.

7. Select **Bitmap** for the file type. Click **Save**.

8. Key the beginning of page 2 of a report shown below. Insert the map picture where indicated. Place a source line under the image.

9. Proofread and correct all errors before printing the page.

2

The United States House of Representatives has 435 congressional districts. About 600,000 people are included in each district. Census Bureau data are used to set the number of congressional districts within each state. Congressional District (insert number) of (insert your state name) is shown below in Figure 1.

B. *Pie Chart and Column Chart*

Your coworker is creating a report related to the company's order system. You have been asked to prepare two charts to place in the report.

1. Create a pie chart.

   - Use **ORDER METHODS 20--** for the chart title. (Use the current year for the date.)

   - The percentages for each order method for the current year are:

Internet	70%
Telephone	20%
U.S. Mail	10%

- Use a chart legend or label the pie chart pieces with the method name.

- Show the values for each pie chart piece.

2. Create a column chart that compares the order method values for this year with those from last year.

- For the chart title, use ORDER METHODS COMPARISON.

- The percentages for each order method for last year were:

Internet	55%
Telephone	25%
U.S. Mail	20%

- Use a chart legend and show the values for each column.

3. Print both charts.

C. Memo with Table

1. Key the following memo in correct format. Create a table to show the data clearly. Center the table and leave one blank line before and after the table.

2. Proofread and correct all errors.

To: All Employees

From: Anna Anderson, Benefits Manager

Date: October 20, 20--

Subject: Health Care Plan Enrollment

The open enrollment period for employee health care plans will be November 1 through December 15, 20--. The three plans that are available and their costs are shown in the table below. Details of the plans are in the attached pages.

HEALTH CARE PLANS

	Employee Cost Per Month		
Plan	Single	Single + One	Family
Plan A	$150	$200	$300
Plan B	$100	$125	$200
Plan C	$175	$225	$300

If you have any questions about the plans, contact me for more information. Complete and return the attached enrollment form by December 15 to ensure that your coverage will be active on January 1.

Attachments

D. Table and Charts

You need to include information about hospitals and their staff in a report.

1. The data for the hospitals are shown below. Create a table to show the data clearly. Use an appropriate title and column headings.

   Hyatt Charity Hospital has 80 nurse's aides, 120 licensed vocational nurses (LVNs), 86 registered nurses (RNs), and 40 doctors.

   Parker Children's Hospital has 86 nurse's aides, 124 LVNs, 89 RNs, and 52 doctors.

   City Hospital has 94 nurse's aides, 142 LVNs, 90 RNs, and 63 doctors.

2. Construct a multiple-line chart that shows the health care providers at those three hospitals.

   - Use an appropriate title.
   - Use a chart legend to identify each line.
   - Use a different color for each line.

3. Construct a bar chart that shows the health care providers at those three hospitals.

   - Use an appropriate title.
   - Use a chart legend to identify each bar.
   - Use a different color for each bar.
   - Show values for the bars.

4. Which of the two charts is better for displaying this data? Why?

E. Flowchart Symbols

When creating flowcharts, writers often use different shapes for different parts of a process. The shapes make understanding the flowchart easier.

1. Work with a classmate to complete this application. Access the Internet and go to a search engine. Search the Web using the keywords *flowchart symbols*.

2. Review several of the sites in the search results list to learn about flowchart symbols.

3. Create a table that shows the shape, name, and purpose of several flowchart symbols. (Flowchart symbols can be inserted into a *Word* table using the Insert, Shapes command.) Include a source line for the table data.

INTERNET

TEAMWORK

Editing Activity

Open and edit the *Word* file *CH10 Editing* from the student data files. Correct all spelling, punctuation, and grammar errors.

Profit Reporting

Thomas Carson is the vice president of the Electronics Division of a large company. One of his duties is to prepare a year-end report for company managers. The report summarizes sales income, costs, and profits for the year for his division. If the division meets its profit goals, Thomas will receive a 20 percent pay bonus.

Near the end of the year, Thomas began gathering data for the report. He found that the division was close to reaching its profit goals. To be sure the division would achieve its goal, Thomas instructed the Invoicing Department to bill for an order in December that would not be shipped until the first week of the next year. This placed the sales income for the order in the current year, allowing the division to reach its profit goal. However, the costs associated with the order will be recorded the following year when the order is shipped. This way of recording the sales and costs will make next year's profits lower.

Thomas received his pay bonus, which was his immediate concern. His motto is "Deal with next year next year."

1. Does the report Thomas prepared show a realistic picture of the division's performance for the year? Why or why not?

2. Did Thomas behave ethically? Why or why not?

Communication for Education and Training

Chris Austin is the director of the Health and Wellness Education Department at a health-care facility. One of his main duties is to schedule 15 to 20 classes every quarter. Scheduling involves deciding what classes to offer. Once the classes have been selected, a timetable is worked out. Then, Chris must find qualified people to teach the courses. After matching instructors with courses and adjusting times, he finalizes the schedule. He also develops the promotional materials that go out to the community.

A recent brochure includes course descriptions, meeting times, and other necessary information. The classes will be held October through December. Chris placed the classes in a table. He used appropriate class titles, such as Heart Health, Family Growth, Childcare, Fitness, and Nutrition.

In the classrooms, several options are available for visual aids. Chris knows that the instructors are very knowledgeable about their topics. However, they seem to know little about using visual aids in teaching. He wants to schedule a one-hour training session. In this session, he will discuss using flip charts, overhead projectors with transparencies, and electronic slides.

1. Should visual aids be part of the presentation Chris gives? If so, how should he use them?

2. How important are graphics and other visual aids in the brochures Chris sends to people in the community?

3. How important are communication skills in a job such as the one Chris holds?

CHAPTER 11
Technical Communication

11.1 *Writing to Instruct*

11.2 *Writing to Describe*

Improving a Process

Ramon Ruiz works in the Shipping Department of a large publisher. When customers return damaged books, the damage often is not obvious to the clerks who unpack them. Therefore, they sometimes place these books on the warehouse shelves. The damaged books are then shipped out again to the next customer who orders the books. That customer finds the damage, returns the damaged books, and usually complains about the inconvenience.

Ramon thinks the company could avoid shipping out damaged books by creating labels that identify the books as damaged. The company could send the new labels to customers who want to return damaged books. When the damaged books arrive back at the warehouse with the new labels stuck to them, the clerks would know to give the customer credit for the return and then destroy the damaged books.

Ramon's supervisor, Ms. Simpson, likes the idea and has had the new labels made. She asks Ramon to write a letter to customers explaining how to use the labels. She also decides that he should write a complete set of instructions for returning books. These instructions would prevent customers from shipping by the wrong method, sending the books to the wrong address, and so on. She also asks Ramon to write a description of the return process for the staff in other departments because they often ask questions about it.

Ramon has read many sets of instructions and assumes that a description of the return process would be very similar. He thinks he probably could just give other staff members a copy of the instructions he writes for the customers. He often talks with staff members on the phone. He knows they are very busy and tend to be impatient. They may not read the instructions. Some may be annoyed at even receiving them.

Questions

1. What questions should Ramon ask himself before he begins writing the customer instructions for returning books?

2. How can Ramon make the instructions look easy to follow?

3. Should Ramon give the customer instructions to the staff instead of writing a process description for them? Why or why not?

11.1 Writing to Instruct

OBJECTIVES

After completing Section 11.1, you should be able to:

1. Explain the purpose of instructions and manuals.

2. List the parts of effective instructions.

3. Write and edit effective instructions.

4. List the parts of effective manuals.

Key▶Point

A manual should allow users to find instructions quickly and understand them easily.

The Purpose of Instructions and Manuals

Do you always read the instructions before tackling a task? Do you find most instructions to be confusing, incomplete, or tedious? Instead of reading the instructions, many people use a trial-and-error approach in trying to program a DVD player, use jumper cables to start a car, or complete some other task. They may glance through the instructions, looking for information that can help them complete the task quickly. As a result, they may complete steps in the wrong order or skip some steps entirely. Only after other approaches fail will they resort to reading the instructions.

Instructions tell readers how to do something. **Manuals** are sets of instructions combined with explanations, descriptions, definitions, and other related information. Both instructions and manuals should provide all of the guidance readers need to carry out tasks. The writer's challenge is to create instructions and manuals that are so well organized that people can find instructions they want quickly and understand them easily.

Parts of Effective Instructions

Instructions should be clear, well organized, and geared to the intended receivers. They must include the information that receivers need—not too much and not too little. Instructions should use words that receivers understand. In addition, instructions should look inviting to read.

Effective instructions include the following parts:

1. A clear and specific title

2. An introduction and a list of any needed tools, equipment, and materials

3. Numbered steps in logical order

4. A conclusion

Figure 11-1 on page 395 shows a set of instructions with the parts labeled.

Figure 11-1 Instructions

How to Use a Respirator

All employees are required to wear a respirator when working in the shop area. For a respirator to protect you, you must put it on properly and test the fit each time you use it.

Put on the Respirator

1. Place the respirator over your nose and mouth.

2. Place the headband on top of your head.

3. Fasten the two bottom straps together behind your neck.

4. Adjust the faceplate and straps to achieve a comfortable, secure fit.
   - *The faceplate should rest on the bridge of your nose and against your chin.*
   - *To adjust the straps, use the metal slides.*

Check the Fit

5. Cover the exhalation valve loosely with the palm of your hand.

6. Exhale.
   The faceplate should bulge slightly. If you feel air on your face, there is a leak. Readjust the faceplate and straps and test again.

7. Place your hands gently over the cartidges.

8. Inhale.
   The faceplate should collapse slightly. If you feel air on your face, there is a leak. Readjust the faceplate and straps and test again.

When you have successfully completed the checks in Steps 5-8, you may enter the shop area.

WARNING
If you cannot get the respirator to fit correctly, **do not enter** the shop area.
Go to your supervisor.

BRAND X PICTURES/JUPITER IMAGES

Following clear instructions makes completing a task easier.

Clear and Specific Title

The title for a set of instructions should name the topic. It may also imply what the reader will do with the topic. The title should be specific enough for readers to know what it does and does not cover. Compare these titles:

Unclear and too broad	Hoses
Clear and specific	How to Load a Hose Bed
	How to Deploy Hoses

Key ▶ Point

The introduction explains what the instructions should accomplish and states who should follow the instructions.

Introduction and Needed Items

Readers need a brief orientation—two or three sentences—before they begin following a set of instructions. Writers tend to skimp on introductions because they want to get started writing the steps of the instructions. However, readers need to know when and why they should follow instructions. The introduction should explain what the instructions should accomplish (if that is not obvious). It should state who should follow the instructions and perhaps when and why to follow them. For example, suppose instructions tell how to order replacement parts. The introduction should explain who is responsible for ordering the parts and when the parts should be ordered.

List any needed items, such as tools, equipment, and materials, so readers can gather them before beginning the steps. Include any of the following sections that are needed.

Key ▶ Point

The introduction should include skills needed, a time frame for completion, and cautions or warnings related to the process.

- **Special skills or knowledge required.** If you expect readers to have special skills or knowledge, point that out. Otherwise, readers may attempt to follow the instructions without the necessary background knowledge. Refer readers to an appropriate source for any additional information they may need.

- **Time frame.** Tell readers how long the entire task or individual steps should take if that information would be helpful to them.

- **Cautions.** Warn readers about possible injury or other hazards. If necessary, repeat the warnings in the steps.

- **Definitions.** Define any terms that might not be familiar to readers, such as *initialize* and *airway*. Try to avoid using unfamiliar terms. They may discourage people from reading the instructions.

Numbered Steps

Detailed guidelines for writing numbered steps appear on page 399. To begin, think carefully about what your intended readers need to know in order to accomplish the task. What do they already know about the procedure? Have they completed similar tasks? How is this task different?

Key ▶ Point

Consider what readers already know when writing numbered steps.

Your goal in writing steps is to provide everything readers need without overwhelming them with details or unneeded information. One way to streamline your instructions is to avoid including obvious steps, such as "Seat yourself in front of the computer."

Conclusion

In the last section of your instructions, describe the expected results. The conclusion will help readers determine whether they have successfully completed the procedure. If your instructions are lengthy, you might summarize the major steps. You might tell readers where to find more help if they need it. The conclusion may simply be a sentence or two that follows the steps and has no separate heading of its own.

check point 1

1. What is the purpose of instructions and manuals?

2. What parts do effective instructions include?

Check your answers in Appendix C.

Writers should create clear instructions that avoid vague and general terms.

STOCKBYTE/GETTY IMAGES

Writing and Editing Guidelines

Writing specific, detailed instructions and descriptions is called **technical writing**. The following guidelines apply to all types of technical writing.

- Be specific and precise. Avoid vague or general terms.

Instead of	beside the strut
Write	next to the right side of the strut
Instead of	wash thoroughly
Write	wash for at least 20 seconds
Instead of	near the top of the page
Write	1 inch from the top edge of the page

- Use language the readers will understand.

Instead of	radiotherapy
Write	X-ray treatment
Instead of	remanded
Write	sent back to the trial court
Instead of	ARM's
Write	adjustable rate mortgages

When choosing what terms to use, consider your audience. General readers might not understand the term *radiotherapy*. However, if you were writing for medical personnel, the term would be appropriate.

- Be objective. A description for a brochure might require subjective terms, such as practical, attractive, good, poor, awkward, difficult, or impressive. However, in most technical writing, writers avoid subjective terms that reflect opinions, not facts.

Instead of	too high
Write	11/2 psi above normal

Instead of	attractive hairstyle
Write	French twist

Instead of	long workday
Write	ten-hour workday

Writing Steps

The following guidelines will help you write clear, easy-to-follow steps for instructions.

- Number each step and start it with a verb. The verb should name an action the reader will complete.

Instead of	1. Menu and Select are pressed at the same time.
Write	1. Press Menu and Select at the same time.

Key ▶ Point
Number steps for instructions and place them in logical order as they should be completed.

- Put the steps in sequential order—the order in which they should be completed.

Instead of	1. Open the drain valve after turning off the power.
Write	1. Turn off the power.
	2. Open the drain valve.

- Describe each step separately so readers will not overlook a step.

Instead of	1. Draw blood samples at 60 minutes, 120 minutes, and 180 minutes.
Write	1. Draw the first blood sample at 60 minutes.
	2. Draw a second blood sample at 120 minutes.
	3. Draw a third blood sample at 180 minutes.

- Indent any explanations under the appropriate step. Do not number explanations because the reader may think they are steps. You may also put the explanations in italics or enclose them in parentheses. Do not confuse explanations with warnings. Explanations are comments that help the reader understand the steps. Warnings are cautions that alert the reader to possible dangers or serious problems.

Key ▶ Point
Place explanations under the related step and do not number them.

Instead of	1. After you click Login, the Partner Home Page will be displayed.
Write	1. Click Login.
	(The Partner Home Page will be displayed.)

- If a step should be carried out only under certain conditions, describe the conditions first. If you do not immediately alert readers to a special condition, they might complete the step before they realize it should be done only at certain times.

| Instead of | 1. Enter the order number in Field 6 if the order will be filled by our warehouse. |
| Write | 1. If the order will be filled by our warehouse, enter the number in Field 6. |

- If you have many steps or several procedures, group them under sub-headings, such as those used in Figure 11-1 on page 395.

- Use single spacing (1 or 1.15) for the information within a step. Leave a blank line (10 or 12 pts.) between steps.

- Include diagrams or other graphics whenever they will clarify the instructions. Place the figures as close to the relevant steps as possible. Add arrows, numbers, or letters to link the steps to the areas of the figures that you are discussing.

- Create a clear, inviting format by using numbers, letters, indentation, bold, and a large amount of white space. **White space** is a blank area that does not contain text or images. Make each step stand out.

- Highlight warnings so readers do not overlook them. For example, you might print a warning in a different color, in a box, or in a large font. Place the warning in a position where the reader will see the warning in time to avoid the danger or problem to which the warning relates.

Editing Instructions

Editing is an important step in preparing instructions. During the editing phase, make sure that the steps are clear, complete, concise, correct, and courteous. Ask the questions listed in Figure 11-2 to help you evaluate the steps.

Ethics

Include source notes for graphics if they are not original. Obtain permissions to use the images if needed.

Figure 11-2 Evaluate instructions to be sure they are correct and complete.

EVALUATING INSTRUCTIONS
• Are the steps worded clearly?
• Do the steps include everything the reader needs to know?
• Is any unnecessary information included that should be deleted?
• Are the steps in the correct order?
• Are the illustrations appropriate?
• Are the warnings highlighted so that the reader will not overlook them?
• Are figures placed as close to the relevant steps as possible?

To check the accuracy of the steps, work through the instructions. Be careful not to follow the steps from memory, but to carry them out exactly as written. Have a printed copy of the steps before you on which to note any corrections you need to make. Write corrections immediately to make sure you will not forget them. Check the figures to be sure that they are in the right place to illustrate steps correctly.

As a further check for accuracy and completeness, ask another person to work through the steps. Ask the tester to write down problems and to suggest ways to improve the steps. If you are present during the testing, the tester can ask questions and give you comments directly. Be prepared to take notes.

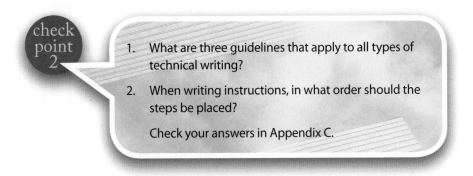

check point 2

1. What are three guidelines that apply to all types of technical writing?

2. When writing instructions, in what order should the steps be placed?

Check your answers in Appendix C.

Parts of Effective Manuals

A manual, as shown in Figure 11-3 on page 402, provides guidance in completing several related processes. For example, a manual might include entering a customer order, setting up shipping, and verifying that the order was packed and shipped. A manual might explain how a machine works and how to use, maintain, and repair it. Manuals often combine sets of instructions for completing various tasks with statements of policies or procedures. They may be written for experienced or inexperienced readers—or for both.

An effective manual should have the following parts:

1. A clear and specific title
2. A detailed table of contents
3. An introduction
4. Logical divisions of material, such as sections or chapters
5. Clear and complete steps in correct order in each section or chapter
6. Figures and illustrations, as needed
7. A glossary of terms, if needed
8. An appendix for supplementary material, if needed
9. An index (usually needed only for long manuals)

Key ▶ Point

When working through instructions, be careful not to follow the steps from memory. Do the steps exactly as written.

Key ▶ Point

Manuals often combine instructions for completing tasks with statements of policies or procedures.

Figure 11-3 Manual Pages

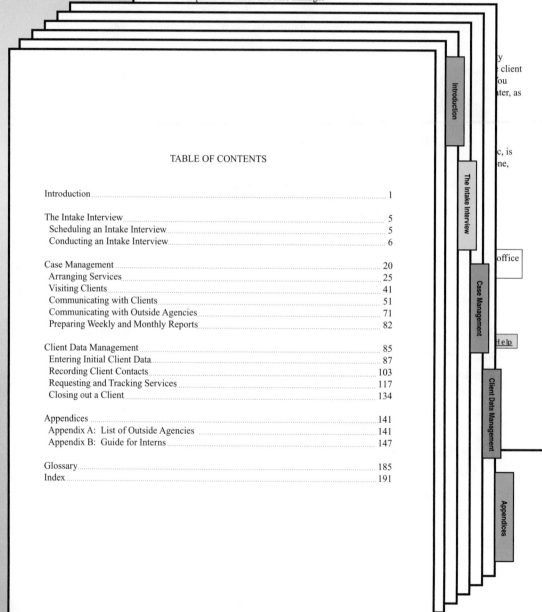

The Intake Interview

The intake interview is your first personal contact with a client. The goals of an intake interview are as follows:

➤ Determine whether the client is eligible for the program
➤ Provide an overview of the program and the client's rights and responsibilities
➤ Acquaint the client and case manager

TABLE OF CONTENTS

Introduction 1

The Intake Interview 5
    Scheduling an Intake Interview 5
    Conducting an Intake Interview 6

Case Management 20
    Arranging Services 25
    Visiting Clients 41
    Communicating with Clients 51
    Communicating with Outside Agencies 71
    Preparing Weekly and Monthly Reports 82

Client Data Management 85
    Entering Initial Client Data 87
    Recording Client Contacts 103
    Requesting and Tracking Services 117
    Closing out a Client 134

Appendices 141
    Appendix A: List of Outside Agencies 141
    Appendix B: Guide for Interns 147

Glossary 185
Index 191

Title, Table of Contents, and Introduction

Like a set of instructions, a manual should have a clear and specific title. The title should state the topic and imply reasons for using the manual.

Few people read manuals from the first page to the last. Instead, many readers use manuals as a reference when they complete a procedure for the first time. Readers might turn to a manual when they have problems with a procedure they know how to perform. For those reasons, information in a manual must be easy to locate. A table of contents allows users to find topics and figures easily.

The table of contents should include all of the headings and subheadings in the manual. Page numbers should be included to make it easy for readers to locate specific topics. The table of contents should also list by title related items in the manual, such as figures, tables, and diagrams. If the manual contains many figures or diagrams, they can be placed in a separate list.

The introduction to a manual may be longer than the introduction for a set of instructions, but it should include the same kinds of information. It should explain how the manual is organized, how it can be used and by whom, and what processes or procedures it covers. Each section of a manual might also have its own short introduction.

> **Key▶Point**
>
> Many readers use manuals as a reference when they complete a procedure for the first time or when they have problems with a procedure.

Sections, Steps, and Figures

The manual should be well organized. Manuals are typically divided into sections or chapters, one for each main procedure or process. A tab on the first page of each section can make the sections easy to locate. Colored tabs are used in the manual shown in Figure 11-3 on page 402. Colored pages that serve as dividers also help readers find the section they want.

Begin each section with a short introduction and follow with the steps needed. Follow the guidelines presented earlier to write clear, complete, correct, concise, and courteous steps. Edit the steps by working through them or having a tester work through them as described earlier.

Use illustrations wherever they would be helpful to readers. For example, a drawing could show how machine parts should be attached. A flowchart could trace the path of an order through a system. An organization chart might show how the company staff is organized. Tables might provide codes, contact numbers, temperatures and pressures, or other information that readers will need.

> **Key▶Point**
>
> Manuals are typically divided into sections or chapters, one for each main procedure or process.

Glossary, Appendix, and Index

A manual may have a **glossary**, which is a list of terms and abbreviations with definitions. The glossary might be placed at the end of the introduction or at the end of the manual. The glossary should be listed in the table of contents so readers can find it easily.

> **Key▶Point**
>
> A manual may have a glossary, which is a list of terms and abbreviations with definitions. These definitions aid the reader in understanding instructions.

OCCUPATIONAL SUCCESS

Creating Manuals Efficiently

Working efficiently contributes to occupational success. You can use several features of word processing software to help you create manuals efficiently.

Heading styles can be used to format headings and subheadings in the manual. Using heading styles ensures that each heading of the same level will be formatted in the same way.

When you use heading styles to format headings, you can have the program generate a table of contents automatically. Creating the table of contents this way is much faster than keying and formatting it manually. The table of contents can be updated easily if you add, delete, or move sections or figures in the document.

Create different sections in the document by inserting section breaks. Each section can have its own header and footer. For example, you might include the section or chapter name and the page number in a footer in each section. This footer would aid readers in locating specific sections of the manual.

When the manual includes illustrations, you can use the caption feature to add captions, such as *Figure 1* or *Table 1*, to the illustrations. The captions can be added as you insert images or later after all images are in place.

When you use the captions feature to insert figure captions, you can generate a table of figures, which is similar to a table of contents. The table of figures can be updated easily if you move figures within the document.

Refer to the Help entries in your word processing software if you are unfamiliar with how to use any of these features.

A manual might also include an appendix with supplemental material at the end of the manual. An appendix might contain forms, floor plans, district maps, company branch locations, suppliers, guides, or specifications.

Each appendix should have a descriptive title and should be listed separately in the table of contents. For example:

Appendix A: Examples of Order Forms. 34
Appendix B: Addresses of Branch Offices. 36

A manual might include special instructions for readers with little experience related to the topic. Basic step-by-step instructions for certain procedures might be placed in an appendix. A note in the instructions might say, "For more information on completing this process, see Appendix C."

Long manuals often include an index at the end of a manual. An **index** is a detailed listing of the topics and subtopics the manual covers and the pages on which the topics can be found. An index can help readers locate specific information quickly.

Use the checklist below to help you write effective instructions and manuals.

Diversity

Additional instructions may be included in an appendix for people with no background on the subject or for whom English is a second language.

check point 3

1. What parts should be included in an effective manual?

2. What information is included in a glossary for a manual? in an index?

Check your answers in Appendix C.

CHECKLIST FOR INSTRUCTIONS AND MANUALS

❑ Have I considered what my readers need to know in order to perform this process?

❑ Is the title clear and specific?

❑ Does the introduction explain who should follow these instructions, when, and why? Does it list needed tools, materials, skills, and knowledge?

❑ Have I worked through the instructions while editing them?

❑ Are the steps organized logically, numbered, and clearly written?

❑ Do the steps start with a verb? Are explanations indented below steps and not numbered?

❑ For a manual, have I made it easy for readers to locate specific information and included a detailed table of contents?

❑ Have I adapted the manual for readers with different experience levels?

Section 11.1 *Applications*

A. *Revise Instructions*

Rewrite the instructions so that they are clear and easy to follow. Replace each vague word or phrase with a more precise one. Place any explanations below the related steps. Make up details, as needed.

1. A small amount of gel should be applied to the electrode, and it should be placed above the left collarbone.

2. View the tape after removing the recording tab.

3. Enter the customer's name. After you enter the customer's name, the screen will display the customer's purchase history.

4. Turn the screw that is located near the panel.

5. When the mixture is cool, add it to the dry ingredients.

6. Clean the area with some bleach and water.

7. Turn the screw a few times to the right.

8. Move the lever up a little bit.

9. Sand the area with fine sandpaper.

B. *Evaluate Instructions*

1. Bring to class a set of instructions for some task or process. The instructions might be for assembling a toy, programming a cell phone, or some other process. If you do not have a printed set of instructions, search the Internet to find a set of instructions and print them. The instructions should be no longer than two pages.

2. Working with a classmate, review the instructions. Do the instructions include the parts listed in this chapter? If not, what parts are missing?

3. Do the instructions follow the guidelines given in this chapter for writing instructions? If not, which guidelines should have been followed and were not?

4. If there are figures in the instructions, are they helpful to the reader? Why or why not?

5. How could the instructions or figures be improved?

REAL WORLD

TEAMWORK

Writing to Describe

Types of Description Writing

A **description** is a verbal and/or visual picture of something. You might be asked to write a description of an object or a mechanism, usually as part of a report or a manual. An **object** is something inanimate that is natural or synthetic and can be seen or touched, such as an apple, a coffee cup, or a pencil. A **mechanism** is a type of object that consists of parts working together to perform one or more tasks. A mechanism can be as simple as a pencil sharpener or as complex as a computer.

You might also be asked to write a process description. A **process** is a series of events that take place over time and results in a change or a product. A process description explains how something works. Figure 11-4 is a process description for how a coal-fired power plant produces electricity.

Figure 11-4 A Verbal and Visual Description of a Process

Source: Tennessee Valley Authority, "Coal-Fired Power Plant," accessed June 12, 2008, available http://www.tva.gov/power/coalart.htm.

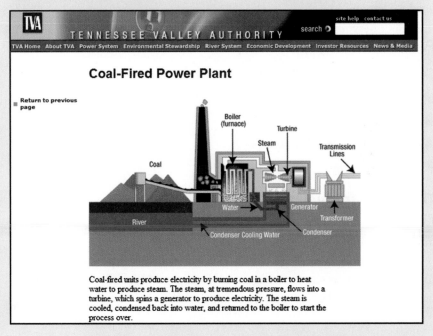

A process may be controlled by humans, or it may be a natural event, such as the eruption of a volcano. While a set of instructions explains how to perform a task, a process description explains how something happens. A process description might include a description of a related object. Many descriptions have photos, diagrams, or other figures. Together the verbal and visual pictures help readers visualize an object and understand how it looks and/or works. Descriptions are used in product brochures, proposals, and instructions.

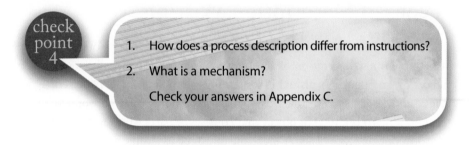

check point 4

1. How does a process description differ from instructions?

2. What is a mechanism?

Check your answers in Appendix C.

Object Descriptions

A description can range from an informal one-paragraph explanation to a formal report. Consider the needs and backgrounds of your readers as you plan a description. Consider what your readers already know about the object or process. Determine how they will use the description. For example, will they use it to assemble a car seat or to evaluate its safety? These questions will help you determine how much detail is needed and the terms you need to define.

Diversity

Education, gender, culture, and experience may influence what a reader knows about a topic. Consider the needs and backgrounds of your readers as you plan a description.

Parts of an Object Description

Object descriptions usually include the following parts:

- Title
- Introduction and overview
- Part-by part description (body)
- Conclusion

Title and Introduction

Like instructions, descriptions should begin with a clear, specific title. An informative title tells what the description covers.

In the introduction, begin with the definition and purpose of the object to orient readers, as shown in Figure 11-5 on page 410. Follow with other basic information. For example, you may describe what the object looks like,

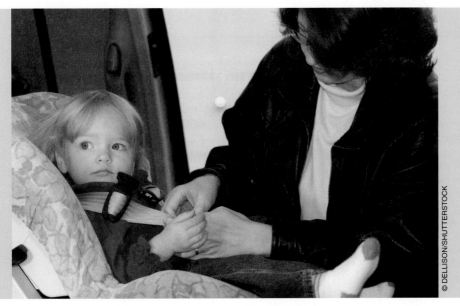

Consider the background and experience of readers when writing an object description.

give a general idea of how it works, and list its principal parts. Do not state the obvious, such as telling readers that a copier makes copies. Include a labeled illustration in the introduction or in the part-by-part description.

Part-by-Part Description

In the body, describe each part of the object separately, as shown in Figure 11-5 on page 410. Explain each part's appearance and function. Describe any subparts (parts of parts) as necessary. List the parts in a logical sequence. For example, you might start with the most important or most obvious part. You might begin at the top and progress to the bottom. You might begin with the main parts and move to the peripheral parts. You might move from the outside to the inside. Label the parts on one large illustration or include an illustration of each part. You might include a cutaway or a cross-sectional diagram of internal parts.

For a mechanism, you might describe how it looks when it is not functioning, what each part looks like and how the parts work together, and/or how the parts fit together.

Conclusion

Longer object descriptions require a brief conclusion to summarize what the main parts are and how they work together. The conclusion of a mechanism description might describe one operating cycle. The conclusion of a short description may be a brief paragraph without a separate heading.

Key ▶ Point

In an object description, describe each part of the object separately in a logical sequence.

Figure 11-5 Mechanism Description

The Hand Drill

The hand drill is the most basic type of drill used in woodworking. It is most often used when fine carpentry work is required or when a power drill is not available. Hand drills are suitable for drilling holes up to 1/4 inch in diameter in light metal or up to 1/2 inch in diameter in wood.

Hand drills are generally 15 inches long or less. A hand drill consists of a frame, a handle, a pinion gear, a chuck, a detachable drill bit, a wheel gear, and a crank.

- The **frame** is the main shaft of the drill. It holds the handle, pinion gear, and chuck. The frame is made of metal.

- The **handle** is used to position the drill and hold it steady. It is made of wood or plastic and is contoured to fit the user's hand. The handle sometimes doubles as a storage place for drill bits.

- The **pinion gear** is a small gear on the main shaft of the drill. It is made of metal.

- Below the pinion gear is the **chuck**, a metal device with jaws that holds the drill bit. Twisting the chuck or turning a key loosens or tightens the jaws. Chucks come in 1/4-inch, 3/8-inch, and 1/2-inch sizes.

- The **drill bit** is made of steel. It consists of a central core with a thread wrapped around it. Drill bits come in many sizes. A hand drill might come with five different drill bits, ranging in size from 1/8 inch to 1/4 inch.

- The **wheel gear** is made of metal. It is attached to the frame of the drill.

- The **crank** is made of wood or plastic and is attached to the wheel gear.

The user positions the drill vertically so the drill tip touches the place where he or she wants to bore a hole. The user holds the handle in one hand and turns the crank clockwise with the other hand, applying light pressure. Turning the crank turns the wheel gear. The turning force of the wheel gear is transferred to the pinion gear. As the pinion gear turns, the chuck and drill bit do, too. The end of the drill bit is a wedge that forces its way into the material. Each time the user turns the crank, the thread on the screw cuts deeper. The corkscrew shape of the drill bit helps carry away the drilled material.

Writing Object Descriptions

When writing an object description, use specific, precise language. Use words that readers will understand, and be objective in your writing style. Describe the object or part by its shape, dimensions, size, color, texture, position, and/or material. To describe an object's shape, you might use words such as *L-shaped*, *threadlike*, or *concave*. In describing its size, you might include the height, width, depth, area, and weight. Measure accurately. Your readers might use the data to determine whether certain parts will fit together. Compare the unfamiliar to the familiar. For example, you might compare the compound eye of an insect to the mirror of a telescope. Both objects have many facets.

Edit the description to be sure it is clear, complete, correct, concise, and courteous. If possible, have a coworker read the description and provide feedback. Proofread carefully and correct all errors.

Ethics

When writing an object description for a product ad, be objective and give accurate information. Do not overstate the value or features of the product.

READING SKILLS

Reading Manuals and Instructions

Reading a manual or instructions is required for many work tasks. You can use skills you learned earlier, skimming and careful reading, to use manuals effectively. Usually, you will not read a manual from beginning to end, as you would read a letter or a report. Instead, you will read the part of the manual that provides help or information for a certain task or policy.

To locate information you need quickly, skim the table of contents or the index of the manual to find the pages that relate to the topic. Go to the page in the first reference. Skim the page to see if it contains the material you need. If it does, read the material carefully. If it does not, go to the page in the next reference. Repeat the process until you find the information you need.

When you read instructions for a task, read all the steps before beginning the task. Instructions should be written with clear steps in logical order. However, not all instructions are written this way. Reading all the instructions first will acquaint you with the entire process and help you spot steps that may be out of order or incomplete.

Open the *Word* file *CH11 Reading* from the student data files. Follow the directions to practice finding and reading material in a manual.

check point 5

1. What parts are usually included in an object description?

2. What information should be included in the body of an object description?

Check your answers in Appendix C.

Process Descriptions

Key ▶ Point

A process description explains how something works. It does not explain how to perform a process.

A process description explains how something works. It does not explain how to perform a process; that is the function of instructions. For example, it might describe a department or business process, such as requesting copies or explaining how a reporting process works. The description might be a separate document or part of a larger document, such as a repair manual or a sales brochure.

Often, a writer prepares a process description and then a set of instructions for the same process. For example, the writer might explain how blood test orders are processed and then how to order blood tests.

Parts of a Process Description

Most process descriptions include these parts:

- Title
- Introduction and overview
- Part-by part description (body)
- Conclusion

Title and Introduction

A process description should have a clear and specific title. The title should tell readers what the process description covers. Contrast the specific title "Telephone Order Process Description" in Figure 11-6 on page 413 with a more general title, such as "Orders." The title also may suggest the technical level of the process description.

Key ▶ Point

The introduction of a process description should define the process and give an overview of its use.

The introduction should define the process and give an overview of its use. It also might explain why or how the process is used, who or what performs it, and where or when it takes place. If the process can be divided into steps, they might be listed in the introduction. The brief introduction in Figure 11-6 tells what a telephone order is, who handles telephone orders, and when the orders are processed.

Figure 11-6 Process Description

Telephone Order Process Description

Introduction
A telephone order is a sale made when a customer calls with a request to purchase items. Telephone orders are processed by sales associates who answer customer calls. Telephone orders are processed during regular business hours (from 8 a.m. to 6 p.m.) Monday through Saturday. Telephone orders are not taken on Sundays and on some holidays when the business is closed.

Steps in the Telephone Order Process
The following steps occur in processing a telephone order.

1. The telephone order process begins when a customer call is answered by a sales associate.
2. The sales associate inputs the customer's contact information and a shipping address, if needed.
3. The sales associate inputs the customer's payment information (credit card data).
4. The customer's payment information is verified. If the payment is accepted, the process continues. If the payment is not accepted, the customer is informed and given the opportunity to use another payment method or abandon the order.
5. If shipping is needed, a shipping label is printed.
6. The package is assembled and shipped. (For some items, such as clip art or music files, no shipping is needed. The customer downloads the items from the company Web site.)
7. An e-mail is sent to the customer confirming the order and giving shipping information, if needed.

Conclusion
Telephone orders are an important part of the company's business. About 25 percent of the company's orders are telephone orders. A flowchart showing the telephone order process is shown on the next page. Detailed instructions for completing each phase of the telephone order process are provided in this manual, beginning on page 98.

96

Figure 11-6 Process Description Continued

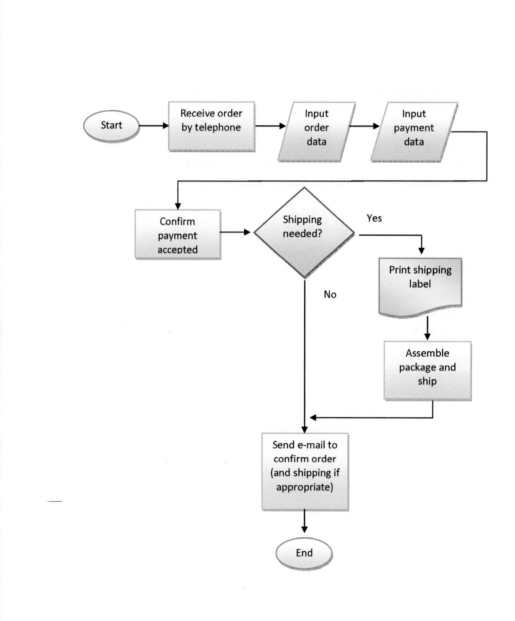

Figure 12   Telephone Order Process

97

Step-by-Step Description

Describe the process in order, much as you would describe the steps in a set of instructions. If the process occurs in a continuous cycle, begin with a major step. In a process description, the steps may be numbered as they are in a set of instructions if the steps are short. However, if the process is lengthy, each step might have its own subheading. Make sure you explain the relationships between the steps: how one step leads to or causes another.

Include illustrations that would be helpful to the reader. For example, the telephone order process description on pages 413 and 414 includes a flowchart of the process.

Use the present tense to describe a process that is ongoing or repeated. Use the past tense to describe a process that was completed in the past.

| Present Tense | The printer is copying and collating pages. |
| Past Tense | The harvesting machine cut and thrashed the wheat. |

The Society for Technical Communication (STC) provides training and support for professional technical writers. Other writers can also benefit from information provided by the STC.

Go to the STC Web site. A link to the site is provided on the Web site for this book that is shown below.

1. Read the *About STC* page. What is the mission of STC?

2. What resources are described on the site that would be helpful to people doing technical writing?

www.cengage.com/school/bcomm/buscomm

Key▶Point

Include illustrations in the body of a process description to help readers understand the process.

Conclusion

As with object descriptions, a long process description may require a paragraph summarizing the process and perhaps discussing its uses or advantages. The conclusion in a short process description might simply be the final paragraph.

Writing Process Descriptions

The first step in writing a process description is determining your readers' needs and levels of experience and knowledge. You must also find out how your description will be used so you know what details to include and how to present them.

When writing process descriptions, use specific, precise language. Choose words that readers will understand. Be objective and factual in your writing style. Describe the process completely from beginning to end. Include enough details for your readers to get a complete picture. Compare the unfamiliar to the familiar. For example, you might compare the process of converting sunlight into electricity with a solar panel to a green plant converting sunlight into energy through photosynthesis.

Edit the description to be sure it is clear, complete, correct, concise, and courteous. If possible, have a coworker read the description and provide feedback. Proofread carefully and correct all errors.

Use the checklist below to help you write effective object and process descriptions.

check point 6

1. What parts are usually included in a process description?

2. What information should be included in the body of a process description?

Check your answers in Appendix C.

CHECKLIST FOR OBJECT AND PROCESS DESCRIPTIONS

❏ Have I considered what my readers need to know, their level of expertise, and how they will use this description?

❏ Is the title clear and specific?

❏ Does the introduction give an overview of the object or process, including its purpose or function and the principal parts?

❏ Are the parts of the object or the steps of the process clearly described in a logical order?

❏ Is the conclusion appropriate?

❏ Have I edited the description to be sure it is clear, complete, correct, concise, and courteous?

Section 11.2 *Applications*

A. *Object Description for an Adult Audience*

Identify an object with at least two moving parts. Suppose you were going to write a description of the object for an adult who had never seen it and did not know what it was used for.

1. What would be a logical way to describe the parts of the object? For example, would it be best to start with the most important part or to start at the top and progress to the bottom?

2. What parts does the object have that you would need to describe? List the parts you can see and any internal parts you know of.

3. What words could you use to describe the object? List at least six words that describe its color, size, dimensions, texture, position, composition (what it is made of), or other features.

4. Using your answers to help you, write a description of the object. Include a title, introduction, body, and conclusion.

5. Ask a classmate to read your description and give feedback on how to improve it.

6. Make changes, as needed. Proofread and correct all errors.

TEAMWORK

B. *Map and Directions*

1. Work with a classmate to complete this application. Draw a map of the route from your school to your home.

2. Write a set of directions someone could follow from the school to your home.

3. Put your map out of sight and exchange directions with a partner.

4. Use your partner's directions to draw a map from the school to his or her home while your partner does the same with your directions.

5. Compare maps with your partner. Are the maps from each home to the school similar? If not, was the problem in the written directions?

6. Make any changes to the directions that would have helped your partner draw a more accurate map.

TEAMWORK

Chapter *Summary*

11.1 Writing to Instruct

- Instructions tell readers how to do something.

- Manuals are sets of instructions combined with explanations, descriptions, definitions, and other related information.

- Effective instructions include a clear and specific title, an introduction, a list of items needed, numbered steps in logical order, and a conclusion.

- Technical writing should be specific, precise, and objective and should use language readers can understand.

- Editing is an important step in preparing instructions. To check the accuracy of the steps, work through the instructions.

- A manual provides guidance in completing several related processes.

- A manual may include a glossary of terms, an appendix with supplementary information, and an index to aid in locating topics.

11.2 Writing to Describe

- A description is a verbal and/or visual picture of something.

- An object is something natural or synthetic that can be seen or touched, such as an apple, a coffee cup, or a pencil.

- A mechanism is a type of object that consists of parts working together to perform one or more tasks.

- Descriptions are often written for mechanisms and other objects to place in instructions or manuals.

- A process is a series of events that take place over time and results in a change or a product. A process description explains how something works.

Vocabulary

Open the *Word* file *CH11 Vocabulary* from the student data files. Complete the exercise to review the vocabulary terms from this chapter.

description	mechanism
glossary	object
index	process
instructions	technical writing
manuals	white space

Critical Thinking Questions

1. Suppose someone follows instructions you have written and makes a mistake. The person says, "But I thought you meant…." What might the problem be?

2. Is it easier to describe an object or a process? Why?

3. Think of a set of instructions you have read within the past week. Were the instructions effective? Why or why not.

4. The manual for your new cell phone discusses eight different procedures, such as downloading ring tones and using voice mail. All the procedures are listed under one heading, *Phone Operations.* Is this an effective way to organize the manual? Why or why not?

CRITICAL
THINKING

Chapter *Applications*

A. *Illustration*

1. Create a figure to illustrate a set of instructions, a manual, a mechanism description, or a process description. You may draw by hand, take a photograph, use clip art, or create the image using software tools.

2. Key a title for the figure in a word processing file.

3. Insert the image in the word processing file. Key a sentence that tells what the figure illustrates.

B. *Instructions for a Task*

REAL WORLD

1. Choose a simple task that you know how to perform well, such as how to make a music CD, lift a patient, change the oil in a car, make lasagna, or cut drywall.

2. Write a set of instructions for performing the task. Your audience is your classmates.

3. The instructions should follow the guidelines given in the chapter. Make sure your instructions include:

   - A title
   - An introduction with a list of any needed tools, equipment, and materials
   - Numbered steps in logical order
   - A conclusion

C. *Object Description for a Child*

TEAMWORK

1. Choose an object, such as an apple, a ladder, a coat, or a crayon.

2. Write a description of the object. Include a title, introduction, body, and conclusion. Use simple words, large type, an illustration, and any other features you think would be helpful to your audience.

3. Ask a classmate to read your description and give feedback on how to improve it.

4. Make changes, as needed. Proofread and correct all errors.

D. Mechanism Description

1. Choose a simple mechanism, such as a nutcracker, an eggbeater, a doorknob, a faucet, or a mechanism used in work that interests you. The mechanism can be one part of a machine.

2. Write a description of the mechanism for a teenager. Include a title, an introduction and overview, a part-by-part description, and a conclusion. Include an image of the mechanism, if possible.

3. Ask a classmate to read your description and give feedback on how to improve it.

4. Make changes, as needed. Proofread and correct all errors.

TEAMWORK

E. Process Description

1. Select a process that you understand well but that is unfamiliar to some people. You might select a process such as one of the following

    - Creating personalized letters using your software's mail merge feature
    - Taking a patient's blood pressure
    - Changing the oil in a car

2. Write a description of the process you selected. Your audience is the general public. Make sure your description includes the four parts of a process description and follows the guidelines given in the chapter.

REAL WORLD

Editing Activity

Open the *Word* file *CH11 Editing* from the student data files. Edit the set of instructions as directed below.

1. The title is not clear and specific. Edit to enter a better title.

2. The introduction does not include a list of needed tools, equipment, and materials. Add such a list.

3. Revise the numbered steps so that they all begin with a verb.

4. One step includes an explanation that should appear in an earlier step and should be indented under the step. Make that correction.

5. One step should be separated into two steps. Make that correction.

6. Identify the warning statement and place it where it should appear. Format the warning statement in a way that will make it stand out.

7. Identify and correct a misspelled word.

Contacting a Customer

Maggie Ryder has been hired as a consultant at a local company. For the past two years, the company sales have declined. Talented employees have been leaving the company. The president, Lu Kim, reviewed customer comments and employee exit interviews. He identified communications as a major problem area. Ms. Ryder examined the organization's employee procedures and customer publications. She quickly understood Mr. Kim's concerns.

For many tasks that employees must perform, there are no written procedures. As a result, those tasks are performed in a variety of ways or not at all. For other tasks, the guidelines are written so poorly that Ms. Ryder had trouble understanding them. Documents that go outside the company are not much better. Guides for customers on using the company's products and services are difficult to follow. They are so technical that they seem to be written for experts.

1. What suggestions could Ms. Ryder give for improving employee procedures?

2. What suggestions could Ms. Ryder give for improving product guides that are written for customers?

Communication for Science, Technology, Engineering, and Mathematics

Mr. Thomas is a chemistry teacher at Valley High School in south Texas. He loves chemistry and teaching. His students appreciate the way he brings real-world examples into the classroom to make lessons interesting. Because of his expertise in crop growth in arid climates, a national company employs him to do experiments at a local research site.

Today, besides teaching his classes, Mr. Thomas has two objectives to achieve. First, he must write a lab assignment for one of his advanced classes. He must write this assignment thoughtfully. If students mix the chemicals improperly, there could be a "foul smelling" result. His second objective is to write a report on one of his experiments at the research site. This report will be sent to fellow scientists at the head research facility in Kansas City.

1. When writing an assignment for the students, what type of writing will Mr. Thomas do? What writing techniques could Mr. Thomas use to write a successful lab assignment?

2. When writing the report on his experiment, what type of writing will Mr. Thomas do? What writing techniques could Mr. Thomas use to write the report on his experiment?

3. Should the recipients of Mr. Thomas' lab assignment and the recipients of the report on his experiment affect his writing? If so, how?

CHAPTER 12

Technology in the Workplace

12.1 Computer Hardware and Software

12.2 Other Technologies

12.3 Workplace Safety and Ergonomics

Outdated Agency

Martha Rodriguez is a real estate agent who has been working for Coleman Real Estate for several months. At one time, Coleman Real Estate had a reputation as one of the best agencies in town. However, in the past few years, it has been losing a lot of business to other agencies.

To Martha, the reasons for lost business are clear. The eight agents, a receptionist, and a secretary are using woefully outdated technology. The office has four aged desktop computers, a black and white printer, and a fax machine. The agency does not have access to the Internet and does not have a Web site. Voice mail is also not available. However, four of the eight agents that work for the company have cell phones.

Walt Coleman, the owner, is a very conservative businessman. He is not computer literate and has been hesitant to invest in a computer system. However, he knows that he needs to do something to regain the business his company has lost. Since Martha's previous job was at a very successful agency, he has asked for her ideas on how to update the company.

Questions

1. What updated technology could Martha recommend for the company?

2. How would the new technology allow the company to serve its customers better than it presently does?

3. What training for company employees could Martha recommend?

12.1

Computer Hardware and Software

Technology at Work

Technology is the application of scientific knowledge to practical tasks. The word *technology* also refers to tools, machines, and other inventions that make work faster, easier, or safer. Technology saves time and effort. For example, a dishwashing machine makes cleaning dirty dishes easy. Using a router makes building a set of kitchen cabinets faster. For employers, technology can save money and improve the quality of products. It allows people to accomplish more work in less time.

Being able to use technology in your work and to learn and adapt to new technologies are useful skills. This chapter provides an overview of common workplace technologies.

Computer Hardware

A **computer** is a machine that processes data according to a set of instructions in order to perform tasks. Computers range in size from supercomputers, which may take up several rooms, to computers that fit in the palm of your hand. A **personal computer** (PC) is a small, relatively inexpensive computer designed for an individual user. Personal computers are also called microcomputers. PCs may be linked together to form networks. A **network** is a group of devices, such as computers and printers, connected in order to share data and/or tasks.

The physical parts of a computer and related devices are called **hardware**. The part of a computer that does the actual computing is the microprocessor. A microprocessor is a silicon chip the size of a fingernail. Microprocessors provide the computing power for many products that people use every day. Cell phones, music players, microwave ovens, TVs, and cars use microprocessors.

A typical computer workstation consists of a computer, monitor, keyboard, and mouse (and desk and chair). A workstation also may include a printer, scanner, or fax machine. Often, though, that equipment is placed in a central location for use by a group of workers. The computer usually is connected to other computers in a network. The network allows users to communicate and share resources such as printers and data.

To keep computer hardware working properly, protect the computer from dust, heat, static electricity, and moisture. Remove the dust from your computer with a small vacuum. To protect the computer from heat, use it

OBJECTIVES

After completing Section 12.1, you should be able to:

1. Give examples of how technology benefits workers.

2. Describe personal computers and types of software commonly used in the workplace.

3. Describe storage options and organization for computer files.

4. Explain the purpose of printers, scanners, and fax machines and services.

Key ▶ Point

A personal computer (PC) is a small, relatively inexpensive computer designed for an individual user.

THINKSTOCK IMAGES/JUPITER IMAGES

only in a well-ventilated area. Use a surge suppressor to protect the computer from power spikes that may cause damage. Keep liquids that may be accidentally spilled away from the computer.

Desktop Computers

A desktop computer is a personal computer that fits on a desk but is too large to carry easily from place to place. It is designed for use in an office or at home. On a desktop computer, you can accomplish many different kinds of tasks. You can send and receive e-mail and instant messages. You can also access networks and the Internet.

Laptop Computers

A laptop computer is a portable personal computer—small enough, as the name *laptop* implies, to sit on your lap. Laptops typically weigh from 2 to 7 pounds and also are known as *notebooks*. They have the same uses as a desktop computer. Laptops can be plugged into any standard electrical outlet. They can also run on batteries that are recharged by simply plugging in the computer. A laptop can have all of the features of a full-sized computer, including CD and DVD drives and e-mail and Internet access.

Laptops are useful for employees who travel or who work away from a desk. Because of their size, laptops have a smaller keyboard than a desktop computer. They have a trackball or other pointing device that allows you to move the cursor instead of a mouse. Many laptops have a small touch pad. You move your finger on the touch pad to move the cursor on the screen and press or tap to select items. Most laptops allow you to attach a conventional keyboard or mouse for use with the laptop.

Key▶Point

A laptop computer has the same uses as a personal computer. However, it is small and portable for use away from an office.

Diversity

A tablet computer allows data entry by handwriting. It provides an easy way to enter data for people who do not have good keyboarding skills.

Tablet Computers

A tablet computer is a portable personal computer that allows users to enter text by keying or handwriting. Depending on the model, you use your finger or a special digital pen to "handwrite" text. You also use your finger or a digital pen in place of a mouse to navigate the screen, select items, and give commands. Otherwise, tablets offer the same features as other personal computers.

A tablet is smaller and lighter than a laptop, about the size of a legal pad and roughly an inch or two thick. The screen rotates and folds down over the keyboard or detaches from it. When detached, the computer screen is sometimes called a *slate*. Tablets are useful for taking notes when you are at a meeting or away from the office. They also are useful for writing in situations where using a laptop is awkward. Nurses, for example, can use a tablet in place of a pen and paper medical chart to make notes. Tablets are useful for people who prefer handwriting to keying. Because they can be held easily, tablets can make reading on the computer comfortable.

Handheld Computers

A handheld computer, also called a *palmtop*, is a personal computer that weighs a pound or less and fits in the palm of your hand. The most common type of handheld is the personal digital assistant, or PDA, which serves as a personal organizer. PDAs and other handhelds may be loaded with software for various uses. PDAs generally include a date book, an address book, a task list, a memo pad, e-mail, and a calculator. As on a tablet, you use a digital pen or your finger to navigate or make selections; and you can handwrite data.

A handheld computer provides personal organizer and other types of programs.

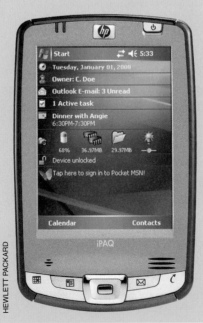

HEWLETT PACKARD

Handheld computer users can also key data using the unit's small keyboard. The keyboard may be on-screen or a physical part of the unit. With some handheld computers, users can connect a standard full-size keyboard or a folding keyboard. Folding keyboards are flexible, full-sized keyboards that can be folded into a small unit for travel or storage.

Handheld computers allow users to synchronize data with other computers. This process allows the computers to update one another. For example, a legal secretary can schedule appointments for an attorney on a desktop computer. The attorney can synchronize his PDA with the computer to keep his schedule up to date. Figure 12-1 shows a screen from *Microsoft ActiveSync*®, a program used to update computers.

Handheld computers permit you to beam (transmit) data to another nearby handheld computer or to a printer. The data is sent through a wireless connection. For example, you can beam a list of contacts to another handheld computer. You may also be able to synchronize a handheld with another computer using a wireless connection. The receiving computer must be equipped to receive data in this way.

Handhelds are inexpensive compared to larger computers. They are popular among students, professionals, and others who need to take notes, store and access information, and manage schedules. A few popular features of handhelds are word processing and spreadsheet software, e-mail, and Internet access. Many other features are available.

Key▶Point

Users can synchronize data between a handheld and another computer to keep both up to date.

Figure 12-1 Data can be updated by synchronizing a handheld computer with a desktop computer.

If you are thinking of buying a handheld computer, consider questions such as these in addition to the cost:

- Is the computer comfortable to carry around?
- Is it easy to use? Try the keyboard, for example, and see whether you can use it easily.
- How will you use it? Does it need to be compatible with other users' computers? Make sure the model you buy has the features you need.
- Can it synchronize with your desktop or laptop computer?
- What is the battery life?

check point 1

1. In general, how does technology benefit workers? Give two examples of how technology benefits workers.

2. List and briefly describe four types of personal computers.

Check your answers in Appendix C.

Computer Software

A computer processes data according to a set of instructions to perform a specific task. Without instructions, a computer cannot do anything. It gets some of the instructions from you, through the keyboard and mouse; but it gets most of them from software. Computer **software**, also called programs, consists of step-by-step written instructions. Programs are written in special languages a computer can understand. Software can be grouped into three types: operating system software, applications software, and utility software.

Operating System Software

The operating system is software that performs the computer's most basic operations. For instance, it handles the transfer of data and files. It controls equipment such as the keyboard, monitor, and printer. It also manages and allows you to use all the other software on the computer.

The operating system provides the interface of the desktop, windows, and other features that make working with the computer easy. You use the operating system when you add, remove, open, and close programs; switch from one program to another; and move, copy, or delete files. *Microsoft Windows*®, *Mac OS*®, and *Linux*® are operating systems.

Application Software

Application software is used to perform work tasks. For example, word processing software is used to create letters, reports, and other documents. *Microsoft Word* is an example of a word processing program. Database software is another type of application program. It allows users to store data, such as customers' names and addresses. The data can be searched, retrieved, and organized in useful ways. Some examples of database programs are *Microsoft Access*®, *dBase™ Plus*, and *FileMaker*® *Pro*.

Spreadsheet software is an application program used to work with numbers. Users can perform calculations, sort data, and create charts with ease. It is one of the most popular types of business software. Some examples of spreadsheet programs are *Microsoft Excel*®, *Lotus*® *1-2-3*, and *Corel Quattro Pro*®. E-mail and IM software (discussed in Chapter 7) are also types of application programs.

Utility Software

Utility software is used to manage and secure data on a computer. For example, virus protection software, which is used to block, detect, and remove viruses, is a popular utility program. Backup software can be used to make a copy of the data on a computer hard drive. The backup copy can be used to restore files that are damaged or accidentally deleted. *Norton 360™*, shown in Figure 12-2, is a program that provides scanning, backup, and other features. Some utility programs come with the operating system software. For example, the *Windows Vista* operating system includes utility programs that allow users to set the computer's security status, uninstall programs, optimize the display, change the time zone for the computer, and complete other tasks.

Figure 12-2 Norton 360 is a popular utility program.

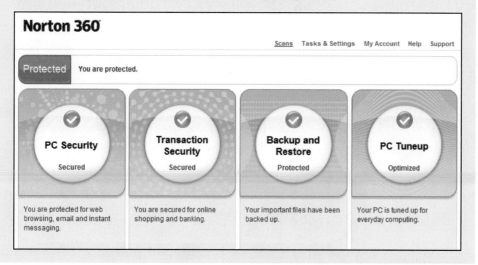

Section 12.1 Computer Hardware and Software

431

Using Software

If you use a computer at work, you will use some of the software discussed in this section. Knowing how to use specific software and being ready and willing to learn new software are valuable assets for many jobs. Whatever software you need to use, you may find the following tips helpful.

Key▶Point

Software tutorials and the Help feature can be used to learn how to complete tasks with the software.

- Many programs used in the workplace have a similar look and operate in a similar way, which helps when you are learning to use a new program. They use menus, toolbars, and icons—sometimes the same ones in several programs—and many of the same basic features.

- Many programs have a Help feature that you can use to learn how to perform tasks. The Help feature, which often includes an online manual, provides valuable information about the software.

- Some programs offer tutorials for common tasks. One type of tutorial, called a *wizard*, takes users step-by-step through a process. For example, writing a letter, creating a legal pleading, or doing a simple query may be covered in a tutorial.

- Software designers work hard to make your work easy. Word processing software, for example, includes features that check spelling and grammar and correct common keying errors. Get to know the user-friendly features of your software.

- When selecting software programs for purchase, make sure you have the computer hardware, memory, and storage needed to run the program. Also, make sure that the program works with your computer's operating system and version.

Programs designed to work together easily are often grouped together in a software suite. For example, *Microsoft Office Professional Edition* has word processing, spreadsheet, database, presentation, personal information management, and desktop publishing software. Integrated software packages have several advantages. The programs have the same look and operate in a similar way. Programs in suites are designed to work well together, and information from one program often can be readily used in another.

check point 2

1. List and briefly describe three general types of computer software.

2. Which of the three types of software is required so that the other two types can be used?

Check your answers in Appendix C.

File Storage and Management

When you save computer files, you generally save them on an internal hard drive on your computer. Besides saving your files there, you need to back them up. To back up files means to make a copy of them on a secondary storage disk or device. Backing up files provides you with a copy of the file that you can use if the file stored on the hard drive is destroyed or deleted.

At many companies, copies of files are routinely saved to a computer on the company network or to another device. This backup may happen automatically when users log off the network. If your company does not follow this practice, you are responsible for backing up the files you create. You would be wise to back up at the end of each workday any files you created or modified that day.

Storage Options

Your company may have a shared network drive to which employees can back up files. As an alternative, your company may provide you with an external hard drive that plugs into your computer. External hard drives are a good choice for backing up files. As with an internal hard drive, they can hold large amounts of data. Files can be organized into folders and can be deleted, copied, or moved as needed. Some drives come with software that makes backing up files quick and easy. Other storage options include compact disks (CDs), digital video disks (DVDs), and flash memory.

© GALUSHKO SERGEY/SHUTTERSTOCK

CDs and DVDs can be used to save copies of computer files.

Compact Disks

A **compact disk (CD)** is a thin platter that can have computer data recorded on it in optical form. CDs can hold about 700 megabytes (MB) of data. A megabyte of storage can hold, for example, about 15 to 20 image files or 500 double-spaced text pages. CDs are a popular media for backing up files. *CD-R* stands for *compact disk—recordable.* You can write files only once to a CD-R. You cannot erase the disk and reuse it or copy revised versions of files to it. *CD-RW* stands for *compact disk—rewritable.* You can reuse a CD-RW, saving files to it many times.

To use CD-Rs and CD-RWs, your computer must have a special drive used to read and save data to CDs. The required software is often included with computers that have the drives. A CD-RW drive lets you use both CD-Rs and CD-RWs.

CDs should be stored in a sleeve or case to prevent damage from scratches or spilled liquids. CDs should be labeled to indicate the data they hold and arranged in a logical order to aid in retrieving the data.

Key▶Point

CDs and DVDs are popular media for backing up files. A special drive is required to store data on a CD or DVD.

Digital Video Disks

A **digital video disk (DVD)** is a thin platter that can be used to store large amounts of computer data in optical form. A DVD is the same physical size as a CD, but it can hold much more data. A single-layer DVD can store 4.7 gigabytes (GB) of data. A dual-layer disk can store 8.5 GB. One gigabyte is equal to 1,000 megabytes. You will need a special drive to store data on a *digital video disk—rewritable* (DVD-RW). Many rewritable DVD drives can be used to create CDs as well. As with CDs, DVDs should be labeled and stored properly.

Flash Memory

Flash memory is a type of storage where data can be electronically saved, retrieved, and erased. A flash memory device can keep stored information without needing a power source. Flash memory devices, such as flash cards and drives, have no moving parts. This makes them resistant to shocks and vibrations that can cause problems with other storage devices.

Flash memory devices offer the advantage of small size (from postage stamp to credit card size). The devices have a storage capacity of 128 MB to 16 GB or more. Flash drives that can be used with the USB port of a computer are popular for transferring and backing up data. They allow fast access to stored data. Files can be organized into folders and can be moved, copied, or deleted as needed.

Flash memory cards and drives are durable and operate with different kinds of devices. For example, flash memory serves as the "film" in a digital camera. If the batteries run down, the images inside the camera remain. Flash memory is used in a variety of other appliances, including cell phones, video games, music players, and video cameras.

Flash memory drives are popular for backing up computer data.

File Compression

File compression software can be used to reduce the size of a file. The smaller size file can be sent to other users more quickly, for example, as an e-mail attachment. Smaller files also allow you to fit more files onto a storage medium. You must use the compression software again to restore the files to their original size before the files can be opened and used.

File compression software is quick and easy to use. Some computers come with this software. It also can be purchased or obtained for free.

WinZip® is a popular compression software. In addition to compressing a single file, this program allows you to create one zipped (compressed) file that contains the data for several files. For example, suppose you have a Word file that contains a report, a *PowerPoint* file that contains a related presentation, and an *Excel* file that contains a related spreadsheet. With *WinZip* you can create one zipped file that contains compressed versions of all three files. You can then e-mail the zipped file to a coworker. The coworker would use *WinZip* to unzip the files to their original format. Sending the zipped file would be faster than sending the three separate files.

File Management

Many companies have a system for naming and organizing computer files for employees to follow. If your company does not, create your own logical system to help you find files quickly and easily.

The operating system of a computer has its own system for organizing the computer's files. You can use that system to organize your files, too. Using folders is a good way to keep files organized. Suppose you want to organize your files for school. You might create a folder for each of your classes. You could create more folders within the class folders. For example,

Key ▶ Point

File compression software can be used to reduce the size of a file. Having smaller files allows you to fit more files on a storage medium.

Figure 12-3 Folders can be used to organize computer files.

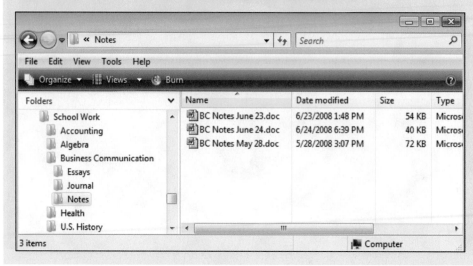

your *Business Communication* folder could contain three folders: one for class notes, one for essays, and one for journal entries.

Use meaningful names for your files and be consistent in how you name files. For example, class notes for Business Communication might be named *BC Notes May 1*, *BC Notes May 2*, etc.

A logical folder arrangement is shown in Figure 12-3. Folders for five classes are in the *School Work* folder. Three folders are in the *Business Communication* folder. Three documents are shown in the *Notes* folder.

You can move, copy, and delete folders and files. You can arrange and view your files in alphabetic order, by most recent date, and in other ways. You can use the Search feature to find files by name, type, date created, text within the file, and other ways. The Search feature can be very helpful when you cannot remember the exact name of a file. Use the tutorials or Help information that comes with the software if you need help working with files or folders.

Key▶Point

The Search feature can be very helpful when you cannot remember the exact name of a file. You can use the Search feature to find files by type, date created, text within the file, and other ways.

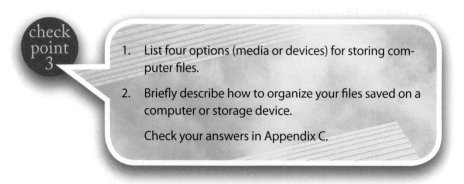

check point 3

1. List four options (media or devices) for storing computer files.

2. Briefly describe how to organize your files saved on a computer or storage device.

Check your answers in Appendix C.

Peripherals

Peripherals are devices that work with your computer to help you accomplish tasks. Printers, scanners, and fax machines are common computer peripherals.

Printers

After you have prepared a document, you can select an option in the software to send the document to a printer. Some printers print in black and white only; others print in color. A document displayed in color on your screen will not print in color unless you have a color printer.

Two types of printers are used in the workplace: inkjet and laser. Each printer produces a printed page in a different way. With an inkjet printer, liquid ink is sprayed onto the paper. With a laser printer, a laser "draws" the page on a drum, which is coated with a dry ink called *toner*. As the paper passes under the rolling drum, it picks up the toner. Both printers generate high-quality documents. Quality is measured in terms of *resolution*, or the number of dots per inch (dpi) the printer is capable of producing. The higher the resolution, the better the page looks.

Ethics

Often, several people in an office share a printer or fax machine. Ethical behavior requires that you do not read printed or faxed documents that are not yours or addressed to you.

© IZAOKAS SAPIRO/SHUTTERSTOCK

Inkjet printers are popular peripherals for home and office use.

You need to know how to do some basic tasks related to printers. Some of these tasks are listed below. You can learn to do those things from another employee or from the printer manual.

- Load paper into the paper trays
- Change paper trays if you are printing on a different size paper
- Clear paper jams
- Change the ink or toner cartridge

Be courteous when sharing a printer. If you run out of paper, load the machine for the next user. If you select any special print features, such as a larger tray, restore the normal settings when you are finished. If you need to print a very long document, check first with other employees about their printing needs.

Scanners

A **scanner** is a machine that creates a computer file from a paper copy. Sheets of paper and pages in books, newspapers, and magazines are examples of items that can be scanned. Some scanners also create images of photos, slides, film, and transparencies. Figure 12-4 shows options for one scanner.

A scanner is a tool for getting text and images into a computer file so you can work with them. Some scanners simply make a picture of the page. The image can be placed in a document, but text on the page cannot be edited. Some scanners work with optical character recognition software (OCR) to "read" the scanned page. These scanned documents can be opened in a word processing program and edited. Scanning text in this way is easier and faster than keying it.

figure 12-4 Scanners offer several options for scanned files.

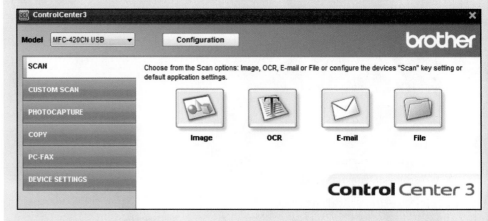

This flatbed scanner, which also has a document feeder, can be used to convert paper documents to image files.

Another purpose for scanning is document storage. Some businesses scan paper documents to create computer files, which require less storage space than paper files.

Many companies use desktop scanners, which come in two types—flatbed and sheetfed. With a flatbed scanner, you place the item to be scanned on the glass plate surface of the scanner and close the cover. The scanning mechanism moves across the document. This process works well for pages in a book. The other type is the sheetfed scanner. You feed the paper sheet into the scanner. The scanning mechanism is stationary.

Pen scanners are gaining in popularity with students, business travelers, and others that take notes from written materials. Most pen scanners are the size of a large marker. You move the scanner slowly across the page as if you were using a highlighter. The scanner may have a small screen that displays the scanned text. Scanned files can be transferred to a computer. Some pen scanners translate or pronounce and define words as they scan.

Scanned files can be large. If size is an issue (for example, if you are e-mailing the file) and you do not need the whole page, you can use the scanner's preview feature to select the part you want. You also can experiment to see whether a lower-resolution scan will meet your needs. The lower the resolution, the smaller the file size will be.

The file format in which you save the scanned image can also affect the file size. Different file formats, such as GIF, JPEG, and PNG, use different compression methods. The file size for an image (at the same size and resolution) can vary in different file formats. You should determine which file formats will be appropriate for the intended uses of the scanned image.

Key▶Point

Some pen scanners translate or pronounce and define words as they scan a page.

The quality of the copy to be scanned can affect the quality of the scanned text or image. Unusual fonts, small text, or broken characters yield occasional text errors. A smudged image may scan poorly.

Fax Machines

A **fax machine** is a device that sends and receives electronic documents over a phone line. It consists of a scanner, which creates an electronic version of the document, and a printer, which prints documents that are received. A telephone connection is required for sending a document by fax machine.

Several other options exist for sending faxes. Your computer may have a fax modem. This device interacts with fax machines and other fax modems to send and receive documents. Your company may have a fax server, a computer that handles all outgoing and incoming faxes via one or more fax modems.

Internet or Web faxing is offered by a number of online service providers. This service provides delivery and receipt of fax messages over the Internet. *Microsoft Word* provides a menu option for sending a document by Internet fax, as shown in Figure 12-5.

Depending on the service, you can send faxes in several ways. One way is to use fax software provided by the service. A second method of Internet faxing is to send an e-mail, attaching the document you want faxed. The service provider turns the attachment into a fax. A third method is to access a Web site and send your fax from there. An advantage of this method is that you can send a fax from any computer. For all methods except fax machine, you will need a scanner if you want to send a printed document.

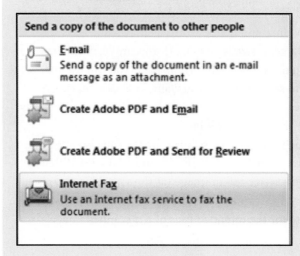

Figure 12-5 Microsoft Word provides easy access to Internet fax service.

Internet faxes can be received on fax machines or on a computer with a fax modem and software. They can also be received as e-mail attachments and on a Web site provided by a fax service. With some online services, you can call a number and get a list of the faxes you have received. You can then route the documents to a fax machine. Your company's Web site may be set up to send and receive faxes.

Always include a cover sheet with a fax. A fax cover sheet is shown in Figure 12-6. The cover sheet should include the following information:

- Date the fax is being sent
- Name, fax number, and phone number of the sender
- Name, fax number, and phone number of the recipient
- Number of pages in the fax

Key ▶ Point

A fax cover sheet that provides contact information for the sender and recipient should be included with every fax.

check point 4

1. What are two types of printers commonly used at work?

2. What is the purpose of a scanner? What are three types of scanners commonly used at home or work?

3. What is the purpose of a fax machine? What other methods (besides a fax machine) can be used to send a fax?

Check your answers in Appendix C.

figure 12-6 A fax cover sheet should accompany each fax.

FAX

To:	Mr. Juan Alvarez	**From:**	Ms. Alma Park
Fax:	606-555-0124	**Fax:**	606-555-0046
Phone:	606-555-0124	**Phone:**	606-555-0045
Re:	Project Bid	**Pages:**	3
		Date:	June 26, 20--

☐ Urgent ☒ For Review ☐ Please Comment ☐ Please Reply ☐ Please Recycle

Comments:

Please review this updated bid, which reflects the changes we discussed.

Section 12.1 *Applications*

A. *Technology Inventory*

You probably use technology in many ways in your personal, school, or work activities. Take an inventory of the technology items that affect your activities.

1. Make a list of the technology items you or your family have or use at home. List each item and give a brief description of it. Tell how the item makes completing tasks faster, easier, or safer. If the item is used for entertainment, explain how it is used.

2. Make a list of the computers, peripherals, and other technology items you use at school. Include items such as computers that you may use in the library, as well as items you use in classes. Consider sports, music, drama, and other extra-curricular activities as you look for technology items.

B. *Software Inventory*

When you use a computer, you use the operating system software and application programs. You may also use utility programs.

1. Make a list of the software programs you use at home, school, or other places.

2. For each program, tell whether it is operating system software, application software, or utility software. (Games are considered to be application software.)

3. For application and utility programs, tell the main purpose of the program.

C. *Software Tutorial*

1. Use the Help feature of a computer program, a wizard, or a tutorial to do something in the software that you did not know how to do. For example, you might use the Search feature of your operating system software to search for a file.

2. Write a set of instructions for completing the task.

12.2 Other Technologies

The Connected World

Technology allows people to be connected to others around the world. Over half of American households have Internet access. Homes, schools, neighborhoods, businesses, and even entire cities run wireless networks. Makers of all kinds of devices, from PDAs to cell phones to headsets to printers, are building in wireless technology.

As you learned in Section 12.1, a network is a group of devices, such as computers and printers, connected together in order to share data and/or tasks. The devices may be linked physically by wires or cables. Instead, they may be linked through wireless connections. The parts of a network also have in common a language or set of rules that allows them to exchange data. For example, hypertext transfer protocol (HTTP) is the set of rules that enables computers to read Web pages.

In a local area network (LAN), the computers are physically close together. They may be in the same building or group of buildings. In a wide area network (WAN), the computers are farther apart. A company might have LANs for each office in Boston, New York, and Tokyo and a WAN that connects the LANs. When a LAN works like the Internet, it is called an *intranet*.

A third type of network is a personal area network (PAN). PANs span even shorter distances than LANs, up to about 30 feet. They can be used to access a larger network. They can also enable computers, cell phones, and other electronic devices within a person's general area to interact.

Bluetooth is a popular technology for PANs. Devices that use Bluetooth send data via radio waves. They have their own set of rules for communicating. You will find Bluetooth technology in some computers, cell phones, music players, scanners, and other products. With Bluetooth, you can send a document from your handheld to a printer. You can transfer files from your handheld to your desktop PC. You can also connect to the Internet so you can send e-mail on your PDA—all without wires.

You probably have seen people using laptops at schools, libraries, bookstores, or other public places without physically connecting their computers to a phone jack. Perhaps you have done so yourself. A popular technology that makes that possible is Wi-Fi. Like Bluetooth, Wi-Fi uses radio waves and its

OBJECTIVES

After completing Section 12.2, you should be able to:

1. Identify different types of computer networks.

2. Discuss how the Internet is used by workers.

3. Discuss security threats and solutions for computers and networks.

4. Identify options for transmitting documents.

5. Describe how to use voice mail, VoIP, and digital devices, such as cell phones and cameras, effectively.

Key▶Point

A LAN connects computers that are physically close together. A WAN connects computers that are far apart.

own set of standards. However, Wi-Fi works at greater distances—up to 1,000 feet. Wi-Fi is used for wireless LANs at work and home.

Wi-Fi is increasingly available in public places, including hotels, airports, and restaurants. Places that offer wireless Internet access are known as **hotspots**. Some places charge a fee for access; in others, access is free.

The Internet

The **Internet** is a vast network that connects millions of computers worldwide. Using the Internet, a student in Athens, Ohio, can do research at a library in Hamburg, Germany. An employee at a factory in West Monroe, Louisiana, can purchase parts from a supplier in Spokane, Washington. A worker in Brisbane, Australia, can e-mail a colleague in London.

Computers on the Internet communicate in different ways. On the **World Wide Web**, which is one part of the Internet, computers use hypertext transfer protocol. When you access a Web site, you are accessing a set of related Web pages stored on a server, or host computer. Web pages are documents written in a computer language called hypertext markup language (HTML). HTML permits the use of audio, video, and graphics. The Web is often called the graphical portion of the Internet. HTML also allows the use of **hyperlinks**: text or graphics that, when clicked, take the user to another location.

With a Web browser program, such as *Internet Explorer*® or *Netscape Navigator*, you can access the Internet and display Web pages. To visit a Web site, you key its address, which is known as a **uniform resource locator (URL)**, in the browser. The URL for NASA, for example, is *http://www.nasa.gov*.

Places that offer wireless Internet access are known as hotspots.

© VASILIY KOVAL/SHUTTERSTOCK

Many people use the Internet on the job for purposes such as the following:

- Send e-mail or instant messages
- Do research
- Purchase products or services
- Get help for using products
- Make travel reservations
- Take courses or classes

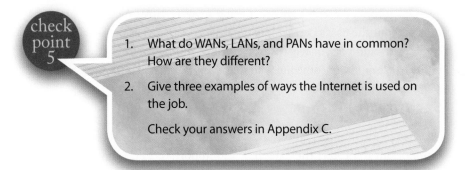

check point 5

1. What do WANs, LANs, and PANs have in common? How are they different?

2. Give three examples of ways the Internet is used on the job.

Check your answers in Appendix C.

Security

While the Internet offers useful services and information to users, it can also pose security threats to computers and networks. Computer viruses, worms, and Trojan horses can do serious damage. Companies and individuals can take steps to protect against these security threats.

Security Threats

A **computer virus** is a program that can infect data files or programs without the knowledge or permission of the user. It can destroy files or corrupt them so that they are no longer usable. Some viruses can steal data and transmit the data to another computer. Viruses may reach a computer or network when files are retrieved from storage devices or shared via a network, such as the Internet.

A worm is a program that is designed to damage programs or networks. A worm can make copies of itself and send those copies to computers on a network. Some worms are designed to be attached to e-mail messages. Other worms can be acquired though instant messaging programs, chat rooms, and shared network folders. Worms can delete files, transmit data, overload storage, or create an entrance to a network.

A Trojan horse is damaging software designed to look like something useful. Trojan horses may appear to be useful or interesting programs, but they are harmful when run. They can erase, corrupt, or overwrite data and transfer files.

They can also log keystrokes for the purpose of stealing information. Stolen passwords or credit card numbers can be used for identify theft.

Unauthorized access to a computer or network is also a security threat. The threat may come from a person with no special expertise. For example, an employee may see a coworker enter a password or store a password on a slip of paper. The coworker's password may be stolen and used to gain entrance to confidential files.

The threat may come from a hacker. A **hacker** is a person who uses computer expertise to break into computer networks. A hacker may steal, delete, or alter files. For example, credit card numbers may be stolen and used to make purchases illegally. Hacking is a crime in the United States.

Unauthorized access may occur using spyware. Spyware is a program that runs without the user's permission. It gathers data, such as e-mail addresses or credit cards numbers, or records places visited on the Internet. The data is sent in the background to someone who may use it for illegal purposes.

Security Solutions

Because so much information is created and stored on computer systems, it is important to protect the data. It is also important to prevent unauthorized access to computer systems.

Companies and individual computer users can take steps to protect against security threats. Some of these steps are described in the following list.

- Back up and carefully store important data. If the data is destroyed or deleted, the copy can be used to restore the data.
- Create and use effective passwords. Use different passwords for different programs or services. Use a combination of letters, numbers, and symbols in passwords. Do not use data as a password that would be easy for someone who knows you to guess. For example, do not use your name, birth date, or address or those of your family members as passwords. Change passwords periodically.
- Log off your computer or network when you leave your desk. This helps prevent others from using your computer to access information.
- Do not open a file or program received as an e-mail attachment unless the file is one you are expecting from a trusted source.
- Use software that checks incoming files for viruses, worms, Trojan horses, and spyware. Update the checking software regularly.
- Use software that scans the computer and removes viruses and other unwanted programs, such as spyware, regularly.
- Do not respond to an e-mail message that appears to be from a bank or other financial institution and requests your bank account numbers or other personal data. A legitimate business will not request your personal data in this way.

Ethics

Using another person's password to gain access to confidential data is unethical.

- When buying online, make sure the site is secure and that your credit card data will be encrypted. Encrypted data is scrambled so that it will be unreadable to an unauthorized user.

- Use a firewall to protect your computer or network. A **firewall** is hardware and/or software that restricts access to computers or networks. Firewalls can protect against computer viruses and other dangerous files. They also can control the Web sites network users may access and the information users can send outside the network. A firewall program and other security measures are included in *Microsoft Windows*, as shown in Figure 12-7.

Key▶Point
Firewalls can protect against computer viruses and other dangerous files.

In addition to using passwords, some companies use a security method called two-factor authentication. With this method, a password and another item are needed to gain access to a computer or network. For example, a user might be required to pass a security badge though a scanner or place a finger on a fingerprint scanner. Some systems use a retinal scan of the user's eye to identify the user.

Anti-virus programs and anti-spyware programs can be used to remove viruses and other harmful or unwanted programs. Data recovery programs can be used to try to recover files that have been corrupted. The process is not always successful.

If you become aware that your credit card numbers or other vital data have been stolen, contact law enforcement agencies. You should also contact the

Figure 12-7 Microsoft Windows includes a firewall program.

credit card providers. If your Social Security number is stolen, you should contact the Social Security Administration. The Federal Trade Commission (FTC) provides an ID Theft Hotline and an online ID Theft Complaint form. It also provides a Web site with up-to-date information about how to work with credit bureaus and law enforcement agencies to reclaim your identity.

check point 6

1. What are four types of programs that can pose a security threat to computers or networks?

2. What is the purpose of a firewall?

Check your answers in Appendix C.

Document Transmittal

At work, you may need to send letters, reports, or other documents to coworkers, supervisors, or customers. Traditional means of sending documents—hand delivery, interoffice mail, the U.S. Postal Service, and private carriers—are still widely used. You also can fax a document, send an e-mail attachment, or post a document on an internal network or company Web site.

Many office networks have a public directory where people can post documents for others to access. Posting provides quick access and prevents the need for repeat mailings. It also permits employees to update files easily, so everyone has access to current information. For similar reasons, documents may be posted on a company Web site for downloading by visitors. When choosing how to send a document, consider the following factors:

Diversity

Consider the recipient and the delivery method that will be most acceptable to him or her when selecting a method for sending a document.

- **Speed.** When does the recipient need the document?
- **Cost.** How much will this method of sending the document cost?
- **Need.** Consider the recipient's preferences and needs. Does the recipient have easy access to a fax machine? Does she or he dislike e-mail or need a paper copy?
- **Security.** Fax and e-mail are less secure than other methods of transmittal. Does the recipient's computer system have a firewall that blocks e-mail attachments?
- **Format.** Fax or physical delivery is a good choice when the format of the document must stay the same.

Pagers

A **pager** is a handheld device that alerts receivers that they have a message. Pagers are small, suitable for slipping in a pocket, clipping on a belt, or stowing in a purse. Pagers are useful for people who are away from their office but who might need to be contacted.

Like telephones, pagers have numbers that distinguish them from other pagers. When placing a call to a person who has a pager, dial the number of the pager. When the connection is made, you simply enter the number the receiver is to call. You could also enter an agreed-on numeric code for a particular message (44 for "call the office," for example). With some pagers, you also may include a brief text or voice message.

When you are using a pager and a message comes in, the pager will alert you by vibrating, beeping, or lighting up. Often you can choose the alert you want to use. The pager displays the number you are to call or the message code, and you can read or hear any message. Two-way pagers allow people to send as well as receive messages.

Key▶Point

Pagers are useful for people who are away from their office but who might need to be contacted.

PHOTODISC/GETTY IMAGES

A pager alerts you to an incoming message by vibrating, beeping, or lighting up.

Voice Mail

Voice mail is a computerized system that answers telephone calls. It allows a caller to leave a recorded message if the receiver is not available when the call comes in. Many organizations provide voice mail for their employees. It is also a common cell phone feature.

If your company uses voice mail, you may need to record a personal greeting that callers will hear in your absence. In some systems, you record only your name; the system supplies the rest of the greeting. In others, the entire greeting is automated. Systems may offer personal and automated options from which you can choose.

When you receive a message, the voice mail system notifies you. There may be a light blinking on your phone or a distinct dial tone that you hear the next time you pick up the receiver to let you know you have a message. You might also receive an alert on a pager or PDA or by e-mail. To retrieve messages, you call the voice mail access number and enter a code or password. You also may need to enter your voice mail box number. Many systems allow you to forward messages to another phone number or to check for messages remotely from a different phone.

With some systems, you can have messages forwarded to your e-mail in-box or to voice mail software that functions like e-mail. You also can retrieve messages from the voice mail system's Web site. Messages may be delivered as audio files that you can hear, or they may be converted to text messages. You have the option of replying by e-mail.

You should answer your messages promptly and delete messages as soon as you have responded to them. You will learn about recording voice mail greetings and messages in Chapter 14.

check point 7

1. What factors should you consider when choosing how to send a document?

2. What is the purpose of a pager?

3. What is the purpose of a voice mail system?

   Check your answers in Appendix C.

Cell Phones

A **cell phone** is a portable, wireless telephone, which changes antenna connections during travel from one radio reception cell to another. Cell phones are a popular way to communicate for business and personal use. A cell phone is basically a two-way radio. The name *cell phone* comes from the division of a service area into cells. Each cell has its own tower or antenna and radio equipment. When you place a call on your cell phone, the call travels through standard phone lines to the phone you are calling or to a long-distance carrier. When you are moving—driving, for example—your call is transferred from one cell to another.

Cell phones come in a variety of shapes and sizes. A *candy bar phone* is the size and shape of a candy bar. A *flip phone* or *clamshell* flips open so you can make calls. In a *slider*, the screen slides up to expose the keypad. In a *swivel*, the screen rotates 180 degrees to reveal a keypad.

Features

To use a cell phone, you need a carrier—a phone company that provides service. Basic features offered by most cell phones and carriers are shown in Figure 12-8.

Key ▶ Point

Cell phones come in a variety of shapes and sizes. They are a popular way to communicate for business and personal use.

Figure 12-8 Cell Phone Basic Features

BASIC FEATURES OF CELL PHONES	
Feature	**Description**
Phone book	Lists phone numbers of contacts
Voice mail	Answers calls when you are not available
Speed dial	Lets you call a number by pressing a single key
Redial	Dials the last number you called
Voice dial	Lets you dial a number from your phone's contact list by speaking the name
Call forwarding	Lets you forward calls to another number
Transfer	Sends your call to another phone
Call waiting	Informs you of incoming calls while you are on the phone
Call hold	Lets you put a call on hold to answer a second call
Caller ID	Displays the phone number of the caller
Multiparty calls	Allows you to converse with two or more other parties
Speakerphone	Lets you talk and hear at a distance from the phone
Text messaging	Allows you to send and receive short text messages
Voice messaging	Lets you send voice messages
Reminder	Lets you set an alarm to remind you of tasks

Key ▶ Point

Cell phones may have special features such as a digital camera or Internet access.

In addition to the basic features described previously, some phones offer a variety of special features such as a headset, Internet access, and a camera that takes digital still or video pictures.

If you plan to buy a cell phone, read reviews from sources such as *Consumer Reports*. Talk to people at work, as well as family members, friends, and neighbors. How do they like their phone? Is their service reliable? Have they had other phones or services they did not like? Try different phones—your friends', your coworkers', and model phones at stores. If you cannot make a call, at least handle the phone and try some of the features. Doing so will help you assess the features and quality of the phone.

Understand the terms of the contract when buying a phone or service plan. Many carriers require you to sign a contract for one or two years. There may be a sizable fee for canceling the service early. Consider a phone with a prepaid plan. You buy a phone and a certain number of minutes. More minutes can be added to the phone as needed. You can stop using the phone whenever you want without paying a penalty.

Smart Phones

A smart phone adds the features of a handheld computer to a cell phone. Smart phones are more expensive than other cell phones. They are popular with business users, however, and their sales are growing. In addition to the features described previously, smart phones include features such as:

- Address book, calendar, and tasks list
- Handwriting recognition
- High-speed data transfer
- A keyboard
- GPS device
- Software such as word processing and spreadsheet programs
- Voice record feature
- Synchronize feature

Key ▶ Point

A smart phone combines the features of a cell phone and a handheld computer.

A smart phone combines the features of a handheld computer and a cell phone.

Developing technology includes hybrid phones that switch from cell phone service to Wi-Fi. This change can save money and improve reception and data transfer.

Text messaging, also called short message service (SMS), is a method of sending brief written messages over cell phones or other devices. It is a quick, convenient, and low cost means of communicating. To compose a text message, you use the device's keypad. Most services set a character limit on messages. As a result, senders often use abbreviations, such as the numeral *4* for the word *for* or *G2G* for *Got to go*.

Text messaging is useful for brief exchanges, such as sending short reminders. Text messaging also is useful in situations when the receiver finds it difficult to accept a phone call; in a meeting, for example. Text messaging is popular in many parts of the world, including Europe, Central Asia, Australia, Iran, and Armenia.[1]

Cell Phone Courtesy and Safety

The widespread use of cell phones and pagers means that people are almost always within reach, whether they are at the office or in other places. These technologies make you more accessible. If you carry a cell phone or pager while meeting with others, however, certain rules of etiquette apply.

If you have a cell phone, ask yourself whether you must receive calls while you are with other people. Consider how a customer you are meeting with will feel if you use his or her time to talk to someone else. Receiving a call while meeting with a customer sends the nonverbal message that the unknown caller is more important than your customer. Instead of taking calls while in a meeting or discussion, send calls to voice mail or turn off your phone. Do not accept a call unless it is urgent or pertains to the business you are presently conducting. If you must accept a call, politely excuse yourself. Take the call privately and make the conversation as brief as possible.

Exercise common sense and common courtesy in your cell phone conversations. Even if your business is not strictly private, avoid discussing it in public places. Choose a location where you will not be overheard or will not disturb the people or events around you. Speak in moderate tones. Use similar restraint when sending text messages on your cell phone. A meeting, conference, or social occasion is not the place for extended text-message exchanges.

Remember that cell phone conversations are not necessarily private. Think of cell phones as mobile radio telephones. Because the message travels via radio waves, other people may be able to pick up your conversations on various electronic devices.

[1]Golnaz Esfandiari, "Text Messaging Takes World By Storm," Radio Free Europe, Radio Liberty, accessed June 30, 2008, available from http://www.rferl.org/content/article/1064083.html.

Diversity

Text messaging is popular in many other parts of the world, including Europe, Central Asia, Australia, Iran, and Armenia.

Key ▶ Point

Turn off your phone when in a meeting unless you are expecting a message or call that pertains to the business you are presently conducting.

When in public, move away from others to use your cell phone.

Be safety conscious when you use cell phones. Do not become so distracted when talking that you do not observe your surroundings. Do not use your cell phone when you are driving. If you need to make a call, find a place to stop the car safely and then make the call. Do not try to conduct business on the phone while you are driving. You need to attend to your driving. Also, the person with whom you are talking may feel (and rightly so) that he or she does not have your complete attention.

VoIP

Instead of a conventional telephone system, your company may use Internet telephony, or **VoIP** (voice over Internet protocol). With this digital phone service, calls go through a high-speed Internet connection rather than a conventional phone line. The main reason that companies choose VoIP is cost savings. VoIP is less expensive than traditional phone service. VoIP is also available for home users.

Most Internet phone services use a standard phone that is linked via an adapter box to an Internet connection. Making a phone call works just as it does with traditional phone service. You pick up the phone, hear a dial tone, and dial the number. You can call any phone number in any location.

For some Internet phone services, your computer serves as the phone. You dial by making menu selections. You talk using a microphone and the computer's speakers or a headset. With some plans, you can place calls only to other PCs and only to people who use the same Internet phone service. With others, you can call any telephone number.

Key▶Point
The main reason that companies and individuals choose VoIP is cost savings.

check point 8

1. How does a smart phone differ from other cell phones?

2. How does VoIP differ from traditional phone service?

Check your answers in Appendix C.

Digital Cameras

A digital camera works very much like a film camera. The main difference is that a digital camera records images in digital form, on a sensor chip instead of film. The images are stored on a reusable memory card in the camera. They can be uploaded to a computer or Web site, e-mailed, or printed. Images are available immediately; no film processing is required. Some companies give employees digital cameras to use in their work. Using digital cameras can save time, money, and effort.

Key ▶ Point

Images created with a digital camera can be uploaded to a computer or Web site, e-mailed, or printed.

- Graphic designers can work with digital images directly in graphics software, without developing or scanning pictures.

- Claims adjustors and appraisers can photograph property damage. They can upload photos directly to their laptop or to the company's Web site.

- Real estate agents can take pictures of a property. They can post them quickly and easily in the company's online listings. They can also create flyers using the images.

- Visiting nurses can send a digital photograph of a skin rash to a doctor, who can recommend a treatment.

- Landscapers can take pictures of a site and use them to develop a landscaping plan.

Global Positioning Systems

People who travel in their work often find a **global positioning system (GPS)** helpful. GPS is a worldwide navigation system consisting of satellites and ground stations. The system allows a GPS receiver to identify its location anywhere on Earth. GPS has been available for commercial use for several years. It is now available to individual users. With GPS, you can determine exactly where you are located. Usually, a GPS device includes software that displays the location on a map for the user's convenience.

A digital camera creates images in a format that can be used on a computer.

IMAGE 100/JUPITER IMAGES

A GPS system can plot the most efficient route for a trip and instantly update directions if you make a wrong turn. It can even provide detailed information, such as when to change lanes for a left exit and what side of the street an address is on. With a locator service, a GPS device can identify popular local spots. For example, restaurants, hotels, gas stations, and ATMs may be indicated.

GPS is used to track the delivery of goods and services and to manage vehicle fleets. It is used in cars, ships, boats, airplanes, helicopters, and construction equipment. It is used by business travelers, service technicians, truck drivers, police officers, firefighters, rescue workers, and many others.

GPS receivers are sold as dedicated (single-purpose) units, often the size of a small radio. GPS is also a feature of some handheld computers, cell phones, laptops, and cars.

Key▶Point

A GPS system can determine exactly where you are located and plot the most efficient route for a trip.

check point 9

1. What are some advantages of using a digital camera over using a traditional film camera?

2. How can a GPS unit be helpful to users?

Check your answers in Appendix C.

Conference Technologies

A company's employees may work in different offices, and some may work at home. Employees and customers may be in different parts of the country or around the world. It is sometimes not practical or too costly to bring people together in one place to discuss business matters. For this reason, remote conferences are popular. In such conferences, people can talk as if having a telephone call or face-to-face conversation.

A teleconference allows people at different locations to talk with one another by telephone. A date and time are planned for the conference. One person may begin the teleconference by calling each person and adding him or her to the conference call. In another method, participants may call a special telephone number to join the conference. Attendees can use a telephone or a speakerphone.

A video conference allows people at different locations to see and hear each other. Sound and images are sent over telephone lines or a computer network. Images are displayed on monitors or computer screens. A video broadcast may be followed by an audio question-and-answer session. If some people do not have access to video equipment, they may go to a videoconferencing center to use equipment there.

A Web conference takes place over an Internet connection. Web conferences may be handled in several different ways. The simplest is for the participants to key text messages in a chat room or use instant messaging. A teleconference using VoIP is a second option. Depending on the equipment used, attendees may be able to send video instant messages. They may be able to view parts of the conference and share documents being discussed.

Training Technologies

Many jobs require on-the-job training. Training is a major expense for some companies. Companies invest in training because it yields benefits. Training can increase worker productivity. It can help keep employees up to date with job skills and knowledge and help improve job performance.

Company supervisors, private consultants, training firms, government agencies, schools, colleges, and business associations all provide training. Training is provided in areas such as these:

- Certification
- Computer literacy
- Continuing education
- Cross-training
- Customer service
- Diversity awareness

Technology Vocabulary

Learning words and terms related to your work will help you improve your reading comprehension. Many special words and terms are related to computers, networks, storage devices, and software. Knowing these terms will be helpful in any job in which you use computers. The career area in which you work will likely have technology terms as well. For example, if you work in the health care field, you will need to learn terms related to medical equipment and tests. Knowing technology terms related to your chosen field will help you communicate clearly and understand materials you read.

Open the *Word* file *CH12 Reading* from the student data files. Follow the directions in the exercise to build your technology vocabulary.

- Health and safety
- Interpersonal skills
- New methods and procedures
- New worker orientation
- Problem solving
- Production or equipment
- Supervisory skills
- Teamwork and leadership

Many formal employee training courses are presented in classrooms by instructors. However, some consist of online learning. Some companies use a blend of traditional methods and online instruction. As an employee, you may receive training that uses one or more of the following technologies:

- **Computer-based training.** Computer-based training is delivered via software, CDs, and DVDs. Often, this type of training is interactive. Employees work through materials on computers at their own pace or in a classroom setting with an instructor.

- **Mobile learning.** With mobile learning, training information is delivered via PDAs, smart phones, MP3 players, tablets, and laptops. Mobile learning usually takes place at the employee's own pace whenever and wherever he or she chooses.

Key▶Point

Computer-based training and mobile learning often allow employees to work through materials at their own pace.

- **Online training.** As the name implies, online training is delivered online through an organization's network or on the Internet. Online training can consist of working with software, sharing text messages, and watching video, CDs, or DVDs. Online training often is interactive.

- **Training videos.** Training videos or DVDs are presented to groups of employees in a classroom setting.

- **Training conferences.** The same technologies used for meetings with employees or customers also are used for training. An advantage of this type of training is that it helps employees focus on the training, away from normal work duties. Another advantage is that employers can be sure that employees in different locations receive the same training at the same time.

check point 10

1. What do a teleconference and a video conference have in common? How do they differ?

2. List five technologies that may be used to deliver training to employees.

Check your answers in Appendix C.

Section 12.2 *Applications*

A. *Computer Networks*

For each situation described below, indicate the type computer network involved: WAN, LAN, or PAN.

1. The computers are physically close together in the same building or group of buildings.

2. The devices are linked physically by wires or cables.

3. The network connects devices in several cities.

4. The network works like the Internet and is also called an *intranet*.

5. Devices in the network use Bluetooth to send data via radio waves.

B. *Security Threats Article*

1. Access the Internet and use a search engine to find articles about computer or network security threats. Use search terms such as *computer virus, worm, Trojan horse, spyware,* or *identity theft.*

2. Select an article on which to report.

3. Give the article name and complete source information. Write a summary of the main points of the article.

INTERNET

REAL WORLD

C. *Document Transmittal Methods*

For each situation described below, indicate the factor that is most important to consider when selecting a method for transmitting the document.

1. A contract is needed at its destination the following day.

2. A project bid contains confidential information.

3. A promotional flyer should be sent by the most economical means.

4. A technical drawing must be delivered exactly as prepared by the designer.

5. The recipient wants to edit the document in a particular software program.

12.3 Workplace Safety and Ergonomics

Workplace safety

OBJECTIVES

After completing Section 12.3, you should be able to:

1. Identify major causes of work-related injuries in offices.

2. Describe the actions of a safety-conscious worker.

3. Understand health and safety issues associated with computer use.

Workplace safety is a major concern for both employers and employees. Many accidents and injuries happen in the workplace. Knowing how to handle accidents and how to prevent them are both important.

Employers are responsible for providing a safe and healthy workplace for their employees. This duty is set out in the Occupational Safety and Health Act of 1970. The Occupational Safety & Health Administration (OSHA) is a U.S. government agency. Its role is to promote the safety and health of American workers. It provides education and sets standards that promote workplace safety and health.

The OSHA Web site provides information on safety standards and how to report safety concerns. It also provides advice for preventing injuries as shown in Figure 12-9.

FIGURE 12-9   OSHA PROVIDES SAFETY TIPS FOR WORKING WITH COMPUTERS.

Source: U.S. Department of Labor, Occupational Safety & Health Administration, available from http://www.osha.gov/SLTC/etools/computerworkstations/positions.html.

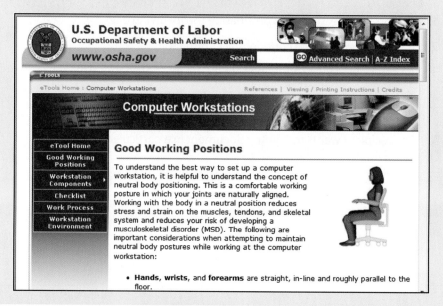

Causes of Injuries in Offices

Although an office is a relatively safe place to work, accidents and injuries do happen. Because of new office technology and equipment, office workers are faced with more hazards than in the past.

Falls are the most common accident in offices.[2] Improper use of stools and ladders leads to many falls. Unstable office chairs and improper use of office chairs also cause many falls. Other causes of accidents and injuries in offices include:

Key ▶ Point
Falls are the most common accident in offices.

- Strains from heavy lifting and repetitive motion tasks
- Crushing injuries from being struck by objects or caught between objects, such as filing cabinets
- Burns from fires, spilled hot liquids, and toxic chemicals
- Shocks from electrical equipment
- Tripping over cables, cords, or open file drawers
- Eye strain from poor lighting
- Tension and stress from noise
- Respiratory problems due to noxious gases or fumes given off by machines (photocopying chemicals)
- Cuts or punctures from improper use of tools such as paper cutters, scissors, shredders, and electronic hole punches
- Injuries caused by irrational or malicious behavior of coworkers or others

Attitudes that Affect Safety

Employers have a duty to set in place reasonable safety rules and procedures. However, safety rules and procedures can be effective only if employees follow them. As an employee, your attitude toward safety will have a big effect on your safety in the workplace. The safety of those around you can also be affected by your actions.

A healthy attitude toward safety procedures is shown by how a worker behaves. Safety-conscious workers are alert to hazards and look for ways to make their work areas and tasks safer. A few examples of how to be safety-conscious at work are given in the following list.

- Read and follow all safety warnings and procedures related to work.
- Wear safety gear or clothing as required.
- Use tools and devices for approved purposes.

Ethics

Employers have a duty to set in place reasonable safety rules and procedures for the workplace.

Key ▶ Point
Safety-conscious workers are alert to hazards and look for ways to make their work areas and tasks safer.

---

[2]"Office Chairs Do's and Don'ts," North Carolina Department of Environment and Natural Resources, accessed June 26, 2008, available from http://daq.state.nc.us/employee/safety/chairs.pdf.

- Do not take shortcuts that may compromise safety to save time.
- Keep work areas free of scraps, trash, or other objects that may cause a hazard.
- Take precautions to see that clothing and jewelry worn at work do not become entangled in equipment.
- Know where fire extinguishers and first-aid kits are located.
- Know whom to call when an accident or emergency happens.
- Know where emergency plans are located and how to follow them.

Emergency Plans

Emergency plans are a vital part of the safety procedures of a company. An emergency plan typically includes information such as the following:

Diversity

Emergency procedures and evacuation routes should be posted in several languages, if needed, so that all employees can read them.

- Safe evacuation routes in case of fire, tornadoes, or other emergencies
- Safe places to take shelter in time of emergency
- Where first-aid kits and fire-fighting equipment are located
- People in charge of key activities, such as calling the fire department, giving first aid, using fire-fighting equipment, or handling a toxic spill

Ask your employer about emergency plans for your office if you are not told about them when you begin a new job.

check point 11

1. List five causes of work-related injuries in offices.
2. Describe five actions of a safety-conscious worker.

   Check your answers in Appendix C.

Computer Use and Ergonomics

Ergonomics is the study of the relationship between people and their working environment. The aim of ergonomics is to make it easier and safer for people to use tools and other objects.

Lifting a patient the correct way and choosing a lightweight tool that fits your hand are examples of applying ergonomics. Applying ergonomic guidelines when performing a task can reduce the chance of certain illnesses or injuries.

Key▶Point

The aim of ergonomics is to make it easier and safer for people to use tools and other objects.

Repetitive Stress Injuries

Keying on a computer can cause repetitive stress injuries (RSI), which are also called repetitive strain injuries. These terms refer to a group of conditions caused by placing too much stress on a joint. Repetitive stress injury happens when the same action is performed repeatedly.[3]

Symptoms of RSI include pain, numbness, a tingling sensation, swelling, and loss of flexibility or strength. RSI can cause damage to muscles, nerves, tendons, and other soft tissues. RSIs are common and costly conditions for Americans. They result in lost wages, lower productivity, and missed work time.

Vision Problems

Computer users also may experience eye strain and related vision problems, sometimes called computer vision syndrome (CVS). Some symptoms of CVS are given in the following list.

- Difficulty shifting focus from the computer screen to more distant objects
- Pain, discomfort, or fatigue in the eye area
- Blurred vision
- Dry, irritated, sore, or burning eyes
- Sensitivity to light
- Headaches, neck aches, backaches, and muscle spasms

Key ▶ Point

Eye strain and other vision problems may result from computer use.

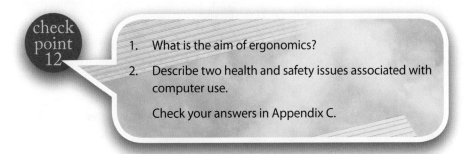

check point 12

1. What is the aim of ergonomics?

2. Describe two health and safety issues associated with computer use.

   Check your answers in Appendix C.

Ergonomics and the Computer Workstation

To work safely and comfortably at a desktop computer, arrange your work area properly. Do warm-up exercises and use the proper keyboarding position. Take frequent breaks to rest your body.

---

[3]"Repetitive Stress Injury," The Arthritis Society, accessed June 26, 2008, available from http://www.arthritis.ca/ types%20of%20arthritis/repetitive%20stress%20injury/default.asp?s=1.

Arrange the Work Area

Follow these steps to arrange your work area comfortably. Figure 12-10 shows a properly arranged work area.

Key ▶ Point

To key in correct position, place the keyboard at elbow height directly in front of your chair. The front edge of the keyboard should be even with the edge of the desk.

- Position the keyboard at elbow height directly in front of your chair. The front edge of the keyboard should be even with the edge of the desk.

- Place your mouse on the same level as the keyboard, as close to your body as possible.

- If you are keying from a document or book, place it near the monitor in a position where you can read and switch your gaze from the monitor to the printed page easily.

- Set your monitor at a distance that makes seeing and reading comfortable—about 18 to 30 inches. The top of the screen should be at or below eye level.

- Adjust lighting to reduce glare on your computer screen. Close blinds and use a desk light if needed.

- Adjust the contrast and brightness on your monitor so text is comfortable to read. Keep the screen free of dust.

Figure 12-10 A properly arranged work area helps users avoid injury.

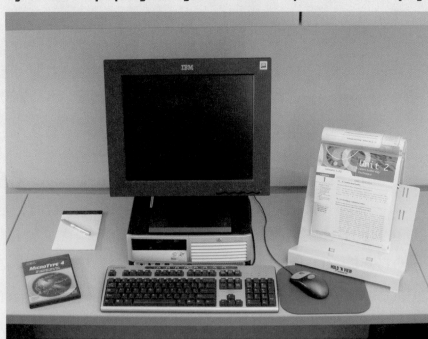

CENGAGE LEARNING

Do Warm-up Exercises

Before you begin a keying session, spend a few minutes doing two or more of the following warm-up exercises:

- Exercise 1. Open your hands with the fingers wide and the muscles tense. Close your fingers into a tight fist with thumb on top. Relax your fingers as you straighten them. Repeat ten times.

- Exercise 2. Clench your fingers briefly and then extend them, relaxing the muscles. Repeat several times.

- Exercise 3. Place the fingers and thumb of one hand between two fingers of the other, and spread the fingers as much as possible. Repeat for all fingers of both hands.

- Exercise 4. Interlace the fingers of both hands together. Wring your hands, rubbing the heel of the palms vigorously.

- Exercise 5. Spread the fingers of both hands as much as possible, hold the position for a moment or two, and then relax the fingers and lightly fold them into the palm of the hand. Repeat slowly several times.

- Exercise 6. Rub your palms with your thumbs. Then rub your fingers, the back of the hands, and your wrists vigorously.

Key▶Point

Doing warm-up exercises can help prepare your hands for a keying session.

Check Your Keying Position

The following list describes the proper keying position, which is illustrated in Figure 12-11 on page 468.

- Keep your feet flat on the floor. If you cannot reach the floor, adjust your chair or use a footrest. If a proper footrest is not available, use a box, a telephone book, a backpack, or another suitable object.

- Keep your body erect. Sit back in the chair with your lower back supported. If the chair does not have a back support, use a small pillow, rolled towel, or piece of clothing. The support should fit the inward curve of your lower back.

- Keep your fingers curved and upright over the *home keys*—**a, s, d, f, j, k, l, ;**

- Keep your wrists and forearms low but not touching any surface.

- Keep your forearms parallel to the keyboard.

- Keep your arms near the sides of your body in a relaxed position. Your shoulders should be relaxed.

If you have never taken a keyboarding class, consider enrolling in one. You will learn the proper keying position so you can key comfortably and reduce your risk of injury. You may also learn to key more quickly with fewer errors, a skill that is useful in many jobs.

Key▶Point

To avoid fatigue, sit up straight and keep your feet flat on the floor when keying.

© FRANKSITEMAN.COM 2007

Take Frequent Breaks

If you work on a computer for extended periods, take frequent breaks. A three- to five-minute break every 20 to 40 minutes is recommended. You can plan some breaks to coincide with established break times. For others, you can plan to accomplish work away from your computer. For example, walk to a printer to collect documents or to the central files to store documents.

Avoid Vision Problems

Arranging your workstation properly can help to prevent and ease vision problems. So will the following additional steps:

■ Make a conscious effort to blink.

■ Shift your gaze away from the screen from time to time.

■ Take at least one break every two hours that takes you away from looking at the screen.

■ If you wear glasses or contact lenses, keep your prescription current.

Other Computers

Applying ergonomics to the use of laptop computers can be challenging. The laptop's keyboard is not detachable and is very close to the monitor. Users frequently must hunch down or set the computer above lap level to see the monitor properly. The small keyboard and pointer device—often positioned at the front of the keyboard so people have to reach past it to key—also pose problems. With that set up, it is difficult to use good keyboarding techniques. It is especially hard to keep your arms at the right height and your wrists straight. Similar concerns arise with tablets, though to a lesser extent because of the option of alternating keying with handwriting.

If you have a laptop, consider investing in a docking station. A docking station allows you to use the laptop as a desktop computer. It includes a full-size keyboard, mouse, and monitor. Another alternative is to use the laptop screen with a full-sized keyboard and standard mouse that plug into your computer. As much as possible, ergonomically arrange the places where you work with your laptop. Take a break every 20 to 30 minutes.

Key ▶ Point

If you have a laptop, consider using a full-sized keyboard and standard mouse that plug into your computer.

Ergonomic Equipment

Padded wrist rests placed in front of the keyboard and mouse are a good investment if used properly. You should not rest your wrists on a wrist rest while keying or using the mouse. Doing so puts pressure on the wrist, which could lead to injury. The real purpose of a wrist rest is to help keep users from bending their wrists. A wrist rest also protects the wrists from the hard, sharp edge of the table or desk. Finally, a wrist rest is a good place to rest the heels or palms of your hands when you are not keying.

Ergonomic keyboards are designed to improve hand posture and make keying more comfortable. Generally, they have a split design with left and right banks of keys. Some people find them more comfortable than standard keyboards.

NET Bookmark

The Human Factors and Ergonomics Society (HFES) provides training and resources for educating people about ergonomics.

Go to the HFES Web site. A link to the site is provided on the Web site for this book that is shown below.

1. Go to the *Information for Students* page. Students make up about what percentage of the HFES membership?

2. Go the *Publications* page. What three publications do members receive as benefits of membership?

www.cengage.com/school/bcomm/buscomm

The mouse, touch pad, and digital pen are all popular pointing devices.

© ANNA DZONDZUA/SHUTTERSTOCK

Diversity

Arranging a computer workstation correctly for children or people who are shorter or taller than average height may be a challenge. Try to adjust the height of desks, chairs, keyboards, and monitors for comfortable and safe keying.

The mouse is available in several different designs. Some are contoured to the shape of the hand. Other pointing devices are joysticks, digital pens, touch pads, and trackballs. Choose a mouse or other pointing device that you find comfortable to use.

An adjustable keyboard tray may help in getting the keyboard at the right height. If you buy a tray, make sure it is large enough to hold a mouse as well. An adjustable footrest is a good purchase if your workstation arrangement does not allow you to put your feet flat on the floor.

You may experience headaches, blurred vision, and other problems associated with using a computer monitor. If so, consider investing in a pair of glasses specifically designed for computer work.

check point 13

1. Describe briefly what you can do to work safely and comfortably at a desktop computer.

2. Describe one warm-up exercise you might do before a keying session.

Check your answers in Appendix C.

Section 12.3 *Applications*

A. Ergonomic Working Position

OSHA provides a checklist for evaluating working position and parts of a computer workstation. Use this form and work with another student to check each other's keying position.

1. From the data files, open the Evaluation Checklist found in the *Word* file *CH12 Checklist*.

2. Print the checklist.

3. Ask a classmate to observe as you sit at the computer and key. Your classmate should then complete the first section of the checklist, Working Posture.

4. Observe your classmate as he or she sits at the computer and keys. Complete the first section of the checklist, Working Posture, for your classmate.

5. Write a paragraph that describes how you can improve your working position.

TEAMWORK

REAL WORLD

B. Ergonomic Workstation

1. Use the Evaluation Checklist found in the *Word* file *CH12 Checklist*, which you printed earlier.

2. Complete the remaining sections of the checklist to evaluate the seating, keyboard, monitor, work area, and accessories.

3. Write a summary detailing any parts of the workstation that need changes or improvement.

REAL WORLD

C. Material Safety Datasheet

Material safety datasheets are used in the workplace to inform employees and others about dangers related to handling substances. Datasheets are often posted on the manufacturer's or distributer's Web sites.

1. Use an Internet search engine to find sites that have material safety datasheets. Use *material safety datasheet* as the search term.

2. Find the material safety datasheet for one product or substance. Print the datasheet.

3. Write a paragraph that tells the name of the substance and the type of information found on the sheet. Include source information for the sheet.

INTERNET

REAL WORLD

Chapter *Summary*

12.1 Computer Hardware and Software

- Technology is tools, machines, and other inventions that make work faster, easier, or safer.

- A computer is a machine that processes data according to a set of instructions in order to perform tasks. Computer software, also called programs, consists of step-by-step written instructions that tell a computer how to operate.

- Users should create a logical system for naming and storing files that allows them to be found quickly and easily.

- Printers, scanners, and fax machines are common computer peripherals.

12.2 Other Technologies

- Technology allows people to be connected to others around the world. WANs, LANs, and PANs are types of computer networks. The Internet is a vast network that connects millions of computers worldwide.

- Computer viruses and other threats can do serious damage to computers and networks. Steps can be taken to protect against these security threats.

- Pagers, voice mail, cell phones, VoIP, digital cameras, and global positioning systems are other technologies related to communication.

12.3 Workplace Safety and Ergonomics

- Workplace safety is a major concern for both employers and employees.

- As an employee, your attitude toward safety will have a big effect on your safety in the workplace.

- Ergonomics is the study of the relationship between people and their working environment. The aim of ergonomics is to make it easier and safer for people to use tools and other objects.

Vocabulary

Open the *Word* file *CH12 Vocabulary* from the student data files. Complete the exercise to review the vocabulary terms from this chapter.

cell phone	Internet
compact disk (CD)	network
computer	pager
computer virus	peripherals
digital video disk (DVD)	personal computer
ergonomics	scanner
fax machine	smart phone
firewall	software
global positioning system (GPS)	uniform resource locator (URL)
hacker	voice mail
hardware	VoIP
hotspots	World Wide Web
hyperlinks	

Critical Thinking Questions

1. Why do employers value workers who can use technology in their work and can learn and adapt to new technologies?

2. Why do software developers provide extensive tutorials and Help features to teach users how to use features of a software program?

3. Do you think fax machines will become obsolete since Internet fax services are now available? Why or why not?

4. What rules of etiquette might participants in a teleconference follow?

5. Ergonomic equipment and guidelines have been developed for many different tasks. Yet people sometimes do not use them. Why do you think that is so?

CRITICAL
THINKING

Chapter *Applications*

A. *Technology Article*

INTERNET

1. Access the Internet and use a search engine to find a current article about one of the following devices:

   - Digital camera
   - Pager
   - Cell phone
   - Smart phone
   - GPS device

2. Select an article on which to report.

3. Give the article name and complete source information. Write a summary of the main points of the article.

B. *Ergonomic Equipment*

INTERNET

Falls from office chairs are a common accident in offices. Chairs also affect how comfortable and productive a worker at a computer station can be.

1. Use the Internet or other sources to find a current article about what to look for in a chair that is ergonomically correct.

2. Write a summary that describe the features a chair should have.

3. Search the Internet for suppliers of chairs. Find a chair that you think would be a good choice for use at a computer workstation.

4. Provide the name or model number of the chair and a source where it can be purchased. Describe the features that make this chair a good choice.

C. *Cell Phones and Driving Safety*

CRITICAL THINKING

Many people talk on a cell phone while driving for business purposes. California has a law that requires drivers to use a hands-free device to talk on the phone while operating a vehicle. Drivers under the age of 18 may use an electronic device while driving only in emergency situations. Other states, such as Connecticut, New Jersey, New York, Utah, and Washington, and the District of Columbia have similar laws.[4]

---

[4]"New California Cell Phone Laws Take Effect 7/1," Find Law, accessed June 30, 2008, available from http://commonlaw.findlaw.com/new_ york/index.html.

Write a short position paper to give your thoughts on this communication and safety issue. In your paper, answer the following questions.

- Do you think state governments should require that drivers who talk on cell phones while driving use a hands-free device? Why or why not?

- Do you think a law such as the one described will improve traffic safety? Why or why not?

- Do you think employers should have a policy on the use of cell phones while driving on business? Why or why not? What points might be included in such a policy?

D. Home Emergency Plan

Schools, businesses, and other public facilities typically have an emergency plan as described earlier in this chapter. Although it may not need to be as long or detailed, your family should also have a plan for how to proceed in case of various emergencies.

1. Identify the types of emergencies your family may face. For example, a fire or tornado may occur.

2. Write an emergency plan that could be used for the two or three most serious emergencies that may be likely to occur. In the plan, include information such as the following:

   - Ways to exit the house safely

   - Where to meet if the family must leave the house

   - The safest place to take shelter in case of bad weather

   - Emergency numbers to call for aid

   - Location of safety and first aid equipment

   - Who will be responsible for each small child or an adult who will need help in relocating or taking shelter

CRITICAL THINKING

REAL WORLD

Editing Activity

Dan Viera is a middle school teacher. He is composing a rough draft of a committee report on whether the school should seek funding for tablet computers. When he traveled home to visit his parents last weekend, he lost the computer file. However, he has a printout of the file that he has scanned. Part of the scanned file appears below.

Open the *Word* file *CH12 Editing* from the student data files. Edit the text to make it clear and concise. Fix the occasional text errors that may have occurred in the scanning process. Add a topic sentence to the last paragraph.

Ergonomics in Action

Doris Roberts works as a customer service associate for a software company. She answers customer calls and provides help with using program features. Aside from two short breaks, Doris sits at her workstation all morning and all afternoon. Her chair is not the right height for comfortable keying, so she often slumps in her chair. Her keyboard is placed at an angle (not directly in front of her body) to make room for a mouse and pad on the keyboard tray. In order to key with both hands, Doris often holds the telephone receiver between her neck and shoulder as she speaks with customers. On many days, her job literally becomes a "pain in the neck."

1. What problems might Doris have as a result of improper chair height and keyboard placement?

2. What injuries could be the result of keying most of the day with few breaks?

3. What changes to her workstation and work habits can Doris make to improve her productivity and her health?

Communication for Information Technology

Ray Xu moved to the United States four years ago. Because English is his second language, he has difficulty reading and speaking English. Presently, he owns six small stores that cater to tourists in the Orlando, Florida, area. These businesses are very successful, and, as a result, Ray needs to implement a computer system. This system will help keep an inventory of items that tourists purchase and help him with his accounting records. Ray is a little worried about buying a system because he knows very little about computers, much less a computer system.

Two weeks ago, Ray contacted Effective Computer Systems. He asked for a proposal on the computer system that he needs. Michelle Goodman is a sales supervisor for this company. Michelle's job requires her to be very computer literate. She must keep up with new equipment and developments in the computer industry. She must also understand the needs of her customers. Her ability to meet the customers' needs is critical to her job success.

Michelle has a proposal that a staff member has written for Ray and must deliver it to him tomorrow. The proposal includes a lot of technical language, computer jargon, and long, complex sentences.

1. If Michelle gives the proposal to Ray as it presently is, what would you expect his reaction to be?

2. What basic principle of audience analysis has the person who wrote the proposal violated?

3. What can Michelle do to improve the proposal for Ray?

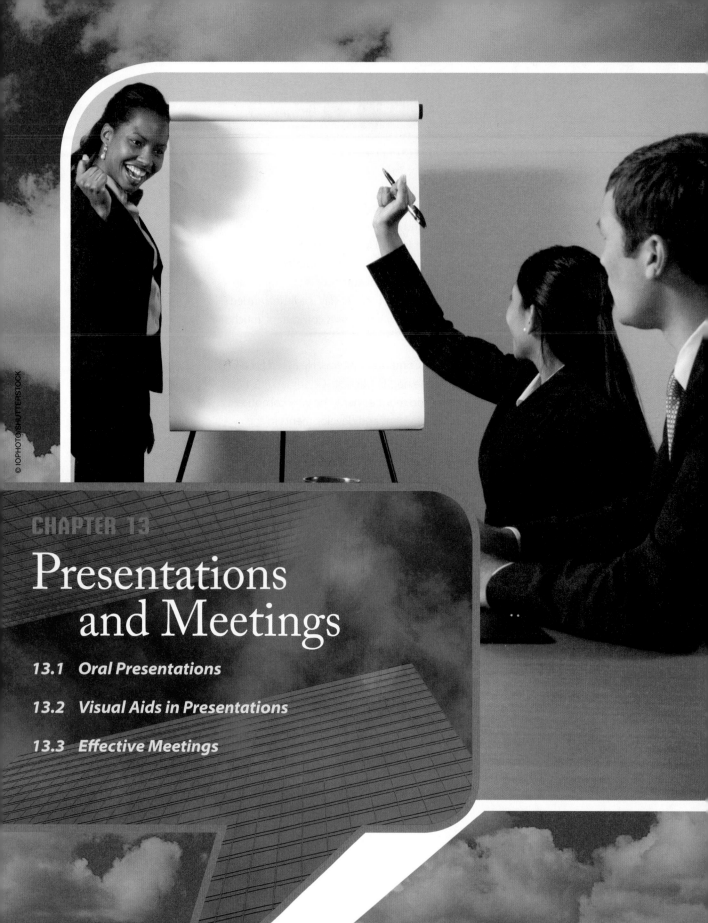

CHAPTER 13

Presentations and Meetings

13.1   Oral Presentations

13.2   Visual Aids in Presentations

13.3   Effective Meetings

Salu's Presentations and Meetings

Salu Alufopho has worked for Computer Systems, Inc., for about four years. Last month he received his third promotion. Now he is working at the first level of management and has found his new duties quite challenging. Oral communication skills play an important role in his new position.

Salu meets often with project managers. After receiving the status of the projects for which he is responsible, Salu meets with his supervisors and briefs them on each project. Occasionally he is part of a team that presents a proposal to a prospective client.

Although he had a speech class at his business college, Salu does not feel prepared for all the presentations he has to give. He has noticed that Ms. Lynn, one of his supervisors, is impressive during her presentations. She maintains interest by using quotations, anecdotes, questions, humor, and statistics.

Salu also has questions about briefings. He knows little about this type of oral presentation and had never seen one before his promotion to management. He also wonders what he could do to plan and organize formal presentations better.

Salu has attended many meetings, but he has received no training on how to organize meetings or make them effective. As Salu analyzes the meetings he has attended, he knows that some were more successful than others. He wonders what a leader does to help ensure the success of a meeting.

Questions

1. How can Salu find answers to his questions about meetings and presentations?

2. What do you think makes a meeting successful?

3. How do you think a briefing would differ from other types of presentations?

13.1 Oral Presentations

Short Oral Presentations

Oral communication is a common business activity. The types of oral presentations you give will depend on your job position. If you supervise others, you may conduct training programs. If you work in a Human Resources Department, you may conduct new employee orientation programs. If you become a high-level executive, you may make presentations to the board of directors, stockholders, media, and civic organizations.

Most oral presentations are simple, straightforward, and short—15 minutes or less. Typical short speeches are introductions and briefings. They should begin with an opening that creates interest and prepares the audience for what will follow. Then they should provide details in the body and summarize the main points in the closing—if needed.

Introducing Speakers

When planning an introduction of a speaker, determine if you should follow a specific format. Many organizations provide guidelines for introductions to keep them short and uniform. If no formal guidelines exist, consider adapting the suggestions discussed in the following paragraphs.

Obtain Information about Speakers

Often, you will be given a resume or other information about the speaker. If possible, find out what the speaker would like you to mention. Your purpose is to prepare the audience to accept the speaker and the speech. Too much information causes restlessness in the audience.

Key▶Point

When introducing a speaker, your purpose is to prepare the audience to accept the speaker and the speech.

Introduce Speakers and their Presentations

When introducing a speaker, mention information about the speaker along with the speaker's name. State the title of the presentation and tell what the speech is about if that is not obvious from the title. Provide information that the audience can relate to and that will create interest in the speech. When giving an overview, do not give too many details that will take away from the speech.

An effective introduction prepares the audience to accept the speaker and the speech.

Briefings

A **briefing** is a short presentation given to bring people up to date on business activities, projects, programs, or procedures. Briefings are usually given at a meeting or a conference. Because briefings are short, highlight key points and provide a few details to support each point. You could use a visual aid that lists the key points.

Key▶Point

The purpose of a briefing is to give current information on activities, projects, programs, or procedures.

check point 1

1. What is your purpose when introducing a person who will make a speech?

2. What is the purpose of a briefing? Where is a briefing usually given?

Check your answers in Appendix C.

Formal Oral Presentations

Preparing formal oral presentations is challenging. A formal speech may last from 20 minutes to more than an hour. It may require that you do research to find the content you need to present. You may need to prepare visual aids to help the audience understand the points you wish to make. You should think about questions the audience members may have and how you will answer them.

Planning the Presentation

Key ▶ Point

Planning is essential for an effective formal presentation.

Planning an oral presentation is like planning a written report. Oral presentations have an introduction, a body, and a closing. They may include visual aids such as tables, charts, graphs, and photos. The following steps are involved in preparing for a formal presentation.

1. Determine the objective of your speech.
2. Analyze the audience.
3. Determine the time available for the speech.
4. Gather information for the speech.
5. Determine the appropriate mode of delivery.

Determine the Objective

What do you want to communicate to an audience? Answering this question will help you determine the objective or purpose of your presentation. Generally, the objective for a work-related speech will be to persuade or inform. The objective for other speeches may be to entertain. Write a sentence that states the objective clearly, as shown in the following examples.

> The objective is to teach marketing managers about new products and sales goals.

> The objective is to persuade a customer to place an order with us because we have a quality product and fast delivery.

Analyze the Audience

Diversity

The age, gender, culture, education, and experience of listeners affect how they receive your message.

Analyze the expected audience in terms of size (number of people), knowledge level, age, gender, culture, and needs.

- How do you want your audience to react to your presentation?
- How much does your audience already know about the topic?
- Is the audience's attendance voluntary or involuntary?
- What do the listeners need to learn or what action do you want them to take?

The size of the audience determines the approach you take for delivery. If the audience is small (20 or fewer people), you may be able to have more audience interaction. If the audience is large, you need a good sound system and some way to make visual aids visible to the entire audience.

If the audience has little or no knowledge of the subject, you need to provide background information and explain words or terms related to the subject. If the audience is familiar with the topic, you may begin talking about the subject directly and give little background information.

Knowing the demographics of the listeners can help when preparing your speech. **Demographics** are characteristics of a group of people, such as gender, age, race, culture, education level, occupation, marital status, and income. Ask questions about the audience members such as those listed below:

- What is the range of ages?
- How many are men and how many are women?
- What is their educational level?
- What are their occupations and income levels?
- Where do these people live or work?
- What cultures or ethnic groups are represented?
- What will be their attitudes toward the topic of your presentation?

Determine Time Available

Speakers often are given a specific amount of time to speak. You need to determine how much of this time to spend on different parts of the speech. For example, suppose you have 30 minutes in which to make a presentation. You might decide to spend 3 to 5 minutes on opening remarks and 15 to 20 minutes to develop the main points. You might allow 5 to 10 minutes for conclusions or a summary and questions. To make sure you stay within the appropriate timeframe, practice your presentation several times, noting its length. *Microsoft PowerPoint* has a timer feature that will help you time your speech as you practice. See Figure 13-1.

Key ▶ Point
You should practice your speech to make sure you can deliver it within the allotted time.

Figure 13-1 Practice your speech so you can keep it within the allotted time.

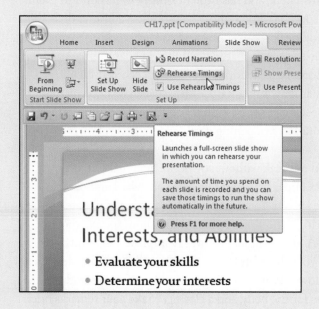

Gather Information

Information for an oral presentation is gathered in much the same way as data for a formal written report. Two sources of data are available—primary sources and secondary sources. Primary research involves gathering new data. Secondary research involves locating data that already have been gathered and reported. Refer to Chapter 9 page 315 to review information on gathering data.

Determine Mode of Delivery

Key ▶ Point

Talking from notes is the most effective mode of delivery for a formal presentation.

Talking from notes is the most effective mode (way) of delivery. Using this method, you prepare an outline or notes and use them as a reference while talking. *Microsoft PowerPoint* has a notes feature that allows users to enter notes related to each slide in a slide show. These notes can be used while practicing or delivering a speech. This method requires practicing beforehand until you can deliver your remarks smoothly. It may seem challenging to have to practice and not to read a speech word for word. However, this method engages the audience in a way that reading a speech cannot. Since you are looking at your outline or notes only occasionally, you can make eye contact with the audience. Your listeners believe you are talking directly to them, and they pay attention. Making eye contact while speaking gives an impression of interest and competence on your part. In addition, it allows you to observe your audience's reactions and to adjust your remarks accordingly.

Two methods of delivery are not recommended. The first is reading a written copy of a speech. When a speaker reads from a manuscript, he or she can make eye contact only occasionally. The speaker's facial expressions and voice are less expressive. Listeners tend to become bored or annoyed. In addition, the speaker risks losing his or her place in the manuscript, has little opportunity to observe listeners, and has little flexibility to respond to them.

Reciting an entire speech from memory is also not recommended. This method allows for a good deal of eye contact. However, working from a memorized speech gives the speaker little flexibility to adapt remarks to the audience's reactions. Moreover, memorizing a long speech is difficult for many people. The speaker may forget parts of the speech or become flustered. A memorized speech can sound stilted and formal, not like natural talk. Memorizing a quotation or opening or closing remarks, however, can be effective.

Key ▶ Point

You might make an impromptu speech to accept an award or thank a group of people.

When you are asked to speak without any notice, you make an **impromptu speech**. For example, you might be given an award and need to make a short acceptance speech. You might be asked to give an update on the progress of a project during a meeting. Even an impromptu speech, though, can be planned quickly. A little planning can vastly improve the results. Take a few moments to gather your thoughts before speaking. Sketch your ideas on a piece of paper if time allows. Avoid rambling by deciding on an introduction, two or three main points for the body, and a closing. Make your remarks brief.

Take a few moments to organize your thoughts before you give an impromptu speech.

Organizing the Presentation

All presentations, formal and informal, should have three main parts: an introduction, a body, and a closing.

Introduction

The introduction to a speech should contain an attention-getter, your topic, your purpose, and a preview of your main points.

Attention-getters hold the audience's attention during a long presentation. Use reliable attention-getters in the opening and throughout your speech. Common attention-getting techniques include:

1. Quotations. Use a quotation to illustrate a point. If possible, memorize the quotation and cite the source.

2. Anecdotes. An **anecdote** is a short account of an interesting or humorous incident. A story related to the audience or the topic is often a good way to begin. People enjoy hearing stories and often understand a point better when they hear a related anecdote.

3. Humor. A little humor can relax a serious business atmosphere and make an audience more receptive. Many speakers warm up an audience with a joke and then proceed to a serious topic. However, humor should be used with discretion and care. Be careful not to offend listeners.

4. Statistics. Cite an interesting or unusual statistic when appropriate. People like some details, but not too many.

5. Questions. Ask a question. A good question can help your audience focus on your topic or make it eager to hear the answer.

Ethics

Be sure to cite the source of a quotation you use in a speech.

Body

The main part, or body, of a presentation should present the main points. Use the same organizational plans as those used in writing reports—direct or indirect. Limit the number of main points and arrange them in a logical sequence. As you progress in the speech, summarize previous points and preview information to come. When you shift topics, provide a transition from one idea to the next.

Add variety to presentations to hold the audience's attention. You can vary the pace of a presentation by using visual aids, asking questions, and using examples to illustrate key points.

Closing

Close a presentation by reviewing or summarizing the main points. State a conclusion, if appropriate, or tell listeners again what you want them to do. Your objective is to make sure the audience understands the topic and possibly takes some action as a result of your presentation.

For many work-related presentations, including a question-and-answer session is appropriate. Allow time for questions and answers in the allotted time for your talk. Think about the questions that may be asked and form answers to them ahead of time. This will allow you to keep the question session moving along. If the group is large, repeat a question before answering it so that all listeners can hear the question as well as your answer. If you do not know the answer to a question, be honest and state that you do not know. Offer to find the answer and contact the person later if appropriate.

Outlining the Presentation

An outline can be a valuable tool when planning any speech. An outline is essential for long, complex speeches. Develop the outline according to the plan used for the speech—direct or indirect order. Use direct order (main idea first) when you expect the audience to be receptive to your ideas. Use indirect order (main idea later) when you expect the audience to be skeptical or unreceptive. Use indirect order when you will be persuading listeners or delivering unwelcome news.

If you plan to deliver your remarks from your outline, prepare it as a **topical outline**. Using a few words to describe each topic rather than complete sentences will help you avoid the temptation to look down and read directly from your outline.

Include "prompts" in the margin for where you are going to use visual aids, cite a source, or even pause. If you are using electronic slides, you can create your outline in the software. Figure 13-2 shows an outline for a speech created in *PowerPoint*. You can also create your outline in *Word* and import it into *PowerPoint* when you are ready to create slides.

Ethics

Speakers can use long, poorly organized speeches to confuse or cloud positions on issues or policies. Such actions may be self-serving, but are they ethical?

Key ▶ Point

Preparing an outline is essential for long, complex speeches.

Figure 13-2 This speech outline was prepared in Microsoft PowerPoint.

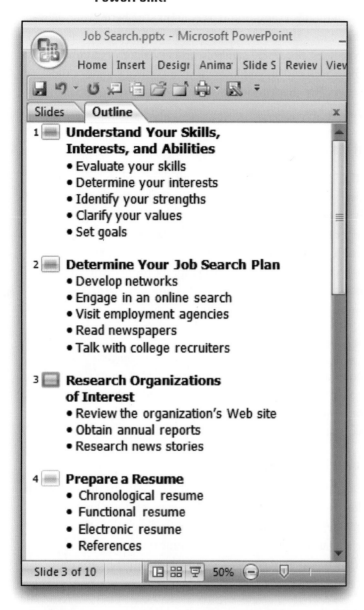

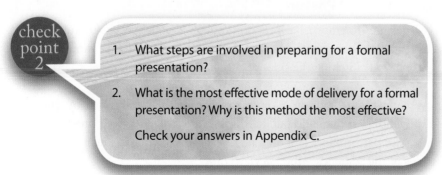

check point 2

1. What steps are involved in preparing for a formal presentation?

2. What is the most effective mode of delivery for a formal presentation? Why is this method the most effective?

Check your answers in Appendix C.

Delivery of Oral Presentations

Key ▶ Point

Delivery of a speech is as important as the content. Effective delivery increases the chance of achieving the goal of the speech.

Delivery of a presentation is as important as content. The better your delivery, the greater the chance that you will achieve the objective of your presentation. Voice qualities, nonverbal symbols, and visual aids can enhance or inhibit delivery. Feedback can let you know if your audience understands and accepts your message. The checklist on page 492 provides suggestions for delivering effective speeches.

Voice Qualities

Your vocal qualities should make you appear confident and competent. Speakers who speak softly give a nonverbal message that they are insecure or shy. Speak loudly enough for everyone to hear while still sounding natural. To achieve appropriate volume, look at the person farthest away and project your voice as though you were speaking to that person.

Speak at a moderate pace. If you talk too rapidly, the audience may not have time to consider all your points and may become confused. Also, you may give the impression that you are nervous.

Nonverbal Symbols

Nonverbal symbols add to or detract from an oral presentation. They indicate how the speaker feels about the situation—relaxed, nervous, or confident. Important nonverbal symbols during speeches include eye contact, facial expressions, gestures, and posture.

Eye Contact and Facial Expressions

Key ▶ Point

When delivering a speech, make eye contact with the listeners. Use appropriate facial expressions and gestures to communicate with the audience.

Maintaining eye contact with members of the audience keeps them involved in your speech. Focus on members of the audience to let them know you want to communicate with them and to read the feedback they give you.

Use appropriate facial expressions to communicate with your audience. A smile, a frown, a look of concern, or a look of surprise can convey a message.

Gestures and Posture

Use gestures to emphasize important points in your speech. Gestures can also indicate that you are nervous. Repeatedly saying "ah" or "um," tapping fingers, and clutching the sides of a lectern indicate nervousness.

Though you may be nervous about giving a speech, the key is to hide or overcome that nervousness. You can overcome this nervousness by gaining experience at speaking in public. Think positively about your presentation and your performance as a presenter. Focus on the needs, interests, and concerns of the audience—the *you* viewpoint.

Use nonverbal symbols, such as a smile, to put listeners at ease.

Send the right message with your posture. Good posture indicates self-confidence, an interest in your topic, and respect for the audience. Poor posture indicates the opposite. Stand up straight in a comfortable position with your feet about hip distance apart. Do not slouch or lean on a desk or podium. Walk at a natural pace (not too slow or hurried) if you move around on the stage. Be careful to stand in a position that does not block the audience's view of visual aids. Listeners should be able to see you and the visual aid.

Visual Aids

Visual aids should be used to emphasize, explain, or illustrate points of your presentation. Transparencies, flip charts, chalkboards, whiteboards, slides, and videos are examples of visual aids. Visual aids for presentations are discussed in the next section of this chapter.

Feedback

Some oral presentations allow immediate feedback to the speaker in the form of questions from the audience. Feedback is important in determining whether the audience has understood or accepted your message. When taking questions is appropriate, allow time at the end for questions and answers.

For some presentations, such as those at conferences or seminars, you may benefit from formal feedback about the session. A questionnaire or evaluation form can be used to gain audience feedback.

Key▶Point

Feedback is important in determining whether the audience has understood or accepted your message.

If the group is very small, you might encourage comments or questions during the presentation. If the group is large, ask the audience in your introduction to hold questions until after the presentation.

An evaluation form should include items such as the following:

- The name and date of the presentation
- The name of the presenter
- Statements regarding the session that the listener can rate or agree/disagree with
- Space for other comments or suggestions for improvement

An evaluation form for a presentation is shown in Figure 13-3.

OCCUPATIONAL SUCCESS

Presentation Tips

Giving effective presentations can be important to your occupational success. The following tips will help ensure that your planning and practice pays off with an effective and smooth delivery.

- Go to the presentation room and practice your speech, using your visual aids. Make sure the audience will be able to see you and your visual aids.
- Arrange for any equipment you will need and for furniture to be moved, if necessary.
- Make a checklist of items that should be taken care of so the room is properly prepared, as well as items you need to bring.
- The day of the speech, pay careful attention to dress and good grooming. Check your appearance in strong light in a full-length mirror.
- Run through your checklist before leaving home.
- Arrive early. Look again at your checklist to make sure everything is arranged properly. Check to see that your visual aids are ready.
- Start on time. Keep track of your time as you talk. If you fall behind, adjust your remarks as needed so you end on time.
- Before you begin to speak, take a deep breath, scan the audience for friendly faces, and smile.

figure 13-3 An evaluation form can provide valuable feedback from the audience.

PRESENTATION EVALUATION FORM

Presenter Name _____ Date _____

Title of Presentation _____

Please indicate the appropriate response for each statement. Thank you for your feedback.

	No	Yes	Somewhat
1. The presenter seemed professional and knowledgeable about the topic.			
2. The content of the presentation will be helpful to me.			
3. The visual aids were helpful and appropriate.			
4. The handouts were helpful and appropriate.			
5. Enough time was allowed for questions and answers.			
6. The overall time allowed for the presentation was appropriate.			
7. The room was comfortable.			
8. I would recommend this presentation to others.			

Comments:

---

check point 3

1. Why are voice qualities and other nonverbal symbols important when delivering a speech?

2. Why is getting audience feedback on a presentation important?

Check your answers in Appendix C.

CHECKLIST FOR POSITIVE OR NEUTRAL MESSAGES

- ❏ Keep the objective of the presentation in mind.
- ❏ Keep the listeners' needs in mind.
- ❏ Know the subject of the presentation well.
- ❏ Practice your speech until you can present it comfortably.
- ❏ Record your speech to provide feedback for improving your delivery.
- ❏ Dress appropriately and be well groomed.
- ❏ Start and finish your speech on time.
- ❏ Use your voice effectively. Speak clearly, project your voice, vary your tone, and use correct grammar.
- ❏ Use nonverbal gestures effectively.
- ❏ Maintain eye contact with the audience.
- ❏ Speak with enthusiasm and conviction.
- ❏ Keep your energy level high.
- ❏ In the closing, summarize the main points or review the action you want listeners to take.

Section 13.1 *Applications*

A. *Plan a Formal Presentation*

1. Identify a topic or problem to be researched and studied for a formal presentation. Ask your teacher to approve the topic.

2. Write a statement that identifies the objective of the presentation.

3. Determine the scope of the speech. Decide what related areas will and will not be included in the speech. The speech should take 10 to 15 minutes, including 2 or 3 minutes for questions.

4. Develop a timeline for completing the speech. Start with the date your teacher gives you for completing the speech. Work backward from that date to create a timeline. (Allow plenty of time to practice the speech.)

CRITICAL THINKING

B. *Research and Write a Presentation*

1. Do research for the speech you identified in Application A. Decide whether primary research, such as collecting data from a survey, or secondary research is appropriate for the speech. You might want to do both types of research.

2. Gather the data. Evaluate each source of data that you use to determine whether it is relevant, accurate, current, reliable, and unbiased.

3. Create a bibliography note and one or more research notes for each secondary data source you use.

4. Decide on an order (direct or indirect) for the speech and create a topic outline.

5. Write extensive notes that you can use to practice the speech. Organize the notes by the parts of the speech—introduction, body, and closing—according to your outline.

6. Identify visual aids that you might use in the presentation. You will create the visual aids, practice the speech, and deliver the speech in Section 13.2.

INTERNET

REAL WORLD

Visual Aids in Presentations

Types of Visual Aids

1. Choose an appropriate visual aid that will help the receiver better understand your message.

2. Prepare visual aids that are well received.

3. Use visual aids in a professional manner during an oral presentation.

Key▶Point

Posters are an effective visual aid that can be prepared ahead of time.

Effective use of visual aids can make speakers appear better prepared and more credible than speakers who did not use visuals. To determine whether you need visual aids in a presentation, consider these three questions:

◼ Will visual aids help clarify the message?

◼ Will visual aids add interest to the presentation?

◼ Will visual aids help the audience remember what was said?

If you answer *yes* to any of those questions, you should use visual aids in your presentation. Many types of visual aids can be used. In Chapter 10, you learned about creating charts and graphs and using digital pictures and maps in reports. These visual aids can also be used in presentations. Visual aids can be displayed using posters, flip charts, transparencies, slides (film or electronic), whiteboards, and other means.

Posters and Flip Charts

Posters and flip charts are similar in size, and both generally are displayed on an easel. For posters, prepare your visuals ahead of time. For flip charts, either prepare your visuals ahead of time and flip through the pad as you speak or draw or write your visuals as you speak.

When using a flip chart, think about the data you are presenting. The data should be easy to read and well organized. To achieve those goals, use appropriate headings and color. Make sure your writing is easy to read. Stand to the side (as much as you can) when writing on the flip chart during a presentation. Stand beside the flip chart (not in front of it) when talking about the data on the flip chart.

Transparencies, Slides, and Computer Presentations

Generally, the content of transparencies and slides is very similar. They may both be created using a software program such as *Microsoft PowerPoint*. The difference lies in how your audience views the visual aid.

◼ With transparencies, images are transferred to clear acetate film and projected on a screen, using an overhead projector.

- With film slides, images are transferred to 35 mm film. The slides are placed in a slide carousel and projected on a screen, using a slide projector.

- With electronic slides, images are created using computer software. They are then saved to a file. When giving the presentation, you open the file and show the images one at a time. As your slides appear on a computer monitor, your audience sees the projected image enlarged on a screen.

Figure 13-4 illustrates one option for projecting a computer presentation using a laptop computer, a projector, and a projection screen.

Computer software allows you to create a **multimedia presentation**. The presentation can include features such as sound and animation. **Animation** is the technique of making text or visuals appear to move in film or computer graphics. Short pieces of video may also be included. **Video** is the transmission of moving pictures to a monitor or television. Music can be used effectively with transitions from one slide to the next. By adding those special features, you can create a visually stimulating presentation.

Be careful not to overuse music, sound, or video. For example, if you use sound too often or if the sound is too loud, audience members may lose their focus on the content of the presentation. They may focus instead on the irritating sounds.

Diversity

If some audience members are hearing impaired, you may need to arrange for an interpreter to deliver the message in American Sign Language.

Figure 13-4 Electronic slides created on a computer can be projected onto a large screen for viewing during a presentation.

DIGITAL VISION/GETTY IMAGES

Objects

The audience can view three-dimensional objects presented from the front of the room or passed among audience participants. This method works well provided the object is large enough and the crowd is small enough. With smaller objects and larger audiences, however, the object should be projected on-screen. A visual presenter, such as the one shown in Figure 13-5, can be used for this purpose. A visual presenter has a color video camera mounted on a movable arm. Items are placed on a base or stage. Some presenters have side or bottom lights to illuminate the objects placed on the base. The camera can show an image of the entire object or it can zoom in for close-up views.

Chalkboards, Whiteboards, and Electronic Whiteboards

Key ▶ Point

An electronic whiteboard is a device that can scan text and images written on it and send the images to a computer or printer.

A familiar visual aid used in schools, the blackboard, now comes in an electronic version. Just as chalk is used to write on a green or black erasable hard board, colorful markers can be used to write on an erasable whiteboard.

An **electronic whiteboard** is a device that can scan text and images written on it. The scanned text and images can then be sent to a computer, printed, or faxed. Some electronic whiteboards work with projectors and allow users to write notes that are projected on a screen.

Figure 13-5 A visual presenter can be used to project an object.

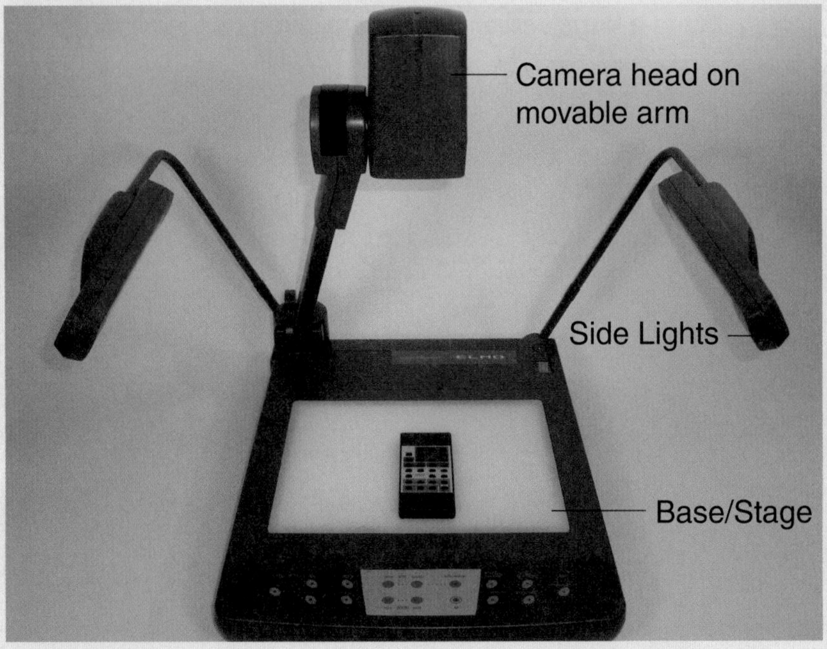

Camera head on movable arm

Side Lights

Base/Stage

PHOTO PROVIDED BY: ELMO USA CORP WWW.ELMOUSA.COM

Handouts

You may want to give handouts to audience members. A **handout** is a page(s) that contains text or images related to a presentation or other topic. Handouts can be given to the audience members at various times. If you plan to give the handout at the beginning of the presentation, include only brief points and a place to take notes. Do not include all the points in the presentation. If all the points are included, audience members may start looking at the handout instead of listening to your talk.

A handout given during a presentation can be used to provide detailed information about a particular point you are making. A handout distributed at the end of a presentation can be used to supply reference materials for your audience to use later.

Ethics

Remember to include the proper source citations for any material in handouts that is not your original material. Permission may be required for some material.

check point 4

1. List five types of visual aids that may be used in a presentation.

2. Which type of visual aid is useful for providing detailed information to audience members?

Check your answers in Appendix C.

Choosing Appropriate Visual Aids

When planning a presentation, you must decide which visual aids would be the best choice. Equipment available, audience needs, and preparation time are factors you should consider.

Equipment Available

Consider the equipment you have available where you will be making your presentation. Some options, such as electronic slides or an electronic whiteboard, require that you have access to special equipment. If you are using posters, you will need an easel or display board. Before you make your visual aids, check that everything you will need is available.

Audience Needs

Consider the options that will be best in helping your audience understand and remember your message. You might prefer to use a chalkboard to display notes. However, if some other option would help your audience understand and remember your message, then use the more appropriate visual aid.

Diversity

Consider the needs of your listeners when creating visual aids. For example, do they need terms defined or are they familiar with the basics of the subject being discussed?

Consider the number of people who will be in your audience and the room size. If you will be speaking to a small group, a poster or flip chart might be appropriate. For larger audiences, use other options. In most situations, computer presentations are a good choice.

Determine the amount of detail your audience needs. Consider using more than one type of visual aid. If you have a lot of detail to present, you might use transparencies or slides to present the main points. You might use handouts to provide more details.

Preparation Time

Determine how much time you have to prepare your visual aids. Time can be a limiting factor. If you have little time to prepare, writing key points on a whiteboard as you speak may be your only option. However, if you have the time, you may want to prepare transparencies or electronic slides.

check point 5

1. What factors should you consider when planning visual aids for a speech?

2. How does the size of the audience affect your choice of visual aids for a speech?

Check your answers in Appendix C.

Preparing Visual Aids

You should use enough visual aids to keep the audience's attention but not so many that the audience is overwhelmed. For most cases, visual aids (other than handouts) should simple and brief. Detailed and complex visual aids that are displayed on a screen will be hard for the audience to understand. Visual aids should be concise, easy to read, and interesting.

Number of Visual Aids

Prepare an acceptable number of visual aids. Do not use so many visual aids that your audience gets overwhelmed with them or so few that your audience gets bored. If, for example, you show a new slide every 12 seconds for the 20 minutes, your audience may quickly become burned out. As a general rule, present a new visual about every two minutes.

Limit the number of visual aids needed by placing only the main points of the speech on a slide or transparency. For example, instead of writing out a

Key ▶ Point
As a general rule, present a new visual about every two minutes.

complete sentence for one of your points, use key words to convey its meaning. Your oral explanation should provide the necessary details. When you have a complicated concept to present, break it down into smaller parts. Present the information in two or more parts instead of one.

Size, Color, Motion, and Sound

Visual aids should be large enough for the audience to see and read easily. Set up your visual aids in the front of the room in which you will be making your presentation. Then sit in a back seat in the room. If you can comfortably see everything (text, pictures, labels on graphics, objects, etc.), your visual aids are fine. If you have to strain to see anything, redo the visual aids so everyone in the audience will be able to see them.

Key▶Point
Visual aids should be large enough for the audience to see and read easily.

Use color for emphasis and interest. Audience members will expect colorful visual aids. Color scanners, color printers, and color markers allow you to add color to your visuals easily. Select colors carefully. The improper use of color can become a distraction or make visuals hard to read. For example, yellow text written on white poster board cannot be seen clearly from a distance.

A common problem in slides is caused by the misuse of color. In general, contrasting colors work well—that is, dark letters on a light background or light letters on a dark background. Bullet points can be set to turn gray or another light color as you move to a new point. This method emphasizes the point being discussed, as shown in Figure 13-6.

Figure 13-6 Color can be used to add interest to visual aids.

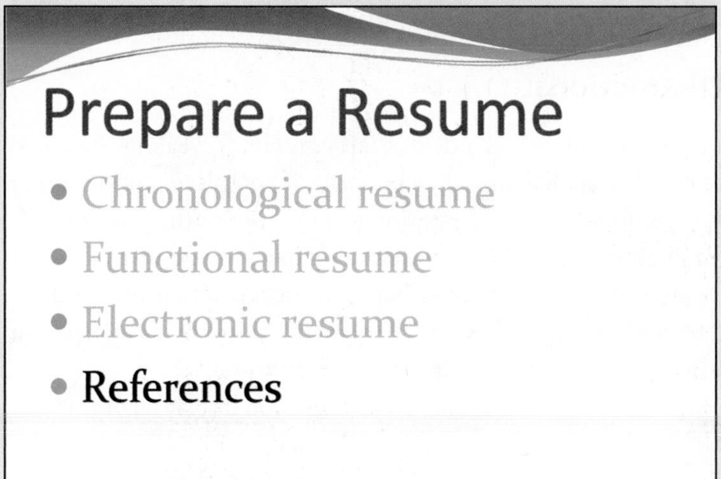

Prepare a Resume
- Chronological resume
- Functional resume
- Electronic resume
- **References**

6

Avoid colors that do not project well; red, for example. As explained earlier, you should view the visuals in the room where they will be used (or a similar setting) to make sure they are easy to read.

Use motion and sound in visuals to add interest and provide content not easily supplied by other means. For example, you might include a short video of the company president welcoming new employees in an employee orientation meeting. You might use sound to signal an important transition or conclusion in your speech. Bullet points on electronic slides can be animated to appear one at a time. This method is helpful when two or more points are on one slide, but you want to discuss them one at a time.

check point 6

1. How can you determine the number of visual aids to use when delivering a speech?

2. How can you determine whether the size and colors used on your visual aids are effective?

Check your answers in Appendix C.

Presenting Your Visual Aids

Following some simple guidelines will help you be effective as you use visual aids during your presentation. You want the visual aids to enhance your speech—not be a distraction for listeners. You need to practice with your visual aids until you can use them smoothly.

Prevent Distractions

Know when to reveal your visual aids or their content. Revealing the content too soon can distract listeners. For example, if you place a poster on an easel at the beginning of your presentation but do not use the poster until after the introduction, some audience members may become distracted by the poster during your introduction. A better approach is to use a blank poster board to cover the poster. Remove the blank poster board when you are ready to display the one behind it.

A visual aid also can become a distraction when you display all of the points on it before you are ready to talk about them. For example, if a slide has three bulleted points that make up the outline of your presentation, do not display all the points as you begin talking about the first point. Because all three points are visible, some audience members will begin looking ahead to see what comes next. Instead of revealing all three points at once, reveal only

Key ▶ Point

A visual aid can become a distraction when you display all of the points on it before you are ready to talk about them.

Reading Onscreen

Much of the information used for research or general information is available in electronic format. Users read e-mail messages, blogs, Web sites, and other documents on computer monitors. Reading onscreen is somewhat different from reading a printed document. For example, the line lengths used in an onscreen document may be much longer than those typically used in a printed document. The text size may be much smaller or larger than in printed documents. You may need to look away from the text to click a scroll bar or a button to move to a new section of text. Returning to the exact spot where you were reading can be difficult. You may need to scan a paragraph to find your place. All these factors can make reading onscreen more difficult than reading printed documents.

You can overcome some of the difficulties of reading onscreen. For example, in a word processing program or a Web browser, you can change the zoom or the font size to one that is larger or smaller to make reading easier. You can resize the window or reset the margins to control the line length. You can place your pointer on the scroll bar arrow or the Next button before beginning to read so that you do not have to look away from your reading. If a page is very hard to read onscreen because of design elements or annoying popup windows or banners, you may be able to copy and paste the text into a word processing program and read it there—without the distractions. You could also print the document.

Open the *Word* file *CH13 Reading* from the student data files. Follow the directions in the exercise to practice adjustments for reading onscreen.

the first point. Reveal each remaining point as you talk about it. In a computer presentation, set the animation so that your bulleted points come in one at a time. If using a transparency, use a sheet of paper to cover part of the page.

Practice Using Visual Aids

You need to have a dress rehearsal for a speech, particularly if you are using visual aids. Go to the room where you will speak, if possible. Practice your speech, using your visual aids. Make sure you know how to turn all equipment on and off, to focus the image, and to position equipment so everyone in the

PHOTODISC/GETTY IMAGES

Face the audience when using visual aids in a presentation.

room can see the visual aids. If you are going to use equipment, such as an electronic whiteboard or slides, make sure all of the equipment is working and that all of the equipment works together. You do not want your audience to wait while you try to get the equipment up and running.

Face the audience when using your visual aids. Audience members prefer to see the front of you. Also, when you speak, the audience can hear you better when you are facing them rather than a screen. When using a pointer, hold the pointer in the hand closest to the visual aid. By holding the pointer in that hand, you avoid turning your back to the audience. When using transparencies, read while facing an overhead projector, rather than turning around to read from the screen. Likewise, when using electronic slides, read from your computer monitor rather than turning toward the projected image.

Key ▶ Point

Face the audience when using your visual aids. The listeners can hear you better when you are facing them rather than a screen.

check point 7

1. Why it is important to make sure all the equipment you will use is working properly well before you begin the speech?

2. Should you look at the screen at the front of the room or at your audience when discussing a visual aid? Why?

Check your answers in Appendix C.

Section 13.2 *Applications*

A. *Prepare Visual Aids*

1. In Section 13.1, you planned visual aids for a formal presentation. Review that plan and determine if you want to make any changes based on what you have learned in this section.

2. Create the visual aids for the presentation.

3. View the visual aids from the back of the room where you will give the presentation (or a similar setting).

4. Make updates to the visual aids, if needed.

B. *Create an Evaluation Form*

1. Create an evaluation form that you can use to gain feedback on your presentation. See Figure 13-3 on page 491 for an example form.

2. Print several copies of the form, one for each person who will hear your presentation.

C. *Deliver a Presentation*

1. Practice the presentation you have prepared, using the visual aids. If possible, video tape your presentation and then review the tape.

2. As further practice, deliver your presentation to one or two classmates. Ask for feedback for improving your delivery.

3. Deliver the presentation to the class or to a group of your classmates.

4. Ask your classmates to complete the evaluation form you prepared earlier, giving feedback on your presentation.

5. Review the feedback you received. Write a paragraph that highlights the strong points of your presentation and lists areas you need to improve in future presentations.

TEAMWORK

Effective Meetings

Types of Meetings

Meetings are an important part of business operations. There are staff meetings, training sessions, and conferences with clients. A meeting may take place with a supervisor and one employee, a group of colleagues, or employees and clients. Many companies have adopted a team approach. Employees from different departments (and even from different locations) work together to solve problems, exchange ideas, and share responsibilities.

In the workplace, you may take part in various kinds of meetings. You may belong to several committees within your organization. For instance, you may belong to a **standing committee**, such as a customer relations committee. This type of group is a permanent part of the organization and meets regularly. You also may be part of an **ad hoc committee**. This temporary group meets for a specific purpose, such as planning a holiday party. A **task force** is a group charged with completing a specific job within a certain time. For example, a task force might write new procedures for business travel.

Employees meet with clients to discuss business projects.

PHOTODISC/GETTY IMAGES

You have learned that many companies now use teleconferences or Web conferences. These meetings are conducted for attendees at different locations via telephone, video, and computer. Teleconferences save on travel time and expense.

Meeting Documents

Two documents that you will use and that you may need to prepare for meetings are agendas and minutes.

Agendas

An **agenda** is a document that lists the topics to be discussed during a meeting. The person who calls or organizes the meeting usually prepares the agenda. The agenda is often distributed in advance so people can prepare for the meeting. Sometimes the tasks of preparing and distributing the agenda are done by an assistant. Groups that meet more than once may appoint a secretary who composes and sends the agenda.

The agenda may be sent as an e-mail attachment or as hard copy. It may be included with the initial message that tells attendees about the meeting or sent later. The meeting announcement is usually by e-mail, memo, or fax and includes the date, time, length, and location of the meeting. Agendas help keep people focused on the scheduled topics for a meeting. Both the leader and participants can use the agenda as a guide.

Plan and Organize Agendas

To plan an agenda, you must know the objective of the meeting. You also need a list of topics to be discussed. For each topic, note the name of the person or group that will lead the discussion. Ask that person how long the discussion will take. If your group includes committees, contact the head of each committee. Ask whether the committee has anything to present and how much time it needs. If your group has met previously, look at the minutes from the last meeting. Determine whether there was any unfinished business from that meeting that needs to be addressed in this one.

Agendas are organized in different ways depending on the objective of the meeting. Very formal meetings follow *Robert's Rules of Order*. These rules are a set of guidelines for parliamentary procedure. In business, meetings with such a high level of formality are rare. Still, many organizations use certain features of *Robert's Rules of Order* to keep meetings orderly. For instance, a meeting often begins with a call to order and ends with adjournment. When a group of people meets for the first time or when new people are added to the group, the leader should review the meeting rules that everyone should follow.

Key▶Point

An agenda lists the topics to be discussed during a meeting and is usually prepared by the person who calls the meeting.

Key▶Point

Very formal meetings follow *Robert's Rules of Order,* a set of guidelines for parliamentary procedure.

An agenda is used as a discussion guide as well as a planning document. It should include every topic that will be discussed during the meeting. When you have all of the information, total the time estimates. If you will not have enough time for all of the items, you may need to postpone items or ask some attendees to be prepared to discuss their topic in less time.

Format Agendas

Some organizations have a preferred format for agendas. If yours does not, use the format shown in Figure 13-7 on page 507. Use two inches for the top margin and default side margins. Use the Title and Subtitle styles (or manually set fonts) for the title and subtitle. Note that leaders are used between the topic and the name of the person leading the discussion. Generally, an agenda includes the following information:

1. A heading that gives the general topic of the meeting, the date and time, and sometimes other information such as the location

2. A list of topics to be discussed, with the name of the person who will lead the discussion and the amount of time it will take for each one

3. Attachments that provide information about some of the topics

Minutes

Minutes are the official record of the proceedings of a meeting. The most common type of minutes, action minutes, summarize topics discussed, decisions made, and actions to be taken. Minutes are sent to people who attended the meeting and to people who were invited but could not attend. On occasion, minutes also are sent to others, such as senior managers or peers, whose work is affected by decisions made during the meeting.

Plan and Organize Minutes

Before the meeting takes place, decide who will take notes at the meeting. For groups that meet more than once, the group may appoint one member to record the minutes. The content of minutes varies depending on the group. Minutes for most meetings consist of a summary of the discussions or action taken.

If you will be preparing minutes, find out before the meeting how detailed they should be. Use previous minutes as a guide. If none are available, talk with the person who has called the meeting. If everything said at the meeting must be recorded, arrange for an audio recording. After the meeting, transcribe the recording or have someone else do it. If you are summarizing and not recording, take careful, detailed notes. Use your best active listening skills and have a copy of the agenda in front of you. Note any items that are discussed out of order.

Key ▶ Point

Action minutes summarize topics discussed and decisions made at a meeting. They also list actions to be taken.

Figure 13-7 Meeting Agenda

Alumni Council

Meeting Agenda, May1, 20--, 6:30 p.m., North Meeting Room

6:30 – 6:35	Call to Order	James Kepler
6:35 – 6:40	Approval of Minutes from April Meeting	James Kepler
6:40 - 7:00	Trustee Report	James Kepler
7:00 – 7:15	Annual Fund Update	Melisenda Vega
7:15 – 7:30	Nominating Committee Report	Madison Tesco
7:30 – 7:50	Upcoming Events	
	Business Lunch – June 6	Arao Kato
	Senior Dinner – June 1	Nina Williams
7:50 – 7:55	Announcements	James Kepler
7:55 – 8:00	Adjournment	James Kepler

Prepare the minutes within a day or two after the meeting so you are less likely to forget items. Issuing minutes promptly gives recipients information that may affect their work. Minutes may be sent as a printed document, as an attachment to an e-mail, or faxed.[1]

Confidential information may be discussed at a meeting and noted in the meeting minutes. Do not send minutes that contain confidential information as an e-mail attachment. Use caution when sending such minutes by fax. Make sure the person who should see the minutes is waiting to receive the fax so that it will not be read by others.

Format Minutes

Some organizations have a preferred format for minutes. If yours does not, use the format shown in Figure 13-8 page 509. Use two inches for the top margin and default side margins. Use the heading styles or manually set fonts for the title, subtitle, and body headings. For minutes that are more than one page, use an appropriate heading on the other pages. For example, use the title of the meeting and the page number. Minutes usually include the following information:

1. The general topic, date, time, and place of the meeting
2. The names of the presiding officer or meeting leader and attendees
3. Summaries of topics discussed and actions to be taken, in order of discussion
4. Attached handouts and meeting materials (optional)

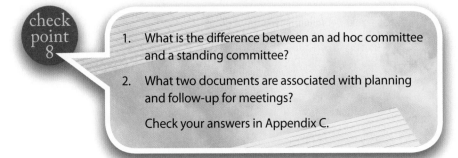

check point 8

1. What is the difference between an ad hoc committee and a standing committee?

2. What two documents are associated with planning and follow-up for meetings?

Check your answers in Appendix C.

Participation in Meetings

You should show interest and take an active part in meetings you attend for work. Be aware that your conduct in meetings—what you do, what you say, and how you say it—sends a message about your attitudes, abilities, and competence. This section of the chapter discusses communicating in meetings. Meetings are most likely to yield good results when they have active participants, organization, and effective leadership.

[1]Susie H. VanHuss et al., *Keyboarding & Word Processing: Complete Course* (Cincinnati: Thomson/South-Western, 2006), 504–506, 508–509.

Figure 13-8 Action Minutes

Technology Advocacy Group

Meeting Minutes, March 24, 20--

Call to Order

The Technology Advocacy Group met on March 24, 20--, in Conference Room B. The meeting was called to order at 8:30 a.m. Kurt Beckley chaired the meeting. Other team members present were Aileen Dumont, Shanyou Han, Janelle Mahoney, Matthew Armando, and Danni Winters.

Minutes

The minutes of the previous meeting were read and approved with no changes.

Blogs and Personal Web Sites

Danni raised the issue of setting standards for appropriate content in student blogs and personal Web sites. She noted that other schools have had problems recently with content on blogs and Web sites. The group discussed the issues of privacy and freedom of expression. The group voted to have Janelle conduct a focus group with five students from each class. The purpose of the focus group is to get input from the students on possible changes to the standards.

Tablet Conference

Aileen reported on the tablet conference that was held last Friday. Attendees liked the hands-on approach used at the conference. Aileen remarked that more support personnel would be helpful for setting up the conference room. The group voted to ask three students to help provide support at future conferences. Before the next conference, the group will give Aileen the names of students who might be asked to help.

Aileen reported that the remaining three conferences for this year are already filled. The group voted to recommend adding two more conferences to be held this year in September and October. Shanyou will draft a memo to Dr. Stribling requesting the extra conferences. He will send the memo to group members for comments by e-mail before sending the final document to Dr. Stribling.

Adjournment

The meeting was adjourned at 9:45 a.m. The next meeting is scheduled for April 20, 20--.

_____

Kurt Beckley, Group Chairperson

Prepare to Take Part

Some meetings require preparation before the meeting. When you receive the agenda for the meeting, review it carefully. Write down any questions you would like to ask. If you need some background on an agenda item, do research to educate yourself. Read any attachments to the agenda.

If a meeting has been called to make a decision, be ready to support your point of view. Disagreeing with others in a meeting is acceptable behavior. Few managers want people who have no opinions of their own. Instead, they want people who voice thoughtful opinions and who bring up points the group should consider. Write down the things you want to say so you will remember them. Come to a meeting prepared—ready to listen as well as to speak—and remain focused on the objective of the meeting.

Arrive on Time

Strive to be on time for meetings. Timeliness sends a nonverbal message that you are dependable and that you believe the meeting is important. Tardiness sends the opposite message. Make a habit of arriving early. Do not allow work, unexpected conversations, or other factors to delay you.

If you are not familiar with the location of a meeting, get directions beforehand. Find a place where you know you can park for as long as necessary at the time of day of the meeting. Allow yourself extra time that day in case traffic is heavier than you anticipated or you make a wrong turn. If you must arrive late for a meeting, notify the leader. When you enter, take your seat without interrupting.

Responsible employees take an active part in meetings.

COMSTOCK IMAGES/JUPITER IMAGES

Improve Decision Making

When members of a group are reluctant to make a decision, the group needs to find the source of the reluctance and move the discussion forward. One way to do that is to ask a probing question, such as "Does anyone need more information about the software?"

Sometimes a group gets bogged down in the process of making a decision. People ask for more information or get sidetracked on unimportant issues. When such things happen, the meeting leader should try to close the discussion and refocus members on the present task. The leader should be tactful but firm. For example, say something like, "Now that we have all of the information we need about the software, we can proceed to costs." Another example is: "Janet has brought up some important concerns that we can look at closely the next time we meet. Today, though, we need to make a decision about costs."

The opposite problem occurs when the group is preparing to make a decision before it is ready. In that case, express your concerns directly or ask questions that will yield information or raise matters you think should be considered. You could say, "I've listened carefully to everything the committee has told us, but I still have some questions. Edith, tell me again why you think the software will help us maintain inventory." Even if the group does not agree with you, your hesitation probably will create more discussion.

One pitfall that groups need to guard against is *groupthink*. This phenomenon was studied by psychologist Irving L. Janis. Groupthink occurs when the members of a group tend to suppress their own ideas. They desire agreement more than quality decisions.[2] As a group member, you have a duty to listen to and consider different points of view. You also have a duty to state your own point of view when you think a decision is wrong.

Make a Positive Impact

The following suggestions will help you make a positive impact on any group of which you are a part.

- Be willing to listen. Groups work best when participants are open to new information and points of view.

- Speak briefly and directly. Speak in a clear, organized manner so others will want to hear.

- Do not have a private conversation with someone during the meeting. Speak to the group and focus on the agenda topics.

- Do not take phone calls during a meeting unless they relate to the business of the meeting.

[2]William Safire, "The Way We Live Now: 8-8-04: On Language; Groupthink," *The New York Times*, accessed July 7, 2008, available from http://query.nytimes.com/gst/fullpage.html?res=9C01E2DD173CF93BA3575BC0A9629C8B63&sec=&spon=&pagewanted=1.

Key▶Point

The leader of the meeting should keep the group focused and lead them through the decision-making process.

Diversity

People with different backgrounds or education may have very different ideas about an issue. Be willing to listen and consider other points of view.

■ Discuss ideas. To discuss is to exchange ideas; to argue is to become emotional and unreasonable. Arguments often start when participants put their ideas ahead of group objectives and refuse to listen to differing points of view.

■ Avoid personal attacks. Mutual respect is a key to group functioning.

■ Engage in fair play. Give everyone the opportunity to speak; do not dominate the discussion.

■ Use body language to your advantage. Make eye contact when you begin speaking, speak slowly and calmly even when excited, and make sure your posture communicates authority and confidence.

■ Take notes that will help you remember what is said, complete tasks, and prepare for any future meetings. Even if the group has a secretary who takes minutes, you still need to take notes on matters of importance to you.

Figure 13-9 summarizes do's and don'ts for meeting participants.

Figure 13-9 Guidelines for Meeting Participation

MEETING PARTICIPATION	
DO'S	**DON'TS**
Prepare.	Show up with no background for the meeting.
Arrive on time.	Arrive late.
Focus on the topic.	Be inattentive or spend much time on side issues.
Be concise.	Ramble.
Participate actively.	Remain uninvolved.
Help the group arrive at sound decisions.	Keep to yourself when the group has trouble deciding on issues.
State positions clearly.	Speak in an unorganized way or choose not to share your views.
Follow the agenda.	Raise issues whenever you want to talk about them.
Discuss ideas willingly.	Argue or refuse to listen to different points of view.
Engage in fair play.	Dominate the discussion or act unfairly.
Support group decisions.	Complain about or keep bringing up issues once a decision has been made or a course of action selected by the group.

check point 9

1. How can you prepare to take part before a meeting?

2. What is *groupthink,* and how can it prevent meetings from being productive?

Check your answers in Appendix C.

Organize Productive Meetings

When considering holding a meeting, determine whether a meeting is the best way to accomplish your goals. When a meeting is needed, you can help make it productive by defining the objective, determining the type of meeting to hold, choosing participants carefully, and taking care of related details.

Define the Objective

An effective leader recognizes what a group can and cannot do. For example, entry-level managers do not develop company policy. Corporate directors develop company policy, but they do not gather routine information. That job usually is done by employees at a lower level. Look carefully at the purpose of the meeting. Determine what the group should accomplish. Plan to state the objective clearly at the beginning of the meeting.

Trying to do too much makes meetings frustrating, disorganized, and unproductive. Set a reasonable time limit for the meeting. Begin and end the meeting on time. Restrict the content of a meeting to its stated purpose. Although, under certain conditions, a meeting can have two or more purposes, you should generally call separate meetings in such instances. The rule is "one objective—one meeting." Do the same when a task is too large to accomplish in a single meeting. Divide the task into workable parts and plan separate meetings.

Key ▶ Point
An effective leader states the objective clearly at the beginning of a meeting.

Determine the Type of Meeting

With your objective in mind, consider again whether a meeting is the best way to accomplish the objective. For example, can employees be informed of a new company policy in a memo rather than in a meeting? If a meeting is needed, identify the type of meeting.

With the objective identified, you can easily determine what type of meeting to hold. Meetings can be held to inform, develop new ideas, make decisions, delegate work, collaborate, and persuade. Determining the type of meeting makes organizing it easier.

To Inform

Meetings are often held to inform people about work-related issues. For example, employees might be told about benefit options for the coming year. Handouts that meeting participants can study after the meeting may be provided. Questions may be answered about materials that were given out before the meeting.

When a meeting is held to inform, determine whether direct or indirect order is best for discussing the topics. When you think the meeting participants will readily accept the ideas or decisions being presented, use direct order. Use indirect order when you want to present supporting information before presenting the main idea.

To Develop New Ideas

Meetings may be held to develop or improve procedures, programs, or products. A common technique used in such meetings is brainstorming. **Brainstorming** is thinking of every possible idea about a topic. The goal is to generate ideas. No one criticizes anyone's ideas. The ideas are not evaluated until after the brainstorming session. If you decide to use brainstorming, invite a diverse group of people. Plan to state ground rules before brainstorming begins and appoint someone to record ideas.

Key▶Point

When brainstorming, do not take time to evaluate ideas. The goal is simply to generate many ideas.

To Make Decisions

Decision-making meetings bring people together to discuss an issue and raise points that should be considered. When planning this type of meeting, you may find it useful to ask for information beforehand. The information can be provided with the agenda. As the leader, you should establish ground rules for the discussion. Deciding by consensus—with all members taking part and accepting the decision—is an effective method. At some meetings, a person in authority will make the final decision after hearing discussion on the issue.

To Delegate Work

Meetings to **delegate** are held to assign tasks to people or groups. Although you can assign tasks over the telephone or by e-mail, you may need to hold a meeting to clarify details. You might want to get volunteers or determine who would be best at handling each task. Meetings to delegate often are followed by informational and decision-making meetings.

Key▶Point

Collaborative efforts succeed only when people work together as a team.

To Collaborate

Meetings held to **collaborate** are sessions in which people work together to accomplish a task. For example, they might organize a complex report. Collaborative efforts succeed only when people work together as a team. For this type of meeting, make sure that whatever supplies and equipment the team needs to work together are provided.

Meetings are held to develop new ideas and make decisions.

To Persuade

When meeting to persuade, people attempt to gain support for a course of action. For example, an engineer may try to convince company managers to develop a new product. A manager may try to convince employees to follow safety procedures.

Choose Participants Carefully

Communication in a meeting works best when everyone has a reason for attending and can contribute to the discussion. When more than one person has the same expertise or point of view, choose only one to join the group. If you can choose, select people you know will be effective participants.

Company policies may affect who should be invited to a meeting. In some companies, meetings usually are attended by people on the same organizational level. In other companies, people from various levels may take part in the same meeting.

Handle Meeting Details

Many details must be handled to have a successful meeting. They include various tasks, such as scheduling the meeting, creating an agenda, and securing equipment and supplies. Taking care of meeting details shows attendees that you value their time and appreciate their input.

Schedule for Convenience

Schedule a meeting at a date and time that is convenient for participants. One way to do that is to offer a selection of dates and times. Ask people to indicate which two or three dates would be best for them. Some companies

Key▶Point

Meetings are more productive when everyone present has a reason for attending and can contribute to the discussion.

✚
Ethics

Do not purposely schedule a meeting when a person who opposes your views cannot attend. To do so would be unethical.

have calendaring software that makes employees' schedules and appointments available to coworkers. Coworkers can look at the schedules of the people they want to attend a meeting to see when people are free. This method is very helpful in selecting two or three possible dates for a meeting. *Windows Calendar*, shown in Figure 13-10 on page 517, allows users to publish a calendar to the Internet, a network location, or a computer.

Early morning and right after lunch are popular meeting times. Many businesspeople hold working breakfasts, lunches, or dinners with food served at the meeting.

Invitations are usually extended by e-mail or phone. Advantages of e-mail are that participants have a written record of the invitation. They can take time in consulting their calendars and replying. When you need an immediate reply or are inviting only a few people, phoning may be a better choice. If you write, include a date by which people should let you know if they can attend. When that date arrives, call anyone who has not responded.

Create an Agenda

Creating an agenda was discussed earlier in the chapter. When composing the agenda, contact people who may have something to present to find out how much time they will need. Send the agenda and any background materials well in advance of the meeting. Plan to bring extra copies to the meeting in case anyone needs them. If you do not have a person who takes minutes regularly, arrange for someone to take minutes. Make sure that person understands what information to record.

Select an Appropriate Site

Key ▶ Point

Select a meeting location that provides the amount of space needed and that is convenient for the group.

A meeting may be held in an office, in a conference room, or at an outside location. Select a location that provides the amount of space needed and that is convenient for the group. For example, you may need a table to hold papers or a projector that is available only in a conference room. If most of the people who will attend the meeting work in one location, it makes sense to schedule the meeting at that location. A room with new furniture or a scenic view provides a pleasant working environment.

Arrange the Furniture

Arrange the furniture sensibly for all concerned. Often, everyone, including the leader, sits around a table. Check that presenters will be able to see the audience and will have the space they need. Ensure that each person will be able to see the presenter and everyone else. Make sure visual aids can be seen clearly from any seat. If you plan to offer refreshments, place them so people will not have to cross in front of others.

Figure 13-10 Windows Calendar allows users to publish a calendar to be viewed by others.

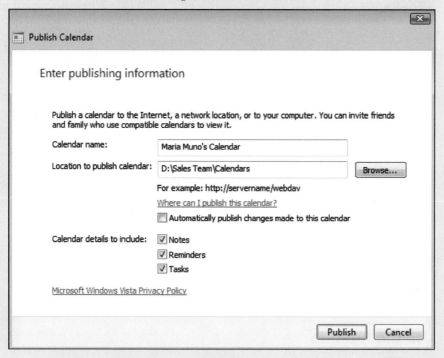

Secure Equipment and Supplies

Make sure the room is equipped with everything that participants will need and that equipment is working properly. Some examples of equipment and supplies that you might require are a speakerphone, computers, a whiteboard, a projector, microphones, an audio recorder, notepads, name tags, and pens or pencils.

Provide for Comfort

The last step in meeting mechanics is to provide for the comfort of participants. Make water, juice, coffee, and tea available. If you are meeting early in the morning, consider bringing in doughnuts, bagels, and muffins. For working breakfasts, lunches, or dinners, choose a vendor whose food and service you know is good from personal experience or who is recommended by someone reliable. Try to anticipate the needs and preferences of the various people who will be attending. For example, if the meeting will include lunch or dinner, vegetarian or kosher offerings might be appropriate. Plan for breaks during long meetings.

Key▶Point
Make sure the meeting room is equipped with everything that participants will need and that equipment is working properly.

check point 10

1. What are six types of details or tasks that must be handled to organize a successful meeting?

2. What strategy can you use to find a meeting date and time that will be convenient for everyone attending the meeting?

Check your answers in Appendix C.

Lead Meetings Effectively

How a leader conducts a meeting has a great deal to do with how successful the meeting will be. The leader should begin the meeting on time. If some participants do not know each other, the leader should introduce them or ask people to introduce themselves to the group. The leader should state the objective of the meeting and the tasks to be accomplished.

Use the Agenda

Key▶Point

Follow the agenda to ensure that topics are discussed in order and within the time allotted.

Use the agenda to ensure that topics are discussed in order and within the time allotted. As each agenda item is dispensed with, summarize points of agreement and disagreement. Outline any actions that will be taken.

A common problem is for participants to stray from the topic. Their attention drifts to other issues, or they begin telling personal stories. Remain polite and friendly, but keep the group on track. When people ramble, a good approach is to summarize what you think they meant to say and to ask a question that will point them in the right direction.

Another common problem is spending too much time on an agenda item. If it looks as though a presentation or discussion will exceed the time allotted, decide whether extra time is needed. If it is not, tell the presenter or group how much time remains and request a summing up or conclusion within that time. If more time is needed, you must decide whether to take time from other agenda items or to revisit the topic at another meeting.

Encourage Participation

Encourage people to share their thoughts. If a discussion is slow getting started, try posing an open-ended question, one that requires more than a simple yes or no answer. For example, you might ask, "What sorts of changes can we make to our basic shop operations to reduce pollution?"

Encourage quiet people to join in by asking direct, specific questions such as, "Gino, will adding this program overload the existing computer system?" When people talk about an area they know well, their shyness often disappears. Although you cannot force people to participate, you can provide a positive setting.

Make sure that ideas are communicated clearly and that everyone understands them. Be alert for puzzled looks and other signs of confusion. When participants do not grasp a concept, restate in your own words what you think the speaker is saying. "I believe Ramon is telling us that, according to these surveys, there is not enough interest among our customers to justify offering this product." If you are not sure what the speaker means, ask a clarifying question. For example, you might say, "Heather, I don't understand what a proxy server does. Can you explain it to us?"

NETBookmark

Several Web sites provide tips and articles for effective presentation and meetings. Go to one of these sites, such as Effective Meetings.com. A link to the site is provided on the Web site for this book that is shown below.

1. Review the articles available about meeting planning and presenting.

2. Select one article on which to report. Give the article name and complete source information. Write a summary of the main points of the article.

www.cengage.com/school/bcomm/buscomm

Key ▶ Point

In a meeting, make sure that ideas are communicated clearly and that everyone understands them.

Handle Difficult People

Handling difficult people is the greatest challenge any meeting leader faces. Sometimes a person is being difficult because he or she is unable to express a concern. This person may think the group has not understood or considered the concern adequately. If you think a difficult person has a legitimate concern, ask questions to try to identify the problem. Be respectful, listen actively, and keep an open mind.

If the behavior persists, keep your composure. Do not respond to the person's arguments point for point. As one consultant suggests, "Act rather than react." Keep your remarks brief and focus on the issue or areas of agreement rather than on personalities.[3] A good strategy is to use the agenda or a technical point to move the discussion to another topic.

Sometimes one person wants to dominate the conversation. To discourage an overly eager contributor, you could say something like, "Chris, we

---

[3]Barton Goldsmith, "Managing Difficult People," *Successful Meetings* 53, no. 2 (February 2004): 32.

Key ▶ Point

A meeting leader should not allow one person to dominate the discussion.

have a lot to cover. We can spend only five more minutes on this topic." If Chris continues to talk, interrupt and redirect the discussion to another person. Say, for example, "Your experiences point to the need to communicate with consumers. Kelly, can you fill us in on the advertising plan?"

Be Professional

The leader sets the tone for the meeting through fairness, work ethic, and control. The following steps show your ability as a leader.

- Recognize everyone's contributions. Participants who believe that their insights are valued will continue to contribute. Even if a proposal has problems, focus on the positive aspects and lead the group forward.

- Maintain high standards. Do not accept poor work or opinions that are stated as facts. When participants do not have information the group needs, postpone the meeting, if possible.

- Maintain order. Make sure the meeting follows the agenda. Allow only one person to speak at a time and discourage private conversations.

End Appropriately

At the end of a meeting, summarize what has been covered and move the group ahead to future action. List items that need further consideration. Review assignments and deadlines for future work. If the group must meet again, explain that you will communicate with everyone soon regarding the date and time. Finally, thank participants for their time and efforts.

Diversity

An effective meeting leader recognizes that everyone has something to contribute.

check point 11

1. How can an agenda be used during a meeting?

2. What strategies can you use to handle difficult people during a meeting?

Check your answers in Appendix C.

Section 13.3 *Applications*

A. *Meeting to Develop Ideas*

1. Form a group with three or four other students. The group will serve as a Fundraising Committee.

2. You have been appointed to record minutes. (In a real meeting, only one person would prepare minutes. In this application, each person will prepare minutes as a learning exercise.)

3. Hold a brainstorming session to come up with ideas for a fund-raiser that students in your school could do to benefit a local charity. Think of as many ideas as you can in five minutes. Everyone should contribute at least one idea.

4. Evaluate the ideas offered and select the two best ideas for further consideration at a later meeting. Select a charity to receive the money that is raised.

5. Key the minutes from your notes taken during the meeting.

TEAMWORK

B. *Meeting Details and Agenda*

You are planning a follow-up meeting in which you will assign tasks for the fund-raiser from Application A.

1. Determine the objective and type of meeting.

2. Plan the details.

3. Send an e-mail to the members of the committee and your teacher with the meeting information and an agenda.

C. *Handling Difficult People*

Difficult people cause other problems in meetings besides those discussed in the text. For example, they may make inappropriate or abusive comments.

1. Choose one negative behavior a difficult person might show at a meeting. You might draw on your experiences with clubs, sports teams, or other groups.

2. Explain how an effective leader can manage this poor behavior.

CRITICAL THINKING

Chapter *Summary*

13.1 Oral Presentations

- Typical short speeches are introductions and briefings.

- A formal speech may last from 20 minutes to more than an hour and may require that you do research to find the content you need to present.

- All presentations, formal and informal, should have three main parts: an introduction, a body, and a closing.

- An outline can be a valuable tool when planning any speech. An outline is essential for long, complex speeches

- Delivery of a presentation is as important as content. Voice qualities, nonverbal symbols, and visual aids can enhance or inhibit delivery.

13.2 Visual Aids in Presentations

- Effective use of visual aids can make speakers appear better prepared and more credible than speakers who do not use visuals.

- When planning a presentation, you must decide which visual aids would be the best choice. Equipment available, audience needs, and preparation time are factors you should consider.

- You should use enough visual aids to keep the audience's attention but not so many that the audience is overwhelmed.

- You should practice with your visual aids until you can use them smoothly.

13.3 Effective Meetings

- Meetings are an important part of business operations.

- Two documents that you will use and that you may need to prepare for meetings are agendas and minutes.

- You should show interest and take an active part in meetings you attend for work.

- You can help make a meeting productive by defining the objective, determining the type of meeting to hold, choosing participants carefully, and taking care of related details.

- How a leader conducts a meeting has a great deal to do with how successful the meeting will be.

Open the *Word* file *CH13 Vocabulary* from the student data files. Complete the exercise to review the vocabulary terms from this chapter.

ad hoc committee	electronic whiteboard
agenda	handout
anecdote	impromptu speech
animation	minutes
brainstorming	multimedia presentation
briefing	standing committee
collaborate	task force
delegate	topical outline
demographics	video

Critical Thinking Questions

1. What may happen if you do not practice your speech so you can deliver it within the allotted time?

2. What may be the result if you do not consider your audience when planning a speech?

3. Why is trying to deliver a speech that you have memorized word for word not a good idea?

4. What type of visual aid do you think is most effective when giving a presentation to a small group (ten or fewer people)? Why?

5. Think of a meeting you have attended that was not very productive. Explain why you think the meeting was not productive.

CRITICAL
THINKING

Chapter *Applications*

A. *Prepare a Speech Outline*

INTERNET

1. Prepare a topical outline of a speech on the topic *Leading Meetings Effectively*. The speech should take 5 to 7 minutes to deliver. Your audience is your classmates.

2. Use the information in this chapter and articles you find on the Internet for the content of the speech. Record source information for the articles.

B. *Prepare Visual Aids*

INTERNET

1. Prepare visual aids for the speech you outlined in Application A. Use a program such as *Microsoft PowerPoint* to prepare electronic slides.

2. Include a title slide and one slide for each main point in the speech.

3. Use slide transitions and animate the bullet points to come on screen one at a time.

4. Use at least one photo, one piece of clip art, and one sound clip in the presentation. These items can be downloaded from the Internet.

C. *Prepare Minutes*

REAL WORLD

1. Visit a local civic organization or government meeting or view a meeting of the group on television. For example, you might watch a meeting of the city council on your local TV cable channel.

2. Take notes during the meeting to use in preparing minutes of the meeting.

3. Prepare minutes of the meeting using your notes. Format the minutes similar to the minutes shown in Figure 13-8 on page 509.

D. *Create a Visual Aids Web Page*

1. Open and print the *Word* file *CH13 Visual Aids* from the student data files. This file contains handwritten text that you will use to create a Web page.

2. Open a new *Word* file. Use default margins. Use the default font and spacing.

3. Key the title *Visual Aids* in all caps and apply the Title style.

4. Format the paragraphs after the first paragraph as bullet points.

5. Insert a photo or piece of clip art that relates to the content of the page.

6. Select an attractive background for the Web page. Add other appropriate elements, if you wish, to create an interesting and attractive page. Do not include links. Assume that the appropriate links will be added when the page is posted on the company network.

7. Save the file as a single file Web page.

8. View the file in a browser program to check the format.

9. Open the file in *Word* and make changes to the format, if needed, for an attractive page.

E. Create a Digital Photo

Digital cameras and many cell phones and handheld computers can be used to create digital photographs. These photos can be used to enhance documents and create visual aids for presentations.

1. Identify an item that you own and might want to sell, such as a bike, musical instrument, or DVD player. Use a digital camera to take a photo of the item.

2. Create an advertisement offering to sell the item that you could post online. Describe the item and include the digital photo. Provide complete information, such as the price and how you can be contacted. Proofread carefully and correct all errors before printing the ad.

Editing Activity

Open the *Word* file *CH13 Editing* from the student data files. Edit the topical outline for a presentation contained in this file. Correct all spelling errors. Make the points for each slide parallel so that they all begin with a noun or they all begin with a verb.

Team Meetings

Terry Woo started working as a member of the computer programming team at his company immediately after graduating from Gonzales Technical College. At his first team meeting, he was surprised at how little the team accomplished. They started out by discussing a project and their various ideas, but arguments arose. After about 15 minutes of arguing, the team leader closed the meeting by saying, "Well, that's enough for today."

At the second team meeting, the same thing happened. This pattern continued until yesterday when Terry found out that his team leader had been fired. Now Terry has been asked to take charge of the team temporarily. The supervisor explained that other team members are too emotionally upset with each other and that the team leader needs to be seen as neutral. The supervisor asked Terry to write a memo to her before the first team meeting explaining what he would do to improve team meetings.

Terry did not dare turn the supervisor down, but he is very concerned about what he should do to help his team. He wants to be sure that his meetings are effective.

1. What approach—direct or indirect—should Terry use for the memo?

2. What strategies can Terry use to improve the team meetings?

Communication for Manufacturing

Kitty Lindsey is very excited. She is applying for a job as a welder at Unique Bikes in Paso Robles, California. This company is one of the premier shops in the USA that customize motorcycles. The employees work on thousands of motorcycles in a year.

As is the case with most welding positions, a high school diploma and training and experience in welding is required. The more experience, the better her chance of getting the job. As you can imagine, the welds on customized motorcycles must be neat, strong, and well done. Most of the welds will be steel to steel, but some will be specialized metals. These welds will require special training and expertise.

Kitty has a high school diploma and has completed a training course in welding. However, she is concerned because she has little experience—mainly at part-time jobs she held during high school or in the summer. However, she is a very enthusiastic, outgoing person and has some knowledge and experience with welding specialized metals. She also realizes that she is applying in a job area where most of the employees are men. Nevertheless, she wants this position and is going to the company today for an interview.

1. What roles will types of communication (oral, written, nonverbal) play in Kitty's interview?

2. Of the three types of communication, which one will be the most important in her work if she gets the job?

3. If she gets the job, what challenges will Kitty face while at work?

ABLESTOCK/JUPITER IMAGES

CHAPTER 14

Communicating with Customers

14.1 Customer Service

14.2 Face-to-Face Communication

14.3 Telephone Communication

Customer Service at a Minimum

In her job as sales support associate, Toni helps six busy salespeople at a company that sells flooring, cabinets, and countertop materials for kitchens and bathrooms. The company, More Than Floors, has two locations in San Antonio.

All the salespeople have cubicles, though they spend most of their time making sales presentations in people's homes. Toni's job is to process the sales orders. When a problem—such as a back order—comes up, she puts paperwork back on the appropriate person's desk. Toni has not learned how to solve the problems, nor has anyone suggested that she do so. She sometimes runs out of things to do. When that happens, she waits in a cubicle until something comes up.

In the showroom, the receptionist, Elena, also has a cubicle. Elena answers all incoming calls. The phone rings 10 to 20 times per hour. Most calls are for the salespeople. Elena takes messages (usually just a name and number) for the absent salespeople. If showroom customers have a question, they often must wait until Elena is between phone calls. Sometimes, if a caller is not someone Elena knows, she puts the call on hold and answers a question with the phone resting on her shoulder.

Once in a while, customers in the showroom approach Toni with a question. Most of the time she just replies, "Sorry, I'm not a salesperson; I can't help you." At other times, Toni tells them they will have to wait for Elena or make an appointment with one of the salespeople. The salespeople, however, do not have cell phones; and Elena does not schedule appointments for them.

Questions

1. How would you feel if you were a potential customer and had a question but could not get an answer?

2. What message does Toni's behavior send to customers? What message does Elena's behavior send to customers?

3. What could the company do to improve customer relations?

4. How could the company use technology more effectively?

14.1 Customer Service

Importance of Customer Service

OBJECTIVES

After completing Section 14.1, you should be able to:

1. Explain the importance of customer service.

2. Identify external and internal customers.

3. Describe effective strategies for dealing with customers.

4. Describe ways to deal with difficult customer situations.

The goal of a business is to make a profit. To make a profit, a company must have more income than expenses. A major source of income for many companies is the sale of products or services to customers. Without customers to buy products or services, many companies could not stay in business. Non-profit organizations also have customers. For example, the people who visit a non-profit museum are its customers.

Organizations use several strategies to attract customers. They advertise products and services, offer sales or discounts, and provide attractive product displays. However, according to marketing experts, "retaining your key customers is more cost-effective than trying to attract new ones."[1] One way to retain customers is to offer quality customer service. **Customer service** is the performance of activities to ensure customer satisfaction. Satisfied customers are more likely to be repeat customers.

When you think of customers, you probably think about people who, for example, want to buy a car or have a roof repaired. Each of these is an example of an external customer. An **external customer** is someone from outside the organization who receives benefits or information or purchases a product or service. As an employee, you may or may not work with external customers. However, you will have internal customers. An **internal customer** is another employee who works for the same company as you do. You provide services to these internal customers. Thus, quality customer service should be of concern to all employees.

Consider an example of internal customer service. Suppose Lisa Morales from the Accounting Department approaches you and asks you to give her a rundown on a project budget. She is asking for a service and is your customer. Your job is to provide the information Lisa needs. You want her to walk away feeling confident that she can come to you for reliable information whenever she needs it. If she does so, you have provided quality service to an internal customer. Workers may have many or only a few internal customers depending on their job duties.

Key▶Point

One way to keep customers is to offer quality customer service.

---

[1] "Marketing Tips, Retain, Attract and Expand Your Customers," Marketing for Business Success, accessed July 9, 2008, available from http://www.m4b.com.au/marketing-tips-customers.htm.

DIGITAL VISION/GETTY IMAGES

External customers are people outside the company to whom you provide products or services.

check point 1

1. Why is providing quality customer service important for businesses?

2. Who are external customers? Who are internal customers?

Check your answers in Appendix C.

Customer Service Culture

Companies that make customer service a priority have a strong customer service culture. In such a culture, the company's policies make it easy for employees to satisfy customers. Employees are allowed to use their own initiative in solving customer problems and are rewarded for doing so. Many companies provide training in customer service to help employees be successful in this vital area.

Key▶Point

Many companies provide training in customer service to help employees be successful in this vital area.

Policies and Procedures

Many companies have policies that govern how employees serve their customers. You should be aware of your company's policies and act accordingly.

In some cases, a company's policies may limit what you can do for a customer. For example, a customer service associate may not have the authority to offer a free replacement for a defective product. A sales associate may need a supervisor's signature before accepting a large amount of cash from a customer. Some policies, as in the latter example, exist to protect the customer or the company from fraud.

Customer Contact

Customer contact is any meeting or communication you have with a customer. Talking with a customer in person and answering e-mail messages are examples of customer contact. With every contact, you make an impression on that customer. At every point of contact, you should provide courteous, professional service. Building trust with customers is important. If the customer trusts you, he or she is more likely to remain a customer.

Be Accessible

To provide good customer service, you need to be accessible to your customers. **Accessibility** is the ease with which customers can contact you. To make sure that you are accessible to your customers, give them at least two ways to reach you. For example, provide an office telephone number and an e-mail address. You may also wish to provide a cell phone number. Assure customers that you will respond to messages quickly and follow through on this promise.

Give Knowledgeable Responses

Knowing your product or service well makes it easy to give knowledgeable responses to customer inquiries. Do not guess when giving customers information. Verify prices, stock availability, size, or other data. You may need to simplify technical or complex issues so the customer can understand.

Sometimes you will not be able to answer a question. Do not be afraid to say, "I don't know." However, do not let the contact end there. Let that customer know you will find the answer and get in touch at some specific time in the near future.

During the initial contact, you should be clear about when the customer can expect something to happen. Indicate whether information will be given in a telephone call, in an e-mail message, or by mail. If the follow-up work takes longer than expected, contact the customer. In general, make the customer feel as if your answering the inquiry promptly and accurately matters to you. Figure 14-1 on page 533 shows how a poor customer service provider communicates with a client. A quality customer service provider, however, has much more contact with the customer.

Diversity

Your customers may have certain expectations because of their cultural background. Be aware of the needs that might arise because of the diversity of your customers.

Key ▶ Point

Do not guess when giving customers information. Verify that the information is correct.

Figure 14-1 Two Views of Customer Service

INADEQUATE CUSTOMER CONTACT							
Mon.	Tues.	Wed.	Thurs.	Fri.	Sat.	Sun.	Mon.
Customer A makes an inquiry.		Customer A wonders what is happening.		Customer A calls another company.			You answer the inquiry too late.

QUALITY CUSTOMER CONTACT							
Mon.	Tues.	Wed.	Thurs.	Fri.	Sat.	Sun.	Mon.
Customer B makes an inquiry.	You consult a coworker.	You call Customer B to reassure her.		You call Customer B with part of the answer.	Customer B waits for more information.		You answer Customer B's inquiry.

Use E-mail Effectively

Many of your customers are likely to have access to e-mail. There is a tendency to be somewhat informal in e-mail, perhaps because many people use e-mail for personal messages. In e-mails to customers, your messages should be businesslike in tone and style. Follow the guidelines below to use e-mail effectively for customer service.

Key▶Point

In e-mails to customers, your messages should be businesslike in tone and style.

- When you receive an e-mail that requires a reply, respond promptly.
- Identify yourself and your company fully. Do not leave it for the customer to figure out from your e-mail address.
- State the purpose of your message clearly.
- State who will take the next action, what that action should be, and when it should occur. In other words, make it clear what the customer can expect.
- If you must transmit a lengthy document, send it as an attachment to an e-mail message rather than in the body of the message.
- Edit the message to make it clear, concise, correct, complete, and courteous. Ask yourself if you have covered the five Ws (who, what, where, when, and why) in the message.
- Key an e-mail message in standard format, using upper- and lowercase letters. Avoid sarcasm or humor that might be misunderstood in print.
- Proofread your message. As always, business correspondence should be error-free.

Respond to Web Site Visitors

Your company may provide customer service on a Web site. You should treat visitors to your Web site with the same care and respect as you would visitors to your office. Some guidelines for a customer-friendly Web site are listed below.

■ Make the site visually appealing and easy to read.

■ Post a list of frequently asked questions (FAQs) along with complete, concise answers.

■ Provide access to as much information as is practical. Everyone who visits the site should be able to find something useful.

■ Organize information logically and effectively. Think about what visitors will want to know and how they will navigate the site.

■ Provide current and accurate information on the Web site. Review the information on the Web site on a regular basis to verify that the information remains current or to update the information, if needed.

■ Respond to e-mail messages from site visitors promptly. Follow the guidelines given earlier for effective e-mail correspondence with customers.

■ If the site has a live chat feature, use it to help customers politely and efficiently, as you would in person.

Key▶Point

You should treat visitors who come to your Web site for customer service with the same care and respect as you would visitors to your office.

check point 2

1. How would you describe a company that has a strong customer service culture?

2. What is a customer contact? Give two examples.

Check your answers in Appendix C.

Customer Interaction

Consider the following scenario. A customer walks into a store. Two salespeople lean on a counter at the back of the store. They are chatting and do not look up when the customer enters. The customer looks around for several minutes, then leaves. The customer did not speak to the salespeople, so she must not have needed any help.

This scenario is an example of customer interaction. In this case, the salespeople failed to interact. Perhaps they did not realize that customer interaction begins the moment the customer enters the store. If service providers do not make contact, customers will form their opinions and, more than likely, move on.

Key▶Point

If company employees do not make contact with customers, they may feel ignored and not do business with the company.

Truth on the Web

An unhappy customer will likely tell several people about a bad experience. A satisfied customer, on the other hand, *might* tell one other person. The effects of "bad press" become even more daunting as the Internet makes communicating easy.

Unhappy consumers can now post their stories on the Internet for thousands of readers to see. Many newsgroups and blogs allow posting of consumer stories. A **newsgroup** is an online discussion group that focuses on a specific topic. Readers can view comments posted by others and post replies. A **blog** is an online journal posted on a Web site. Some blogs allow readers to reply to postings on the site. On both newsgroups and blogs, some entries tell of good customer service. However, many postings tell of rip-offs, unfair practices, and poor customer service in general.

These Web forums raise the issue of **credibility** (being believable or trustworthy). On some sites, anyone can post a comment, and no one checks the truthfulness of it. What is to stop a company from planting false stories about competitors to ruin their business? Perhaps a company that wants to generate some "good press" may plant a false account of good customer service on one of these sites. How do site visitors know that what they are reading is true?

As long as the Web remains relatively unmonitored, the possibility exists that false stories will be posted. Consumers must exercise caution and good judgment when reading blogs and newsgroup postings. As with all information found on the Internet, consider the source. Is the person, company, or group posting the information reliable and unbiased? Is the information accurate and current? Answers to these questions should guide you in evaluating the postings you read.

Make a Good First Impression

First impressions *do* count. Job interviewers—and interviewees—know it. Salespeople and customers know it, too. Customers want to be favorably impressed from the moment of contact with a customer service provider. They want to be in pleasant surroundings. They want to feel welcome. Certain actions and behaviors can help make the first meeting with a customer a favorable one. Be ready to receive customers. Give them prompt attention and greet them cheerfully.

Give Customers Prompt Attention

Make sure that both you and the area for which you are responsible are ready for customers. Dress appropriately for work and pay attention to good grooming. Keep your work area neat and organized so it gives a good impression.

Customers come to get advice, receive help, or to make a purchase. If they do not receive prompt attention, they may take their business elsewhere. Your organization may have a policy for approaching external customers. For example, at some stores, salespeople are required to greet customers as they walk in the door. In other jobs, employees decide when to approach customers.

Some customers like to browse on their own. Others want attention right away. You should observe each customer carefully as he or she enters. Decide which customers want to be approached and which do not. Consider a policy of making eye contact with every customer and smiling pleasantly. By doing so, you show that the customer is welcome and that you are ready to be of help.

When you make contact with a customer, give the person your full attention. If you are sorting tools, for example, stop sorting and look directly at the customer. Setting your work aside and focusing on the customer gives the right impression—that the customer has your full attention.

Sometimes customers have to wait. The sales floor might be busy or the waiting room full. When service will be delayed, explain why if the reason is not obvious. "One of Dr. Malone's patients had an emergency this morning, and that has pushed his appointments back. We are running about 30 minutes behind schedule." If you can give customers an idea of when they will receive service, do so. If the time frame changes, keep customers informed. Be ready to make alternative arrangements for those who cannot wait.

Greet Customers Cheerfully

A pleasant, cheerful greeting goes a long way. Look at the customer, give him or her a real smile, and say something appropriate in a pleasant tone of voice.

"Good morning. May I help you?"

"Hodges Company. How may I direct your call?"

"Hi, Jess. What can I do for you?"

You probably have encountered people who do not look at customers. Perhaps they carry on a conversation with a coworker or friend while serving someone. They may seem bored or occupied with their own thoughts, and do not smile or even say hello. Be aware of the poor impression such employees convey and do not be one of them.

Key ▶ Point

Make eye contact with every customer and smile pleasantly to show that the customer is welcome and that you are ready to be of help.

Diversity

Remember, people appreciate a greeting based on their culture. Learn how to greet your frequent customers appropriately.

Provide Quality Service

Providing quality customer service means different things to different people. In every case, though, quality customer service involves courtesy, careful listening, and individualized treatment. The key is to combine these elements in every customer contact.

Be Courteous

You have the ability to set the tone of your customer contact. Think of your customers as guests, and treat them accordingly. For example, instead of saying, "I need those papers," you can say, "May I have those papers, please?" Remember that what is considered courteous can vary from person to person and from culture to culture. As best you can, show courtesy and respect to your customers in the way that they understand.

If you are dealing with a dissatisfied or angry customer, try to remain calm. As a professional, you should provide friendly service, even if you are tired or the customer is being unpleasant. True professionals put forth their best effort with every customer, every time.

Listen Carefully

Listen carefully to everything the customer has to say. Do not assume that you know what he or she wants or needs. Consider the customer's tone of voice and look for nonverbal cues. A client who leans back in a chair probably feels comfortable and relaxed. A client who clasps his or her hands or clutches the arms of the chair probably is nervous.

Diversity

Politeness and formality in business transactions are valued highly by people from many cultures. Make an effort to learn the codes of proper conduct if you interact with customers from different cultures.

DIGITAL VISION/GETTY IMAGES

Make eye contact and greet customers when they enter your area.

Key ▶ Point

Show the customer that you are listening attentively. Maintain eye contact and nod or smile as the customer speaks.

Diversity

Be sensitive in dealings with people who do not speak English well or who are deaf or hard of hearing. Speak clearly and make sure the customer understands.

Show the customer that you are listening attentively. Maintain eye contact. As the customer speaks, nod, smile, or look concerned. Ask questions if you do not understand. An alternative is to say something like, "Let me make sure that I understand your concerns." Then restate what you understood the customer to have said.

You may need to fill out a form or enter data on a computer while talking with a customer. If so, explain or ask politely before beginning. As you work, make sure the customer remains the focus of your activity.

Make Sure the Customer Understands You

Make sure the customer understands what you say. Speaking too rapidly, particularly on the telephone, is a common problem. When people are very busy, they tend to speak more quickly and try to hurry things along. Never convey that you are too busy for a customer or attempt to rush the customer through a transaction. Besides showing disrespect, speaking too quickly frequently results in repeated questions, wrong information, and misunderstanding.

Determine the Customer's Needs

Remember that every customer is an individual with individual preferences and needs. Listen to customers carefully and try to identify their particular needs. Show respect by not attempting to sell them products or services that do not meet their needs.

For businesses that rely heavily on repeat customers, treating customers as individuals is especially important. Consider this scenario: Remi is a hair stylist. She and her partner, Jarrod, have a clientele that has stayed with them for many years. They frequently gain new customers through word-of-mouth referrals. Remi and Jarrod are experts at knowing their customers' likes and dislikes. They make notes of personal preferences such as favorite hair treatments and styles. They ask about their customers' children by name and cut their hair at a discount. They talk about work, pets, travel, books, or movies. They know which customers are usually in a hurry, which ones are often late, and which ones are likely to forget an appointment.

When asked what matters most in customer service, Remi replied, "Two things. First, treat every customer as your only customer. Second, although you are trying to get new customers, always remember your loyal customers."

Deal with Customers Ethically

Ethics

To gauge your ethical behavior, ask yourself: Am I treating customers as I would want to be treated?

Be ethical in your dealings with internal and external customers. One way to gauge your own professional, ethical behavior is to ask yourself this question: Am I treating my customers as I would want to be treated? If the answer is no, then you need to change your behavior. Being fair and honest is a good place to start. Make sure that you fully disclose all the information your customers need to make informed decisions. You can advise a customer, but make sure that your advice fits the customer's needs, not your own.

Ethical business communication includes maintaining confidentiality. Carry out transactions with customers quietly and discreetly. This action is important whether you are a bank teller, a washing-machine salesperson, or an advertising consultant. The customer's business is no one else's business. When you use tact and discretion, your customers learn to trust you. If they trust you, they are more likely to keep coming back.

check point 3

1. What two things can you do to make a good first impression on customers?

2. List five things you can do to provide quality customer service.

Check your answers in Appendix C.

Managing Challenging Situations

Employees sometimes must deal with challenging customer situations. You may have to say no to a customer or respond to complaints. On other occasions, you may encounter difficult customers. Customers who are angry or upset may require your best communication skills. This part of the chapter offers guidelines for managing those situations.

Refuse Requests Gracefully

Employees cannot grant every customer request. A customer may ask for a cash refund for a CD player. However, your company does not allow cash refunds after 30 days. A supervisor may want you to finish a project by Friday, but there is too much work to complete in this time.

When you need to refuse a request, use an indirect approach. If appropriate, begin with an apology. Explain the reasons for the refusal and state or imply the refusal. Tell the customer what you can do, as shown in the following example. If you cannot do anything to help the customer, try to close the conversation in a positive way.

> I'm sorry this player didn't work out for you. We provide cash refunds for our products up to 30 days after purchase. Because the 30 days has passed, I can give you a store credit that you can use in any of our stores within the next year.

Key▶Point

When you need to say no to a customer, use the indirect approach. First, give reasons for the response and then give the negative response.

Key ▶ Point

When dealing with customer complaints, use positive words that show empathy.

Note that the first statement in the example is not an admission of fault. It merely expresses understanding of the customer's situation. When you must refuse a customer request, use positive words that show empathy.

Say	I can understand the problem you are having.
Instead of	The software is not intended for that kind of use.

When you explain the reasons for the refusal, do not simply state company policy. The customer is not interested in your company's policy. Instead, give a fair reason for the refusal.

Say	For their safety, we require that small children remain in the play area or in the lobby if they are accompanied by a parent.
Instead of	Our policy is not to allow small children in the gym.

When you need to refuse a coworker's request and you can offer a solution, do so. When you cannot, admit it frankly and ask your coworker to help you problem-solve the situation.

> The project has involved more work than we planned. With my current workload, I estimate I'll need another ten days to finish. Could we push back the delivery date? If not, I know I could finish on time if you asked Ming or Vincent to do some of my regular duties.

Resolve Complaints Effectively

Key ▶ Point

Companies view legitimate complaints as a way to learn about problems with their products.

A young mother found her baby playing with a piece of plastic torn from his diaper. She wrote immediately to the manufacturer. The manufacturer was grateful. The woman had identified a dangerous problem with the product. The manufacturer recalled the diapers and redesigned them.

Legitimate complaints are welcomed by most companies. They view such complaints as ways of learning about problems with their products and services, as well as about customers' wants and needs. Follow these steps to resolve a customer's complaint:

1. Make sure you understand the complaint.

2. If an apology is in order, offer one.

3. If an error was made, assure the customer that you will correct the error and explain how.

4. If no error was made, try to close the conversation on a positive note.

Key ▶ Point

Ask questions to help you understand a customer's problem or complaint.

Listen carefully when the customer explains the complaint. Ask questions and take notes if necessary. Disregard side issues and stick to the main point. While taking time to listen to the customer, move quickly to resolve the issue.

Listen carefully when a customer explains a complaint.

Mistakes happen in dealing with customers. When they do, acknowledge the mistake by apologizing. You need not accept personal blame, nor should you blame someone else. Apologizing is a way to get past the mistake and begin to rectify the situation. Always follow an apology with a statement that assures the customer that you will fix the mistake or correct the error. If someone else needs to address the problem, make sure it is brought to the attention of the appropriate person. An apology can be as simple as the following statements.

I'm sorry that happened, sir. Let me order a new product for you.

Thank you for bringing this to my attention. We'll send you a corrected order tomorrow morning.

Match the Solution to the Problem

When customers make complaints, they sometimes ask for resolutions that are not reasonable. For example, a customer whose $30 sweater was lost by a dry cleaner might demand $100. Unreasonable requests may be prompted by anger over the problem or a disagreement about what is fair.

Even companies that follow the policy "the customer is always right" place reasonable limits on what a customer can receive. Know what you can and cannot do for customers. If you have the authority to make your own decisions in resolving problems, strive for a solution that is fair or a little more than fair to the customer. For example, if you worked at the dry cleaner, you might offer the customer $50 or $50 worth of free dry cleaning.

Key▶Point

When dealing with customer complaints, place reasonable limits on what you offer to do for the customer.

Deal Appropriately with Difficult Customers

Key ▶ Point

When dealing with a difficult customer's complaints, remain professional and do not take the customer's criticisms and attitude personally.

Fortunately, truly difficult customers are rare. Often, an angry, irrational customer becomes calm and reasonable when he or she realizes that someone is serious about resolving the problem. Follow these guidelines when dealing with a difficult customer:

■ Begin by trying to identify the problem.

■ Use your best listening skills and show empathy and respect.

■ Recognize that the customer may be emotional or irrational for reasons you know nothing about.

■ Do not show anger. Remain professional and do not take the customer's criticisms and attitude personally.

Some customers may be unwilling to accept a reasonable solution or explanation. Others may become abusive. If you find yourself losing your composure in such a case, ask a supervisor to assist you in resolving the problem.

check point 4

1.   What steps can you follow to resolve a customer's complaint?

2.   Describe actions you can take to deal with difficult customers.

Check your answers in Appendix C.

Section 14.1 *Applications*

A. Serving an Internal Customer

You are an associate in the Human Resources Department. An internal customer sent you the e-mail message shown below.

1. Read the message from your internal customer.

2. Open the *Word* file *CH14 Policy* from the student data files. Use the policy provided in the file to find the information the customer needs.

3. Send a reply e-mail providing the requested information. (Send the e-mail to your teacher or save and print the message but do not send it.)

TO:	Human Resources Associate
FROM:	Keiko Wong
DATE:	June 12 , 20--
SUBJECT:	Drug Testing Policy

Please provide some information about the company's drug testing policy.

1. Who is subject to drug testing by the company?

2. When may testing of these individuals be required?

3. Who will have access to the results of employee drug tests?

B. Customer Service Policies

1. Work with a classmate to complete this activity.

2. Use an Internet search engine to find the Web sites of several companies that sell products or services to consumers, such as Amazon.com, Overstock.com, Lands' End, Allbrands.com, or Macy's.

3. Visit the Web sites for several companies and read the returns policy.

4. Identify at least one company that you think has a returns policy that is favorable to customers. Give the company's name, Web address, and types of products sold. Tell what makes the returns policy favorable.

5. Identify at least one company that you think has a returns policy that is unfavorable to customers. Give the company's name, Web address, and types of products sold. Tell what makes the returns policy unfavorable.

REAL WORLD

TEAMWORK

Face-to-Face Communication

OBJECTIVES

After completing Section 14.2, you should be able to:

1. Recognize voice qualities that can affect communication.

2. Identify parts of a conversation.

3. Describe the factors that lead to successful face-to-face communication.

Communication and Your Voice

Your voice qualities, as well as the words you choose, can have a big impact on how successful you are in communicating with others. For example, using an appropriate volume and pleasant tone can encourage people to listen to you.

Voice Qualities

The quality of the human voice varies in a number of ways. Though you may think otherwise, you can control how your voice sounds. In fact, you do it every day. Have you ever listened to yourself? Record your speaking voice and listen. You might be surprised at what you hear.

The **pitch** of your voice is its highness or lowness. Most of us prefer to listen to voices that are neither too high nor too low. Television and radio broadcasters are taught to speak with a somewhat low pitch. A voice that has a high pitch or a pitch that is too low can be unpleasant to hear.

In your everyday speech patterns, you change the pitch of your voice. For example, you raise the pitch of your voice at the end of a question. If you are talking confidentially to someone, you probably talk in a low, steady pitch. If you are excited or enthusiastic about something, your pitch may rise. A person who speaks in a monotone (having no variation in pitch) may be considered boring and may quickly lose the attention of the listener.

Another quality of your voice that you can control is its volume. Use an appropriate volume level for each situation. If you are addressing a dozen coworkers sitting around a conference table, speak loudly enough for everyone to hear. Your listeners will think you lack confidence if you speak too quietly. If you are talking to a customer, only you and the customer need to hear what you have to say. Keep your volume at a conversational level.

The tone of your voice may be the voice quality that customers remember the most. **Tone** is the attitude toward your listeners that is implied by your choice of words and pitch of your voice. When you say, "May I help you?" is your tone courteous or impatient? Do you sound bored or truly concerned when you say, "I understand" to a customer? Even if you feel bored or impatient, you can alter the tone of your voice to send a more positive message. Your success as a customer service provider may depend on it.

Key▶Point

Tone is the attitude toward your listeners that is implied by your choice of words and the pitch of your voice. The tone of your voice may be what customers remember the most.

The tone of your voice sends a message to your listeners.

DIGITAL VISION/GETTY IMAGES

Speech Clarity

Using proper enunciation and correct pronunciation will assure clarity of speech. **Enunciation** is the way in which you say each part of a word. Clear, correct enunciation makes your speech easy to understand. Poor enunciation makes your speech difficult to understand. For example, do not say *hafta* for *have to*, *gonna* for *going to*, and *workin'* for *working*. The speed at which you speak affects your ability to enunciate. It is important not to talk too fast, especially on the telephone or when leaving voice messages.

Pronunciation is the way a word is spoken. For example, a person might say very clearly, "Place the dirty dishes in the *zink*." However, *zink* is a mispronunciation of the word *sink*. Incorrect pronunciation is distracting to your listeners. It is especially important to pronounce people's names correctly. Do not be afraid to ask someone to repeat a name if you do not catch it the first time or if you simply are not sure how to pronounce it.

Most of us probably take our voices and speech patterns for granted. Keep in mind that your speech plays a large role in the impression you make on people. Pay attention to how you speak. Listen to others. What qualities do their voices have? Are they agreeable or unpleasant? Analyzing others' vocal qualities, as well as your own, will help you speak with a voice that is easy and pleasant to listen to.

Key▶Point
Pronunciation involves saying a word correctly. Enunciation involves saying each part of a word clearly.

check point 5

1. List three voice qualities that can affect communication.

2. Give one example of incorrect pronunciation of a word and one example of poor enunciation of a word or term.

Check your answers in Appendix C.

Parts of a Conversation

Face-to-face communication is sharing messages with someone in person. Talking to a friend over lunch, reporting on work to your boss, and giving information to a customer are examples of this type of communication. Sending messages through words and body language is critical to making yourself understood. In turn, you must interpret a speaker's words and non-verbal cues to receive and understand messages.

Whether a conversation is brief or lengthy, it follows a pattern. Think of a conversation as a process that has a beginning, a middle, and an end. More precisely, it has these five parts, or stages: greeting, introduction, exchange, summary, and closing.

1. **Greeting.** Whether it is a nod of the head, a brief "Hi," or a more formal "Good morning, Mr. Lopez," a greeting begins every conversation. The tone of a greeting should match the nature of the conversation. For example, a cheerful greeting followed by the delivery of bad news would be inappropriate.

2. **Introduction.** Think of the introduction as a transition from the greeting to the topic of the conversation. An introduction may use a direct or indirect approach. Many workplace conversations use a direct introduction: "Are you ready to meet with me about that report now?" An employee who would like some help from a coworker might use an indirect approach. For example, she or he might say, "How's your workload this week?" This question would then lead to the real purpose of the conversation, which takes place in the next stage.

3. **Exchange.** The exchange usually is the longest stage of a conversation. During the exchange, the parties give and receive information. Both speakers must use their oral communication skills as well as their listening skills effectively to make the conversation meaningful. Non-verbal cues, such as gestures, facial expressions, and posture, contribute to sharing information during the exchange stage.

Key ▶ Point

A conversation begins with a greeting and an introduction of a topic. An exchange of information follows.

Reading Aloud

In the workplace, there may be times when you need to read aloud. You learned in an earlier chapter that reading documents aloud helps with proofreading and editing. In this situation, the volume of your voice should be low so as not to disturb nearby coworkers. You should read slowly and give attention to each word.

Reading aloud to others requires that you consider the tone and volume of your voice and the rate at which you speak. For example, during a telephone call with a customer, you might need to read a product description to the customer. In a meeting, you might need to read the minutes from the last meeting.

When you read aloud to others, strive to pronounce words correctly and enunciate clearly. Use an appropriate volume—loud enough to be heard but not so loud as to be annoying. Your tone should convey interest in the topic and a desire to be helpful, especially when giving information to a customer. Be careful not to speak too fast. Use a moderate, relaxed rate of speech. When possible, read the document silently before you need to read it aloud to others.

Open the *Word* file *CH14 Reading* from the student data files. Follow the directions in the exercise to practice reading aloud.

4. **Summary.** During the summary, the sender and receiver may briefly restate what they have discussed. They may state an agreement they have come to, or they may just give a sign that the conversation is almost over. "That sounds good. Let's do that," is a summary that both indicates agreement and signals that the conversation is ending. If the summary reveals that the speakers do not have a common understanding, the speakers may need to go back to the exchange stage for further discussion.

5. **Closing.** The closing should be pleasant. Whether it is formal or informal depends on the relationship between the speakers. A handshake, a wave, or a pat on the shoulder may accompany a closing. A closing may also involve verifying what is to happen next, as in, "I'll put that file on your desk. See you tomorrow."

check point 6

1. What are the five parts of a conversation?

2. In which part of a conversation are the main ideas shared?

Check your answers in Appendix C.

Guidelines for Success

Despite the use of electronic methods of communication, talking with customers in person is still an important form of customer contact. To create the impression you need for success, follow these guidelines for face-to-face communication:

- **Relax.** Though you need to be aware of the message you are sending, being too focused on how you speak can make you tense. Instead, relax and exhibit confidence. Focus on sharing information. If you are relaxed, the person you are talking to is more likely to relax.

- **Think before you speak.** Whether you are delivering good news or bad news, consider how the information will affect your listener and deliver the message accordingly. Speak in a way that your listener will understand. Choose your words carefully and moderate the speed and volume of your speech.

Key ▶ Point

Whether you are delivering good news or bad news, consider how the information will affect your listener and deliver the message accordingly.

Relax and exhibit confidence when talking with customers.

DIGITAL VISION/GETTY IMAGES

- **Listen carefully and actively.** Listening carefully sends the message that you care what the other person has to say. It also fosters a trusting relationship with the receiver. Watch the listener's facial expressions and other body language to get the complete message. Your customer, Gloria, may say, "That's fine," but her body language may reveal that she is uncomfortable with the solution you have suggested. By recognizing the discomfort, you can provide more information that will put her at ease.

- **Use names.** Learn your coworkers' and customers' names, remember them, and use them. When you meet new customers, use their surnames, particularly if they are older than you. This sign of respect can go a long way toward building a relationship with a customer.

- **Make eye contact.** Making eye contact is one sign that you are paying attention to—and interested in—what a speaker is saying. It also helps you and the speaker focus on the conversation rather than on nearby distractions. Failing to make eye contact sends the message that you are nervous, uncomfortable, or perhaps untrustworthy. None of those messages will win customers.

- **Use a pleasant tone of voice.** Be pleasant and courteous in your speech, even in a hectic environment or even if a customer becomes unpleasant or hostile. Do not speak in a way that indicates you are bored, upset, or impatient.

- **Be honest and sincere.** Customers value honesty and sincerity. They do not want to feel that you might be hiding something from them. If they trust you—if they believe that you are being honest—they are more likely to listen to your ideas.

Diversity

The use of surnames and appropriate titles is especially important to people from other cultures. A business person from Germany or Japan, for example, might be offended if a business acquaintance used his or her first name.

check point 7

1. List guidelines you can follow for successful face-to-face communication with customers and others.

2. Why is making eye contact important when talking with customers?

Check your answers in Appendix C.

Section 14.2 *Applications*

A. *Voice Qualities*

Indicate whether pitch, tone, enunciation, or pronunciation is creating a barrier to communication in each situation.

1. "I gotta check with my supervisor about that, sir," said the clerk helpfully.

2. "Please hold, ma'am, while I verify your account number," squeaked the telemarketer.

3. "Your 'realitor' can advise you about home inspections," offered the loan officer.

4. "Who's next? Please step up," ordered the clerk at the returns desk, glancing at the clock.

TEAMWORK

B. *Customer Conversations*

Work with a partner to plan and role-play the following situations. The student who assumes the part of the customer service provider should model good customer service by using an appropriate tone of voice and making eye contact. In each situation, include the five parts of a conversation: greeting, introduction, exchange, summary, and closing.

1. A customer is opening a new account at a bank and is transferring a large sum of money from another bank to the new account. The customer, a senior citizen, is sitting across a desk from a bank officer who is entering information on a computer.

2. A sales associate is visiting a couple who claims that the floor they just had installed is defective. The sales associate can tell right away that the floor is indeed defective. She informs the customers that there must have been a manufacturer's error. The couple is gratified to hear the news. However, they are still upset by the problem. The sales associate proceeds to reassure them and to tell them what will happen next.

Telephone Communication

Effective Telephone Communication

Although e-mail and Web sites are used increasingly to communicate with customers, telephone communication remains an important way to reach and help customers. Talking with customers by telephone is more personal than sending an e-mail message. A phone call can give customers instant feedback for their questions or concerns. Since most businesses and individuals have a telephone, almost everyone can be reached by phone.

A person working in a typical office may spend one or more hours a day on the telephone. For this reason, communicating effectively by telephone is important. Listening carefully, paying attention to nonverbal cues, speaking clearly, being courteous, and learning to handle difficult callers are strategies you can use for effective telephone communication.

Listen and Observe Verbal Cues

Telephone communication requires the same listening skills, attention to verbal cues, and preparation as does face-to-face communication. You cannot see the expression on the caller's face. You are completely dependent

STOCKBYTE/GETTY IMAGES

The telephone is an important tool for business communication.

on what you hear. The caller is completely dependent on what he or she hears from you. Because you cannot see the person to whom you are speaking, you should be very careful about listening and attending to verbal cues.

Speak Clearly

Because your recipient must rely only on what he or she hears, speak clearly and perhaps a little more slowly on the telephone than you would in person. Your enunciation of words is especially critical on the telephone. Make sure you speak directly into the mouthpiece.

Use a pleasant, low pitch of voice. Your voice conveys your personality, even over the telephone. Talking in moderate pitch makes your listeners more comfortable than using very high or low pitch.

Be Courteous

Open and close conversations cordially. *Thank you* is always appropriate to say to a customer or other caller. If there will be further contact with the person, make sure that she or he knows when and how it will occur. Then close with something pleasant, such as, "Good-bye, Mr. Simms. Have a nice day." Always let the caller hang up first.

Be aware of your surroundings and the volume of your voice when talking on the telephone. Do not speak so loudly that you disturb others or that confidential information may be overheard. When using a cell phone away from the office, try to find an area away from others to place and take calls. Set your cell phone to a silent alert and let it accept messages when you are meeting with customers or are in area where calls may disturb others, such as in a theater or a seminar.

Handle Difficult Callers

As when dealing with customers in person, a customer may become angry or upset during a call. When dealing with a difficult caller, try to remain calm and professional. Often the caller is upset with your company's actions, not with you personally. Follow these guidelines to deal with difficult callers:

Key ▶ Point

When dealing with a difficult caller, remain calm and professional.

- Speak with a friendly and courteous tone.
- Try to identify the reason that the caller is angry or upset.
- Tell the caller how you can help.
- Transfer the caller to someone else in the company who can provide help if appropriate.
- If the caller becomes abusive or uses profanity, end the call quickly. Offer to help the caller later when he or she has calmed down.
- Inform your supervisor or follow your company procedures regarding keeping a record of abusive calls.

check point 8

1. List strategies you can use for effective telephone communication.

2. List some guidelines you can follow to deal with difficult callers.

Check your answers in Appendix C.

Outgoing Calls

You will make outgoing calls to customers and coworkers as you complete your job duties. Planning and organization are important for successful outgoing calls.

Plan Calls

As with other types of messages, identify the objective of the communication. Decide whether a direct or indirect approach will work best to accomplish your objective. Consider the listener's needs as well as his or her background, experience, and culture when planning a call. Before you dial, plan a list of points to cover during the call. Make sure you have all the information you need. You do not want to have to interrupt the call to get something from the other side of your office. If you are shuffling papers while you talk, the caller may think that you are disorganized or simply not paying attention.

Consider the time zone for the location you are calling. You may want to place an important call to a customer the first thing when you arrive at work at 9 a.m. However, if you work in New York and the customer is in Los Angeles, you are not likely to find the customer at work at this time. You can use a Web site, such as the one shown in Figure 14-2 on page 554 to find the time zone for a location.

Take Part in the Conversation

When your call is answered, you may need to ask a receptionist or someone else to connect you with the person to whom you wish to speak. When you have reached that person, greet her or him by name and identify yourself immediately. A greeting is the first step in a phone conversation just as it is in a face-to-face conversation.

After the greeting comes the introduction part of the conversation. Briefly state the purpose of your call. Ask whether this is a good time for the recipient to talk if the call will take more than a few minutes. If you have caught the

Key▶Point

When planning a call, identify the objective of the message and the approach (direct or indirect) to use.

Diversity

Learn to greet frequent callers in their first language. For example, you might greet a frequent caller from Mexico in Spanish.

Figure 14-2 The Official U.S. Time Web Site

Source: The Official U.S. Time, accessed July 13, 2008, available from http://www.time.gov/.

recipient at a bad time, arrange to speak later. Be sure to say whether you will call again or whether the recipient should call you.

If this is a convenient time for the recipient to talk, you are ready for the exchange part of the conversation. Have a document file open on your computer or a pen and paper at hand to take notes of important points discussed during the call. If the exchange is long or important commitments are made, summarize the main points of the conversation before ending the call. You may also consider sending a letter or e-mail message to summarize and document the call.

As in a face-to-face conversation, the closing should be pleasant. If further contact is needed, indicate what action will happen next. For example, you might send supporting documents by mail or arrange a time for a later call.

Leave Effective Messages

In Chapter 12, you learned about voice mail systems. This technology makes leaving messages convenient for callers. There is an art to leaving a message on an answering machine or voice mail. You may have received messages that were hard to understand. Callers sometimes speak too softly,

Figure 14-3 An effective voice mail message is courteous and provides the needed information.

GUIDELINES FOR AN EFFECTIVE MESSAGE	
Message Steps	**Example**
Greet the recipient.	Hello, Mr. Chang.
Identify yourself. If you are calling someone outside your company, identify your company.	This is Sherry Marconi from LX Systems.
Briefly state your purpose for calling.	I am calling to confirm our meeting tomorrow in your office at 9 a.m. I have the design documents ready.
Explain how the recipient may contact you.	To speak with me before then, call 555-0129.
Close the message in a friendly manner.	Have a nice day.

too quickly, or at such length that their messages are cut off. Figure 14-3 suggests what to say and how to say it when leaving voice mail messages.

Voice mail is best used to maintain contact or to provide brief answers to questions. Lengthy voice mail messages can be inconvenient and hard to understand. Recipients might have to listen to a long message several times to get all of the information. If your message is long, complicated, or confidential, do not provide the information on the phone. Instead, ask the recipient to return your call.

When leaving a message, remember to think of your audience and apply the principles of business communication. Messages should be brief, clear, and complete. They should focus on the receiver, not the sender.

Key ▶ Point

Voice mail is best used to maintain contact or to provide brief answers—not for lengthy messages.

check point 9

1. What activities are involved in planning an outgoing call?

2. What steps are involved in leaving an effective voice mail message?

Check your answers in Appendix C.

Incoming Calls

You will receive incoming calls from customers and coworkers. When answering calls, try to answer by the second ring. This sends the message that you want to talk to the caller and that you value the caller's time. Identify yourself and your organization.

When you need to transfer a call, do so efficiently. Make sure you know how to transfer calls correctly. When doing so, tell the caller to whom you are transferring the call and why. Offer the caller your colleague's number or extension, so that the caller can call that person directly next time.

Record Voice Mail Greetings

If you use voice mail, you will need to provide a greeting for callers who reach your voice mail recording. An effective greeting includes the following elements:

- Your name
- A statement explaining that you are not available to take the call
- Clear, specific instructions on how to leave a message
- A statement telling when the call may be returned

An example message is shown below:

Hello, this is Isabel Trevino. I will be out of the office on Wednesday, January 19, but will be checking my voice mail. Please leave your name, number, and a brief message at the tone. I will return your call later today.

If you think that callers may need to talk to someone else in your absence, your message should include contact information for that person.

The example explains that Ms. Trevino will be out of the office all day but that she will be checking voice mail periodically. Such specific information is very helpful to callers. It tells them why you are not available and when they may expect you to return their call. When possible, record personalized greetings that provide useful, current information for callers.

When you record your greeting, speak clearly and a little more slowly than you do in conversation. Play back your greeting and listen. Make sure it provides all the information callers need and can be understood easily.

Take Messages

You have learned how to record greetings and leave messages using a voice mail system. However, some companies do not have voice mail. Even when voice mail is available, some people prefer to leave a message with a person rather than record a message. There may be times when you need to refer

Diversity

If you frequently get calls from people who speak a particular language other than English, leave an alternate message in that language.

a caller to someone else who can provide the information needed. In cases such as these, you need to take a message for a coworker or supervisor. A telephone message should contain the following pieces of information:

- Name and organization of the caller
- Telephone number and extension of the caller
- Date and time of call
- An appropriate message
- Your initials or name as the message taker

Many companies provide paper forms on which to record messages. In other companies, employees send messages to coworkers by e-mail as shown in Figure 14-4.

Screen Calls

Screening calls is a procedure used to learn who is calling and sometimes the reason for the call. You may be asked to screen calls for a supervisor or a coworker. For example, your manager, Mr. Park, may be in an important meeting. He may be expecting a call related to the work of the meeting. He instructs you to let him know when that call comes in but to take messages from other callers.

Diversity

Some companies thoughtfully provide an option to speak to a person on their voice mail systems. This option is helpful to people who are not comfortable leaving a recorded message.

Key▶Point

Be tactful, yet direct when screening calls to learn the caller's name and the purpose of the call.

Figure 14-4 Telephone Message

TO:	Robert Johns
FROM:	Mary Alexander
DATE:	June 12 , 20--
SUBJECT:	Phone Message

Date and Time: June 12 at 1:35 p.m.

Caller: Mr. Al York of York Industries

Caller's Telephone Number: 606-555-0124

Message: He wants to discuss changes to the project bid you submitted.

Action Required: Please return his call.

Be tactful, yet direct when screening calls. To learn the caller's name, ask questions such as, "May I ask who is calling?" or "May I tell Ms. Perez who is calling, please?" Often, the caller will state his or her name and the name of the person to whom she or he wishes to speak.

You may also need to learn the purpose of the call. You can ask questions such as, "May I tell Ms. Perez why you are calling?" If a caller refuses to give a name or reason for calling, follow your company's policy regarding how to handle such a situation. In some companies, callers who will not give a name or reason for calling are politely told that the company cannot help them without this information.

check point 10

1. What elements are included in an effective voice mail greeting?

2. What information should you record when taking a telephone message for a manager or coworker?

3. What is the purpose of screening calls?

Check your answers in Appendix C.

Section 14.3 *Applications*

A. Voice Mail Greeting

You will be on vacation next week and will not be checking voice mail. Use the following information to compose an appropriate voice mail greeting for the time of your absence. Make up any needed details, such as the dates of your vacation.

- Your assistant, Grant Goff, will handle routine inquiries in your absence.

- Grant will telephone you if anything urgent arises.

- Grant's extension is 229.

B. Voice Mail Message

Prepare a voice mail message for the members of your roofing crew. Include the following information and make up any needed details, such as your phone number.

- The crew will not be working at the Whitakers' tomorrow.

- The crew should report at 9 a.m. to Ichiro Sako's home at 1412 Overbrook Avenue.

- Crew members can call you if they need directions or have questions.

C. Cell Phone Etiquette

1. Work with a classmate to complete this activity.

2. Use the Internet or other sources to find and review articles regarding cell phone use.

3. Create a list of guidelines for considerate and professional use of cell phones.

4. Include an appropriate title and complete source information for the articles.

TEAMWORK

INTERNET

Chapter *Summary*

14.1 Customer Service

- Customer service is the performance of activities to ensure customer satisfaction. Satisfied customers are more likely to be repeat customers.

- Companies that make customer service a priority have a strong customer service culture. In such a culture, the company's policies make it easy for employees to satisfy customers.

- Customer contact is any meeting or communication you have with a customer. At every point of contact, employees should provide courteous, professional service.

14.2 Face-to-Face Communication

- Your voice qualities, such as pitch, volume, and tone, can have a big impact how successful you are in communicating with others.

- A conversation has these parts: greeting, introduction, exchange, summary, and closing.

- To create a favorable impression in face-to-face conversations, relax and think before you speak. Listen attentively, use names, and make eye contact. Use a pleasant tone of voice and be honest and sincere.

14.3 Telephone Communication

- Telephone communication is an important way to reach and help customers.

- Listening carefully, paying attention to nonverbal cues, speaking clearly, being courteous, and learning to handle difficult callers are strategies you can use for effective telephone communication.

- Planning and organization are important for successful outgoing calls.

- Using a proper greeting, taking accurate messages, and screening calls effectively are important for handling incoming calls.

Vocabulary

Open the *Word* file *CH14 Vocabulary* from the student data files. Complete the exercise to review the vocabulary terms from this chapter.

accessibility

blog

credibility

customer service

enunciation

external customer

internal customer

newsgroup

pitch

pronunciation

screening calls

tone

Critical Thinking Questions

1. Why is providing good customer service important to the success of many businesses?

2. Is providing good customer service important to the success of non-profit organizations? Why or why not?

3. What is the most important thing you can do to help make your face-to-face communications successful?

4. Many people do not like to receive phone calls from sales associates. Given this fact, why would a person choose to be a telemarketer—someone who makes sales calls?

CRITICAL
THINKING

Chapter *Applications*

REAL WORLD

A. *Customer Service Log*

You may have contact with letter carriers, receptionists, bus drivers, telemarketers, coworkers, or any number of other types of service providers.

1. Keep a log of the experiences you have with customer service providers for one week. In a three-column table, identify the customer service provider in the first column. In the second, indicate whether your impression of each service provider was positive or negative. In the third column, note what the person did to create that impression.

2. Write a paragraph that describes your best or your worst customer service encounter during the week.

B. *Rating Telephone Customer Service*

1. Review items in a mail-order catalog, and find a product that you want to know more about. Perhaps you need to know its dimensions, or exactly what material it is made of.

2. Use the catalog's toll-free number to call the company and make an inquiry about the product. Thank the customer service provider for his or her time. Take notes during the conversation.

3. Summarize your notes. Then rate the customer service provider's response to your inquiry as excellent, good, or poor. Give specific reasons for your rating.

C. *Role-Playing Conversations*

At a home improvement store, a sign in the paint department claims that "WE CAN MIX OR MATCH ANY COLOR." The sales associates who work at the paint desk have a computer they can use to match items that customers bring in. For example, a customer might bring in a pair of curtains or a pillow from a sofa. The only criterion is that the object whose color is being matched be at least one square inch.

One customer wants to match a narrow stripe in a piece of wallpaper. She says, "I'd like to match this color," pointing to the quarter-inch-wide stripe. The young employee responds, "Can't help you." In fact, what the employee meant was that the wallpaper stripe was too small a sample to be able to use the computer to match the color. The customer, a bit surprised and put out by the employee's lack of helpfulness, says, "Okay, I'll go somewhere else," and leaves the store.

Work with several classmates to develop the following role-plays in connection with this scenario.

1. Role-play the scene just as described.

2. Now suppose that the employee's supervisor witnessed the exchange. Role-play a conversation in which the supervisor gives some constructive criticism to the employee.

3. Role-play the initial exchange between the employee and the customer as it *should* have occurred.

D. Evaluating Telephone Communication

Rate the following methods of telephone communication as good or poor. Consider the employees' attitudes as well as what they say. For poor ratings, tell how the communication methods could be improved.

1. LaToya prides herself on her speedy customer service. She answers customers' questions as briefly as possible, assuming that the customers just want to be done with their business quickly. She closes her telephone calls by saying, "Okay. Bye."

2. Marly covers the phones whenever the company receptionist is away from her desk. She dislikes this part of her job and thinks that she is much too busy to be bothered with it. If her colleagues are not available to take their calls, she takes the caller's name and number. She does not bother to record a message.

3. Sarin works at a bank. She answers customer inquiries about account balances, account statements, and various transactions. She hopes to become a bank loan officer in time. She always asks her customers, "Is there anything else I can do for you today?"

Editing Activity

Open the *Word* file *CH14 Editing* from the student data files. The file contains the body of an e-mail message from a conference organizer to a person who has registered for the conference. Edit and proofread the message. Correct all errors and use effective principles of communication.

Dealing Ethically with Customers

The sales associates at an appliance store earn a salary plus commission. This means that they earn a certain percentage of the sale price of each item they sell. This amount is paid in addition to a base salary that remains the same each month.

Commissions vary depending on the price of each appliance. In general, the basic models of appliances cost less and give associates a lower commission than the more expensive models. For that reason, the sales associates convinced the sales manager *not* to display the most basic models. Technically, the basic appliances are still available to customers. However, the sales associates do not mention the basic models unless customers ask about them.

1. Do the sales associates at this store exhibit good customer service practices? Why or why not?

2. Is displaying only the more expensive models of appliances unethical? Why or why not?

Communication for Human Services

The Your Image salon is a well-established, full-service salon that caters to a steady client base. The owner, Jan Claymore, feels lucky that she has had very little staff turnover in the last two years. The cosmetologists, (more informally called stylists), four women and two men, all seem content with their jobs and with the atmosphere at the salon.

Jan's newest stylist, Steve Edgerton, joined the salon about four months ago when Jan expanded her staff. Steve came well recommended. In addition, quite a number of his former clients followed him to Your Image. Jan is glad to have gotten both a good employee and some more steady clients. Steve seems to enjoy working with all types of customers, from the kids right on up to the older men and women. As a result, clients have been giving Jan good feedback about her newest stylist.

In the back room, however, where the stylists relax and take their breaks, Steve seems to do nothing but complain. Whether it is the weather, the clients, or the stale coffee, he seldom has anything good to say about anything. Some of the other stylists have begun to refer to Steve as "Bad News Steve." They try to take their breaks while Steve is busy so they do not have to listen to his complaining in the break room.

Everyone has noticed that Steve's attitude changes as soon as he is in the presence of a client. The employees all wish that the pleasant Steve would stay, and the "Bad News Steve" would not bother to come into the salon.

1. As Steve's coworker, there are things you would like to say, but you are not comfortable speaking to him directly. You wish you could just leave a flyer in the break room from a "How to Be a Good Coworker" seminar. What would such a flyer say? Remember that you are trying to change someone's behavior, not his personality.

2. As his employer, what should Jan do or say to make Steve aware that he needs to pay attention to his internal customers as well as to his external customers?

CHAPTER 15

Getting a Job

15.1 *Job Search*

15.2 *Resume*

15.3 *Application Letter and Form*

15.4 *Interview and Follow-Up Messages*

Brad's Job Search

Brad Adams is excited. Next week he will graduate from Jackson City High School near White Fish, Montana. He took as many business courses as he could and is looking for a teller's position at a bank in nearby Missoula.

Even though he is excited about graduation, he is also concerned. The economy around Missoula is good, but he does not yet have a job. The problem is that he does not know how to go about getting a job.

He wanted to start his job search five weeks ago but did not know how to begin. His friend, Hannah Young, suggested that he go to the library and get a textbook with a resume to use as a pattern. Brad thought that sounded good, so he did what Hannah suggested. He went to the library, found a book, checked it out, and wrote a resume listing his qualifications for any job.

Two weeks later, he mailed out the resumes along with copies of job advertisements from a local paper. No luck! No interviews and no job.

Questions

1. How well does Brad understand the process of getting a job?

2. How good was Hannah's advice?

3. Did Brad start his job search process soon enough?

4. Based on his method of writing a resume, do you think Brad's resume is well written?

15.1 Job Search

Your Goals

OBJECTIVES

After completing Section 15.1, you should be able to:

1. Write personal and career goals.
2. Identify your job qualifications.
3. Identify job opportunities.

A **job search** is the process of finding job openings and applying for jobs. Whether you are just starting your career or are reentering the job market, finding a job requires preparation and planning. Before you begin a job search, consider your personal and career goals.

Personal Goals

When preparing for a job search, identify your personal and career goals. Thinking about your personal goals will clarify what is important to you. Writing personal goal statements that answer these questions will help you identify your personal goals.

- What do I most enjoy doing?
- What are my interests?
- How important to me is material success and fame?
- Where do I want to live—in the city, suburbs, or country?
- In what kind of environment do I want to work—in an office or in the field, for example?
- Do I want to work mainly with people? with animals? with machines? with ideas?

Key ▶ Point

Thinking about your personal goals will clarify what is important to you.

Add any questions that will help you identify your personal goals. Consider the answer to each question and write a goal statement. For example, if you most enjoy playing a musical instrument, your goal statement might be, "I want to have a job in which I can play the piano." If material success is important to you, your goal statement might be, "I want to have a job that pays well and allows me to lead a comfortable lifestyle." Put your goal statements in order of importance.

Career Goals

Just as you did with your personal goals, take time to think through what you want out of your career. Consider short-term and long-term goals. Think about the age at which you would like to be able to retire.

Consider your personal goals and career goals when planning a job search.

Writing career goal statements that answer the following questions will help you identify your career goals.

- What job do I want to be doing ten years from now?
- How far do I want to advance in my career field?
- What is my ideal balance between personal and work obligations?
- Do I prefer steady, fixed work hours or a varied, flexible work schedule?

Add any questions that will help you clarify what you want from a career. Consider the answer to each question and write a goal statement. For example, if you want to be working as an attorney ten years from now, your goal statement might be, "I will complete college and law school to prepare me to pass exams and be licensed as an attorney." Prioritize your career goals by listing them from most important to least important. Compare the list to your list of personal goals to understand what you want from life and work.

Key▶Point

Prioritize your career goals by listing them from most important to least important.

check point 1

1. What is a job search?

2. Why should you consider your personal and career goals before beginning a job search?

   Check your answers in Appendix C.

Job Qualifications

Qualifications are skills, abilities, experience, and training that prepare a person to do a job. Identifying your qualifications gives you the information you need to prepare a resume and to market yourself during a job interview. A **job interview** is a discussion of a job and your qualifications with an employer. Reviewing your qualifications may also help you see skills or education that you need to acquire for a job.

Experience

Key▶Point

When identifying your qualifications, include temporary, part-time, and nonpaying jobs as well as paid work experience.

Work experience and other achievements can help prepare you for a job. When identifying your qualifications, list all your work experience. Include temporary, part-time, and nonpaying jobs as well as paid work experience. Make a list of information such as the following:

- Name, address, and telephone number of each employer
- Job title
- Names of supervisors
- Salary history
- Dates of employment
- Major tasks, duties, and skills that you completed or refined for each job
- Military experience
- Unpaid volunteer activities (such as raising funds for charity)

In addition to work experience, list your other achievements and activities. For example, if you served as treasurer of a club or an organization, were captain of the tennis team, or won a local contest for your artwork, list that information.

Skills and Education

Employers want to know about your skills and education related to a job. List specific skills that relate to your intended career and any special courses or programs you have completed. Include high school information only if you have no postsecondary education. For each school, list the following:

- Name of the school
- City and state of the school
- Dates attended or expected graduation date
- Certificates or degrees earned or courses completed
- Honors or awards received

Both paid and volunteer work can help prepare you for a job.

Personal Traits

Think about your personal traits, such as honesty, creativity, and enthusiasm. Then consider how your personal traits can be used on the job. Employers are interested in applicants with computer, communication, problem-solving, and decision-making skills.

To help you think about your personal traits, answer the following questions:

- Do I have leadership ability?
- Do I meet deadlines?
- Do I work well under pressure?
- Do I enjoy learning new skills? Do I enjoy teaching others?
- What are my personal strengths and weaknesses?

Having an understanding of your skills and personal traits will help you select a career area in which you can be successful.

Career counselors are available who can help you with a self-analysis by arranging for you to take aptitude and personality tests. The Internet is another source for self-assessment tests. Self-analysis can help you determine what you want, what you have to offer, and what career is right for you.

Career Portfolio

Begin by creating a file that contains information about your skills, abilities, experience, and training. This file becomes the basis of your career portfolio. A **career portfolio** is a computer file, file folder, notebook, or small briefcase

Diversity

Each person has unique personal traits. Try to find a job where you can make use of your strong points.

containing samples of your work, transcripts, letters of recommendation, and other related items. A career portfolio can also be posted on your personal Web site or a career Web site.

Some items that you might include in your portfolio are described in the following list.

- Samples of your work, completed projects, or research
- Academic transcripts, certificates, or diplomas of coursework completed
- Test scores
- Letters of recommendation and awards (from school, work, or organizations)
- Copies of job application forms
- Copies of resumes

Ethics

Display only your own work and do not overstate skills or accomplishments in your career portfolio.

check point 2

1. What areas should you consider when listing your qualifications for a job?

2. What is the purpose of a career portfolio?

Check your answers in Appendix C.

Job Opportunities

After you have identified your personal and career goals, you are ready to identify job opportunities. You can locate job openings in several ways:

- Ask for information at school placement offices
- Check with personal contacts in your job search network
- Look in newspapers and professional magazines
- Search the Internet
- Use employment agencies

Some companies offer internships to students. An **internship** allows a student to work for a company for a set period of time as part of a learning experience. Usually, the student is paid for his or her work. If you have worked as an intern with a company, check with your contacts there about job openings. Student interns are sometimes offered a permanent position with the company.

Key▶Point

An internship can lead to a permanent job position.

School Placement Offices

Many postsecondary schools provide job placement services. Placement offices assist employers and student applicants by providing opportunities for both to meet. School placement offices also may have access to job banks that enable you to search for openings or send resumes to employers.

Job Search Network

An informal but often effective way to locate job openings is to talk with people you know—family, friends, and acquaintances. This is called **networking**.

Many of the best jobs are never advertised. Instead, they are given to someone who learned about the job through networking. Therefore, it pays to build a strong job search network. Let the people in your network know that you are looking for a job and the type of job you want. Ask them to let you know about openings they learn about. When you find a job, thank the people in your network who have given information to you and let them know you have found a job.

Publications and the Internet

Job ads may appear in your local newspaper as well as in regional and or national newspapers. Many professional and industry publications also contain job listings. The job listing may or may not state the name of the company advertising the job. If the company name is given, do research to learn information about the company that can help you write an effective response. Respond to ads found in these publications as quickly as possible, and make sure you follow the instructions in each advertisement.

Another source of job openings is the Internet. Specific Web sites allow organizations to list job openings. Most of these sites organize the openings based on location or job title. Through these sites, such as Monster.com and CareerBuilder.com, thousands of job listings from all over the country can be reviewed. The federal government and state governments also have Web sites that show job openings. The Web site in Figure 15-1 on page 574 shows the State of Oregon Jobs Page.

NETBookmark

Several Web sites provide free career self-assessment tools. Go to a search engine such as Google. A link to Google is provided on the Web site for this book that is shown below. Search for *career self-assessment*. Go to one of the sites in the search results and complete a free self-assessment activity to help you review your interests, skills, values, and personal traits.

1. What is the name of the self-assessment tool you used?

2. What did you learn about your personal traits, skills, interests, or values from using this tool?

www.cengage.com/school/bcomm/buscomm

Key ▶ Point

Job ads can be found in newspapers and magazines and on Web sites.

Some job sites allow users to create job search agents. These search agents can review job postings for the user and find jobs that meet the criteria set by the user. For example, the job agent might find jobs for accountants in the greater Cincinnati area. Using job search agents can save time when looking for job postings that meet your needs.

Employment Agencies

Both public and private employment agencies are available to match job seekers with job opportunities. State employment agencies frequently have listings of jobs. To contact state employment agencies, refer to the government section of your telephone directory under your state's name.

Private employment agencies charge a fee to the employer or to the applicant. Before signing an agreement, find out who pays the fee and how the fee is calculated. Do not sign an agreement you may not wish to keep.

Many organizations use temp agencies to provide workers needed only temporarily—perhaps for a short-term project. A temp agency provides workers for a project as required by an organization. Working through a temp agency can be a good way to gain work experience and meet potential employers. Workers in temporary positions are sometimes offered full-time positions with the company.

Key▶Point

Before signing an agreement with an employment agency, find out who pays the fee and how the fee is calculated.

Figure 15-1 State of Oregon Jobs Page

Source: State of Oregon, "State of Oregon Jobs Page," accessed on July 22, 2008, available from http://www.oregonjobs.org/.

Working in a temporary position is a good way to get work experience.

Researching Organizations

Doing research on specific organizations is important to your success in getting the job best suited for you. This research can help you decide whether you think you would like to work for the company. Interviewers are more likely to hire someone who knows something about their company than someone who has not taken the time to do basic research.

To research an organization, visit a local or school library or go online. Many companies have Web sites that provide information about the company. Check publications, such as company annual reports and *The Wall Street Journal*, for company information. You also can find articles on companies in paper or electronic indexes such as *Business Periodicals Index* and *Business NewsBank*.

In addition to conducting secondary research, try to talk with people who are familiar with the company. Employees and customers can be good sources of information.

Figure 15-2 on page 576 lists data that job applicants should know about a prospective employer. You may not be able to find all the information listed about each company. Finding information about small businesses may be more difficult than finding information about large companies. A local chamber of commerce may be able to provide some information about a small business.

Ethics

Learn all you can about a prospective employer's reputation and practices. You may not be comfortable working for a company if you do not agree with its policies.

Figure 15-2 Do Research to Learn About Prospective Employers.

EMPLOYER INFORMATION	
Organization Identification	• Name, city, and state of the home office • Local address and telephone number • Internet address • Name of the person responsible (if possible) for the department with which you will interview • Name and title of the person with whom you will interview
Organization Classification	• Business, government, or charitable organization • Unique company features
Organization Activities	• Production, sales, service-oriented, or a combination • Any brand names associated with the company • Company's competition
Organization Size	• Number of employees, which indicates the size of the organization • Annual sales or production output
Location of Facilities	• Location of the company's branch or regional offices, plants, or outlets • Location where you would prefer to work

check point 3

1. List five ways a person could learn about job openings.

2. What types of information should you try to learn about a prospective employer?

Check your answers in Appendix C.

Section 15.1 *Applications*

A. *Personal and Career Goals*

1. Write five or more personal goals that will affect or be affected by your job or career choices.

2. Write five or more career goals that will affect or be affected by your personal goals.

3. Identify any personal and career goals that seem to clash or not support one another. Decide which of the goals is more important to you.

B. *Your Job Qualifications*

Make a list of your job qualifications. Consider the following areas as you make your list:

- Work experience
- Volunteer experience
- Internship experience
- Awards or achievements
- Education and training
- Special skills
- Personal traits

C. *Job Opportunities*

1. Find at least three job openings in a career area of interest to you. Use any of the methods described in the chapter to find the job openings.

2. For each job opening, list the following information:
   - Job title
   - Organization name and location
   - How you found the job opening
   - Experience, education, and skills required for the job

REAL WORLD

INTERNET

Resume

Preparing a Resume

You have considered your personal and career goals and learned ways to find job opportunities. The next step in the job search process is to write a resume. A **resume** (sometimes called a *data sheet*) is a concise summary of an applicant's qualifications for a job. An effective resume helps you get an interview. This section focuses on how to organize, format, and write an effective resume—a tool that you use to market yourself to employers.

Employers receive many resumes and must scrutinize each of them quickly. Your resume should highlight skills and abilities that the prospective employer needs. Based on the resume's appearance, the reader forms a first impression. For that reason, a resume should be easy to read and attractive.

Use the following guidelines when preparing a printed resume:

- Use margins of at least 1 inch on all sides.

- Print the resume on high-quality, 20-lb. bond paper. Use light colors that are appropriate to business, such as white, off-white, and gray. Use matching envelopes. Generally, you should avoid pastels.

- Use distinctive headings to emphasize different parts of the resume.

- Limit your resume to one page (unless you have extensive job-related experience).

- Format your resume attractively on the page, using white space effectively.

- Use parallel structure in headings and listings.

- Do not use the pronoun *I* as the first word of a sentence on a resume. Instead, use action verbs. For example, say, "Filed correspondence" rather than "I filed all correspondence."

- Correct all spelling, grammar, and punctuation errors.

- Use a word processor to prepare your resume so you can easily make adjustments to content and format.

Resume content may be general or specific. Use a general resume if you are applying for a variety of jobs. Use a specific resume if you have one particular job or type of job in mind.

Key▶Point

Your resume should highlight skills and abilities that the prospective employer needs.

DIGITAL VISION/GETTY IMAGES

An effective resume helps you get an interview.

Many resumes contain the following sections, which are discussed in more detail later in the chapter:

- Heading
- Job objective
- Special qualifications
- Education
- Work experience
- Activities, interests, and achievements

Think about the content you put in those sections. Make sure you omit any information that might cause a negative reaction. For example, if you have an interrupted work history, omit dates when listing work history. Too frequently, job applicants provide information that creates questions and prevents them from getting a job interview. Be prepared to answer questions about your job history and give dates during a job interview when you explain your interrupted work history.

When you organize your resume, think about its role as a selling tool. Choose an organizational plan that highlights information that will impress employers. Your resume can be organized in one of three ways: reverse chronological order, functional order, or a combination of the two. Use the order that presents your qualifications in the best light.

Key▶Point

Choose an organizational plan for your resume that highlights information that will impress employers.

Reverse Chronological Order

A resume organized in reverse chronological order presents the most recent work experience first and works backward to earlier jobs. Most resumes are organized this way. If much of your work experience is relevant to the job for which you are applying, organize your resume in this order. It can be used to illustrate your career progression. A resume in reverse chronological order is shown in Figure 15-3 on page 581.

Functional Order

A resume may be organized in functional order. In this order, your accomplishments or skills are listed in order of their importance. The most important or impressive skills are listed first. This technique will emphasize your strengths.

After listing your job objective, include a heading such as "Professional Skills" or "Qualifications." Use separate paragraphs to emphasize each skill category. For example, if a job requires strong communication skills, you might organize your skills under headings such as "Writing" and "Public Speaking."

Key ▶ Point
A functional resume works well for people who are just entering the job market or those who are changing careers.

Many people organize their resumes in functional order. This order works well for people who are just entering the job market or those who are changing careers. People who are looking for work after a long period out of the job market may also use this order. A resume for a high school student that is organized in functional order is shown in Figure 15-4 on page 582.

Parts of a Resume

Software products, such as *Resume Maker*, are available to help you write a resume. You also can access templates online or use word processing templates to create a resume. Typically, those resources include the sections of a resume that are shown in Figure 15-3 on page 581.

Contact Information

The heading section provides the information the receiver needs to contact you. This contact information should include your name, address, and a telephone number where you can be reached. An e-mail address may also be provided. Place your contact information at the top of your resume. Be aware that many employers will be turned off by unprofessional e-mail addresses. For example, *coolchick@hotmail.com* does not sound professional. Use an e-mail address that sounds professional, such as *janerogers@hotmail.com*. You may wish to open an e-mail account that you use just for your job search. All messages related to your job search can be sent from and received to that account. Using a separate account will decrease the chances of missing a message. A separate account can be particularly helpful if you receive a large number of junk mail messages to your other e-mail account.

Figure 15-3 Resume in Reverse Chronological Order

Elena Torres

Address: 145 Crabapple Road | Richmond, IN 47374-2187
Telephone: 765-555-0148   **E-mail:** edelrio@sunset.net

CAREER OBJECTIVE	To obtain a position as a legal secretary at a large law firm with opportunity for advancement
EDUCATION	Associate of Applied Science, June 2008, Waynesboro Junior College, Waynesboro, Indiana

Received Rotary Scholarship
Major: Office Technology   GPA: 3.6

Related Courses and Skills:
- Advanced Word Processing (MS Word)
- Text input at 70 wpm
- Shorthand at 100 wpm
- Dictation transcription at 60 wpm
- Spreadsheet (Excel) and Database Management (Access)
- Business Law
- Business Applications Software
- Business Management
- Business Communication

EXPERIENCE

Carlton E. Ballard, Attorney-at-Law, Richmond, Indiana. Full-time legal secretary, August 2005 to present.
- Format and edit legal documents using computer and word processing software; transcribe from machine dictation
- File documents with the courts
- Post to client accounts and make bank deposits
- Answer telephone, greet clients, make appointments, and file correspondence.
- Developed familiarity with software developed especially for law firms.

Carson's Department Store, Richmond, Indiana. Sales clerk, September 2000 to August 2005.
- Operated computer terminal and handled customer transactions
- Set up displays and stocked merchandise

VOLUNTEER WORK

Special Olympics volunteer in 2005 and 2006.
- Oversaw coaching sessions.
- Scheduled practices.

REFERENCES   References and transcripts are available upon request.

Figure 15-4 Resume in Functional Order

Harry Kim

Address: 145 Maple Street, Richmond, IN 47374-0145
Telephone: 765-555-0149   **E-mail:** harrykim@richmond.net

CAREER OBJECTIVE   To obtain a position as a stockroom clerk

QUALIFICATIONS   **Receiving and Delivering Stock**

- Experienced at using a computer to record locations of incoming stock and to locate stock in inventory
- Proficient at using an electronic scanner to identify and pull stock for customer orders
- Experienced in delivering stock to specific locations within the building

Creating Displays

- Able to arrange stock in appropriate and creative displays
- Familiar with safety precautions related to creating safe displays

Helping Customers

- Able to greet customers in a friendly manner
- Able to help customers by locating requested stock in an efficient manner

Handling Stock

- Physically strong and healthy
- Able to bend or reach to shelves
- Able to lift up to 60 pounds and push/pull up to 300 pounds using a dolly
- Familiar with safe techniques for bending and lifting to handle stock

EXPERIENCE   CarZone Parts Company, Richmond, Indiana. Part-time stockroom clerk, August 2008 to present.

Volunteer athletic equipment organizer at Jackson High School, Richmond, Indiana, 2007 to present.

EDUCATION   Jackson High School, expected graduation date June 2009. Honor roll with current GPA 3.6. Received good citizenship award in 2008.

REFERENCES   References are available upon request.

Job Objective

The **job objective** (or career goal) is a brief statement that describes the type of position for which you are applying. The job objective lets employers know whether your interests match their needs. Employers also can use this section to screen you out if your objective does not fit their openings. When you are unsure of exactly what the employer is seeking, you may want to omit the job objective.

Special Qualifications

A brief statement or listing of your main qualifications may be placed at the beginning of your resume (after the contact information and objective). This placement helps ensure that a prospective employer will notice them. This section should cite your strengths that relate to the job, as shown in the following example.

> Microsoft Certified Application Professional. C++ Certification. Know Java and Visual Basic Script programming languages.

Education

If you are still in school, your education may be your strongest qualification. Begin with the most recent postsecondary school you have attended. List each school, the degree or certificate earned, the major area of study, and completion dates (month and year). Include credit and noncredit workshops, seminars, and classes if they relate to the job objective.

If you are in high school or have not attended postsecondary schools, list the name and location of your high school. Give your graduation date or the expected date of graduation. List the courses you completed that prepared you for a job.

Include any scholarships, educational awards, and academic honors you have received. If your grade point average (GPA) is good—at least 3.0 on a 4.0 scale—include it on the resume. List GPA as an overall average or as an average in your major. If you have served in the military, include brief information on your military service.

Experience

The section on work experience should describe (in the order that makes you look best) all work experience you have had that relates to the job you are seeking. For each job, list the name the company or organization you worked for. Give the city and state of the organization. Give the job title and a description of your responsibilities and accomplishments. The dates of employment are often included but are not required. Include increases in responsibilities or pay if possible. When writing this section, use action verbs such as those listed in Figure 15-5 on page 584.

Ethics

Ethical behavior requires that all the information included on your resume be true. Do not list skills or training that do you not have in order to appear qualified for a job.

Key▶Point

Work experience may be presented on a resume by date, by company, or by job title.

Work experience may be presented by date, by company, or by job title. Figure 15-3 contains a good example that describes work experience listed by date and by skills. Briefly mention summer and part-time jobs that are unrelated to your job objective if space allows. The following example shows how to list your work experience by employer:

Telesystems Corporation, Park City, Utah. Technician from March 2000 to present.

- Prepare repair estimates, and answer customer inquiries.
- Operate testing equipment and repair cellular phones.
- Analyze repair records, schedule customer repairs, and order parts.

The next example shows how to list work experience by job title.

Cashier. Wheeler's Variety Store, Laramie, Wyoming, from July 2001 to May 2005.

- Assisted customers in making purchases and returns.
- Operated electronic cash register
- Completed cash, check, and credit card transactions

Key▶Point

Employers value initiative, leadership, and teamwork skills. On your resume, list activities that reflect those skills and qualities.

Activities, Interests, and Achievements

Employers are looking for people who are willing to work hard. They value initiative, leadership, and teamwork skills. On your resume, list activities that reflect those skills and qualities. Refer to your self-analysis (Section 15.1) for relevant information to include in this section.

Figure 15-5 Use action verbs to describe work experience.

ACTION VERBS			
administer	design	operate	revise
advance	develop	order	set up
analyze	direct	organize	supervise
calculate	increase	produce	supply
complete	initiate	provide	train
create	key	recommend	verify

Truthful Resumes

A resume is an important tool that you can use to market your skills to employers. Including keywords related to the job description can get your resume noticed by a person or a resume tracking program. You want your resume to give the best possible impression of your skills and abilities. Be careful, though, about what you include on your resume. Consider the following situation:

> Jason found several job openings that seemed like good opportunities. He revised his resume for each job, including keywords that related specifically to that job. One job posting included the phrase "Knowledge of Java helpful." Jason included "Knowledge of Java" in the skills listed on his resume. However, Jason has had no experience with Java. He plans to do some reading on the topic if he gets called for an interview with the company.

Has Jason acted in an unethical way? Why or why not? What do you think might happen if Jason is asked about his experience with Java at an interview?

The following are possible headings for this section, based on the particular information you are including:

- Achievements, Awards, and Honors
- Volunteer Work
- Activities and Achievements
- Additional Interests and Qualifications
- Professional Associations

References

A **reference** is a person who can attest to your character or qualifications for a job. Generally, you do not include references on a resume. Instead, you should prepare a separate reference sheet that includes the following information about your references: name, title, address, and contact information. You may wish to indicate on your resume that references and transcripts are available upon request.

Some employers are interested only in work-related references. Others are interested in both employment and academic references. Some employers may want a character reference.

Before you include the names of people as references, ask for permission to use them as a reference. Select only those people who will give you a good reference. If they agree to be a reference for you, let them know what kind of job you are applying for so they can describe their experiences with you appropriately. You might want to provide each reference with a copy of your resume.

check point 4

1. List types of information typically included in a resume.

2. Explain how a resume organized in functional order differs from a resume organized in reverse chronological order.

Check your answers in Appendix C.

Alternative Resumes

A traditional resume is prepared in print format. A print resume can be hand delivered or sent via regular mail or fax to the receiver. You may also need to prepare resumes in alternative formats. Scannable print resumes, electronic resumes, and Web resumes are formats with which you should be familiar. When you are providing a resume for a company, be sure to ask what type of resume is appropriate.

Scannable Print Resumes

Because some companies scan resumes into a database, you may want to give a receiver a scannable print resume. A **scannable resume** is in print form. It is designed so that it can be easily scanned into an electronic file using OCR software.

Many companies scan the resumes they receive and store the information, using keywords. Then when a position becomes available, a computer program identifies all resumes that have "hits" in the keywords. Using keywords in a resume is critical to a successful job search. For example, if a company is looking for an accountant, the keywords used in the search might be *accounts receivable*, *accounts payable*, *payroll*, or *journals*. If a company is looking for a human resources manager, the keywords used in the

---

Key ▶ Point

Before you include the names of people as references, ask for permission from each person to be used as a reference.

Key ▶ Point

Scannable print resumes, electronic resumes, and Web resumes are alternate resume formats you may want to prepare.

Key ▶ Point

A computer program can search electronic resumes looking for keywords related to a job.

search might be *salary and benefits administration*, *recruitment and selection*, *training and development*, or *affirmative action*.

When creating a scannable print resume, follow these guidelines:

- Send only originals or copies made on a good laser or ink-jet copier.
- Use high-quality white or off-white paper.
- Mail flat resumes. Do not fold them because creases may result in the scanner misreading the resume.
- Do not staple the resume; staples must be removed before scanning.
- Position your name at the top on a line by itself.
- Place each part of your contact information on a separate line below your name.
- Use keywords that employers might use to find applicants for the job you are seeking.
- Use a sans serif font, such as Arial, Calibri, or Courier, in sizes 11 through 14 point. Use a short line length—typically 80 or fewer characters.
- Avoid using bold, italics, underscores, boxes, columns, graphics, and shaded areas that may cause problems with the scan. Use hyphens or asterisks to replace bullets.
- Left-align all text, including headings. Format section headings in all caps.
- Avoid short vertical lines and slashes that the computer may try to read as a letter.
- If a second page is needed, key a heading on the second page. Include your name and *Page 2* in the heading.
- Proofread carefully and correct all errors.

The resume in Figure 15-6 on page 588 is an example of a scannable print resume.

Key▶Point

In a scannable resume, avoid using bold, italics, underscores, boxes, columns, graphics, and shaded areas that may cause problems with the scan.

Electronic Resumes

An **electronic resume** is one that is saved in a computer file, typically in ASCII format. In an ASCII file, all word processing codes are removed, resulting in a very plain-looking document.

An electronic resume contains the same data as a print resume. It might be sent by e-mail or posted on an Internet site. Employers can place the electronic resume into a resume-tracking program. A resume-tracking program can scan resumes to look for keywords that match a particular job. Using an electronic resume saves the employer the step of scanning the resume.

Figure 15-6 Scannable Print Resume

ELENA TORRES

Address: 145 Crabapple Road, Richmond, IN 47374-2187
Telephone: 765-555-0148
E-mail: edelrio@sunset.net

CAREER OBJECTIVE

To obtain a position as a legal secretary at a large law firm with opportunity for advancement

EDUCATION

Associate of Applied Science, June 2008, Waynesboro Junior College, Waynesboro, Indiana
Received Rotary Scholarship
Major: Office Technology   GPA: 3.6

Related Courses and Skills:
* Advanced Word Processing (Word)
* Text input at 70 wpm
* Dictation transcription at 60 wpm
* Spreadsheet (Excel) and Database Management (Access)
* Business Law
* Business Applications Software
* Business Management
* Business Communication

EXPERIENCE

Carlton E. Ballard, Attorney-at-Law, Richmond, Indiana. Full-time legal secretary, August 2005 to present.
* Format and edit legal documents using computer and word processing software; transcribe from machine dictation
* File documents with the courts
* Post to client accounts and make bank deposits
* Answer telephone, greet clients, make appointments, and file correspondence.

Carson's Department Store, Richmond, Indiana. Sales clerk, September 2000 to August 2005.
* Operated computer terminal and handled customer transactions
* Set up displays and stocked merchandise

VOLUNTEER WORK

Special Olympics volunteer in 2005 and 2006.
* Oversaw coaching sessions.
* Scheduled practices.

REFERENCES

References and transcripts are available upon request.

Web Resumes

A **Web resume** is a resume that is written in HTML. It can be viewed on the Web using a browser program, such as *Internet Explorer*. This type of resume may use links to other screens. It can support stylish elements, such as sound clips, animation, graphics, and video clips.

Using a Web resume is a good way for an applicant to show his or her HTML skills. Those applying for high-tech jobs commonly use a Web resume. You should consider creating this type of resume in addition to a print and electronic resume.

In a Web resume, the data does not need to be confined to one page. For example, as part of work experience, the prospective employee might provide detailed job descriptions, drawings of blueprints, or other items from a career portfolio. Look at Figure 15-7 on page 590 for an example of the first page of a Web resume.

Key▶Point

A Web resume can be viewed in a browser program and can contain links to an electronic portfolio.

check point 5

1. What are three types of resumes that may be used in addition to or instead of a traditional print resume?

2. What are some advantages of using a Web resume?

Check your answers in Appendix C.

Figure 15-7 First Page of a Web Resume

Norman DeLozier

9396 Elton Hollow Drive
Des Moines, IA 50319
Telephone: 555-555-0108
E-mail: norman.delozier@hotmail.net

Contact
Information

Professional
Profile

Education

Experience

References

Portfolio

PROFESSIONAL PROFILE

- Technology expert with 16 years' experience in the management of systems, systems design, and administration. Expertise in the following:

- Planning, implementing, and managing systems, their programs, and their procedures

- Using technology to improve procedures, reduce costs, and attain goals

- Consulting and working with users, solving problems, and meeting users' needs

- Overseeing development in Web infrastructure, database administration, system architecture, and e-commerce

EXPERIENCE

- Iowa State Department of Justice, Des Moines, Iowa

- Systems Analyst, 1999 to present

- Determined users' needs for new software applications and developed software.

- Developed new system, including hardware and software, for a new division of the Iowa State Tax Division, which included researching and analyzing tax laws and statutes.

- Trained and provided technical support for user of the new system.

Section 15.2 *Applications*

A. Print Resume

1. Assume that you will soon be graduating from high school and you want to apply for a job. Identify a job for which you are qualified. Use any of the methods of locating job openings described earlier in the chapter. If you cannot find a current job opening, identify a job you would be qualified to do if there were an opening.

2. Create a resume that you could use when applying for the job you identified. Use the functional order for your resume.

B. References

1. Identify three people who you think would be willing to serve as job references for you. These people should be able to attest to your character or your job qualifications.

2. Contact each of the three people and ask each one to serve as a job reference for you. If one of the people does not agree to serve as a reference, find another person who will serve as a reference for you.

3. Create a References sheet. Key the title REFERENCES at the top of the page. For each reference, list the person's name, job title, and contact information.

REAL WORLD

C. Scannable Resume

1. Revise the print resume you created earlier. Format it as a scannable resume. Print the resume.

2. Scan the resume using a scanner with OCR software. Identify any problems or errors that occurred with the scan.

3. Revise the scannable resume, if needed, to change elements that did not scan properly.

15.3 Application Letter and Form

Application Letter

OBJECTIVES

After completing Section 15.3, you should be able to:

1. Describe the parts and content of an application letter.
2. Write an application letter.
3. Complete an application form.

Key▶Point

A solicited application letter is written to apply for a specific job opening that has been advertised.

The next step in the job search after writing your resume is to write an application letter. An **application letter** is a message written to an employer that expresses interest in a job and asks for an interview. This type of letter is also called a cover letter. An application letter is sent with a resume. Learning to write an application letter is essential to a successful job search.

Like resumes, an application letter is a sales tool that markets you. It may be either solicited or unsolicited. A solicited application letter is written to apply for a specific job opening that has been announced or advertised. An unsolicited application letter is written to apply for a position that has not been advertised or announced and may or may not be open. Every application letter has three basic parts: an opening, a body, and a closing.

Opening Paragraph

In the opening of an application letter, you must capture the reader's attention so the remainder of your letter will be read. Include the following information in your opening paragraph:

- Indicate that you are applying for a position.
- Name the position for which you are applying.
- Tell how you learned of the opening (solicited letter).
- Identify your abilities (unsolicited letter).

If you are writing in response to an advertisement, you might open your letter as follows:

> Please consider me as an applicant for the management trainee position you advertised in the October 12 issue of the *Daily Leader*. My degree in management and my work experience as an assistant store manager qualify me for this position.

In the opening paragraph of an unsolicited application letter, focus on the position in which you are interested. You might open your letter in the following way:

> If you have an opening for an experienced truck mechanic, please consider me as an applicant.

Your application letter should capture the reader's attention.

Body Paragraphs

The body of the letter comes after the opening paragraph. The paragraphs in the body should convince the employer that you are the right person for the job. Instead of just repeating the facts presented in your resume, interpret those facts for the reader. This second paragraph and possibly a third one should illustrate your education, experience, and other qualifications for the job.

When you respond to a published job opening, explain how your qualifications meet those that are requested. Here is an example of an effective body paragraph that focuses on the requirement of work experience:

> As a quality control inspector, I worked closely with the plant manager to improve quality and reduce costs. During my year in this position, my department was rated Number 1 in quality, and costs were down 8 percent.

If you have not had much work experience, focus on other qualifications. Your education, related activities and honors, ability to learn quickly, or enthusiasm could be stressed. Note the wording of the following paragraph:

> During my first year of college, I was awarded an academic scholarship. While working toward my associate degree in business administration,

Key ▶ Point

The paragraphs in the body of an application letter should convince the employer that you are the right person for the job.

I was elected vice president of the school's Phi Beta Lambda chapter. As vice president, I organized and hosted a fund-raising event for leukemia research.

You should also explain any information in your resume that may raise questions or cause a negative reaction. (Of course, do not include information that will cause a negative reaction unless you must do so.) For example, if you took a long time to complete your education, you should explain why in your letter. Consider the following example:

While attending college, I worked full-time to support my family and to pay for my school expenses. I took two courses each semester and completed my associate degree in three years.

Closing Paragraph

Key▶Point

The closing paragraph of an application letter should ask for an interview and tell how you can be contacted.

The closing paragraph should have a confident tone and ask for an interview. Make it easy for the employer to contact you for an interview by providing your telephone number again. (It also should appear in the heading of your resume.) Avoid the overused phrase *at your convenience*. Note the following closing paragraph:

As my enclosed resume illustrates, my education and my experience qualify me for this position. May I have an interview with you to discuss my qualifications for the job? You can reach me at 555-0177 between 8:30 a.m. and 4:30 p.m. any weekday.

If you are writing to an out-of-town company, mention if and when you will be in the area for an interview. For example:

Will you meet with me to discuss my qualifications while I am visiting San Antonio next week? On Monday, I will call your office to see if we can meet.

Figure 15-8 on page 595 shows a sample solicited application letter. Figure 15-9 on page 596 provides a sample of an unsolicited application letter.

Application Letter Guidelines

An employer will form a quick first impression of you from your application letter. You can make your application letters more effective by following these general guidelines:

- Address the application letter to a specific person rather than just to the company.

- Enclose a resume with your letter and refer your reader to the resume in the body of the letter.

- Print your letter on the same high-quality, 20-lb., white, off-white, or gray bond paper you used for your resume. Use a matching business-size envelope.

Figure 15-8 Solicited Application Letter

506 Northwest Highway
Clovis, NM 88102-0506
April 30, 20--

Mrs. Hazel Minnifield
Director of Human Resources
Mountain Finance, Inc.
32 Commerce Way
Portales, NM 88130

Dear Mrs. Minnifield

Please consider me as an applicant for the accounts receivable clerk position that you advertised in *The Chronicle* on April 29. My bookkeeping experience and college degree in Administrative Technologies have prepared me for this position.

As a bookkeeper for a busy sales office for more than two years, I have gained valuable work experience. To broaden my skills, I recently completed an advanced workshop on collection techniques. The skills I gained from the workshop will help me work effectively with Mountain Finance customers.

As you can see from the enclosed resume, my background fits all the requirements mentioned in your job advertisement. May I meet with you to discuss my qualifications for this position? After 2 p.m. on weekdays, you can reach me at (505) 555-0129.

Sincerely

Arman Diaz

Arman Diaz

Enclosure

Figure 15-9 Unsolicited Application Letter

175 River Road
Hartford, WI 53027-0175
November 10, 20--

Dr. Alan Park
Director of Medical Services
Atlantic Manufacturing
902 Cedar Street
Hartford, WI 53027-0902

Dear Dr. Park

The Hartford News recently reported that Atlantic Manufacturing is expanding its medical services center. With this larger facility scheduled to open next month, will you have an opening for a physical therapist?

The skills I developed from my coursework and hands-on experience during a six-month internship will enable me to assist employees who require physical therapy due to work injuries. While earning my degree, I also completed a research project on work-related injuries.

As an intern at Hartford Clinic, I learned to use hydrotherapy, electrotherapy, and chest physical therapy to treat a variety of conditions. My studies with registered physical therapists gave me insight into the nature and treatment of assembly line injuries.

My education, experience, and desire to meet new challenges would make me an asset to your company. After you have reviewed the enclosed resume, could we meet to discuss my qualifications? Please call me at 555-0133.

Sincerely

Margie Monaco

Margie Monaco

Enclosure

1. What are the two types of application letters? Describe each type.

2. What information should be placed in each part of an application letter?

Check your answers in Appendix C.

Application Forms

Many companies require job applicants to complete an application form. An **application form** is a document provided by an employer that you complete. On the form, you give your contact information, education, work history, and other information. A company can use application forms to compare the qualifications of different job applicants. Some employers use computers to read and store completed application forms. Applications forms can be searched by the computer when the employer is seeking candidates with particular skills. Qualified applicants may be invited for an interview.

Using Sample Application Forms

If possible, fill out a sample application form for practice. If you have none, look at a copy of a form you have completed for a previous job. This sample should include information such as your social security number, work experience (dates, addresses, supervisors, salaries), education (dates, schools, possibly GPAs), and references (names, addresses, telephone numbers, and e-mail addresses). If you have certifications or licenses, include the date granted and the number assigned for each.

If you obtain a copy of the company's application form in advance, make a photocopy and practice on it. Type or print neatly. Make a photocopy of the completed form for your job search file.

Completing an Application Form

When you visit an employer, take all the information needed to complete an application form. Take with you a copy of your resume and your sample application form. Follow these suggestions to complete an application form:

- Use a pen that writes clearly and sharply with blue or black ink.
- Skim through the application form before filling in any information to get an idea of the kinds of information you need to supply.

Ethics

Some application forms require applicants to certify that they have not omitted any significant information. Before you sign your form, check once more to make sure you have not omitted anything significant.

A job application form includes contact information and qualifications of an applicant.

©KHZ/SHUTTERSTOCK

- Read all instructions before you start to write on the application form.

- Answer all questions on the application form. If a question or section does not apply to you, write N/A (for not applicable).

- Sign the application form to certify that all information is correct.

- Research the market so that you are aware of the salary range for the job. Some application forms have questions about desired salary.

- If the application form has space for references, list the names from the reference sheet you prepared earlier.

- Take time and care in completing the application form to increase your chances of being offered the job.

check point 7

1. What is an application form?

2. How is an application form used by an employer?

Check your answers in Appendix C.

Section 15.3 *Applications*

A. *Application letter*

TEAMWORK

1. Identify a job opening in a career area of interest to you. You can use one of the jobs you found for Section 15.1 Application A or a different job.

2. Write an application letter for the job. Use an Enclosure notation and refer to your resume in the body of the letter.

3. Ask a classmate to review the letter and offer suggestions for improvement. Revise the letter as needed.

B. *Updated Resume*

1. Review the functional resume you created in Section 15.2 Application A.

2. Update the resume to make it appropriate to send with your application letter.

C. *Application Form*

1. Open and print the *Word* file *CH15 Form* found in the student data files. This file contains a job application form.

2. Complete the application form using your information. Assume you are applying for the job from Application A.

15.4 Interview and Follow-Up Messages

The Job Interview

OBJECTIVES

After completing Section 15.4, you should be able to:

1. Discuss the purpose of a job interview.

2. Explain how to prepare for a job interview.

3. Write a thank-you letter after a job interview.

4. Write an acceptance letter for a job offer.

Employers generally do not hire solely on the basis of a resume. They want to talk with job applicants to determine if they are qualified for the position and if they are a good fit for the company. As a job applicant, you can use the interview as an opportunity to determine if you want to work for a particular company.

Interviews may last anywhere from 20 minutes to several hours. An interview may take place on a single day or over several days. During the interview process, you may be interviewed by one person or by a group. How you present yourself is crucial—as with resumes, first impressions are very important.

Preparing for a Job Interview

Your success in an interview depends in large part on your preparation. Before the interview, find out information about the company. Review the research you conducted before applying for the job and fill in any gaps. You should also think about questions that may be asked and prepare questions you want to ask. Nervousness during an interview is natural. Preparing to answer typical questions will help relieve your anxiety. Expect to be asked about your work experience, education, goals, self-concept, and relationships with others. Figure 15-10 on page 601 provides a list of frequently asked questions.

During the interview, you may be asked if you have any questions. Be prepared to ask questions. Your questions should help you learn more about how you fit with the position and the company. Remember, you are trying to determine if you want to accept this position. Keep your questions related to the job and the company. Until you are offered a position, avoid asking questions about salary or benefits. Here are some questions you might ask:

Key▶Point

During an interview, be prepared to ask questions about the job or the company if given the opportunity.

■ What would my major responsibilities be?

■ What qualities are you seeking in the person for this job?

■ Does your company have training programs?

■ What is the typical career path for someone in this job?

Figure 15-10 Sample Interview Questions

COMMONLY ASKED INTERVIEW QUESTIONS	
Education	• Why did you major in _____ ? • Which courses did you like best? least? Why? • What motivated you to seek a college education?
Work Experience	• What kind of work did you do at your last job? What were your responsibilities? • Describe a typical day on your last (or present) job. • What was the most difficult problem you encountered on your last (or present) job? How did you handle it? • What did you like best about your previous positions? least? • Why did you leave (or want to leave) your last job? • What do you know about our company? • What aspects of this job appeal to you most?
Human Relations	• What kind of people do you enjoy working with? • How do you get along with other students? with instructors? with coworkers or supervisors? • In your previous jobs, how much did you work as part of a team? • Are you a team player?
Goals	• What are your career goals? • Why do you want to work for our company?
Self-Concept	• What are your greatest strengths? weaknesses? • What would you like to tell me about yourself? • Why do you think you are qualified for this job? • What have your supervisors complimented you on? criticized you for? • What rewards do you look for in your career? • Do you work well under pressure?

If possible, ask someone to create a visual and audio recording of you in a mock interview. Viewing the interview will help you assess your interview skills, particularly your nonverbal skills (body language), and improve them. You can analyze your answers and then make any needed changes.

Take to your interview an extra copy or two of your resume and list of references. Bring other items you may need, such as pens, a small notebook, a small calendar, and your portfolio. If the interviewer asks questions related to the items in the portfolio, you can indicate that you brought them with you and offer to show them.

Follow these pointers when interviewing:

- Dress conservatively; avoid flamboyant styles or colors.
- Wear a business suit in navy, gray, black, or brown when interviewing for office or professional jobs. If you do not have a suit and you are a man, wear a sport coat and tie; a woman, wear a dress and jacket or a skirt and jacket.
- Avoid heavy fragrances and flashy jewelry. Women also should avoid bright nail polish, frilly clothes, and heavy makeup.
- Choose a conservative, attractive hairstyle.
- Make sure you are well groomed—good deodorant; clean clothes; polished shoes; clean nails; and freshly brushed teeth.

Those clothing guidelines apply only to professional positions. When interviewing for other positions, dress appropriately. Make sure you are well groomed and clean. For example, if interviewing for a beautician or automobile mechanic position, you would not dress in a suit. You would wear clothing appropriate for someone working in that job.

If you are unfamiliar with the interview location, travel there before the day of the interview to learn the route. Locate a place that you can park on the day of the interview. Consider whether traffic will be heavier and more travel time will be required at the time you go to the interview. Allow plenty of travel time on the day of the interview. You must be on time for the interview to create a favorable impression.

Taking Part in a Job Interview

At the interview site, you may be introduced to the interviewer by a receptionist or an assistant. As you wait in the reception area for the interview to begin, conduct yourself in an appropriate manner. The receptionist may have an influence on whether you are hired. Here are some points to remember:

- Do not smoke.
- Do not chew gum.
- Greet the receptionist cordially.
- Do not bring friends or relatives to the interview.

Diversity

Dress appropriately for an interview. The attire considered appropriate for an interview will vary by industry, job, and geographic location.

Key▶Point

Do not smoke or chew gum during an interview or while waiting to be interviewed.

Chapter 15 Getting a Job

Make eye contact and greet the interviewer with a smile.

Greet the interviewer with a smile and make eye contact. Use the interviewer's name in a greeting such as, "Glad to meet you, Dr. Wanamaker." When you reach the interview room, wait to be seated until you are invited to sit down. Then let the interviewer begin the interview and direct the discussion.

Your nonverbal skills are very important during the interview. From the time you meet, the interviewer will be assessing you for the job. Use non-verbal cues to your advantage. Use good posture and make eye contact often with the interviewer. Display a pleasant expression on your face that indicates you are interested in what the interviewer is saying. Also, listen effectively so you can answer questions and gather appropriate information.

During the interview, you will be expected to answer questions so the interviewer can get to know you and your abilities. Speak clearly and distinctly as you answer the questions and use good grammar.

Many interviewers will begin with ice-breaker questions such as "I see that you were in the school band. What instrument did you play?" Those questions are intended to put you at ease. Answer them naturally and be yourself.

During the next stage, the interviewer gathers information about you by asking questions such as those in Figure 15-10 on page 601. Listen to each question carefully and pause to gather your thoughts before answering. Often, a simple *yes* or *no* is not enough. Use each answer as an opportunity to convince the interviewer that you are the best person for the job.

Key ▶ Point
Speak clearly and distinctly as you answer interview questions and use good grammar.

Reading Job Announcements

Reading skills are important for locating and getting a job that is right for you. When you read a job announcement, pay attention to the requirements or qualifications listed. Make a note of keywords you can use in your resume and application letter to link your skills and experience to the job requirements.

Open the *Word* file *CH15 Reading* from the student data files. Read the job announcement and identify keywords, qualifications, and skills related to the job.

Look at the following dialogues. In the first situation, the applicant can talk about only one topic (weakness). In the second example, the applicant can talk about all of his or her strengths.

Interviewer: "What is your biggest weakness?"

Applicant: "My biggest weakness is a fear of public speaking. But to overcome this weakness, I have joined Toastmasters and am giving as many speeches as I can."

Interviewer: "Why should we hire you?"

Applicant: "There are several reasons you should hire me. For example . . ."

You may be asked personal questions that are illegal or potentially discriminatory. You can answer the question if you wish. The best way to handle illegal questions may be to deflect them courteously, while providing some useful information, if possible. For example:

Interviewer: "How will your children be taken care of while you work?"

Applicant: "If you are asking whether I will arrive on time and do a good job, the answer is definitely yes. I have reliable childcare. Also, you can check my current job performance and attendance record. They are excellent."

Interviewer: "Do you have a stable personal life?"

Applicant: "Because my career is very important to me, I won't let anything interfere with it. I will be able to provide the results you want."

Key ▶ Point

The best way to handle illegal interview questions may be to deflect them courteously, while providing some useful information.

If you are asked an illegal question, maintain your composure and be ready to provide information if the interviewer can show you that the question is job-related.

Interviewer:	"What church do you attend?"
Applicant:	"I don't understand how that question relates to my performance on the job. Can you explain?"
Interviewer:	"Are you married?"
Applicant:	"My marital status is not related to my ability to do the job, what job-related information can I give you?"

Figure 15-11 provides examples of illegal interview questions. Look them over and decide how you would answer these questions if you were asked them in an interview.

If the interviewer asks your salary requirements early in the interview, indicate that you require the standard salary for the position in question. You can also say that you require a salary that is appropriate for your education and experience. Letting the interviewer make a salary offer rather than naming a figure yourself puts you in a better position to negotiate.

Key▶Point

Letting the interviewer make a salary offer rather than naming a figure yourself puts you in a better position to negotiate.

Figure 15-11 Illegal Interview Questions

ILLEGAL INTERVIEW QUESTIONS

- Are you married? single? divorced? widowed?
- Do you have small children? Do you plan to have children?
- What is your date of birth?
- Have you ever been arrested?
- Where were you born?
- How much do you weigh?
- Where does your husband (wife, father, mother) work?
- Are you pregnant?
- Do you belong to a religious group? If so, which one?
- Which religious holidays do you observe?
- Do you rent or own your home?
- What is your maiden name?
- Do you smoke?
- Do you have a girlfriend/boyfriend?

The interviewer will provide both verbal and nonverbal signals that the interview is over. Stand up, smile, and shake hands firmly. Typically, a job is not offered at this point. However, asking the interviewer when a decision will be made is appropriate.

check point 8

1. What is the purpose of a job interview?

2. How can you prepare for a job interview?

Check your answers in Appendix C.

Follow-up Messages

A job applicant should know how to write two types of follow-up messages. The first follow-up message is a thank-you letter that should be sent shortly after the interview. This type of message also brings your name before the interviewer again. The second type of message should be sent to accept or reject a job offer that the applicant has received.

Thank-You Letter

Key▶Point

Within two days after the interview, you should write a brief follow-up letter thanking the interviewer.

Within two days after the interview, write a brief follow-up letter to the interviewer. Thank him or her for the interview. If you are sure you want the job, indicate your interest. You also may decide to send your follow-up message by e-mail. Follow-up messages should be courteous and thoughtful.

Organize the letter or e-mail like a goodwill message—as the following example illustrates. Refer to Figure 15-12 on the next page for an example of a thank-you letter.

Main Idea	Thank you for giving me the opportunity to interview yesterday for the position of legal secretary. After talking with you and seeing the office operations, I am convinced that I would like to join Powell and Sutton's legal secretarial staff.
Supporting Information	During the interview, we discussed my availability for the Bayside office. After further consideration, I am happy to say that I would be able to work in any of the firm's locations in the city.
Helpful Closing	My education and experience make me confident that I would be able to perform the duties of the position well. If you need further information about my qualifications or have any questions, please call me at 555-0111.

Figure 15-12 Thank-You Letter

884 Peyton Lane
Apartment 29
Quincy, MA 02169-0884
March 24, 20--

Ms. Alicia Perez, Vice President
Lions Department Store
439 East Sassafras Drive
Quincy, MA 02169-0439

Dear Ms. Perez

Thank you for meeting with me yesterday to discuss the opening of accounts manager at the
Lions Department Store on Mid Hollow Drive.

After having some time to think about the position and its responsibilities, I am sure that my
experience at Turnbrook Motors would help me succeed in this position.

Ms. Perez, I am excited about the opportunities of the accounts manager position and look
forward to hearing from you soon.

Sincerely

Joe Wong

Joe Wong

A thank-you letter lets the interviewer know that you appreciate having had the opportunity to interview for a job.

BLEND IMAGES/JUPITER IMAGES

Acceptance or Rejection Letter

When you are offered a job, you should formally accept or reject the offer in writing. Address the letter to the person with whom you interviewed or who gave you the job offer. If you want to accept the job, say that you are pleased to accept the job offer. State your understanding of the job position, start date, and other details that you want to verify. Indicate what you are looking forward to about the job. Ask any questions that you need answered. For example, you might ask, "Do I need to come to the office to complete any paperwork before my work start date?"

If you do not want to accept a job that is offered to you, send a letter to the person who offered you the job. Politely decline to accept the offer. Give a reason for declining the offer that does not put the company in a bad light. Try to keep the goodwill of the interviewer. You might want to apply for a different job at this company at a later time.

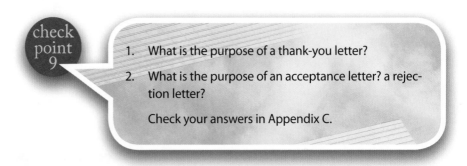

check point 9

1. What is the purpose of a thank-you letter?

2. What is the purpose of an acceptance letter? a rejection letter?

Check your answers in Appendix C.

Section 15.4 *Applications*

A. *Interview Questions*

1. Identify a job opening in a career area of interest to you. Assume that you have been invited to interview for the job.

2. Select ten questions from the various categories in Figure 15-10 on page 601. Write sample answers to the interview questions.

3. Select two questions from Figure 15-11 on page 605. Write sample responses that you could give to these illegal interview questions.

B. *Thank-You Letters*

1. Identify a job opening in a career area of interest to you.

2. Assume that you had an interview for the job yesterday.

3. Write a confirming thank-you letter to the interviewer.

   - Make up a name for the interviewer.

   - Use the real name and address of the company, if known. If you do not have a real company name and address, make up the needed details.

   - Thank the interviewer and indicate that you are definitely interested in the job. Provide a few supporting details.

4. Now assume that after learning more about the position, you do not think the position is right for you. Write a thank-you letter to the interviewer.

   - Thank the interviewer.

   - Indicate that you are no longer interested in the job. Give one or two reasons why you are no longer interested.

   - Try to keep the goodwill of the interviewer. You might want to apply for a different job at this company at a later time.

C. *Acceptance Letter*

1. Assume that you have been offered the job for which you interviewed in Application B.

2. Write an acceptance letter to the interviewer.

Chapter *Summary*

15.1 Job Search

- A job search is the process of finding job openings and applying for jobs.
- Before you begin a job search, consider your personal and career goals.
- Identifying your qualifications gives you the information you need to prepare a resume.
- A career portfolio contains samples of your work, transcripts, letters of recommendation, and other related items.
- You can locate job openings through school placement offices, personal contacts, newspapers, the Internet, and employment agencies.

15.2 Resume

- A resume is a concise summary of an applicant's qualifications for a job.
- A resume may be organized in reverse chronological order or functional order.
- A reference is a person who can attest to your character or qualifications for a job.
- Scannable print resumes, electronic resumes, and Web resumes are alternatives to a traditional print resume.

15.3 Application Letter and Form

- An application letter is a message written to an employer that expresses interest in a job and asks for an interview.
- An application form is a document provided by an employer that you complete. It gives your contact information, education, work history, and other information.

15.4 Interview and Follow-Up Messages

- In a job interview, an employer talks with a job applicant to determine whether the person is qualified for the position and a good fit for the company.
- Within two days after an interview, the applicant should write a thank-you letter to the interviewer.
- A job offer should be formally accepted or declined in writing.

Vocabulary

Open the *Word* file *CH15 Vocabulary* from the student data files. Complete the exercise to review the vocabulary terms from this chapter.

application form	job search
application letter	networking
career portfolio	qualifications
electronic resume	reference
internship	resume
job interview	scannable resume
job objective	Web resume

Critical Thinking Questions

1. Which is more important to identify first—your personal goals or your career goals? Why?

2. Why is it important to tailor your job objective and other parts of your resume to each job opening for which you apply?

3. Would a functional resume or a resume organized in reverse chronological order be best for you? Why?

4. Why is it important to write a follow-up letter to an interviewer even if you have decided you do not want the job for which you interviewed?

5. Is writing an unsolicited application letter a good use of your time? Why or why not?

CRITICAL
THINKING

Chapter *Applications*

A. *Job Search Plan*

1. Identify the method(s) of finding job openings that you think is likely to work best for you.

2. Write an explanation of how you would conduct a job search. For example, would you search first on the Web or would you seek only jobs listed with an agency or in the newspaper? Explain why you have chosen your particular search strategy.

B. *Interview Role-Play*

TEAMWORK

1. Work with two classmates on this project.

2. Each person will serve in each position—as interviewer, an observer, and as job applicant. Complete these steps to prepare for the interview:

   - Identify a job position for which you will apply when you are the applicant and share this information with your classmates.

   - Write a list of questions you will ask the applicant when you are the interviewer.

   - Write a list of items you will watch for when you are the observer.

3. Participate in two interviews (as an applicant in one and as an interviewer in the other). Be an observer in a third interview. Make notes as you watch the interview when you are the observer. Be certain to point out both the strengths and the weaknesses of the applicant's performance.

C. *Company Research*

REAL WORLD

INTERNET

1. Select two companies or organizations for which you would be interested in working.

2. Do research to find the following information for each company:

   - Company name

   - City and state of the home office

   - Address and telephone number of the location nearest you or where you would want to work

   - The name of the director of the Human Resources Department or the head of a department in which you would want to work

   - City, state, and country locations of other plants or offices

   - Internet address

- Industry and products made or services offered

- Size (number of employees and dollar amount of sales per year)

- Activities or events in the current news related to the company, if any are available

D. Unsolicited Application Letter

1. Select one of the companies for which you conducted research in Application C.

2. Identify a job position at the company. Write an unsolicited letter of application to the company for that job position.

3. Address the letter to the person in charge of the department you want to join or the director of the Human Resources Department.

E. Career Portfolio

You have created several items that can be used to create a career portfolio. In this application, you will select a format for your portfolio and organize the materials.

1. Select a format for your career portfolio. The items can be placed in computer files, file folders, a notebook, or a small briefcase.

2. Collect or create the following items and place them in your portfolio:

- Traditional print resume
- Scannable resume
- Electronic resume
- Web resume (optional)
- Sample solicited letter of application
- Sample unsolicited letter of application
- Sample thank-you letter
- Sample acceptance letter

- List of references
- Letters of recommendation from references
- List of work history
- Copies of awards or honors you have received
- Copies of diplomas and transcripts
- Samples of work or project descriptions

Editing Activity

Open the *Word* file *CH15 Editing* from the student data files. Edit the application letter, breaking the text into appropriate paragraphs. Correct all errors and rewrite, as needed, to improve the letter.

Completing an Application Form

Nancy Russell had just finished a successful interview with ParData Computer Services of Dallas, Texas. She was pleased with the situation, for the job would provide a good salary and full benefits. Carson Weir, the interviewer, gave Nancy an application form and asked her to fill it out.

As Nancy looked over the form, she realized that she had a pen with her but it had green ink. The form required Nancy to provide four references. She knew who her references were, but she did not have their addresses, telephone numbers, or e-mail addresses.

The application form also asked for her work experience and the dates of her employment. Nancy could provide a record of her experience, but she was unsure of the dates.

1. Under the circumstances, what should Nancy have done? Should she have filled out the form as best she could? Should she have asked for a pen with blue or black ink? Should she have asked for permission to take the form home, fill it out, and bring it back the next day?

2. What should Nancy have done to be better prepared?

Government & Public
Administration

Communication for Government and Public Administration

Holly Galleon is the director of the local office of the Department of Motor Vehicles. People who want to register their automobiles or transfer ownership of an automobile come to this office. Individuals can also get a driver's license or renew a driver's license at this office. The office is open Monday through Friday, 8 a.m. to 4:30 p.m. The office is closed on all holidays. Registration of automobiles and transfer of ownership cannot be done over the telephone or via the Internet.

When customers come into the office, they take a number and sit down to wait for their turn to be helped. In the office, there are plastic chairs for customers to sit in while they wait. The clerks who work in the office have a desk with a plastic chair beside it for the customer. The clerk's computers are connected to the state's mainframe computer. Responses to their input are almost immediate.

Most of the time customers have to wait 20 to 40 minutes to be helped. When the office is extremely busy, customers may have to wait an hour. Clerks are advised not to apologize for the long wait. Holly thinks an apology would only remind the customer of his or her long wait. Nevertheless, customers are commonly impatient because of their long wait.

Walls are painted a soft gray and neon light fixtures line the ceiling. There are a few posters on the walls that give people information about the documents they will need when registering an automobile or transferring ownership of an automobile.

1. Are the customers of this office being treated in a friendly and efficient manner? Why or why not?

2. What could be done to improve customer service?

Communication for Arts, A/V Technology, and Communication

Kyle Rogers lives in New York City and is an aspiring actor. He loves the stage and being in front of people. He loves the challenge of acting like someone else. He also enjoys being the center of attention. Obviously, he has a personality that fits an actor well. However, Kyle realizes that he also needs talent and experience to succeed as an actor.

To prepare himself for an acting career, Kyle participated in high school plays and was president of the school's drama club. He also belonged to a local theater group and has had lead roles in several of the group's productions. Last month, he hired an agent and is presently taking acting lessons. To pay for his acting lessons, Kyle had to borrow money. These lessons are expensive, but they seem necessary if Kyle is to succeed as an actor.

Kyle's life is hectic and tiring. During the day, he is taking acting lessons and trying out for acting roles. He is working evenings in a restaurant as a server. Kyle feels discouraged when he is rejected for acting parts. Each time he tries out for an acting role, he feels a great deal of pressure. He also realizes that if he gets an acting role in a play, he may have to quit his job at the restaurant.

1. What type of resume, reverse chronological or functional, would you recommend for Kyle? Why?

2. In the acting profession, how important is nonverbal communication?

3. Do you think Kyle places more value on his personal goals or his career goals? Explain your response.

Appendices

Appendix A *Glossary*

Appendix B *Proofreaders' Marks and Documentation Styles*

Appendix C *Checkpoint Answers*

Appendices **617**

Appendix A

Glossary

A

abbreviation A shortened form of a word or a group of words

accessibility The ease with which someone can be contacted

acknowledgment A message that tells a sender that a message or item has been received

active listening Hearing and trying to understand and remember a message

active voice The condition in which the subject of a sentence is doing the action

ad hoc committee A temporary group that is formed to accomplish a specific task

adjective A word that describes a noun or pronoun

adverb A word that describes a verb, an adjective, or another adverb

agenda A document that lists the topics to be discussed during a meeting

alternative A possible solution or course of action that may be selected from those available

analytical report A report that analyzes a problem, presents facts and conclusions, and makes recommendations

analyze To examine, closely study, or evaluate in order to better understand something

anecdote A short account of an interesting or humorous incident

animation The technique of making text or visuals appear to move in film or computer graphics

apostrophe An internal punctuation mark used to indicate possession or the omission of letters in a word

appendix Supplementary materials that are placed at the end of a document or book

application form A document provided by an employer that an applicant completes to give contact information, education, work history, and other information

application letter A message written to an employer that expresses interest in a job and asks for an interview

appositive A noun or phrase that renames and refers to a preceding noun

attachment notation Text that indicates that a separate document is attached to the letter or memo

audience analysis The process of creating a profile of the intended receivers of a message

B

bar chart An image used to compare different groups of data to each other through the use of bars of different lengths

bias A belief or opinion that hinders fair and impartial actions or judgments

bibliography A list of sources used in preparing a report or other written work

blind copy notation Text that indicates that a copy of the message is being sent to the person(s) named without the recipient's knowledge

blog A journal posted on a Web site that may allow readers to reply to postings on the site

body The part of a document (memo, e-mail, letter, or report) that contains the paragraphs of the message

brainstorming Thinking of many ideas about a topic without evaluating the ideas

briefing A short presentation given to bring people up to date on business activities, projects, programs, or procedures

business communication Sending and interpreting messages related to products, services, or activities of a company or an organization

C

capitalization Using uppercase letters in writing

career portfolio A computer file, file folder, notebook, or small briefcase containing samples of your work, transcripts, letters of recommendation, and other related items

casual listening Hearing and understanding a message but not trying to remember the message in the long term

cell phone A portable, wireless telephone, which changes antenna connections during travel from one radio reception cell to another

channel The mode or form used to send a message, such as speaking person-to-person or sending an e-mail

claim A message that requests a refund, an exchange, or a discount on merchandise or services

clause A group of words with a subject and a predicate

clear message A message that is specific, precise, and complete

clip art A drawing or image that has been saved as an electronic file

collaborate Work with other people to accomplish a task

collection message A message that tries to persuade a customer to pay a past-due bill

collective noun A word that represents a group that usually acts as a single unit

colon An internal punctuation mark that directs the reader's attention to the material that follows it

column chart An image used to compare different groups of data to each other through the use of columns of different lengths

comma An internal punctuation mark used to separate items in a sentence and to provide clarity

communication The process used to send and interpret messages so they are understood

communication barriers Things or conditions that interfere with the communication process

compact disk (CD) A thin platter that can have computer data recorded on it in optical form

complete message A message that contains all the needed information

computer A machine that processes data according to a set of instructions in order to perform tasks

computer virus A program that can infect data files or programs without the knowledge or permission of the user

concise message A message that is brief and to the point but includes enough information to achieve its objectives

conclusion An opinion that is based on research findings or studying data

confidential information Data that should be kept private or secret

conflict A disagreement or quarrel

conjunction A word that joins words, phrases, or clauses

contacts list A group of people with whom you communicate

contradictory Inconsistent or opposing

copy notation Text that indicates that a copy of the message is being sent to the person(s) named

copyright The legal right of someone, usually the author or artist, to use or reproduce a work

correct message A message that does not contain errors or omit needed information

courteous message A messages that is positive, considerate, and bias-free

credibility The quality of being believable or trustworthy

credit refusal A message that denies credit to an applicant

cross-cultural communication Sharing messages verbally, nonverbally, or in writing with people from different cultures

culture A set of beliefs, attitudes, practices, and social customs that distinguishes a group of people

customer service The performance of activities to ensure customer satisfaction

D

dash An internal punctuation mark used to show a sudden change of thought

declarative sentence A sentence that makes a statement

delegate Assign tasks or duties to others

demographics Characteristics of a group of people, such as gender, age, race, culture, education level, occupation, marital status, and income

description A verbal and/or visual picture of something

digital video disk (DVD) A thin platter that can be used to store large amounts of computer data in optical form

direct address Speaking directly to someone, usually calling the person by name

direct object A word or phrase that helps complete the meaning of a sentence by receiving the action of the verb

discrimination Unfair treatment of a person or group on the basis of prejudice

diversity The presence of a wide range of variation in qualities or attributes of people or things

documentation A method of identifying sources used in a report

E

editing Reviewing and revising a message to improve it

electronic resume A resume that is saved in a computer file, typically in ASCII format

electronic whiteboard A device that can scan text and images written on it and send the images to a computer, printer, or fax machine

e-mail An informal message that is written, sent, and received on a computer; more formally called electronic mail

emoticon A combination of keyboard characters or icons, such as a smiley face, used in messages to indicate emotion

empathy Understanding another's point of view or feelings without necessarily sharing them

emphatic listening Hearing and trying to understand the speaker's point of view, attitudes, and emotions

enclosure notation Text that indicates that a document is included with a memo or letter but not attached to it

enthusiasm Showing excitement or a lively interest

enunciation The way in which each part of a word is said

ergonomics The study of the relationship between people and their working environment with the aim of making it easier and safer for people to use tools and other objects

ethics Principles of right and wrong that govern behavior

ethnicity The division of people into groups that share a common ancestry, history, or culture

etiquette A set of rules of behavior for a particular place or situation

evaluative listening Hearing and judging the importance or accuracy of what a speaker is saying

exclamation point An external punctuation mark that shows strong emotion

executive summary A brief overview of a report; also called a synopsis or an abstract

external communication barriers Things or conditions outside the receiver or the sender that hinder the communication process

external customer Someone from outside the organization who receives benefits or information or purchases a product or service

F

fact A statement that can be proved to be true or correct

fax machine A device that sends and receives electronic documents over a phone line

feedback The response of a receiver to a message

firewall Hardware and/or software that restricts access to computers or networks

flame An angry or insulting e-mail message or to write such a message

flowchart An image that shows a step-by-step diagram of a procedure or process

fragment An incomplete sentence that may or may not have meaning

friendliness Being supportive, helpful, or kind

G

gesture The use of your arms and hands to express an idea or feeling

global positioning system (GPS) A world- wide navigation system consisting of satellites and ground stations that allows a GPS receiver to identify its location anywhere on Earth

globalization The integration of activities among nations in areas such as commerce and culture

glossary A list of terms and abbreviations with definitions

goodwill A positive feeling or attitude toward others; the positive reputation or image of a company

goodwill message An acknowledgment or a friendly message designed to build relationships

grapevine An informal communication channel in an organization

graphic A table or chart that helps the audience or reader understand data or concepts

H

hacker A person who uses computer expertise to break into computer networks

handout A page(s) that contains text or images related to a presentation or other topic

hardware The physical parts of a computer and related devices

hotspots Places that offer wireless Internet access

hyperlinks Text or graphics on an electronic page that, when clicked, take the user to another location

hyphen An internal punctuation mark used after some prefixes and in forming some compound words

hypothesis A possible solution to a problem or situation that can be tested

I

identity theft Stealing and illegally using a person's private data

impromptu speech A short, informal talk given with little advance notice or preparation

inclusion Seeing and valuing the contributions of everyone and treating everyone fairly

index A detailed listing of the topics and subtopics covered in a book, manual, or other written work

indirect object A word that receives the action that the verb makes on the direct object

informational report A report that present facts and includes very little analysis

informative listening Listening to obtain specific information or understand a message

instant messaging (IM) A means of communicating electronically via text messages with one or more people in real time

instructions Steps that tell readers how to do something

interjection A word that expresses surprise or strong feeling

internal communication barriers Things or conditions within the receiver and the sender that hinder the communication process

internal customer An employee of your company to whom you provide information or services

Internet A vast network that connects millions of computers worldwide

internship An arrangement in which a student works for a company for a set period of time as part of a learning experience

interview A conversation between two or more people for the purpose of gaining facts, ideas, or opinions

intranet A communications network within an organization that is meant for the use of its employees or members

invoice A bill for items or services purchased from a company

J

job interview A discussion of a job and your qualifications with an employer

job objective A brief statement that describes the type of position for which an applicant is applying; also called a career goal

job search The process of finding job openings and applying for jobs

L

landscape orientation Positioned with the long edge (of an image or page) at the top

leadership Providing guidance and inducing others to act

legend A chart feature that identifies the items that the pieces, columns, bars, or lines in the chart represent

letter A document used to send a formal written message to someone outside or inside an organization

line chart An image that shows changes in quantity or value over time

listening The process of hearing and focusing attention to understand an oral message

M

manuals Sets of instructions combined with explanations, descriptions, definitions, and other related information

mechanism A type of object that consists of parts working together to perform one or more tasks

memo An informal document that is sent to someone within your organization; more formally called a memorandum

message An idea expressed by a set of symbols

message environment The physical and social setting in which a message is sent or received

minutes The official record of the proceedings of a meeting

mixed punctuation A format style that has a colon after the salutation and a comma after the complimentary close in a letter

multimedia presentation A speech in which computer software is used to combine several kinds of visual and/or audio aids

multinational company A company that conducts business in at least two nations

N

netiquette A set of informal guidelines for behaving courteously online

network A group of devices, such as computers and printers, connected together in order to share data and/or tasks

networking Building relationships with people who can help in an activity, such as a job search

neutral opening Statements that do not imply a positive or a negative response to the receiver

newsgroup An online discussion group that focuses on a specific topic

nonrestrictive element A phrase or clause that gives information that is not essential to the meaning of the sentence

nonverbal communication Messages sent without or in addition to words

nonverbal symbols Actions or conditions that express a meaning

noun A word that names a person, place, or thing

number expression The way numbers are written—as words or numerals

O

object Something inanimate that is natural or synthetic and can be seen or touched

objective A goal or an outcome to be achieved

observation Watching or monitoring people or things in an effort to learn something

obstacle Something that hinders or prevents progress or achieving a goal

open punctuation A format style that has no punctuation after the salutation or complimentary close in a letter

opinion A view held by or a conclusion reached by someone

order A request that the receiver sell goods or services to the sender

organization chart An image that shows the relationships of employees, positions, and departments

outline A listing of topics in a logical order

P

pager A handheld device that alerts receivers that they have a message

paralanguage Nonverbal symbols, such as voice pitch, rate of speech, laughing, and sighing

parentheses Internal punctuation marks used in pairs to set off nonessential words, phrases, or clauses

passive voice The condition in which the subject of a sentence is receiving the action

period An external punctuation mark used to signal the end of a sentence or indicate an abbreviation

peripherals Devices that work with a computer to help you accomplish tasks, such as printers, scanners, and fax machines

personal computer A small, relatively inexpensive computer designed for an individual user

personal space The nearby area around a person or the area the person considers his or her territory

persuasive message A message that tries to convince the reader to take an action

phrase A group of related words with no subject or predicate

pie chart An image that shows how the parts of a whole are distributed

pitch The property of a sound, such as a voice, that describes it as high or low

plagiarism The act of claiming someone else's words or ideas as your own

portrait orientation Positioned with the short edge (of an image or page) at the top

possessive noun A noun that shows ownership

postscript A sentence or paragraph at the end of the letter that reinforces the message or adds information

posture The way a person stands or sits

predicate Everything said by, to, or about the subject in a sentence

prejudice A bias that prevents objective thought about a person or thing

preposition A word that connects a noun or pronoun to other words in the sentence

primary appeal The most convincing point in a persuasive message

primary research Gathering new data for a report or other purpose

process A series of events that take place over time and result in a change or a product

project bid A document that describes work to be done, completion times, charges, and related details

pronoun A word that takes the place of a noun

pronoun antecedent The noun or noun phrase that is replaced by a pronoun

pronunciation The way a word is spoken

proofreaders' marks Words and symbols used to mark edits on printed documents

proofreading Reviewing and correcting the final draft of a message

proposal A formal document that describes a problem or need and recommends a solution

publish Send a message to a receiver or make a message available to a receiver

Q

qualifications Skills, abilities, experience, and training that prepare a person to do a job

question mark An external punctuation mark used after a direct question

quotation marks Internal punctuation marks that indicate a direct quotation, a definition, nonstandard English, or a title

R

race The division of people into groups based on physical characteristics such as skin or hair color

reading The process of seeing and interpreting written words and other symbols

receiver A person who hears, sees, or reads symbols and interprets a message

recommendation A suggestion of what should be done

redundancy Needless repetition

reference A person who can attest to your character or qualifications for a job

reference initials The initials of the person who keyed a memo or letter

reflective listening Hearing, understanding, and restating the speaker's message

report A document that provides facts, opinions, or ideas about a specific topic or problem

request denial A message that does not grant or approve an item or action

request for proposal (RFP) A document that outlines needs or problems to be solved and solicits solutions

restrictive element A phrase or clause that gives information that is essential to the meaning of a sentence

resume A concise summary of an applicant's qualifications for a job

routine request A message that asks for information or action that the sender thinks will be given or done willingly

S

sales message A message that tries to persuade a potential customer to purchase a product or service

scannable resume A print resume formatted so that it can be easily scanned into an electronic file using OCR software

scanner A machine that creates a computer file from a paper copy, film, slide, or transparency sheet

scanning Reviewing material to get a basic understanding of the objectives and the important points of material you are going to read

scope The boundaries of the report—what will be included and what will not

screening calls A procedure for incoming calls that is used to learn who is calling and sometimes the reason for the call

secondary research Locating data that already has been gathered and reported for a report or other purpose

self-confidence Belief in yourself and your abilities

semicolon An internal punctuation mark that is used to denote a pause and that is stronger than a comma

sender A person who creates and shares a message

sentence A group of related words that contains a subject and a predicate and expresses a complete thought

sincerity Being open and genuine or earnest

smart phone A device that combines the features of a cell phone and a handheld computer

soft sell A subtle or low-pressure appeal used in an attempt to sell a product or service

software Step-by-step instructions written in special languages a computer can understand; also called programs

source line Text that tells the location from which data has been taken

spam Unsolicited electronic junk messages

standing committee A group that is a permanent part of an organization and meets regularly to consider a problem or issue

stereotype An oversimplified belief about a group of people

subject The person who is speaking, the person who is spoken to, or the person, place, or thing spoken about in a sentence

subject line A document part that states the topic of the message in a memo, e-mail, or letter

survey A set of questions or statements used to learn facts or opinions

synergy The interaction of people or things that creates or accomplishes more than the sum of the individual efforts or parts

T

table An arrangement of data organized in rows and columns

table of contents A list of what is included in a report, book, or other document

task force A group charged with completing a specific job within a certain time

teamwork Two or more people acting together to achieve a goal

technical writing Writing specific, detailed instructions and descriptions

timeline A schedule that lists the dates by which each task and phase of a project must be completed

tone The attitude toward your listeners or the topic discussed that is implied by your choice of words and the pitch of your voice

topical outline An outline that uses a few words to describe each topic rather than complete sentences

trade secret Information that gives a business a competitive advantage and that it makes reasonable efforts to keep secret

transition A word or phrase that connects sentences or paragraphs to one another

U

uniform resource locator (URL) An Internet address

V

verb A word or phrase that describes the action, state of being, or condition of the subject of a sentence

verb tense An indication of the time an action takes place

verbal symbols Words used in a spoken or written message

video The transmission of moving pictures to a monitor or television

virtual team A group whose members do not share a physical workspace but work together using communications technology, such as telephone and e-mail

visual aid An object, picture, drawing, map, poster, chart, or other image that helps the audience or reader understand data or concepts

voice mail A computerized system that answers telephone calls

VoIP A digital phone service in which calls go through a high-speed Internet connection rather than a conventional phone line

W

Web resume A resume that is written in HTML and can be viewed in a browser program

white space Blank area in a document that does not contain text or images

wildcard A symbol, such as an asterisk (*) or a question mark, used in conducting data searches

World Wide Web A part of the Internet consisting of computers that use hypertext transfer protocol documents

Proofreaders' Marks and Documentation Styles

Proofreaders' Marks

PROOFREADERS' MARKS

SYMBOL		MARKED COPY	CORRECTED COPY
‖	Align	$298,000 $117,000	$298,000 $117,000
∼∼∼	Bold	The meaning is important.	The **meaning** is important.
≡	Capitalize	bobbie caine	Bobbie Caine
◡	Close up space	Use con cise words.	Use concise words.
ℒ	Delete	They are happpy.	They are happy.
∧	Insert	Please make *a* copy.	Please make a copy.
#	Space	Show alot of examples.	Show a lot of examples.
___	Italicize	The Sacramento Bee	The *Sacramento Bee*
stet	Ignore correction	He is an *stet* effective writer.	He is an effective writer.
/	Lowercase	Sincerely Yours	Sincerely yours
◯	Move as shown	I am only going tomorrow.	I am going only tomorrow.
⊏ ⊐ ⊓ ⊔	Move left, right, up, or down	Mr. Herschel King 742 Wabash Avenue Skokie, IL 60077	Mr. Herschel King 742 Wabash Avenue Skokie, IL 60077
¶	Paragraph	¶The file is attached.	The file is attached.
sp	Spell out	7209 E. Darrow Avenue	7209 East Darrow Avenue
∿	Transpose	The down up and motion	The down and up motion
⌐	Use initial cap only	FORMATTING A MEMO	Formatting a Memo

Documentation Styles

Whenever you use someone else's material you must document your sources. Sources should be documented in a manner that makes it easy for readers to locate additional information about the material and in an acceptable citation style.

Types of Citations

Most source documentation falls within two categories: that which appears within the text and that which appears at the end of a document. The in-text reference provides immediate identification of the source of the material and makes it easy for the reader to locate more detailed information at the end of the report.

Reference lists, **works cited lists**, and **bibliographies** appear at the end of a document. All three lists contain the information necessary for the reader to locate the original source material. Reference lists include only information used to support the material discussed in the document. A works cited list must include all the works cited within the report. Work cited lists are sometimes labeled as Literature Cited, Works Consulted, or Bibliography. A bibliography is not as limited as a reference list. A bibliography may include related material, background information, and additional readings. It is also acceptable to annotate a bibliography.

Citation Styles

Three of the most widely used documentation styles are from the American Psychological Association (APA), the Modern Language Association of America (MLA), and the University of Chicago Press' *The Chicago Manual of Style*. Following is a brief description of each group's citation guidelines.

APA

The APA style is the style most often used in reports produced by individuals in the social and physical sciences. For in-text citations, the APA style calls for a simple author-date format (Means, 2004). An APA-style bibliography or reference list is alphabetized by the author's last name. Figure B-1 on page 627 shows the presentation of references using the APA style.

MLA

The MLA style is the standard for many writers in business, industry, government, and the media. In the MLA style, in-text citations refer the reader to a comprehensive Works Cited List at the end of the document. The format of the in-text citation is author-page (Means 365). Figure B-2 on page 628 shows acceptable reference format using the MLA style.

Figure B-1 References using the APA Style

REFERENCE TYPE	REFERENCE FORMAT
Annual report	Willamette Company, Incorporated. (2004). *2004 Annual Report*. Seattle, WA: The Willamette Company, Incorporated.
Book, one author	Logan, P. (2002). *Small Winners*. New York: Stallings Publishing Co.
Book, two authors	Parker, Erica M., and T. M. Gauge (2002). *Winning Is Not the Only Thing*, Phoenix, AZ: McDougle Press.
Book, edited	David, Gill A. (Ed.) (2003). *The Horse that Won the World*. Kansas City, MO: Lopes and Kinner Publishing.
Brochure	Collision Center. (2004). Accidents Do Happen. [Brochure]. Ruston, LA: Louisiana's Collision Center.
CD-ROM encyclopedia article, one author	Lee, Tyler (2001). Filing Systems. *FileProof 2000* [CD-ROM]. Silcon Valley, CA: FoolProof Systems, Inc.
Encyclopedia article, one author	Callens, Elizabeth (2003). Database systems. *The Computer Users' Encyclopedia*, Dallas, TX: Automated Press.
Film, videotape, or audiotape	*Successful Computer System Projects*. (2003). [Film]. Atlanta, GA: Systems Development Resource Center.
Government publication	U.S. Department of Defense. (2004). *The Cost of the B-1 Bomber*. Washington, DC: National Press, Inc.
Internet, Web	Combining ethics and your travel. (2003). *Ethnic-o-Travel*. [On-line]. Available: **http://www.travelsites.com/dogood.htm**. Cited 2003 May 13.
Interview	Susanboy, Martha, professor, Clever City State (2001, January 12). Interview by author. Clever City, UT.
Journal article	Jiang, J. J. (2002). Systems success and communication. *The Journal of Computer Intelligence 9*, 112–117.
Magazine article	Johnson, K. (2002, April 10). Losing and the loser psychology. *Successful Challenging*, 43–45.
Newspaper article, no author	"Is the weather really cyclical?" (2002, December 28). *Ruston Daily Journal*, p. B–7.
Newspaper article, one author	Marks, Amy. (2002, December 21). "Successful weddings in Modesto." *Modesto Daily Times*, C–12.
On-line newspaper	Adams, B. M. (2003, February 10). "The exciting international lawyer." [On-line]. *Lawyers Journal 34*, 23–26. Available: **http://www.alajournal.com/realworld.htm.**

Figure B-2 References using MLA style

REFERENCE TYPE	REFERENCE FORMAT
Annual report	Willamette Company, Incorporated. *2004 Annual Report*. Seattle, WA: The Willamette Company, Incorporated.
Book, one author	Logan, P. *Small Winners*. New York: Stallings Publishing Co., 2002.
Book, two authors	Parker, Erica M., and T. M. Gauge. *Winning Is Not the Only Thing*. Phoenix, AZ: McDougle Press, 2002.
Book, edited	David, Gill A. (Ed.). *The Horse that Won the World*. Kansas City, MO: Lopes and Kinner Publishing.
Brochure	Collision Center. (2004). *Accidents Do Happen*. [Brochure]. Ruston, LA: Louisiana's Collision Center.
Encyclopedia article, one author	Callens, Elizabeth. "Database Systems." *The Computer Users' Encyclopedia*. 2003 ed.
Film, videotape, or audiotape	*Successful Computer System Projects*. Film. Atlanta, GA: Systems Development Resource Center, 2003.
Government publication	U.S. Department of Defense. *The Cost of the B-1 Bomber*. Washington, DC: National Press, Inc., 2004.
Internet, Web	"Combining Ethics and Your Travel." *Ethnic-o-Travel* (2003). On-line. Internet. Available: **http://www.travelsites.com/dogood.htm**. 13 May 2003.
Interview	Susanboy, Martha. Personal Interview. 12 January 2001.
Journal article	Jiang, J. J. "Systems Success and Communication." *The Journal of Computer Intelligence 9* (2002): 112–117.
Magazine article	Johnson, K. "Losing and the loser psychology." *Successful Challenging* 10 April 2002: 43–45.
Newspaper article, no author	"Is the Weather Really Cyclical?" *Ruston Daily Journal* 28 December 2002: B–7.
Newspaper article, one author	Marks, Amy. "Successful weddings in Modesto." *Modesto Daily Times* 21 December 2002: C–12.

The Chicago Manual of Style

The Chicago Manual of Style is the reference guide for most publishers and editors. *The Chicago Manual of Style* supports both a documentary-note style and an author-date style. Figure B-3 shows examples of both styles. In the documentary-note system (see the Newspaper reference in Figure B-3), the writer provides notes and retrieval information about the source information in a parenthetical note. This style can eliminate the need for a comprehensive bibliography. Similar to the in-text reference style of the APA, the author-date in-text style of *The Chicago Manual of Style* provides a relatively unobtrusive pointer to a more detailed reference list at the end of the document.

For More Information

Style guidelines for the three sources referenced in this appendix cover almost every aspect of writing and editing. To learn more about each, you may want to check your local bookstore or the World Wide Web. How do you choose which style to use? As the notes on these styles indicate, different subject areas may have different conventions for crediting source material. For example, the American Mathematical Style has its own set of conventions for presenting citations and other information. You should use the style most acceptable to your subject area or organization.

Figure B-3 References Using the Chicago Manual of Style

Book, one author

Logan, P. 2002. *Small winners*. New York: Stallings Publishing Co.

Book, two authors

Parker, Erica M. and T. M. Gauge. 2002. *Winning Is Not the Only Thing*. Pheonix, AZ: McDougle Press.

Journal article

Jiang, J. J. 2002. Systems success and communication. *The Journal of Computer Intelligence 9*: 112–117.

Magazine article

Johnson, K. 2002. Losing and the loser psychology. *Successful Challenging*, 10 April, 43–45.

Newspaper

This type of citation is commonly incorporated into the text of the report; for example,

An article in the *Modesto Daily Times* of December 21, 2002 describes recent weddings in the Modesto area. Common elements in these weddings included . . . .

Unpublished interview

Susanboy, Martha. 2001. Interviewed by author. Clever City, UT, 12 January 2001.

Appendix C

 Chapter 1 Answers

Checkpoint 1

1. The communication process involves five elements: a message, a sender, a receiver, a channel, and feedback.

2. A receiver must interpret the meaning of the verbal and nonverbal symbols used by the sender.

Checkpoint 2

1. Four purposes for business communication are to obtain or share information, to build goodwill and image, to persuade, and to build relationships and self-esteem.

2. When people feel goodwill toward a company, they are more likely to share information, grant requests, or offer support in other ways. When a company has a positive image, the public is more likely to buy products or services from the company.

Checkpoint 3

1. A letter from the company president to employees is an example of a formal communication.

2. Reasons why using written communication may be appropriate include:

   • Written messages provide a record of information exchanged. For example, a price quoted in a written bid cannot be disputed.

   • The message can be revised until it is logical and clear. Revision is especially important when complex data must be explained.

   • A written message allows the receiver to read the message and refer to it as many times as necessary.

   (Students are to provide two reasons.)

Checkpoint 4

1. Conditions outside the receiver and the sender that hinder communication are called external communication barriers. Poor lighting, heat or cold, humidity, uncomfortable seating, and noise are examples of these barriers.

2. Conditions within a receiver or sender that hinder communication are called internal communication barriers. Examples are a receiver's background, education, biases, and emotional state.

Checkpoint 5

1. When creating an audience profile, you should consider the receiver's age, gender, background, education, experience, interests, concerns, attitudes, and emotional state.

2. Interpreting feedback can help senders overcome communication barriers.

Checkpoint 6

1. The receiver's duties in the communication process are to read and to listen effectively.

2. A written message may be read several times if needed to gain understanding. A spoken message might be heard only once with no opportunity to ask questions.

Checkpoint 7

1. Reading is important for workplace success because any career or job you choose will require reading. You must be able to read effectively to interpret messages from coworkers and customers, follow instructions, and complete procedures. Doing research and using data to make decisions and solve problems also require reading.

2. Ways reading is used in the workplace include reading to stay informed, follow procedures, handle transactions, provide customer service, and gather data for use in making decisions and solving problems.

Checkpoint 8

1. Scanning is an attempt to get a basic understanding of the objectives and the important points of the material you are going to read. Scanning helps improve reading comprehension by giving you an overview of the material you plan to read.

2. Answers will vary. Three things you can do to help improve your careful reading skills may be any of these:

   • Select a location that is conducive to reading. If a room is not comfortable or has distractions, you cannot focus on what you are reading.

   • Scan the item you are to read. Getting an overview of the information will help improve your understanding of the material.

   • Use a dictionary to look up words you do not know. Building your vocabulary will help improve your reading speed and comprehension.

   • If you are a word-for-word reader, try to learn to read in groups of words. Silently pronouncing each word slows reading speed. Try to grasp the meaning of phrases and clauses without focusing on individual words.

- Find the main idea in every paragraph. The rest of the sentences in a paragraph usually provide additional details about the main idea.

- Recognize the order of events in a situation. This understanding will allow you to reconstruct the entire situation if necessary.

- Take notes or highlight information while reading. Study your notes to help you recall what you read.

- To check your understanding and create a frame of reference, compare the information you read to what you already know.

Chapter 2 Answers

Checkpoint 1

1. Diversity refers to the presence of a wide range of variation in qualities or attributes of people or things.

2. A diverse workforce makes employers better able to meet the needs of growing global markets and an increasingly diverse U.S. population. Having a diverse workforce enhances the reputation of a company. It also helps the company attract talented employees and keep customers. Diverse work groups may be more creative and innovative than groups that are not diverse.

3. Employees who believe that their employer is indifferent or is hostile to workers "like them" may seek jobs elsewhere. Companies that do not have a diverse workforce may not understand what a diverse group of customers wants or needs. This can result in missed opportunities for new markets and loss of customers. Failing to recognize workers' differences and needs can result in lower productivity and low morale.

Checkpoint 2

1. The U.S. population is becoming more diverse.

2. The United States has more female citizens than male citizens.

3. By 2012, African-American, Latino, and Asian-American people will make up about 30 percent of the U.S. workforce.

4. The U.S. workforce as a whole is getting older.

Checkpoint 3

1. Three differences in culture that may be barriers to communication are language, body language, and personal space.

2. Answers will vary. A sample answer is provided here.

- The *OK* gesture used in the United States would likely be perceived as poor manners by someone from France, where it signifies *worthless* or *zero*.

- The way people indicate yes and no differs significantly in some cultures. To say yes, a Greek may tilt his or her head to either side. To say no, the person may nod upward slightly or just lift his or her eyebrows.

Checkpoint 4

1. Etiquette is a set of rules of behavior for a particular place or situation. Following proper etiquette is important for improving communication and relationships.

2. A stereotype is an oversimplified belief about a group of people. Prejudice is a bias that prevents objective thought about a person or thing. Both stereotypes and prejudice can hinder communication because senders or receivers prejudge other people.

Checkpoint 5

1. A person who has a professional attitude:

- Refrains from making judgments about others

- Keeps an open mind

- Does not make assumptions or jump to conclusions

- Keeps emotions in check

- Is slow to take offense

- Gives others the benefit of the doubt

2. Having a professional attitude helps you communicate successfully by avoiding communication barriers.

Checkpoint 6

1. To learn about other cultures, you can read articles on the Internet, books, and magazines. You can take courses on diversity and talk with people from other cultures.

2. You should avoid acronyms, idioms, slang, and jargon in cross-cultural messages because people from other cultures are not likely to understand them.

3. Answers will vary. A sample answer is given here.

Avoid politics, religion, and other potentially sensitive topics. Avoiding these topics may prevent offending someone.

Checkpoint 7

1. Ethics are principles of right and wrong.

2. Personal ethics are influenced by your experiences and the culture and society in which you learn and grow.

3. Employees should be aware of the code of ethics of their employers because they are expected to respect their company's code of ethics while doing business for the company.

Checkpoint 8

1. Follow these guidelines to help ensure that your statements to customers are truthful ones.

- Learn about the products or services your company offers.

- Inform yourself about company policies and procedures. Know the rules of your organization. Learn exactly what you can and cannot do for clients.

- Offer facts, not opinions. Remember that facts can be proven with evidence to be true.

2. Types of information that are often confidential include:

- Patient medical records

- Information a person shares with his or her attorney

- Clients' financial data
- Some court records
- Trade secrets

Checkpoint 9

1. It is important to keep computer passwords secret so that others cannot use your password to access private information.

2. You should not make a comment in an e-mail or instant message that you would not put in a printed letter. E-mail and instant messages are not always private and may be monitored by an employer or others.

Checkpoint 10

1. Avoiding plagiarism is easy. While doing research, note the source of any information that you think you might use. Put quotation marks around text you have written down word for word or copied from the Internet. Check your final draft against your sources to be sure you have not used another writer's words or ideas without giving credit to the source.

2. Copyright is the legal right of someone, usually the author or artist, to use or reproduce a work. Copyright protection lasts many years but not forever.

 **Chapter 3 Answers**

Checkpoint 1

1. Nonverbal symbols may reinforce, contradict, or substitute for verbal symbols. They may also regulate the verbal part of a message.

2. Answers will vary. An example answer is given here.

   You may say, "That's fine." However, if your voice is strained and you look away from the receiver, your behavior indicates that you are not in agreement.

Checkpoint 2

1. The appearance and correctness of a written document send critical nonverbal messages. Color, pictures, graphics, and errors can also send nonverbal messages in a written document.

2. Examples of nonverbal symbols sent in spoken messages include body language, touching, space, time, and paralanguage.

3. When judging attitudes, people often give more importance to how words are spoken than to the words themselves.

Checkpoint 3

1. Important aspects of your image are based on level of confidence, eye contact, friendliness, enthusiasm, sincerity, and appearance.

2. Having the right amount of self-confidence is important because having too much or too little confidence can hurt your image.

3. Your clothing should be appropriate to your work setting because being poorly groomed or dressed in a way that is not appropriate can create a negative impression.

Checkpoint 4

1. The listening process involves hearing a message, focusing attention on the message, understanding the message, and remembering the message.

2. Hearing is simply detecting sounds. Listening involves hearing and also focusing attention, understanding, and remembering.

Checkpoint 5

1. Casual listening involves hearing and understanding a message but not trying to remember the message in the long term. Active listening is hearing and trying to understand and remember a message. Active listening may be informative, evaluative, emphatic, or reflective.

2. Four types of active listening are given in the following list.

   - Informative listening is used to obtain specific information or understand a message. Doctors use informative listening to learn about their patients.

   - Evaluative listening involves judging the importance or accuracy of what a speaker is saying. Listening to a presidential candidate's speech is an example of evaluative listening.

   - Emphatic listening involves trying to understand the speaker's point of view, attitudes, and emotions. A support associate listening to a customer's complaint is an example of emphatic listening.

   - Reflective listening involves understanding and restating the speaker's message. A guidance counselor may use reflective listening when talking with a student about career goals.

Checkpoint 6

1. Eight barriers to effective listening are listed below.

   - Deafness or a partial hearing loss
   - Attitudes about the speaker
   - Attitudes about the topic
   - Prejudices or differing opinions
   - Assumptions made about the message
   - Environmental distractions
   - Physical discomfort
   - Divided focus

2. Note-taking techniques can create a divided focus. The listener is dividing his or her focus between listening and recording information. While writing notes about one point, the listener may miss the speaker's next point.

Checkpoint 7

1. Four techniques for improving listening skills include:

   - Focus on the main idea
   - Evaluate the message

- Provide feedback
- Take notes

2. Notes taken during listening can be organized in an outline with main points followed by details. Notes can also be organized in two columns with main ideas on the left and supporting details on the right.

3. To practice active listening in a small group, listen for both ideas and feelings. Use effective eye contact and body language that indicate to others that you are listening. Check your understanding by asking questions or restating ideas as appropriate.

Checkpoint 8

1. Workplace relationships include employee and manager relationships, coworker relationships, and customer relationships.

2. A manager is in a position of authority. You should respect this authority by being an honest and loyal employee. Your manager should expect that you will do your work to the best of your ability, keep confidential information secure, and support the efforts of your company and workgroup. Part of keeping a good relationship with your manager is respecting lines of authority in communicating with other employees.

   Your manager should provide you with the appropriate direction and support to do your job well. Your manager should treat you with respect and give you regular feedback about your work and how well you have completed your duties. Your manager should not expect you to do anything that is illegal or unethical.

3. Follow these guidelines for dealing with coworkers.

   - Be fair and honest in your dealings with coworkers. However, remember to keep confidential information secure, even from coworkers.

   - Be helpful. If a coworker requests your help with a rush project, give your help if you can do so without creating problems for other projects that have a higher priority.

   - Be tactful when communicating with coworkers. If work has errors or must be redone, state this information in a positive and constructive way.

   - Acknowledge your mistakes. Do not attempt to hide your mistakes or blame others for your errors.

   - Show appreciation and acknowledge good work done by others. Try to resolve conflicts with coworkers before the problem becomes serious.

Checkpoint 9

1. Workplace teams may include:

   - Manager and employee teams
   - Department teams
   - Workgroup teams
   - Special teams or committees

2. Using teams to achieve goals can have several advantages. Members of a team bring different skills and

knowledge to the group. Team members who work well together often create a synergy and are more creative and productive than the individuals would be working separately. Team members may be able to help one another if a part of the project is behind schedule or not working as planned. A team with culturally diverse members may be better able to understand the needs of culturally diverse customers.

Using teams to achieve goals can also have disadvantages. If the team is disorganized or the members do not understand their goals or tasks, the team may accomplish little. Poor communication among team members can also be a problem that limits the team's accomplishments.

Checkpoint 10

1. Guidelines teams can follow to help them be successful are listed below.

   - Identify the goals of the team. State clearly what the team plans to accomplish. State how the team will know when the goals are achieved.

   - Determine tasks or steps needed to accomplish the goals. The team may need to break large tasks into small parts.

   - Identify resources needed to complete the tasks. Get any approvals that are needed before proceeding.

   - Assign duties and tasks to team members. Set times for when each task should be accomplished.

   - Communicate regularly with team members about the progress of tasks.

   - Resolve conflicts that arise. Do not let prejudice and assumptions that may be incorrect hinder communication.

   - Brainstorm ideas for solving problems that arise.

   - Evaluate procedures. Periodically, look at how the work has progressed. Individual team members should reflect on the procedures used and ways to improve them. The team should consider how well the members work together and how procedures and relationships can be improved.

   - Celebrate success. When significant parts of the project or an entire project is completed, recognize efforts of group members.

2. Things you can do as a team member to contribute to team success are listed below.

   - Set aside personal goals and focus on the team's goals.

   - Do your work as well as you can. Be reliable and responsible.

   - Contribute your ideas and opinions to team discussions.

   - Find roles that you can fill and be ready to step into other roles, including leadership roles, when you are needed.

   - Be supportive of your team members. Keep the team's affairs confidential.

   - Do not take it personally when others disagree with you or criticize your ideas.

Chapter 4 Answers

Checkpoint 1

1. Adverb
2. Conjunction
3. A noun names a person, place, or thing. *Car, girl,* and *clock* are examples of nouns. A pronoun takes the place of a noun. *She, he,* and *they* are examples of pronouns.

Checkpoint 2

The simple subject is shown in italics and the simple predicate is shown in bold.

1. *Brandon* **ran** three marathons this year.
2. *Lucille* **is** a trained nurse.
3. *Ramon* and *Maria* **work** at this company.
4. *We* **have been** to every store in the mall.
5. *Elena* **will finish** her report on time.

Checkpoint 3

The independent clause is shown in italics and the dependent clause is shown in bold.

1. *She took many pictures on her trip,* **which lasted a month.**
2. *The report* **that you wrote** *contains valuable information.*
3. *I will go* **if I am invited.**
4. **Since John will be out of town,** *he will not attend the meeting.*
5. *The work will be completed* **as soon as time allows.**

Checkpoint 4

1. Simple
2. Complex
3. Compound
4. Complex
5. Simple

Checkpoint 5

1. A noun is a word that names a person, place, or thing.
2. A proper noun names a specific person, place, or thing. Examples of proper nouns are *Mary Ann, Seattle,* and *Pepsi.* A common noun is a word that identifies a person, place, or thing in a general way. *Girl, team, rock,* and *car* are examples of common nouns.
3. women, cats, brushes, facilities, sisters-in-law, district attorneys
4. A collective noun is a word that represents a group that usually acts as a single unit. Examples of collective nouns are *tribe* and *jury.*
5. men's, dog's, tables', sister-in-law's, district attorney's

Checkpoint 6

Corrections are underlined.

1. These are <u>their</u> books.
2. Buy extra pencils for Jane and <u>me</u>.

3. Give the report to <u>whomever</u> you find at home.
4. Correct
5. Correct
6. Gloria and <u>I</u> went to the movies.

Checkpoint 7

Corrections are underlined.

1. Alice Wong delivered <u>her</u> speech well.
2. The manager and employees read <u>their</u> bulletins.
3. Each of the boys ate <u>his</u> lunch.
4. Bill or Ray can complete <u>his</u> assignment.
5. Mr. Lau and I took <u>our</u> seats on the airplane.

Checkpoint 8

Corrections are underlined.

1. Kim is <u>more efficient</u> than Robert.
2. Of the three books, the first one is the <u>best</u> one.
3. Your performance was <u>more nearly excellent</u> than mine.
4. Her daughter is <u>a</u> pretty child.
5. Correct

Checkpoint 9

Verbs are underlined.

1. Since joining the restaurant, he <u>has worked</u> as a chef. Past tense
2. Our local high school <u>will play</u> in the basketball tournament. Future tense
3. I <u>am</u> happy about the change. Present tense
4. My team <u>won</u> the race. Past tense
5. She <u>is</u> our new teacher. Present tense

Checkpoint 10

Corrections are underlined.

1. Ben or Jan <u>needs</u> to finish the report.
2. Fifty dollars <u>is</u> the amount we paid.
3. The team members <u>race</u> to the finish.
4. Malloy and Moss <u>manufactures</u> toys. (*Malloy and Moss* is a company name.)
5. A number of bills <u>are</u> past due.

Checkpoint 11

Adverbs are underlined.

1. The children read <u>quietly</u>. *Quietly* modifies the verb *read.*
2. The car was traveling <u>very fast</u>. *Fast* modifies the verb *was traveling. Very* modifies the adverb *fast.*
3. The <u>really</u> big dog chased the cat. *Really* modifies the adjective *big.*
4. He watched the movie <u>today</u>. *Today* modifies the verb *watched.*
5. The work has <u>already</u> been completed. *Already* modifies the verb *has been completed.*

Checkpoint 12

Prepositional phrases are underlined.

1. Effective reading is important <u>for workplace success</u>.
2. The item was found <u>under the desk</u>.
3. Please finish this work <u>for me</u>.
4. <u>Before eating</u>, always wash your hands.
5. Come <u>into the garden</u> and <u>through the back gate</u>.

Checkpoint 13

Conjunctions and interjections are underlined.

1. <u>Oh!</u> This is a lovely present. Interjection
2. Mario <u>and</u> Jill attended the basketball game. Conjunction
3. <u>Help!</u> The house is on fire. Interjection
4. <u>Although</u> I would like to go, I must stay here. Conjunction
5. <u>Both</u> Raji <u>and</u> Kapoor ran for office. Conjunction

Chapter 5 Answers

Checkpoint 1

1. The team won the game by a narrow margin.
2. Return all borrowed equipment to the proper location.
3. Will you please close the door on your way out.
4. Mr. and Mrs. Levi arrived on time.
5. Dr. Patel is on vacation.

Checkpoint 2

1. When will the project be completed?
2. Have you already eaten lunch?
3. Have you keyed the report? the letter? the flyer?
4. Will you return before noon?
5. Can she lift the box?

Checkpoint 3

1. Oh no! I forgot my keys!
2. Help! The store is being robbed!
3. Surprise! Happy birthday!
4. Great! I knew you could do it!
5. Hold on! We're falling!

Checkpoint 4

1. After lunch, we will continue our meeting.
2. The item in the package was broken, and I refused delivery.
3. Please remember, I need the data this afternoon.
4. He played and I sang.
5. The reports, all of which were late, supported his plan.

Checkpoint 5

1. I see, Maria, that you have completed the report, the letter, and the memo.
2. The fast, quiet printer was a welcome addition to the office.
3. Tom Wilson, Sr., talked with Ms. Mendez from Boston Cards, Inc.
4. Grammar, punctuation, spelling, etc., will be counted on the test.

Checkpoint 6

1. The meeting will end at noon; lunch will be served after the meeting.
2. She planned to leave work early; however, her boss asked her to work late.
3. The seminars will be held in Lexington, Kentucky; Cincinnati, Ohio; and Knoxville, Tennessee.
4. I ordered a printer, a fax machine, and three ink cartridges; but I received only a printer.
5. The quilters chose a variety of block patterns; for example, lone star, log cabin, flying geese, and birds in the air.

Checkpoint 7

1. Each camper will need the following items: a sleeping bag, a pillow, a backpack, and a rain tarp.
2. The game will begin at 1:30 p.m.
3. The copier's special features are these: fast printing speed, reduction mode, and duplexing.
4. The group is well-traveled: they toured Europe last year.
5. This horse is fast: he set a track record.

Checkpoint 8

1. Do you believe that—yes, I guess you do.
2. Bobby Chin—he's the one in the red shirt—is our best player.
3. The park's attractions are these—swimming pools, tennis courts, picnic tables, hiking trails.
4. One key element is missing—money.
5. Dallas, Houston, and San Antonio—all are important markets for us.

Checkpoint 9

1. Watch this station for up-to-the-minute reports.
2. My father-in-law is retired.
3. Margie is the co-coordinator for the project.
4. One-fourth of the building has been painted.
5. Please keep the team up to date on your progress.

Checkpoint 10

1. She asked, "Will you be home early?"
2. Did he say, "I was home alone"?
3. "I agree," said the teacher, "that your work has improved."
4. She wrote the article "The New Math" for the school newspaper.
5. A "hacker" is someone who accesses a computer network without authorization.

Checkpoint 11

1. The vast majority (95 percent of the members) voted to accept the contract.
2. Homonyms are words that sound alike but have different meanings. (See a dictionary for word definitions.)
3. The American Marketing Association (AMA) has thousands of members.
4. On the report title page, include (a) your name, (b) your class, and (c) the date.
5. Refer to Chapter 4 (page 56) to review this information.

Checkpoint 12

1. Last year's rainfall exceeded this year's rainfall.
2. Jamal's plan has the best chance of success.
3. My mother was born in '55.
4. I don't think the children are in school today.
5. The jury's verdict was delivered earlier today.

Checkpoint 13

1. Mr. Brown will meet with Miss Vega.
2. Albert P. Jones, Jr., is the first member to volunteer.
3. Dr. Anna Sanchez is in charge of this case.
4. The patient lives at 6 Elm Avenue.
5. Come to the family reunion, which will be held in Texas.
6. The FBI will review the case.
7. The balance to which I referred earlier in this letter has been paid.
8. Retrieve invoice No. 398, and check the payment date.
9. The merchandise was purchased wholesale.
10. Thank you for agreeing to speak to our group on Monday, December 7.

Checkpoint 14

1. Joe and I left work early.
2. "We hope you will visit us soon," Will said, "after you recover from your illness."
3. On Monday, Alicia will leave for a cruise on the Pacific Ocean.
4. Is Mom home yet?
5. Dr. Roberts and Ms. Thomson are in room 3.
6. The South is having a severe drought.
7. Please turn to page 34 and read about French cuisine.

Checkpoint 15

1. I ordered 15 cartons of paper.
2. The four new employees were assigned network passwords.
3. The box held 4 rulers, 11 notebooks, and 20 rolls of tape.
4. Nan's birthday is April 15.
5. I sent the order to One Maple Street.
6. Lemonade costs 50 cents per cup.
7. The meeting begins at 10 a.m. and will last 2 1/2 hours.
8. She will get 50 percent of the $3 million prize.

Chapter 6 Answers

Checkpoint 1

1. The four steps in planning a message are: identify the objective, determine the message's main idea, choose supporting details, and adjust the message for the receiver.
2. Adjusting the message for the receiver involves putting yourself in the place of the receiver. For example, you should consider the knowledge, experience, and education the receiver has about the subject of the message.

Checkpoint 2

1. When a message has only good news, direct order should be used for the message.
2. When a message has both good news and bad news, direct-indirect order should be used for the message.
3. When a message has only bad news, indirect order should be used for the message.

Checkpoint 3

1. Courteous messages are positive, considerate, and bias-free.
2. Writers should avoid biases related to gender, race, age, and disability.

Checkpoint 4

1. Correct messages are those that do not contain errors or omit important information.
2. Answers will vary. A sample answer is given here.

   If you make an error in a date on a project bid, your company's employees may have to work overtime to complete the project on time.

Checkpoint 5

1. Concise messages are brief and to the point. They do not contain unrelated material that can distract the reader from the important points of the message.
2. A redundant expression is an unnecessary repetition of words. For example, the expression *past history* is redundant because all history is in the past.

Checkpoint 6

1. Clear messages are specific, precise, and complete. They provide all the information needed for receivers to understand the message. They do not contain contradictory information.
2. Answers will vary. A sample answer is given here.

   The copier is fast.

   The copier prints 15 pages per minute for color copies.

Checkpoint 7

1. Complete messages contain all the information needed to achieve the objectives of the sender.
2. Complete business messages should include the five Ws: who, what, where, when, and why.

Checkpoint 8

1. The five stages in the writing process are planning, composing, editing, proofreading, and publishing messages.

2. The purpose of editing a message is to improve it. The writer may check to make sure the message is courteous, correct, concise, clear, and complete.

Checkpoint 9

1. Proofreading differs from editing in that it mainly involves looking for errors or omissions rather than improving writing style or tone.

2. Proofreaders' marks are words and symbols used to mark edits on hard copy documents. The symbols can be written quickly, and they take up very little space.
   The symbols are standard, so you can understand proofreaders' marks made by other people and they can understand yours.

Checkpoint 10

1. Sending an e-mail message, mailing a letter, and posting a page on a Web site are examples of ways to publish a message.

2. Paper of the same quality should not be used for all printed business messages. Letters and other important documents should be printed on high-quality paper to make a good impression on the receiver. Less expensive paper should be used for routine documents, such as memos to coworkers.

Chapter 7 Answers

Checkpoint 1

1. Memos and e-mail are both informal, internal documents. They are different in that memos are sent as printed documents and e-mail messages are sent electronically by computer.

2. E-mail messages are the most commonly used type of document for internal business messages.

3. A letter is more formal than a memo.

Checkpoint 2

1. The purpose for a business message may be to:
   - Promote goodwill
   - Provide a record
   - Advise, direct, or state a policy
   - Inform
   - Request information or reply to requests
   - Persuade

2. Answers will vary. An e-mail might be sent to inform an employee about a change in a meeting date and time.

Checkpoint 3

1. The five Ws that you should consider when planning the details for a message are *who, what, where, when*, and *why*.

2. When the supporting information appears before the main idea in a message, indirect order is being used.

Checkpoint 4

1. A distribution list consists of names of persons to whom a memo is sent. It should be used when a memo is sent to several people.

2. To make the heading for a two-page memo appear only on page 2, suppress the heading on page 1. You may also be able to select an option such as *Different first page* that creates a different header for page 1 (which would be blank).

Checkpoint 5

1. A subject line indicates the topic or main idea of the message. An effective subject line is short, specific, and clear.

2. Selecting names from an address book can reduce errors in addresses on the To line. You can use an address book to create customized e-mail lists to send messages to groups of people.

Checkpoint 6

1. Some companies use IM to communicate with clients, customers, and suppliers. Most often, IM is used at work to communicate with coworkers.

2. The primary IM netiquette rule is to be considerate of others.

Checkpoint 7

1. The standard parts of a letter are the date, letter address, salutation, body, complimentary close, writer's name and title, and reference initials.

2. For a business letter, begin the date at about 2 inches from the top of the page or center the page vertically. Use default side margins.

Checkpoint 8

1. A business letter may include one or more of these optional parts: attention line, reference or subject line, company name, enclosure or attachment notation, copy or blind copy notation, and postscript.

2. A postscript is a sentence or paragraph that reinforces the message of the letter or provides additional information. A postscript is placed at the end of the letter below the last notation.

Checkpoint 9

1. Block and modified block styles are used for business letters.

2. The envelope letter address format recommended by the U.S. Postal Service uses all capital letters and no punctuation. Traditional letter address format uses initial capital letters and punctuation.

Chapter 8 Answers

Checkpoint 1

1. The steps in planning a message are:
   a. Identify the objective.
   b. Identify the main idea.
   c. Determine the supporting details.
   d. Adjust the content to the receiver.

2. Messages with neutral or positive news should be organized in direct order.

Checkpoint 2

1. Two types of letters that contain neutral messages are routine requests and claims.

2. A claim is a message that requests a refund, an exchange, or a discount on merchandise or services.

Checkpoint 3

1. Examples of documents that contain positive messages are orders, positive responses to requests, friendship messages, and acknowledgments.

2. An acknowledgment is a message that tells a sender that a message or item has been received.

Checkpoint 4

1. Messages that deny requests, decline to supply information, refuse credit, or reject a proposal are examples of a negative message.

2. When using indirect order for a negative message, follow these steps:

   a. Begin with a neutral opening.

   b. Explain the reasons for the negative news.

   c. State or imply the negative news.

   d. Close on a positive note; if possible, offer an alternative.

Checkpoint 5

1. Two types of letters that contain negative news are messages that deny a request and messages that refuse credit.

2. A message that contains both positive and negative news should be organized with the positive news in the opening. The positive news is followed by the reasons for the bad news and then the bad news itself.

Checkpoint 6

1. Answers will vary. A letter that tries to convince a customer to buy a product is an example of a persuasive message.

2. The purpose of the supporting details in a persuasive message is to give information that will convince the receiver to do as you request.

Checkpoint 7

1. Most persuasive messages are organized in indirect order.

2. To organize a persuasive message in indirect order, follow these steps:

   a. Gain the reader's attention.

   b. Show the reader that he or she has a need or will benefit from fulfilling the request.

   c. Explain your solution to that need—in other words, your request.

   d. Present the supporting information.

   e. Ask for a specific action.

Checkpoint 8

1. A sales message tries to persuade a potential customer to purchase a product or service.

2. The purpose of a collection message is to persuade a customer to pay a past-due bill.

3. Collection messages have four stages as listed below:

   a. The reminder stage

   b. The strong reminder stage

   c. The discussion stage

   d. The urgency stage

Checkpoint 9

1. A proposal is a formal document that describes a problem and recommends a solution.

2. Most, but not all, proposals contain the following elements:

   a. Introduction

   b. Background

   c. Need

   d. Scope of project

   e. Action plan

   f. Schedule

   g. Cost

   h. Qualifications

   i. Call for action

   j. Supporting information

check point Chapter 9 Answers

Checkpoint 1

1. An informational report presents facts but includes very little analysis.

2. An analytical report analyzes a problem, presents facts and conclusions, and makes recommendations.

Checkpoint 2

1. Seven planning steps for creating a report are:

   a. Identify the problem or topic.

   b. Decide on areas to investigate.

   c. Determine the scope of the report.

   d. Plan ways to gather data.

   e. Collect the data.

   f. Develop a preliminary outline.

   g. Analyze the data, draw conclusions, and make recommendations.

2. Scope refers to the boundaries of the report—what will be included and what will not.

Checkpoint 3

1. Primary research involves gathering new data. Secondary research involves locating data that already have been gathered and reported.

2. Three methods that can be used to do primary research include interviews, surveys, and observations.

3. When using data from secondary sources, ask these questions to help evaluate the information you find:

   - Is the information relevant to the topic or problem?
   - Is the information true and accurate?
   - Is the information reliable? Is it provided by a reputable source?
   - Is the information current or useful?
   - Is the information biased?

Checkpoint 4

1. Five ways the outline for an informational report can be arranged include:

   - Chronological order
   - Order of importance
   - Logical sequence
   - Category
   - Geographical order

2. The outline for an analytical report can be arranged by hypotheses or by alternatives.

3. A discussion outline provides more information about the topics and the subtopics than a topical outline provides.

Checkpoint 5

1. Direct order should be used for a report when the report is routine (a weekly sales report, for example) or when the reader is expected to respond favorably.

2. Indirect order should be used for a report when you expect an unfavorable response or when the receiver may need persuasion to accept the main idea.

Checkpoint 6

1. Informal reports usually are written in a relatively personal style. Personal pronouns and contractions are often used in this style.

2. An impersonal writing style should be used if a report is about a serious problem or if it is going to a senior manager.

3. An impersonal writing style makes a report seem more objective than a personal writing style.

Checkpoint 7

1. Informal reports have three main parts: the opening, the body, and the closing.

2. For informal short reports written in direct order, the opening may include the following information:

   - The subject and purpose of the report (the reason the report is important)
   - Recommendations
   - A preview of the sections of the report
   - The summary of findings or the conclusions

Checkpoint 8

1. Formal reports, rather than informal reports, are used only when absolutely necessary because of the amount of time required to write formal reports.

2. Formal reports usually are written in an impersonal style because these reports need to sound impartial and professional.

Checkpoint 9

1. Preliminary report parts include a letter or memo of transmittal, a title page, a table of contents, and an executive summary. They are placed before the report body.

2. A bibliography and an appendix are supplementary parts that follow the report body.

Chapter 10 Answers

Checkpoint 1

1. Using graphics and other visual aids in the communication process is important because visual aids help readers and listeners understand and remember information.

2. Examples of visual aids include objects, pictures, drawings, maps, posters, and charts.

Checkpoint 2

1. When placing a graphic in the body of a document, place the graphic on the same page as its reference, if possible. When that placement is not possible, place the graphic on the next page following its first reference.

2. A numbering system, titles, and source lines can be used to identify or provide information about graphics in a document.

Checkpoint 3

1. An organization chart shows lines of authority and relationships among employees in a company.

2. A map shows geographic regions such as cities, states, or countries.

3. A flowchart shows the steps in a procedure or process.

Checkpoint 4

1. Tables are a valuable visual aid in reports and other documents because they show data in a way that is easy to understand.

2. Tables can be created in word processing or spreadsheet programs.

3. The goal is to use a format for the table that makes the data easy to read and understand.

Checkpoint 5

1. An organization chart shows the relationships of employees, positions, and departments. It shows lines of authority and communication in a company.

2. The purpose of a flowchart is to show a step-by-step diagram of a procedure or process.

3. When you make a pie chart, arrange the data in some logical order. For example, by company department, by regions, or by amounts (highest to lowest).

Checkpoint 6

1. A line chart shows show ups and downs or trends over a period of time.

2. In a bar chart, bars extend from left to right. Items or categories being compared are placed on the vertical axis. Values are placed on the horizontal axis. In a column chart, columns extend vertically from the bottom to the top of the chart. Items or categories being compared are placed on the horizontal axis. Values are placed on the vertical axis.

Checkpoint 7

1. A map shows geographic relationships.

2. A photograph is used to provide a realistic view of a specific item or place.

3. A drawing is useful for showing details or a procedure that cannot be shown in a photograph.

 Chapter 11 Answers

Checkpoint 1

1. The purpose of both instructions and manuals is to provide the guidance readers need to carry out tasks.

2. Effective instructions include the following parts:
   a. A clear and specific title
   b. An introduction and a list of any needed tools, equipment, and materials
   c. Numbered steps in sequential order
   d. A conclusion

Checkpoint 2

1. The following guidelines apply to all types of technical writing.
   • Be specific and precise.
   • Use language the readers will understand.
   • Be objective.

2. When writing instructions, put the steps in sequential order—the order in which they should be completed.

Checkpoint 3

1. An effective manual should have the following parts:
   a. A clear and specific title
   b. A detailed table of contents
   c. An introduction
   d. Logical divisions of material, such as sections or chapters
   e. Clear and complete steps in correct order in each section or chapter
   f. Figures and illustrations, as needed
   g. A glossary of terms, if needed

   h. An appendix for supplementary material, if needed
   i. An index (usually needed only for long manuals)

2. A glossary is a list of terms and abbreviations with definitions. An index is a detailed listing of the topics and subtopics the manual covers.

Checkpoint 4

1. A set of instructions explains how to perform a task. A process description explains how something happens.

2. A mechanism is a type of object that consists of parts working together to perform one or more tasks. A mechanism can be as simple as a pencil sharpener or as complex as a computer.

Checkpoint 5

1. Formal descriptions usually include the following parts:
   • Title
   • Introduction and overview
   • Part-by part description (body)
   • Conclusion

2. In the body, describe each part of the object separately. Explain each part's appearance and function. Describe any subparts as necessary. List the parts in a logical sequence.

Checkpoint 6

1. Most process descriptions include these parts:
   • Title
   • Introduction and overview
   • Part-by part description (body)
   • Conclusion

2. In the body, describe the process in order. If the process occurs in a continuous cycle, begin with a major step. If the process is lengthy, each step might have its own subheading. Relationships between the steps should be explained. Illustrations that would be helpful to the reader should be included.

Chapter 12 Answers

Checkpoint 1

1. In general, technology benefits workers by making work faster, easier, or safer. For example, a dishwashing machine makes cleaning dirty dishes easy. Using a router makes building a set of kitchen cabinets faster.

2. Four types of personal computers are listed below.
   • A desktop computer is a personal computer that fits on a desk but is too large to carry easily from place to place. It is designed for use in an office or at home.
   • A laptop computer is a portable personal computer that is small enough to sit on your lap. Laptops typically weigh from

2 to 7 pounds and also are known as *notebooks*. They have the same uses as a desktop computer.

- A tablet is a portable personal computer that allows users to enter text by handwriting. Otherwise, tablets offer the same features as other personal computers.

- A handheld computer, also called a palmtop, weighs a pound or less and fits in the palm of your hand. As on a tablet, you use a digital pen or your finger to navigate or make selections; and you can handwrite data.

Checkpoint 2

1. Three general types of computer software are listed below.

   - Operating system software performs the computer's most basic operations. It handles the transfer of data and files; controls equipment such as the keyboard, monitor, and printer; and manages other software on the computer.

   - Application software is used to perform work tasks. For example, word processing, database, and spreadsheet programs are application software.

   - Utility software is used to manage and secure data on a computer. For example, virus protection software and backup software are utility programs.

2. Operating system software manages and allows you to use all the other software on the computer.

Checkpoint 3

1. Computer files can be saved on an internal hard drive or on CDs, DVDs, and flash memory devices.

2. Using folders is a good way to keep files organized. You could create a folder for each topic to which your files relate. More folders can be created within the main folders to organize files further. You can use meaningful names for your files and be consistent in how you name files.

Checkpoint 4

1. Two types of printers commonly used at work are ink jet printers and laser printers.

2. The purpose of a scanner is to create an electronic image of a page or other printed item. Three types of scanners commonly used at home or work are flatbed scanners, sheetfed scanners, and pen scanners.

3. The purpose of a fax machine is to send or receive an electronic image of a document. A fax can also be sent using a computer with a fax modem or by using an Internet fax service.

Checkpoint 5

1. WANs, LANs, and PANs are all types of computer networks. They differ in the area covered. A WAN connects computers and devices that are great distances apart, such as in different cities. A LAN connects computers and devices that are closer together, such as in one city. A PAN connects computers and devices that are close together, such as in a home or other building.

2. Many people use the Internet on the job for purposes such as the following:

- Send e-mail or instant messages

- Do research

- Purchase products or services

- Get help for using products

- Make travel reservations

- Take courses or classes

Checkpoint 6

1. Four types of programs that can pose a security threat to computers or networks are computer viruses, worms, Trojan horses, and spyware.

2. A firewall is hardware and/or software that restricts access to a network by outsiders. Firewalls can protect against computer viruses and other dangers files.

Checkpoint 7

1. Factors should you consider when choosing how to send a document include:

   - Speed. When does the recipient need the document?

   - Cost. How much will this method of sending the document cost?

   - Need. Consider the recipient's preferences and needs.

   - Security. Fax and e-mail are less secure than other methods of transmittal.

   - Format. Fax or physical delivery is a good choice when the format of the document must stay the same.

2. The purpose of a pager is to alert receivers that they have messages.

3. The purpose of a voice mail system is to allow a caller to leave a recorded message if the receiver is not available when the call comes in.

Checkpoint 8

1. A smart phone adds the features of a handheld computer to a cell phone. Smart phones are more expensive than other cell phones.

2. With VoIP, phone calls go through a high-speed Internet connection rather than a conventional phone line. VoIP is often less expensive than traditional phone service.

Checkpoint 9

1. Advantages of using a digital camera over using a traditional film camera include no film processing fee, images that are available for use instantly, and images that can be used in computer files.

2. A GPS unit can be helpful to users by allowing them to:

   - Determine exactly where they are located

   - Plot the most efficient route for a trip and instantly update directions

   - Identify popular local spots, such as restaurants, hotels, and gas stations

Checkpoint 10

1. A teleconference and a video conference both allow people at distant locations to meet electronically. In a teleconference, participants can hear one another. In a video conference, participants can hear and see one another.

2. Five technologies that may be used to deliver training to employees include:

   - Computer-based training
   - Mobile learning
   - Online training
   - Training videos
   - Training conferences

Checkpoint 11

1. Causes of work-related injuries in offices include:

   - Falls from improper use of stools and ladders and unstable office chairs
   - Strains from heavy lifting and repetitive motion tasks
   - Crushing injuries from being struck by objects or caught between objects such as filing cabinets
   - Burns from fires, spilled hot liquids, and toxic chemicals
   - Shocks from electrical equipment
   - Tripping over cables, cords, or open file drawers
   - Eye strain from poor lighting
   - Tension and stress from noise
   - Respiratory problems due to noxious gases or fumes given off by machines (photocopying chemicals)
   - Cuts or punctures from improper use of tools such as paper cutters, scissors, shredders, and electronic hole punches
   - Injuries caused by irrational or malicious behavior of coworkers or others

   (Students are to list five causes.)

2. Actions of a safety-conscious worker include:

   - Read and follow all safety warnings and procedures related to work.
   - Wear safety gear or clothing as required.
   - Use tools and devices for approved purposes.
   - Do not take shortcuts that may compromise safety to save time.
   - Keep work areas free of scraps, trash, or other objects that may cause a hazard.
   - Take precautions to see that clothing and jewelry worn at work do not become entangled in equipment.
   - Know where fire extinguishers and first-aid kits are located.
   - Know whom to call when an accident or emergency happens.
   - Know where emergency plans are located and how to follow them.

   (Students are to list five actions.)

Checkpoint 12

1. Ergonomics is the study of the relationship between people and their working environment. Its aim is to make it easier and safer for people to use tools and other objects.

2. Two health and safety issues associated with computer use are repetitive strain injuries and vision problems.

   - Repetitive stress injury happens when the same action is performed repeatedly. Symptoms of RSI include pain, numbness, swelling, and loss of flexibility or strength. RSI can cause damage to muscles, nerves, tendons, and other soft tissues.
   - Computer users may experience eye strain and related vision problems, sometimes called computer vision syndrome (CVS). Some symptoms of CVS are pain, discomfort, or fatigue in the eye area; blurred vision; and sensitivity to light. Headaches, neck aches, backaches, and muscle spasms may also occur.

Checkpoint 13

1. To work safely and comfortably at a desktop computer, arrange your work area properly. Do warm-up exercises and use the proper keyboarding position. Take frequent breaks to rest your body.

2. One warm-up exercise you might do is: Clench your fingers briefly and then extend them, relaxing the muscles. Repeat several times. (Exercise descriptions will vary.)

check point **Chapter 13 Answers**

Checkpoint 1

1. When introducing a speaker, your purpose is to prepare the audience to accept the speaker and the speech.

2. A briefing is a short presentation given to bring people up to date on business activities, projects, programs, or procedures. Briefings are usually given at a meeting or a conference.

Checkpoint 2

1. The following steps are involved in preparing for a formal presentation.

   a. Determine the objective of your speech.
   b. Analyze the audience.
   c. Determine the time available for the speech.
   d. Gather information for the speech.
   e. Determine the appropriate mode of delivery.

2. Talking from notes is the most effective mode of delivery for a formal speech. This method engages the audience and allows you to make eye contact with listeners. In addition, it allows you to observe your audience's reactions and to adjust your remarks accordingly.

Checkpoint 3

1. Voice qualities and other nonverbal symbols are important when delivering a speech because they create an impression of the speaker. They may make the speaker seem confident and competent or nervous and unsure of the topic. Speakers that seem confident and competent are more likely to achieve the goals of the presentation.

2. Getting audience feedback on a presentation is important in determining whether the audience has understood or accepted your message.

Checkpoint 4

1. Visual aids that may be used in a presentation include:

   • Posters

   • Flip charts

   • Transparencies

   • Slides

   • Computer presentations

   • Objects

   • Chalkboards or whiteboards

   • Electronic whiteboards

   • Handouts

   (Students are to list five aids.)

2. Handouts are useful for providing detailed information to audience members.

Checkpoint 5

1. When planning visuals for a speech, you should consider the equipment available, audience needs, and preparation time.

2. The size of the audience determines, in part, which visual aids can be used effectively. If you will be speaking to a small group, a poster or flip chart might be appropriate. For larger audiences, slides, transparencies, or a computer presentation may be required.

Checkpoint 6

1. You should not use so many visual aids that your audience gets overwhelmed with them or so few that your audience gets bored. As a general rule, present a new visual about every two minutes.

2. Set up your visual aids in the front of the room in which you will be making your presentation. Then sit in a back seat in the room. If you can comfortably see everything (text, pictures, labels on graphics, objects, etc.), your visual aids are fine. If you have to strain to see anything, redo the visual aids so everyone in the audience will be able to see them.

Checkpoint 7

1. It is important to make sure all the equipment you will use is working properly well before you begin the speech because delays can result if the equipment is not working. Audience members may lose interest and even leave the session if they must wait while you try to get equipment working. If you must spend several minutes to get the equipment working, you may not have enough time remaining to present all the points in your speech as planned.

2. Face the audience when using your visual aids. Audience members prefer to see the front of you. Also, when you speak, the audience can hear you better when you are facing them rather than a screen.

Checkpoint 8

1. An ad hoc committee is a temporary group that is formed to accomplish a specific task. A standing committee is a permanent part of the organization and meets regularly to address some issue or task.

2. An agenda and minutes are two documents associated with planning and follow-up for meetings.

Checkpoint 9

1. There are several steps you can take to prepare before a meeting, as listed below.

   • When you receive the agenda for the meeting, review it carefully.

   • Write down any questions you would like to ask at the meeting.

   • If you need some background on an agenda item, do research to educate yourself.

   • Read any attachments to the agenda.

   • If a meeting has been called to make a decision, be ready to support your point of view.

2. Groupthink occurs when the members of a group tend to suppress their own ideas. They desire agreement about quality decisions. Groupthink can prevent meetings from being productive because members do not offer new ideas or solutions for problems.

Checkpoint 10

1. Details or tasks that must be handled to organize a successful meeting include:

   • Schedule for convenience

   • Create an agenda

   • Select an appropriate site

   • Arrange the furniture

   • Secure equipment and supplies

   • Provide for the comfort of those attending

2. One strategy is to offer a selection of dates and times. Ask people to indicate which two or three dates would be best for them. Some companies have calendaring software that makes employees' schedules and appointments available to coworkers. Coworkers can look at the schedules of the people they want to attend a meeting to see when people are free. This method is very helpful in selecting two or three possible dates for a meeting.

Checkpoint 11

Checkpoint 11

1. Use the agenda to ensure that topics are discussed in order and within the time allotted. As each agenda item is dispensed with, summarize points of agreement and disagreement. Outline any actions that will be taken.

2. If you think a difficult person has a legitimate concern, ask questions to try to identify the problem. Be respectful, listen actively, and keep an open mind. If the behavior persists, keep your composure. Do not respond to the person's arguments point for point. Use the agenda or a technical point to move the discussion to another topic.

check point Chapter 14 Answers

Checkpoint 1

1. Providing quality customer service is important for businesses because it helps businesses retain customers. Without sales to customers, many companies could not stay in business.

2. External customers are people (or companies) outside the organization to whom products or services are provided. Internal customers are people inside the organization to whom products or services are provided.

Checkpoint 2

1. A company that has a strong customer service culture makes customer service a priority. The company's policies make it easy for employees to satisfy customers. Employees are allowed to use their own initiative in solving customer problems and are rewarded for doing so.

2. A customer contact is any meeting or communication you have with a customer. Talking with a customer in person and answering e-mail messages are examples of customer contact.

Checkpoint 3

1. To make a good first impression on customers, give customers prompt attention and greet customers cheerfully.

2. Five things you can do to provide quality customer service are:
    *   Be courteous.
    *   Listen carefully to customers.
    *   Make sure the customer understands you.
    *   Determine the customer's needs.
    *   Deal with customers ethically.

Checkpoint 4

1. Follow these steps to resolve a customer's complaint:
    a. Make sure you understand the complaint.
    b. If an apology is in order, offer one.
    c. If an error was made, assure the customer that you will correct the error and explain how.
    d. If no error was made, try to close the conversation on a positive note.

2. To deal with a difficult customer, begin by trying to identify the problem. Use your best listening skills and show empathy and respect. Recognize that the customer may be emotional or irrational for reasons you know nothing about. Do not show anger. Remain professional and do not take the customer's criticisms and attitude personally.

Checkpoint 5

1. Pitch, volume, and tone are three voice qualities that can affect communication.

2. Saying "zink" instead of "sink" is an example of incorrect pronunciation. Saying "hafta" instead of "have to" is an example of poor enunciation.

Checkpoint 6

1. The five parts of a conversation are the greeting, introduction, exchange, summary, and closing.

2. The main ideas are shared in the exchange part of a conversation.

Checkpoint 7

1. Guidelines you can follow for successful face-to-face communication with customers and others include:
    *   Relax.
    *   Think before you speak.
    *   Listen carefully and actively.
    *   Use names.
    *   Make eye contact.
    *   Use a pleasant tone of voice.
    *   Be honest and sincere.

2. Making eye contact is important because it shows that you are paying attention to what a speaker is saying. It also helps you and the speaker focus on the conversation rather than on nearby distractions.

Checkpoint 8

1. Listening carefully, paying attention to nonverbal cues, speaking clearly, being courteous, and learning to handle difficult callers are strategies you can use for effective telephone communication.

2. Follow these guidelines to deal with difficult callers:
    *   Speak with a friendly and courteous tone.
    *   Try to identify the reason that the caller is angry or upset.
    *   Tell the caller how you can help remedy the situation if that is appropriate.
    *   Transfer the caller to someone else in the company who can provide help if appropriate.
    *   If the caller becomes abusive or uses profanity, end the call quickly. Offer to help the caller at a later time when he or she has calmed down.
    *   Inform your supervisor or follow your company's procedures regarding keeping a record of abusive calls.

Checkpoint 9

1. Planning an outgoing call involves these steps:

   - Identify the objective of the call.

   - Decide on a direct or indirect approach for the message.

   - Consider the needs, background, experience, and culture of the recipient.

   - Make a list of the points you want to discuss during the call.

   - Consider the time zone for the location you are calling.

2. These steps are involved in leaving an effective voice mail message:

   - Greet the recipient.

   - Identify yourself. If you are calling someone outside your company, identify your company.

   - Briefly state your purpose for calling.

   - Explain how the recipient may contact you.

   - Close the message in a friendly manner.

Checkpoint 10

1. An effective voice mail greeting includes the following elements:

   - Your name

   - A statement explaining that you are not available to take the call

   - Clear, specific instructions on how to leave a message

   - A statement telling when the call may be returned

2. A telephone message should contain the following pieces of information:

   - Name and organization of the caller

   - Telephone number and extension of the caller

   - Date and time of the call

   - An appropriate message

   - Your initials or name as the message taker

3. Screening incoming calls is a procedure used to learn who is calling and sometimes the reason for the call.

check point Chapter 15 Answers

Checkpoint 1

1. A job search is the process of finding job openings and applying for jobs.

2. Thinking about your personal goals will clarify what is important to you. Prioritizing your career goals and comparing the list to your list of personal goals will help you understand what you want from life and work.

Checkpoint 2

1. When listing your qualifications for a job, consider work experience, volunteer experience, skills, education, and personal traits.

2. A career portfolio is a computer file, file folder, notebook, or small briefcase containing samples of your work, transcripts, letters of recommendation, and other related items that you can use to demonstrate your job qualifications to an employer.

Checkpoint 3

1. Ways a person could learn about job openings include:

   - Ask for information at school placement offices

   - Check with personal contacts in your job search network

   - Look in newspapers and professional magazines

   - Search the Internet

   - Use employment agencies

2. Types of information you should try to learn about a prospective employer include:

   - Organization identification

   - Organization classification

   - Organization activities

   - Organization size

   - Location of facilities

Checkpoint 4

1. A resume typically includes information such as:

   - Contact information

   - Job objective

   - Special qualifications

   - Education

   - Experience

   - Activities, interests, and achievements

2. A resume organized in functional order presents your accomplishments or skills listed in order of their importance. The most important or impressive skills are listed first. This technique emphasizes your strengths. A resume organized in reverse chronological order presents the most recent work experience first and works backward to earlier jobs.

Checkpoint 5

1. Three types of resumes that may be used in addition to or instead of a traditional print resume are a scannable resume, an electronic resume, and a Web resume.

2. Advantages of using a Web resume include:

   - The resume does not need to be limited to one page.

   - The resume may use links to other screens, such as those in a career portfolio.

- The resume can support stylish elements, such as sound clips, animation, graphics, and video clips.

Checkpoint 6

1. Two types of application letters are solicited letters and unsolicited letters. A solicited letter of application is written to apply for a specific job opening that has been announced or advertised. An unsolicited letter of application is written to apply for a position that has not been advertised or announced and may or may not be open.

2. An application letter has three basic parts: an opening, a body, and a closing. The opening paragraph should indicate that you are applying for a position, name the position, and tell how you learned of the opening (solicited letter) or identify your abilities (unsolicited letter). The paragraphs in the body should discuss your education, experience, and other qualifications for the job. The closing paragraph should have a confident tone, ask for an interview, and tell how you can be reached.

Checkpoint 7

1. An application form is a document provided by an employer that you complete. It gives your contact information, education, work history, and other information.

2. An employer can use application forms to compare the qualifications of different job applicants. Some employers use computers to read and store completed application forms. Applications can be searched by the computer when the employer is seeking candidates with particular skills. Qualified applicants may be invited for an interview.

Checkpoint 8

1. Job interviews allow an employer to talk with job applicants to determine if they are qualified for the position and if they are a good fit for the company. As a job applicant, you can use the interview as an opportunity to determine if you want to work for a particular company.

2. Before the interview, find out information about the company. Review the research you conducted before applying for the job and fill in any gaps. You should also think about questions that may be asked and prepare questions you want to ask.

Checkpoint 9

1. The purpose of a follow-up letter is to thank the interviewer and indicate your continued interest in the job, if that is the case.

2. An acceptance letter is written to accept a job offer. A rejection letter is written to decline a job offer.

Index

A

abbreviations, 143, 161
   commas, 148
   informal use in e-mail messages, 234
   miscellaneous, 163
   parentheses, 157
absolute adjectives, 121
abstract, 341
acceptance letter, 608
accessibility, 532
achievements, 584–585
acknowledgments, 271
acronyms, 47
action plan, 297
action verbs, 108, 123
active listening, 80
active voice, 125, 188, 196
activities, 584–585
ad hoc committee, 504
address book, 229, 231
address format for business envelopes, 246
adjectives, 106, 119–121
   articles, 119–120
   modifying, 128–129
   renaming, 109
   using comma between, 147
Adobe Photoshop, 372
advanced searches, 318
adverbs, 106, 128–129
affirmative action coordinator, 42
agendas, 213, 505–506
   creation, 516
   usage, 518
agreement in number, 126
alternative, 322
alternative resumes
   electronic resumes, 587
   scannable print resumes, 586–587
   Web resumes, 589
analytical reports, 312
analyzing data, 324–325
anecdotes, 485
animation, 495
antecedents, 117–118
anti-spyware programs, 447
anti-virus programs, 447

apology, 541
apostrophes, 142, 158–159
appendix, 341, 352–353
   manuals, 401, 404–405
   visual aids, 365–366
application forms, 597–598
application letters, 592–594
applications, 431
   electronic format, 200
appositives and dashes, 153
area charts, 377
articles, 119–120
assumptions, 83
attention-getters, 485
attention line, 243
attitudes about speaker and topic, 82–83
attorney-client privilege, 55
audience analysis, 12–13
audience profile, 12–13

B

backing up files, 433
backup software, 431
bar charts, 369–370, 378
bar graphs. *See* bar charts
barriers to effective listening, 82–83
Better Business Bureau (BBB), 270
bias-free words, 184–185
bibliography, 341
bibliography notes, 319–320
blind carbon copy (Bcc), 229–230, 233
blind copy notation, 225
block letter example, 240
block letter format, 246
blogs, 535
Bluetooth, 443
body
   e-mail messages, 228
   letters, 242
   memos, 222–223
   presentations, 486
body language, 41, 70–71, 512
Boolean operators, 318
brainstorming, 514
briefings, 481
buddy list, 235

bulleted lists, 223, 242
business communication, 6
   direction, 8
   ethics, 52–59
   formal communication, 7
   honesty, 53–54
   informal communication, 7
   oral communication, 9
   written communication, 8
business correspondence
   e-mails, 210–211
   letters, 211–212
   memos, 210–211
   other documents, 213
business documents, 213
   advising or directing employees, 214
   explaining procedures, 214
   informing, 215
   recording events, 214
   stating policy, 214
business envelopes, 246–248
business letters, 211–212
   block letter format, 246
   folding, 248
   modified block format, 246
   optional parts, 243–245
   postscripts, 245
business messages
   empty phrases, 188
   goodwill, 176, 182
   persuading, 215
   promoting goodwill, 216
   purpose, 258
   redundancies, 188
   supporting details, 186
   unnecessary elements, 187–188
Business NewsBank, 575
Business Periodicals Index, 316, 575
businesses, ethical guidelines, 52
Business.Gov web site, 55
buyers and sellers, disputes between, 270

C

call for action, 298
capitalization, 163–164
carbon copy (Cc), 229–230, 233

career goals, 568–569, 583
career portfolio, 571–572
CareerBuilder.com, 573
careful reading, 23, 411
casual listening, 80
category axis, 369
CD-ROM collections, 382
cell phones, 14
    camera, 452
    candy bar phone, 451
    carriers, 451
    clamshell, 451
    contracts, 453
    courtesy and safety, 454–455
    features, 451–453
    flip phone, 451
    headset, 452
    Internet access, 452
    slider, 451
    smart phones, 453–454
    swivel, 451
cells, 451
Center for Immigration Studies, 36
chain letters, 296
chalkboards, 496
challenger, 94
channels, 5, 15
charts, 370, 373
    area charts, 377
    bar charts, 378
    category axis, 369
    column charts, 378
    comparison over time, 369
    flowcharts, 375
    landscape orientation, 375
    legend, 369, 376
    line charts, 377
    misleading, 380
    numerical data, 223
    organization charts, 374
    pie charts, 376
    portrait orientation, 375
    reading, 369
    spreadsheet programs, 372
    statistical information, 223
    value axis, 369
chat window, 236
The Chicago Manual of Style, 338
claims, 263
clauses, 109, 111
clear messages, 188–189
clip art, 366–367, 372–373, 383
ClipArt&More 3.5Million, 382
closed climate, 11
closing paragraphs, 190
closings
    acknowledgments, 271
    claims, 263
    conversation, 547
    friendship messages, 270
    goodwill, 278
    ineffectively written, 279

negative messages, 278–279
offering receiver another option, 278
orders, 264
outgoing calls, 554
positive messages, 264
positive responses, 267
presentations, 486
routine requests, 260
sincere tone, 278
soft sell, 279
well-written, 279
code of ethics, 52
collaborate, 514
collection messages, 293, 295
collective nouns, 115
colons, 151–152, 156
color printers, 437
columns, 373
commas, 142, 145–148
committees, 91–92
common nouns, 114
communication, 4
    downward, 8
    effective, 45–50
    formal, 7
    horizontal, 8
    informal, 7
    lateral, 8
    oral, 9
    purposes of, 6–7
    upward, 8
    voice, 544–545
    written, 8
communication barriers, 11, 40–41
communication process, 4–5
compact disks (CDs), 434
companies, guidelines for dealing with
        clients and coworkers, 49
comparative degree, 120–121
complaints, resolving effectively, 540–541
complete information, 179
complete messages, 189–190
complete paragraphs, 190
complete predicates, 107–108
complete sentences, 109, 143
complete subject, 107
complex sentences, 112
complimentary close, 242
compound adjectives, 120, 154
compound antecedents, 118
compound-complex sentence, 112
compound nouns, 114
compound plural nouns, 115
compound predicates, 108
compound pronouns, 116
compound sentences, 112, 145
compound subjects, 107, 127
compound words, 154
compressing files, 435
computer-based training, 459
computer presentations, 494–495
computer software, 372–373, 430–432

computer viruses, 445
computer vision syndrome (CVS), 465
computers, 426
    desktop computers, 427
    handheld computers, 428–430
    hardware, 426
    laptop computers, 427
    microprocessors, 426
    tablet computers, 428
    unauthorized access, 446
    unethical use, 451
    use and ergonomics, 464–465
concise messages, 187–188
conclusions, 325, 350
condition linking verbs, 123
conference technologies, 458
conferences and listening, 87
confidence, 74
confidential information, 9, 55
    customer interaction, 539
    keeping secure, 90
    medical information, 54
    minutes, 508
    protecting, 56
    reports, 331
conflicts, 90
conjunctions, 106, 131, 147
conjunctive adverbs, 112, 129
Consumer Reports, 452
contact information, 580
contacts list and instant messaging (IM), 235
content errors, 194
contractions, 158–159
contracts, dates and money amounts, 186
contradictory information, 189
conversations, 546–547
coordinate conjunctions, 112, 131
    preceding with comma, 145
    semicolons, 150
copy notation, 225
copyrights, 58, 320
Corel Quattro Pro, 431
CorelDRAW Graphics Suite, 372
correct messages, 186
correlative conjunctions, 131
correspondence, 214–216
court records, 55
courteous messages
    bias-free words, 184–185
    disability bias, 185
    gender bias, 184
    neutral words, 184–185
    positive words, 182–183
    proper titles, 183–184
    race and age bias, 185
courteous request, 142
cover letters, 592
coworkers, 90
credibility, 535
credit refusal, 280
critical listening, 81
cross-cultural communication, 46–48

cultural differences, 40
    body language, 41
    coworkers, 90
    customs, 43
    etiquette, 43
    nonverbal symbols, 41
    personal space, 42
    small group, 87
cultures, 35
    assumptions about, 47–48
    different use of time, 54
    establishing need, 290
    facial expressions and gestures, 71
    nonverbal communication, 46
    nonverbal symbols, 70
    soft sell in closing of letter, 259
    times and places for discussing
        business, 14
customer interaction
    confidentiality, 539
    courteousness, 537
    determining customer's needs, 538
    ethically dealing with customers,
        538–539
    first impressions, 535–536
    greeting cheerfully, 536
    listening carefully, 537–538
    making sure customer understands
        you, 538
    prompt attention, 536
    quality service, 537–539
customer relationships, 91
customer service, 22
    apology, 541
    difficult customers, 542
    fair reason for refusal, 540
    importance, 530
    matching solution to problem, 541
    refusing requests gracefully, 539–540
    resolving complaints, 540–541
customer service culture
    accessibility, 532
    customer contact, 532–534
    effective use of e-mail, 533
    knowledgeable responses, 532
    policies and procedures, 531–532
customers
    accessibility, 532
    carefully listening to, 537–538
    contact with, 532–534
    dealing effectively with difficult, 542
    e-mails, 533
    external, 530
    eye contact, 536
    internal, 530
    nonverbal cues, 537
    retaining, 530
    satisfied, 535
    strategies to attract, 530
    treating as individuals, 538
    unhappy, 535
customs, 43

D

dashes, 142, 153
data
    analyzing, 324–325
    bias, 319
    collecting for reports, 315–321
    drawing conclusions, 325
    evaluating sources, 319
    organizing, 325
    primary research, 315
    searching online, 318
    secondary research, 316–320
data recovery programs, 447
database services, 316
database software, 431
Date line in memos, 221
dates and letters, 239
dBase Plus, 431
decision making, 22
decision-making meetings, 511, 514
declarative sentences, 142
delegating work, 514
demographics, 483
demonstrative pronouns, 116–117
denying request, 280
dependent clauses, 109, 111–112, 157
descriptions, 407–409
developmental paragraphs, 190
difficult callers, 552
Digital Age, 19
digital cameras, 382, 456
digital information, 19
digital video disks (DVDs), 434
direct-indirect order, 180
direct objects, 108
direct order, 179–180, 217
    formal reports, 338
    informal reports, 327–328, 331
    meetings, 514
    presentations, 486
direct questions, 143
direct quotation and capitalization, 163
disability bias, 185
discrimination, 35, 49–50, 185
discussion format, 323
discussion-stage collection message, 295
distribution list, 220–221
diverse workforce, 34
diversity
    benefits, 34–35
    challenges, 35
    overview, 34–35
    population predictions, 36
    terms related to, 35
    trends, 36–37
    workforce, 36–38
divided focus, 83
docking station, 469
document storage, 439
document transmittal, 448
documentation, 319–320

documents
    appendix, 365–366
    body, 365, 366
    default margins, 200
    formatting guidelines, 200
    meetings, 505–508
    referencing graphics, 365–366
    visual aids usage, 365–368
doer, 94
downward communication, 8
drawings, 370, 383

E

e-mail, 56, 210–211
    address book, 231
    attachments, 224, 232, 446, 448, 505
    body, 230–231
    Cc and Bcc lines, 229–230
    Date line, 230
    draft, 232
    effective use of, 533
    Forward feature, 233
    From line, 230
    To line, 228–229
    netiquette, 233–234
    priority, 233
    proper order, 216–217
    Reply and Reply All, 233
    return receipt feature, 233
    sensitive or confidential data, 198
    signature file, 231
    spelling checker, 232
    Subject line, 230
    work-friendly features, 231–233
e-mail addresses, 229, 231
e-mail lists, 231
e-mail software, 231, 431
editing
    memos, 226
    messages, 192–193
education, 570, 583
effective communication
    cross-cultural communication, 46–48
    fairness, 49–50
    professional attitude, 45
    sensitivity, 49–50
    strategies, 45–50
effective instructions, 394–397
effective manuals, 401–405
effective messages, 182
EffectiveMeetings.com Web site, 519
electronic resumes, 587
electronic rights, 56
electronic slides, 373, 495
electronic whiteboards, 496
emergency plans, 464
emoticons
    business e-mails, 234
    instant messaging (IM), 237
empathy, 177
emphatic listening, 81

employee and manager relationships, 89–90
employees
    honesty with clients, 54
    managing challenging situations, 539–542
    refusing requests gracefully, 539–540
employment agencies, 574
empty phrases, 188
enclosure notation, 224
English as second language
    visual aids, 365
enthusiasm, 75
enunciation, 545
Envelope feature, 246–247
environment, 77
environmental distractions, 83
Equal Employment Opportunity (EEO)
        officer, 42
equipment and ergonomics, 469–470
ergonomics
    arranging work area, 466
    computer use and, 464–465
    equipment, 469–470
    ergonomic keyboards, 469
    footrest, 470
    frequent breaks, 468
    keyboard tray, 470
    laptop computers, 469
    mouse, 470
    padded wrist rests, 469
    pointing devices, 470
    proper keying position, 467
    repetitive stress injuries (RSI), 465
    tablets, 469
    vision problems, 465, 468
    warm-up exercises, 467
    workstations, 465–470
ethics
    clip art use without permission, 366
    communicating in ethical way, 53–58
    confidential information, 54–56
    copyright, 58
    electronic rights, 56
    fair and honest dealing with claims, 263
    fair use, 58
    honesty, 53–54
    personal, 52
    plagiarism, 57–58
    privacy, 56
    protecting confidential information, 9
    sexual harassment, 71
    shared principles, 52
    tactful, honest response, 276
    truthful resumes, 585
Ethics (features)
    chain letters, 296
    charts that mislead, 380
    computer and networks use, 451
    providing complete information, 179
    truth on the web, 535

ethnicity, 35, 165
etiquette, 43
Eudora, 228
evaluative listening, 81
exchange, 546, 554
exclamation points, 142, 144, 156
executive summary, 341, 345
experience, 570, 583–584
external barriers, 11, 16
external customers, 530, 536
external hard drives, 433
external marks, 142
eye contact, 71, 76, 484
    customers, 536
    face-to-face communication, 549
    oral presentations, 488
eyes, 71

F
face-to-face communication
    eye contact, 549
    guidelines for success, 548–549
    honesty and sincerity, 549
    listening carefully and actively, 549
    names, 549
    parts of conversation, 546–547
    pleasant tone of voice, 549
    relaxing, 548
    thinking before you speak, 548
    voice, 544
facial expressions, 70
    cultures, 71
    oral presentations, 488
facts, 277
fair use, 58
fairness, 49–50
falls, 463
favorable messages, 179
fax machines, 440–441, 448
Federal Trade Commission (FTC), 448, 558
feedback, 5
    oral presentations, 489–490
    seeking, 15
    sender, 17
feminine nouns, 117
feminine pronouns, 117
file compression software, 435
file formats, 439
file management, 435–436
FileMaker Pro, 431
files
    backing up, 433, 446
    compression, 435
    meaningful names, 436
    organizing, 433, 435–436
    saving, 433
    storage options, 433–434
film slides, 495
financial companies, 55
findings and analysis, 347–349
firewall, 447

Fireworks, 372
first impressions, 535–536
first-person pronoun, 117
five Ws (who, what, where, when, and
        why), 189–190, 216
flames, 234
flash memory, 434
flip charts, 494
flowcharts, 369, 375
folders, 435–436
follow-up messages, 606–608
following procedures, 21
footrest, 470
formal business letters, 199
formal communication, 7
formal oral presentations, 481–486
formal reports, 312
    appendix, 341, 352–353
    bibliography, 341
    body, 341
    complexity, 338
    conclusions, 350
    direct order, 338
    executive summary, 341, 345
    findings and analysis, 347–349
    formats, 313
    formatting, 338, 353–354
    headings, 353–354
    impersonal style, 338
    indirect order, 338
    introduction, 346
    letter of transmittal, 339–340, 342
    memo of transmittal, 339–340
    organizing, 338
    parts, 339–354
    planning, 313
    recommendations, 350
    style manual, 353
    summary, 350
    table of contents, 340, 344
    title page, 340, 343
    visual aids, 354
    works cited, 351
    writing style, 338
formatting
    formal reports, 338, 353–354
    informal reports, 331–336
Forward feature, 233
fragments, 110
free career self-assessment tools, 573
frequent breaks, 468
friendliness, 75
friends list / instant messaging (IM), 235
friendship messages, 270–271
From line
    e-mail messages, 230
    memos, 221
functional order, 580
Future Business Leaders of America
        (FBLA), 95
future perfect tense verbs, 125
future tense verbs, 124

G

gender bias, 184
gender-neutral pronoun, 117
gestures, 71, 488–489
global positioning system (GPS), 456–457
globalization, 37–38
glossary in manuals, 401, 403
goodwill, 6, 176, 182
    acknowledgments, 271
    closing, 217, 259, 278
    closing paragraph, 190
    messages, 270
    promoting, 216
Google, 367, 573
grade point average (GPA), 583
grammar checkers, 196
grapevine, 7
graphics
    audience's attention, 364
    avoiding dividing, 366
    clear and accurate picture of data, 380
    computer program creation, 372–373
    importance, 364
    large amounts of data, 364
    numbering system, 367–368
    referencing, 365–366
graphs, 223, 369. *See also* charts
greetings, 546, 553
group e-mail addresses, 231
groupthink, 511

H

hackers, 446
handheld computers, 428–430
handouts, 497
handshakes, 71–72
hard copy and proofreading, 195
hardware, 426–430. *See also* computer hardware
headers in e-mail messages, 228
headings, 353–354
    Date line, 221
    From line, 221
    To line, 219–221
    second page, 225–226
    styles, 404
    Subject line, 221–222
Health Insurance Portability and Accountability Act of 1996 (HIPAA), 54
hearing, 79
hearing-impaired employees, 16
Help feature, 432
helping verbs, 110
honesty
    business communication, 53–54
    sincerity and, 549
horizontal communication, 8
hotspots, 444
humor, 48, 485
hyperlinks, 444
hypertext markup language (HTML), 444

hypertext transfer protocol (HTTP), 443
hyphens, 142, 154
hypothesis, 322

I

ID Theft Hotline, 448
ideas, developing new, 514
identity theft, 55
idioms, 47
illustrations
    See also graphics
    manuals, 404
    process description, 415
image and nonverbal symbols, 74–76
impromptu speech, 484
inclusion, 35
incoming calls, 556–558
incomplete sentences, 236
indefinite pronoun, 119, 159
indefinite pronoun agreement, 119
independent clauses, 109, 111–112, 150, 152
index
    manuals, 401
    skimming, 411
indirect objects, 108
indirect order, 180, 217
    formal reports, 338
    informal reports, 327–328, 331
    meetings, 514
    presentations, 486
indirect question, 142
informal abbreviations, 234, 236
informal communication, 7
informal document, 210
informal message, 211
informal reports, 312
    analyzing problem, 327
    body, 331
    closing, 331
    direct order, 327–328, 331
    formats, 313
    formatting, 331–336
    impersonal style, 329
    indirect order, 327–328, 331
    letter reports, 331–333
    main idea, 327
    manuscript reports, 332, 335–336
    memo reports, 332, 334
    opening, 331
    organizing, 327–328
    outlines, 328–329
    parts, 331
    past tense, 330
    personal style, 329
    planning, 313
    present tense, 330
    requested information, 327
    supporting information, 327
    writing style, 329–330

information
    digital form, 19
    obtaining or sharing, 6
Information Age, 19
informational reports, 312
informative listening, 81
informing, 176, 215, 514
inkjet printers, 437
instant messaging (IM), 56, 235–237
instant messaging (IM) software, 431
instructions
    accuracy and completeness, 401
    cautions, 397
    clear and specific title, 394, 396
    conclusion, 394, 397
    definitions, 397
    describing steps separately, 399
    diagrams or graphics, 400
    editing, 400–401
    effective, 394–397
    evaluating, 400
    highlighting warnings, 400
    introduction and needed items, 394, 396–397
    listing conditions, 399–400
    numbered steps, 394, 397, 399
    objective, 399
    purpose, 394
    reading, 411
    skills or knowledge required, 397
    source notes for graphics, 400
    spacing, 400
    subheadings, 400
    technical writing, 398
    time frame, 397
    understandable language, 398
    verbs, 399
    white space, 400
    writing steps, 398–400
intensive pronouns, 116
interests, 584–585
interjections, 106, 133
internal barriers, 11, 16, 77
internal customers, 530
internal marks, 142
internal memos, 199
International Listening Association (ILA), 85
Internet
    access, 443
    blogs, 535
    chain letters, 296
    faxing messages over, 440–441
    job opportunities, 573–574
    newsgroups, 535
    purposes for using, 445
    World Wide Web, 444
Internet Explorer, 444
internships, 572
interoffice mail, 211
interrogative pronouns, 116–117
intervening phrases, 126
interviewers, 602–603, 606

interviews, 315
intimate zone, 72
intranets, 198–199, 443
intransitive verbs, 125
introducing speakers, 480
introduction, 297
    conversation, 546
    manuals, 401, 403
    outgoing calls, 553–554
    presentations, 485
    process description, 412
introductory elements, 146
invoice, 213
irregular plural nouns, 115

J

Janis, Irving L., 511
jargon, 47
job ads, 573
job announcements, 604
job interviews, 570
    answering questions, 603
    asking questions, 600
    clothing guidelines, 602
    follow-up messages, 606–608
    interviewer, 602
    nonverbal skills, 603
    personal questions, 604–605
    preparing for, 600, 602
    salary requirements, 605
    sample questions, 601
    taking part in, 602–606
job objective, 583
job opportunities
    employment agencies, 574
    Internet, 573–574
    internships, 572
    job search network, 573
    publications, 573–574
    researching organizations, 575–576
    school placement offices, 573
job qualifications, 570–572
job search
    career goals, 568–569
    job opportunities, 572–576
    job qualifications, 570–572
    personal goals, 568
    reading, 19
job search agents, 574
job search network, 573

K

keyboard tray, 470
keyboards, ergonomic, 469
keywords, 316–317

L

landscape orientation, 375
language, 40, 46–47
laptop computers, 427, 469

laser printers, 437
lateral communication, 8
leader, 94
leadership, 95
learning and cross-cultural
        communication, 46
legal documents, 157
legend, 369, 376
legitimate complaints, 540
letter of transmittal, 339–340, 342
letter reports, 331–333
letterhead, 212, 226
letters, 198
    address, 239, 241
    attention line, 243
    body, 242
    complimentary close, 242
    date, 239
    editing and publishing, 245–248
    folding, 248
    optional parts, 243–245
    postscript, 245
    proper order, 216–217
    reference initials, 242
    reference line, 243
    request information, 215
    salutation, 241
    standard parts, 239–242
    subject line, 245
    writer's name and title, 242
    writing, 239–245
line charts, 369–370, 377
linking verbs, 109, 123
Linux, 430
listeners, attaching meaning to what
        was said, 84
listening, 16–17
    actively, 48, 80
    assumptions, 83
    attitudes, 82–83
    barriers to effective, 82–83
    carefully and actively, 549
    casual, 80
    conference setting, 87
    divided focus, 83
    effectively, 84–87
    emphatic, 81
    environmental distractions, 83
    evaluative, 81, 85
    external barriers, 16
    focusing attention, 79
    focusing on main idea, 84–85
    hearing, 79
    informative, 81
    internal barriers, 16
    overcoming poor habits, 86
    physical discomfort, 83
    prejudices or differing opinions, 83
    process, 79–80
    providing feedback, 85
    reflective, 82
    remembering, 79

    sharing responsibility, 84–86
    specific situations, 86–87
    taking notes, 85–86
    telephone communication, 551–552
    understanding, 79
lists, 143, 158
local area network (LAN), 443
logging off computer, 446
long quotations, 152
Lotus 1-2-3, 431

M

Mac OS, 430
mail merge, 247
main idea, 177, 186, 217, 259
    acknowledgments, 271
    claims, 263
    focusing on, 84–85
    friendship messages, 270
    orders, 264
    positive messages, 264
    positive responses, 267
    routine requests, 260
main verbs, 110
managers, 89–90
managing files, 435–436
manual pages, 402
manuals
    appendix, 401, 404–405
    clear and complete steps, 401
    clear and specific title, 401
    combining instructions, 401
    creating efficiently, 404
    figures and illustrations, 401, 403
    glossary, 401, 403
    heading styles, 404
    illustrations, 403–404
    index, 401
    introduction, 401, 403
    logical divisions, 401
    purpose, 394
    reading, 411
    section breaks, 404
    sections or chapters, 403
    table of contents, 401, 403
    title, 403
    used as reference, 403
manuscript reports, 332, 335–336
maps, 370, 381
margins, 353
masculine nouns, 117
masculine pronouns, 117
mechanical errors, 194
mechanism, 407, 410
medical information, 54
meetings
    ad hoc committee, 504
    agendas, 505–506, 516, 518
    appropriate site, 516
    arriving on time, 510
    body language, 512

brainstorming, 514
clarifying question, 519
collaborate, 514
decision-making, 514
defining objective, 513
delegating work, 514
details, 515–517
discussing ideas, 512
documents, 505–508
dominating conversation, 519–520
effectively leading, 518–520
encouraging participation, 518–519
ending appropriately, 520
equipment and supplies, 517
identifying type, 513–515
improving decision making, 511
informing, 514
invitations, 516
minutes, 213, 506–508
objective, 505
participants, 515, 517
participation, 508, 510–512
persuading, 515
phone calls during, 511
preparation before, 510
productive, 513–517
professionalism, 520
scheduling, 515–516
standing committees, 504
taking notes, 512
task force, 504
teleconferences, 505
time limit, 513
Web conferences, 505
workplace, 504
memo of transmittal, 339–340
memo reports, 332, 334
memos, 210–211
    attachment notation, 224
    blind copy notation, 225
    body, 222–223
    bulleted and numbered lists, 223
    copy notation, 225
    Date line, 221
    default side margins, 219
    distribution list, 220–221
    editing and publishing, 226
    enclosure notation, 224
    headings, 219–222
    From line, 221
    To line, 219–221
    line spacing, 219
    notations, 224–225
    proper order, 216–217
    recording plans or discussions, 214
    reference initials, 224
    requesting information, 215
    second page headings, 225–226
    sharing confidential information, 215

Subject line, 221–222
tables, graphs, and charts, 223
templates, 226
writing, 219–226
messages, 4–5
    active voice, 188
    channels, 5
    clear, 188–189
    closing, 259
    complete, 189–190
    concise, 187–188
    correct, 186
    courteous, 182–185
    editing, 192–193
    effective, 182
    environment, 13–14
    errors, 194
    evaluating, 85
    favorable, 179
    feedback, 5
    goodwill, 270
    main idea, 186
    negative, 274–279
    neutral, 179, 258
    organizing, 179–180, 216–217, 259
    passive voice, 188
    persuasive, 286–301
    planning and organizing, 176–178, 216–217
    positive, 179, 258
    positive and negative news together, 283
    proofreading, 194–197
    publishing, 198–200
    receivers, 5
    routine, 179–180
    sender, 5
microprocessors, 426
Microsoft Access, 431
Microsoft Excel, 372, 431
Microsoft Office Professional Edition, 432
Microsoft Outlook, 228
Microsoft PowerPoint, 373, 484, 494
Microsoft Windows, 430, 447
Microsoft Word, 372, 431, 440
minutes, 506–508
misleading charts, 380
mixed punctuation, 241–242
MLA Handbook, 353
mobile learning, 459
Modern Language Association (MLA) style, 353
modified block format, 246
modified block letter example, 244
Monster.com, 573
Monthly Labor Review, 36
mouse and ergonomics, 470
MSN Messenger, 235
multimedia presentations, 495
multinational company, 38
music, 495
mutual respect, 512

N
names, 549
NASA Web site, 444
National Atlas Web site, 381
National Do No Call Registry, 558
need, 297
negative messages, 217
    closing, 278–279
    denying request, 280
    effective opening, 275–276
    indirect order, 180
    ineffective opening, 275–276
    negative news itself, 277–278
    neutral opening, 275
    objective, 274
    order for information, 275
    organizing, 275–279
    planning, 274
    reasons for negative news, 276–277
    refusing credit, 280
    softening, 277–278
    tone, 274
    writing, 280
negative news, 276–278
negative thinking, 75
Net Bookmark
    Better Business Bureau, 270
    Career self-assessment tools, 573
    clip art, 367
    effective presentations and meetings, 519
    Equal Employment Opportunity Commission (EEOC), 50
    Federal Trade Commission (FTC), 558
    Human Factors and Ergonomics Society (HFES), 469
    International Listening Association (ILA), 85
    memo templates, 226
    Modern Language Association style (MLA), 353
    Online Writing Lab (OWL), 190
    reading tests, 23
    Society for Technical Communication (STC), 415
netiquette
    e-mail message, 233–234
    instant messaging (IM), 237
Netscape Navigator, 228, 444
networking, 573
networks, 426, 443
    unauthorized access, 446
    unethical use, 451
neutral messages, 179
    checklist, 272, 492
    claims, 263
    goodwill closing, 259
    main idea, 259
    organizing, 259
    planning, 258
    routine requests, 260

neutral messages (*continued*)
  supporting details, 259
  writing, 260–263
neutral nouns, 185
neutral opening, 217, 275
neutral pronouns, 185
neutral words, 184–185
newsgroups, 535
nominative case pronouns, 116
nonessential elements
  commas, 145
  dashes, 153
  parentheses, 157
nonrestrictive elements, 146
nonstandard English, 155
nonverbal communication roles,
  68–69
nonverbal cues, 546
nonverbal messages, 75, 77
nonverbal skills, 603
nonverbal symbols, 4, 14–15
  body language, 70–71
  contradicting verbal message, 69
  cultures, 41, 70
  degree of importance, 68
  eye contact, 76
  handshakes, 71–72
  image and, 74–76
  interpreting, 68
  opinions based on, 68
  oral presentations, 488–489
  paralanguage, 73
  personal space, 70, 72–73
  posture, 76
  regulating verbal message, 69
  reinforcing verbal message, 68
  self-confidence, 74–75
  spoken messages, 70, 72–73
  substituting for verbal message, 69
  time, 73
  touching, 71–72
  written messages, 70
North American Free Trade Agreement
  (NAFTA), 37
Norton 360, 431
notations, 224–225
notes, 85–86
nouns, 106–107, 114–115
  neutral, 185
  objects functioning as, 108
  used as adjectives, 120
number expression, 165–167
numbered lists, 223, 242
numbers, 127, 148, 157

O

objective case pronouns, 116
objectives, 176, 407
objects, 108, 408–409, 496
observation, 315
obstacles, addressing, 290

Occupational Outlook Handbook, 42
Occupational Safety & Health Administration (OSHA), 462
Occupational Safety and Health Act of
  1970, 462
Occupational Success
  creating manuals efficiently, 404
  leadership, 95
  presentation tips, 490
  searching for data online, 318
  using mail merge, 247
  work/life balance, 38
omission of words, 148
online purchases, 447
online research, 316–318
online training, 460
open climate, 11
open punctuation, 241
opening paragraph, 190
operating system
  organizing files, 435–436
  software, 430
opinions, 277
optical character recognition software
  (OCR), 438
oral communication, 9, 480
oral presentations
  See also presentations
  analyzing audience, 482–483
  briefings, 481
  delivery, 488–490
  demographics of listeners, 483
  determining objective, 482
  feedback, 489–490
  formal, 481–486
  gathering information, 484
  introducing speakers, 480
  mode of delivery, 484
  nonverbal symbols,
    488–489
  planning, 482
  primary research, 484
  secondary research, 484
  short, 480–481
  time available, 483
  visual aids, 489
  voice qualities, 488
orders, 264
organization charts, 369, 374
organizing
  files, 435–436
  messages, 179–180, 216–217
  negative messages, 275–279
OSHA Web site, 462
outgoing calls, 553–555
outlines, 321–323
  informal reports, 328–329
  presentations, 486
overcoming barriers
  receiver's duties, 15–17
  sender's duties, 12–15
OWL web site, 190

P

pagers, 449
palmtop, 428
paper, 199–200
paragraphs, 190, 192–193, 259
paralanguage, 73
parallel construction, 133
parallel talk, 82
paraphrasing, 17
parentheses, 142, 157–158
parts of conversation, 546–547
parts of speech, 106
passive listening, 80
passive voice, 125, 188, 196
passwords, 446
past perfect tense verbs, 124
past tense
  informal reports, 330
  process description, 415
past tense verbs, 124
peer group teams, 93
perfect tenses, 124–125
periods, 142–143, 156
peripherals
  fax machines, 440–441
  printers, 437–438
  scanners, 438–440
personal area network (PAN), 443
personal business letters, 212, 246
personal computer (PC), 426
personal contact, 48
personal digital assistant (PDA), 428
personal ethics, 52
personal goals, 568
personal pronouns, 115, 278
personal space, 42, 70, 72–73
personal traits, 571
personal zone, 72
persuading, 7, 176, 215, 515
persuasive messages
  addressing obstacles, 290
  adjusting content to receiver, 286
  asking for specific action, 292
  chain letters, 296
  checklist, 301
  collection messages, 293–295
  direct order, 287
  emphasizing primary appeal, 291
  explaining solution, 290
  gaining reader's attention, 287
  identifying objective, 286
  including deadline, 292
  indirect order, 287
  introducing topic, 287
  main idea, 286
  organizing, 287–292
  planning, 286
  proposals, 296–300
  sales messages, 292–293
  showing need, 290
  supporting details, 286, 290–291

writing, 292–301
photographs, 366–367, 370, 373, 382
phrases, 110
physical discomfort, 83
physical environment, 14
pie charts, 369–370
pitch, 544
plagiarism, 57–58, 320
planning messages, 176–178, 216
plural nouns, 114, 117, 126
plural pronoun, 117
pointing devices, 470
population predictions, 36
portrait orientation, 375
positive degree, 120–121
positive messages, 179
    acknowledgments, 271
    adjusting content to receiver, 258
    checklist, 272, 492
    closing, 264
    details, 264
    friendship messages, 270
    goodwill closing, 259
    goodwill message s, 270
    main idea, 258–259, 264
    objective, 258
    orders, 264
    organizing, 259
    planning, 258
    positive responses to request, 267
    supporting details, 258–259
positive responses, 267
positive words, 182–183
possession, 159
possessive nouns, 115
possessive pronouns, 116
posters, 494
postscript, 245
posture, 76, 488–489
predicate adjectives, 123
predicate nominatives, 116, 123
predicates, 107–108
prejudice, 43, 49, 83
preliminary parts, 339–341
prepositional phrases, 110, 131
prepositions, 106, 131
present perfect tense verbs, 124
present tense
    informal reports, 330
    process description, 415
present tense verbs, 124
presentation software, 373
presentations
    See also oral presentations
    attention-getters, 485
    body, 486
    closing, 486
    direct order, 486
    eye contact, 484
    impromptu speech, 484
    indirect order, 486
    introduction, 485

    multimedia, 495
    organizing, 485–486
    outlining, 486
    practicing, 483–484
    tips, 490
    visual aids, 494–502
primary appeal, 291
primary research, 315, 484
printers, 437–438
privacy, 56
private employment agencies, 574
problems, matching solution to, 541
process, 407
process description, 407, 412, 415–416
productive meetings, 513–517
professional attitude, 45, 49
professions, ethical guidelines, 52
programs. *See* software
project bids, 186
project team, 92
prompt attention, 536
promptness, 73
pronoun-antecedent agreement, 117–118
pronouns, 106, 115–117
    neutral, 185
    used as adjectives, 120
pronunciation, 545
proofreaders' marks, 196–197
proofreading
    comparing drafts, 195
    content errors, 194
    hard copy, 195
    mechanical errors, 194
    methods, 194–195
    multiple proofreaders, 195
    proofreaders' marks, 196–197
    spelling and grammar checkers, 196
proper keying position, 467
proper nouns, 114
proper titles, 183–184
proposals, 297–298
protecting confidential information, 56
public zone, 72
Publication Manual of the American
    Psychological Association (APA), 338
publications, 573–574
publishing memos, 226
publishing messages, 198–200
punctuation, 142
    apostrophes, 158–159
    colons, 151–152
    commas, 145–148
    dashes, 153
    exclamation points, 144
    external marks, 142
    hyphens, 154
    internal marks, 142
    parentheses, 157–158
    periods, 142–143
    question marks, 143–144
    quotation marks, 155–156
    semicolons, 150–151

purchase orders, 264
purposes of communication, 6–7

Q

qualifications and career portfolio,
    571–572
quality service, 537–539
question marks, 142–144, 156
questions, 485
quotation marks, 142, 155–156
quotations, 155, 485

R

race, 35
race and age bias, 185
Reader's Guide to Periodical Literature, 316
reading, 15–16
    aloud, 195, 547
    carefully, 23
    customer service, 22
    decision-making, 277
    effective, 195
    English as second language, 24
    external barriers, 16
    following procedures, 21
    handling transactions, 21–22
    importance, 17, 19–22
    improving skills, 23–24
    improving speed and comprehension, 24
    internal barriers, 16
    on the job, 20–22
    job search, 19
    making decisions, 22
    overcoming internal barriers, 77
    scanning, 23
    secondary research, 324
    skimming, 23
    solving problems, 22, 277
    speed and comprehension, 217
    staying informed, 20
    types, 23
Reading Skills
    building vocabulary, 42
    checking understanding, 17
    confused and misused words, 217
    facts or opinions, 277
    reading aloud, 547
    reading charts, 369
    reading for comprehension, 77
    reading for research, 324
    reading goals, 195
    reading job announcements, 604
    reading manuals and instructions, 411
    reading onscreen, 501
    technology vocabulary, 459
receivers, 5
    adjusting message for, 177–178
    background and experiences, 6
    duties, 15–17
    emotional state, 13
    knowing factors about, 12

receivers (*continued*)
    listening, 16–17
    reading, 15–16
recommendations, 325, 350
recording, 176
redundancies, 188
reference initials, 224, 242
reference line, 243, 245
references, 158, 585–586
reflective listening, 82
reflexive pronouns, 116
refusing credit, 280
regular adjectives, 120
reinforcing verbal message, 68
rejection letter, 608
relationships
    building, 7
    customer, 91
    employee and manager, 89–90
relaxing, 548
remembering, 79
reminder message, 293
repetitive stress injuries (RSI), 465
reports
    alternative, 322
    analytical, 312–313
    analyzing data, 324–325
    body, 341
    collecting data, 315–321
    confidential data, 331
    copyrights, 320
    crediting source of information, 320
    defining, 313–314
    developing timeline, 314
    drawing conclusions, 325
    formal, 312
    formats, 313
    hypothesis, 322
    identifying problem or topic, 313–314
    informal, 312, 327–336
    informational, 312
    interviews, 315
    introduction, 346
    making recommendations, 325
    observation, 315
    outlines, 321–323
    plagiarism, 320
    primary research, 315
    processing data, 321–326
    purpose, 312–313
    research notes, 320
    scope, 314
    secondary research, 316–320
    styles, 312
    surveys, 315
    types, 312–313
request for proposal (RFP), 297, 298
requests, 176, 215, 280
research
    bibliography notes, 319–320
    Boolean operators, 318
    broadening, 318
    documentation, 319–320
    evaluating data sources, 319
    inside company, 317
    interviews, 315
    keywords, 316–317
    narrowing, 318
    notes, 320
    observation, 315
    online, 316–318
    print, 316
    reading, 324
    secondary, 316–320
    surveys, 315
    U.S. government, 317
researching organizations, 575–576
resolution, 437
respect, 49
restrictive elements, 146
Resume Maker, 580
resume-tracking program, 587
resumes
    achievements, 584–585
    activities, 584–585
    alternative, 586–590
    contact information, 580
    education, 583
    electronic format, 200
    experience, 583–584
    functional order, 580
    general, 578
    interests, 584–585
    job objective, 583
    keywords, 586–587
    paper, 199
    parts of, 580, 583–585
    preparing, 578–586
    printed guidelines, 578
    references, 585–586
    reverse chronological order, 580
    sections, 579
    special qualifications, 583
    specific, 578
    truthful, 585
return address, 246
return receipt feature, 233
reverse chronological order, 580
Robert's Rules of Order, 505
routine messages, 179–180, 186
routine reports, 199
routine requests, 260
rows, 373
rules, 374
rumors, 7

S

safety rules and procedures, 463
sales messages, 292–293
salutation, 241
satisfied customers, 535
scannable print resumes, 586–587
scanners, 382, 438–440

scanning, 23
schedule, 297
school placement offices, 573
scope, 297, 314
screening calls, 557–558
search engines, 573
    advanced searches, 318
    free clip art, 367
    keywords, 316–317
second page headings, 225–226
second-person pronoun, 117
secondary research, 324
section breaks, 404
security
    anti-spyware programs, 447
    anti-virus programs, 447
    backing up files, 446
    e-mail attachment, 446
    e-mail requesting personal data, 446
    hackers, 446
    logging off computer, 446
    online purchases, 447
    passwords, 446
    solutions, 446–448
    spyware, 446
    threats, 445–446
    Trojan horses, 445–446
    two-factor authentication, 447
    unauthorized access, 446
    virus checking software, 446
    viruses, 445
    vital data stolen, 447–448
    worms, 445
self-analysis, 571
self-confidence, 74–75
self-esteem, 7
semicolons, 112, 142, 150–151, 156
senders, 5
    audience analysis, 12–13
    duties, 12–15
    feedback, 15, 17
    message environment, 13–14
    nonverbal symbols, 14–15
    selecting channel, 15
    verbal symbols, 14–15
sensitive topics, 48
sensitivity, 49–50
sentence structures, 111–112
sentences
    capitalization, 163
    clauses, 109
    complete, 109
    declarative, 142
    fragments, 110
    objects, 108
    parallel construction, 133
    phrases, 110
    predicate, 107–108
    subject, 107
    subject complements, 109
sexual harassment, 71
shared network drive, 433

sharing printers, 438
short message service (SMS), 454
short oral presentations, 480–481
signature blocks, 231
signature file, 231
simple predicates, 108
simple sentences, 111
simple subjects, 107
simple tenses, 124
sincerity, 75
single quotation mark, 155
singular nouns, 114, 117, 126
singular pronouns, 117
skills, 570
skimming, 23, 411
slang, 47, 155
slate, 428
slides, 494–495
small groups, 87
smart phones, 453–454
Social Security Administration, 448
social setting, 14
social zone, 72
Society for Technical Communication
    (STC), 415
soft sell, 259
    closings, 279
    positive responses, 267
software, 430–432
software suite, 432
solution, matching to problem, 541
solving problems, 22
sound, 499–500
source lines, 368
source notes, 400
space zones, 72
spacing, 353
spam, 230–231, 234
speakers, 84–85, 480
speaking clearly, 552
special qualifications, 583
special teams, 91–92
specific actions, 292
specific resumes, 578
speech clarity, 545
speed reading test, 23
spelling checkers, 196, 232
spoken messages and nonverbal symbols,
    70–73
spreadsheet programs, 372–373
spyware, 446
standard form, 213
standing committees, 504
state employment agencies, 574
state-of-being linking verbs, 123
state-of-being verbs, 109
State of Oregon Jobs Page, 573
statistics, 485
STC Web site, 415
stereotypes, 43
storage options, 433–434
strong reminder message, 293

style manual, 353
subject, 107, 109
subject complements, 109
subject line
    letters, 245
    memos, 221–222
subject-verb agreement, 126–127
subordinate conjunctions, 131
summary, 350, 547
superlative degree, 120–121
supplementary parts, 341, 353
supporter, 94
supporting details, 177, 186, 259
    negative news, 276
    orders, 264
    persuasive messages, 290–291
supporting information, 217, 298
surveys, 315
synergy, 92
synopsis, 341

T

table of contents, 340, 344
    heading styles to format headings,
        404
    manuals, 401, 403
    skimming, 411
table of figures, 404
Table Styles, 372
tables, 223, 369
tablet computers, 428, 469
task force, 504
teams
    decision-making, 94
    ground rules and procedures, 93–94
    guidelines for success, 94–95
    peer group, 93
    problem solving, 96
    project, 92
    recorder, 94
    roles, 93, 94
    special, 91–92
    standout members, 96
    synergy, 92
    virtual, 93
    workgroup, 91
    working effectively, 93–96
teamwork
    workplace relationships, 89–91
    workplace teams, 91–93
technical writing, 398
technology, 426
    Bluetooth, 443
    cell phones, 450–455
    computer hardware, 426–430
    computer software, 430–432
    conference technologies, 458
    connecting world, 443–444
    desktop computers, 427
    digital cameras, 456
    document transmittal, 448

    file storage and management, 433–436
    global positioning system (GPS),
        456–457
    handheld computers, 428–430
    Internet, 444–445
    laptop computers, 427
    pagers, 449
    peripherals, 437–441
    security, 445–448
    tablet computers, 428
    training, 458–460
    vocabulary, 459
    voice mail, 450
    voice over Internet protocol (VoIP), 455
    Wi-Fi, 443–444
teleconferences, 455, 458, 505
telephone communication
    courteousness, 552
    difficult callers, 552
    effective, 551–552
    incoming calls, 556–558
    listening, 551–552
    outgoing calls, 553–555
    preparation, 551–552
    speaking clearly, 552
    verbal cues, 551–552
temp agencies, 574
templates for memos, 226
text messaging, 454
thank-you letter, 606
thinker, 94
thinking before you speak, 548
third-person plural pronouns, 126
third-person pronouns, 117
third-person singular pronouns, 126
time, 73
    abbreviations, 161
    colons, 152
    number expression, 167
timeline, 314
title page, 340, 343
Title VII of the Civil Rights Act of 1964, 49
titles
    instructions, 396
    manuals, 401, 403
    pie charts, 376
    process description, 412
    tables, 373
to be verbs, 123
To line
    e-mail message, 228–229
    memos, 219–221
tone, 544
toner, 437
topic sentence, 190
topical format, 323
topical outline, 486
touching, 71–72
trade secrets, 55
training conferences, 460
training technologies, 458–460
training videos, 460

transactions, handling, 21–22
transitions, 192–193
transitive verbs, 125
transparencies, 494–495
Trojan horses, 445–446
tutorials, 432
two-factor authentication, 447

U

understanding, 79
unhappy customers, 535
uniform resource locator (URL), 444
unnecessary elements, 187–188
unrealistic expectations, 75
unwritten code of conduct, 52
upward communication, 8
urgency-stage collection message, 295
U.S. Census Bureau Web site, 317
U.S. Equal Employment Opportunity
    Commission (EEOC), 50
U.S. government, 317
U.S. Mail, 296
USAJOBS web site, 19
utility software, 431

V

value axis, 369
verb phrase, 110
verbal cues, 551–552
verbal messages, 68–69
verbal symbols, 4, 14–15
verbs, 106
    action, 123
    active voice, 125
    complete predicate, 108
    future perfect tense, 125
    future tense, 124
    indirect object, 108
    intransitive, 125
    linking, 123
    modifying, 128–129
    passive voice, 125
    past perfect tense, 124
    past tense, 124
    perfect tense, 124–125
    present perfect tense, 124
    present tense, 124
    simple tenses, 124
    tenses, 124–125
    transitive, 125
vertical lists, 143
video, 495
video conference, 458
virtual team, 93
virus checking software, 446
virus protection software, 431
viruses, 445
vision problems, 465, 468
visual aids, 48
    acceptable number, 498–499

audience, 364, 497–498
bar charts, 370
chalkboards, 496
charts, 374–380
choosing appropriate, 369–370,
    497–498
color, 499–500
column charts, 370
computer presentations, 494–495
distractions, 500–501
document usage, 365–368
drawings, 370, 383
ease of creation, 364
electronic whiteboards, 496
English as second language, 365
equipment available, 497
flip charts, 494
flowcharts, 369
formal reports, 354
handouts, 497
identifying, 367–368
importance, 364
line charts, 370
maps, 370, 381
motion, 499–500
numbering system, 367–368
objects, 496
oral presentations, 489
organization charts, 369
photographs, 370, 382
pie charts, 370
placing, 365–367
posters, 494
practicing using, 501–502
preparing, 498–500
presenting, 500–502
size, 499–500
slides, 494–495
sound, 499–500
source line, 368
tables, 369, 373–374
titles, 367–368
transparencies, 494–495
types, 494–497
whiteboards, 496
visual presenter, 496
vocabulary, 42
voice, 544–545, 549
voice mail, 450
    leaving effective messages, 554–555
    lengthy messages, 555
    recording greetings, 556
    speaking to person, 557
voice over Internet protocol (VoIP), 455
volume, 544

W

The Wall Street Journal, 575
The Wall Street Journal Index, 316
warm-up exercises, 467

Web browsers, 444
Web conferences, 458, 505
Web pages, 444
Web resumes, 589
Web sites, 444, 448
    credibility, 535
    free career self-assessment tools, 573
    free clip art, 367
    information about company, 575
    photographs, 382
    responding to visitors, 534
    tips and articles for effective
        presentation and meetings, 519
white space, 200, 400
whiteboards, 496
Wi-Fi, 443–444
wide area network (WAN), 443
wildcard, 318
Windows Calendar, 516
Windows Vista utility programs, 431
WinZip, 435
wizard, 432
word processing programs, 431
    clip art, 372
    custom dictionary, 196
    default margins, 200
    Envelope feature, 246–247
    mail merge, 247
    memo templates, 226
    spelling and grammar checkers, 196, 232
    tables, 373
words, confused and misused, 217
work experience, 583–584
work/life balance, 38
workers and discrimination, 35
workforce, 34, 36–38
workplace
    discrimination, 185
    meetings, 504
    relationships, 89–91
    safety, 462–464
workplace teams
    advantages and disadvantages,
        92–93
    guidelines for success, 94–95
    special teams, 91–92
    standout members, 96
    workgroup teams, 91
    working effectively, 93–96
works cited, 351
workstations, 426
    arranging work area, 466
    ergonomics, 465–470
World Wide Web, 382, 444
worms, 445
writing process stages, 192
written communication, 8

Y

you approach, 177